A Great and Lasting Beginning

A Great and Lasting Beginning

The First 125 Years of St. Ambrose University

By
George William McDaniel

To Dr Ross McFadden

thank you for helping St Ambrose

George William McDaniel

St. Ambrose University has reached its 125th year through the efforts of thousands of Ambrosians who are numbered among those who love her: students, faculty, staff, alumni, and friends. This is ultimately their story, and it is to them that a *Great and Lasting Beginning* is dedicated.

Table of Contents

Preface

Father Charles Griffith, a professor of history and later spiritual director of the seminary, was fond of speaking of St. Ambrose by quoting Daniel Webster who had said of his alma mater, Dartmouth College, "It is, sir, a small college, and yet there are those who love it." Count me among those who love St. Ambrose. I transferred in as a student in 1963 and graduated in 1966. I was ordained in 1970 and after four years as a parish priest, I returned to St. Ambrose in 1974 as dean of students. After a stop in the development office and graduate school, I found my way to the Department of History and Geography, which has been my home for nearly twenty-five years.

This book is the story of the school Bishop John McMullen founded in 1882. He had a vision for a school for boys, and he had definite ideas about the purpose of education. He hoped that St. Ambrose would be the vehicle for realizing that vision and that those boys would carry it forward in their lives after leaving St. Ambrose. He did not live long enough to see anything but a glimpse of his vision, so it was left to later generations of Ambrosians to carry it forward. This book is the story of all of us Ambrosians as much as it is a story of that school for boys.

It is also a story of change. St. Ambrose has changed a great deal in its 125 years of existence, and sometimes it is difficult to find evidence of McMullen's vision. However, I contend it is still here. The Roman Catholic Church has also changed and those changes, especially since Vatican Council II in the 1960s, have affected St. Ambrose. Higher education in the United States has changed and the Catholic sector of it has had to adapt in ways with which its leaders were not always comfortable. But as one observer noted, it is this "willingness to adapt" that has made it possible for Catholic higher education, St. Ambrose included, to "not just survive, but flourish." The world has changed and Ambrosians were not immune to the forces at play half-way around the globe. They were changed and their school was changed by those forces.

I am not the first to write about St. Ambrose, and I am indebted to all of those who have gone before me. Their work is an integral part of my work. Father Griffith was the first to write about St. Ambrose in the 1920s and 1930s. Monsignor U. A. Hauber was the greatest of us. He came to St. Ambrose as a student in 1901, and except for four years in major seminary, he remained at St. Ambrose until his death in 1956. He was regularly elected historian of the Alumni Association and wrote about St. Ambrose in a column titled "In Retrospect," in the *Ambrosian Alumnus* from 1949 until his death. Some of the early columns were published in a pamphlet, *Oaks and Acorns from the College Campus*. Monsignor Sebastian Menke, a student, faculty member, and president from 1926 to 1973, wrote an unpublished memoir, "Memoirs and Reflections of Sebastian G. Menke," which was helpful for those years. The Reverend Anthony Gorham Farrell's centennial history, *Bees and Bur Oaks: 100 Years of St. Ambrose College*, was a great help as a reference and guide. I also benefitted from *Seasons of Growth, History of the Diocese of Davenport 1881-1981*, by Sister Madeleine Marie Schmidt, CHM.

One of the problems of writing about an institution over a long period of time is that often names change. The group now called the Board of Directors began as the Board of Trustees, later was called the Board of Control or the Corporation Board or the Board of Managers. I have tried to refer to it using the name appropriate to the time.

In January 1883, the *Iowa Messenger* began publication. For the next fifty years it changed its name several times before settling on the *Catholic Messenger* in 1936. For the sake of clarity, I refer to it in the text and the endnotes by its current name, the *Catholic Messenger* or just the *Messenger*.

St. Ambrose began as a high school and in time became St. Ambrose Academy. I refer to it as the academy throughout, because that is what everyone remembers it being called.

I based the enrollment figures for the first three years on the names in the cash ledger. After that I used the list printed in the annual catalogue. There was no official reporting day in those earlier years, and there is no good way to tell at what point in the year the list was compiled for the printer. It is possible that some students were not accounted for because they came at the beginning of the year but left before the list was compiled. But by using that list consistently, I provided for reliability in statistics. Later, the registrar's office published official enrollment figures and I relied on those.

The book of Ecclesiastes reminds us that "writing books involves endless hard work," and that "much study wearies the body." That is true, but my work and study was made much easier by the support of friends and colleagues. The archives in O'Keefe Library was a valuable resource. When I began, John Pollitz, the library director at the time, gave me a key to the Ambrose Room and the archives so I could come and go at will. I found the archives filled with valuable information, but the greatest resource was Kathy Byers, whose official title is administrative assistant, but who also serves as archivist. She and her student helpers did a wonderful job of organizing and cataloguing the archives and she was always on the lookout for more information for me. The entire staff of the library and its new director, Mary Heinzman, had a hand in this book, but I mention especially the people in interlibrary loan and the reference desk who found obscure information cheerfully and quickly. I thank them all.

At the Diocese of Davenport, the archivist, Arnie Wieser, gave me a desk to use, showed me where things were, and was a congenial companion in the business of history. The Richardson-Sloane Special Collections Center of the Davenport Public Library was a treasure. Amy Groskopf, the Special Collections Department manager, and librarians Mary Ann Moore, Karen O'Connor, and Sarah Wesson never failed to answer my questions or point me in the direction of the answer. Sister Joan Sheil, CHM, archivist for the Congregation of the Humility of Mary, was helpful with questions about the Congregation and Marycrest College.

I am grateful to President Edward J. Rogalski who commissioned me to do this book and agreed to my requests for half-time teaching and a one-year leave to complete the work. Dr. Edward Littig and Ms. Linda Wastyn of the Office of Advancement at St. Ambrose have provided support, both financial and moral, during the years the book was in process. The cover of the dust jacket was their idea, and a great one. Production of the book was done by the *Quad-City Times*. Terry Wilson, Director of Sales Support, Marketing and Research, has been a calm and supporting colleague throughout. Becky Heidgerken laid out the book and was patient with my requests to move a picture from one page to another. Tom Heidgerken scanned the images and used the magic of the computer to make some older photos look like new. Some of the images in the book are courtesy of the Communications and Marketing Office. I thank Linda Hirsch, Sal Paustian, and Darcy Duncalf for helping me find just the right picture. Other images are courtesy of the *Buzz* and I thank Alan Sivell, the advisor, for granting me access to the paper's photo archives. Images by Father Edward Catich are published courtesy of the Catich Gallery.

My colleagues in the History department have been supportive, from rearranging our course schedules to accommodate my leave, to offering supportive comments and patiently listening to me talk about my latest discovery in the library. Professor emeritus Richard Geiger and the Reverend Monsignor Drake Shafer read the entire work and offered friendship and helpful comments. Many other Ambrosians never failed to answer my questions or to share their memories and impressions of our history.

Some of the earliest research was done when I held the Baecke Chair of Humanities in 1993, and some of the writing was supported by the Baecke Chair in 2006. Faculty development grants made research trips possible to the Hesburgh Library at the University of Notre Dame and the Fraser-Hickson Library in Montreal, Canada. The faculty reimbursement program also helped with a research trip to the library at the University of Illinois.

My greatest thanks, however, go to my editor, Laurie Boyce-Steinhauser. This is a better book because of her work. She corrected my grammar, gently asked if I really wanted to say something, or suggested a paragraph might be better somewhere else or eliminated altogether. She offered solace and support when the whole thing seemed impossible. With great patience and good will, she walked this journey with me and I will be forever grateful. She is now an Ambrosian.

Portions of the Introduction appeared first as the Richard E. Geiger History Lecture in 2002 and were later published as, "'A Great and Lasting Beginning': Bishop John McMullen's Educational Vision and the Founding of St. Ambrose University," *Catholic Education: A Journal of Inquiry and Practice* 9, no. 1 (September 2005).

Portions of Chapter One first appeared as an essay, "They Were the Sons of Immigrants," at the Contemporary Club in 2004.

Portions of Chapter Ten first appeared as the Baecke Chair of Humanities Lecture in 1993 and were later published as "Catholic Action in Davenport: St. Ambrose College and the League for Social Justice," *The Annals of Iowa* 55, no. 3 (Summer 1996).

Portions of Chapter Eleven were first given as "The Chapels of St. Ambrose University," the Arts and Sciences Lecture in 2003.

Bishop John McMullen

In the spring of 1882, Bishop John McMullen, who had been in the new Diocese of Davenport for about six months, met with the Reverend Henry Cosgrove, the pastor of St. Marguerite's (later Sacred Heart) Cathedral. "Where shall we find a place to give a beginning to a college?" McMullen asked. Cosgrove's response was immediate: "Bishop, I will give you two rooms in my school building." "All right," McMullen said, "let us start at once."[1]

Introduction

McMullen's desire to found a college was not as impetuous as it may have seemed. Like many American Catholic leaders in the nineteenth century, McMullen viewed education as a way for a growing immigrant Catholic population to advance in their new country. Catholic education would also serve as a bulwark against the encroachment of Protestant ideas that formed the foundation of public education in the United States. And Catholic higher education would provide future lay leaders for both church and society and provide for an American-trained clergy to serve Catholic parishes. From 1861-1866, as president of St. Mary of the Lake University in Chicago, McMullen had worked to make that institution a means to achieve those goals. But when it was abruptly closed in 1866, his hopes for his vision were dashed. Now, as bishop of Davenport, he had the authority and the opportunity to begin again to realize his vision.

John McMullen was born on January 8, 1832, in Ballynahinch, County Down, Ireland, the sixth of twelve children of James and Alice McMullen. The next year the McMullen family left Ireland and moved first to Megantic County in southern Quebec, Canada, and then, after three years to Prescott, Ontario, on the banks on the St. Lawrence River. But a fire soon destroyed their house, so James McMullen sold the land, and in early 1837, moved his family to Ogdensburg, New York. Here young John McMullen began to attend the local public school and quickly developed a love of learning; he even refused to go out to recess, preferring to spend the time reading. John attended public school only because there was no Catholic parish or school in the community. To remedy this situation, neighbors sent James McMullen to New York City to ask Bishop John Hughes for a priest to serve the growing Catholic community at Ogdensburg.

In 1843, the McMullen family moved once again, this time to Joliet, Illinois. Here they became members of St. Patrick Parish and on Christmas Day 1843, John McMullen made his first communion.[2] Within a year, however, they moved to Chicago, where James became a hotel keeper.[3] Once in Chicago, John became an altar boy at St. Mary's Cathedral and it was there that he first met the new bishop of Chicago, William Quarter.[4]

Bishop Quarter arrived in Chicago in May of 1844 and immediately began to recruit candidates for the priesthood to come to Chicago. When he became bishop, there were twenty-four priests in Illinois, but when the new Diocese of Chicago was created, most of those men returned to their own dioceses in Indiana and Missouri. Within a short time, Bishop Quarter and his brother, the Reverend Walter Quarter who came with him from New York, were the only two priests in the city of Chicago.[5]

Although an immigrant himself, Quarter realized that American Catholics would be best served by American priests trained in the United States. On June 3 he opened St. Mary's College in his own house where he taught his first six recruits and ordained them as quickly as possible. This "school" became the "germ" of St. Mary of the Lake College, which Quarter formally organized that same year.[6]

The first Catholic college in the United States was Georgetown in Washington, D.C., founded in 1789 by Bishop John Carroll. Carroll hoped that Georgetown would "unite the means of communicating Science with an effectual provision for guarding and preserving the Morals of Youth."[7] Although Georgetown was open for all students, Carroll hoped that it would be a "nursery for the seminary."[8]

There were sixteen Catholic colleges for men when the bishops of the United States met at their Second Provincial Council in 1833. There they declared that Catholic education for the "rising generation" was a "subject of first importance." Catholic colleges would give them the "best opportunities of literature and science, united to strict protection of their morals and the best safeguards of their faith."[9] Seven years later the bishops once again addressed the question of education. They wrote and urged Catholics that for the "sake of your children, your country and your religion," help the bishops "provide for the literary, moral and religious education of one sex as well as the other."[10] Moreover, at the 1833 Provincial Council, the bishops reinforced a directive of the sixteenth-century Council of Trent which called for a seminary under the direction of the bishop in every diocese.[11]

Two trends that began in the 1830s and 1840s increased the need for Catholic education to safeguard the faith of the rising generation. The first was a program of education reforms that encouraged the formation of a public school system. Since many of those education reformers came from a Protestant tradition, schools frequently used the King James Bible as a principal text. Not surprisingly, Catholics viewed this public education system as a threat to the faith of their children and so they formed their own schools.

The second trend was the flood of immigrants, many of whom were Catholic, that began to enter the United States in the mid-1840s. The

A Great and Lasting Beginning

church would have to expand rapidly to take care of the religious needs of these new Americans. Moreover, the response by non-Catholic Americans to these immigrants was a virulent nativism that in its extreme forms led to scurrilous literature, and church and convent burnings.

Those two trends made the preparation of American priests even more urgent. The rising generation of Catholics needed to be ready to take their place in a more hostile society; priests would show them the way. Those two trends also tended to isolate Catholic higher education from the remainder of higher education in the United States. Charged with defending the Catholic faith, educating priests, and committing its resources to care for immigrants, American Catholic higher education became more polemical than intellectual. One critic of those years noted that "seminary intellectual life was anything but exciting. Frequently, the besetting sin was not anti-intellectualism, but non-intellectualism, not a downright hostility toward mental improvement, but a vague apathy and indifference."[12] Once the nativist attacks of the 1840s and 1850s subsided, Catholic education maintained what the historian the Reverend Monsignor John Tracy Ellis called a "self-imposed ghetto mentality." The long-term consequence to Catholic higher education was what historian Professor Richard Hofstadter called "its cultural impoverishment, its non-intellectualism."[13]

Those trends were even more obvious in seminary education. When the Council of Trent called for a seminary in every diocese, the purpose, in part, was to take seminary education away from the large universities of the day and place it directly under the supervision of the local bishop. Those episcopal seminaries were to provide pastoral education to aspiring priests, and while "literary education seems to have been presupposed," it was "not demanded." In those seminaries, the young men would be isolated from the temptations that were present in the more open atmosphere of the universities.[14]

This model of a separate seminary was introduced in the United States when Bishop John Carroll invited priests of the Society of St. Sulpice to begin St. Mary's College in Baltimore.[15] For the next forty years, St. Mary's Seminary was the only seminary for the exclusive training of priests in the United States. One bishop wrote that he preferred that his students go to an exclusive seminary where they would be "free of the distractions so characteristic of the mixed college-seminary."[16] This attitude would remain an important influence in American seminary education.

St. Mary of the Lake was the thirtieth Catholic college for men in the United States, although six of the twenty-nine colleges that preceded it had already closed.[17] Quarter said that it was a "small college" begun in a "very humble way," but he hoped to find the means to have it "carry . . . on more extensively" to educate Catholic men for whatever career path they chose, including the priesthood. Quarter also hoped that the school would be much more than a small college and seminary. He had a "far-eyed vision" that Chicago could become the center of Catholicism in the growing midwestern states and that his school would play an important role in that vision.[18]

Quarter traveled throughout Illinois and as far as New York to raise funds for a building to accommodate what he hoped would be a growing student body. His persistence paid off and classes began in the new build-

ing on July 4, 1846.[19] Still the school continued to struggle for funds, so that in December, Quarter wrote a pastoral letter to the people of the diocese. He painted a stark picture of what the consequences would be to their families if there were not enough priests to serve them: no religious instruction for their children, no one to administer the sacraments, the poor would be neglected, and the faith would not be handed down. To prevent that he urged each Catholic family to contribute one dollar a year to the school. In a separate letter to the priests, he asked them to form devotional societies among the people to encourage vocations to the priesthood.[20]

Fourteen-year-old John McMullen was serving Mass in December 1846 when he heard Bishop Quarter's pastoral letter read from the pulpit. From his family's experience in New York, he knew the importance of a priest and parish for the Catholic immigrant. He said it was at that moment that he determined to become a priest, so he entered St. Mary of the Lake and began his studies for the priesthood.[21]

McMullen excelled in school and he soon became a tutor for the younger students. He was a study hall monitor, taught religion classes to the elementary students in the parish school, and continued to serve Mass in the parish church. During these years, McMullen began what would be a life-long commitment to publishing when he and another student began the campus newspaper, the *St. Mary's Weekly Collegiate*.[22]

With the founding of St. Mary of the Lake, Bishop Quarter seemed to be on his way to realizing his far-eyed vision, when in April 1848, he suddenly died. Even in death, however, Quarter continued to serve the needs of his fledgling university when he left his estate to the school.[23] Bishop Quarter and his ideas about education had a lasting impact on the young John McMullen. Thirty-four years later, when Bishop John McMullen opened his own school that he hoped would play an important role in the life of Catholics of his state and the Midwest, he never forgot Bishop Quarter's far-eyed vision.[24]

In the meantime, McMullen continued his education at St. Mary of the Lake. He graduated in 1852 and was ready to begin the study of theology that fall, but was forced to suspend his studies because of illness. He was not idle, however, and he used the time to regularly write articles for Catholic newspapers. He published a few articles in the *Truth Teller*, a New York newspaper, but most of his writing was for the *Western Tablet*, a diocesan newspaper founded by Quarter's successor, the Most Reverend James Van de Velde.[25] Some of these articles reported on events around the diocese or on national issues such as anti-Catholicism, the church and the state, attempts to control the sale of alcohol, and two articles about the public schools as exponents of Protestantism and the use of taxes paid by Catholics to support the public schools.

In the fall of 1853, McMullen expected to return to St. Mary of the Lake, but instead Van de Velde told him he would be going to study at the Urban College of the Propaganda in Rome.[26] The Urban College had been founded by Pope Urban VIII in 1627 to train priests to serve in missionary lands like the United States in the nineteenth century.[27] So John McMullen, and his friend and eventual biographer James McGovern, left Chicago in

August. After the Atlantic crossing and a long journey across Europe, the two Chicago students arrived in Rome on October 15, 1853, and began their studies two days later.[28]

The Rome in which McMullen and McGovern arrived was an extraordinary place. The Most Reverend John Lancaster Spalding, the bishop of Peoria, wrote that during those years, "the Pope was also king, Rome was still the city of the soul, and religion there was clothed in power, in majesty, in splendor and beauty, such as elsewhere it has never worn." Spalding continued that "to live in such environment, to kneel at the tombs of saints, to dwell amid the ruins of the mightiest works of man, to look on the face of pure religion illumined by whatever of most divine human genius has wrought, is to have all that is noblest in one's being, stirred and thrilled; and they who return from this fountainhead of what on earth is greatest and most holy, unregenerate and unraised, must surely be hopelessly common or altogether frivolous."[29] McMullen was taken with this power of the Roman church. After witnessing the Holy Week ceremonies, he wrote that he "indulged in a secret inexpressible joy" as he realized that "the true religion must yet reign triumphant in the new world."[30]

The next year Chicago's new bishop, the Most Reverend Anthony O'Regan, came to Rome and met with his students. O'Regan told McMullen to study church history, which he said was the "indispensable key" to the rest of his studies. He urged McMullen to visit the Christian antiquities around Rome which would give him "a broader and clearer light to the history of the Church and her doctrines." McMullen took his bishop's advice and began to visit religious and historical sites. He found in the Christian antiquities "a fund of theological lore in the original expressions of the early Christians." McMullen used his research to write a major work that was reportedly a "summary of the rites and institutions of the Church." He also began to build his own theological library which McGovern said was McMullen's "great treasure, his only earthly possession."[31]

During McMullen's years in Rome, he grew to understand the universality of the church. At the Urban College, he studied with men from all over the world. Once he attended a series of lectures given at the Academy of Languages where he heard presentations in forty-four different languages.[32] Moreover, he learned to appreciate the long history of Rome. As someone from a frontier community that was receiving hundreds of immigrants each month, and where its oldest residents could remember when it was a small village, the antiquity and continuity of Rome was a profound lesson.

McMullen continued to send articles to Catholic newspapers in the United States.[33] He also found a new outlet for his writings when Thomas Darcy McGee, the publisher of the *American Celt*, a newspaper which was directed to Irish and Irish-American audiences, asked McMullen to write letters from Rome. McGee asked McMullen for "fortnightly" letters and emphasized that "everything that happens in Rome is of interest to us."[34] McGee claimed to have a circulation of 10,000 subscribers in North America, so McMullen was now writing for a much wider audience than in the past.[35]

In the February 11, 1854, edition of the paper, McGee told his readers to expect a "series of letters" from Rome that would be of "additional interest" to the readers. McMullen wrote seven letters between February and July which were published as "Our Roman Correspondence," and talked about a wide variety of subjects. He wrote about the renovation of Roman churches, as well as excavations around Rome and the discovery of Roman antiquities. He told his readers about the celebration of Lent and Holy Week in Rome, and the celebration of St. Patrick's Day at the Irish College. He cultivated an interest in Roman art and expressed a concern that so much of it was being sold and taken out of the country. He described the beatification and canonization of saints and talked about life in his college. He wrote about the political climate of Rome and the presence in the city of the French army on its way to the Crimean War, as well as the failure of the Rothschild family to repay a loan.

On June 20, 1858, following five years of study, John McMullen was ordained a priest.[36] Walking back to his rooms at the college following the ordination ceremony, he said, "I thought I should feel like quite another person after ordination, but I am still only John McMullen."[37] McMullen and the other newly ordained priests then observed the custom of the Urban College and celebrated Mass for the community, each in his own "peculiar rite." Over the next few days each student changed "his college habit . . . for the secular dress of the country for which he [was] destined" and departed "to struggle in the great cause in which each [was] enlisted."[38]

McMullen's "struggle" in the cause would have to wait, however, because Bishop O'Regan asked him to remain in Rome to take the examinations for the Doctor of Divinity Degree. He passed the examinations in July with the highest praise; one examiner called him a "great theologian."[39] Now, finally, the Reverend Dr. McMullen could return to Chicago. When he arrived home in October, a new bishop for Chicago, James Duggan, was about to be installed.

McMullen's first assignment was as an assistant pastor at his old parish, St. Mary's. He was delighted to offer Mass on the altar where he had first served as an altar boy, and to preach from the same pulpit used by his mentor, Bishop Quarter. After a few months at St. Mary's, he was moved to St. Louis Parish in Chicago.[40] He plunged into the work of being a parish priest. He celebrated the sacraments and preached regularly. In addition to his sermons, he also delivered a series of lectures about the church.[41] He visited the sick and took care of the poor, often out of his own pocket. Later, when his friends presented him with two new suits, he immediately gave one away to a priest who had none.[42]

Concern for the plight of those with social needs continued throughout his priesthood. McMullen visited the local prisons to take books and newspapers to the inmates. One prison, the City Bridewell, housed prostitutes, many of whom were Irish and Catholic.[43] Concerned about the fate of these women once they left Bridewell, McMullen borrowed money from his brother James, and used it to start a shelter called the House of the Good Shepherd.[44] McMullen hoped it would be a place for women to return to a more productive life, as well as a place of refuge for women in "danger of entering upon such a career."[45] He also wanted to build a Catholic reform school for boys, but that effort was met with strong opposition by proponents of the reform school already being run by the city of Chicago.

McMullen's efforts were not without critics. In August 1859, the building that was under construction for the House of the Good Shepherd

A Great and Lasting Beginning

burned in a fire that McMullen suspected was arson. He redoubled his fund-raising efforts in Chicago and throughout Illinois, and began to build again.[46] Other critics of his efforts said that the church should just build churches and teach catechism. McMullen said that while, for Catholics, those were "the greatest works of our day," institutions such as "Colleges, Orphan Asylums, Reform Schools," benefitted the whole community, not just Catholics.[47] In 1881, just before he left Chicago for Davenport, McMullen opened the St. Vincent Infant Asylum for pregnant, unmarried women, their children, and foundlings.[48]

In early 1861, McMullen was assigned as rector of Holy Name Cathedral. At the same time he also served mission parishes in Arlington Heights, DeKalb, and the nearby towns of Sycamore and Lodi (now Maple Park), in each of which he built a church.[49] Later in the spring of 1861, the appointment as the president of St. Mary of the Lake University was added to his other duties.[50] It seemed as if his whole life had been a preparation for this assignment, "Here is the place of my work," he said. His delight in being back at his old college was evident when he declared, "If Saint Mary of the Lake is worth anything, she shall have all I can bestow upon her."[51]

The university had fallen on hard times since McMullen had graduated nine years before. In 1856, Bishop O'Regan had asked members of the Congregation of the Holy Cross to operate the school. The agreement between the bishop and the Holy Cross fathers required them to invest money in repairs to the two buildings that comprised the school. But the Panic of 1857 and the depression that followed had made it difficult to find the resources to maintain the school. So at the end of the school year in 1861, the Holy Cross fathers left and McMullen became president.[52]

One historian wrote that with McMullen's appointment, "a second spring appeared to dawn on the sorely tried institution."[53] When McMullen took over the school in the summer of 1861, only thirty-seven of 156 students were classified as collegiate; it was essentially an advanced high school with courses in the classics and natural sciences.[54] The faculty consisted of four laymen and McMullen, who taught metaphysics and history, in addition to his duties as president.[55] A few months later, McMullen reported to his friend, James McGovern, that he was beginning to make improvements so it could open with "decency."[56]

One who knew McMullen described him as of "medium stature, stout, but with no loose flesh, he looks a sturdy, self-reliant, dignified, thoughtful and modest man." He had "gray, keen eyes" and a "thin mouth" with "firmly set" lips that "no sunshine [would] melt, no storm make tremble." His manner could be brusque but never with the "sick, the miserable and the poor."

He talked "as one having something very clearly in his mind to say and very clearly will he say it. He is a man without a superfluity of any sort."[57] A long-time friend commented on his "singleness of purpose" and an "energy which was bounded only by the impossible."[58] McMullen's friend, Peoria Bishop John Lancaster Spalding, recognized his "perfect sincerity, his complete honesty." Spalding said, "As you stood before him the thought arose, here is a man, a very piece of nature, fixed and firm-set as though infinite forces working through endless time had converged to stamp and mark him as with God's own hand."[59] McMullen would need to call upon all of those

characteristics as he faced the challenges of building St. Mary of the Lake into the kind of university Bishop Quarter had dreamed of and McMullen hoped to build.

When McMullen took charge of St. Mary of the Lake, most Catholic colleges were little more than high schools. One critic doubted whether any Catholic college existed whose "sole object . . . was to impart a collegiate education, in its strictest sense." There was a need for a "numerous and well-educated clergy" and a "large class of educated seculars [and] for this we need colleges devoted primarily to secular studies, to the rearing and training of a generation of scholars that can more than match, in all the branches of a liberal education, the best scholars educated in the country."[60]

To create that kind of college, the curriculum expanded into separate ecclesiastical, classical, commercial, and scientific courses, and professional curricula such as medicine and law were added.[61] These reforms would enable Catholic universities to "send out living men . . . inspired with faith and genius, who will take the command of their age . . . inform it with their own love of truth, and raise it to the level of their own high and noble aspirations."[62]

That kind of university became McMullen's goal. He issued a prospectus which noted the necessity for knowledge to meet the challenges of the "vast . . . complicated commercial transactions" demanded by a growing city like Chicago. He said that St. Mary of the Lake would provide a thorough education to prepare its graduates to meet those challenges. Its faculty would "leave nothing undone to lay a basis of religious, mental, and physical education which will render the pursuits of the sciences and the arts both easy and pleasant" in the years after graduation.[63]

When McMullen became president, the university was housed in two inadequate buildings. Now he began to raise funds to erect a new, larger building for the school. He also contributed all of his own financial assets to the project. The cornerstone was laid in July 1863, and the first wing of the new building was put into use the following January.[64]

McMullen began to enlarge the faculty and the curriculum. He secured several more faculty members with doctorates who could teach courses in business and the sciences. He established a medical school where St. Mary of the Lake students would be taught by the faculty of Rush Medical School. And he began a law school in a lecture hall close to the court house.[65]

Next he turned his attention to the seminary, which had been Bishop Quarter's first school and the "germ" of the university. By the time McMullen became president, financial pressures and the difficulty of finding a faculty had forced many American bishops to close their diocesan seminaries.[66] Earlier the American bishops had hoped to form a national seminary, but that plan had failed.[67] Following this, some bishops relied on newly formed regional seminaries, many of which were put in rural settings that the bishops believed would serve as "buffers to the lay culture beyond the seminary." Other American bishops began to send their seminarians to the new American College in Rome, or the American College in Louvain, Belgium. This was controversial, however, as some bishops did not want a Roman-trained clergy because, with the high degree of anti-Catholic nativism in the 1850s, they were afraid of the reaction these priests would receive upon their return to the United States.[68] Still others sent their men to the scholasticates of various religious orders in the United States.[69]

McMullen rejected these alternative models and he also rejected the idea that seminarians should be isolated from lay students and the rest of society. He believed that seminarians should be educated in their own diocese, alongside non-seminary students. He wrote that being "educated with the youth of his own country," and coming into "contact with the prevalent opinions and modes of thinking of the people," was the best preparation for a seminarian.[70]

Like Catholic colleges, American seminaries were also perceived to be of inferior quality and that was unacceptable to McMullen, so he made plans to add to the seminary curriculum. In 1863, armed with his Doctor of Divinity Degree, his friend, the Reverend James McGovern, returned from Rome and was placed in charge of the seminary.[71] With the addition of a third priest with a doctorate, McMullen hoped to have St. Mary of the Lake declared a pontifical university so it could grant degrees in theology, but the authorities in Rome denied his request.[72]

McMullen wanted his students to be exposed to the issues of their own time, as well as the classics. Previously, he had encouraged the activities of the university discussion club, the Lyceum.[73] Now in January 1865, he began to publish the *Monthly*, a journal filled with articles of "general interest in Literature, Science and Art as concern Catholics throughout the country."[74] Each issue contained essays on various current topics, poetry, short news items about Catholicism and religion in general, and fiction that was serialized over several issues. McMullen wrote a major essay for nearly every issue on such diverse topics as slavery, the Missouri Compromise, the Fenian Society, the Catholic Church and the Civil War, a recent papal encyclical on church and state, and the Christian missions. The journal was well-received, and had enough subscribers to meet its expenses. But the pressures of running the university, and a growing dispute with Bishop Duggan led McMullen to suspend publication of the *Monthly* after only twelve issues.[75]

Another important part of the intellectual climate of the university came through McMullen's long-standing friendship with Eliza Allen Starr, a poet and artist who lived near the university and regularly lectured on art.[76] McMullen had developed an interest in art during his years in Rome. Now, Starr's home became a salon where McMullen, McGovern, and other priests from the university would come to discuss art, as well as a wide variety of other subjects. McMullen respected and encouraged Starr's publishing career and attended her lectures whenever he could. According to Starr, McMullen, and a "few others like [him], are the leaven of literature in this country."[77] Starr and McMullen remained friends until his death.

By 1866, McMullen would need all of his friends to support him in increasingly difficult times. Although the number of students at the university continued to grow, there were still financial problems. The diocese had been carrying a debt of $6,000 on the university. In January of 1866, Duggan told McMullen that he would no longer do so and that the school would be closed. A tearful McMullen informed the faculty of the bishop's

decision, and a few days later, Duggan closed the university.[78] Two years later Duggan would just as suddenly close the seminary, marking an "inglorious end" to the "only viable effort during the [nineteenth century] to make theological training for the diocesan clergy an integral part of university education."[79]

It is difficult to find a precise reason why Duggan abruptly closed the university. The $6,000 debt does not seem to be a great amount of money and it had been carried for several years. There may have been growing tension between the bishop and the priests at St. Mary of the Lake, in part because of the independence of the university. Perhaps "some unrevealed trouble between Duggan and McMullen" had led to the closure.[80] All of those reasons may have been exacerbated by the mental illness that would eventually hospitalize Duggan.

The abrupt closing of St. Mary of the Lake was a blow to McMullen. Starr said it was not a "personal disappointment," but that McMullen felt the closing was a "loss to religion and education."[81] McGovern, however, was probably closer to the mark when he noted McMullen's tears, and said that for the "first time" in McMullen's life, he "was disappointed in his hopes."[82]

McMullen had made Bishop Quarter's far-eyed vision of a Catholic university in Chicago his own. It would educate men for service as priests, prepare many more Catholic men to take their places in society, and would serve as a place where ideas could be debated. McMullen's "vision of the magnificence of the field which Chicago offered" and his own desire to carry out Quarter's far-eyed vision, would have to wait.[83]

In the next few years, McMullen tried to put aside his disappointment about the university. He continued to teach at the seminary until it was closed in 1868, and he also served in a number of parishes in Chicago. His first post-university assignment was as pastor of St. Paul's Parish in Chicago.[84] The church was located in the "most unpromising" part of the city and the appointment was widely viewed as Duggan's way of "degrading the doctor."[85]

Those were also years of more conflict with Duggan. The bishop's mental health continued to decline and there were questions about his ability to continue to serve. In the hopes of regaining his health, Duggan went to Europe for a rest. While he was away, McMullen and three other priests pressed Rome for Duggan's removal. When Duggan returned from Europe and discovered their actions, he suspended the four priests. McMullen went to Rome himself to present the evidence directly to the appropriate officials. While he was there, Duggan had a complete breakdown and was taken to a mental institution in St. Louis, where he remained until his death in 1899.

When McMullen returned from Rome in July 1869, he was sent to St. Rose of Lima Parish in Wilmington, south of Joliet. While he was there he began a new parish in the nearby coal mining community of Braidwood. He continued to write articles about church history and polity, and he traveled around northern Illinois and as far west as Rock Island to deliver lectures. Believing that priests should continue their intellectual pursuits, McMullen lamented that too often priests were "engrossed in the temporal progress" of their ministry and that, therefore, there was a "great deal of intellectual ability lying torpid which ought to be brought out."[86]

In 1870, Duggan's successor, the Most Reverend Thomas Foley, vindicated McMullen by appointing him as the rector of Holy Name Cathedral and later, vicar general of the diocese.[87] Any joy he felt in returning, however, was dashed in October 1871, when Holy Name Cathedral, the buildings that had housed the university, his earlier parishes, Eliza Starr's home, and the Good Shepherd home were among the thousands of buildings lost in the Chicago fire. Gone were all of McMullen's personal belongings, including the library he had begun to build when he was a student in Rome and the manuscript he had written in Rome about the early church.

The next few years saw McMullen attend to the needs of his parishioners who had lost their homes and businesses in the fire. He lived and ministered in the "Shanty Cathedral," a temporary wooden structure erected soon after the fire, while he oversaw the plans to build a new Holy Name Cathedral.[88] To ensure that the educational needs of the parish were met, he built a new grade school.

With the death of Bishop Foley in 1879, Chicagoans began to wonder who their next bishop would be. Following the removal of Bishop Duggan, McMullen had been frequently named as a likely successor, and he was again mentioned as the next bishop. But he was not destined to remain in Chicago. Instead, on May 9, 1881, it was announced that there would be a new Diocese of Davenport, Iowa, and John McMullen would be its first bishop.[89]

Over the next few weeks, McMullen busied himself with winding up his affairs in Chicago and preparing to become the bishop of Davenport. Soon the time came for McMullen to leave the Chicago in which he had grown up, been educated, and served as a priest for twenty-three years. McMullen endured a round of farewell celebrations, the most poignant of which was from his parishioners at Holy Name, held in the new school building McMullen had built. The man chosen to speak on behalf of the parish told him it was appropriate to have the event in the school, which would "stand as an enduring monument to [McMullen's] untiring energy, unyielding perseverance, and determined Christian spirit." As a parting gift, the priests of Chicago gave him a purse of $4,000 in gold. McMullen set this money aside as a foundation for the college he hoped to begin in his new diocese.[90]

The *Chicago Times* published a profile of McMullen that used an image that would turn out to be more apt for the founder of St. Ambrose University than the author could have known. He told of the ballad of the "Oak and the Ivy," where an ivy vine grew around the gnarled trunk of a huge oak tree. A storm tore the leaves of the ivy to shreds, but within a few days the plant began to grow new leaves because the vine had been protected by the trunk of the oak tree. He said that externally, McMullen was the oak, sometimes "knotted and gnarled" but that within was a "gentle and noble" spirit, "quick in sympathy, lofty in aim, humble in feeling, robust, steadfast, and sincerely Christian."[91]

McMullen arrived in Davenport on July 30 and was greeted with similarly effusive speeches and gifts. For the time being, he moved into the rectory of St. Marguerite's Parish, which he had named his cathedral, until a permanent residence could be found.[92] The following Sunday he presided at his first pontifical Mass in his cathedral. Preaching about the unjust steward from the gospel, McMullen may have been speaking to himself. He reminded the people that they would all be held accountable for their stewardship of the goods they had been given. McMullen enjoyed the day, in spite of the pomp of the ceremonies, but he took special delight in the Gregorian Chant that the church choir sang.[93]

In his first weeks in Davenport, he visited the churches and institutions of the city. One of his first visits came at the end of August when he laid the cornerstone of a new church for St. Joseph's Parish. He spoke briefly and told the people that this was the "day of Church building," a time for the parish to "renew the faith cherished in the schools and exhibited in the generosity of Christian charity."[94] McMullen had written that all Catholic parents should "provide a sound and adequate Catholic education" which would prepare their children "for intellectual contact with their fellow-men in the sphere of life they may be called to occupy."[95]

He reinforced this message in early September when he sent a pastoral letter to the priests of the diocese and told them that he had already accepted "several" students to study for the priesthood and that he expected to accept more soon. He urged the priests to ask the people to contribute to the support of these seminarians.[96]

On September 20, the bishop began a six-week trip through his diocese which included the four lower tiers of Iowa counties and stretched from the Mississippi River to the Missouri River. He met his priests and people and administered the Sacrament of Confirmation to nearly 2,900 of them.[97] In every parish he visited, he asked the pastor how the parish school was doing. If there was a school, he met with the students and praised the efforts of the people to maintain it.[98] If the pastor replied that he had no school, McMullen would suggest that he start one. If he sensed some reluctance, the bishop would say, "Well, try, there is no harm in trying."

Throughout his travels, he also expressed a concern about the number of boys not continuing beyond grade school and he talked about starting a "boys school for them." His efforts to encourage education were already being noticed. When he arrived in Council Bluffs at the end of October, the mayor welcomed him and commented on McMullen's "zeal and efficiency in the course of Catholic education."[99]

In subsequent trips around the diocese, his message remained the same: try to start a school. Then in the spring of 1882 he took his own advice and had his conversation with Father Cosgrove about where to locate his school. Now he could take Bishop Quarter's far-eyed vision, and his own dashed hopes that St. Mary of the Lake would be a great Catholic university for the Midwest, and make them a reality in his own diocese.

McMullen's school began as simply as Quarter's had thirty-six years before as a combination of preparatory school, college, and seminary. McMullen had a great vision for the university: St. Ambrose was to be a place where ideas were important and the life of the mind was valued; a place where the classics, the arts, the humanities, and commerce informed each other; a place where seminarians and lay students would study side by side; a place from which its graduates were challenged to resist torpidity and continue to learn throughout their lives; and finally, a place where its graduates were encouraged to engage their world as moral, faith-filled people. Through his teaching, lectures, articles, interest in the arts, and ministry,

Bishop McMullen embodied that vision. He had wished those ideals to be the University of St. Mary of the Lake, but when that failed, those hopes transferred and became St. Ambrose University.

Although McMullen lived just long enough to see his far-eyed vision begin, he knew that he had begun something important. In December 1881, when he had been in Davenport for only five months, McMullen wrote Eliza Allen Starr to tell her about his long autumn of visits throughout his diocese. "This is a great country," he wrote, "and when I am gone, will be a great Catholic country, for a great and lasting beginning is already here."[100] Within a few weeks of that letter, Bishop McMullen and Father Cosgrove would have their conversation, and St. Ambrose University would become part of McMullen's "great and lasting" contribution to the Diocese of Davenport and Catholicism in the Midwest.

A Great and Lasting Beginning

"St. Ambrose," by Leslie Bell.

T he rising generation of American Catholics are a hardy, stalwart, labor-loving race, with as much talent and ingenuity as were ever possessed by the youth of any country. The young Irish American is found everywhere. . . . They are found in every grade, in every station, putting forth an energy, and manifesting a spirit of enterprise, not easily rivaled, and certainly not surpassed. Their ability and learning are felt in the halls of legislation, adorn the forum, are displayed in the pulpit and the press, and shine brilliantly in the various posts of danger and responsibility in our armies. They are the proprietors of the soil in the west, and are met in the busy marts of commerce in the east. They are, in a word, numerous amongst those who deserve to be called the pride and hope of our country, numerous among her best citizens and bravest defenders.

– Father John McMullen, c. 1865

❧ Chapter One ❧

O n September 4, 1882, a day with a clear sky and the temperature in the high 60 degrees, thirty-three boys walked into two classrooms of St. Marguerite's Cathedral grade school at Eleventh and Iowa Streets in Davenport, Iowa. They were the first students, on the first day, of St. Ambrose Seminary. There was no public notice that something lasting had begun that day. There had been no advertisement in the newspaper announcing the opening of a new school for boys; apparently the news had spread from the pulpits of local Catholic parishes. And there was no news story in the days following saying that school had begun. The first mention of the school came in October when Bishop John McMullen, who had been away, was interviewed by the local newspaper.

The thirty-three boys who walked in that morning were just that, boys. They ranged in age from twelve to twenty-three but most were between thirteen and sixteen. Most lived in the Cork Hill neighborhood of the school, so called because of the large number of Irish immigrants in the area. One boy lived on West Sixth Street, another lived on Mitchell Street (now Fillmore), and still another lived out on North Gaines, two were from DeWitt, one was from Joslin Station, Rock Island County. All thirty-three of them had one thing in common: they were the sons of immigrants.[1]

The thirty-three students were born in the United States, almost all of them in Iowa. At least one of the parents of Charles Bairley, Herman Bartemeyer, William H. Harrison, Francis J. Huot, Mattias Koch, Bernard Mackin, Edward McCormick, Henry Motie, brothers Edward and Peter O'Shaughnessey, and Edward Woeber, was born in the United States, two in Iowa, the rest in New York, Pennsylvania, Ohio, Indiana, or Missouri. Only three of the students, Ed McSteen, and the brothers Edmund and Scott Stackhouse, had both parents born in the United States. Forty-five of the parents were foreign-born. Both parents of Cornelius Buckley, Edward Butler, John Doyle, Frank Lew, John Malone, Andrew McGee, the brothers Edward and Maurice McNamara, Edward Miniter, Thomas O'Brien, George O'Dea, Thomas O'Donnell, John Reid, James Renihan, and John Ryan were from somewhere in Ireland: Cork, Kilkenny, Wicklow, Wexford, Tipperary, Louth, Longford, Offaly, Clare, Meath, Galway, Kerry, Dublin, Waterford, Limerick, or Connaught. Eight of the parents were from some-

where in present-day Germany: Baden, Westphalia, Wurtenberg, Hanover, Bavaria, Hesse Cassel, or Prussia. Joseph Jacobs' father was born in Bohemia; John Otten's parents were born in Hanover; John Quinn's father was born in Ireland, his mother in Canada; John Ruhl's father was born in Hesse Cassel, his mother in Prussia; Edward Woeber's father was born in Bavaria; and Francis Huot's mother was born in France. All of the immigrant parents had arrived in the United States by the Civil War.

Immigrants of this generation left Europe for a variety of reasons, economic opportunity being the most common. But the Germany and Ireland of the 1840s and 1850s were also awash with social and political conflicts. In Ireland, groups like Young Ireland and the Fenians were fighting for independence from England. In Germany, various groups, including the "48ers," were fighting for liberal reform. The turmoil of these conflicts and the possibility of being drafted into someone's army drove immigrants to leave their homelands. So for many reasons immigrants came to Davenport. In 1885, in the city of Davenport with a population of 23,830, 25.7 percent of the population had been born in Germany and 4.6 percent had been born in Ireland.

Once in the United States, these immigrants sought to accommodate themselves to the burgeoning capitalism of Antebellum America and the Gilded Age. Many of the Davenport immigrants were craft workers: carpenters, bricklayers, stonemasons, plasterers, or excavators who provided well for their families and were proud of their position in the community. Considered by some to be the "aristocracy of labor," they sometimes called themselves middle class to distinguish themselves from less successful workers. Perhaps that is why the craft workers among the fathers identified themselves to census takers and in city directories as "contractors." Other immigrants chose entrepreneurship as the way to the middle class. They opened small stores, or sold real estate, or operated a manufacturing firm, or began a wholesale operation.

The immigrant fathers of the thirty-three new St. Ambrose students exemplified that. Five were farmers. Many of the town dwellers were clearly working class. There were expressmen, teamsters, laborers, a night watchman, and many were construction craftsmen. Several worked for the Rock

A Great and Lasting Beginning

Island Railroad, one was a claims agent, another worked in the shops, and two were engineers.

Other immigrant fathers had occupations that put them in the rising middle class of the era. Three were grocers and one of these later became a banker and a large land owner. Another had a contract with the Union Pacific to build trestles and bridges and he used the money he made to invest in Davenport real estate. Still another was the Davenport city clerk and later sold insurance. Others worked for a wholesale hardware company. There were two grain brokers and the last was a manufacturer.

The fathers bequeathed to their sons a legacy of work and striving. They also bequeathed to them a legacy of commitment to community, religious, social, and political groups. Many were active in their churches as trustees or ushers or were active in the Gentlemen's Sodality, a group that gathered for fellowship and prayer. One who had seen service in the Civil War was a member of the Grand Army of the Republic, the Civil War veterans organization. A number were members and leaders of Division 1 of the Ancient Order of Hibernians. There was a Davenport city street commissioner and a rural school district director. A number of the fathers were members of the Roman Catholic Mutual Protection Society, an insurance and burial society. Others were members of the Irish National League, which advocated independence for Ireland.

Less plentiful information is available about the immigrant mothers, identified by the census only as "housewives." They are not listed in city directories. Their obituaries often identify them by their husband's name and typically do not include as much information as their husbands' obituaries do. As housewives they occupied an important niche in the dynamic of the family. Typically they played an important role in sustaining the ethnic traditions of their family. They would likely have been the religious center of the home, teaching their children prayers and seeing to their religious upbringing. For most of the women, the parish and its various committees gave them their principal activity outside their homes. Moreover, it provided them with a network for support that was so important for all immigrants.

Whatever dreams these fathers and mothers had for their St. Ambrose sons, education was a key to realizing those dreams. McMullen expressed some of those hopes when he wrote thirty years earlier, that it was the "paramount" duty of parents to provide a Catholic education that would "respect faith and morals, but which at the same time . . . fit its subject for intellectual contact with their fellow-men in the sphere of life they may be called to occupy."[2] Certainly as immigrant parents they hoped the education their sons received at St. Ambrose would better prepare them to take advantage of the opportunities offered in the United States and become members of the rising middle class.

St. Ambrose Seminary was the 145th Catholic college for men established in the United States since 1789 when Bishop John Carrroll founded Georgetown. But of those schools only seventy-eight were still open the day the first thirty-three boys entered St. Ambrose, and a number of those seventy-eight would close in the next decades. About three-fourths of those colleges were founded by religious orders and the remainder, like St. Ambrose, were established by a diocesan bishop.[3] In those colleges the

diocesan bishop became the "central figure" whose "educational views and administrative attitudes" would determine whether the college would "prosper or wither."[4] At St. Mary of the Lake, McMullen experienced the "administrative attitudes" of a non-supportive bishop, so while he gave full support to his college, McMullen was aware of the challenges he, his successors, and the administrators of the school would face to keep St. Ambrose open.

St. Ambrose began at a time when American educators, religious and secular, were beginning to question the proper curriculum of a college. For most of the early part of the century, college curricula emphasized the basic liberal arts. Catholic colleges "endeavored by means of a religious training, mental discipline, and liberal culture, to produce the complete Christian character."[5] In the years following the Civil War, however, American secular colleges began to develop curricula for studies in medicine, law, and engineering. Although McMullen was determined to be a part of that trend by establishing a law school and medical school at St. Mary of the Lake in the 1860s, most Catholic institutions like St. Ambrose continued to emphasize the "purpose of higher education was mental discipline" that would prepare its graduates to assume any position in life.[6] Other than seminaries, there were only a handful of professional programs in Catholic colleges.

An allied issue was the very term college. Although it began as St. Ambrose Seminary, as early as 1885, the school would often be referred to as St. Ambrose College.[7] For most of the nineteenth century, the term college was loosely applied to any schooling beyond grade school. However, during the later years of the nineteenth century, the secular educational system began to distinguish between three or four years of secondary work at an academy or high school and then another three to four years at a college. The high school would be viewed as a preparation for life, not for college, and would be separated in curriculum and sometimes, space, from the college.

But in the Catholic system there was very little distinction between secondary and college curricula. It was often a seven year course of studies undertaken by twelve- to fourteen-year-olds who were "sufficiently advanced in elementary branches to give hope of their profiting by academic studies."[8] Since the same teaching staff taught at all levels, this provided a "pedagogical continuum" for the students.[9]

Still another challenge to the success of St. Ambrose was to put it on a firm financial footing. The school was founded in good economic times in Davenport. An economic report published in early 1883 indicated that there was prosperity in various sectors of the local economy. Manufacturing was the "best" in the history of Davenport with prices that were "firm and well sustained, collections generally good," and the report listed a number of factories that had added manufacturing capacity.[10] But most of the students were from working-class families who would struggle to pay the tuition of $30 per semester. Additionally, Catholics as a group were not generous contributors to their colleges. In the late nineteenth century, they were significantly outpaced in college giving by Protestants who gave generously to their denominational institutions.[11] These Presbyterians, Methodists, Baptists, and Congregationalists had been in the country longer, were better-established in the middle class, and were better able to give more. Unlike their Catholic neighbors, they were not also supporting a

St. Marguerite's School.

system of grade schools.

With tuition as the only source of income for most Catholic colleges, these schools had to accept anyone who could pay tuition with no regard to academic entrance requirements; they were "compelled to admit 'any lad not absolutely a criminal.'"[12] But just how to meet all the challenges of definition, curriculum, and the financial question were all subjects of national debate and discussion during the first quarter of the twentieth century. Although reforms were initiated by some Catholic colleges, St. Ambrose would be slow to change and at the beginning of the twentieth century, it could be described as "small, in constant financial difficulty, academically inferior, static in educational philosophy, traditional in curriculum and pedagogy, rigid in discipline and student life, clerical in faculty administration, and isolated almost completely from the mainstream of American higher education."[13] It would remain so until after World War I.

At St. Ambrose such debates were in the future, and all the thirty-three students of the new St. Ambrose Seminary understood was that summer was over and school had started. As they entered the building that morning, the boys were greeted by two faculty members, the twenty-four-year-old Reverend Aloysius J. Schulte, the president of the school, and twenty-year-old Joseph Halligan.

Born in 1858 in Fort Madison, Iowa, Schulte had attended seminaries in Milwaukee, Collegeville, Minnesota, and Dubuque, and had been ordained as the first priest of the new Diocese of Davenport the previous December.[14] A colleague described Schulte as "Apt in his studies . . . adding a fine mind to an exquisitely good character, he evinced that rarest of all acquisitions, sagacity and good common sense."[15] A former student said that he was "capable of being gruff at times, but not so as a rule. [He was] a strict disciplinarian, very much down on smoking and chewing. He was one of the grandest men that ever lived."[16]

Bearing an "unlimited capacity for work," in addition to his duties at St. Ambrose, he also served as the assistant pastor of the Cathedral Parish, and celebrated Mass at the Immaculate Conception Academy (ICA), a school for girls run by the Sisters of Charity of the Blessed Virgin Mary (BVM) from Dubuque.[17] Later he would become the pastor of St. Peter's Parish in Buffalo, just down river from Davenport.

Schulte understood McMullen's vision for St. Ambrose. He believed that since human beings were both body and soul, education must join natural science, the knowledge of nature acquired by observations, with spiritual science, the knowledge of God's law imprinted in the heart or revealed by God. Both were an "integral part" of Christian education. Therefore, proper education must include the sanctification of the soul, the development of the intellect, and the promotion of physical welfare. The job of the educator was to "develop, train and cultivate all the faculties, moral, intellectual and physical," which would form students into Christian men and women ready to take their place in the world. According to Schulte, the fact that human beings were made for God was the core principle of education.

A Great and Lasting Beginning

Speaking in 1901, he said, "Religious teaching, impressions, and observances should penetrate all branches of education and instruction, of which they are not merely a part among other parts, but the soul and spirit diffused through the whole system. Religion does not merely run parallel to the course of secular studies, but like a vitalizing sap, should enter into and pervade every fiber of them." To Schulte the teaching of history, art, literature, and science were windows to understand "God's dealing with mankind." Religion (theology) and its "handmaid," philosophy, were the core of this learning and as such they "lay down the fundamental principles of law, government and social order," which were necessary in "active as well as speculative pursuits, law and morals, to guide us in politics, in the liberal professions and in the business of everyday life."[18]

The curriculum Schulte developed tried, as much as possible with only a faculty of two, to put those principles into practice at St. Ambrose. So Schulte taught the classics, but he also taught geology. He had no formal training in science, but he taught himself, found ways to equip a science laboratory, often from his own pocket, and worked to find other science teachers. Along with Francis B. Huot, one of the members of the first class, he built a geology collection of over 2,000 specimens, which was reportedly "one of the finest collections of geological specimens in the west."[19] A later observer said that Schulte had "great plans for the future" of St. Ambrose. His style "back in the eighties, was distinctly of the progressive type; he did not confine the curriculum to the traditional classical training; there were up-to-date courses in modern science as well."[20] He also visited other schools, studied their curricula, and familiarized himself with the latest trends in education.[21] Schulte had a hand in every aspect of the early St. Ambrose. Years later he remembered, "If there were some cockleburs on the campus you might picture me pulling them up. We spent most of the first few years pulling up cockleburs."[22]

The other member of the faculty was Mr. Joseph Halligan. Born in Davenport in 1862, Halligan graduated from St. Marguerite's school and then attended St. Vincent's College in Cape Girardeau, Missouri, where he studied for the priesthood. He left the seminary but continued his studies and received a Bachelor of Arts Degree in 1881.[23] At St. Ambrose Halligan taught commercial courses, including typewriting, stenography, and bookkeeping. He also taught Latin.

Rev. A.J. Schulte (later photograph).

A former student remembered Halligan as a "brilliant man" who was an "excellent teacher, though some complained that he often talked over" the heads of students. And although he may have sometimes been a difficult teacher, he reportedly had a "good disposition . . . [and] was quite lenient with the students."[24] Another person remembered Halligan as "ever the considerate Catholic gentleman."[25] Like Schulte, Halligan understood that St. Ambrose was a place where "every element of secular education is thoroughly imparted and in addition that preeminent element of moral training" is available.[26]

The boys were not greeted on the first day by Bishop McMullen. At the time McMullen and Cosgrove had their conversation in the spring of 1882 about finding a place for a school for boys, the bishop had already contracted cancer. Just before the bishop's long diocesan tour in the fall of 1881, Cosgrove had commented that McMullen's "health seems not to be good."[27] That tour in the fall, and a second tour in the early winter of 1881-1882, had "aggravated the disease that ended his life, for he was never in good health after."[28] Writing a friend in January 1882, McMullen admitted that "I find that I have no longer the vigor of other days. At times I feel that my earthly pilgrimage is coming to a close . . . this winter has been very severe on me. . . pray that I may bear patiently whatever comes in the way of bodily infirmities and accept all with sincere resignation." Three months later McMullen wrote Eliza Allen Starr, "If the weather had been warmer I should be better now, but it is chilly and I am not so well."[29]

McMullen appeared at commencement ceremonies at the Immaculate Conception Academy on June 29, 1882. He was too ill to stand and speak, so he offered his congratulations to the graduates from his chair. He told them he had hoped to invite them all to his house for a picnic, but that would have to wait until another time. According to Michael V. Gannon, the principal speaker that day, he also said he intended to start a school for boys, which may have been the first public announcement about the beginning of St. Ambrose.[30]

By August 1882, his health had declined so much that his doctors prescribed an ocean voyage and a visit to the spas of Europe. McMullen left in mid-August and was in New York City on the day classes began at St. Ambrose. By the time he arrived in New York, however, he realized that an ocean voyage

*Mr. Joseph Halligan
(later photograph).*

would be too much for him, so he stayed in the east and finally returned to Davenport at the end of September.[31]

In his absence, Cosgrove, Schulte, and Halligan opened the school, originally named St. John's College, in honor of the bishop. When McMullen returned, however, he objected, saying that while St. John was a great apostle, he was not an educator. Since this would be an educational institution, McMullen said, "I think we shall call it St. Ambrose," for the fourth-century bishop of Milan and Doctor of the Church.[32]

McMullen likely came to appreciate St. Ambrose during his days as a student in Rome. While there he wrote the manuscript about the rites and institutions of the early church which may well have included a section on the Ambrosian liturgical rite and Ambrose's role as a leader of the early church.

Ambrose was born in Trier in 339, where his father was a Roman governor. Educated in Rome, Ambrose began service as a Roman official in a variety of posts, and in 370, was named governor of Amelia-Liguria, with its capital at Milan.[33] Ambrose became governor in the midst of a religious controversy between the Arians who denied the divinity of Jesus, and Catholics who accepted the Creed of Nicea. In 373, when the See of Milan was open following the death of an Arian bishop, there was a contentious struggle between the Arians and Nicean Catholics for the position. One day the controversy broke out into a public confrontation between the two factions and Governor Ambrose arrived to quell the disturbance. Seeing him there, a child in the crowd shouted, "Ambrose for bishop." Although Ambrose was not a baptized Christian, his skills as a leader and his reputation for honesty made him a popular choice for bishop. At first Ambrose demurred, but when the people insisted, he agreed to accept the office. Within a span of eight days, Ambrose was baptized, confirmed, ordained a priest, and then ordained a bishop.[34]

As bishop of Milan, Ambrose was responsible for the church in all of northern Italy as far south as Pisa and Ravenna. He celebrated the liturgy and preached daily with an eloquence presaged when, according to legend, a swarm of bees had settled on his face when he was an infant. One biographer commented that even if the legend was not true, nevertheless, bees are a "propitious symbol, suggesting community . . . diligence, selflessness and, of course, sweetness."[35] His preaching brought converts to Christianity, including most notably, Augustine, whom Ambrose baptized. Ambrose rebuked the rich for ignoring the poor with an intensity that was rare in the other western fathers, and he reportedly gave away all his personal wealth when he became bishop. He wrote commentaries on the scriptures, introduced congregational singing to the liturgy, and maintained a wide correspondence. He began to build a series of large basilicas outside the walls of the city in an architectural style that became known as Ambrosian.[36] He defended the divinity of Jesus against the Arians. And in what one historian has called "perhaps his most striking contribution," he challenged the emperor and defined a "distinction between Church and state where one had hardly existed before."[37]

As bishop, teacher, administrator, educator, church builder, musician, scholar, and preacher, Ambrose engaged the world and in the process

St. Ambrose, early 5th century, St. Ambrose Basilica, Milan.

A Great and Lasting Beginning

became "the outstanding figure of his time—respected, consulted, and obeyed, as no bishop of the period" had been.[38] It was this Ambrose that Bishop McMullen saw as a model for the students of his university. And, in important ways, as an educator, a church builder, a preacher, a writer, a commentator on his times, and with a deep concern for the poor, it was also the kind of man McMullen was.

Upon his return to Davenport, McMullen gave a newspaper interview where he described the career of St. Ambrose as a "patron of education" and a "writer, architect and composer." He also discussed his own expansive, far-eyed vision to have St. Ambrose be a university for the entire upper Mississippi Valley, under the patronage of all the dioceses of the region. He stated that within the next year he hoped to find a larger, more centrally located site on which to erect a new building that would, with additions, accommodate hundreds of students.[39]

The name of the school was St. Ambrose Seminary, but the number of students studying for the priesthood would always be a small percentage of the total student body. Only two of the first thirty-three students, Bernard Mackin and James Renihan, would be ordained, but this too fulfilled McMullen's vision. In an earlier essay, "Clerical Seminaries," McMullen advocated the view that it was important that seminary students study alongside students preparing for other careers. He had put that into practice at St. Mary of the Lake, and now he continued that model of a diocesan seminary-university at St. Ambrose, whose mission was to "impart to its students a thorough mental and moral culture, so as to enable them to fill any position in life."[40] Nevertheless, the education of priests remained an important part of that mission.

Many bishops and seminary officials disagreed with McMullen's vision but it also had supporters. A later president of St. Ambrose, the Monsignor Ulrich A. Hauber, commended McMullen's vision. Hauber wrote that it was good when future priests "rubbed shoulders" with lay students and he said that St. Ambrose "may be proud of the fact that it pioneered in this policy of coeducating priests and laymen."[41] Another observer urged that seminarians "come into personal contact with atheism and agnosticism and existentialism and positivism, with technology and science—even with women!" In that way, he said, seminarians could see that "the life of the intellect is not simply theory," and that while ideas can "move the world" they must "first move" the seminarian.[42] Commenting on this suggestion, American Catholic historian John Tracy Ellis observed that at St. Ambrose, this had been the practice "for some years."[43]

There were two courses of study from which the students could choose, or more likely, into which they were assigned by Schulte and Halligan. The first was a five-year Classical curriculum that included Latin, Greek, English, literature, rhetoric, poetry, elocution, history, geography, mathematics, natural philosophy, and Christian doctrine. The other course of study was a two-year Commercial curriculum which included arithmetic, grammar, letter writing, geography, United States history, reading, spelling, penmanship, bookkeeping, commercial law, and Christian doctrine. Additional courses in German, French, physiology, chemistry, geology, and

botany were optional. The students seemed to be equally divided between the two curricula.[44]

Within two years the curriculum expanded to four courses of study. The five-year Classical course and the two-year Commercial course remained the same. There was a new three-year Collegiate course that allowed the student to choose from both the classical and commercial curricula. And finally, students not ready to enter any of the other three courses could enter the Preparatory department, "provided they know the multiplication tables and are able to read and write."[45] In spite of the names "collegiate" and "classical," the curriculum at St. Ambrose was essentially a high school curriculum and, except for a few men who would go on to seminary for philosophy and theology, students left St. Ambrose after a year or two to pursue their life's work.

The students settled into their first year at St. Ambrose. Since they represented a wide variety of levels of preparation and ages, the challenge for Schulte and Halligan was great. They had the two rooms of St. Marguerite's school, but that was often not enough space to accommodate students at different levels of study. Sometimes they took one group of students into the hallway for recitations while other students remained in the classroom to study quietly. When he was able, McMullen visited the school and listened to the lessons the students had prepared.

The first semester ended in January with examinations conducted by Cosgrove, Schulte, and Halligan. The results reportedly gave "entire satisfaction" to the examiners who now looked forward to the second semester.[46] When classes began again, three of the original students, Eddie McSteen, Henry Motie, and George O'Dea did not return. But eight others entered as new students: Henry Malone, John Dolan, brothers George and William Nevin, Dan McMullen, Frank Dwyre, Martin McNamara, and Henry Maniett. These new students also enlarged the area served by the school: McMullen was from Charlotte in Clinton County, Malone was from Des Moines, McNamara was from Ireland and had recently come to Long Grove, Iowa, and Maniett was from Chariton in central Iowa. Their presence served to emphasize the diocesan mission of the school.

Throughout the spring, life at St. Ambrose was tempered by the declining health of Bishop McMullen. He had left Davenport again in mid-December for the desert west where he remained until the beginning of March. When he returned to Davenport, he told his doctor that he knew he was dying, but, he said, "My books are balanced and I am ready for the journey. . . my time is now devoted to the entertainment and instruction of my friends."[47] He visited the school when he could, and although by the end of April it was reported that he was "improved," he was "still very feeble." In mid-June he was able to go to Chicago to see old friends and family in what they, and he, must have known was a farewell visit. McMullen was on his deathbed when examinations took place in late June, and in deference to his condition, there was no commencement ceremony at the end of the year. However, there was not really anyone to "commence." Following examinations, several students were singled out for honorable mention but there were no degrees or diplomas granted.[48]

McMullen died at age fifty-one on July 4, 1883, just after the school year ended. He left the school his vision of education and his hopes that St.

Ambrose would play a significant role in the life of the church in his diocese and the upper Mississippi Valley. There was a sense of loss beyond the usual grief at a death. One priest who knew him said the bishop was "idolized" and that he "would have been the most remarkable bishop" in the United States.[49] The students also noticed his absence. Writing a year later, one student said that during the second year they had "missed our kindly Father, his smiling face no more illumed (sic) the gloom of our study hall, there was a void within our hearts–a dark and dreary void–the ties of love were broken. The things went on as were before, but the Father dear was dead."[50]

It is not possible to speculate what the first years of St. Ambrose would have been like had McMullen been in good health and able to apply his energies to developing the school. He was a determined man, one who, having been defeated once in his attempt to build a great university, would not let that happen again. His death in July, and the naming of Cosgrove as the next bishop a year later, resulted in a different level of commitment to the school.

Following the death of Bishop McMullen, Cosgrove was named the administrator of the diocese. Born in 1834 in Pennsylvania of Irish parents, Cosgrove had been ordained in 1857 for the Diocese of Dubuque. He was assigned to St. Marguerite's Parish in Davenport and spent all his years there. When McMullen became bishop, he had appointed Cosgrove as his vicar general; now Cosgrove was head of the diocese, but not with all the powers a bishop would have. He remained as administrator until July 1884, when it was announced that he was to be the second bishop of Davenport; he was consecrated in September 1884.

At the end of the first year, Cosgrove and Schulte were faced with a less than favorable financial situation. Income from tuition for the year amounted to $852 and expenses totaled $1,137. The largest expense was for the salaries of the two faculty members: Schulte received $88.20 a month and Halligan was paid $40 a month. But since most of the students paid their tuition in monthly installments, or whenever they could, there was often not enough money available to pay the salaries. Many times Schulte did not receive a salary, or he was paid by the bishop from diocesan funds. Often Halligan did not receive his full salary at the end of each month; throughout the year the cash ledger would show a "past due salary" entry for Halligan.

The rest of the expenses went for supplies to begin the school: desks, bookcases, books, wastebaskets, and sundry items like paper and pencils. St. Ambrose did not pay rent to the cathedral parish for the use of its school rooms, but it did contribute to the coal budget for the building. The budget was balanced only because of two gifts from McMullen totaling $285, a pattern which his successor bishops would follow. The *Messenger* noted with pride the success of the first year, and urged

Bishop Henry Cosgrove.

that before they sent their sons elsewhere, parents look at the advantages of St. Ambrose, among which was its size, which allowed instructors to "devote time to each student, which is an impossibility in the old overcrowded" schools in the East.[51]

When school opened for the second year, the *Messenger* noted, "Everything, in and around the school looks clean, neat and cool. The rooms are high, the air pure, and everything looks inviting. The stairs have been carpeted, new books added to the fast growing library," and it predicted that St. Ambrose would "be the beacon light for the Catholic youths of the Diocese."[52]

To attract more new students, the tuition was lowered to $25 per semester and it was announced that scholarships were available in the Commercial department.[53] However, in spite of the positive image projected by the *Messenger*, and the lower tuition, only twenty-eight students began the year. Nineteen had returned from the first year and there were eight new students; six more students would come for the spring semester. New this year were students from Iowa City and Washburn, near Waterloo.

Although the numbers were lower, Schulte hired Timothy J. Mullen, a

A Great and Lasting Beginning

seminarian, to teach in the spring semester of 1884. Halligan continued to teach the business courses and Schulte continued to teach and administer the school. Schulte was given credit for much of the early success of St. Ambrose, so when it was rumored in late 1884 that he was leaving Davenport for another assignment, the *Messenger* said this was cause for "regret," because his work "in and for St. Ambrose Seminary is proven in its success."[54]

Cosgrove's generosity in offering Bishop McMullen two rooms in his parish school enabled St. Ambrose to begin, but it also added more pupils to a building which was growing more crowded with grade school students. In October 1882, McMullen had stated that he wanted to build a large building for his school; this was at once an expression of his hopes for a larger college and also a realization that the St. Marguerite's school building had limited space. But his death and the long period with no bishop meant that nothing was done about a new building for St. Ambrose.

Discussion about a new building intensified after Cosgrove became the bishop of Davenport on September 14, 1884. The need for space was exacerbated in that fall when forty-six students entered St. Ambrose, combined with an increase in enrollment in St. Marguerite's grade school which used the rest of the building. Commenting at the end of the fall semester in January 1885, the *Messenger* noted that "room, at present is very limited," and that it hoped that through the "great zeal of our beloved Bishop, to see the new St. Ambrose rear its turrets to the sky."[55] But first the bishop would have to locate a site for the proposed new building.

Several sites were under discussion. One was near the reservoir located on Scott Street between Fifteenth and Sixteenth Streets; another was an unspecified site in northeast Davenport. Cosgrove's choice was a site at Eighth and Ripley Streets.[56] As discussion proceeded, however, attention focused on a site on West Locust Street in an area known as Noel's Grove. What had formerly been a large tract of land covered with a grove of oak trees had by now been divided up among many land owner-developers.

The land for the proposed new St. Ambrose campus was a ten acre tract owned by Henry G. Marquand of New York City. Marquand had purchased the land in 1855 from Adam and Susan Noel for $4,000, apparently as an investment. Cosgrove knew Noel's Grove well since years earlier St. Marguerite's Parish held picnics there.[57] But Cosgrove worried that the Locust Street site would be too far away for students to travel to and from school each day. However, Cosgrove set aside his reservations, and in April 1885, he purchased the ten acres from Marquand for $6,800.[58] Marquand reportedly lowered the price from $12,000 because the land would be used for a religious institution.

The property was bounded on the south by West Locust Street, on the east by Scott Street, on the west by Western (approximately where the current driveway at the west end of Ambrose Hall is located) and on the north by High Street (approximately where the drive behind Christ the King chapel is located). The purchase of the land and the subsequent building were made possible, in part, by using the $4,000 in gold that the priests of Chicago had given McMullen when he left Chicago and which he had saved for his school.[59]

Schulte remembered that the new campus "seemed out in the country"

and the *Messenger* commented that the site was so big that the "students will enjoy all the quiet and comforts of country life."[60] But it was hardly isolated. There were houses on Gaines Street to the west and a few houses on Western to the north. Mercy Hospital was located a few blocks west on Lombard Street. There were no houses on Locust Street across from campus, but Halligan remembered that there were onion fields.[61] There were houses on Locust Street east of campus and on Scott and Ripley Streets. Casper Fries had a wagon and blacksmith shop on the corner of Locust and Harrison. There were other businesses on Harrison Street south of Locust and a public school on Locust between Harrison and Main. Streetcars ran up Brady Street and stopped on Locust and another streetcar line went west from Brady on Sixteenth Street, two blocks south of Locust. Still, Locust was a deeply rutted mud street and, according to the *Messenger*, a "disgrace to the city," so bad that "four horses and a mule could not draw a baby cab along" the street. It pointed out that St. Ambrose and Mercy Hospital to the west would "add greatly to that section of the city, advance the price of property and increase population" and urged the city fathers to see that the street was improved.[62]

Construction of the new building began almost immediately. The architect was Victor Huot. Born in France, Huot had come to the United States in 1842 and settled in Cleveland where he had worked as a builder. He moved to New Orleans where his parents and brothers had settled. In the mid-1850s, he and his brothers came to Davenport. As an architect and builder, Huot was responsible for designing and building houses for some of Davenport's most prominent families, as well as Mercy Hospital, the Immaculate Conception Academy, and several churches.[63] He already had a connection with St. Ambrose since his nephew, Francis Huot, was in the first class and was still a student.

The bishop asked Father Schulte to oversee the design of the new building. When Huot presented the first set of drawings, Schulte told him it was too small and to enlarge it.[64] Huot's final design was for a four-story building with a mansard roof and a central tower with provisions for wings to be added to the building as needed. This was exactly the kind of "expandable" building McMullen had hoped to build. It would include everything needed for the school: classrooms, offices, storage rooms, a library, study hall, and a laundry. Huot's plan called for residence rooms for students and faculty members, as well as a gymnasium on the fourth floor. But the decision was made to finish only the first two floors, so for the time being St. Ambrose would remain a day school, and the few students from outside the city of Davenport would room in homes in the neighborhood.[65] Curiously, probably because there were no resident students, there was no provision for a chapel in the building.

The decision not to finish the interior of the upper two floors saved a considerable amount of money, since labor, materials, and the furnishings that the additional space would have required did not have to be purchased. The fact is there was not enough money to finish the building. The estimated cost of the building was $11,000. The bishop had received two cash donations to assist in paying for the project: a $100 donation from a James Slattery of New York; and a $1,000 donation from John L. Miles, a Davenport loan agent and insurance man. For the rest Cosgrove had to borrow large sums of money which created a debt which would plague him for the next several years.[66]

Although the attention of everyone was focused on the building going up on Locust Street, the third year of St. Ambrose Seminary ended at St. Marguerite's with graduation on June 30, 1885. There had been no graduation in 1883 because of McMullen's health, and there was apparently no ceremony at the end of the 1884 year. However, the college catalogue listed John Ryan, one of the original students, as the lone graduate in the Commercial department, making him the first student to receive a diploma of graduation from St. Ambrose.

Typical of nineteenth-century graduations, the 1885 program was filled with music, drama, and speeches performed by the students. It began with an overture played by the Second Regiment Band, followed by a salutatory written by Martin McNamara and delivered by Frank Balluf. A student cast performed Molière's *Le Bourgeois Gentilhomme*. This was followed by more music and finally the conferral of diplomas on nine graduates.

The principal address was delivered by Michael V. Gannon. Born in Dublin, Ireland, in 1846, Gannon had immigrated to Davenport in 1866. He taught at St. Marguerite's school in the 1870s, and was admitted to the bar in 1873. He had been with McMullen in 1882 when the bishop announced that he was going to start a boys' school. At the time he delivered the commencement address, he was the district attorney for the local judicial district. Later he practiced law in Omaha and Chicago and served for a time as the president of the Irish National Land League. He would be a frequent visitor and speaker at St. Ambrose events. In his speech to the graduates of 1885, Gannon congratulated Davenport Catholics for establishing St. Ambrose for it made it possible for its graduates to occupy "any station in life." The ceremony ended with the students singing, "Ere We Part."[67]

Five days later, on Sunday, July 5, under threatening skies, clergy, civic leaders, Catholics from the city, and Bishop Cosgrove gathered to bless the cornerstone of the building. They processed around the building as the bishop sprinkled it with holy water. The cornerstone was then cemented into place and the building dedicated to "Almighty God and the ever blessed Virgin Mary under the invocation of St. Ambrose." A copper box was placed in the cornerstone with a copy of the dedication program, the first and second prospectus of the institution, and copies of the current editions of Catholic and Davenport newspapers.

Davenport Mayor Ernst Claussen reminded the crowd that the oldest among them could remember when Indians "roamed in [the] beautiful grove" that was now St. Ambrose. He commented on the importance of "universal education" to the maintenance of self-government, and he said that with the Immaculate Conception Academy and Mercy Hospital, Catholics in the area already had a record of institutions that would "elevate the character . . . purify the mind . . . improve the sentiment and cultivate all that is good and noble in the hearts and minds of our growing generation." He said that now St. Ambrose college "bids fair to become the third in the galaxy of beneficial institutions" in Davenport. He noted that it would draw students from the area and the adjoining states and he urged all the citizens of Davenport to "extend to them the right hand of fellowship, to help, to assist, and to encourage them in all possible ways."[68]

The principal speaker of the day was the Reverend James P. Ryan, assistant pastor of the cathedral. Taking as his text the command of Jesus to "Go therefore and teach all nations," Ryan said that was what had motivated Bishop McMullen to found the institution. Following a long rehearsal of the importance of education in the history of the church, Ryan noted especially that American Catholics founded schools because of the sectarian nature of common schools which attempted to separate religion from education. "The institution whose cornerstone has been laid here today," he proclaimed, "is intended to educate, not the head apart from the heart, but the head and the heart together. This is to be a Catholic College where secular and religious education will go hand in hand." Ryan said the goal of the college would be to "Send forth from its halls thorough going scholars, thorough going Americans, and above all, thorough going Catholics." The speeches concluded, the rain which had threatened all day came in torrents, sending the people to construction sheds and the porches of neighboring houses.[69] The hope was to have the building completed in time for school in September, but it would not be ready for classes until November 1.[70]

The school took an important step on October 5, 1885, when it filed articles of incorporation with the State of Iowa which declared that St. Ambrose Seminary was under the "patronage, control, direction and supervision of the ecclesiastical body of the Roman Catholic Church" in the person of the "Bishop of the Diocese of Davenport." Bishop Cosgrove, the Reverend Michael Flavin, vicar general, and Schulte, as president of St. Ambrose, were the officers of the corporation and the "board of managers" with full power and authority. The articles stated that "no particular religious faith shall be required of any person to entitle him to admission as a student of said seminary."

As early as 1798 Georgetown College admitted non-Catholics for instruction "in the sciences and morality." Separate living quarters were provided for them, but there was no classroom discrimination and they were not obligated to participate in religious services. This custom of open admissions continued in most Catholic colleges in the nineteenth century. The reasons were no doubt based on educational philosophy about the universality of knowledge, but they were also practical. In an era of strong anti-Catholic sentiment, Catholic colleges could not be perceived as practicing the same kind of discrimination that was used against them. Moreover, most struggling Catholic colleges, like the incipient St. Ambrose, could not afford to turn any students away.[71]

The fall semester of 1885 began at St. Marguerite's, but the students eagerly looked forward to moving to the new building. With the cornerstone laid, one student wrote that when the building was finished, there would "gather within its walls a larger number of students than before, wherein heart and will working in a happy unison will generate true wisdom into good. Our hopes for the next year are of the highest order. With a new and commodious institution, . . . we can predict a proud and successful year."[72] The unnamed student no doubt expressed the hopes of the bishop and the administration of St. Ambrose that the new building would draw more students which would mean more income from tuition, which was the only source of money to keep the school in operation.

A Great and Lasting Beginning

On November 1, fifty-five students moved to the new building. Six of them had been among the first thirty-three students and thus could make the claim that they had attended St. Ambrose at both of its campuses. Schulte continued as president and prefect of studies, and Halligan continued as principal of the Commercial department. Three students were also listed as members of the faculty: Charles O'Reilly was the prefect of discipline and Herman Kempker and Martin McNamara were his assistants. It would be the practice for a number of years to put older students, often those who were studying for the priesthood, in charge of discipline. O'Reilly was also in charge of the library.

They were joined at the new building by the Reverend John Thomas Aloysius Flannagan as vice president and disciplinarian. Flannagan was born in Haverhill, Massachusetts, in 1860. His family moved to Iowa City when he was a young boy. In July 1885, Flannagan was ordained a priest and that November he began his service at St. Ambrose. In addition to his administrative duties, Flannagan taught the classics and rhetoric.

The Commercial department had the largest number of students and with more classroom space available in the new building, Halligan was able to add telegraphy, typewriting, and shorthand to the curriculum. The additional space also made it possible to add to the library, which was characterized as a "splendid" library with "choice and selected reading." By the spring of 1887, St. Ambrose received a significant gift of books, valued at $10,000, from the estate of the Reverend Maurice Howard of Keokuk. The collection included works on history, science, and art and included multi-volume sets of the works of St. Thomas Aquinas and St. Augustine. Howard's bequest brought the total number of books in the library to nearly 4,000.[73]

The new building and its furnishings had put a strain on the financial resources of the diocese. St. Ambrose was struggling and there seemed to be a question, at least in the mind of Cosgrove, whether it should continue to exist. On May 25 and 26, 1886, the bishop met with his bishop's council, a group that included the Reverend Andrew Trevis, the vicar general, and senior pastors whom the bishop occasionally called together for advice. For this meeting Cosgrove had an agenda of fourteen items of diocesan business and the first item was St. Ambrose. In presenting his agenda, he asked the council to discuss three questions about the college. First, should St. Ambrose be "enlarged or restricted?" His second question concerned the faculty: Who else besides Schulte might be appointed as president, and was Schulte "assured of his office?" This suggests that Cosgrove may have lacked confidence in Schulte. The rumors two years earlier that Schulte was leaving and Cosgrove's questions now, may also indicate that Schulte was not happy and wanted to leave. In light of subsequent events, however, it seems more likely that Cosgrove had some dissatisfaction with the college and perhaps Schulte. Cosgrove also asked the council if assistant professors for the college should be priests or laymen or both, and he raised the issue of their salaries. Cosgrove's third question involved whether the upper floors of the building should be finished for boarding students, or at least whether rooms should be provided for one or two professors.

Cosgrove presented a financial report on the college that showed expenses of $6,800 for the purchase of the land, and $8,843.11 already paid for

construction of the building. Another $2,500 was due on the building. Because that figure had not been paid, Victor Huot had obtained a mechanics lien against Cosgrove at the beginning of 1886. There was one other small bill due in the amount of $136.62 for total expenses of $18,279.73. Cosgrove reported receipts of $1,000 from John Miles, $100 from James Slattery, $46.80 collected at the cornerstone ceremony, and a legacy of $50 for total receipts of $1,196.80. The remaining debt, and no doubt the reason for the meeting, was $17,082.93.

Since the agenda was so large, the bishop asked two councilors to consider the questions and present recommendations to the council. They met overnight and presented their recommendations the next day. First they said that since the college was in debt for $17,000, it would be "imprudent" to increase that debt by "making further improvements." After discussion, all the councilors except Trevis, who argued that they should create rooms for at least one professor, voted to approve that recommendation. Next, they suggested that no change be made in the college until the debt was paid, or at least greatly diminished. And finally, they said that there should be an annual collection in the diocese to pay off the debt. These last two recommendations were approved unanimously by the council.[74]

That fall classes began with fewer students than the year before. Although the *Messenger* noted that "prospects were extra good" for a successful year, the fact that enrollment had not increased with the new building was a matter of some concern.[75] So in May 1887, Cosgrove announced that the upper two floors of Ambrose Hall would be finished so the school could begin to accept boarding students in the fall. There were already a number of students from out-of-town who were staying in local homes and boarding houses and, according to Cosgrove, this was a matter of some concern to their parents. Cosgrove was confident that the Catholics of the city of Davenport would fund the estimated $5,000 cost to finish the building.[76]

A month later the bishop's council met for their first meeting in a year. In the face of the bishop's announcement the month before, they began by moving to dispense with the reading of the rather lengthy minutes of the previous meeting, except for the section that related to their recommendations and discussion about St. Ambrose. This was the council's way of reminding Cosgrove that they had advised him not to proceed until the debt had been reduced. The bishop defended his action and "explained the urgent reasons for the present work of completion of the college building." He said that students were not coming to St. Ambrose because their parents did not want them boarding in private homes in town. It seemed clear to Cosgrove that boarding facilities on campus would increase the number of students and increase college income. He also said that the priests of the diocese needed a place for their annual retreat and that boarding facilities on campus would provide that. Finally, he said he thought that the means to pay for this could be found in the city of Davenport. The only action the councilors took was to recommend that the bishop appoint two priests to travel to the "principal parishes" of the diocese to raise money to retire the debt.[77]

Schulte had been waiting outside the room during this discussion. Now that they had completed their business, the councilors called him into the meeting where he spoke at length about St. Ambrose.

The next month Cosgrove sent a pastoral letter to the priests and people of the diocese with the same announcement. Here he emphasized the necessity to give St. Ambrose "a more definite character of stability" by adding boarding students. He said that the purpose of the addition of boarding students was not just to make it a "financially profitable institution," although that certainly would be an important consequence, but to provide the education necessary for seminarians, and a Catholic education for those who wanted to "pursue a business career in the world" in a setting which would provide "daily and continual religious influence during their years of study." He assured parents who were reluctant to send their sons to Davenport that they would be "properly cared for by the reverend professors, who [would] keep a constant watch over each and every one." Finally, he said that to pay off the current debt, he was sending Schulte and the Reverend James Davis, pastor of St. Michael's Parish in Holbrook, through the diocese to take up a collection.[78] Their efforts met with some success: the debt was

At the end of five years of existence, St. Ambrose had taken some small steps toward realizing Bishop McMullen's vision. In large and small ways it was already impacting the lives of those who had spent some time studying there. When classes began on September 6, 1887, only one of the original thirty-three students remained. The stories of the post-St. Ambrose lives of those thirty-three students illustrate that although the United States offered opportunities to immigrants and their sons, health, family obligations, or the lack of luck sometimes mitigated against success.

Over half the class remained in the area. Cornelius Buckley returned to the family farm near Joslin, but early in the century he moved to Rock Island where he would have a successful career with a company that manufactured plumbing supplies, and later he worked in real estate. Thomas O'Brien also moved to the Illinois side of the river where he worked as a salesman for various firms, including the Singer Sewing Machine company. In Davenport John Otten worked as a contractor. John Quinn

reduced but not retired. It would remain a problem for the bishop for the next few years, and even lead him to consider a radical step.

During this time work began on finishing the third and fourth floors of Ambrose Hall. By early July the plasterers completed their work and the furniture was purchased from the Knostman and Son furniture store.[79] The third floor contained a large hallway that included the stairwell, with a dormitory on the west side and the chapel on the east side. The fourth floor was a large, open dormitory area which in time would come to be called "the Irish Village." The library and the museum for Schulte's geology collection on the lower floor now had more space.[80] All was in readiness for classes to begin on September 6. McMullen was gone, but in the lives of the students and alumni of St. Ambrose, his vision and his hopes for his school continued.

and John Malone were laborers. Matthias Koch joined the family real estate business. Andrew McGee was a draftsman.

Frank Lew joined the Davenport police force and rose to the rank of captain. Two of his sons would graduate from St. Ambrose, be ordained priests, and serve on the faculty of the college. Two other members of the class worked for local government. Francis Huot became the city assessor and Scott Stackhouse was the district court clerk.

The entrepreneurs included John Reid, who was one of the owners of the Reid, Mohr, and Kloppenburg printing firm. Herman Bartemeyer joined his father in the grocery store at Fourteenth and Harrison, and ran the business until he retired in 1932. The O'Shaughnessey brothers also joined their father in the grocery store. Peter became the bookkeeper and Edward clerked. Within a decade, however, both of them had left the business, and the city directory listed them both as laborers. Edward died in 1906 and Peter in 1907, each at age 39, and each probably from

A Great and Lasting Beginning

consumption.

The grocery business gave John Ruhl his start. He worked as a grocer until 1898 when he went into real estate and insurance. In 1919, with two of his sons, he formed Ruhl and Ruhl. Four years later he died of heart disease at age 55.

William Hudson Harrison's life could have been written by Horatio Alger. As a student he had worked in the news stand at the Burtis House. Later he purchased a news stand at the Kimball Hotel. Over the next few years he managed hotels in Davenport, Rock Island, and Chicago. Eventually he and a partner built and operated the Davenport Hotel.

St. Ambrose began as a seminary, but only three of the thirty-three students went on to study for the priesthood. Francis Huot stayed at St. Ambrose for five years, then went to St. Mary's Seminary in Baltimore, but left before ordination and came home to work for the city. James Renihan attended St. Ambrose for five years and then went to St. Vincent's Seminary in Cape Girardeau, Missouri. Ordained in 1891, he served a number of parishes in the diocese. An excellent student, he delivered lectures around Iowa on subjects ranging from King Lear to Ireland. But in July 1909, he developed laryngitis, which developed into pneumonia and he died on July 25.

Bernard Mackin came from a farm in DeWitt and entered St. Ambrose at age 23, by far the oldest student in the class. He stayed at St. Ambrose for two years, then went to St. Mary's Seminary in Baltimore, and was ordained in 1888. He first served at Sacred Heart Cathedral and was involved in the construction of the present church. His last assignment was at St. Paul's Parish in Burlington. His health declined in the last two years of his life and he died on July 28, 1909, three days after his classmate, the Reverend James Renihan.

Edward Woeber had already lost both parents and was living with his brother at the time he entered St. Ambrose. He left after one year and led a rather aimless life, working at a number of jobs. After a few years his health began to fail. He sought a cure by traveling to Lourdes, but it did no good and he died in 1892 at the age of 26.

Maurice McNamara clerked for three years in the Michael V. Gannon and McGuirk law offices, then in 1887, took a job with the Northern Pacific Railroad and moved to Montana. Within a year, however, he had contracted consumption so he returned to Davenport, and died at age 23 in 1889. Ed McCormick also died young. After St. Ambrose, he worked in the machine shop at the Rock Island Arsenal until he died of the effects of asthma at age 27. John Doyle was a mattress maker who was 29 when he died following a long illness.

Others in the class found that opportunity lay in places much farther away from the Quad-Cities. Charles Bairley stayed at St. Ambrose for five years, and then joined his family who had moved to Santa Barbara, California. He worked in a livery stable for a while, but most of the rest of his life he worked as a carpenter and he died in California in 1949. George O'Dea moved to Oklahoma and sold real estate. Thomas O'Donnell went to Kansas City and became the national organizer for the Fraternal Order of Eagles. After living in several places, Ed Stackhouse ended up in Minneapolis where he was a salesman. Ed Butler moved to St. Louis where he became a real estate developer.

Eddie McSteen left St. Ambrose after only one semester. He studied telegraphy, and by age fifteen, he was one of the youngest telegraphers on the Rock Island Railroad. According to the *Messenger*, he served as an example "for hundreds of boys in Davenport who are wasting their time and running the street." He eventually moved to St. James, Minnesota, where he became a dispatcher for the Omaha Railroad until his retirement in 1938.

Ed Miniter also worked for the railroad. He went to St. Ambrose for two years and then, in 1884, moved with his family to Marshalltown, Iowa. Ed got a job as an engineer for the Northern Pacific Railroad and lived in Missoula, Montana, when he died at age 40 in 1908. Two members of the class, Edward McNamara and Joseph Jacobs left Davenport and their fate remains unknown.

The two longest-lived members of the class left Davenport for Chicago. Henry Motie moved there in 1890 with his widowed mother. He became a policeman, later worked as a motorman, and still later worked as a mechanic in a factory. John Ryan read law with Gannon and McGuirk in Davenport, studied at the University of Iowa Law School, and returned to Davenport where he joined the practice of E. M. Sharon. When he moved to Chicago, he worked in the Cook County Recorder's Office. Motie and Ryan were not only classmates, they were related; Motie married Ryan's sister and for a time Ryan lived with the Moties. Henry Motie died on February 16, 1950. Five months later, on July 16, his classmate and brother-in-law John Ryan died.

Like their parents the students were active in their community and church. They served on parish committees and were members of the Holy Name Society, the Catholic Order of Foresters, and the Knights of Columbus. Francis Huot was one of the founders of St. Alphonsus Parish. He maintained his connection to St. Ambrose by caring for the geological collection he and Fr. Schulte had begun when Huot was a student. Ed Miniter, John Ruhl, and William Harrison were members of the Elks; Ruhl was also a member of the Davenport Turners; Harrison served one term on the Davenport City Council; and Miniter was active in the Brotherhood of Locomotive Engineers.

Those thirty-three students represent the thousands of students who followed them to St. Ambrose. Years later Joseph Halligan wrote with pride about the lay graduates of St. Ambrose: "Here in Davenport we have scores of them, prominent in banking, commercial and professional life, in offices of public and private trust, citizens of upright life, a credit to their church and their state. Of alumni from outside the city, I have heard a similar recital."[81]

It is a common belief that the children of immigrants do better than their parents. If the "contractors" of the parental generation hoped for the middle class, for the most part their sons achieved that. Part of that rise included the time they spent at St. Ambrose. Even though their experience at St. Ambrose may have been brief, the school and the vision remained with them.

In 1893, when the first St. Ambrose Alumni Association was formed, John Ryan and Ed Stackhouse were elected officers. In 1914 when the association reorganized, three members of the first class were charter members and more joined later. And when they died, their families remembered their St. Ambrose experience too: some of their obituaries read, "He was a member of the first class at St. Ambrose College."

GENERAL REGULATIONS

All the pupils will be required to observe the strictest punctuality and cleanliness in all things.

All discussions on religion, politics, and nationality are strictly prohibited.

No pupils will leave the College grounds without previous permission.

All correspondence will be subject to the inspection of the Faculty.

No newspapers, periodicals, etc., are permitted in the house, except such as may meet with the approval of ecclesiastical authorities. Should exceptions be made for seniors they will not pass the papers to juniors. Newspapers, etc. not approved of, will not be delivered to the pupil. The use of intoxicating liquors, tobacco, fire-arms and other dangerous weapons is prohibited.

Students are required to observe silence in all places at all times except during the hours of recreation.

All communication between House Pupils and Day Scholars is prohibited.

Pupils are not permitted to enter private rooms without express permission.

Improper language and behavior is not tolerated.

The College assumes no responsibility concerning the religious practice of Day Scholars outside the school, and parents will see to their sons in this respect.

Each student, at his entrance, receives a printed copy of the Regulations of the Institution.

❧ Chapter Two ☙

If the parents were to see that their sons went to church on Sunday, and presumably monitor the rest of their out-of-school behavior, the rules printed in the catalogue for 1887 made it clear that the college would act *in loco parentis* (in place of the parents) while the students were on campus. Similar lists of regulations were common in nineteenth-century Catholic colleges. However, if even critics of the day suggested that self-discipline was a better preparation for life beyond college than an imposed discipline, most schools, St. Ambrose included, opted for imposing discipline. There were no doubt rules of behavior while the college was at St. Marguerite's and in the first years on Locust Street. But now that St. Ambrose had become a boarding school, rules and regulations became even more important. Each student received a copy of the regulations, and some of the more important of those were framed and hung in the study hall, "as a constant reminder to all, that 'the wicked standeth in slippery places.'"[1]

It is not surprising that the General Regulations cite rules on deportment, the use of alcohol and fire-arms, language, and a wonderful Victorian sense that for peace in the house, religion, politics, and nationality should not be discussed. It is also not surprising that there are rules to provide for quiet to enable study.

It is surprising that there is nothing in the General Regulations about religious observance on campus. In another place, the catalogue says that students were to be "carefully instructed in the doctrines and practices of their holy religion," that time would be "set aside" for spiritual reading and prayer, and that all students "must approach the sacraments at least once a month." In 1910 a regulation would be added stating that non-Catholics "enjoy the same rights and opportunities as Catholics," and that their "reli-

gious views must not be unduly interfered with." The 1910 Regulations say that all students, Catholic and non-Catholic, must be present at "the religious exercises of the community." Years later there would be vigorous debates about whether there should be mandatory attendance at Sunday and daily Mass and at retreats, but in the 1880s, apparently once a month was sufficient.

It is curious that the regulations say that there should be no "communication" between house pupils (resident students) and the day scholars (commuters). It is disturbing to modern sensibilities that there would be censorship of newspapers and magazines and that the students' mail would be inspected by the faculty, although this latter regulation was dropped a few years later.

Father Flannagan had been the disciplinarian when he arrived in November 1885, and most certainly he was the author of the General Regulations. Over the next few years, discipline was the responsibility of a succession of senior students or newly ordained priests, but clearly the tone was set by Flannagan. He has been described as a "cultured American gentleman reared in the atmosphere of the Victorian – or shall we say Puritan? – behavior pattern." As such he was opposed to drinking, smoking, dancing, and sporting events on Sunday.[2] He was also formal in his manners and dress and he expected the students to follow his example. He insisted that the students wear a coat and tie in the refectory, and any infraction of good manners was met with an immediate reprimand. This formality would continue after Flannagan became president in 1891.

The day-to-day responsibility for enforcing the Regulations and monitoring the activities of the students fell to the prefects of discipline, later

A Great and Lasting Beginning

called proctors, and still later, resident advisors. In the early years, the prefects were older students, almost always chosen from among those studying for the priesthood. Depending on the number of students, at least one prefect was responsible for the resident students and another for the day students. Since the prefects represented authority, not just of the school but also because of *in loco parentis*, there was some friction between the students and them. However, a level of respect also developed which was apparent when, in 1887, the students surprised their prefects with Christmas gifts. Accompanied by appropriate remarks of gratitude, the resident students gave their prefect, Daniel Mulvihill, a gold-headed cane, and the day students gave their prefect, James Crosby, a gold pen.[3]

One of the General Regulations for students at St. Ambrose forbade the use of "intoxicating liquors." Controversy about the issue of liquor in Iowa went back to territorial times and over the decades two attitudes developed among Iowans. One was represented by those who wanted strict regulation of personal behavior, including liquor consumption. For them the state would be an agent of enforcement of personal morality. The other attitude was that such issues were best left to individual decisions.

In 1882, the year St. Ambrose began, Iowans had voted on whether to add a prohibition amendment to the state constitution. The measure had carried in the state with 55 percent of the vote, but in Scott County, the vote was nearly 78 percent against; only Dubuque County had a higher percentage against. But a year later the Iowa Supreme Court ruled that there had been procedural irregularities in the amending process and overturned the vote. In 1884, the Iowa General Assembly passed a prohibition law that its proponents hoped would make Iowa dry. The law, however, was widely ignored especially in river towns like Davenport.[4]

The tone of the response in Davenport to these anti-liquor laws was set by Mayor Ernst Claussen who declared that the citizens of Davenport would not obey "such an infringement on personal liberties."[5] This attitude was borne out when the 1885 state census indicated that Scott County was first in the state in the value of the output from breweries, with 26 percent of the brewery output of the entire state.[6] Another indication of the liquor situation came from its opponents: Carrie Nation, the anti-liquor crusader from Kansas called Davenport "that beer-besmeared, whiskey-soaked city." It was clear that civil government was not going to enforce the prohibition laws in Davenport and Scott County, so religious leaders, including Bishop Cosgrove and the pastors of the city parishes, would have to undertake a moral crusade. Cosgrove warned against sitting still while Davenport went "to the devil," and Father

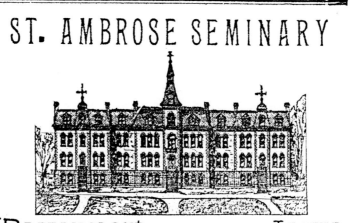

ST. AMBROSE SEMINARY

Davenport, - - - - Iowa

Established by the late Rt. Rev. John McMullen, D. D. Bishop of Davenport, September 4 1882, for the education of the Catholic youth of the Diocese. Full CLASSICAL, COLLEGIATE, COMMERCIAL AND PREPARATORY Course. Next Term begins September 4th. 1888. Send for a Descriptive Catalogue, to

REV. A J SCHULTE, President

James P. Ryan, the pastor of St. Mary's Parish, urged the Knights of Columbus to undertake a crusade against liquor abuse "in defense of our young and innocent."[7]

Among the young and innocent people who needed to be protected from the abuses of liquor were the students at St. Ambrose. In early 1885, the St. Marguerite's Total Abstinence Society was organized with Schulte as its president and Halligan on the program committee. Students were encouraged to become involved in the society. Temperance activity continued on the St. Ambrose campus, and in 1895, it was reported that almost three-fourths of the boarding students signaled their intention to form a temperance society on campus. That same year the "pledge," a promise not to drink alcohol, was administered to a "large number of students."[8] No doubt this kind of *in loco parentis* monitoring of their sons' activities was precisely what parents wanted when they sent them to the priests at St. Ambrose.

Another addition to the catalogues of 1886 and 1887 that can be attributed to the new boarding school status is a list of belongings the students should bring with them when they came to school. This included two suits, preferably black, six shirts, two night-shirts, six towels, six napkins, four pairs of drawers, stockings, overshoes, slippers, hats or caps, one napkin ring, a knife, fork, tea and table spoons, comb and brush, blacking and brush, soap, and enough collars, cuffs, and neckties "sufficient for daily use."

Tuition remained at $25 per semester for the Commercial and Classical courses, and $15 for the Preparatory course. The new boarding students paid a fee of $95 for board, tuition, bed, bedding, washing, and mending. There was also a $25 fee for half boarders, those who would take only noon-time dinner at the college.

The domestic chores of the new boarding school were handled by three Sisters of the Congregation of the Humility of Mary of Ottumwa: Sister Mary Peter Orienz, Sister Mary Benedict Smith, and Sister Mary Dechantel O'Reilly. These sisters and the many Humility sisters who succeeded them over the next decades did the cooking, baking, cleaning, laundering, mending, and caring for the sick in the infirmary. They also provided a feminine, motherly presence to an all-male school. Since finances were limited, they became ingenious in making slim ends meet in order to feed and care for dozens of teen-aged boys, as well as the resident priests.[9]

In addition to their classroom work, there were other opportunities, both formal and less formal, for the students to gather for a common purpose. The first student organization at St. Ambrose was the Sodality of the Immaculate Conception of the Blessed Virgin Mary. Sodalities were common organizations for men and women in nineteenth-century parishes. They usually met once a month and emphasized Mass attendance, frequent reception of Holy Communion, and Christian service. The Sodality members would act as sacristans in the chapel and provide servers for liturgical services. In the mid-1890s, this latter function was taken up by the Acolythical Society which trained its members to assist at Mass.

Another type of early organization at St. Ambrose was the literary society. Literary societies were common in nineteenth-century American colleges, so that as one scholar noted, even at the most "poverty-stricken and primitive" school, two rival literary societies would form shortly after classes began. In the years after the Civil War, literary societies were the "most popular and powerful student organizations," and since they were often the only extracurricular activity, they claimed a virtual monopoly on a student's time. They were organized to enhance the debating and public speaking skills that students would need in their post-collegiate careers.[10]

The first of these was the St. Ambrose Literary and Debating Society formed in the 1883-1884 year to help the students learn the "self-possession so befitting a true gentleman, and that eloquence and readiness for speech so necessary for the orator."[11] Since many of these literary societies built libraries for their own use, another purpose was "the acquisition of sound knowledge, and a taste for literary studies."[12] Membership in the St. Ambrose Society was limited to students in the upper classes. Early on, Schulte appointed Joseph Halligan to be the president.

A year later, with Schulte as its president, the St. John's Literary and Debating Society was organized for the younger students "to afford its members every opportunity for mental improvement, and make use for this end of original essays, selected readings, declamations and debates." A committee was appointed to draft rules, officers were elected, and the debate topic and essay assignments were made for subsequent meetings. Usually at a meeting, someone would read a famous speech by a politician or an essay on some topic. But the focal point of the evening was the debate. Over the years the topics were recycled, but they were varied: "That to Columbus alone belongs the honor of having discovered America; that the Indians had a full right to America; that theoretical bookkeeping is necessary for a businessman; that a street car line over the Government Bridge would be beneficial to the city of Davenport; that a mechanic is more useful to the country than a farmer; that there is more science in the game of football than in a game of baseball; that the prohibition law is beneficial to the state of Iowa; that the statesman is more worthy of esteem of the people than the soldier."[13] Rarely, however, did the literary societies at St. Ambrose debate issues directly related to the campus.

The members took themselves very seriously and often spent a good deal of time discussing their own rules and regulations. Each society had a program committee which would give members a notice a week or two before the meeting that they were expected to engage in a debate or present an

Awarded to W.B. McDonough, Elocution.

St. Ambrose Seminary, Davenport, Iowa, June 26, 1888.

essay. But the minutes often indicate that when a scheduled member was absent, a substitute would quickly be found who would take his place. This would often work to the advantage of the purpose of the societies: to help their members develop the skill of talking "on their feet" at a moment's notice. If the format was a debate on some local or national issue, each side would present its arguments and the members would decide which side prevailed.

The literary societies served as a means to reinforce basic classroom work in grammar and public speaking. They were extracurricular activities that gave the students opportunities for expression that the curriculum did not provide. Often in these literary societies, students had a greater degree of academic freedom than they would in their classes. They also served as an outlet for the energies of teen-aged boys; it is probably no accident that these societies usually met on Friday evenings. In time, however, the popularity of literary societies declined as athletics, music clubs, drama clubs and other specialized organizations formed. In the twentieth century, many of the functions of the literary societies were made part of the regular curriculum.[14]

At the commencement ceremony at the end of each year, honor students were recognized and the name of the best students in every class was published in the catalogue. Local priests provided gold medals for the best essay on the catechism, or for the best work in the class on humanities, or for the best essay in rhetoric, or for the best historical essay. The award that came to have the greatest prestige was the gold medal in elocution. The literary societies served as a "training ground" for the senior students to prepare for the elocution contest. The annual elocution award took on special significance in 1892 when the Reverend Albert M. Nodler, the vice president and disciplinarian, created an elocution contest. A number of students performed dramatic readings or declaimed speeches from history. The winner that first year was William P. Shannahan, later a president of St. Ambrose, who performed an argumentative oratory which, according to the *Messenger*, was "forceful, impressive." The paper also noted that Shannahan exhibited a "fine presence," with a "natural, clear, distinct delivery," and "graceful emphatic gestures."[15] A panel of judges led by Bishop Cosgrove, several local pastors, and the publishers of the *Messenger* awarded Shannahan the Reldon Gold Medal in Elocution, which had been donated by Nodler (his name spelled in reverse). Within a few years the elocution contest became a major and elaborate event in the late spring.

Another activity closely allied with the literary and debating societies were dramatic societies, the first of which was the St. Aloysius Dramatic Association, formed with twenty-one members in the 1885-1886 year. Schulte, whose first name was Aloysius, was president and a strong supporter of the activities of the association. Students filled the other officer

A Great and Lasting Beginning

The cast of King Arthur. *Standing left to right: William P. Shannahan '96, Bert Cavanaugh '90, Thomas Brennan '89. Seated, J.M. Hanson '92, Frank Kottenstette '96, Dennis Sullivan '89.*

positions and there was a student committee on dramas.[16]

The productions were elaborate with sets and costumes. Their purpose was not to train the students for a career on the stage, but to provide an outlet for student expression. The first production of the Dramatic Association came at the end of that school year when the students put on *The Hidden Gem*, a two-act play attributed to Cardinal Wiseman, at the Burtis Opera House in downtown Davenport. In 1888, the students staged *Atonement or Malediction*, a three-act drama by Joseph Lyons, also at the Burtis Opera House. Two years later they produced Henry van Rensselaer's *King Alfred*, once again at the Burtis. The next year they moved to the Grand Opera House for *More Sinned Against Than Sinning*, by John L. Carleton.

Like the literary and debating societies, dramatic societies would cease to exist, only to emerge later under a new name. After 1893, when an addition to Ambrose Hall created more room, there was much more dramatic activity and the plays would regularly provide an opportunity for students to perform and bring the general public to campus as their audiences.[17]

Another annual celebration was the feast of St. Ambrose in December. Sometimes in the first years, the bishop came to campus to celebrate Mass for the feast day of the college's patron. At other times in those early years, there was little formal notice of the day at all. In 1894 after the first class of the day, the students petitioned the president for a free day and he granted it. Nothing special was planned; nevertheless, the day was a "source of happiness and mirth to professors and students alike" and "was joyously spent and for time to come its recollection will be intensely pleasant and desirous."[18] The following year, the day was celebrated with a formal program where the bishop, local pastors, and the sisters joined the students. The program included music from the band, glee club, and Mandolin Club, and essays from students including a sketch of the life of St. Ambrose. The highlight of the program was a long poem on St. Ambrose written and delivered by Edward Weil which told how "St. Ambrose trod life's thorny way," and concluded: "May Ambrose patron of our school/Direct its youth and guide its rule./And lead us on to useful ages/To be the sires, and saints, and sages,/Of homes, and states, and nations wise/Whose worth shall pierce the very skies./And when our mortal course is run/And Heaven's will on earth is done/May we tread the path that he has trod/The way that leads the soul to God."[19]

The other saint who was celebrated each year was St. Patrick. After all, the college was founded by a man born in Ireland and many of the early faculty and students were of Irish descent, or as it was remarked, if they did not have "Irish blood in their veins [they] had at least, sympathy for suffering Ireland in their hearts." Like the celebration of St. Ambrose, some years St. Patrick was toasted informally and other years with a program. One of the first elaborate celebrations came in 1892. In the morning the St. Ambrose students joined with the students of the Immaculate Conception Academy, a girl's school on Main Street, and attended Mass at the cathedral. That afternoon the students presented a program which included remarks by Flannagan. Toasts to the day, to the United States, to the music of Ireland, to Catholics in the United States, and to Irish patriot Daniel O'Connell were given by students named Hanson, Shannahan, Condon, Loftus, and Donohoe. The double quartet, consisting of Gaule, Gallagher, Cotter, O'Reilly, Walsh, Patton, Condon, and Gillespie, sang "Marching Through Georgia," "Down on the Farm," and "The Dear Little Shamrock of Ireland." Father James Davis, now the pastor of the Cathedral Parish, was the main speaker of the afternoon. Born in Kilkenny and educated at Carlow College, Davis served at St. Marguerite's Parish and was a frequent and popular visitor to campus. Davis told the students, "Everybody should celebrate St. Patrick's Day; not only the Irish but everybody that ever met an Irishman. Unfortunately, some carry it too far; it is St. Patrick's Day in the morning; and before evening it is somebody else's day. Although the habit does not make the monk, neither does the green make the Irish. But it shows there is a liberal and generous heart beneath." He praised the "noble spirit" of the students and urged them to love their country but not to "forget" Ireland, the land of their forefathers.[20]

Sports also played an important role in campus life. In the late nineteenth century when St. Ambrose was beginning, the faculty left the organization of sports and games to student groups. Some faculty objected to the violence of football or the free spirit displayed on the playing field. But a scholar of American collegiate sports observed, "Even a rigidly religious faculty could likely see that it was less harmful, and maybe even beneficial, to allow a certain degree of indecorous physical mayhem on campus than to try to subdue it completely."[21]

St. Ambrose students, however, did not depend on an organization in order to play a game. Depending on the season, the game would be football or baseball. Not only the students participated. A story from the second year of the school tells of how Timothy Mullen, a seminarian who taught that year, kicked a football over the belfry of the fire department Hose House located nearby. This was apparently a test of athletic prowess in the neighborhood of the school. Another story relates that Halligan kicked a football onto the roof of the school where it lodged in the drain pipe.

When the students played football, windows were sometimes broken in the school and rectory. But if the faculty hoped that with the end of the football season, parish windows would be safe, those hopes were dashed when Mullen appeared with a baseball and bat. Baseball was the "dominant" sport in most nineteenth-century American colleges, including St. Ambrose, where it was the "big college sport." In those first years there were no baseball uniforms, no gloves or mitts, often the players were barefoot, and now not only were the parish windows broken, but windows were broken in homes across the street as well.[22]

Within a year the students began to organize inter-class baseball games and soon the "St. Ambrose Seminary Base-Ball Associations" were organized. The stated purpose of the associations was to provide "both pleasure

and exercise to the students." Membership was open to "all wishing to participate in America's popular amusement."[23] The Ambrosians organized themselves into two teams: the Collegians and the Metropolitans, each with a president, secretary, treasurer, and captain. As the number of students at St. Ambrose grew, more teams were organized. By the late 1880s, they were organized into boarding school teams and day school teams, and a variety of names like the Maroons, Giants, Athletics, Grays, Davenports, Stars, Ansonians (named for Chicago Cubs first baseman and manager Cap Anson), and the Shamrocks were used, and often reused. These inter-class contests served to create community as well as provide an outlet from the in-school discipline of the classroom and the *in loco parentis* rules of the campus.

The move to Locust Street with its ten acres of land created opportunities for outdoor activities. In addition to space, another asset was that the neighbors' windows were well beyond the reach of long fly balls. Ambrose Hall was built on high ground at the south end of the site. Behind the building, the land sloped down and this lower, flat area became the site of playing fields for baseball and eventually football and other sports. The site was not without problems, however. First trees had to be cleared away in the area behind Ambrose Hall for a proper diamond to be laid out. But the best area behind the building was crossed by an old creek, and it would not be until the mid-1890s before the area would be tiled and the old creek covered.[24] Another part of the field was laid out so students could play croquet or quoits, a game which involved tossing a ring over a peg.

In the winter the baseball field was flooded with water to create an ice rink which was used for skating. The students used a combination of 500 feet of hose and pipes to get water to the site. The ice rink was used when the weather cooperated. One winter the warmer weather had "wrought havoc with the skating rink. The 'home base' and the catcher's 'footprints' are plainly visible where the ice ought to be."[25]

Winter weather brought other opportunities for recreation. When the snow cover was great enough, a horse-drawn sleigh was rounded up and as many piled in as possible for a ride around the neighborhood. One evening in February, the students and faculty joined together for a sleigh ride. The glee club came along and accompanied the ride with songs. Their efforts reportedly brought forth "applause, groans and snowballs, the last being decidedly in the advance." When the ride was over, Father Davis gave the leader of the glee club a box of cigars which was passed around to accompany the lunch that had been provided to end the evening.[26]

The snow-covered hills behind the building were a natural site for sledding and sliding. The boys used a "hobby," a "new-fangled nineteenth-century invention" which was a cross "between a butcher's block and a Japanese slipper" made of "barrel-staves and sundry other pieces of wood." It apparently worked well as a sled, but it also "filled their 'trouseroons' with holes."[27]

With a boarding school of high school-aged students, recreation took many forms and each season found new enthusiasms. One year checkers would be "the game." Another time the rage was Rip Rap, a card game with complicated rules, one object of which was to make the opponent "go down."[28] After an addition to the building in 1893, a billiards table became

The Play Hall (far right), the first gymnasium, was located behind Ambrose Hall.

the center of attention for indoor recreation.[29]

During those years there was no Thanksgiving vacation, so homesickness was a problem. There would be a traditional dinner for the faculty and students, and during the years Flannagan was on campus, a curious game evolved. Led by Flannagan, after dinner, the faculty would assemble with a barrel of apples in the study hall overlooking the front of the campus. When the students were assembled on the lawn, the priests threw the apples and watched the students scramble to retrieve them. It is not clear whether the students or the faculty enjoyed the game more. Even the usually staid Flannagan enjoyed the anarchy of this "game."[30]

The opportunity for indoor games increased in 1888 when a new building, the second on campus, was erected, largely with money furnished by Cosgrove. Referred to as the Play Hall, the building was about twenty-five by fifty feet, with a high roof looking very much like a wooden barn. It was located behind the west end of Ambrose Hall (about where later students would remember the chimney stood). There was room for pommel horses, horizontal bars, a trapeze, and other exercise equipment, as well as a handball court.[31]

When the building was finished, Schulte called a meeting of the students for November 7, 1888, and announced that the administration of the Play Hall would be turned over to them. The students then met and formed the Athletic Society. They elected officers, all of whom were students, and appointed a committee to draw up a constitution and by-laws for the society and for the use of the Play Hall. The constitution stated that the object was "to afford both amusement and exercise," and it declared that "every lawful means of exercise" was permitted. All boarding students were eligible for membership and all members were expected to "act with propriety, and exercise charity towards his fellow members." In other words, to "act as becomes a gentleman." The constitution provided for a president, vice president, secretary, treasurer, sergeant-at-arms, and the master of games. The sergeant-at-arms was given the responsibility to see that everyone abided by the rules and that the Play Hall was swept twice a week. The master of games was to take charge of all the equipment and to notify the Society if

anything became unfit for use. The by-laws provided that all accidental damage would be paid for by the Society, but other damage would be the responsibility of the member who caused it. Prefects of the boarding area would retain their authority in the Play Hall and any business that could not be settled by the membership would be referred to the faculty.[32]

On two occasions the student members could not settle an issue and had to refer the matter to Schulte. Once the students wanted to place an electric light in the Play Hall. Since that would be an expense larger than the Society could manage, a committee was appointed to "wait upon" Schulte on the matter. He apparently turned them down because at the next meeting the members defeated a motion to purchase a light for the building. Later however, they voted to assess themselves five cents a member to pay for the light. Another time the members met to discuss a common Play Hall problem, broken windows. A committee had failed to discuss the matter with Schulte as they had been assigned to do, so the meeting recessed while they sought him out. Schulte told them that the school would pay half the cost and they would be responsible for the rest.[33] The members assessed themselves ten cents each to pay for the windows.

When the Society was established, membership was limited to boarding students, but within a year, a day school group was formed with its own officers. There was periodic discussion, however, on the relationship of the day scholars and the Athletic Society and whether the two branches of the organization should be merged. Once again the officers were to "wait upon" Schulte on the matter. In time the membership was open to all St. Ambrose students.[34]

The Athletic Society seemed to work well under student leadership during its first years. But as colleges moved into the twentieth century, two important changes occurred and the St. Ambrose experience illustrated those changes. First, the inter-class games were overtaken by intercollegiate games. Second, the faculty began to take over the student-organized athletic societies and form boards of control made up of faculty and administrators. Later student and alumni representatives would be added to these boards of control of athletics.[35]

In September 1889, the *Messenger* noted that St. Ambrose entered its eighth year "under the most desirable auspices," with attendance above average. The newspaper, which was owned and operated by the Irish-American Sharon family, noted that "it is a pleasing fact to chronicle that more of our Irish-American boys are taking a collegiate course, and are competitors for academical honors now, than ever before in the history of our state."[36]

The sixty-eight students who enrolled that year may have been above the average number of previous years, but it was still five fewer than the year before. However, the number of students coming from greater distances in the late 1880s increased. Now there were students from Cascade, Muscatine, Fort Madison, Riverside, Burlington, Des Moines, Council Bluffs, and Holbrook, all in Iowa, as well as Rockford and Quincy in Illinois. However, the total number of students did not increase at a dramatic rate. It would not be until 1892 that there would be more than eighty students; in 1898, there would there be more than ninety; finally in 1902, twenty years after St. Ambrose opened, the number of students would be greater than 100. Over the decade about 60 percent of the students would be boarding students.

The failure of the enrollment to increase more rapidly and the impact of those numbers on the income of the college was a continuing matter of concern to Bishop Cosgrove. One major issue was that through the years of the late 1880s and into the 1890s, the college rarely ended the year in the black. The only source of income was the tuition paid by the students, and each year there were always a few who could not pay. These annual deficits usually amounted to only a few hundred dollars, but in a budget of only a few thousand dollars, deficits of those amounts quickly added up.

The second, and in the short term, more vexing problem, was the bishop's growing frustration with the continuing debt. In May of 1887, Cosgrove had announced that Schulte and Davis would solicit funds throughout the diocese to pay for finishing the upper two floors of Ambrose Hall and to pay down the debt. Over the next year, their solicitations and money from collections in parishes they did not visit realized over $4,300. Added to that were contributions of $500 from the bishop, $1,000 from John L. Miles who had previously given the same amount to the building fund, and a $100 contribution from Mrs. Nicholas Fejevary, a Davenport women involved in many charitable projects. This helped, but not enough.

On August 18, 1888, Cosgrove raised the issue of the continuing college debt at a meeting of the bishop's council. The discussion centered around the annual seminary collection begun by McMullen in September 1881.[37] In the years since then, the annual contributions had averaged $5,000 each year. From this fund the bishop paid for the education of seminarians who were studying around the country and abroad, as well as those who were studying at St. Ambrose. Cosgrove also used it to pay part of the salaries of Schulte and Flannagan. Now he wanted to know from his councilors if he could use the surplus of this fund to pay down the St. Ambrose debt. Following a discussion, the councilors unanimously passed a resolution that it "should not be considered an alienation of seminary funds to use some of the surplus for paying college debt."[38] Realistically the seminary fund rarely had a significant surplus for the bishop to use; by the time he paid for the education of seminarians, there was little left.

A week later Cosgrove discussed the debt at the Quasi-Synod, a meeting of the priests held each year following the annual priests' retreat. The bishop told the priests that there was still a debt of almost $11,000, and he appealed to them to help him cancel the debt. It was moved and accepted unanimously that the priests would make two-year pledges for that purpose. The bishop led off with a pledge of $500, and within a short time, the sixty priests present had made pledges that brought the total to $5,000.[39]

There was another source of pressure on Cosgrove. In his first five years as bishop, the number of Catholics in the diocese increased to over 56,000, and he had created twenty-three new parishes to serve them. At the same time the number of priests serving the diocese had only increased from seventy-five to eighty-one. In 1889, four of those priests were at St. Ambrose, and although the number of students at the college was slowly growing, the prospect that he would need to assign more priests to the college was very apparent.

It is difficult to know the level of commitment Cosgrove had to St. Ambrose. When Bishop McMullen asked him where he could find a place for his school, it would have been hard for Cosgrove to refuse him two rooms in the cathedral grade school. Cosgrove may well have believed that having done that much, McMullen would take responsibility for opening the school and maintaining it. But McMullen was ill and left Davenport a few weeks before school began. Then, with McMullen's untimely death, Cosgrove had the full responsibility for St. Ambrose.

Later opinion about Cosgrove and St. Ambrose is mixed. The Reverend Monsignor U. A. Hauber, who was a student in the early years of the twentieth century, remembered the bishop's visits to the school during that time. Hauber said that Cosgrove "had a deep and sincere interest in the college of which he was co-founder."[40] That interest led him to be generous with donating his own money and using diocesan funds to support the school. But Joseph Halligan, who was there at the beginning, said that although St. Ambrose got a "good start," it was not "pushed" by Cosgrove "the way it should have been pushed."[41] Still, whatever his personal enthusiasm about St. Ambrose, in the late 1880s, Bishop Cosgrove had the responsibility for a school that was barely holding its own, largely through his own generosity and the generosity of the priests and people of the diocese and a few friends in the city of Davenport.

Even with the generosity of these people, the debt remained at St. Ambrose and the bishop would have to continue to assign priests to its faculty. So sometime in mid-1889, Cosgrove and Father Andrew Trevis, vicar general of the diocese and vice president of the Board of Trustees of St. Ambrose, began corresponding with "distant churchmen" with an offer that might have solved the financial and staffing problems of St. Ambrose and "which would have been far-reaching in their effects on St. Ambrose College."[42]

Trevis wrote an official of the Christian Brothers, a religious order whose principal ministry was education, to see if the order would be willing to take over the administration and staffing of St. Ambrose. Trevis was told that the order would make no commitment but would consider the matter.

On December 6, 1889, the bishop wrote Brother Romuald, the former

A Great and Lasting Beginning

Brother Visitor (Provincial), reminding him that Trevis' correspondent had promised to consider the matter. Cosgrove described St. Ambrose as a school with boarders and day students who were taught by diocesan priests. He said that the school was "beautifully located," yet "removed from the noise and bustle" of the city. Although it was called a seminary, "properly speaking it is only a high school for our Catholic boys who have advanced too far or are too large for our parochial schools." He said he would like to "give it in charge to the Christian Brothers" and he was confident that in a "short time" it would be a "very prosperous school." Finally he invited Romuald to visit the school, but asked that if he did come that he not speak of why he was there to anyone, "lest perhaps it might disturb the priests who are conducting the school."[43] Cosgrove received a prompt response to his invitation from Brother Paulian, the current Brother Visitor in St. Louis, who told him that the order did not have enough brothers to take on St. Ambrose. Paulian assured Cosgrove he would not mention the matter to "any party."[44]

On January 21, 1890, Cosgrove met with his bishop's council. Without mentioning what he and Trevis had been doing, Cosgrove asked about the "advisability of placing [St. Ambrose] in charge of some order of brothers." The councilors told him they thought it would be difficult, but possible, to get a staff of brothers who could "make his college a success." However, they expressed some reservations about the Christian Brothers who had recently failed in an attempt to found an academy at Prairie du Chien, Wisconsin. They said that "though the brotherhoods contain many excellent men yet very many of them are not what they should be." They reminded the bishop that he could "more easily exercise his right of appointment" if the college was staffed by his own priests, whereas with the brothers, he would not always be able to control who was teaching on his campus. Finally they said they only "mention these facts" and they declined "either to approve or disapprove of the proposed change."[45]

If the bishop's councilors were not willing to suggest a course of action, Trevis was, and he continued to pursue the Christian Brothers. Trevis had been traveling in the east for several months and had not been at the January meeting of the bishop's council. It is not clear whether he knew of the recommendation the bishop had received. In April 1890, Trevis wrote Cosgrove from Baltimore to say that he had met with Brother Patrick, the assistant to the superior general of the order in Paris, who was visiting Christian Brother houses in the United States. Trevis said he had made the case for the brothers to take over St. Ambrose and pressed Patrick to reverse the negative decision Cosgrove had received the previous December. Although Patrick mentioned the difficulty of finding men to do the job, Trevis left the meeting "hopeful" that Patrick would write the brothers in St. Louis to visit the campus, or even that Patrick could visit himself, if his travel schedule permitted it. Finally, Trevis told Cosgrove that he did not "suppose you have concluded any arrangement for St. Ambrose with any other parties," and urged him to issue an invitation to the Christian Brothers in St. Louis to visit St. Ambrose.[46]

Cosgrove wrote immediately to Paulian to say that if anyone wanted to visit St. Ambrose to let him know so that he would be there. But the response from Paulian was the same: he had no men to send and he would not "think of accepting even the most generous offer for some three or four

years to come."[47]

The other parties to whom Trevis referred was the Society of Mary or Marianists. Sometime in late 1889, Cosgrove had written the Reverend Landelin Beck, the provincial superior of the Marianist Province of America in Dayton, Ohio. On February 8, 1890, Beck replied that the superior general wanted "more precise" information about St. Ambrose. Beck asked Cosgrove to supply information about the organization of the college, in what condition the Marianists would receive it, the number of day students and boarders, a copy of the prospectus, and his opinion about prospects for success. He also asked for a "photographic view of the buildings."[48] Cosgrove told them it was a classical and commercial institution housed in one building but that "two others were to be put up." The bishop said there were good prospects for the success of St. Ambrose since it was the only Catholic high school for boys in Davenport.[49]

Meeting on February 19, 1890, the Marianist provincial council discussed the information Cosgrove had supplied and had two questions: Was he willing to sell the college to the Marianists, or was his intention to turn over the operation of St. Ambrose and pay the Marianists a salary?[50] Beck wrote Cosgrove on February 18 to say that the Reverend Joseph Weckesser, SM, the president of St. Mary's Institute, would visit St. Ambrose in the coming weeks to talk with Cosgrove and get this additional information.[51]

Following this visit to Davenport sometime in early March, the provincial council was told that the building was too small to accommodate the combination of classical and commercial pupils who attended. An even bigger problem, however, was that the bishop could not sell the school without permission from Rome, a long and complex process, and he could not afford to pay the kind of salaries the Marianists wanted. After discussion, the council decided that it could not accept Cosgrove's offer.[52]

The question of whether to turn the operation of St. Ambrose over to a religious order, however, did not go away. In June of 1891, Cosgrove once again raised this issue at a meeting of the Bishop's Council. Cosgrove said that St. Ambrose was still "not self-sustaining," and he asked the councilors to discuss what could be done "to make it more successful." Cosgrove may have implied that one option would be to close the school because the councilors' first recommendation was that St. Ambrose "be kept going." They said that the bishop could use funds from the seminary collection to make up the "annual deficit." They also recommended that he open a new parish "around the college" and that a religious order be invited to "take charge of both" the parish and the college. They pointed out that the area to the west of the college was growing rapidly and that a new parish would provide an "incalculable" benefit to the people moving into the area.[53]

Not easily dissuaded, Cosgrove tried one last time to get the Christian Brothers to take over St. Ambrose. In March of 1893, he wrote Brother Paulian and reminded him that he said he would reconsider the issue in three years. Cosgrove said that the college was still conducted by priests of the diocese, and he added, "I must say [it] has been very flourishing." But, that for the reasons he had given him in 1890, Cosgrove preferred "to have it conducted by Christian Brothers." Just what Cosgrove had told Paulian in 1890 is not clear, but the answer from the Christian Brothers was clear: they would not take over St. Ambrose College.[54]

The various attempts by Cosgrove to turn St. Ambrose over to a religious order were born of his frustration with the continuing annual deficit and the debt which remained from buying the property and building Ambrose Hall. There is no indication that he wanted to close the school, although the possibility was there. If he did not want to close the school, neither did he want the burden of supporting it. He would have been happy to have a Catholic college in his diocese, but he did not share McMullen's vision that it be a diocesan school serving Catholics of the upper Mississippi Valley.

In the midst of the discussions about securing a religious order to take over St. Ambrose, two personnel changes took place at the college which did have far-reaching effects. First, Joseph Halligan left the school at the end of the 1891 spring semester to found the *Davenport Daily Leader* newspaper. Halligan's leaving not only marked the departure of one of the original faculty members, but it marked a change in the lay presence on the faculty: for the next fifteen years, priests would be in charge of the Commercial department. In the mid-1890s, local music teachers were hired part-time to teach at St. Ambrose, but it would not be until the fall of 1904 that another layman would become a full-time faculty member at St. Ambrose when William L. Doyle came to teach chemistry.

The other change with a far-reaching effect for St. Ambrose came in September 1891, when Father Schulte left to become the pastor of St. Mary's Parish in Iowa City.[55] The late 1880s were full years for Schulte. In addition to teaching at St. Ambrose and the responsibilities of being the chief administrator, at one time or another he also assisted at the Cathedral, said Mass for the sisters and students at the Immaculate Conception Academy, and was the pastor of St. Peter's Parish in Buffalo. Added to those duties were his travels through the diocese to raise money for St. Ambrose.

It also is clear that although Schulte was president of the college and secretary treasurer of the Board of Trustees, he was not a part of the discussions among the bishop and his councilors about the future of St. Ambrose. Cosgrove's insistence that the Christian Brothers keep the matter a secret lest they "disturb the priests" at St. Ambrose indicates that Schulte was not a part of those negotiations. Nevertheless, since the bishop was discussing the matter with his councilors, and given the nature of clerical culture, it seems likely that Schulte was aware of what was going on.

The strain of work began to tell on Schulte and sometime in late 1889, he was taken ill and spent several weeks under care at the bishop's house; he was still there in February 1890 when the *Messenger* published a brief notice of his illness.[56] Years later Halligan said that Schulte had "a sort of breakdown in health, perhaps some heart trouble."[57] Schulte's illness coincided with the exchange of letters between Cosgrove and the Christian Brothers and Marianist Brothers, as well as Cosgrove's discussion with his councilors concerning the future of St. Ambrose. The continuing problem of the operating deficits at St. Ambrose would also have been a burden to Schulte.

In time he regained his health and with the beginning of school in the fall of 1890, he was back in the classroom. Whatever his standing with the bishop might have been, Schulte still had the esteem of his colleagues and the students. On March 19, 1891, the feast of St. Joseph (Schulte's middle name was Joseph), they gathered in his classroom where first prefect Joseph Hanson spoke to Schulte on behalf of all the students. Hanson said the students had noticed Schulte's many acts of kindness, and perhaps acknowledging the strains of the past year, he said they had also "not failed to notice and realize the fact that the cares, the anxieties and the responsibilities of

the President of a Seminary, when accompanied by the duties of priest and professor, are by no means a light or insignificant task." Hanson noted Schulte's "zeal" for religion and education since the school opened nine years before, and his continuing willingness to do whatever was necessary to satisfy the needs of the students.

In response Schulte told them he thought they had "overdrawn the picture" of his virtues and talents. He exhorted them to "persevere faithfully in their studies and to endeavor in every way to become good and useful citizens," and he wished them success in whatever they did in the future. At the end of the program, Joseph Hanson asked for a free day which Schulte granted immediately.[58]

Graduation was held on June 23, 1891, in Ambrose Hall. The room was decorated with evergreens and flowers, with pictures of McMullen and Cosgrove and the Sacred Heart and the Blessed Mother on either side of the stage. Opposite the entrance to the room was a life-sized picture of St. Ambrose. The ceremony had the usual music, readings, and declamations by the students, and the valedictory address, delivered by Joseph Hanson. The bishop awarded certificates of graduation in the Commercial department to John J. Condon of Davenport and John M. Walsh of Riverside, and delivered the closing address. Schulte was not present.[59]

A week after commencement, Cosgrove convened the meeting of the bishop's council that discussed whether to build a parish near the college and turn both over to a religious order. If Schulte knew about that, it could have been the last straw in his decision to leave St. Ambrose. In any case Schulte was scheduled to take up his duties in Iowa City on September 17. Two days before he left, Schulte was given a farewell dinner attended by the bishop, Trevis, and the college faculty.[60] With that, the Schulte era at St. Ambrose ended.

Schulte's move to Iowa City seemed to have a certain logic to it. The state university was located there and St. Mary's Parish was on the edge of the campus. Schulte had experience in college education and therefore, he seemed the best choice for pastor.[61] But there was much more to it than that. Schulte's vision and his hopes for St. Ambrose clashed with the bishop's. Schulte wanted St. Ambrose to be a more progressive institution, teaching more science and other subjects which was the growing trend in American higher education. But those things cost money, and money was one thing St. Ambrose and the bishop did not have. What innovations Schulte was able to bring about, like the geology collection, were often paid for out of his own pocket. All the while, the bishop had to reach into diocesan funds to keep the college in the black. Schulte and Cosgrove had different hopes for the college and when the opening occurred in Iowa City, Cosgrove took advantage of it and removed Schulte from St. Ambrose. In his sermon for Schulte's funeral fifty years later, Hauber, who would be among the next generation of progressive leaders of St. Ambrose, said that Schulte's "removal in 1891 was a great loss to St. Ambrose College, from which it did not easily recover for many years."[62]

Bishop McMullen was dead, all thirty-three of the original class had left St. Ambrose and gone on with their lives, Halligan and Schulte departed in the summer of 1891, and now Cosgrove was the only one left of those who were there at the beginning. It would be a reluctant Bishop Cosgrove, and a new president, who would shepherd the school in the years ahead.

A Great and Lasting Beginning

ST. AMBROSE SEMINARY

LOCUST ST. BETWEEN SCOTT AND WESTERN AVE.
DAVENPORT, IOWA

The institution was founded by the late Rt. Rev. John McMullen, D. D., first Bishop of Davenport, in the year 1882

INCORPORATED UNDER THE LAWS OF THE STATE OF IOWA, OCT. 6, 1885

The Seminary is under the supervision of the Rt. Rev. Ordinary of the Diocese, the Rt. Rev. H. Cosgrove, D. D.

The object of the Institution is to impart to the Catholic Young Men attending, a thorough Mental and Moral Culture,

The Course embraces the CLASSICAL, COMMERCIAL, SCIENTIFIC AND PREPARATORY COURSE.

TERMS: Boarding School, - per year $190 00
Day School, - - " " 50.00

Instruction in music given at terms arranged with Professor

❧ Chapter Three ❧

As the *Catholic Messenger* announced in late October 1891, the new president of St. Ambrose was Father J. T. A. Flannagan, who had been vice president since 1885. Father Albert A. Nodler who had come to St. Ambrose the year before as disciplinarian, now added the office of vice president. Two other priests, both newly ordained, joined the faculty, the Reverend Arthur J. Zaiser, who taught music, languages, and mathematics, and the Reverend John J. Cassidy, an 1887 graduate of St. Ambrose, who became the principal of the Commercial department. The *Messenger* article also noted the growth in the number of boarding students, improvements made to the grounds, and baseball, which was the most important sport on campus, although a rival, football, would rise to challenge it in the 1890s. There was one other change that year: the tenth annual catalogue dropped the title Seminary, and now called the school St. Ambrose College.

There were no summer sessions at St. Ambrose so that was a time for maintenance on the building and grounds. The improvements noted by the *Messenger* in the summer of 1891 included new sidewalks through the campus, a new baseball field, remodeling of some of the rooms in the building, painting and plastering in other areas, some new furniture, and "a general renovation throughout."[2] But more serious changes for the campus were already under discussion.

The enrollment was increasing each year. There had been sixty-three students in the fall of 1887, the first year that boarding facilities were available: thirty day students and thirty-three boarders. The next year the number of boarding students had increased to forty-two, and that fall Schulte had told a visitor that if that rate of increase continued, it would not be long before an addition would have to be made to the building to accommodate more students.[3] The fall of 1891 saw an increase to seventy-one students: twenty-four day students and forty-seven boarders. With the prospect of even more students the following year, the pressure for an addition to the building was becoming greater.

Cosgrove discussed the matter with his council in July 1892. He told them that the debt from the building was still not paid off and that there was still an annual budget deficit, over $800 for the 1890-1891 year, and several hundred dollars for the 1891-1892 year.[4] The councilors recommended that the St. Ambrose professors visit parishes throughout the diocese to preach on higher education and that they take up a collection to support St. Ambrose. The councilors also discussed the need for more room at the college and told the bishop that when he deemed it "prudent" he

should begin planning for an addition to the building. They also said that "if possible," he should raise the salaries of the professors. They told the bishop that at an "opportune time" he should appeal to the diocesan clergy for personal contributions to St. Ambrose.[5] The bishop accepted those recommendations, and that summer Flannagan, and the pastor of the cathedral parish, Father James Davis, a strong supporter of the college, toured the diocese.[6]

For years Cosgrove had relied on his councilors for advice about diocesan affairs, including what to do about St. Ambrose. Along with the councilors, there was a Board of Trustees of the college, made up of the bishop, the vicar general, and the president of the college. The vicar general was also a councilor and thus part of the discussions about the college, but the two presidents, Schulte and now Flannagan, were not on the bishop's council, and so they were not present for those discussions. In practice, the members of the bishop's council served as trustees of the college. Even though he did not always take their advice, the issues were thoroughly discussed. Up to now the St. Ambrose matters discussed involved paying off the debt, raising money for capital improvements, and whether to turn the college over to a religious order. Now the councilors suggested that the bishop raise the salaries of the St. Ambrose faculty; later, they would suggest curricular changes, both of which were issues that might properly be made by college authorities.

Discussions continued over the next year about an addition to Ambrose Hall and by the spring of 1893, planning was in an advanced stage. But when the councilors met on June 6, 1893, they expressed some misgivings about proceeding. The bishop made the case that the addition was necessary to accommodate the growing number of students. He said that at least $14,500 would be necessary for the construction and furnishing of the addition. The councilors, however, were more concerned about the "feasibility" of building the addition. The college was still not self-supporting, a debt remained, and following several weeks of national economic uncertainty, in early May the stock market had collapsed. Since the councilors were uneasy about undertaking a large financial outlay, they told the bishop that the professors should travel through the diocese to make an appeal for St. Ambrose. If that was successful, then "as soon as possible," the bishop should "proceed to make the improvements."[7]

Apparently Cosgrove took "as soon as possible" to mean immediately, because by early July the excavation for the addition was finished and the foundation walls were completed. The addition was on the east side of the

A Great and Lasting Beginning

original building. The ground floor held a trunk room, laundry rooms, and a gymnasium. The entire second floor was a study hall. The third floor had rooms for two professors, an infirmary, the library and reading room, and a science laboratory. The entire fourth floor housed the chapel. Bath and shower rooms were built on the landing of the staircase which formed the connection between the original

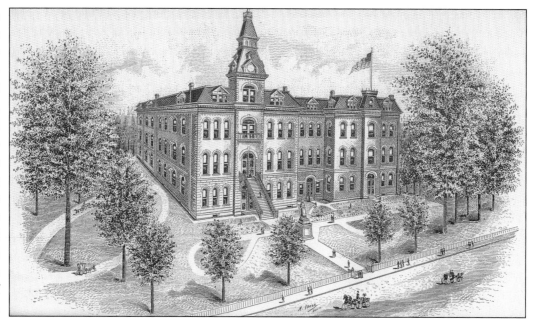

Ambrose Hall, 1893.

diphtheria killed the young and many died from it in Scott County that spring, including three siblings in one family. As soon as a student was diagnosed, he was sent to Mercy Hospital. Several Ambrosians who were sent there with diphtheria eventually recovered. When it became clear that an epidemic was imminent on campus, the healthy students were sent home and school was closed for

building and the new wing (where the elevator is now located). The cost for the addition was estimated to be $20,000.[8]

The new chapel was sixty feet by forty feet and occupied the entire fourth floor. The wooden floor was oiled and the walls were white with varnished woodwork. Six pillars supported the ceiling. Four rows of pews seated about 175 people. The sanctuary, which was seventeen feet wide and fifteen feet deep, was at the north end of the room, and was surrounded by a railing. The main altar in the center of the sanctuary was white with gilt trimming and was donated by St. Anthony's Parish in Davenport. On either side of the sanctuary were two side altars taken from the original St. Marguerite's Cathedral torn down the year before to make room for the new Sacred Heart Cathedral. One side altar was dedicated to the Blessed Virgin and the other altar was dedicated to St. Joseph. Seven double windows provided light which was supplemented by electric ceiling lights. Music was provided by a pipe organ, a gift of Bishop Cosgrove. It was, as one student enthusiastically put it, an "ideal chapel" for "one of the foremost educational institutions of the west."[9]

The new chapel was used for the first time in December 1893. The next spring a new statue of the Immaculate Conception based on the painting by Murillo, was installed on the Blessed Mother's altar. At the same time two statues of kneeling angels arrived, which were placed on either side of the main altar. A third statue of an angel holding a vessel for holy water was placed at the door of the chapel.[10]

The infirmary on the third floor was an important addition to the campus. In a building where several dozen young men were living in an open dormitory, common diseases like colds, influenza, measles, and the mumps spread rapidly. With the infirmary, students who were ill could be provided the possibility of isolation from the remainder of the student body. Still, illness, and sometimes death, would be a part of the rhythm of life during those years at St. Ambrose.

In February 1893, a more serious disease appeared on campus: diphtheria. Two students, Willie Russell of Muscatine and Joseph Tholl of Council Bluffs, died of diphtheria and several others were ill. A virulent disease,

several weeks so that the building could be thoroughly disinfected. That same winter a third student, Herman Stohben, died from pneumonia.[11] Although preventative measures would be taken to avoid epidemic illness, the diphtheria epidemic on campus would not be the only time the school would close and the students would be sent home because of illness.[12]

In the meantime, improvements continued to be made to the grounds. In 1895, a brick sidewalk replaced an earlier plank walk that ran from Ambrose Hall to Locust Street. New stone steps were installed to lead down to a new brick sidewalk which ran along Locust Street for the entire length of the campus. In 1898, the college boasted that it was now under "complete fire protection" since the Davenport Water Company had finished laying pipes with hydrants along Locust Street as far as Gaines Street.[13] One other addition in those years would become a campus landmark. The Reverend Edmund Hayes, the pastor of St. Patrick's Parish in Imogene, Iowa, donated a statue of St. Ambrose which was placed on a pedestal, donated by Father Davis, in front of Ambrose Hall.[14]

Each year also saw improvements on the interior of the building. In January 1894, the library moved into its room in the new wing. The following October new bookcases were installed in the library to replace temporary shelves that had been in use since the addition was built.[15] Two years later an "elegant line of opera chairs with book rest attachments" replaced the old desks that had been used in the "upper recitation room" since the move to Locust Street.[16]

New traditions were added to established events. Bunting in blue and white, the recently chosen school colors, decorated the hall for the annual elocution contest for the Reldon Medal in 1893.[17] Following the contest, several former students remained and met to discuss the formation of an Alumni Association. All former students received notices to attend a meeting to be held following the graduation ceremony on June 21. At that meeting a committee was appointed to draft a constitution creating the Alumni Association of St. Ambrose College, which was "to cooperate in promoting the interests of the college and a fraternal union among the members." Anyone who had studied for one year at St. Ambrose was entitled to membership. Following ratification of the constitution, the members elected the Reverend Henry Maniett as president. Maniett had entered as a student in the second semester of the first year and was now the college vice president. John J. Ryan, elected vice president, Ed J. Stackhouse, secretary, were both members of the original class of thirty-three students in 1882. The Reverend Daniel Molyneaux was named treasurer, and Father John J. Cassidy was elected historian.

The *Messenger* noted that the formation of the Alumni Association was "only another illustration of the kind of men St. Ambrose [was] graduating, men full of push and energy and rapidly making their mark in the world." The college had already produced eleven priests who were serving the diocese, as well as "lawyers, doctors, bookkeepers and laborers in many of the trades." By the next year there were forty members and they made plans to have an annual banquet.[18]

Some of the men full of push and energy got their start while still students at St. Ambrose. The addition of more space with the new building gave those in-house entrepreneurs a greater opportunity to ply their wares. One unnamed student opened a barber shop in the corner of a room on the third floor, and offered "all styles of hair cutting, curling, frizzing and mustache trimming." According to reports, he did a "thriving business, the financial stringency notwithstanding." Another student, Michael J. Riaski, managed the college bookstore which sold text books as well as a supply of candy and other confections. His business was so good he hired two clerks to assist him.[19]

Business may have been good at the college bookstore, but the nation was in one of the "most severe depressions in the country's economic history." The gross national product had declined nearly 12 percent since the beginning of 1893, and national unemployment was about 19 percent. Annual average wages had dropped about 10 percent and many American families "experienced extreme hardship." There are no precise figures for Iowa, but the *Iowa Biennial Report* for 1892-1893 reported that "hundreds of laboring people" in Iowa were unemployed, "largely in the building trades and factory employees."[20] Because of the depression, Flannagan told the bishop that 1893-1894 had "been a hard year," but he assured the bishop that the many past due accounts he reported were "all good," and that "most, if not all" would be paid soon. In spite of that, the college ended the year in the black.[21]

In other ways it had been a good year. The addition was completed and was now in full use. Three of the five priests on the faculty, Henry Maniett,

The original statue, 1895.

the Reverend Daniel Mulvihill, and the Reverend Martin McNamara were graduates of St. Ambrose, meeting one of Bishop McMullen's goals to educate clergy for service in the diocese.

Just before school opened for the fall semester in 1894, Flannagan spoke with the *Davenport Democrat* and gave a cautiously optimistic view of the coming year: "Of course, the unsettled condition of business affairs and the hard times that set in last summer have affected the school as well as every other enterprise that must be supported by money. But here we have felt it less than it has been felt in some quarters, many of our students being the sons of wealthy farmers, who are just now well able to send their sons to school and have not much for them to do at home. So we shall not open with a decreased enrollment, at any rate."[22]

Flannagan may have overstated the prosperity of Iowa farmers who were also impacted by the depression, but he was correct in his assessment about enrollment. That fall there were eighty-four students, five more than the previous year, divided between thirty-six day students, an increase of seven, and forty-eight boarders, a decrease of two.

The session that began in the fall of 1894 saw a significant change in the curriculum. Two years before, the bishop's council agreed that an additional course in Latin should be added so that the seminary students could become "better Latinists."[23] Now two years of philosophy were also added to the five-year Classical course. The impetus for those curriculum changes was a decree by the United States bishops at the Third Plenary Council of Baltimore in 1884, where the requirements for those studying to be priests were strengthened to two years of philosophy and four years of theology.[24] In the years following that decree, St. Ambrose students who were studying to be priests, like Bernard Mackin and James Renihan, left St. Ambrose to study philosophy and theology elsewhere in the country. Now with more Latin and two years of philosophy, those students could remain at St. Ambrose to study philosophy, and then go to major seminary for theology.

The addition of philosophy to the curriculum brought another change to the campus: the Reverend George Giglinger joined the faculty. Born in Bavaria in 1868, Giglinger had studied in Rome at the Propaganda College, the same place young John McMullen had studied over thirty years before. Giglinger earned a Doctor of Divinity Degree and was ordained a priest in 1890. He served in parishes in Ft. Madison and Burlington and came to St. Ambrose in 1894, where along with philosophy, he also taught German, and became the first St. Ambrose faculty member with a doctorate. Recalled as a "simple, humble man" he did not enforce much discipline in the classroom. Later, Giglinger protested that he was not suited to teach philosophy, so in 1901, he turned over philosophy to one of his former students, the Reverend William P. Shannahan, but he continued to teach

A Great and Lasting Beginning

German until 1907.

If he was easy-going in the classroom, Giglinger became a social crusader, very much in the mold of later generations of Ambrose faculty. He organized Our Lady of Lourdes Parish in Bettendorf to serve the Mexican immigrants who worked for the Bettendorf Company. At the request of the bishop, he found the location for and built St. Vincent's Home for orphans. He joined the temperance crusade to dry up Davenport saloons and was so outspoken that occasionally he needed a police escort to get to campus. Later, when he was pastor of St. Mary's Parish in Keokuk, he supported the medical practice of an African-American doctor by giving him rooms in the parish school when the doctor could not find office space elsewhere.[25]

The faculty and senior students in 1893. Bottom row, left to right: unidentified, Michael Riaski '97, Jack Wickham '94. Second row: John M. Walsh '96, John Condon '95, Patrick J. Gaule '95, James W. Gillespie '96, Charles J. Donohoe '96. Third row: unidentified, Rev. John M. Cassidy, Rev. J.T.A. Flannagan, President, Rev. Henry Maniett, Rev. A.J. Zaiser, unidentified. Top row: unidentified, William P. Shannahan '96, Patrick Flynn '93, unidentified.

or whether Iowans should repeal the state prohibition law. But the more common activity of the Philalethic Association was to have a member present an essay for discussion. Charles J. Donohoe won a copy of *Ben Hur* for the best essay describing the chapel that had just been dedicated in the new wing of Ambrose Hall.[29]

The Philalethic Association did not meet in the 1894-1895 year, and it was apparently replaced by Giglinger's Friday night "quiz" classes. But in the fall of 1895, Flannagan reorganized the group with himself as the faculty moderator. The group met irregularly that fall and then suspended and resumed for a few meetings in the fall of 1897. Those meetings were more social than the previous times the

Giglinger augmented his philosophy classes by holding a "quiz" class on Friday evenings. A student would be in charge of the class, but Giglinger would be in attendance. The format was like the literary society format where someone would propound a thesis and the students would argue in opposition.

The philosophy students quickly became the campus elite. Later they would room in a section of Ambrose Hall that came to be called "Wisdom Row," where according to legend, they led a quiet life among books and games of chess.[26] This assumed status may have been the reason for the doggerel which appeared in the *Catholic Messenger* in November 1894: "A little philosopher jolly and fat,/On a keg of powder one day sat;/He scratched a match on the sole of his shoe,/And the gentle zephyrs through his whiskers blew./And now he is a little angel dear,/Many, many miles from here;/And on a golden harp with golden strings,/Angelic songs he often sings./Often sings of college life,/With all its joy, with all its strife./And sings in a voice of the highest soprano,/The praise and goodness of Ambrosiana."[27]

At Thanksgiving time 1893, a group of senior students, many of whom would enter the new philosophy curriculum and go on to be ordained priests, met to form the Philalethic Association (meaning the love of truth).[28] This group had occasional debates, usually on topics current in the news, such as whether the United States should annex the Hawaiian Islands

group existed: an October meeting began with a speech from Julius Caesar, a trombone solo, the reading of Longfellow's "Evangeline," a band concert, and the evening closed with a recitation of James Whitcomb Riley's "Nothin' to Say."[30] The title of the Riley poem may have been prescient, since it appears there were only two more meetings of the group before it disbanded.

One short-lived club, perhaps an outgrowth of the Philalethic Association, was the To-Ka-Lon Club, formed in the spring of 1898 to cultivate careful reading and discussion. Each member was to read ten pages of a book and then relate what he had read to the other members. That spring they were reading Cobbett's history of the Protestant Reformation, the writings of Bishop John Lancaster Spalding, and the lectures of the Reverend Tom Burke. One wag said of them: "Unto the campus they repair/To tread some path alone./And there discuss their theme with care/The boys of To-Ka-Lon." When someone suggested the club had ceased to exist, a member rejoined, "The To-Ka-Lon, the To-Ka-Lon,/Dear friends is still alive./Come rain or shine, or gloomy days,/The Club will still survive."[31] But how alive it was is a matter of some conjecture, since there is no further record of the club, at least under that name. There is no indication as to the meaning of the name of the club.

Twice in the mid-1880s, the topic of debate at the meetings of the St. John's Literary Society had to do with the relative merits of baseball and

Fr. Giglinger and the philosophers of 1896. Standing, left to right: John J. Condon, James W. Gillespie, Francis A. Kottenstette, John M. Walsh, Charles J. Donohoe. Seated: Patrick Gaule, Edward Weil, Fr. Giglinger, William P. Shannahan.

football. The proposition was put one of two ways, either "that there is more science in a game of football than in a game of baseball," or, "that there is more pleasure derived from a game of football than from a game of baseball." In both cases the affirmative side was judged to be the winner.[32] If football was popular with the students at St. Ambrose, it was not popular with the administration.

Football was evolving as a sport in the late nineteenth century. Its roots were in rugby, with its scrummage and its rough, sometimes brutal play. Cosgrove called it "roughby," a game of "unseemly conduct" not suited for gentlemen, and Flannagan thought that parents would not want to see their sons rolling around in the mud.[33] Nevertheless, football had been part of life at St. Ambrose since Tim Mullen kicked a football over the Hose House tower in the days at St. Marguerite's, and it continued to be played informally into the 1890s.

If the president and the bishop did not like football, at least they tolerated its presence on campus. The catalogue of 1893-1894 noted that the spacious campus gave "ample" room to play football, baseball, and other outdoor sports. That same year the Athletic Society listed a football team with James Gillespie as captain, which played a number of games against the city high school, which it claimed it had always beaten. But when Clinton High School, which apparently had a very good team, sent a challenge to play the Ambrosians, they declined, because according to one player, "man is destined to die but once."[34] Still there seemed to be ambivalence

about football at St. Ambrose. The author of "Ambrosiana," a column which appeared regularly in the *Catholic Messenger* through those years, said that "rugby, an inhuman species of physical exercise, is justly becoming unpopular among the students," and that he awaited the day when "this semi-savage sport" would be "declared illegal by appropriate legislation."[35] St. Ambrose students continued to play football through the 1890s, but it would be another ten years before there would be any official recognition of the sport on campus.

If football was the "dominant" sport on other American campuses, at St. Ambrose it was baseball, which the college catalogue called "America's popular amusement," that continued to occupy that position. Baseball at St. Ambrose was a two season game. The first season began as soon as the weather permitted in the spring. In mid-March 1894, the *Messenger* noted that baseball was being played with "all the old time zest." A week later, however, it noted that a recent cold snap had "hushed the melodious voice of the umpire on the diamond."[36] There was also a fall season and the students played as long as the weather allowed. In mid-October 1894, they played what had been billed as the final game of the season, only to have the weather warm up so that several more games were played before the cold stopped them in mid-November.[37]

There continued to be inter-class contests, with as many as a dozen teams organized by various groups of students. But the baseball "season" began with the first game against an off-campus team. By the early 1890s, the best players from all the teams organized as the College Nine and played

A Great and Lasting Beginning

Rev. Flannagan's first band. Seated, left to right: M.J. Miles, R.H. Shillig, Rev. Flannagan, M.M. Loftus, T.P. Murphy. Standing, left to right: C.J. Donohoe, O.H. Mueller, H.A. Knebel, H.J. Hogan, M.J. O'Hearn, J.N. Adam, E.C. McCormack, J.F. O'Callaghan.

Davenport teams from off-campus. The 1894 season began with a game against the local YMCA. Before a crowd of 200 spectators and behind heavy hitting by the Ambrose batters, the college won 15-8. Over the next few weeks, St. Ambrose played Davenport High School, teams of local players put together for a game, and Augustana, whom they defeated, 23-19.

Early the morning of Decoration Day, May 30, Maniett took a group of students to lay flowers on graves at the Catholic cemetery. They returned to campus to watch the younger St. Ambrose team defeat Davenport High School, 22-4, and that afternoon, the college team defeat East Davenport, 22-5. At season's end, the college team had a record of eight wins and two losses.[38]

Handball was another popular sport at St. Ambrose. The Play Hall had a handball alley and the Athletic Society set rules to regulate its use. Tournaments among the St. Ambrose students became a regular part of recreational activities, especially as a part of the celebration of special days on campus. On St. Patrick's Day of 1899, the students played handball all day, and according to one reporter, "Erin's favorite game developed a number of champions."[39] In addition the better players accepted challenges from off-campus teams; in 1896 Ambrosians played a series of handball games against teams from the local YMCA.[40]

In the years since the Athletic Society had been organized in 1888, it had been under the control of the students. It met regularly and maintained control over official sports on campus, which was typical on most American campuses. Nationally, however, control of athletics by students was beginning to disappear as faculty and the administration took more control. Part of the reason for this change was the increasing cost of even the smallest program, so that self-assessment of the members to meet expenses was no longer adequate. Another reason was that sports contests moved from being inter-class to inter-collegiate so administrators felt that better control could be exercised by them than by the students. Finally, as sports became more popular on campus, faculties worried about conflicts with academic values.

At St. Ambrose this movement to faculty involvement and then control of sports began at the fall organizational meeting in 1893, when Mulvihill, the master of discipline, was elected the Athletic Society's president. It is not clear why this happened and there is no indication of any change in the constitution or by-laws to allow it. Rather it seems to have been a pragmatic decision at a time when there was dissension in the group; nevertheless, the students accepted this and reelected him the next February for the spring semester.[41] The next year Mulvihill was elected manager of the Athletic Society, and from then onward there would be a priest-manager. Students once again held the office of president but in 1898, a priest was elected treasurer; after that the treasurer would always be a priest.

In May 1893, another annual custom began with Field Day. All the students participated in a variety of events including races of various lengths, high jump, running jump, standing jump, a sack race, string race, three-legged race, a free-for-all shoe race, and a free-for-all blind race. The day concluded with a baseball game. Field Day became an annual end-of-year event alongside the elocution contest and commencement. Often the bishop would be in attendance, as well as spectators from throughout the city.[42]

The major celebrations of the year, commencement, St. Ambrose Day, the elocution contests were observed with ceremony that included speeches, dramatic performances, and music. Since 1885, music at commencement was provided by the Second Regiment Band. Founded as the German Union Band in 1856 by Jacob Strasser, in 1885, it was affiliated with the Second Regiment, Iowa National Guard and took the name Second Regiment Band.[43] In 1894, that band was not available for commencement, so music was provided by Otto's Orchestra, founded by Ernst Otto, a prominent local music teacher. Occasionally at commencement, a student would perform a piano solo, or a student group would sing a selection, but there was no organized music program on campus.

There was a long musical tradition in Davenport. The German immigrants who began to settle in Davenport in the years before the Civil War brought music with them. In the last half of the nineteenth century, there were a number of popular local concert bands coming from that immigrant tradition which gave frequent concerts throughout the community. There were also many music teachers who formed choral and chamber groups from their students who gave regular performances. For several years in the 1890s, there was a summer opera series performed by local musicians.[44] Local concerts and music programs were one of the places Ambrosians went when they had an opportunity to leave campus in the evening.

Another source of the musical milieu of Davenport came from the river boats which brought music, and especially late in the period, jazz, to Davenport. Finally the railroad bridge which connected Iowa with Chicago meant that touring groups stopped in Davenport for concerts. In the 1890s the John Philip Sousa Band played in Davenport regularly, as did his chief rival, Patrick Gilmore's Band. Other musical groups who appeared regularly included military bands from the United States and Europe, the Chicago Symphony, a touring group from the Metropolitan Opera in New York, and other professional companies.

That musical tradition was the context for a music program at St. Ambrose. Moreover, with a wealth of teachers of all genres of music, Flannagan had a source for a music faculty. The first formal music program at St. Ambrose came in the 1894-1895 year when a Mr. G. E. Griffith was hired to be professor of vocal music. Griffith organized a glee club which began slowly with only a few members, and apparently was in need of a great deal of rehearsal.[45] One wag said that the first rule of the glee club was that "no member will be permitted under any consideration to make use of his vocal organs outside the club room," he could talk but not sing, "unless for money."[46] At its first performance, the glee club provided music for the elocution contest in May 1895, and at graduation the next month. The music tended to the familiar and sentimental: "Tenting Tonight on the Old Camp Ground," and "Home They Brought Her Warrior Dead," based on a poem by Tennyson, were sung at the elocution contest, and "Auld Lang Syne," and "Words of Farewell," at commencement. Griffith spent only one year at St. Ambrose, but the glee club continued for the next few years under student leadership. Vocal music did not receive much support from Flannagan and it would be another ten years before there was another faculty member for vocal music.

Another musical group that performed at the 1895 elocution contest and commencement was the Mandolin Club. Edward C. McCormack, a student from Boone, Iowa, was listed among the faculty in the catalogue for the next three years as teacher of piano, mandolin and guitar. That first Mandolin Club had McCormack as its leader. He and Edward McGorrisk

from Des Moines played mandolin, and Matthew Miles from Cedar Rapids played piano. This group became one of the most popular on campus and within a year it had grown to two banjos, two guitars, three mandolins, and a piano.[47] But when McCormack left St. Ambrose, the Mandolin Club ceased to exist.

Flannagan did not support vocal music, what he wanted was a band. During those years the only organized extracurricular activities were football and baseball. But neither could be played during the winter months. A band would provide a wholesome extracurricular activity that could be pursued year-round, and it could provide music for St. Ambrose events. So sometime in 1895, Flannagan called Mr. Albert Petersen to campus to discuss the formation of a band. Born in Davenport in 1867, Petersen began his musical career when he formed the Davenport Cornet Band in 1882. Later he served as an apprentice in Jacob Strasser's Union Band and in 1895, he became its manager.[48] Flannagan asked Petersen if he could organize a band at St. Ambrose, but Petersen told the president that the prospect was not good for a band, since there were no instruments, and there were no students with any experience playing musical instruments. "We must have a band," Flannagan insisted, "obstacles are to be overcome." Flannagan asked Petersen to make a list of the instruments that would be needed and he ordered them at once from the C. G. Conn Company in Elkhart, Indiana.[49]

The instruments arrived in mid-October and Petersen began the process of matching an instrument to a student. There were four cornets, two altos, a tenor horn, a trombone, tuba, bass drum, and snare drum. Edward McCormack, one of the few students with musical training, was named the leader and played baritone horn.[50] The band made its debut performance at the St. Ambrose Day celebration on December 9, 1895, when it played "America."[51]

Under Petersen's leadership, the band grew over the next few years. It became a part of the campus celebrations of St. Ambrose Day and St. Patrick's Day, the elocution contest, Memorial Day, which often was observed with a concert on the lawn, and commencement. During the year the band or a chamber group made up of band members often played for literary society meetings. The band did not perform off-campus very often, but it did play occasional concerts at the Immaculate Conception Academy and St. Vincent's Home. On a June evening, the band went to Mercy Hospital and gave a concert on the grounds for the sisters and nurses. In June 1896, the St. Ambrose band received statewide attention when it led a parade of the members of the Roman Catholic Mutual Protection Society who had gathered in Davenport for their state convention, as they marched from the Hibernian Hall in downtown Davenport to the Cathedral for Mass.[52] During those years the band, orchestra, glee club, Mandolin Club, and other musical groups fulfilled Flannagan's goal to have wholesome, year-round extracurricular activities.

Through the 1890s, the attention of St. Ambrose students was focused on the various activities on campus, classes, games, religious services, recreation, study hall, society meetings, and the impromptu activities that they created. The students were permitted to officially leave campus only with

A Great and Lasting Beginning

permission, and if the rules were followed about no newspapers or magazines, it would seem that they were shut off from the world. However, the world did intrude in a number of ways. The economic depression of the 1890s impacted the campus. Family responsibilities and crises, such as illness or death, took students away from campus. Even the academic schedule was in some ways dictated by events outside the campus.

Although it was located in a growing city, St. Ambrose still moved to the rhythm of an agricultural economy and had since the first class when farmers had sent their sons to St. Ambrose. The academic year was divided into two five-month sessions, one beginning the first Tuesday of September and ending in January, and the other beginning in February and running until the end of June. Since the beginning, the catalogue had said that a student would only be accepted for a full term of five months (one semester), but that students would be accepted at "all times, their terms dating from time of entrance." This allowed students to arrive for the fall semester after the harvest in October or November and to leave in the spring semester in time to get home for planting. In effect, their five month semester would overlap the two regular semesters. Those students, and their parents, saw this as something to do during the winter months which would provide some basic high school education that would prepare them to return to the farm or to get a job. For those students, a diploma or degree were not important. The catalogue added, however, that students who wanted to take the regular course of study leading to a diploma or degree, would "find it greatly to their advantage to enter at the beginning of a semester."[53]

Recovery from the depression began in 1897 and in the 1898-1899 year, the first full year after recovery, the enrollment jumped dramatically from seventy-four to ninety-three students, the largest increase from one year to the next so far. Included in that increase was the number of boarding students, which rose from forty-three to fifty-seven. By now students came from rural southeast Iowa communities like Long Grove, Villanova, Riverside, Holbrook, Morse, Georgetown, Harper, What Cheer, as well as Neola, near Council Bluffs, Bayard, southeast of Carroll in north central Iowa, and Maloy in southwest Iowa.

The students returned to campus for the semester that began in February 1898 as newspapers across the nation were filled with calls for war to drive the Spanish out of Cuba and free the Cuban peasants from Spanish oppression. Then on February 15, the United States battleship *Maine* blew up in Havana Harbor with the loss of 260 American lives. With public opinion whipped up by American newspapers, Spain was blamed for the explosion, and Americans were urged to go to war to "Remember the *Maine*." At first President William McKinley resisted the war talk but finally, on April 11, he asked Congress to declare war. Now the United States and Spain were engaged in a brief, romantic war that one American official called "a splendid little war," and Theodore Roosevelt, the war's most famous hero, called "a bully fight."

Many Americans viewed the war as a religious crusade by the forces of Christianity against evil and for some that evil was best represented by Roman Catholicism, the predominant religion of Spain. Those nativist Americans questioned the wartime loyalty of American Catholics. At the same time, many Americans of Irish descent were concerned about talk of an American alliance with Great Britain against the Spanish. Centuries of anti-British animus by Irish-Americans led to their opposition to the alliance and they spoke openly against it. In the jingoistic fervor about the war, this opposition by Irish-Catholics exacerbated the anti-Catholicism of many Americans which made them question further the loyalty of American Catholics. The truth was almost all of the American bishops supported the war and American Catholics proclaimed their loyalty by serving in the military. Catholic parishes held events to raise money for the support of American troops. One Iowa newspaper editor said one of those parish fund raisers had made the local pastor and his parish many friends, "especially from well-meaning but mistaken people who have such a prejudice against Catholics."[54]

Shortly after the sinking of the *Maine*, the League of the Sacred Heart, a newly formed religious group on campus, announced that their prayer intention for the rest of the month was the welfare of seamen, but especially on behalf of the victims of the *Maine*. The next month the entire student body marched downtown to St. Anthony's church to attend Mass for the repose of the souls of the American dead. Once war was declared, at least one student went home to see his brother off to war, and Father Giglinger offered his services to the country.[55]

Commencement was held on June 16, just days before Americans landed in Cuba. Bishop Cosgrove sat in the middle of the stage which was decorated with red, white, and blue bunting. The usual student essays and speeches had a patriotic tone. Peter J. Gallagher presented an essay entitled, "Some Thoughts Suggested by the War," and William Guinan delivered a patriotic address, "Catholic Loyalty." The main speaker was Michael V. Gannon who had been the speaker at the first St. Ambrose commencement ceremony in 1885. Gannon congratulated the school on the progress it had made since then. He then discussed the national political situation and the war and he urged the students not to countenance any alliance between the United States and Great Britain, who he said, was an "[Irish] national foe, and an international traitor, and not to be trusted."[56]

By the time the students returned for the fall semester, the war with Spain was essentially over. The United States ended up with Cuba, the Philippine Islands, and Puerto Rico as new territories. For the students at St. Ambrose, the war raised their consciousness about other peoples and parts of the world, but except for that, and the excitement it created, it had little impact on the campus.

The patriotic rhetoric of commencement was forgotten as attention turned to the new students on campus, the fall baseball season, and their studies. The only postscript to the war that was sounded on campus came in October. President William McKinley had announced that the United States should "take" the Philippine Islands as American territory, and "educate the Filipinos, and uplift and Christianize them." American Protestant groups saw this as a call to missionary activity in the former Spanish colonies. American Catholics pointed out that the former Spanish colonials in the Philippines, Cuba, and Puerto Rico were already largely Roman Catholic Christians. Giglinger took note of this and said, no doubt with the same fervor he would use a few years later against Davenport saloon keepers, that those missionaries "had better stay home and be converted themselves."[57]

The chapel in 1902. The main altar was a gift from the Archbishop of Dubuque. The two side altars had been in the original St. Marguerite's Cathedral and were moved to the St. Ambrose Chapel built in 1893, and then moved to this chapel.

The economic depression of the 1890s was in part responsible for a series of national crusades by middle-class reformers, called Progressives, who attempted to correct the economic abuses created by a rapidly expanding industrial economy in the years after the Civil War which, they felt, had contributed to the depression. Other Progressives sought to reform abuses created by rapid population growth in American cities, such as inadequate, unsafe, and unsanitary housing and neighborhoods, and the inability of municipal governments to cope with the problems that growth created. Government, these Progressives thought, should be free of corruption and should efficiently serve the needs of the people. Another group of reformers undertook crusades against the personal immorality that they saw in society; the most vocal of these reformers were the temperance advocates. The efforts of Cosgrove and Giglinger in the early twentieth century to close the saloons of Davenport were a local manifestation of those reforms. Still others became advocates for the rights of American women, especially the right to vote. What all of those reformers wanted was to bring order and efficiency to what they came to view as a chaotic society.

One of the means they used to achieve this goal was the formation of professional associations that would view a problem and propose solutions. Groups like the American Medical Association and the American Bar Association became agencies for setting standards for the education, prac-

tice, and professionalization of their disciplines. Similar standardization efforts took place in education. The National Education Association, which had been founded in 1857 to promote better teaching and to promote public education in the United States, now began to form committees to study the relationship between secondary schools and colleges and to try to establish college entrance requirements. At the first meeting of the North Central Association of Colleges and Secondary Schools in 1895, the members discussed the question, "What Constitutes a College and What a Secondary School?" Based on those discussions, in 1901 the North Central Association established the Commission on Accredited Schools whose task was to define standards for accreditation.[58]

Now Catholic educators began to ask some of the same questions of themselves and their systems. These discussions would lead to an "organizational revolution . . . in Catholic higher education." In 1899, there were ninety Catholic colleges with a total enrollment of 16,000 students, 60 percent of whom were in high school, the remainder of whom were in college or professional studies.[59] That fall, St. Ambrose had ninety-four students, almost all of whom were in high school, which put it well below the national ratio of college to high school students. However, there was little common understanding among Catholic educators about what should constitute a college curriculum, the relationship between the preparatory and

A Great and Lasting Beginning

high school students and the colleges, and the standards that should be set for college teachers.

An early warning that Catholic education could be left behind as public schools changed was sounded by Notre Dame Professor Maurice Francis Egan. Speaking at the 1893 Catholic Columbian Congress, Egan had noted the "crisis . . . in higher Catholic American education" and said that colleges

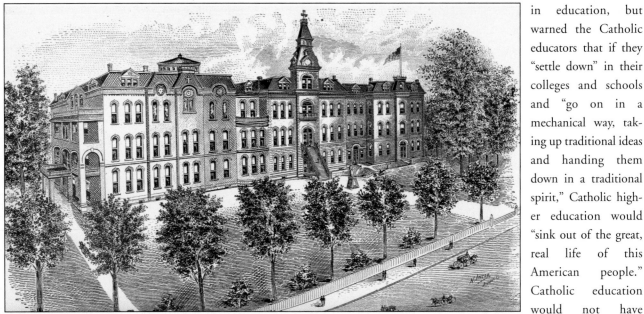

Ambrose Hall 1901-1908 showing the new addition that included the chapel, the porches on the west end, and the porte cochere.

in education, but warned the Catholic educators that if they "settle down" in their colleges and schools and "go on in a mechanical way, taking up traditional ideas and handing them down in a traditional spirit," Catholic higher education would "sink out of the great, real life of this American people." Catholic education would not have "standing" in America unless it became "an intellectual force" and

should "broaden their scope" or remain "small and isolated eddies apart from the main stream." Another speaker said that the parochial grade school system in the United States provided a "solid base," and that with the recent opening of the Catholic University of America there was a "proper roof," but that in between there was a great lack in the "private Catholic colleges and academies spread throughout the land."[60] In 1899, leaders of Catholic education formed the Association of Catholic Colleges which helped lead the reforms that would separate high schools from colleges and establish standards for both levels.

The first meeting of the Association was held in Chicago in the spring of 1899.[61] Fifty-three colleges sent representatives. Flannagan and the Reverend Richard Renihan, who was master of discipline and professor of languages and mathematics, represented St. Ambrose.[62] The attendees listened to papers and discussions on a variety of topics, including: "The Typical Catholic College: What Should it Teach?"; "The Problems of Catholic Education in Our Present Social Needs"; "The Catholic College as a Preparation for a Business Career"; "What the College May do for Preparatory Schools"; "College Entrance Conditions"; "Requirements for College Degrees"; and "The Drift Toward Non-Catholic Colleges and Universities."[63]

The most challenging speech, however, came from someone not scheduled to give a formal presentation, Bishop John Lancaster Spalding of Peoria. Spalding had written and spoken extensively on most of the issues facing the Catholic church in the late nineteenth century, including education. He had been numbered among those church leaders of the period who said that the church should adapt itself to the modern world in which it existed. According to one historian, his influence on Catholic thought in the United States was wide, "probably greater than that of any other American Catholic" bishop.[64]

Spalding told the assembled educators that their gathering together to discuss issues was important. He praised the faith of the American people

that the "curse of our schools, the curse of all schools in ages," had been that they were in the "hands of men who became mere machines, who ceased to learn, ceased to live what they were teaching."[65]

Maniett attended the second meeting in 1900, but there is no record of any representation from St. Ambrose in the next three years. In 1904 many of the leaders of the Association met to form the new Catholic Educational Association (CEA). Flannagan; Shannahan, prefect of studies and philosophy professor; and the Reverend Charles J. Donohoe, master of discipline and teacher of mathematics, Greek, civics and economics, represented St. Ambrose. St. Ambrose remained a member of the CEA but apparently no one attended the annual meetings until 1911 when Shannahan and others began to participate. There would be some reforms at St. Ambrose during those years, led primarily by Shannahan, but for the most part, it seems apparent that the leaders of St. Ambrose were willing to "settle down" with traditional spirit and ideas. Only with different leadership would St. Ambrose begin to reform in the years right after World War I.

As the United States moved into the new century, it had put the economic distress of the previous decade behind it and Davenport and St. Ambrose shared in those better times. The Iowa and Illinois farmers who were sending their sons to St. Ambrose were beginning two decades of the best years American agriculture had ever experienced. Within a few years the city of Davenport, with its 200 factories and other businesses, could boast that it was the "second leading city in per capita wealth" in the nation.[66]

At St. Ambrose there was a steady increase in overall enrollment, but the number of boarding students increased at a faster rate than day students. A brief note in the *Messenger* in February 1900 hinted that another building program was being discussed. Noting that the attendance had increased for the second semester, it said that the boarding school was "filled to utmost capacity," and that the faculty and students hoped that the "much-needed west wing" would soon be a reality.[67] The increase in the number of students was also reflected in the year-end financial reports. Flannagan reported that for the 1898-1899 year, receipts were $10,199 and expenses amounted to $9,901, resulting in a positive balance of $298. The next year receipts went up to over $12,000, and over $11,000 the year after that. Although expenses also increased in each of those years, Flannagan reported that the college was in the black by small amounts in both years and that he was able to deposit $1,800 in the bank during those years.[68]

The money did not stay in the bank for long. Four hundred dollars was spent to put an iron fence along the front of the property on Locust Street. More significantly for the future, however, the bishop spent $1,500 to buy two lots on Locust Street from Mr. and Mrs. Henry B. Armil. The Armil property extended the front of the campus west along Locust Street for another 125 feet and extended north for 150 feet (the area of the circle drive and flag pole on the modern campus). According to the *Messenger*, this additional property would "render the grounds of St. Ambrose greatly enhanced in value and more suitably adapted to outdoor recreation for the students."[69] But more important, it was the first indication that the bishop and the college administration intended the school to grow beyond its original limits.

The question of the addition of a new wing on Ambrose Hall was discussed at the May 1, 1901, meeting of the bishop's council, which now included Flannagan. Prior to the discussion about St. Ambrose, however, the councilors raised the possibility of a division of the diocese. It had been rumored that the western half of the diocese, from Des Moines west to Council Bluffs, would be split off to create a new diocese. The councilors were not enthusiastic about such a division and passed a resolution to "disapprove" the division of the Diocese of Davenport unless the bishops of the region "deemed it best for the good of religion."

Turning to the matter of an addition onto Ambrose Hall, the councilors thought that if the diocese were divided, the present building would be large enough. They worried that students from the new diocese would be less likely to come to St. Ambrose or that a new bishop in western Iowa would start his own college, so they passed a resolution that "the proposed addition be postponed until the matter of the division of the diocese is settled."[70] An even larger issue was the high price of building materials which would make an addition too expensive. This was the "dominating factor in dooming the wing at least for the present." As it turned out, in 1902, the Archdiocese of Dubuque was divided creating the new Diocese of Sioux City, but the Diocese of Davenport remained the same.

In spite of the recommendation of his councilors, the bishop, and probably Flannagan, were not willing to wait until the issue of the division of the diocese was settled. They apparently were not concerned about the price of building materials either, because shortly after the meeting, plans were being drawn for an addition on the west end of the building. The architect they chose was George P. Stauduhar of Rock Island. A graduate of the University of Illinois, Stauduhar had begun the practice of architecture in Rock Island in 1890 and would eventually build dozens of churches and commercial buildings in central and western Illinois and eastern Iowa.

Stauduhar continued Victor Huot's design of the original building. The

ground floor expanded the dining room and included a trunk room, a bath parlor, and toilet rooms. The second floor added more classrooms. The third and fourth floors were to be the new chapel, which the *Messenger* said would be the "neatest of its kind in the West." On the exterior there were two porches and a porte cochere. The original building was connected with the new west wing on the ground floor, which included the refectory expansion, on the second floor by a parlor and hallway, and on the third floor by a hallway. The estimated cost was just under $20,000. The bids were let in mid-July and ground was broken later that month. By the end of August, the foundation had been poured and work on the superstructure had begun with the hope that the building would be ready for use in December.[71]

The students returned for the beginning of the fall semester on September 10. Within a few days, there was a brief pause in the usual activities on campus when word came that President William McKinley had been shot. McKinley had been attending the Pan-American Exposition in Buffalo, New York, when he was shot on September 6. He lingered for a week and died on September 14. Students whose grandparents had told them of the assassination of President Abraham Lincoln in 1865, and whose parents recalled the assassination of President James A. Garfield in 1881, now lived through the latest national trauma. The students and faculty gathered to offer Mass in his memory and the St. Ambrose Day observance that fall included a tribute to the dead president.[72]

The students quickly returned to the routine of classes, games, and a new activity on campus that fall, "sidewalk superintending," as they watched the walls of the addition go up and wondered for what each new room would be used. By November the exterior work was completed, but a lack of sufficient funds slowed the work so the December deadline was not met, and now the hope was that it would be ready for occupancy by February 1.

In December Bishop Henry Cosgrove wrote the priests of the diocese to ask them for money so the addition could be completed. He said he knew he did not have to speak to them about the importance of Catholic education and the American spirit of self-sacrifice that had made it possible. St. Ambrose was now in its twentieth year and had grown in "favor and popularity" due to the "zeal of the efficient and self-sacrificing priests who [had] been at the head of the institution." The cost of the addition was $25,000 and Cosgrove said he had given $10,000 already so that the work "might not be in any way retarded." Now he wanted the priests to donate the remaining $15,000 so that he would not have take out a loan. He appealed to their loyalty to the diocese, their "submission" to their ordinary, and he said he knew that he could rely on their "faithful cooperation."[73] The priests responded with cash and pledges of nearly $3,200, far below what the bishop had hoped for, so in the end he was forced to take out a loan. Once again a St. Ambrose building program had resulted in a debt, which in July 1903, a year after the building was finished, still amounted to $10,500.[74]

Work resumed in January 1902, and the ground floor dining room was put to use in the middle of that month. One by one classrooms began to come into use as they were finished and the entire classroom section of the new wing was turned over to the faculty on March 1.[75] The last area to be finished was the chapel. The hope was that it would be finished in time to dedicate it on April 17, but once again there were delays and that deadline would not be met.

The new chapel was dedicated on April 30. The effect was splendid enough to convince those who saw it that it was the "neatest" chapel in the west. The main altar was white with a panel in front depicting the Last Supper, made by the Dubuque Altar Company and a gift of Archbishop Joseph Keane of Dubuque. The altar rail was white, with a white marble top and was a gift of Col. James P. Donahue, secretary-treasurer of the Davenport Water Company, and his sister, Mrs. Mary F. Thompson. The side altars had been moved from the 1893 chapel. The three arches over the altars were lined with frosted incandescent lights. The walls were light in color with light brown, olive green, and ivory cream accents. A picture of the Immaculate Conception was painted in the dome of the cupola. In addition the dome was surrounded by leaded glass windows in a diamond pattern to bring natural light into the chapel. The oak pews, donated by the local Loras Council of the Knights of Columbus, seated 276 worshipers, but there was still not enough seating for all who wanted to attend the dedication, so only invited guests were admitted.[76]

On the east wall in back, there was a stained glass window with the figure of St. Henry, given by the priest alumni in honor of Bishop Henry Cosgrove. Next to it on the south wall was St. Aloysius, given by the Reverend Michael Nolan in memory of his brother, the Reverend Robert Nolan. Next to it was a window depicting St. John the Evangelist, a gift of Mrs. Catherine Cassidy in memory of her son, Father John J. Cassidy, an 1887 graduate of St. Ambrose who had been ordained in 1892, and had served as principal of the commercial department for one year. Cassidy had died of typhoid fever in August 1900. The next window, dedicated to St. Joseph, was a gift of the Reverend Anton Nierman, long-time pastor of St. Joseph's Parish in Davenport. And at the west end of the wall was a window of St. Ambrose, given by the mother of the Reverend William McDonough, an 1889 graduate who had died in 1899, the first priest alumnus to die. The large central window with a rose window above it represented the Annunciation and the Vision of St. Anthony of Padua. In memory of his parents, this large window was a gift of Frederick H. Bartemeyer, whose son had been a member of the first class. Two smaller rose windows on the south wall depicted the "Ecce Homo" and the "Mater Dolorosa." The classes of 1901 and 1909 donated a rose window over the main altar showing Jesus blessing the little children.[77]

Before the Mass began, Bishop Cosgrove blessed the chapel and the altar. He then took his place on the west side of the sanctuary while Archbishop Keane, who was to preach the sermon, entered, and sat on the east side of the sanctuary. Flannagan was the celebrant of the Solemn High Mass. There was no choir at St. Ambrose, so music was provided by the choir from the Immaculate Conception Academy who sang from the choir balcony over the west doorway, accompanied by members of the St. Ambrose orchestra.

Archbishop Keane took as his text Solomon's prayer in the Book of Wisdom, "Grant me oh God, wisdom that standeth by Thy throne," and used the relationship of Ambrose the teacher and Augustine the student as an example for the students of St. Ambrose College. Keane said that Ambrose taught Augustine to listen not just to his intellect but also to his heart, that it was in both that wisdom, the "appreciation of Him whom you love, that Light of love and Power of Love," could be found. The lesson Ambrose taught Augustine was the lesson that Keane urged the students of St. Ambrose College to learn from their patron saint. The chapel was a place where students could come to "hold silent conversation with God," and that when they were weary they should come to the chapel to "ask for that light of love and beg St. Ambrose to teach [them] the lesson he taught to St. Augustine--the lesson of love." "Here in this chapel," he concluded, "may the spirit of St. Ambrose always be cultivated and may all the blessings [that] come from heaven through his spirit [be] cultivated in this house of prayer."[78]

Following the dedication Mass, lunch was served in the college refectory. Father Davis acted as toastmaster and Flannagan spoke to thank the archbishop for his gift of the altar and for his sermon. Flannagan also thanked the clergy and laity whose donations had made the new wing possible. This was followed by a series of toasts, led off by Father Schulte, whose toast was to "St. Ambrose—Past and Present." Schulte recalled the early days of the college and the role of Bishop McMullen. He said that Bishop Cosgrove had "injected new life" into the school and had given the administration of the college "every possible encouragement" and that he hoped to see the college "continue in the good work and live and flourish for many years to come." Schulte's toast was followed by other toasts appropriate to the day.[79]

For the next fifty years the chapel in Ambrose Hall served the needs of the college. Students celebrated the rhythms of the liturgical seasons. Once a year the priests of the diocese gathered in it for their annual retreat. Students marked the casualties of two world wars and the deaths by accident or disease of their schoolmates. They came to rejoice in victories, good grades, and happy news from home. The first wedding in the new chapel took place in June 1903, when Father Richard Renihan married Dr. L. J. Porstman and May Springmeier of Buffalo, Iowa. Over the years other couples would return to be married in the chapel.[80] Some students were baptized in the chapel and in the first years the bishop confirmed groups of students there. Some graduates returned to be ordained deacons and priests there. And over the years countless weary students heeded Archbishop Keane's advice and came to the chapel to ask for light and to beg their patron to teach them "the lesson of love."

Bishop McMullen's school was now twenty years old, but in some ways it was not too different from the school he knew. The number of students had tripled in size since that September day in 1882, the building that he had hoped to construct had been expanded twice, but the curriculum had not changed significantly since Schulte and Halligan taught there. The faculty was larger, and included some who were graduates of St. Ambrose. But only one had the kind of advanced degree that McMullen had sought for his school in Chicago and would have wanted for St. Ambrose.

Writing fifty years later, the Reverend Monsignor U. A. Hauber called those years a "period of incubation. The little acorn had been planted by men of true vision, but it took time for the roots to sink deep and the crown to find its way through the underbrush before the majestic oak could be perfected. St. Ambrose could not develop as a college for Catholic young men until the foundation had been laid in preparing both a student body and a staff of competent instructors."[81]

The train carrying two ambitious young men, Lou Mueller and the writer, from Iowa City emerged from the Fejervary Park ravine and swung around the curve on its elevated roadbed. We suddenly found ourselves looking out upon a level expanse dotted with working men's homes, plain and severe-looking in their small treeless yards. This was a new world for boys reared in the quiet atmosphere of a university town and the surrounding rural areas. It was a vivid and to us bewildering panorama with its disturbing emphasis on the nature of our modern industrial expansion. The train came to a stop at the old depot at Fifth and Perry and we asked for directions to the College. 'Take a Harrison street car at the corner.' We had never seen a street car. This one was the old summer type, open on both sides the full length, with a motorman and a conductor who swung himself along the outside platform from seat to seat to pick up and ring in our nickels. 'We want to go to St. Ambrose College.' 'Yes, I'll tell you when to get off.'[1]

Chapter Four

When Ulrich Hauber stepped off the Harrison Street car that tenth day of September in 1901, walked the two blocks to campus, and went up the stairs of Ambrose Hall, he walked into the place that would be his home until his death in 1956. For the generations of students who joined him at St. Ambrose during those decades, he would come to represent what was best about St. Ambrose and themselves.

It was the first year of the new century. On the day he arrived, President McKinley lay dying in Buffalo and one of the first events Hauber took part in at St. Ambrose was the memorial mass for the dead president. The new president, the former Rough Rider Theodore Roosevelt, charged into the center of national life and seemed to say that change was afoot and all was possible. Years later Hauber, the biologist and scientist, would recall that a few years before his arrival on campus, radium was discovered which made possible the atomic age he would live to see. The year before he arrived, Mendel's laws of genetics were rediscovered, having been ignored by scientists for decades. "Such events are decisive," Hauber wrote. And at the beginning of the year, while Hauber was still a high school student in Iowa City, Queen Victoria died. She had lived long enough to have an era named for her, and she had become the symbol of the previous century. Nearly fifty years later, Hauber wrote, "Somehow our young minds sensed then and there that important history was being made. We tried to picture the future, our future. Our dreams were wild, but hardly as fantastic as the reality it has come to be."[2]

Born June 28, 1885, in Wilburgstetten, Bavaria, just a few days before the cornerstone was laid in Ambrose Hall, Hauber was five when his family came to the United States and settled in Iowa City. He had just graduated from St. Mary's High School when he came to St. Ambrose. Like the students who entered in September 1882, Hauber was part of the immigrant experience that characterized and defined nineteenth-century America. They came with dreams to an uncertain future, but they were convinced that education was the way to capture the best of that future. Hauber was a first generation immigrant; the students of 1882 were second generation,

which constituted 48 percent of the enrollment in Catholic colleges at the beginning of the century.[3] Within a few years, the college would see members of the third generation when the sons of the students of 1882 began to enter St. Ambrose.

Hauber wrote of the "new world" he experienced in industrial Davenport. Other students had similar experiences when they first saw the city and the college. One student who had arrived from southeast Kansas three years before Hauber told of the student who was so "awe-stricken" at the size of Ambrose Hall that he threw his head back, looked up at the fourth story and said, "Judas Mike, ain't she a whopper!"[4] The city had other challenges as well. Hauber related that when he took the streetcar by himself for the first time, he jumped off before the car had fully stopped, fell backwards, and was nearly run over by a horse and buggy. "Golly but I felt cheap," he wrote in his diary, "everybody looking at me and the conductor giving me a calling down! Well I got a lesson."[5]

The lessons that received the first priority, however, were those learned in the classrooms of St. Ambrose. Many students took the same trip up Harrison Street on the street car. When they arrived they met with Father Flannagan who would assess their academic record and assign them to the appropriate level of study. The fall that Hauber arrived there were 102 students: eighty-six boarders and sixteen day students. Only thirteen of those students, including Hauber, were college students, and all of those were seminarians. The remainder were commercial or preparatory students. Many of those attended from November to April and were called "aggies" by the other students, because they came after the "corn was husked" and left in time for spring plowing.[6] The "aggies" could arrive anytime in the fall; one year ten of them arrived in early December, and then left when they thought it was time for the spring farm work to begin.[7] There was a great deal of fluidity in the student body. The minute book of the St. John's Literary Society often noted that on a given evening, someone who was to present that night had left school, perhaps because he had found a job, or was unable to afford to stay in school, or had scholastic problems.

By early in the twentieth century the number of boarding students was

A Great and Lasting Beginning

Ambrose Hall 1901-1908.

far greater than the number of day students. The General Regulations still contained a rule that "communication between House Pupils and Day Scholars" was prohibited. According to Hauber, during those years the day students, by now called "day-dodgers," were "merely tolerated," and there was a strict separation of the two groups of students except in the classrooms, study hall, and sporting events.[8] Since the inception of the Athletic Society, the position of the day students had been a frequent cause of debate. Although officially the day students could be members of the Athletic Society, there still seemed to be friction. In 1895, for example, there had been a motion that the master of games "should keep day scholars and strangers out of the ball alley."[9] Often intramural contests had a team of boarders against a team of day students, but frequently those contests ended in a free-for-all. Keeping the day students separate from the boarders may well have been an issue of preventing mischief in the dormitory; it may well have been that the day-dodgers, like the aggies, were more likely to leave school when they got a job, and therefore they were not seen as reliable participants in campus activities.

Once they were enrolled, the students settled into the regimented routine of the semester: rise before 6:00, Mass at 6:10, breakfast at 7:00. Following breakfast, most of the community went for a fifteen minute walk. This included the faculty who paced back and forth on a sidewalk near the building, a custom continued by some faculty members for decades. Following this exercise period, the students turned to study and recitations from 8:00 until noon with a ten minute break at 9:25. At noon there was dinner and free time until 1:15, then study and recitations until 4:00, free time until 5:00, study until 6:00, supper and study until 9:00 when there were night prayers, and lights out at 9:30. Wednesday and Saturday afternoons were free. On Sunday the students could go to early Mass in the chapel, to St. Anthony's Parish, or to the cathedral for Mass. But for those who went to early Mass there would be Sunday study period from 9:00 until 11:00, and again from 2:00 until 3:00. Benediction of the Blessed Sacrament would be celebrated at 3:00 on Sunday afternoon and following that, the rest of the day was free.[10] Seats were assigned in the chapel, apparently to help the faculty know who was attending Mass. Those assignments would be changed if a group of students was found to be less than reverent. Students' free time was filled with literary society meetings, sports practice, music practice, additional study, and for some, jobs as waiters in the refectory or as janitors in the building. The students' days were full and highly regulated.

About midway through his first week on campus, Hauber became homesick and debated whether to leave St. Ambrose and go home. But that would have meant failure and disgrace. Once the homesickness passed, he entered into the life of the campus. After a few weeks he wanted to explore Davenport but this desire brought him into conflict with the rules about leaving campus. Normally if a student wanted permission to leave campus it was so he could purchase some necessary personal item. So when Hauber asked the master of discipline to leave campus, he was asked, "What is it you want to get?" Hauber replied that he did not want to buy anything but that he had been in Davenport for six weeks and he wanted to see the city. He received permission, but was told to return by 2:30 that afternoon.

It was a grave problem for the student if he was caught leaving campus after hours. Once Hauber sneaked out and walked to nearby Vander Veer Park. He knew that "to be caught meant expulsion and disgrace [but that] the urge to get away from the 'prison' was too strong." Later in his student years, he discovered a way to leave the building after night prayers by leaving a certain door unlocked or by climbing up the fire escape. One time, however, he and a friend returned to find a light in the room next to the unlocked door. Fearful that their absence had been discovered and that someone was waiting for them, they walked around until 1:00 a.m. When they returned the light was still on, so they decided to "face the music." But no one was in the room and they were able to return undetected. He said later that "the scare cured at least one of the culprits."[11]

The daily regimen was altered during the end-of-semester examinations. Written and oral examinations were given for each subject, conducted by boards of examiners including during the early years, the bishop. The examinations were intended to test the grasp of the subject matter and demonstrate a general proficiency. The examination period extended over several days and the following 1906 schedule is typical: On Monday written examinations were given in Christian Doctrine. Tuesday included tests in German, astronomy, orthography, English literature, commercial law, and shorthand. The mathematics tests were given on Wednesday. Thursday was English, Greek, and geography. On Friday the examinations were given in Latin, bookkeeping, history, and philosophy. On Saturday, Monday, and Tuesday, oral examinations would be given in some of the subjects. Results of the examinations were read out on Wednesday and those students who achieved honors in class were mentioned at commencement, and their names were published in the college catalogue.[12]

The one part of the day the students were sure not to miss was mealtime. One of the first activities at the beginning of the year was to assign the students to tables in the refectory. Like their chapel seats, those assignments would be changed several times throughout the year, especially if the faculty noticed a particular combination of students causing trouble in the refectory. The boarders were served three full meals a day, and the half-boarders ate the noon-time dinner. The menus were plain and basic. Sometimes there would be oatmeal for breakfast, but there was always meat: sausage, beef steak, or wienerwurst. The noontime dinner was meat, potatoes, vegetables, or fish on Fridays. Supper was cold meat, probably left over from dinner, potatoes, and bread. At all meals there was bread, vinegar, mustard, and water on the table; butter was set out for breakfast and supper. Coffee was served for breakfast and tea for supper. Dessert was always a treat and the Sisters of Humility became famous for their pies. Even with the best efforts of the sister cooks, the routine of institutional cooking brought complaints. One wrote in a diary, "Beans for dinner as usual"; another wrote, "We were confronted with indescribable pudding for dinner"; another, "Devlin turns up his nose at the salmon"; and still another wrote, "for the first time in the history of the S. A. C., we have pork chops for dinner."[13]

Most of the students boarded in two large dormitories, one of which was the fourth floor of the original building, the space already named the "Irish Village." What had been the chapel on the fourth floor of the 1893 addition now became a dormitory. Those dormitories were large, open rooms, with rows of beds and lockers along the wall. If there was a larger number of boarding students than those areas could house, they were put anywhere space could be found; one semester beds were set up in the library.

Like all the new students, Hauber was subjected to "mild forms of initiation" by the older students. Years later, freshman initiation would become a highly regulated and ritualized activity, but now it was merely high jinks. Hauber related that one day he went into the library dormitory, sat down on a bed, and began to read. Suddenly he was pummeled with pillows which turned into a general wrestling match. He was told that he was now initiated and would be "let at peace" if he came into that dormitory again. But later he was further "initiated" when a crowd got after him and put shaving lather on his face and sent him away. He said that a "whole lot of fellows got initiated in there" that day.[14] Another form of intimidation was "belly-floggings," described as "retaliatory measures, uproariously and good-naturedly taken against too-frisky companions, to teach them proper humility."[15]

The open dormitories provided the occasion for all kinds of horse play. One common trick was to tie a fellow student's night shirt in knots. When that happened to Hauber, he retaliated in kind against the suspected culprit and he did such a good job of tying the other student's night shirt that he could not untie it and ended up throwing it away. After lights out students would stage attacks on other students in their beds, reaching across the space between beds to pull the covers off, with the offender feigning sleep when the other student tried to find out who had done it. The tricks were not appreciated by all. Once, when someone made a clatter by throwing a hickory nut across the room, the prefect was awakened and all the dorm residents were made to go to the study hall to "write lines" swearing never to do such a thing again.[16]

The faculty continued to monitor other parts of student behavior. The general regulations continued the ban on the use of intoxicating liquors. The early years of the decade were the years of Cosgrove's and Giglinger's crusades against Davenport saloons. So students were closely watched, and if one returned from downtown showing the effects of alcohol, he was dealt with severely, including expulsion if the offense was serious enough. One January, Hauber recorded in his diary that "a great fuss was raised today about boys getting drink from the janitor but no proof could be found." He did not record if there were any consequences for the suspected janitor. Temperance was also a frequent topic at the annual retreat. In March 1909, the retreat master told the students that liquor was a moral, social, and national evil, and he urged the students to take as their motto regarding liquor, "I'll have none of it."[17]

The general regulations also had a prohibition against the use of tobacco products but early in the twentieth century that began to change. In 1902, eighteen-year-old students could smoke if they had the written permission of their parents; two years later the age was lowered to sixteen. Still, students without parental permission, or those too young to have parental permission, found places to smoke and they developed elaborate warning systems when a faculty member approached. In time, smoking became widely accepted and smoking materials were sold in the campus store. In

A Great and Lasting Beginning

the early teens there was even a Smoker's Club which sponsored dances and other social activities.[18]

Literary and debating societies continued to be one of the most common extracurricular activities for the students. The St. Ambrose Society, which had been organized in the mid-1880s, continued to meet. The Philalethic Society went out of existence but in its place the St. Thomas Literary Society formed in January 1900, and would continue to meet sporadically for the next ten years. In the fall of 1903, Hauber was among nine students who met in the philosophy classroom to discuss the formation of another new literary and debating society. The founders were all philosophy students, eight of whom would eventually be ordained and the ninth who would become the Illinois State Banking Commissioner. Hauber was commissioned to write a constitution and by-laws and to select "several long Greek words to present to the members," one of which would become the name of the society. At the next meeting Hauber presented several potential names and the members selected Logomachetean, which means "a war of words." According to its newly adopted constitution, the object of the society was the "free discussion of any subject," the delivery of orations and recitations, and the reading of essays to achieve "fluency of extemporaneous speaking, as well as a knowledge of parliamentary rules."[19] The group adopted a level of formality to its meetings, insisting that members be addressed as "Mister," a rule enforced when a member was "called to order" for using a personal name. As new members were added, they ceremoniously signed their names in the minutes' book.

The issues discussed by the Logomachetean Society were usually related to world events or current national controversies. There were debates about the Russo-Japanese War; the actions of the United States in fomenting revolution in Panama; a discussion about whether immigration was beneficial to the United States; debates about the tariff and whether the federal government should control the railroads, both matters of importance to the farm state economy; a debate about women suffrage. The most frequently debated topic through the life of the society concerned the rights of labor to organize, the benefits of organization, whether labor unions were a "detriment" to the country, and whether child labor should be prohibited, all issues that would continue to be debated on campus over the coming decades. For all their seriousness of purpose, they still maintained a sense of fun. Once in 1904, the issue proposed for debate was whether the hen that laid the egg or the hen that hatched it was the mother of the chicken. A number of members "vehemently objected" to the question because they felt it was not in the "spirit of the society and that the discussion of it would hardly be consistent with decency." The society continued to meet until 1911, long enough for the Reverend Ulrich Hauber, now a member of the faculty, to attend a meeting and congratulate the current members.[20]

In 1908, another literary society was formed when a group of students from the German course organized the *Bonifacius Verein*. All the meetings, as well as the minutes of the meetings, were in German which gave the students an opportunity to practice conversational German. The content of the meetings included discussion of German literature and culture. For several years, the members performed plays in German.[21]

Later in the decade, the college began to bring lecturers to campus from around the country to speak to the students and the public. The topics varied widely, from a lecture on Mexico to one on the four English cardinals, Newman, Manning, Vaughan, and Wiseman who shaped Catholic thought in the nineteenth century, to lectures on socialism. Shakespeare was a common topic; one year the students heard a series of six lectures over two months on themes selected from his plays. Several lecturers appeared more than once over the years but the most frequent speaker before World War I was the Reverend John A. Ryan.

Born in rural Minnesota in 1869, Ryan attended local schools, went to St. Paul Seminary, and was ordained in 1898. He was deeply influenced by Pope Leo XIII's 1891 encyclical, *Rerum Novarum* (On the Condition of Labor), which discussed the rights of labor, criticized socialism and capitalism, talked about the importance of social justice, and became the basis for subsequent Catholic social thought. Ryan studied at the Catholic University of America and his thesis was published in 1906 as *The Living Wage*. He would later write about other justice issues, and in 1919, wrote the "Bishops' Program of Social Reconstruction." In 1920, he was named the head of the Social Action Department of the National Catholic Welfare Conference, a position he held until his death in 1945.

Ryan spoke at St. Ambrose the first time in November 1910 when he delivered two lectures. In the afternoon, he discussed current social problems like child and women labor, alcohol, whether labor was receiving a fair share of the wealth, and how much government regulation was appropriate to achieve justice. That evening he delivered a lecture to the public on socialism and Christianity.[22]

Ryan returned two years later to deliver two lectures. The first, "The Kind of Life That is Worth While," discussed the current efforts to increase material comforts. He urged the rich to "keep their expenditures for the gratification of self within the bounds of reason," which he said would lead to more respect for them and "do much towards removing the prevalent feeling of discontent" among the poor. He said it would be better to aid one's neighbor and observe moderation in material gratification. "The kind of life that is worth while," he concluded, "is the life of the mind and heart, of knowing the best to be known and loving the best to be loved."

Ryan's second lecture, "The Right and Wrong of Labor Unions," introduced a topic that would become one of the principal themes of the advocates of social justice in the years ahead on the St. Ambrose campus. Unions were necessary, he said, because unorganized labor did not have the power to bargain with capitalists: thus "the laborer must work or starve while the employer has sufficient capital to hold off for many days or months." Ryan discussed collective bargaining, the closed shop, boycotts, and injunctions against union activities. Finally, he said that labor unions should be encouraged and they have "already done much for labor. They have taught their members democracy, self-restraint, and willingness to sacrifice something for principle and to work for a cause. . . The important thing," he said, was to make unions a "force for good."[23]

Ryan appeared again on the St. Ambrose campus in January 1915 when he spoke on the minimum wage and the stance of Christianity on the war in Europe which had begun the previous August. His last appearance before the end of World War I came when he delivered the commencement address in June 1915. Ryan criticized the current skepticism against religion as proclaimed by socialism and a growing number of popular publications

The athletic field with the tower of Ambrose Hall visible behind the treeline, 1904.

in the United States. He said that current social evils were not a "collective matter, but individual," and he "warned the graduates not to be dazzled by the brightly lighted snares and pitfalls which the world, with its tinsel and vanity, would place before their eyes."[24]

Ryan had a great influence on the issues that the faculty and students at St. Ambrose would discuss in the decades ahead and which would become the basis for social justice activities on campus. One of those later leaders in social action issues, the Reverend Edward O'Connor, was a student when Ryan spoke on campus. Others, like the Reverend Martin Cone, studied economics and sociology at the Catholic University of America in 1917-1918 where Ryan was on the faculty. Later, the Reverend William O'Connor would come under Ryan's influence at the Catholic University.

In January 1903, Ambrosians were startled to read that their president, Father Flannagan, would leave St. Ambrose at the end of the school year to become the pastor of St. Matthias Parish in Muscatine, Iowa.[25] There was no explanation given for the move but there was speculation that Bishop Cosgrove had intended to bring Father Schulte back as president. If so, it would have been a return to a more progressive attitude about what was needed at St. Ambrose. Schulte might have moved the college more rapidly in the direction that Catholic higher education was going in the nation.

Whatever the bishop's motive was in moving Flannagan, abruptly in June he reversed his decision. In a letter published in the *Catholic Messenger*, he said that when he had appointed Flannagan to Muscatine six months earlier, he had hoped to recognize him for his years of service in a difficult position at the college. At the same time he said he knew it would be difficult to find a successor for him at the college. That had turned out to be more difficult than the bishop had anticipated, so he said that "circumstances became such that I saw but one way out of it–to ask Father

Flannagan to remain at the College." Cosgrove said Flannagan had not asked to be moved but had "acquiesced" to his wish to move, because "the will of his superior was for him the will of God." Finally, Cosgrove said that "Father Flannagan neither directly nor indirectly sought this change: I am wholly responsible for it."[26]

The bishop's letter seems overly defensive in accepting full responsibility for the decisions regarding Flannagan. It was unlikely that another priest would have refused to take the presidency if the bishop had asked. It is possible that Flannagan wanted out of the college, for three years later he would leave the college and be replaced by Shannahan. The incident may be another indication of the ambivalence of the bishop toward St. Ambrose that had led to the attempts years before to give it to a religious order and to remove Schulte from the presidency.

The next year there was more news of change in the diocese and the college when it was announced on October 7, 1904, that Father James Davis, the pastor of the cathedral and vicar general of the diocese, had been appointed coadjutor bishop of Davenport. A coadjutor bishop is one who serves a diocese when the bishop is still in place, but who will succeed the sitting bishop immediately upon his death or resignation. Bishop Cosgrove was now seventy years old and in declining health, and as coadjutor bishop, Davis would take on many of his responsibilities. Davis was a popular choice for that role. The previous year when he had celebrated his twenty-fifth anniversary as a priest, Cosgrove praised his "sound judgement" and his "executive ability" and said that he would be an "ornament to the hierarchy of the church." Another speaker, the Reverend Thomas Mackin of Rock Island, recalled the cries of the citizens of Milan, "Ambrose for bishop," and said that "we in the fullness of heart exclaim, 'Davis for Bishop.'"[27]

Davis was consecrated bishop on November 30, 1904, and made his first appearance at the college as a bishop at the St. Ambrose Day celebration the evening of December 6. Davis had always been a popular figure on campus

A Great and Lasting Beginning

Baseball team of 1907 standing in front of the new grandstand.

and the evening turned into a celebration of his new position. The evening included the usual program of numbers by the band and orchestra and recitations on various topics, but the centerpiece was an address to Bishop Davis by James O'Neill, a student from Council Bluffs. On behalf of the students, O'Neill congratulated the new bishop and said that he hoped that his visits to St. Ambrose would be "more frequent in the future." O'Neill called Davis a "champion" of education who would always "have at heart the interests of St. Ambrose college," that in Davis the students recognized "the man of your time, and as Schiller says, 'The man of his own time is the man of all times.'" Davis thanked the St. Ambrose community for its good wishes and said that his interest in the college was second only to that of his friend, Bishop Cosgrove, who was sitting nearby. He expressed the hope that the college would grow and he urged the students to study the life of their patron, St. Ambrose, and "emulate his learning, his eloquence and piety."[28]

The growth the new bishop hoped for was already underway. Some of it was the work of painting, wallpapering, and plastering that was routine during each summer vacation. Other work, however, involved larger improvement projects. In 1902, for example, new gas lights were installed in the study hall that were said to be four times stronger than the lights in place. The next year three additional fire escapes were added to the building.[29]

In 1905, Cosgrove donated money to build a chemistry laboratory in a large room on the south side of the new west wing of the building. The bishop's gift led to the hiring of William J. Doyle to teach chemistry. Doyle had attended St. Ambrose from 1887-1890 and then went to the University of Iowa. When he was hired, he became the first full-time lay professor since Joseph Halligan.[30]

In 1906 new individual lockers were added to the dormitories so residents could lock their belongings. Although this was expensive, the *Catholic Messenger* claimed that it was the "policy of the college to spare no expense to make things convenient and pleasant for the young men" who attended St. Ambrose.[31] And in 1907, the city of Davenport finally graded Locust Street from Harrison Street to Warren Street to a thirty-eight foot width and paved it with asphalt. The college was assessed $1,919 for its portion of the cost, nearly half of which was paid by the bishop.[32]

Another area of growth involved the ground behind Ambrose Hall. There had been a baseball diamond and a field large enough to play football, but now there was need for more space. When it had been announced in mid-July 1901 that the new west wing would be added to Ambrose Hall, it had also been announced that a new, separate building would be built for a modern gymnasium. The next year when the chapel was dedicated, however, no progress had been made on a gymnasium, but there were still plans to build it.[33]

By 1905 there was still no new gymnasium, but that summer contractors were hired to reshape the area behind Ambrose Hall and create more playing fields. The old Play Hall was moved further west, oak trees were cut down, and over 14,000 cubic yards of earth was moved to create a large flat area for three baseball diamonds and a football field. The field extended north to the northern border of the campus. The surrounding high ground formed a natural amphitheater which provided places for spectators to sit and watch ball games. The total cost of $3,500 for the project was underwritten in part by contributions totaling $1,151 donated by the priests of the diocese at their retreat in 1905.[34]

While the Play Hall was refurbished to create a new handball alley and provide better space for indoor games, a gymnasium was "fast developing into an imperative new requirement," especially for use during the winter months. The 1905 catalogue discussed this need and declared that the "attention of the friends of the College [was] respectfully invited to this matter of a gymnasium." Advocates of a new gymnasi-

Bishop James Davis.

um with all the necessary equipment said it would be an appropriate commemoration of the college's twenty-fifth anniversary in 1907.[35]

In mid-February 1907, as the college baseball team began to get ready for its spring season, it was announced that the Alumni Association had raised over $1,000 to build a grandstand to seat about 350 fans. The structure was to be covered and would sit on the southeast corner of the athletic field (approximately in the position of the Cosgrove Hall cafeteria on the modern campus). The college administration hoped that the new grandstand would provide another benefit to the college. Up to now the cost of the athletic program had been borne by private contributions from the faculty and some friends of the college. With a grandstand the administration could begin to charge admission to athletic events and use the proceeds to help offset the expenses of a growing athletic program.[36] The new grandstand was used for the first time on May 15, when St. Ambrose defeated the Davenport High School team by the score of 3-2, in a fast, one-hour-and-twenty-minute game. All the fans liked the new grandstand, but they noted that the students still preferred to sit on the "banks surrounding the campus."[37]

The twenty-fifth year of the college, 1906-1907, brought a series of changes. The first was the death of Bishop Henry Cosgrove on December 22, 1906. Cosgrove was a link to the history of the founding of Catholicism in Iowa and Davenport. He knew Bishop Matthias Loras, the founding bishop of Iowa. Following his ordination as a priest in 1857, he was sent to St. Marguerite's Parish in Davenport, where he knew Antoine and Marguerite LeClaire, generous supporters of Catholicism in Davenport and the founders the parish, which was named for her. It was at St. Marguerite's

in 1882 that he and Bishop McMullen had their conversation which led to the founding of St. Ambrose. As bishop, Cosgrove moved the college to Locust Street and saw to the construction of the original building and the first two additions. As bishop, Cosgrove and his councilors made the major decisions about expansion, whether to turn the school over to a religious order, when to build and what the shape of the building would be; at times they also discussed curricular issues and the salaries of professors. It was the bishop who raised the money and paid the bills for capital expenditures and it was the bishop who assumed responsibility for the annual operating deficit. However, Cosgrove seemed content to see the school grow slowly and remain essentially what it was at its founding twenty-five years before, a school for boys beyond grade school age.

On February 26, 1907, Bishop Davis met with his councilors to discuss the future of St. Ambrose. First they discussed the possibility of the division of the diocese. The issue had apparently been a concern during the last years of Cosgrove's life, and it was a topic of discussion among those attending his funeral. There the opinion was that with a healthy, younger Davis, there was no need to divide the Diocese of Davenport.[38] But at their meeting in February, Davis told the councilors that there were "persistent rumors" that the diocese would be divided "in the near future." The councilors resolved to write a letter to the apostolic delegate in Washington, D.C., to express their concern about such a move. They told the delegate that "such a division would impoverish both dioceses and materially interfere with the progress and work of religion," including, by implication, the work of St. Ambrose College.[39] What impact their letter had with the delegate is not known, but if it had any impact, it only delayed the division. The new Diocese of Des Moines was created in 1911. This did have an impact on the deliberations about the college.

Next Flannagan made the case for a gymnasium, additional classrooms, and residence rooms at St. Ambrose. He noted that the number of boarding students was increasing and that the dormitories were "overcrowded," the sanitary condition was "poor," that more room was needed "in every way," and that the need for a gymnasium for physical exercise was "more apparent each year." The councilors said they understood the need, but felt that the time was not right for such a project. A motion was made to build an addition at "some future time" with the projected $30,000 cost to be divided equally among the bishop, the priests, and the college. No action was taken on the motion, but after further discussion, they voted to authorize Flannagan to "secure plans" for a gymnasium and to secure figures on the cost of an addition to Ambrose Hall, but they said that building could proceed only after they knew what would happen about the division of the

A Great and Lasting Beginning

St. Ambrose College, Davenport, Iowa.

Ambrose Hall 1909.

diocese.[40]

The bishop began a series of changes at the college. Speaking at the St. Ambrose commencement the previous summer, Davis had told how the "little mustard seed" that was St. Ambrose had now grown to "great proportions." He said that Bishop Cosgrove had been fortunate to have "men of ability" at the college and he singled out Flannagan's "wise direction."[41] Now late in the spring of 1907, in the first signal that change was in the works for St. Ambrose, the bishop announced that he had appointed Flannagan to be the pastor of Sacred Heart Cathedral and vicar general of the diocese.[42]

Although he would leave the school he had served since 1885 as vicar general, Flannagan was vice president of the Board of Trustees of the college and a member of the bishop's council, which was still making the important decisions regarding the college. The college had grown from seventy-one students in Flannagan's first year as president to 127 in his last. The more significant number, however, was the ratio of day students to boarding students. In his first year there were twice as many boarding students as day students, but in his last year as president there were five times as many boarders as day students. To meet the need to accommodate the growing number of boarders, two additions had been put on Ambrose Hall. But when Flannagan left the presidency, most of the students at St. Ambrose were still high school level students and Flannagan, like the late bishop, was content to have it remain that way.

At the twenty-fifth commencement on June 18, Flannagan's last as president, the students chose as a theme, "Some Triumphs of the True." The student speakers talked of various individuals who exemplified the theme in their own time. Bishop Davis sounded the theme when he paid tribute to the twenty-five years of St. Ambrose and he singled out the alumni who were "filling honorable positions in every walk of life, in trade and commerce, in the pulpit and at the bar, in medicine and surgery." He also thanked the alumni for their generosity in contributing nearly $1,000 to build the new athletic field. He congratulated the graduates and told the other students he hoped they would return in September "refreshed" to resume their studies.[43]

When the refreshed students returned in September, they would begin to benefit from the results of the meeting of the bishop's council which occurred ten days after the June commencement. There the councilors discussed the vacancy in the office of president and recommended that the bishop appoint Father William Shannahan, the current vice president, prefect of studies and professor of philosophy, as the third president of St. Ambrose.

Shannahan was born near Ardon, in Muscatine County, Iowa, on February 2, 1870. When he was fifteen, his family moved to Williamsburg, Iowa, then to nearby Holbrook. He attended St. Ambrose for one year in 1888-1889, then returned home where he taught in a country school for two years. In 1891, he returned to St. Ambrose and became one of the first philosophy students when philosophy was added to the curriculum. He also served as a prefect in the study hall, where students remembered that under Shannahan, "We didn't get by with any fooling in the study hall."[44] He graduated in 1896 and went on to study theology. Following ordination in 1899, he studied philosophy for one year at the Catholic University of America, then returned to St. Ambrose to teach philosophy.

Shannahan was remembered as a "tireless worker" who was up early in the morning and worked late into the evening. A genial man, his room became a gathering place where the faculty came in the evening to relax, talk about the day, and exchange ideas. Shannahan was ready to discuss any subject and according to Hauber who was now a junior faculty member, "His ideas were always clear-cut and well-expressed no matter what the topic of discussion happened to be: literature, philosophy, science, economics, politics, the practical problems of running a college–he was at home in all fields."[45] Shannahan would be assisted by Father Charles J. Donohoe as vice president and the Reverend William L. Hannon who became prefect of studies. Shannahan, Donohoe, and Hannon were all from Holbrook, and their hometown newspaper took understandable pride that "perhaps in the whole country there cannot be found another instance where three boys from the same parish meet, in matured days, to fill responsible positions on the faculty of a great college."[46]

On the same page of the *Catholic Messenger* where Shannahan's appointment was announced, came the notice that the bishop's council had decided to build an addition to the campus. This had been the other topic of discussion at the June meeting of the council where they again raised the issue of the need for a gymnasium but now they also called for more residence rooms for the philosophy students. It was reported that each year the college received applications for this kind of private room, and the implication was that enrollment would increase if this amenity were available. These private rooms could also be used to house the "elder priests" of the diocese who came to St. Ambrose for their annual retreat, a point made as much out of concern for the elder priests as it was a way to make the project more attractive to the priests of the diocese who would be expected to support it financially. There was general agreement among the councilors that such an

addition should be built because it would give St. Ambrose students "all the advantages given by other schools." The estimated cost of $30,000, would be borrowed, and the debt would be repaid by raising money from the priests of the diocese.[47]

If anyone doubted the need for more room at St. Ambrose, the 1907 fall enrollment figures made the case. There had been 127 students, 21 day students and 106 boarders in the 1906-1907 year. That fall those numbers increased to 144 students, 119 of whom were boarders. Those numbers may have contributed to discussion throughout the late summer and fall which led to a revision of the original plans for the addition. When the bishop's council met on January 21, 1908, Shannahan and Donohoe were called in to explain the new plans. They said that the college had five needs that they hoped to meet with the addition: more dormitory rooms, a larger study hall, the gymnasium, additional rooms for elder priests during retreat, and an auditorium. The addition of the auditorium to the earlier plans raised the estimated cost to $40,000, to be divided equally among the bishop, the priests, the college, and the parishes of the diocese. The college faculty would visit the parishes to solicit the $10,000 that had been set as their goal. The councilors accepted this plan and the bishop agreed to their request that he be present at the next meeting of every deanery as a way to explain the plan to the priests.[48]

Fund raising for the addition began immediately. College priests visited parishes throughout the spring and summer to raise money and also to urge pastors to encourage the people to send their sons to St. Ambrose. To support their efforts, Bishop Davis wrote a letter to the people of the diocese appealing for funds. He called St. Ambrose the "crowning feature" of the diocesan educational system, the only one on which the entire diocese had a claim and a responsibility. He said the addition and its amenities were

The laboratory on the first floor of 1909 addition. (In 2006, the Admissions Office occupied the space.)

A Great and Lasting Beginning

necessary if St. Ambrose was to compete with other colleges. He described the features of the new addition, explaining that it would cost about $50,000. The college was now self-supporting, and in spite of a higher cost of living, the rates charged were the same as they had been for years: tuition was $20 per semester, where it had been since 1895; full room, board, and tuition had been set at $95 in 1887 and had been raised to $100 in 1901 where it remained. The bishop pointed out that many of their sons had

The auditorium 1909.

sought gymnasium. The main part was a two-story space with a balcony that overlooked the fully equipped gymnasium (later students would know this space as the Bee Hive). At the west end of the gymnasium, there was a locker room and showers. Beneath the balcony there was a two lane bowling alley. There was also a room for table games and a billiard room complete with two tables. The first floor on the front, the same level as the refectory and kitchens of the earlier additions, contained science laboratories and the college laundry. The second floor contained a large study hall, a large classroom, and a new infirmary with five rooms for use by students who were ill. On the third floor in the back was a two-story auditorium that would seat 450 people. The stage at the west end was complete with theatrical lighting and fitted with a drop curtain which showed a scene of the Grand Canal in Venice; there were other drop curtains to provide scenery for plays. The auditorium became the site of plays, the oratorical contest, commencements, music concerts, and public lectures. In the east wall of the auditorium there was an opening through which a motion picture projector could show images, which, according to the *Messenger*, "gives an idea of the up-to-date or rather entirely new and progressive ideas carried out in planning additional facilities" for the learning and entertainment of the students. The remainder of the third and fourth floors were divided into twenty private rooms for students. The central stairway of the new wing was the connection with the 1893 section of the building, and served as a public entrance for events in the auditorium. To emphasize the public nature of the entrance, the exterior featured a stone facing and the interior carried a tiled floor which included a monogrammed "SAC."[51]

already entered professional and business careers following their education at St. Ambrose. But he said that the "great glory" of St. Ambrose was as a "nursery" of priests, and he reminded them that more than one-third of the priests of the diocese had been educated at St. Ambrose. Although he knew the priests of the diocese would contribute generously, he told the people it was their college and asked for their support.[49]

In April the contracts were let for construction of the new wing of Ambrose Hall and work began almost immediately. When guests arrived for the June 17, 1908, commencement ceremony, they found that the foundation was already in place. In his remarks the bishop pointed out that the graduates and their guests were crowded into the study hall which was too small for their numbers but that next year they would gather in the spacious new auditorium. He then surprised everyone when he announced, to great applause, that the priests of the diocese had pledged $15,000 to the project and had promised to raise $10,000 more. The college also needed more students and he said that the priests had promised to find the "bright intelligent young men" in their parishes and encourage them to attend St. Ambrose.[50]

Work on the building continued through the fall of 1908, once again providing students with many sidewalk superintending opportunities. The new building was an L-shaped structure wrapping around the east and north sides of the 1893 wing. The leg of the L on the east side of the 1893 wing, however, was set back from the plane of the rest of the building, a feature that would lead to yet another addition in four years. The earlier additions to Ambrose Hall had continued Victor Huot's French design with its Mansard roof and round topped windows. This addition had flat topped windows and a straight roof line, giving it a cleaner, twentieth-century American look.

The topography of the land meant that the ground floor on the north side was lower than the rest of the building. This area became the long-

The college took possession of the addition after the first of the year. The dedication on February 22, 1909, was held in the glittering new auditorium, which was filled to standing room. The band and orchestra provided music. The three presidents, Schulte, Flannagan, and Shannahan spoke, as did the mayor of Davenport who congratulated the college on the addition and wished St. Ambrose a "brilliant future." The principal speakers were John B. Sullivan, a Des Moines attorney and member of the Iowa House of Representatives, who brought greetings from the Catholic community of Des Moines, and Michael V. Gannon, a perennial speaker at St. Ambrose events. Gannon reminded the audience of his deep connection with St. Ambrose. He had been principal of St. Marguerite's in the years before St. Ambrose began there, and he had been in the audience in 1882 when Bishop

The gymnasium 1909. There was a two-lane bowling alley under the balcony on the left. This area later became the Bee Hive.

McMullen announced he was starting a boy's school, which had now become a college "second to none in the west." Finally Bishop Davis spoke and thanked all those who had made the addition possible. He said that with it, St. Ambrose began another "quarter of a century radiant with hope." Following the dedication ceremony, there was a banquet at the new Davenport Hotel where there were more congratulatory speeches.[52]

At the Quasi-Synod at the end of the annual priests' retreat in June, the bishop thanked the priests and their people for their support of the addition to St. Ambrose. Once again, as he urged them to send students to the school, he noted the large number of priests in the diocese who had graduated from the college, and said he hoped that before long, St. Ambrose would be able to supply all the priests of the diocese. Then he told them that construction of the addition had cost $56,842. The fund raising in the parishes had yielded $9,500, the college had paid $7,500 from its funds, Davis had contributed $10,000, the priests of the diocese contributed $15,500, and he had taken out a loan for the rest, which left a debt of about $17,000. The *Messenger* noted that the generosity of the priests and people boded well for the future and hoped the "munificent" spirit continued.[53]

The next month the annual St. Patrick's Day celebration was held in the new auditorium. The program featured the usual musical selections by the band and orchestra; readings from Shakespeare; an essay entitled, "Were the Dark Ages Dark?" the thesis of which was that they were not; and an oration on the faith of Erin in which the speaker used "glowing word pictures" to tell "the glory of her steadfastness." The highlight of the program was the presentation of the first play presented on campus for many years, "The Old Captain's Idea," written by the Reverend Joseph P. Stahl of the college faculty. The college thespians took full advantage of the new stage, its scenery, and lights, and the audience of 500 was delighted with the result.[54]

The hope that the new addition would bring in more students was real-ized when 178 students, 138 of whom were boarders, enrolled in the fall of 1909, up from 159 with 132 boarders the previous year. The next year enrollment would fall off slightly, but in the 1910-1911 school year, students came to St. Ambrose from fourteen states, and it was reported that there had been inquiries from even more states. The increase in students meant more lockers were installed, more desks were placed in the study hall, and more tables were provided for the refectory which, it was feared, might still be too small.[55]

There was a little noticed, but important, change during those years when the bishop and his advisors amended the articles of incorporation. When St. Ambrose was originally incorporated in 1885, the Board of Trustees consisted of the bishop, the vicar general, and the president, but the important decisions regarding St. Ambrose were made by the bishop's council. They had discussed the governance question at a meeting on April 15, 1907, and suggested that the Board of Trustees be expanded to include the vice president of the college. For whatever reason, however, when the amended articles of incorporation were filed in January 1908, the members of the Board of Trustees remained the bishop, vicar general, and president. For the foreseeable future, the important decisions about the college would remain with the bishop's council. One significant change did take place when the amended articles were filed: the name of the institution now officially became St. Ambrose College, the name it had been calling itself since the early 1890s.[56]

During the first decade of the twentieth century, the curriculum began the process of separation of the academic (high school) program and the

A Great and Lasting Beginning

The 1906 football team photographed behind Ambrose Hall, standing: William Adrian, Donohoe brother, Lawrence Maher, Hugh Sweeney, Edward Barron, Nugent, Edmund Corridan, Edmund Burke, Edmund McDermott, unknown, Roscoe Carney. Seated: Charles Moylan, Frank Buckley, Thomas Smith, unknown, Eugene Waters, Donohoe brother, Robert Fischer, McGuinn.

collegiate program. The leader of this change was Shannahan who became prefect of studies in 1901. Prior to that, the curriculum had included a five-year Classical course, to which seminary students added two years of philosophy; a two-year Commercial curriculum; and an Academic course which blended the two. In 1902, the Classical course was dropped and the remaining courses were realigned. The new Commercial course remained a two-year program, but included a Preparatory course for those students who needed it. A new three-year Academic course corresponded "in large measure" to a regular high school curriculum. Academic students who needed it could also take the Preparatory course with the commercial students. The four-year Collegiate course would be the "equal of similar courses in the best colleges." Completion of the Academic course was a prerequisite for admission to the collegiate course. There was also a four-year German curriculum which could be taken along with any of the regular courses of study.[57]

This curricular change would lead to the eventual separation of what became St. Ambrose Academy from the college, and reflected changes being advocated in Catholic higher education nationally. No one spoke more forcefully for the formation of Catholic high schools apart from colleges than the Reverend James A. Burns, CSC, the president of Holy Cross College at the Catholic University of America. Speaking at the 1901 meeting of the Association of Catholic Colleges, Burns said the "Preparatory departments of our colleges are not a satisfactory substitute for a system of Catholic high schools."[58] Advocates of separation of the high school and college curricula argued that it would strengthen both levels and that a system of Catholic high schools would become feeder schools for Catholic colleges. In 1904, for example, there were 6,000 public high schools and 500 public colleges, but only 200 Catholic high schools and 100 Catholic colleges. Looking at those figures, one observer said that the "critical period" had arrived for Catholic colleges and that the importance of the high school movement had not been "overstated" by Burns. By the end of the decade, Catholic colleges had the choice of continuing the system of a combined six-year high school and college curriculum, or adopting the progressive alternative of moving to the 8-4-4 plan (eight years of elementary education, four years of secondary education, and four years of college) that was rapidly becoming the norm in American public education.[59]

St. Ambrose was moving, albeit slowly, in the latter, progressive direction. In 1910, under the leadership of Shannahan, the college began to delineate more clearly the distinction between the high school and collegiate levels. Since 1885, the college catalogue had said that those who completed the Classical course and had spent at least two years at St. Ambrose were eligible for the Bachelor of Arts Degree, and that with additional study they could receive the Master of Arts or Master of Accounts Degree. There is no record that those degrees were ever awarded; rather the students were given the "Honors of Graduation" or a "Certificate of Graduation."[60] The 1910 catalogue contained an announcement that beginning the next year those who had completed the four-year Academic course (high school) would receive a diploma, and graduates in the Philosophy course would receive the degree of Bachelor of Arts. In 1911, four philosophy students, Thomas C. Donohoe, Carl H. Meinberg, Walter E. Cullinan, and Bart E. Linehan, were awarded the first Bachelor of Arts Degrees from St. Ambrose.

The next year another revision of the curriculum further separated the academy and the college. There was now the two-year Commercial course and a four-year Academic course, which corresponded to the "standard High School course." Evidence of the completion of eighth grade was required for admission to the Academic course. Graduation required four years of Latin, English, and mathematics, two years of Greek, and one year of physics and chemistry; graduates were "qualified to meet the usual college entrance requirements." The new four-year Collegiate course required graduation from the Academic course or its equivalent, and graduates could be admitted to graduate programs at the state university. The former four-year German curriculum was now a five-year course and could be taken in addition to the regular college curriculum.[61]

One consequence of the new gymnasium was that physical education became part of the curriculum with Charles A. McGee as the instructor, while the Athletic Society continued to organize intramural sports. Baseball teams played against each other in round-robin tournaments. The handball courts were always busy. There had been a lawn tennis club for a few years, but even after it ceased to exist, students continued to play tennis.

At a meeting of the Athletic Society on October 12, 1909, the members organized a handball team and elected Martin "Foxy" Rogers as captain. They also organized a bowling team with Michael Phelan as captain. With a suggestion from the faculty advisor that they organize a basketball team, another college sport was added to the athletic program at St. Ambrose.[62]

Eight men turned out for the basketball team that began its season with a game against Augustana College on December 11, 1909. Their coach was E. C. Klafs, the physical education instructor. Through the season which extended into March, the Ambrosians played Wilton, Moline, Clinton High School, Clinton YMCA, and Davenport High School. The team only won one game, a 26-24 overtime victory against Moline High School. The most lop-sided loss was against the "probable" state champion, Davenport High School, who defeated St. Ambrose 65-9. This game cost the team its star forward, Ralph Nettleton, who broke his collarbone. Nettleton's injury was felt across campus since he was also a baseball and football star, a mem-

ber of the orchestra, and leader of the band. A return game against Davenport was cancelled.[63] The next season Ralph McManus took over the team which played seven games; they won the three home games and lost the away games.

The College Nine, made up of the best baseball players on campus, remained the most important spring athletic team. By the middle of the decade, its schedule included games with the local Knights of Columbus team, Augustana College, Davenport High School, a team from the arsenal, as well as occasional games with out-of-town teams like St. Joseph's (Loras) College in Dubuque.

Decoration Day celebrations included a doubleheader, with one game against a local team and the other against a team made up of alumni. There was excitement on campus in 1905 when Jimmy Shields, the star shortstop on the Ambrose team, signed with the Clinton Independents, a semi-pro club, for the season. The Clinton team was so anxious to sign "the popular expert of the College Nine," that the deal was completed by long distance telephone before "any other team could put in a bid for his services."[64]

The Athletic Society continued to organize a football team which played other local teams, but it did not have the same kind of official support that baseball did. Throughout the decade the annual college catalogue listed the various intramural baseball teams and the names of the College Nine, but only once in the decade was a football team and its members listed. The well-known attitudes of the bishop and president toward football may have been part of the reason. It was only after Cosgrove's death and Flannagan's departure as president that football began to have a place on campus. The continuing controversy about football itself may have been another reason. For example, the Logomachetean Society continued to debate the issues of the day, such as whether world naval disarmament was possible, or whether the saloon had caused more misery than the sword, and they also debated football. At their first meeting in 1903, they had discussed whether rugby football produced more beneficial effects or evil effects. Now in 1910 at one of their last meetings before the group disbanded, they debated whether football should be abolished in American schools and universities.[65]

There is no record of the content of the Logomachetean debates about football but they represent the local version of debates that were taking place nationally. By the middle of the first decade of the century, football had become the dominant college sport, but educators were ambivalent about this dominance. To some, like Cosgrove and Flannagan, football "was a cancer because of its brutal side and unethical play"; to others "it was valued for its promotion of character, virility, and esprit de corps." To this latter group, football was a facilitator of manly qualities in an environment where intellectual pursuits were not perceived as manly, and it became a symbol of "college and national virility." A growing number of educators were concerned that football was increasingly perceived as the "most visible sign of college life," a fact that University of Wisconsin historian Frederick Jackson Turner deplored, saying it was "absurd" that football was "the test of the excellence of a university and the proper means of advertising it." Harvard president Charles W. Eliot went so far as to say that football was "unfit for college men."[66]

Another critic broadened the scope of his criticism to college competitive sports in general and claimed that they had an "evil effect" on students because the "win at any cost" attitude of administrators led the students to

A Great and Lasting Beginning

Ambrose Hall 1913.

lying, cheating, and acts of brutality on the playing field. He worried that future leaders of business and politics were being recruited from the "ranks of bright young college men, whose sense of right and wrong has been debauched upon the athletic field."[67]

In response to the critics, in 1906, a new set of rules for football was adopted which had the goal of eliminating the brutal conduct carried over from football's roots in rugby, and which had been the source of the objections of Cosgrove and Flannagan to the sport. Another aim of those rules was to open up the game, achieved in among other ways by making the forward pass legal. The major changes in 1910 included changing the structure of the game from two thirty-five-minute halves, to four fifteen-minute quarters, and having the teams change ends after each quarter.[68]

Reform of the rules of the game satisfied some critics, but many others called for more supervision of sports by college administrators. At St. Ambrose the Athletic Society began in 1888 with student leadership, but by 1894, there was a priest manager and treasurer. Through most of the first decade of the century, the society concerned itself with forming teams and creating schedules for intramural sports. But in the fall semester of 1909, two issues were discussed which were the last, student-led initiatives for athletics on campus. At a meeting on September 17, the students discussed whether to buy new uniforms for the football team. Carl Meinberg, a student from Keokuk, in "one of the best" speeches heard for years, spoke in favor of the new uniforms, arguing to great applause that a col-

Official monogram of S.A.C. 10 in. high. Block Style. Color = white

lege without a football team was not recognized by other schools. A few students said the school should have a better team than the previous year before they would contribute, but most of the students present favored taking up a collection to buy new uniforms. After the students had collected $75.25 toward the purchase of the uniforms they were told that since they had the "good will of the faculty in all athletic sports," the faculty would assist in the effort. The discussion indicates that football had now become more respectable on campus, but not so much so that the administration was willing to fully support it. This attitude continued when three years later, at the last meeting of the Athletic Society, the members decided that the students should be assessed twenty cents to purchase new football jerseys.[69]

In December 1909, the members met again, this time to discuss the creation of a monogram to be awarded to those who took part in at least three games as a member of the first team of football, basketball, and baseball. They noted that such a practice was popular at other schools, that it would bring prestige to the individual player, and it would draw attention to the college athletic program. A committee of five appointed to design the monogram, decided it should be a ten-inch-high white, block A with a small S. The first letters were awarded to the basketball team on April 7, 1910, and to the baseball team at a meeting of the Athletic Society on June 13, 1910. The first football letters were awarded on December 17, 1910.[70]

The place of athletics on campus changed

The science lecture hall. (In 2006, the Admissions Office occupied the space.)

dramatically in the 1909-1910 year with the addition of the Reverend James A. O'Neill to the faculty. O'Neill was a 1905 graduate of St. Ambrose, and in his last year as a student he was president of the Athletic Society. He came to St. Ambrose in the fall of 1909 as master of discipline and professor of English and mathematics. In the spring of 1910, he was appointed the manager and treasurer of the Athletic Society. In this role he addressed the meeting of the Athletic Society on April 16 where he proposed to organize a baseball league. This would be an intramural league, similar to what had been the custom for years, but now O'Neill, in a sign of new support by the administration for athletics, offered prizes of $20 and $10 for the first and second place teams in the league. Up until now, the College Nine had been formed from the best players of the various intramural teams, but now, as another sign of change, a member proposed that the "first team," the varsity players of the College Nine, be excluded from the intramural league teams.[71]

In the fall of 1910, O'Neill was appointed as the first director of athletics at St. Ambrose. One of his first actions was to hire Ralph McManus as the first football coach, and with that the administration took control of football. A football star at Rock Island High School, McManus was the coach of the Moline West Ends, an independent team that had won the Illinois state championship the previous year. McManus was also the sports editor of the *Rock Island Argus* newspaper.[72]

McManus put together a small and inexperienced team which played its first game on October 8, 1910, against Davenport High School at the Three-I League Park, in the west end of Davenport just off Telegraph Road. St. Ambrose lost the game 9-0 when the Davenport fullback drop-kicked a field goal and scored a touchdown and extra point. St. Ambrose fans noted

that in spite of the win, Davenport High made only two first downs and was forced to punt every other time they had the ball. St. Ambrose played five more games that season and won against the Rock Island Socials, Geneseo High School, Muscatine High School, and Hedding College of Abingdon, Illinois. The last game of the season was on Thanksgiving against Rock Island High School, and although the student section urged on the team with a "number of college yells and snappy songs," St. Ambrose lost 6-0, to give the team a 4-2 record for the season.[73] There was also a junior football team, called the Minims, made up of younger students who finished their season 6-0, and were not scored upon all season.

Athletic opportunities increased even more in 1911 when the college spent $10,000 to buy all the pieces of property on the western border of the campus northward from the property it had purchased ten years before (the area from the flag pole north to behind where Lewis Hall sits, and east of Davis Hall on the modern campus). Most of the property was unoccupied, but fences were removed and all but one of the buildings was razed. The remaining building was remodeled for use as an isolation hospital. The rest of the property was graded for additional athletic fields for the younger students, a court for lawn tennis, and to serve the new track and field team.[74]

The 1911-1912 year saw a jump in enrollment from 174 the previous year, to 219 students, 160 of whom were boarders. Football and basketball had now joined baseball as established varsity sports. The literary societies continued to debate weighty and less weighty issues. The band, orchestra, and a new choir provided music for the various on-campus programs. The dramatic society staged two productions: *Half Back Sandy* for the St.

A Great and Lasting Beginning

The Latin study hall.

Ambrose Day celebration in December, and *The Toastmaster* in the spring. In addition, the *Bonifacius Verein* presented *Der Darwinaffe* in May. And the students went to classes, the study hall, the chapel, played intramural sports, crept to the back of the campus to sneak a cigarette behind a tree, and kept one another awake with dormitory horse play.

In the meantime other, smaller changes were taking place on campus. The faculty continued to grow and in 1912, there were nine priests and five laymen. The Commercial curriculum was enhanced with the addition of Actual Business Practice equipment, a laboratory set up with stations where students could transact business and play the role of either customer or clerk. The library continued to expand with gifts by friends of the college like E. M. Sharon, the publisher of the *Catholic Messenger*, who donated 200 books on history, politics, biography, and a variety of other subjects. In 1910, the Reverend Patrick J. O'Reilly began to teach a course in Irish history and a few years later, a course in Gaelic would be added to the curriculum. That same year Sister Mary Peter, who had come to St. Ambrose in 1887 as one of the first sister housekeepers, left to take a position at the mother house of the Sisters of the Humility of Mary.[75]

On April 18, 1912, Shannahan appeared at the bishop's council meeting and presented a report on the state of the college. He told them that enrollment was good, regular maintenance was done, the work on the new athletic fields was completed for a cost of about $500, and the new infirmary for students with "contagious diseases" was open. He was pleased to report that the conduct of the students was "on the whole most gratifying," because only one student had been dismissed for misconduct during the year. Most of the students were "daily communicants," and nearly all went to confession weekly; all were required to go to confession once a month. He said that the recent purchase of the additional property for $10,000 had raised the college debt to $20,000 and that the interest on the debt was being paid out of ordinary college revenues.

With that as prelude, he next told the councilors that yet another addition to the building was needed. When the east wing had been added three years before, the front was set back from the front of the earlier sections of the building. The part that was "uncompleted" was in the "private room section of the building." One reason that section was not built was the

necessity to economize, another was uncertainty about the success of renting private rooms to students. Now there was a demand for more rooms for students and professors, one of whom had to be housed off campus that year.

Shannahan proposed a four-story addition that would extend south twenty feet to make the entire south face of Ambrose Hall on the same plane, and with the same style of architecture designed by Victor Huot twenty-seven years earlier. This addition would provide ten private rooms for students, two rooms for professors, and a general science room for an estimated cost of $12,000. Shannahan admitted that this would increase the college debt, but he pronounced the college financial situation as "satisfactory" and he was confident that the additional debt could be borne. The bishop and his councilors approved the addition, but mandated that the cost be met by an assessment levied against the priests and parishes. Each dean would provide his estimate of what the parishes in his deanery could do and present this to the bishop so he could set fund raising goals.[76]

Construction began before the fund raising began and by commencement in the middle of June, the progress was apparent. The addition was ready in late September when students and faculty moved in. The upper three floors were residences, but the first floor became the new museum where Schulte's geological collection moved and where, thanks to a donation by the Reverend Joseph Tritz of Clinton, a large collection of stuffed hawks, owls, a passenger pigeon, and various birds' eggs also found a home.[77]

When the Quasi-Synod met at the end of the priests' retreat in June, the bishop urged the priests to "take a lively interest in the diocesan college by sending pupils." Although progress had been made to improve the school, for the institution to succeed, it had to "keep abreast of the times." He told the priests that the present addition, for which they and their people had been assessed, would be the "last for many years to come. It completes the work, all ought to feel proud of what has been accomplished in their college."

With the completion of the 1912 addition there may have been a sense that the building was complete, but that confuses the building with the college. It was far from complete, and in the decade ahead, new leadership looked beyond the current footprint of Ambrose Hall and provided for future growth of the college.[78]

The Actual Business Practice room.

Sandy haired Tom Mitchell kept on mowing the grass under the majestic oaks on the front lawn, stopping the while to light the stub of a pipe. The great Doctor of the Church, St. Ambrose, from his pedestal on the front walk was imparting his blessing to passersby. Jim Gaffney was hurling curve balls down on the diamond. Luigi Ligutti was practicing the English language. Groups sat on benches on the hill. The bell in the tower rang out the Angelus. Young men stopped and blessed themselves. And evening came to a spring day at St. Ambrose in Nineteen Hundred Thirteen.

<h1 align="center">❧ Chapter Five ❧</h1>

When David Klise, a 1913 academy graduate, wrote his vignette from the vantage point of fifty years later, it described a college that was still a small world unto itself. He noted that in 1913, "There was no cold war; no world tension . . . there were few automobiles then, no paved highways, no stop and go lights, no radios, no television and no talkie movies . . . Shaves were fifteen cents; hair cuts a quarter . . . there were high button shoes; high stiff collars and hard hats. Life was less complex and people somehow seemed happier than they do today."[1]

Occasionally the idyllic picture Klise painted would be shattered when the tower bell tolled for the death of a student or for victims of war. But for the most part, life at St. Ambrose in the early teens was not that much different from when Father Schulte and Joseph Halligan listened to student recitations, and Father Flannagan tossed apples out of the window at Thanksgiving. During those years, however, the world and Catholic higher education were changing. Soon the work of education reformers at home, and events an ocean away, would reach out and draw Ambrosians into a new world, and change the college in ways that Schulte may have hoped for and Flannagan largely resisted.

That spring the auditorium was filled with a crowd that overflowed into the hallway to witness the thirty-first annual commencement. They heard recitations and speeches from students, music by the band and orchestra, remarks by Bishop Davis, and the commencement address by Des Moines Bishop Austin Dowling. Six college graduates received the Bachelor of Arts Degree, seventeen academy students received diplomas, and ten students received certificates from the Commercial department. Most of the graduates were from the Diocese of Davenport and the new Diocese of Des Moines, but others were from Darlington, Wisconsin; Clark, South Dakota; South Omaha and Pender, Nebraska; and Rock Island and Aledo, Illinois.

The week before Shannahan had treated the college graduates to a five-course dinner at Zum Altendorf, a restaurant in west Davenport. The night before commencement, former students, friends, and some of the faculty joined the academy graduates at the Kimball House Hotel in downtown Davenport, where they dined on little neck clams, broiled live lobster, mushrooms sous clouche, grilled milk-fed chicken, potatoes Delmonico, asparagus tips, fruit salad maraschino, and baked Alaska. Over coffee and cigars, toastmaster David Klise called on his classmates to make speeches and toasts. Ambrose Burke spoke first on the achievements of the class. All in all, it was an grand ending to their St. Ambrose years, and an auspicious beginning of the rest of their lives.[2]

The class of 1913 had more than just their memories to remember their days at St. Ambrose. Sometime that winter, David Klise was among a group of students who decided they should publish a yearbook. They secured faculty approval in February, and set out to find editors and a staff. The students wrote to as many alumni as they could find to urge them to subscribe to the annual. They hoped that it would be the impetus for the revival of the Alumni Association which had not met for many years.

That summer the building was turned over to the painters and decorators who refurbished all of the interior except the new, 1912 addition. Most of the priest faculty left town. Shannahan went to his family home near Williamsburg. With pride, the local paper noted the visit of the "big brainy man" who had not yet "reached his prime," but already had a record rich with the "ripe fruits of matured wisdom and his genius for hard work." The next week Shannahan and Father Stahl, English and science professor, left for a trip to Montreal, New York, and Atlantic City. Three other priest faculty members, William Hannon, Owen McGuire, Patrick O'Reilly, took an extended "educational recreative trip" to Europe.[3]

Other faculty members traveled closer to home on behalf of the college. When he returned from the east, Shannahan visited parishes in Muscatine County, his birthplace. His traveling companion, Stahl, visited parishes in the Keokuk deanery in southeastern Iowa. The Reverend Francis Barry traveled to Monroe County in the western part of the diocese to talk about St. Ambrose to the Irish parishes of Melrose and Georgetown. Hauber went to his home area and visited parishes in the Iowa City deanery. Their message included seeking financial support to pay for the recent addition and encouraging parents to send their sons to St. Ambrose.[4]

School began on September 9 with a record enrollment. As they settled into their dormitories and classes, the students turned their attention to the coming football season. With the leadership of Father O'Neill and the coaching of Ralph McManus, football had taken its place as the primary fall activity on campus. The previous season the team had finished with five wins, one loss, and one tie. At the football banquet at the end of that season, the team had elected Ed Morrissey, from Lovilla, Iowa, as its captain. Morrissey played tackle on defense and fullback on offense, and was the team leader even before his election as captain. Now the campus community expected that Morrissey, and the many other returning players, would have an even better season.

That fall St. Ambrose would be facing some new teams. The year before the college had taken a major step toward an intercollegiate sports program when it joined with Iowa State Teachers College, Ellsworth College, Parsons College, William Penn, Charles City College, Upper Iowa, and St. Joseph's (Loras) to organize the Hawkeye Conference.[5] The new conference established rules for participation in athletic events: athletes must be full-time students doing passing work in class; professional athletes and faculty were barred from participation; athletes could only participate for four years; and each institution had to submit a certified list of participants before each game. The football schedule that fall reflected this change. In addition to perennial foes William and Vashti of Aledo, Illinois, Iowa Wesleyan, and Dixon Normal College, St. Ambrose would now play Iowa State Teachers College and Upper Iowa from the new conference. The conference lasted until 1923 when many of its members, including St. Ambrose, joined the new Iowa Conference.[6]

In the spring Ralph McManus had left the area to pursue business interests, and even as forty players turned out for the first practice on September 15, they were still without a coach. Finally O'Neill hired Victor Littig, who had played on the Harvard College team, to be the coach.[7]

The first game of the season on September 27 was against a team made up of alumni. On the opening kickoff, Ed Morrissey raced down field to tackle the runner, tried to side-step a player, and twisted and broke his leg. He was taken to Mercy Hospital for treatment. The game continued without him and a dispirited St. Ambrose team lost to the alumni 9-0. Morrissey's broken leg was set, but in a few days it became infected and had to be amputated.[8] Morrissey's injury was a shock to the campus. It seemed that the fears of Bishop Cosgrove and Flannagan about "roughby" were being realized, and as he lay in the hospital, the college cancelled the rest of the football season. Over the next few weeks, it was hoped that Morrissey would recover, but he developed pneumonia and died on November 11.

Ed Morrissey's body was brought to the college chapel for a Solemn High Requiem Mass. Bishop Davis preached the funeral sermon and called Morrissey "probably the best physically developed student in college," and he praised his "manly character, his energy, and the thoroughness which he

Ed Morrissey.

had shown in his college career." O'Neill accompanied the body for burial in Morrissey's home of Lovilla.[9] Following his death, football was dropped for the next season as well and would not be resumed until 1915.[10]

There were more changes to the athletic program at St. Ambrose. In January 1914, O'Neill became pastor of St. Mary's Parish in Nichols, Iowa. As the first athletic director at St. Ambrose, he made football and basketball collegiate sports and had hired coaches for both. He was always able to find the necessary funds for sports teams. He took the college into membership in the Hawkeye Conference. He was responsible for completing the process that had begun years before, of moving control of athletics from the student-run Athletic Society to the college administration. Just before he left the college, he created the Board of Directors of the Athletic Society made up of Hannon, the Reverend Henry Takkenberg, and the Reverend William Adrian, who became the new athletic director. In another two years the Athletic Society ceased to exist and the Athletic Board controlled the sports program on campus.[11]

The idyllic world David Klise wrote about was shaken by the tolling of the tower bell to mark the death of Ed Morrissey. In other ways the world came on campus and made the students' world more complex. In the fall of 1914, a new motion picture projector was installed so that movies could be shown in the auditorium. Some of the films were educational, obtained from the Catholic Film Association, or supplied by Iowa State College. More to the students' liking, however, were films supplied by a local theater owner. Through him the students saw films starring Mary Pickford, Charles Chaplin, or William S. Hart, which drew the comment of one student that these were better than an "educational film, 'How to Knit Your Own Socks,' or anything of that kind." Not even all the commercial movies were universally well-received; when the movie, *Quo Vadis*, was shown, one student observed that, "some liked it; others didn't."[12]

Another piece of modern technology brought an even wider world to St. Ambrose. In October 1913, the college purchased equipment to build a wireless radio station which the manufacturer said would bring in signals from 1,000 miles away. When it was installed, however, the farthest signal it received was only five miles away, and that signal was not clear. A new 300 foot loop antenna was installed on the roof of Ambrose Hall, and on November 9, 1915, the 7:55 time signal was heard from Springfield, Illinois. Two nights later a time signal was received from Arlington, Virginia, 1,200 miles away. Not satisfied with that, another antenna was placed on the roof stretching from the cupola on the west end of the building to a tower constructed on the east end. This brought in signals from as far away as Key West, Florida, and San Francisco, California. Takkenberg was the "director-in-chief" of the station and used it in the physics class he taught. Students regularly came to the radio room to listen for weather reports, to try to bring in more stations from even farther away, and put themselves at the beginning of technology that would help transform life in the twentieth century.[13]

If the students were moving into an unknown new world, the alumni were recalling the past. The Alumni Association that had formed in the 1890s had lasted only a few years, and now, in the yearbook published in 1913, there had been a plea to revive it. The faculty sent invitations to all those who had been students since the school began to attend a meeting

Day students 1914.

on June 17, 1914.[14] Over 200 alumni responded and heard Shannahan tell them that an Alumni Association was a way of "renewing and maintaining the friendship and good fellowship which should characterize all those who had received their mental and moral training at St. Ambrose College." Following remarks by other prominent alumni, and the election of officers, the group adjourned for a banquet in the college dining hall. After dinner Flannagan reminded the lay alumni that they could be a "great force for good" in their communities and that as "sterling Catholic laymen, as upright, moral citizens . . . the alumni of St. Ambrose [could] do more good than could be done by books without number."[15]

The next year the alumni adopted a constitution, established a fund to

provide scholarships for needy seminary students, called for an annual homecoming celebration, and provided for the formation of branch associations in other cities. The main speaker of the evening was Judge Maurice F. Donegan. Donegan had attended St. Ambrose in the late 1880s, graduated from Creighton, and earned an MA at Georgetown and a law degree from the University of Iowa. He practiced law in Davenport and currently served as a district court judge. In the 1930s, he would serve as a justice on the Iowa Supreme Court. The judge urged the "sons of St. Ambrose" to take an active role in "the affairs of our Catholic institutions" which he said was necessary for the "salvation of the Church" in the United States as well as the "welfare of our country and the welfare of humanity."[16]

The Alumni Association met again in August 1916. Their numbers were swelled by the state convention of the Knights of Columbus which was meeting in Davenport at the same time. The speaker for the evening was John Hynes, who had been a student and star athletic the decade before and was now practicing law in Des Moines. Hynes had also attended Yale and said that he "would not exchange a single oak on the grounds of St. Ambrose for all the stately elms of Yale; nor would I give our humble, time-worn though inspiring statue of St. Ambrose for all the granite of Harvard."[17] This was the last time the alumni met before its activities were interrupted by World War I.

For the students who lived under the oaks of St. Ambrose, the innovations

A Great and Lasting Beginning

The Manning Club in 1918. Front row: Louis Rohret, Paul Moore, Anthony Jaeger, Edward Cone, John Gerwe. Middle Row: Robert Cullinan, Anthony Wallace, Rigobert Hellweg, Raymond Kinnavey, Newman Flannagan, James Garrity. Top row: Francis Griffith, Edward O'Connor, Francis Simmons, Mark Devlin, George Volz.

of the motion pictures and the wireless were set against the familiar, well-established life at the college. Sunday nights were devoted to the meetings of the literary and debating societies which still played an important part in the extracurricular activities of the students. Several new and reorganized societies, including the St. Thomas, the St. Philip Neri, and the St. Joseph Society were for the younger, academy students and emphasized elocution and public speaking.

One new society, the Bensonian, was organized in September 1915 for commercial students. The society was named for Robert Hugh Benson, a Roman Catholic priest who had ministered to students at Cambridge University in England. He died at age forty-three, the year before the Bensonian Society was organized. The revived St. Ambrose Society and the new St. Patrick's Society were also organized for commercial students. These societies were an attempt to supplement the commercial courses with literature and other liberal arts topics as a way to provide more "liberal education for commerce majors." No matter what they were named, one contemporary observed that in all of them, "floods of immature oratory have been poured forth over the questions debated!"[18]

One new society for philosophy students was organized by former members of the Logomachetean Society. First called the Senior Debating Society, in 1913 the name was changed to the Manning Society, named for the late Cardinal Henry E. Manning of Great Britain. Manning had been

a champion of Catholic education and social reform and had advised Pope Leo XIII as he was writing the encyclical *Rerum Novarum* in 1891. Organized to develop "extemporaneous speaking and forensic oratory among it members," it endeavored "to point out the why, the wherefore, and the what-should-be of everyday problems, social, economic, and political." For the next few decades, the Manning Club, as it came to be called, was the primary organization of the seminary students.[19]

The still relatively new theater was the site of plays, vaudeville shows, and other entertainments. The *Bonifacius Verein* presented its annual play in German, frequently directed by Hauber. Usually the drama society staged two plays each year which were frequently produced, directed, and sometimes written by Stahl. In the middle years of the decade, Mr. L. B. Canterbury, the vocal instructor, took over from Stahl. Then in 1918, Mrs. Helena Bradford Churchill was hired as an instructor in public speaking and dramatic arts, a position she would hold off and on from 1919 until her death in 1939. Churchill was born in New Hampshire in 1873. Her family moved to Augusta, Wisconsin, where she graduated from high school. Widowed at age 27, she studied speech and drama at Winona State Normal School, the University of Minnesota, the Stanley School of Expression in Minneapolis, and received a degree from the Emerson College of Oratory in Boston. Churchill also directed community theater in Davenport and became one of the leaders of the local theater scene. She was one of the first two female faculty members at St. Ambrose hired that year; the other was Miss Elizabeth Arnauld who taught shorthand and typewriting for one year.

Flannagan's band, now Shannahan's band, continued to provide music for major events at the college. Albert Petersen, the first band director, had left St. Ambrose in 1898 and was replaced by Ernst Otto who left after one year and was replaced by a succession of directors. Albert Petersen returned in 1900 to lead the first orchestra. As he had with the band, he had to find instruments and players and slowly build the orchestra. The orchestra gave its first concert at the St. Ambrose Day celebrations on December 7, 1900. Thereafter it shared the duties with the band and appeared at all the major campus events. In 1902, Petersen again took charge of the band and led both groups until 1907, when Otto returned to lead the band, and William Paarman came to take over the orchestra.[20]

The band and orchestra that provided music for David Klise's commencement ceremony in 1913 were still led by Ernst Otto and William Paarman. That year saw the arrival of A. A. Hall as the first vocal music instructor. Hall organized a glee club which became another musical group that performed at St. Ambrose events. Their repertory was mostly popular and religious music, but at the 1914 commencement, they "ventured on a somewhat unusual field" deemed "rather presumptuous on the part of amateurs," when they performed a chorus from Verdi's opera *Ernani*.[21]

There was also a college choir organized by Stahl in September 1912. This new choir sang for the first time at Sunday Mass on September 22.[22] Early in the century, Pope Pius X had issued a series of statements that encouraged greater participation by the laity in the celebration of the liturgy. The starting point of this reform was the restoration of Gregorian Chant, the usual music the St. Ambrose choir sang for religious services. The choir also began to sing new musical settings of the Mass that were being written in response to the pope's directives. The pope had also encouraged congregational singing, and within a few years the college had purchased hymn books for use by the people.[23] The choir was soon singing regularly at Sunday and Holy Day Masses, the Sunday afternoon vespers and Benediction services, and Lenten and May devotions.

Congregational singing was just part of

Mrs. Helena Bradford Churchill.

something of a religious revival on campus. In the fall of 1915, the Sodality of the Blessed Virgin Mary was reorganized after an absence of a few years. There was daily recitation of the rosary in the chapel and the senior classes of philosophy students participated in daily spiritual reading and meditation. There was also a steady increase of daily communicants, another reform encouraged by Pope Pius X.[24]

In 1914, music on campus advanced from an extracurricular club activity to an official place in the college curriculum, when the Reverend Carl Meinberg joined the faculty and became music director. Meinberg was born in Keokuk and had graduated from St. Ambrose in 1911. As a student he had played piano for the orchestra, played the cornet in the band, and sang in a Gregorian Chant quartet. He was ordained in 1914 and came to the college where over the years he taught Greek, scripture, English, and history. He would later serve as college chaplain and much later would be the sixth president. In addition to his duties as music director, he took over the band from Ernst Otto and the chapel choir from Stahl.

Music took another step forward when in 1916, music courses were listed in the catalogue for the academy and college students. There had been private lessons available in the past and those continued, but now students could study music theory and technique and receive credit for it. Erwin Swindell was hired to teach piano, harmony, and composition. Swindell had studied at the Mary Wood Chase School in Chicago and had just come to Davenport to open a studio.[25] With lyricist S. A. Crabbe, Swindell composed the first school song, "The Blue and White," which began: "Where mighty Mississippi flows,/Where o'er the hills the west wind blows,/The oaken boughs swing to and fro,/And spring birds come and sing and go/The old school stands; the old bell rings/Whose echo in my heart still sings."

There were other small but significant changes in the middle years of the decade. In the fall of 1914, the enrollment increased dramatically, which necessitated opening a new dormitory in rooms west of the chapel. More space was created for the Commercial department with a new study room for shorthand and typewriting, complete with fifteen new typewriters. In the fall of 1915, Hauber, who had been teaching Latin and Greek, began to teach biology which would become his

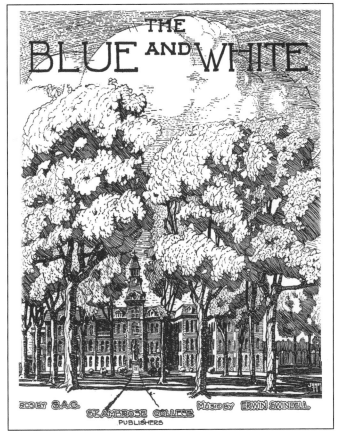

A Great and Lasting Beginning

life's work. The college built a greenhouse west of Ambrose Hall that was used as a laboratory for his courses, but also was used to supply flowers for the chapel.[26]

While he was a student, David Klise could not have known how debates taking place among Catholic higher education advocates would lead to reforms that would change the school he knew and remembered. The debates continued the discussions that had been taking place since the beginning of the century about the creation of Catholic high schools apart from Catholic colleges. The reformers said the first step was to establish standards that defined a college as a "four year course of studies subsequent and complementary to a four year High School," and then ensure that high school students had a curriculum that prepared them to meet those standards.[27] Shannahan had begun this process with the curricular revisions of 1910 and 1911.

Now it was time to go farther, and national figures like Father James A. Burns, who had been leading this movement for over a decade, continued to press the issue. Shannahan and McGuire, the prefect of studies, heard Burns speak at the annual meeting of the Catholic Educational Association in July 1915. Burns noted with some pride that Catholic high schools were "springing up all over the country," and this was a "most significant tendency." He also reiterated a point he had been making for a number of years that the growth of high schools would mean a "great increase" of students to the colleges, and that they should "help the development" of high schools.[28]

National statistics indicated that movement of students from grade school to high school to college was a "speculative rather than a practical problem" since most students in Catholic and public schools still did not advance to the next level. However, that was not the situation at St. Ambrose. Of the nineteen members of the academy class of 1914, seven entered the Collegiate course at St. Ambrose, and five others entered college elsewhere. The remainder entered the work force. The next year it was reported that "nearly all" of the twenty-seven 1916 academy graduates had entered St. Ambrose College.[29]

There were other indications that the separation of the academy and college was occurring at St. Ambrose. Prior to this the varsity athletic teams had contained both academy and college students. Now the new athletic director, Father Adrian, formed separate teams for the college and the academy, as well as a third group, the Midgets, for boys too young or small to play at the other levels. The 1916 catalogue published that summer contained separate sections for the Academic, Collegiate, and Commercial departments, with the requirements for graduation for each department, a division of the curricula by discipline, and a description of each course.

Rev. William Hannon.

While changes were underway that would affect the future St. Ambrose, news came that the old St. Marguerite's school building was to be demolished. The parish had built a new grade school, so the old building was no longer necessary and the space it occupied would be used for a playground. The *Messenger* noted that "to hundreds of old citizens, the removal of the old building will bring pangs of regretful memory. It is the last evidence of the pioneer days in the parish," and the last evidence of the pioneer days of St. Ambrose.[30]

As the old cathedral school building came down, plans were already underway for a new building at St. Ambrose. Shannahan had hired George P. Stauduhar, who had designed the 1901 addition on the west end of Ambrose Hall, to design another addition to be called Senior Hall as a building for the college. As Stauduhar designed it, the first floor was a swimming pool and the second floor was a gymnasium. The third floor, which was connected to the back of the original 1885 section of Ambrose Hall by an archway, had single and double rooms for students, two suites of rooms for professors, and two guest rooms. At the south end there were showers and toilets, and at the north end there was a library. The rooms were constructed around the outside of the floor which left an open, central area where it was envisioned that some of the artifacts from the museum could be displayed. The fourth floor, which was also connected to the main building, would have single and double rooms, two larger rooms to hold seven and eight students, and additional rooms for professors. There were toilets, showers, and a wash room on this floor. The central area would be an open well so that light from a skylight in the roof would illuminate the exhibition space on the third floor. Stauduhar also proposed a design to alter the chapel to increase its seating capacity.[31]

The plans for the $100,000 building were announced in August 1915, and fund raising had already begun in the local parishes. The *Messenger* said the contemplated improvements had "stirred the friends of the school to renewed effort in its behalf and the addition promised and so much needed, has been hailed with enthusiasm throughout the state." However, an announcement in the *Catholic Messenger* the week before that Shannahan was moving from the presidency of St. Ambrose to become pastor of St. Patrick's Parish in Iowa City meant that the building Shannahan and Stauduhar designed would not be built.[32]

Shannahan had been president since 1906 during which time the number of students had doubled. Most of these were high school students but Shannahan had begun some of the curricular reforms that would lead to the separation of the academy and college. The grounds had been enlarged and more playing fields were created. He had been responsible for the large 1908 east wing and the small addition to it built in 1912. But Shannahan was essentially a conservative, and the new Senior Hall he proposed still envisioned a school under one roof.

Whether Shannahan had asked to be moved, or if the move was the

The library in Ambrose Hall 1905.

bishop's idea, the consequences for St. Ambrose were profound. The new president was Father William Hannon who had come to St. Ambrose following his ordination in 1903 and had taught a number of subjects, was prefect of studies, and since 1910 had been the vice president of the college. Both Shannahan and Hannon hailed from St. Michael's Parish in Holbrook; Shannahan had even preached at Hannon's first Mass in their parish church.

Although Shannahan and Hannon shared a parish of origin, their ideas about St. Ambrose could not have been more different. In a very real sense the founder of the modern school, Hannon had a vision of a "greater St. Ambrose" and he was the first president since Schulte to share Bishop McMullen's vision.[33] As soon as he assumed the presidency, Hannon began to plan for a reorganization of the school. He was assisted by the new vice president, Father Stahl, another man with ideas and vision. Together they had the ability to engage their colleagues to help build the greater St. Ambrose. Hannon let it be known that his only priority would be to run St. Ambrose. His predecessors as president had done all the administrative duties and also taught a full schedule of courses. Once he was president, Hannon no longer taught; his plans for the greater St. Ambrose would take all of his time and energy.

Hannon was in tune with the educational reforms that had been debated for years. But contrary to national reformers since the time of Horace Mann in the 1830s, Hannon said that the individual and society were "best served by an education whose atmosphere is permeated and vitalized by religion." Since education is the preparation for life, and no life was complete without God, no "education without religion can in any way be complete." Religion was the "supreme co-ordinating principle of life" and neither art nor science had any meaning without God. Hannon believed that religion and education were not just tools for abstract thinking, they spoke about eternity, but also attitudes about "capital and labor." He said his convictions about the "immortality of the soul have a surprisingly cogent influence on the price I charge for potatoes and coal . . . my hours of labor and my neighbor's pocketbook."[34] During Hannon's years as president, he would undertake a series of reforms to better equip St. Ambrose students to understand the relationship between God, art, science, and their neighbor's pocketbooks.

Hannon's principal goal was to have St. Ambrose become an accredited school. Accreditation was one of the most important issue Catholic educators discussed in the 1912-1915 period. Although they could not agree on what standards should apply, most agreed that it was necessary to establish standards for Catholic schools or someone else, like the government, would do it for them. There was even more urgency when the North

LeClaire Gymnasium.

Central Association of Colleges and Secondary Schools published its first list of accredited colleges in 1913, and Notre Dame was the only Catholic college to be accredited.[35]

Finally in 1915, the Catholic Educational Association (CEA) published the standards necessary for accreditation: sixteen units of high school were necessary for admission to college; 128 units were required for graduation; the college must have at least seven departments which had to include English, history, language, and philosophy, taught by professors with degrees appropriate to the subject they taught. The library had to have at least 5,000 volumes. The college had to have laboratories equipped appropriately for physics, chemistry, and general science. Students had to carry at least sixteen hours per week and professors should ordinarily teach no more than sixteen hours per week.[36]

These standards were a good start, but most Catholic educators noted that they were "not as rigorous" as the standards set by the North Central Association.[37] In 1918, the Catholic Educational Association sent a survey to its 108 member schools, and of the eighty-seven who responded, only fifty-two, including St. Ambrose College and Academy, met the 1915 standards.[38] This recognition by the CEA was a good start, but only a start. Hannon wanted St. Ambrose to be a fully accredited institution by the North Central Association and that would require other, significant reforms, including building Senior Hall for the college students, the com-

plete separation of the college and the academy, sending faculty away for advanced degrees, and creating an endowment to support the work of the college.

To lay a foundation for these reforms, Hannon began to look to the larger Davenport community for support. First, he convinced the bishop to expand the Board of Trustees of the college. The bishop, the vicar general, and the president of the college continued on the board, but now the deans of the five diocesan deaneries, Shannahan, and Monsignor James P. Ryan, were added to the board. Flannagan was the vicar general, Schulte was a dean, and with Shannahan, all the former presidents of the college were now on the Board of Trustees. In addition five prominent Catholic businessmen were added to the board: Henry C. Kahl, a construction and real estate executive; Thomas F. Halligan, president of Halligan Coffee Company; Lee J. Dougherty, an executive with Guaranty Life Insurance; Thomas J. Walsh, president of Walsh Construction; and Fred B. Sharon, the publisher of the *Catholic Messenger* and Davenport postmaster.

Hannon also moved into the intellectual life of the larger community. In 1917 he was invited to become a member of the Contemporary Club, a literary society whose members included newspaper publisher E. P. Adler; congressman F. Dickinson Letts; banker and former congressman Albert Dawson; author Arthur Davidson Ficke; superintendent of public schools Frank L. Smart; department store president Roland Harned;

aviator Ralph Cram; the dean of Trinity Episcopal Cathedral; the minister of the Unitarian Church; the director of the Putnam Museum; and various architects, lawyers, physicians, and businessmen. The members of the Contemporary Club gathered monthly to hear and discuss essays on a wide variety of topics. During his years of membership, Hannon delivered two essays, one titled "Cardinal Mercier," and the other, "The Catholic School." Hannon's membership at a time when St. Ambrose was expanding was an important sign that he wanted the college to be a part of the life of the community and that he hoped for support from that community.

Hannon wasted no time in beginning his reforms, the first of which would change the footprint of St. Ambrose College. In early November, he announced a revision of the plans for Senior Hall. The first two floors of Stauduhar's design would become the gymnasium, and a new Senior Hall would be a separate building west of Ambrose Hall. It would contain private rooms for college students, a library, classrooms, and a chapel. Construction would not begin until after the completion of the gymnasium, but the hope was that it would begin in the summer of 1916 with completion the following spring.[39]

Work began immediately on the gymnasium. The ground was cleared and readied in November 1915, but a harsh winter delayed construction until the next spring. By the end of May, the foundation work was complete and the steel framework was set in place. At the end of August enough work was done that the *Messenger* could publish a photograph of the new building. The redesigned building kept the swimming pool and locker rooms on the ground floor. The main floor contained the gymnasium with a basketball court and room for all the gymnastic equipment. Stauduhar had designed bleachers for the outdoor athletic field that could be moved into the gymnasium during the basketball season. Above the gymnasium was a balcony with a running track, and above that was a rifle range, complete with targets and equipment. Since the first of the year, President Woodrow Wilson had been calling for increased preparedness by the United States in the event it was forced to enter the war that had been raging in Europe since 1914. Then in June 1916, Congress passed the National Defense Act to expand the regular army and the National Guard, and to establish the Reserve Officer Training Corps at colleges and universities. The *Messenger* noted that the rifle range would "give the students a chance to join in the general preparedness crusade now occupying so much attention and to become expert in the use of army equipment."[40]

The building was nearly finished when the college paused to celebrate the feast of St. Ambrose on December 7. In a program following the Mass, Hannon said that for twenty years his dream had been to have a "fine building for recreation," and that the new gymnasium would be that building. He reminded his audience that "we can and should take an interest in athletics, but we must not forget that our mental training is as important as our physical development."[41]

The St. Ambrose community gathered to dedicate the new gymnasium on January 31, 1917. The ceremony began in the pool with a series of races. It then moved to the main floor for a program that included music and speeches from college officials and other dignitaries, including the

mayor of Davenport. It was announced that the gymnasium would be called LeClaire Gymnasium, named for Antoine LeClaire, a founder of Davenport and an early benefactor of the Cathedral Parish and Catholicism in the community. The speeches were followed by two basketball games.[42]

The final cost of LeClaire Gymnasium was over $115,000 for the building and equipment. The priests of the diocese and the bishop had contributed $40,000 and a loan was taken out for the remainder.[43] At a meeting of the priests following their retreat in June 1918, the bishop reported that most of them had paid their pledges and he urged those who had not to do so soon. He also reported that another $5,000 was spent to convert the former gymnasium in Ambrose Hall into a manual training and wood shop department for the academy students. This would benefit those St. Ambrose students who wanted vocational training, and it also gave the opportunity for Catholic grade school students to come to St. Ambrose for this training, rather than to the public school where they had been receiving it. Adrian took courses at the University of Iowa to prepare himself to teach manual training.[44]

As president, Hannon was true to his word that athletics should be encouraged. In the fall of 1915, he brought football back to campus for the first time since the death of Ed Morrissey two years before. The new coach was George W. Jones. A graduate of the College of the Holy Cross, Jones had most recently been in charge of athletics at Worcester Polytechnic Institute. Seven games against Hawkeye Conference teams and others were scheduled that fall, but the inexperienced Ambrosians won only two games. The next year the team recorded three wins, three losses, and two ties. When the 1917 season opened, Jones and most of the football stars of the previous year had entered the service. Under new coach Jimmy Galvin, the team ended the season with a record of five wins and three losses. Because of World War I, there were no varsity sports in the 1918-1919 year.[45]

In spite of the new gymnasium, basketball was still in its developmental stage at St. Ambrose. The most popular sport remained baseball. In the early years of the decade under coach Walter Davis, the team had a mediocre record, best expressed by the comment about the 1915 team that it "did not win all its games but it always gave a fine exhibition of baseball skill." In the 1916 season, Jones took over the team and under his leadership the team won two Hawkeye Conference titles and the Midwest Catholic championship.[46]

World War I, the Great War, the war to end all wars, began with the assassination in Sarajevo of the heir to the Austro-Hungarian throne and his wife on June 28, 1914. Five weeks later all of Europe was engaged in a war to defend national honor and dynastic rights. President Woodrow Wilson declared that the United States would be neutral in thought and deed, but eventually the country would also be drawn into the war. After four years and ten million casualties, the war swept away most of the royal houses of Europe and redrew the map of Europe and the Middle East. It also swept away the assumptions on which people had based their lives, and it would take some time before a new world could be put together. The change was so dramatic that some historians consider World War I as

A Great and Lasting Beginning

Refectory, ground floor of Ambrose Hall. This area later became the business office.

the beginning of the twentieth century, and many consider it the most important event of that century.

When Hannon became president in September 1915, the war in Europe was already one year old and the idyllic world David Klise remembered was already disappearing. Hannon's vision for the greater St. Ambrose swept away the nineteenth-century assumptions about education that had been the norm at St. Ambrose, at least since Flannagan had become president in 1891.

Locust Street was a long way from the battlefields of Europe, yet the war came to St. Ambrose. Bishop Davis had been in Europe when the war began, and upon his return in October 1914, he commented that the "famous institutions of learning" there were already suffering from the "awful devastation of war," and that it was "encouraging" to see that St. Ambrose and other American colleges were "flourishing." In March 1915, the students followed the wishes of Pope Benedict XV and observed "Peace Sunday" with High Mass. The chapel was "thronged" all day with students praying before the Blessed Sacrament to the Prince of Peace. Movie nights in the auditorium now included newsreels of scenes from the battlefields.[47]

Some Ambrosians were already in uniform as members of Battery B,

Iowa National Guard. The unit was mustered into active duty, and in the summer of 1916, they were in training at Camp Dodge, outside of Des Moines. As the unit left for service on the Mexican border in mid-July, the *Messenger* noted that "every one of them is a true son of St. Ambrose . . . of whom the college expects much and will follow with prayerful pride in their loyal service to America."[48]

Ambrosians who graduated that June, many of whom would be in uniform within a year, heard the Most Reverend Henry Tihen, bishop of Lincoln, Nebraska, talk about the "millions of devoted men" who were already battling for the ideal of patriotism in Europe, "enduring hunger, heat and cold, pain and death," without complaint. He asked why his listeners could not endure similar sacrifice. There was never a greater need for "young blood," and he said if his listeners were "upright, faithful until death," the world would admire them and St. Ambrose college would receive "added luster from your many lives and Christian virtues."[49] Before the war ended, over 200 Ambrosians would be in uniform, some of whose "young blood" would be shed on the battlefield.

If the bishop's patriotic fervor and the war news led Ambrosians to focus some of their attention on Europe, they still managed to enjoy their time at St. Ambrose. Classes continued, recreational sports provided relief from their studies, and the lure of off-campus entertainments was always present, unless they had committed some offense and were therefore on the "blacklist," and had to spend time in the college "Leavenworth." For those who could leave campus, they headed for the Royal Marquette Billiard Parlor or the Columbia or Garden Theaters. If there was time they would stop at the Hotel Dempsey for a meal. Others took a series of street cars to Suburban (Credit) Island to go fishing, resulting in many stories about the "fish that got away" in the dormitories at night.

Occasionally on a very nice day, whispers would pass through the refectory at noon that it would be a good afternoon for a free day. One or two philosophy students would be designated to go to the president to ask for a free afternoon and a "general permission" for all to leave campus. Once granted, the students would hurry to shave and dress in their "niftiest suit, wide-spreading tie and cloth-topped shoes" and head downtown. For the price of ten cents, they could sit in the balcony, or for twenty cents, get a seat on the main floor of the Columbia Theater and hopefully have enough money left for a bag of peanuts. There they could see the vaudeville acts in town that day, and then rush to catch the 4:30 streetcar back to campus.[50]

On Halloween of 1917, Ambrosians celebrated in a way to take their minds off the war in Europe, at least for an evening. The philosophers on Wisdom Row ate leftovers they had managed to "forage" from the kitchen. They celebrated "sedately, tho' not shrinkingly" in a "cheerful atmosphere of frugal comfort." The third floor celebration was more "pretentious" with an elaborate meal of oysters, potatoes, fruit, and pumpkin pie, accompanied by speeches and toasts. The "cosmopolitans" on fourth floor had "unpronounceable, tho' perfectly digestible food" that included filet mignon, pommes de terre, halibut, and various desserts. It turned out to be "one of the really pleasant memories of their college days."[51]

The news about the war did not cloud their ability to find humor in their daily lives and to make jokes about it:

History Professor: Please name some notable date in Roman history.
Student: Marc Antony's with Cleopatra.

Father Hauber: Mr. Wagner, can you tell us anything about the spinal column?
Wagner: The spinal column is a long wavy line. I sit on one end and my head sits on the other.

Father Meinberg: Mr. Moore, in what condition was Job at the end of his life?
Moore: Dead.

English Professor: Please give me your idea of life at St. Ambrose College.
Student: Life at St. Ambrose is neither a "Tempest," nor a "Midsummer Night's Dream," but sometimes it is a "Comedy of Errors," in which you can take it "As You Like It," but, taking it "Measure for Measure,"

you find that "All's Well That Ends Well."[52]

The war did not begin well and would not end well. When President Wilson appeared before a joint session of Congress on April 2, 1917, he asked for a declaration of war to make the "world safe for democracy." Two days later the Senate voted for war 82-6, and on Good Friday, April 6, the House of Representatives voted for war 373-50. Following the declaration of war, Wilson announced, "It is not an army that we must shape and train for war, it is a nation." Training the nation for war led to new government agencies to mobilize civilians, calls for sacrifices at home, programs to raise money to pay for the war, and ways to recognize those in service and those who died. All of those things would change the daily lives of Americans and Ambrosians.

The students were on their Easter vacation when war was declared. When they returned the following week, Hannon called a special assembly. He told the students to show their loyalty to the country, "particularly during these times." He urged them to follow closely the events of "the greatest war the world has ever seen." The student body rose to sing "The Star Spangled Banner," followed by "America." As they left the auditorium, they gave nine long "rahs" for President Wilson.[53]

It did not take long for Ambrosians to express their patriotic sentiments in other ways. The 1917 edition of *The Ambrosian* yearbook, issued just weeks after the United States entered the war, featured an American flag and part of a patriotic poem, "America," by Bayard Taylor, which had been written for the centennial of the country in 1876. The sections of the yearbook were introduced with drawings of soldiers from earlier American wars.

The question of military training at St. Ambrose had been under discussion for some time, but now with war, the need for further discussion ended. Two weeks following the declaration of war, the students met to form a cadet corps; 125 students of military age pledged to be a part of military training until they graduated. Hannon told the students he was proud of their actions and Michael V. Gannon explained military service to them. The next week they held the first regular drill in LeClaire Gymnasium. They divided into four squads and practiced marching and saluting. The shooting gallery in the top of the gymnasium now took on added importance. For the time being, they would drill four times a week.[54]

A few days after the declaration of war, the Davenport chapter of the American Red Cross was organized. Hannon served on the local committee and shortly one hundred students were enrolled in the Red Cross. Hannon presented the local chapter $100 on behalf of the students and faculty. On June 23, Battery D of the Iowa National Guard organized and three Ambrose students enlisted. They would eventually see service in France.[55] They were just the first of the 223 Ambrosians who would serve during the war.

The students still on campus were anxious to hear from their colleagues now in the service. Occasionally one would stop by if he was passing through on the train, or was home for a few days' leave, and many wrote letters back to those still on campus. Their concern for those in the fight was obvious, although they often covered it with bravado. Bill Quigley was

A Great and Lasting Beginning

an all-around athlete from Holyoke, Massachusetts; at 5'4" and 135 pounds, he was a fearsome football player and captain of the team. One student wrote "it's a safe and sure bet the Boche that tackles 'Billy' had better carry a clean conscience into battle." The Sodality of Mary prayed for Billy and the others and made their prayer intention for the year the "return of men to the True Faith, for our soldiers at the front, and for an early and victorious end of the war."[56]

Through 1917 and 1918, each week saw more students departing to enlist, or answer draft summons. Some left to contribute to the war in other ways. In May 1918, two students took jobs with the McCarthy Construction Company which was building a war plant in Savannah, Illinois. The usual spring exodus of the "aggies" was intensified that year as students returned home to their farms to replace older brothers who had left for military service.[57]

Students were not the only ones who were in uniform. Coach George Jones enlisted and by October was already in France. The faculty and students sent him cigarettes and newspapers, although he wrote that he wished they would send more local football news. His letters told them of daily life; he said he was mastering French currency and terms for food. "We hear little about the war, and discuss it less," he told them, "feed the army well, and you have removed its chief cause for anxiety." He said that France was a "land of black bread, no sugar, vermin, torture, and wooden crosses." While some of the Americans in France worried that they would not see any action, Jones said that he "should not be at all disappointed" if he did not see any.[58] Other faculty members who served included Father Barry, Edwin Bashe, and Bernard J. Marron.

To mark the participation of Ambrose men in the war, another verse was added to the school song, "The Blue and White": "When Freedom called her sons around/The Colors, and her bugle sound/Had flung a challenge to the foe,/No Ambrose men, with footsteps slow,/Hung back, but with the flag's advance,/They followed on the fields of France."

To pay for the war and encourage civilian support for it, the government issued bonds which were variously called Liberty Loans or Victory Loans. Each state had a quota to sell and in the first drive in May 1917, Iowa did not meet its quota. For the second drive in October, local business leaders created an extensive organization to ensure that each county reached its goal. At St. Ambrose the academy freshmen were the first class to "go over the top" and meet their goal.[59] The next spring students raised money by purchasing thrift stamps at the campus store. They were urged to go "over the top together and pull for our old Uncle Sam." They put a large clock dial on the bulletin board and used the hands to mark their progress. The Manning Club promoted the campaign and its members visited other campus organizations to urge their participation. Under the slogan, "Let your two bits do their bit; help win the war," the students raised over $300.[60]

One of the federal wartime agencies President Wilson created was the Food Administration, chaired by Herbert Hoover. The goal was to encourage farmers to raise more food to feed the troops. Farmers were asked to put more land into production, even to take out fences so one more row of crops could be planted. Banks were encouraged to make low-interest loans to farmers so they could buy more land or new machinery to raise more food. Since farm production became so important, there was even more urgency for Ambrose students to leave home early to help with spring planting.

Another goal of Hoover's Food Administration was to ask Americans to sacrifice some of their food to benefit the troops. Americans learned to live with Meatless Tuesdays, Wheatless Wednesdays, and to cook with recipes created by the Department of Agriculture that substituted other grains for wheat in breads and other bakery products. The students noticed the difference. One wrote that "meatless Tuesday is not so odious to the local consumer as one might suppose. Chicken may not be meat, hooveristically speaking, but 'it is meat for us.'" Another said, "Talk about Hooverizing—we had salmon hash with corn and potatoes in it tonight. Can you beat it?"[61]

As a show of Ambrosian patriotism, a ten foot flagpole was rigged to the radio tower on the roof of Ambrose Hall. The military had ordered the wireless station closed down for the duration, so the flagpole did not interfere with radio reception. Each day Francis Griffith and Paul Moore, two students from Keokuk, would raise the American flag. However, everyone on campus awaited the day they could raise their own service flag. This banner would contain a star for every man in the service, and as more Ambrosians entered the military, the prospect was that the St. Ambrose flag would be "ablaze with stars." The service flag was unveiled at a ceremony in the auditorium on June 10, 1918. As the chorus sang "The Star Spangled Banner," the flag was slowly raised to reveal a Latin cross filled with 175 stars. Sam T. White, the chairman of the Scott County Council of National Defense, urged the students to support the soldiers and the war effort. He said the "time is past when a man could be a hyphenated American; now every one is either all American or a traitor."[62]

The hyphenated Americans of whom White spoke were those of German birth or ancestry. One of the regrettable features of World War I was a virulent anti-German hostility. The dilemma for German-Americans had been expressed on campus two years before by Father Giglinger. In the fall of 1915, Giglinger had traveled to Europe to visit relatives and friends who lived behind the German lines. Upon his return he told the students that although he was "now a staunch American" he had "racial leanings toward his native land."[63] Many Americans thought that German-Americans could not overcome their racial leanings. In response people of German descent changed their surnames, and businesses with German names changed them. In Davenport a German language newspaper, *Der Demokrat*, which had been published since the 1850s, went out of business. One casualty on campus of the anti-Germanism was the *Bonifacius Verein,* which went out of existence during the war.

In May 1918, just before White spoke on campus, Iowa Governor William Harding had issued the so-called Babel Proclamation that declared that English was the only language that could be spoken in Iowa. Harding urged that Iowans call their local sheriff if they heard someone conversing in any foreign language. In Scott County four women were arrested for speaking German on their party-line telephone. Across Iowa, high school German teachers led their students to the school lawn and burned German language books.[64] At St. Ambrose German language courses remained in the catalogues of those years; however, it is not clear whether the classes were actually taught.

By late 1914, the war had settled into a war fought from trenches that stretched for hundreds of miles across France and Belgium. Hundreds of thousands of combatants died of war and disease in the trenches. Then in the spring of 1918, the Germans opened an offensive that pushed the Allies back nearly to Paris. In June large numbers of Americans were engaged for the first time in battle, and through the summer the Allies were able to begin to push the Germans back east. Coach George Jones was now in the trenches, the land of torture and wooden crosses. Now word began to come to campus of death: Frank Seybert from Council Bluffs who had been at St. Ambrose from 1914 to 1916, killed in action; Francis Woods from Massachusetts, a 1916 academy graduate, also killed in action.[65]

When school opened in the fall of 1918, it seemed to "want the attractiveness it used to borrow from old companionships and familiar faces . . . only a dwindling remnant of the 'Old Crowd' staunchly remains to stand for former days and year-worn traditions. Duty, and that of the stern-faced kind, has commandeered the majority of our matured and seasoned veterans."[66]

As Ambrosians in France faced their stern-faced duty in the trenches and died in field hospitals, and Ambrosians on campus drilled on the baseball field, another killer was stalking the fields of Europe, the streets of cities around the world, and the halls of St. Ambrose: Spanish influenza. The influenza pandemic probably began in the spring of 1918 in the United States and spread quickly through military camps. From there it spread to Europe through the military camps and trenches of the war. It appeared in Spain, striking even the king, and because Spanish newspapers reported on the disease, it became known as Spanish flu. Before it subsided a year later, it had killed an estimated 100 million people worldwide, more in one year than the plague of the Middle Ages had killed in a century. It killed quickly: one could become ill in the morning and be dead by nightfall. And unlike other influenzas that struck the very young and the very old, this flu attacked people in their prime, in their teens and twenties and thirties. It spread so rapidly through American cities that one Red Cross worker reported, "a fear and panic . . . akin to the terror of the Middles Ages regarding the Black Plague."[67]

The first cases appeared in Iowa in September at Camp Dodge outside

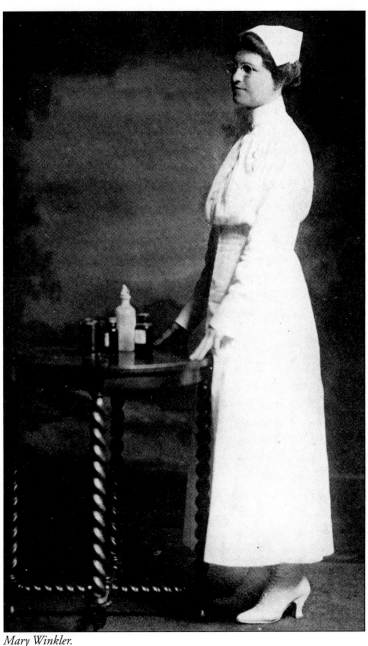

Mary Winkler.

Des Moines, and it spread quickly through the state.[68] It appeared on campus in early October, and the fear and panic the Red Cross worker noted in American cities was evident at St. Ambrose. One student kept a diary of those days:

October 9: Flu breaks out and two fellows go to the hospital. Everybody scared.

October 11: Eight new cases of Influenza. Wisdom Row moves up to the West Dormitory to give the "Flu" a wide berth.

October 12: Flu is increasing rapidly.

October 13: Third floor moves out to accommodate "Flu" patients. Over thirty cases. Some talk of closing school.

October 14: Ten new cases of Influenza. Everybody has a half-sorry, half-hopeful look on his face.

October 15: Two more cases go to the hospital, otherwise the "Flu" seems to be at a standstill.

October 16: School closes.[69]

When the outbreak began on campus, the college moved quickly. Students who showed no signs of illness were sent home. To care for the students on campus, the Red Cross sent nurse Mary Winkler. Born in Keokuk, Winkler had come to Davenport and graduated from the Mercy Hospital nursing program in 1915. Winkler cared for the students in the campus infirmary.

The Davenport Board of Health also moved quickly and on October 16, it issued a number of regulations for public places: street cars had to be disinfected daily; books were germ carriers so the library closed; football games with out-of-town teams were cancelled, although in-town teams could play one another; public meetings were cancelled; grade schools were closed; although cafes could remain open to serve meals, and pool rooms could remain open to sell cigars and tobacco products, most other businesses had to close. Most churches cancelled Sunday services but the Catholic parishes arranged to celebrate Mass on the church lawns.[70]

As the number of students with the flu increased, Hannon announced that St. Ambrose would close on Tuesday, October 15, and the students would be sent home. However, students with colds or any other sign of illness had to remain on campus. If the flu did not develop, they were eventually allowed to leave. The next day newspapers reported 105 more cases of the flu in Davenport, bringing the total to 332 cases since the epidemic began. It also reported one death that day, seventeen-year-old Edward Quigley, a St. Ambrose student from DeWitt. He was taken home for burial, but because of Iowa State Board of Health regulations, the funeral services were "strictly private."[71]

The next week Mary Winkler went to the hospital with the flu where she died on October 22. Ambrosians were deeply touched by her service to them at the sacrifice of her life. The yearbook the next year published her picture with the notation that she was a "Christian soldier who by her charity and devotion to duty, gave her life that those entrusted to her care, during the epidemic last Fall, might live."[72]

The war ended with the armistice which took effect at 11:00 a.m. on November 11, 1918. It was 2:00 a.m. in Davenport when the citizens were awakened by the blast of whistles and the ringing of church bells to let them know the war was over. In spite of the health department regulations about gathering together, the "down-town streets were filled with scurrying automobiles, the sidewalks with happy and excited throngs. Flags were everywhere. There were impromptu parades." School had not resumed at St. Ambrose, so the diarist noted: "November 11, Armistice signed. Nobody here to sign it."[73]

The war had exacted a huge price in human lives. About ten million combatants died of battlefield deaths and disease. Nearly 117,000 Americans died, 3,300 from Iowa, and 131 from Scott County. Two hundred and twenty-three Ambrosians served in uniform and seven men died.

Although the war was over, the dying continued. By mid-November, the flu seemed to have run its course. The Davenport Health Board lifted the closing orders and schools and businesses reopened, including St. Ambrose which resumed classes on November 18. Several former students who had been in the first weeks of training for military service were released and returned to school. To make up for the month that was lost, classes were held all day, Thanksgiving vacation was cancelled, Christmas vacation was cut in half, and there was no Easter vacation. The St. Ambrose community gathered on Thanksgiving Day for a High Mass where they gave thanks for the peace and remembered their colleagues who had died in Europe and at home.[74]

In early December, the flu struck again. The national Public Health Service issued a bulletin that warned that epidemic conditions existed again in "various parts of the country." Iowa, it said, showed a "marked increase" in the number of cases. Davenport was hit especially hard in this new wave of sickness; some suggested the Health Board had lifted the restrictions too soon. Now new restrictions were ordered for the city. One local newspaper reported the flu had taken "over six times as many Davenport lives as all the devilish devices of the bloody Hun."[75]

On December 2, all the day students were sent home. To enable them to keep up their school work, teachers improvised correspondence courses that could be mailed to them. The boarding students were told to stay on campus and not go downtown. There were rumors that once again the school would be closed. Even the students who remained on campus were segregated. Those who lived in the dormitories and those who lived in private rooms went to Mass on alternate mornings. The precautions seemed to work as there were few on-campus cases in the second wave. But this wave of the flu did touch Ambrosians. The Reverend Frank Nugent, a 1901 graduate stationed at the cathedral, died on December 2, and the Reverend Joseph Coughlin, class of 1913, died a week later at St. Anthony's Parish in downtown Davenport. Once again the flu abated and on December 18, the students were allowed to go downtown for the first time in a month, and a few days later they left for a brief Christmas vacation.[76]

The influenza pandemic continued for most of 1919, but St. Ambrose was spared any more serious bouts with it. But the toll had been heavy. In 1918, 6,543 Iowans died from the flu. The city of Davenport reported 4,518 cases of the flu from October through December 1918; 270 people died.[77]

Classes resumed on January 2, 1919, and the day students returned to campus for the first time in a month.[78] Life returned to normal at St. Ambrose. With the end of food rationing the meals improved. On February 21, the diarist noted, "eggs for dinner, the first time in 1919." Then in April, "real eggs for dinner." Meat returned to the diet as well as the staple "beans, as usual for dinner."[79]

The fear evidenced during the flu epidemic had made them more wary of illness. In April two cases of smallpox led to rumors that the school would close again. The next fall, a combination of mumps and colds once again brought rumors that school would close. But most of the ill were sent to the infirmary in Ambrose Hall, or to the "cottage," the name they gave to the isolation house on campus, and returned to classes when they were able.[80]

Throughout the spring their colleagues who had been in service returned for a visit and to talk about their experiences. In May Capt. George Jones returned. He had been a captain of artillery at the front where he had seen the worst of it. For his leadership, he was awarded the Distinguished Service Medal.[81]

Armistice Day 1919, the first anniversary of the end of the war, was observed on campus. Classes ended just before 11:00 and the campus community assembled for a prayer service. Hannon told them they should be grateful to God for the sacrifices made by the men and women who served, including their classmates and friends. Their sacrifice had created a debt the students would be obligated to repay by their lives in future service to the country. He urged them to study hard so they would be prepared in the event a crisis arose in the future. In closing he said, "America, then, is a precious heritage, won and kept for us by those who have gone before us. What are we going to do and what are we doing now to keep it safe for ourselves and those who will come after us?" Because of the war, their world was less certain and serene than the 1913 world described by David Klise. The war had changed everything, and at St. Ambrose the change would continue. But that would be for tomorrow. To continue the Armistice Day celebration, classes were cancelled for the afternoon, and the students were given a general permission to go downtown.[82]

The most important thing in Davenport and the most important factor for the future of Davenport is men. The institution of the city devoting its time to the production of strong-bodied, clear-headed, clean-minded men is St. Ambrose College . . . [which] offers a complete collegiate standard college course and its credits are accepted in full value by all of the leading universities . . . A total investment of $1,000,000 in grounds, buildings and equipment makes St. Ambrose an institution of real importance in Davenport . . . More than $150,000 a year is spent in the operation and maintenance of St. Ambrose college, and naturally at least 90 percent of this money is spent in Davenport. From the business point of view the college is a 100 percent community asset . . . Due to a substantial endowment raised some years ago, [St. Ambrose] has been expanding and growing rapidly in the last decade. The school among the oak trees is now one of the most flourishing colleges of Iowa. The Davenporter who is thinking of sending his boy away to school would do well to consider his home-town school first. Send him to St. Ambrose.[1]

Chapter Six

The endorsement of St. Ambrose published in the Davenport Chamber of Commerce News in October 1929 reflected the reforms made at the college in the decade following World War I. St. Ambrose was still the diocesan college, with the vision of Bishop McMullen to educate priests to serve the diocese alongside laymen who would serve as leaders in their parishes and communities. But now the college was paying increased attention to the larger community outside its parishes and Catholic institutions, to the city of Davenport and the cities and towns where its graduates lived.

The man most responsible for maintaining the original vision for St. Ambrose, making it a creditable educational institution and a community asset, was the fourth president, Father William Hannon. When he became president in 1915, he had an ambitious agenda for making St. Ambrose a true college: accreditation, an endowment, a larger library, a faculty with graduate degrees, and a building to separate the academy and the college. He had barely begun those changes when the disruptions of the war forced him to delay any further activity. Now that the war was over, Hannon could resume action on his plans.

Hannon was successful because he was fortunate to have a faculty who worked alongside him to achieve his goals. He was also fortunate that Bishop Davis allowed progress at the college, even if he did not understand the need for it. When Hannon told the bishop that the college needed an up-to-date library, Davis responded, "Why more books? Most of those in the library have not yet been read." Hannon lost his temper and told the bishop that a first-rate college, an accredited college, had to have a first-rate library. If he was not the education bishop Hannon might have hoped for, Davis did not stand in Hannon's way of achieving his goals for the college.[2]

Throughout his presidency, Hannon would continue to rely upon the priests and parishes of the diocese for financial support. But he also began to move into the Davenport business community to broaden the base of support for the college. During the war Hannon had been called on to make speeches throughout the community. After the war the Scott County Council of Defense, a group of businessmen formed to coordinate local war efforts, named him to be a delegate to a peace conference in St. Louis.[3] Add to that his membership in the Contemporary Club, and Hannon was regularly associating with the larger, non-Catholic Davenport community in ways his predecessors had not done.

Hannon had begun his ambitious agenda for the college when he revised the plans for Senior Hall and announced that it would be a separate building. However, he understood that an endowment would make his other plans feasible. Ten years before, there had been pleas for contributions to create scholarships to help defray the expenses of the seminary students, which resulted in donations of a few hundred dollars each year. In 1908, Bishop Davis had sent a letter to the people of the diocese to appeal for funds to build an addition to Ambrose Hall. In the letter he noted that, unlike most other Iowa colleges, St. Ambrose did not have an endowment. He said that at other colleges money was "constantly pouring in" to fund chairs and scholarships. Now he appealed to "wealthy Catholics" to support St. Ambrose in the same way. But there was no real effort to solicit endowment funds.[4]

The bishop continued to solicit the annual seminary collection begun by Bishop McMullen. It now averaged $5,000 a year, which the bishop used to pay the tuition of seminarians at St. Ambrose and for those studying theology at various seminaries in the United States and Europe. Like Bishop Cosgrove before him, Bishop Davis also used surplus money in the seminary account to fund projects at St. Ambrose. In 1911, for example, he used $6,500 from the fund to purchase additional property for the campus.[5] Although this fund was essentially a scholarship fund for seminary students, as well as for other ad hoc purposes, it was hardly an endowment.

The problem of an annual operating deficit that Bishop Cosgrove had faced continued: tuition income still did not cover annual expenses. In 1915-1916, the deficit was $1,000 and the next year it was $2,950.[6] So in early 1917, Bishop Davis announced that he was establishing an endowment for St. Ambrose using $10,000 from the estate of Margaret T. Dittoe. Her late husband, William T. Dittoe, who had died in 1903, had been the diocesan attorney in the nineteenth century. It was he who negotiated with Henry G. Marquand for the Locust Street property. The bishop pointed out that the priests had responded to his appeal for funds to build LeClaire Gymnasium. But now he would widen his appeal for support of the college by turning to the Catholic laymen of the diocese. The bishop also said that he would approach the Knights of Columbus, the Ancient Order of Hibernians, and other Catholic societies for support.[7]

Davis did apply to the state council of the Knights of Columbus for a loan of $50,000, which was the amount that remained unpaid for the construction of LeClaire Gymnasium. He told them that he had raised funds for the building on a five-year pledge plan, that he wanted to use the Knights of Columbus loan to pay off the debt on the building, and then repay the loan as the pledges were paid. The Knights responded that they had an "iron-clad rule forbidding loans to educational institutions," so they turned Davis down.[8]

On April 12, 1917, six days after the United States declared war, Davis discussed the proposed St. Ambrose endowment with his council. He told them that it was "desirable to have an endowment fund" for St. Ambrose, and he again proposed to use the Dittoe estate as its foundation. The councilors agreed that St. Ambrose should have an endowment "worthy of the diocese," and they said that the college should do a better job of making its work known throughout the diocese. They proposed an annual collection for the college endowment be taken up on the first Sunday of Advent, that the pastors make an "earnest appeal" for the college and the endowment, and that the bishop send a pastoral letter emphasizing the necessity of an endowment. They also said that the bishop, or the president or vice president of the college, should contact the "more wealthy of the various congregations" for "generous donations" to the endowment.[9]

Because of the war, the proposed annual collection was not taken up in 1917, but the idea was not lost. On August 28, 1918, the bishop wrote to the priests of the diocese that they were to read his letter at all the Masses and take up a collection for the college on the second Sunday of September. Davis pointed out the necessity of higher education for the "talented layman." The "pioneer days" of education were gone, and competition and state regulations demanded that St. Ambrose become a modern college. To accomplish that, the college needed a "generous endowment." The priests had supported it since the beginning, but St. Ambrose belonged to all the people of the diocese and he asked for their support.

Wartime prosperity had created good wages, and farmers were having good crop years, so Davis suggested that they share that prosperity. He urged them to donate their Liberty Bonds and to put St. Ambrose in their wills. Once again he asked them to establish scholarships to support seminarians; the income from $5,000 would support one seminarian. Perhaps looking to the end of the war and the changes that would be inevitable because of it, he said that the "future of the Church in this country is dependent largely on the qualities of its educated laymen, and let us prepare to the best of our ability to make the future give us the golden harvest that awaits us." The collection proceeded over the following weeks and by the end of October, it had raised $7,914.[10]

The proposed endowment was one item the bishop discussed with his councilors at a meeting in January 1919. He reported that the final total from the collection of the previous fall was $8,741. That was a good amount, but even if that amount was raised every year, it was clearly inadequate to create the kind of college the bishop wrote about and Hannon envisioned. But they took no action on an endowment. The councilors also discussed the salaries of the priests at St. Ambrose. The consensus was that the salaries were not high enough to be an "inducement" for priests to join the faculty and to encourage them to continue their educations. So they proposed a salary scale that began at $300 a year for the first year and rose incrementally to $800 a year by the fifteenth year of service. The president would be paid $1,000 a year. The professors would also all receive room and board.[11]

The councilors met again in June where the bishop pushed the idea of raising money for an endowment. He said the necessity of one had been explained on other occasions and that the "future of the institution's standard largely depended" on an endowment. A resolution was proposed that a fund drive begin "as soon as possible" and that a committee be appointed for the campaign. Three priests, the Reverend John I. Grieser, pastor of St. Mary's Parish in Muscatine, Father Charles J. Donohoe, former vice president of the college and now pastor of St. Paul the Apostle Parish in Davenport, and Father Schulte, former president and now pastor of St. Mary's Parish in Iowa City, all voted in favor of the resolution. The Reverend Monsignor Edward J. McLaughlin, pastor of St. Mary's Parish in Clinton, and the Reverend Francis J. Leonard, pastor of St. Mathias Parish in Muscatine, voted no. Monsignor James P. Ryan did not vote. Since the decision had been made to raise money for the endowment fund, the councilors decided that the annual collection for St. Ambrose would be discontinued.[12]

It is not clear why the councilors objected to the endowment. The war was over, and as the bishop had pointed out in his letter the previous August, there was prosperity. It was clear at the January meeting that an annual collection would not yield enough money to create a proper endowment that would provide annual funds for the operation of the college. Yet the councilors did not discuss the issue in January and passed it by only one vote in June.

If some of the councilors were hesitant, the bishop was not. First, he selected the Reverend John M. Walsh to chair the committee. Walsh was born in Riverside, Iowa, and came to St. Ambrose as a student in 1889. He graduated in 1896 and was ordained a priest in 1900. Since ordination he had served in a number of parishes and was pastor of St. Mary's Parish in Albia when the bishop asked him to head up the endowment committee. So he could devote full-time to the endowment campaign, the bishop relieved him of his duties at Albia.

With the chair chosen, the bishop next selected a committee of priests from each deanery and invited them to a meeting on August 20. Those in attendance engaged in a wide-ranging discussion of the issues involved in the drive: Should a quota be established for each parish; should individuals be approached for contributions, or should all donations be voluntary; should each pastor determine what his parish could give? Hannon spoke at length about the necessity of the endowment and said that contributions from the parishes had to average $6,000 to reach the $500,000 goal.

Following the discussion, the group said that Walsh should select his own executive committee who could preach on the fund in the parishes. Finally, they thought that the campaign should begin in the "country parishes" which could set an example of generosity for the city parishes.[13]

Walsh set to work immediately, formed his executive committee, and scheduled preachers to go around the diocese. To assist them he provided them with a list of points to stress. The suggestions emphasized the spiritual work of building God's Kingdom on earth through Catholic education. St. Ambrose had to have proper laboratory equipment and an endowment of at least $200,000, which were among the standards necessary to ensure that St. Ambrose could be accredited and its students could transfer to the Iowa state colleges. Finally, the preachers were to explain how pledges could be made and paid off over a period of years and suggestions about how much to give.[14]

To begin the campaign, Bishop Davis issued a letter to the people of the diocese. Most likely the letter was written by Walsh and it emphasized

Drawing by John Bloom, 1923.

ALUMNI

Knights of Columbus in Davenport. Over the next few weeks, priests fanned out through the diocese speaking in parishes and urging the support of the people. Their work paid off, and by the end of November 1919, the fund had $114,997 in cash and pledges.[16]

The campaign in the rural parishes continued through the winter while the planning began to open the campaign in the city of Davenport. Walsh asked Lee J. Dougherty, a former mayor of Davenport and a member of the St. Ambrose Board of Trustees, to chair the Davenport effort with a committee of two laymen from each of the seven city parishes. The bishop and Walsh presided at an organizational meeting on Sunday evening, April 11, 1920, at the Knights of Columbus hall. Bishop Davis began by announcing that over $300,000 had been pledged in the rural parishes. Flannagan and Hannon were among the speakers.[17]

On the eve of the Davenport campaign, set for May 2, the bishop issued another letter. It reiterated the themes from the bishop's earlier statements and it discussed at some length the

the importance of Catholic education as the way to preserve the faith of the "youth of today." The campaign was beginning in the context of widespread, often violent strikes in the United States that many Americans saw as Communist attempts to take over organized labor, and perhaps, the country. So Davis appealed to their patriotism and said that the current "unrest, the strife, the near-anarchy" would be "cured by the infusion into our national life of a new element of real, not sham, democracy—a citizenship of fairness, justice, reasonableness." This, he said, would be accomplished by "citizens with a conscience," formed by the kind of "sound Christian education" available at St. Ambrose. But an endowment was needed to make it possible for St. Ambrose to provide this education. Past efforts had not been adequate; action must be taken now: "Temporizing is futile; makeshift plans will not do. So, I come to the fork in the road. I must have my college up to the standard, or cease to have a college. I must meet State requirements in teachers and equipment, or my collegiate courses will fail of State recognition, and my students' work will not be accepted. To do these things, I must without delay get the college squarely on its feet financially." He said that his "special representative," Walsh, would soon visit their parish, and that he hoped their "Catholicity and . . . patriotism" would be "eloquent in the generous help" of the people.[15]

The campaign began with a gift of $3,000 from the Loras Council of the

issue of accreditation by North Central, the first open discussion of this issue, which suggests that it was written for the bishop by Hannon. That would also explain the intensity of the plea: "To my mind, we are brought face to face with a most serious condition. It is not time to complain. To save our College from falling behind in the onward march of progress, all of us, clergy and laity, must work together to put it where it belongs–in the very front rank."[18]

On May 2, pastors from rural parishes where the drive had already taken place were chosen to preach in the Davenport churches. That afternoon, campaign workers gathered at the Hotel Blackhawk for a dinner where it was announced that there had been lead gifts totaling $60,000. Several dignitaries made speeches which said little about accreditation and the education of the faculty, but stressed the necessity of the college as a place to send boys who would "blossom forth as worthy citizens." The Reverend Loras Enright, the pastor of St. Ambrose's neighboring Holy Family Parish, said that institutions like St. Ambrose are "a light of Americanism, a light of patriotism, teaching men to think not altogether of themselves, but of others."[19]

Two weeks later Walsh reported to an enthusiastic crowd at the Blackhawk Hotel that the people of the Davenport parishes had contributed $177,042. The bishop remarked that the donors had made "it possible for St. Ambrose College to cast off the burden of a struggling

A Great and Lasting Beginning

institution and take its place in a new life." At the end of the evening, Walsh announced campaigns throughout the summer in other cities and towns of the diocese.[20]

The total amount from the diocese continued to rise. At a June meeting of the bishop's council, it was reported to be about $600,000. The councilors instructed the college attorney, Clark Hall, to take the necessary legal steps to revise the college's articles of incorporation so that the fund could be properly administered. They also discussed how to invest the money and decided that part of it would be deposited in various banks around the diocese. The rest would be invested in farm mortgages, which in the summer of 1920 were paying about 7 percent interest.[21]

The endowment campaign was a great success. Walsh reported that on December 1, 1920, the total amount pledged had reached $871,754, about one-fourth of which had been paid, the remainder to be paid in three-to-five-year pledges.[22] Unfortunately, the fund drive was completed at the same time as the beginning of an agricultural depression that made it difficult for many farmers to pay their

Rev. John M. Walsh, chairman of the Endowment Fund.

long-term pledges. Farmers had experienced unprecedented prosperity during the war. To grow more crops to feed the troops, many had gone into debt to purchase additional land or equipment. Commodity prices were high enough, however, for farmers to meet their mortgage obligations. Then in late 1920, a combination of "tighter credit, a sharp decline in European imports, and the eventual onset of the postwar business recession" led to a farm depression that lasted for twenty years. Corn prices fell from $1.97 a bushel in May 1920, to 46 cents a bushel in October 1921. Farmers could not meet their mortgage payments, which led to the bankruptcy of nearly one-half million farmers nationwide. In Iowa, one quarter of all banks failed between 1921 and 1929.[23] As a consequence, the full amount of the pledges would not be realized, but even so, by the middle of the decade, the endowment investments were yielding about $25,000 per year.[24]

The endowment campaign would continue for the next few years, but its success at the beginning was because of the vision of Hannon and the organizational skills and hard work of Walsh. The bishop admitted that he and his council had "long remained inactive and puzzled" about what to do to support the college. He also said that he rejected the term "drive" to describe the fund-raising, "There has been no 'drive' about this in the past, and there will not be now or in the future." Instead, he claimed that all the donations were "freely and gladly given" by people who wanted "sound education" in the diocese.[25] Neither Hannon nor Walsh shared that puzzlement, and they knew that it was a drive; people had to be convinced, and they convinced the farmers of Parnell and Lovilla and the other rural parishes, as well as the businessmen of Davenport and Clinton and the other

towns of the diocese, that investing in St. Ambrose was good for religion, education, and business.

As the endowment campaign proceeded, other parts of Hannon's program were underway. One of those involved graduate study by members of the faculty. In the past, faculty members were generalists, using the degrees they had earned in college or the seminary as the basis to teach whatever was needed. It was not unusual for a faculty member to teach English one year, history the next, and mathematics the year after that. Hannon's goal, and a necessity for accreditation, was that faculty members have advanced degrees in the field they taught. Moreover, it was not just having a degree that was important, it was also necessary to develop a faculty committed to scholarship. As one historian noted, the "imperative need for academic excellence" represented by a scholarly faculty, became the "leitmotif" of Catholic higher education during those years.[26]

The first faculty member with a doctorate was Father Giglinger, who had a Doctor of Divinity (DD) from the Propaganda College in Rome. Another graduate of the Propaganda was Father Henry Takkenberg who came to teach at St. Ambrose in 1913 and had a Doctor of Sacred Theology (STD). In 1919, the Reverend J. B. Culemans with a PhD in philosophy from the University of Louvain, and Dr. William Yancy, with a PhD in physics from Georgetown University, joined the faculty.

Since the mid-teens, faculty members had been attending summer school at the University of Iowa, the Catholic University of America, the University of Chicago, and other schools to work on advanced degrees in their field. Often the bishop used money from the seminary collection to pay for those summer sessions. To emphasize its importance, the 1916 catalogue, the first with Hannon as president, listed the degrees the faculty had earned. Three years later each faculty member was listed with his entire educational vita, the schools he attended, and the degrees earned.

The first two faculty members to benefit from Hannon's program of graduate study were Father Martin J. Cone, with a PhD in sociology from the University of Iowa, and the Reverend Thomas C. Donohoe, who earned a PhD in philosophy at the Catholic University of America. Cone and Donohoe had been on the faculty for several years and finished their degrees in 1921. Another long-time faculty member who benefitted from Hannon's program was Father Hauber, who finished a PhD in biology at the University of Iowa in 1925. Through the 1920s and 1930s, Hannon and his successor presidents would continue to send faculty members away for advanced degrees.

As more faculty earned advanced degrees, the curriculum began to change. Those most responsible for curriculum reform were Hauber, the prefect of studies, and Father Joseph Stahl, the vice president. Later Hauber gave most of the credit for the curriculum reform to Stahl, who had a "zeal for the future," and who laid the ground work for the "final emergence of a first class four year college."[27] Stahl may have done great work on the reforms, but Hauber underestimated his own contributions to the changes at St. Ambrose.

Until 1915, the college catalogues listed the curriculum by class year with the schedule set for each year. The freshmen took Latin, English, German, mathematics, political economy, natural science, and Christian doctrine. There was a similar listing for the other years of the college program. Beginning in 1915, a program for each class year was listed, but the courses were listed by department: religion; philosophy; Latin and Greek; history, economics, and political science; mathematics; biology, geology, and astronomy; physics and chemistry; and French and German. Each department listed several courses, and the students had the opportunity to choose some courses as electives.

From 1915 through 1927, the departmental arrangement remained essentially the same. A basic college curriculum had been established and the only significant changes in those departments were the addition of more courses over the years. One addition in 1915 was a new Department of Education for students who wanted to become teachers. Through the nineteenth century, school teachers were usually self-taught, or had attended a year or two at a normal school, nineteenth-century schools for the training of elementary school teachers. But late in that century, educators came to believe that education "was a science worthy of study in universities."[28] Led by the University of Iowa which established the first permanent college-level education department in the nation, colleges began to add education courses to their curricula. This professionalization of teacher training spread rapidly as the high school movement made the need for teachers more acute.

An education curriculum at St. Ambrose developed slowly. The 1915 catalogue said that to become a "successful teacher" one should receive a "liberal education," "thoroughly" master a subject, and have training in the "principles and methods of pedagogy." There were no courses listed, but if enough students wanted to pursue education courses such as methods of education, the history of education, or child psychology, the courses would be offered. For the next two years education was listed as part of the Philosophy department, then it disappeared from the catalogue. It returned in 1923 as a department with four courses: general psychology, principles of education, school administration and class management, and the history of education.[29]

A few new departments were added in the 1920s. Public speaking and accounting became college departments in 1922 as did commerce in 1926; both had been part of the old Commercial course that had its roots in the origin of St. Ambrose. The remainder of the Commercial courses became part of the St. Ambrose Academy curriculum.

One part of the collegiate core did undergo significant reorganization through those years. In 1916, history, economics, and government were joined together in the Department of Social Science, with the courses taught by a number of faculty members, including Father Cone who taught

economics. In 1918, Cone finished a Master of Arts Degree in political science and economics at the Catholic University of America. Cone studied there during the years Father John A. Ryan used his faculty position to popularize the issues of social justice based on the recent papal encyclicals.

Pope Leo XIII's 1891 encyclical, *Rerum Novarum*, written out of his concern about the alienation of labor from the church, taught that the church was rightly concerned with the economic and social conditions of the people. Leo XIII had defended the right to private property; condemned socialism and the excesses of capitalism; said that labor had the right to organize; and said that the church must teach the principles of social justice and not be "so preoccupied with the spiritual concerns of her children as to neglect their temporal and earthly interests." Leo XIII's successor, Pope Pius X, shared his predecessor's concern about political philosophies that led people away from the church. To combat this he urged bishops to have priests study the social sciences so they could "place them at the opportune time at the helm of . . . works of Catholic action."[30] These were the themes that had been the topic of the several lectures Ryan had delivered at St. Ambrose in the years before World War I.

During the war, the American bishops had formed the National Catholic War Council to coordinate Catholic participation in the war effort. With the war over, various American groups created plans for post-war reconstruction, and the bishops called on Ryan to draft their own plan. Issued in February 1919, the "Bishops' Program of Social Reconstruction" brought the principles of *Rerum Novarum* to the United States in a progressive document that called for reforms in labor legislation including a minimum wage and the right of labor to organize; public housing programs; old age, sickness, and unemployment insurance; controls on business organizations, including monopolies; and greater cooperation between labor and management.[31]

When Cone returned to St. Ambrose in the fall of 1918, social science was reorganized into a department with five courses: the principles of economics, which discussed wealth, land, labor and capital, and a study of the current problems in the economic and industrial life of the nation; exchange, a course about money and banking; governments of the world; principles of sociology; and ethics. With the reorganization of the department, history was removed and not taught at St. Ambrose for three years when it reappeared as a separate Department of History.

Cone continued to study the question of labor and justice in his doctoral program at the University of Iowa. His dissertation, "Labor and National Politics Since 1871," discussed several failed attempts by labor to organize a political party and become a force in national politics.[32] Cone received the PhD in political science in 1921 and returned to St. Ambrose where he continued to revise the social science department. The economics curriculum now included courses in the industrial history of Europe and industrial relations, a course about organized labor and its relationship to management. Cone's goal was to give the students a "correct conception of the industrial questions of the day" which would prepare them for their "responsibilities as a citizen in later life" as members of society, participants in the affairs of government, and as part of the industrial world where they would work.[33]

Enrollment continued to grow through the war years. In 1917-1918,

COLLEGE

after the United States had entered the war, the enrollment increased to 252, thirty-five of whom were collegiate. The next year enrollment increased to 269, but college enrollment fell to fifteen, as most college-aged men were in the service. In 1919-1920, with the war over and the army demobilized, enrollment jumped to 334 students, thirty of whom were collegiate.

One of the post-war students contributed a short article to the humor section of the 1921 issue of *The Ambrosian*, the college yearbook. A headline, "Faculty Offers to Confer with Students," led to the article which read: "June 9, 1920. The faculty of the University of Passemall have a new and up-to-the-minute method of operating their school. Before any rule is put into effect, the Student Council is consulted and allowed to O.K. all such rules. The old rules were found to be a detriment to some students, hence each one is treated individually and shown the best of courtesy. Hail Ye Student Council!"

There was no student council in 1921 and the General Regulations for the post-World War I students, created without student input, were not

Drawing by John Bloom, 1922.

much different from those for students in 1885. There were rules about punctuality, cleanliness, silence for study, rude behavior, and language. Students were limited to the college grounds; newspapers and other outside sources of information had to be approved; parents were responsible for the day students' religious practice; smoking was permitted for those over sixteen if they had their parents' permission; all students had to be present, with respectful decorum, at all religious exercises. The prohibition on communications between the house pupils and day students was deleted in 1910. And the faculty no longer opened the students' mail. The expectation that St. Ambrose students would act like Christian gentlemen still formed the basis of life on campus.

The increase of sixty-five students in the fall of 1919 created a housing crisis, so in September the college purchased the house on the southeast corner of Locust and Gaines Streets and moved fifteen philosophers from Wisdom Row into it. One of them commented that the move was "cruel since we were all settled [in Ambrose Hall] and such great pains were taken to see that the pennants hung evenly." The new residence became known as the Frat House, and according to one source "everything about the place is elite and exclusive."[34] The residents even came up with a Greek letter name for it, Sigma Alpha Chi, or S. A. C. Hauber was the disciplinarian for the Frat House, but he admitted that he was not very good at it. The residents

adopted a dog as a mascot, which they named Geraldine. There was great consternation one day when Geraldine turned up missing, and they suspected that Ambrose Hall residents had kidnaped her. Living in the Frat House increased the sense of sophistication they already possessed as philosophers. Meals became elaborate affairs; at the "first annual banquet," oyster soup was the main course, but they admitted that "next day oysters were not so popular."[35]

The Frat House was only a temporary solution to the overcrowding, and discussions began about building a new residence hall. The new hall would also revive the plans for the Senior Hall that had been part of the original design for the gymnasium building. The first step was to purchase land along Gaines Street on the west side of the campus. The college also added a large tract of land on the north which extended the border to Lombard Street (the site of Timmermann Field on the modern campus), with the purchase of land from Frederick H. Bartemeyer, the father of one of the members of the first class.

In the fall of 1921, a building committee that included Hannon and Schulte hired local architect Arthur Ebeling to draw up plans for a four-story building to house classrooms, laboratories, faculty offices, and student rooms. At a meeting of the bishop's council on January 22, 1922, Ebeling presented his design for a 104-by-44-foot building in a Tudor Gothic design, which was the southern-half of a proposed larger building. The estimated cost of the first half was $109,000, which would be paid out of interest income from the endowment. The council approved Ebeling's plans and then voted unanimously to name it Davis Hall.[36]

Work began immediately and proceeded through the spring and summer. The building was nearly completed in time for students to move in when school resumed in September 1922. The basement contained a recreation room and Hauber's biology laboratory. The college offices and classrooms were on the first floor. The upper two floors contained rooms for the students and professors. Hauber remembered moving into his room on the second floor while the plaster was still wet. The move of the college students into the new building meant that the Frat House was closed. As one resident moved out, he said with mock seriousness, "Hail to you, dear Frat House! You have served your purpose well, and fond memories of you will be cherished by all who made their home with you!"[37]

As the college residence, Davis Hall had its own rules. Students were to

South half of Davis Hall, 1922.

be at Mass every morning and at Benediction on Sunday afternoon. There were study hours and no room visitations; day students were never permitted in rooms at any time. Rooms were to be kept clean, there was no smoking in the hallways, and nothing was to be thrown out of the windows. Students were restricted to campus unless they had permission to leave, and leaving without permission could result in suspension or expulsion. Hauber was appointed master of discipline, and he remembered that while the Science department in the basement "prospered," the same could not be said of discipline because, "Technical training in the laboratory does not make for administrative efficiency."[38]

Davis Hall was dedicated at the homecoming celebration on November 15. The day began with the blessing of the building which was followed by speeches in the auditorium and a football victory against Campion in the afternoon. After a banquet that evening, there were more speeches and a musical program. The *Messenger* said that Davis Hall was a tribute to the bishop and the clergy who had worked to place St. Ambrose "on a sure foundation." The editor of the *Davenport Daily Times* noted that the new college building showed the "increasing importance" of St. Ambrose to the city of Davenport.[39] It was also another step in Hannon's goal for a greater St. Ambrose.

The alumni were another group Hannon wanted to enlist in his effort to create the greater St. Ambrose. The Alumni Association formed in 1914

had last met in August 1916, when they elected Edward J. Dougherty, president of the Citizens' Trust and Savings Bank, as president. Because of the war, the group had not met, but in June 1922, Dougherty and Hannon sent letters announcing the revival of the Alumni Association. Dougherty said that there was "work for us alumni to do" which could be best accomplished by an active association. Hannon told them that the alumni could help "in the making of the Greater St. Ambrose."[40]

Over 400 alumni met on November 15, 1922, for the first St. Ambrose homecoming which was held in conjunction with the dedication of Davis Hall. In florid rhetoric, the *Messenger* noted that the gathering of alumni "was an Epoch marking a larger life, the reaching of the foothills with the summits above, with the Alumni cheering on the workers." The paper said it was "among the first fruits" of the work of the bishop, and it put "a gleam of realization into the idealistic dreams" of the past presidents of the college. The new alumni president, Harry McFarland, thanked the alumni for their contributions to the endowment fund.[41]

The next spring the Alumni Association organized a Tri-City branch with a large gathering in the Gold Room of the Hotel Blackhawk. The Reverend William Lawler, the college registrar, urged the alumni to encourage graduates of local high schools to attend St. Ambrose. At the end of the meeting, the local group elected Judge Maurice Donegan as its president.[42] The next year a local alumni chapter was organized in Chicago.

The enthusiasm of the alumni for St. Ambrose was catching. At the second annual homecoming in October 1923, nearly 600 alumni came to

A Great and Lasting Beginning

campus. The football game against Still College of Des Moines ended in a scoreless tie, but that did not dampen the spirits of the students and alumni. At the banquet that night in LeClaire Gymnasium, the alumni talked about the past, but looked to their role in the future of St. Ambrose. Judge Donegan paid tribute "not to the St. Ambrose of the past, not to the group of buildings we call the college, not to a student body or even to the alumni, but to the St. Ambrose of the future which the alumni is seeking to build."[43] That spirit was exactly what Hannon needed.

One of the earliest religious organizations on campus was the Sodality which had been reorganized by Father Meinberg in 1915. Committed to prayer and also to social action, in 1917, it established a foreign mission unit to raise money to support missionaries. The next year it adopted the missionary work of an Ambrosian, the Reverend Bernard Meyer, a member of the Catholic Foreign Mission Society

The first grotto, 1922.

of America, commonly known as Maryknoll, who was working in China. A 1913 graduate, Meyer had joined the newly formed Maryknoll in 1914, and in 1918, was one of the first four Maryknoll missionaries to go to China. Through the years the St. Ambrose missionary society supported Meyer's work by putting on variety shows, raffles, and other fund-raising activities. In November 1926, Meyer came to St. Ambrose to express his gratitude to the students. He told them he wanted to build a school in China to train catechists. He was presented with $1,000 to establish the school, which he named St. Ambrose in China. The students noted that many people preferred to donate to build a chapel, but Meyer had told them that chapels were empty in China "from the lack of steady instruction." Over the next decade, the students of St. Ambrose College would support the students of St. Ambrose in China and Meyer's work.[44]

During the war, the Sodality had prayed daily for the war to end and when it did, they raised funds to build a shrine to the Blessed Mother in thanksgiving for the peace. But the high cost of materials after the war necessitated postponing the building of the shrine until later. In 1922, Miss Margaret Meek of Keokuk donated a statue of Mary holding Jesus for the shrine. The students raised more money and had a grotto built on the lawn east of Davis Hall. Trees were planted behind it and with other landscaping, it became a place for private prayer.[45]

The Sodality was just one of many clubs on campus during the decade. Some of the old literary and debating societies still met and provided

extracurricular opportunities to supplement class work in rhetoric and grammar. In the 1920s, several new groups were organized that directly related to curricular issues. In 1922, Dr. William Yancy organized the Science Club to make it possible for members to listen to lectures by those involved in the various sciences. This also gave them the opportunity to do advanced work in science and present their results to the public. The next year Hauber organized the Pre-Medic Society for students who planned to go on to study medicine. Later in the decade, the Commonweal Club was organized for students in the social sciences and commerce classes. The Engineer's Club began in 1927 to provide opportunities for pre-engineering students to learn about the profession, and to supplement their class work to better prepare them for entrance into engineering at one of the state universities.[46]

One of the most important of the old groups, the Logomachetean Society, which had disbanded in 1911, reorganized in 1922. During the two years of this incarnation of the Society, the members debated the issues of the day: the Teapot Dome scandal in the federal government, whether immigration laws should be strengthened, whether the State of Iowa should levy a gasoline tax, whether Congress should pass a bonus bill for World War I veterans. Other meetings were taken up with extemporaneous debates on less lofty subjects: why the west side of Davis Hall was the best, why a student should not ditch classes, why there should be no Saturday classes, and whether Andy Gump was America's greatest cartoon.[47] Many of the meetings adjourned having conducted no business.

In 1920, the philosophy students organized the K. E. Club for the purpose of the "deepening and promotion of good-fellowship." No one was ever sure just what the initials K. E. stood for, although someone suggested it meant "Kat Eyes." Clearly adopting the characteristics of social fraternities that were prevalent on secular campuses, the meetings consisted of entertainment of various kinds: boxing matches, feeds, smokers, or theater parties. When Davis Hall opened, the club members moved in and were able to get a room to use for their meetings.[48]

Discussion among members of the K. E. Club led to a new student publication, the *Ambrosian*, a quarterly magazine, which first appeared in March 1923. Each issue contained fiction, poetry, humor, and artwork produced by the students. When the yearbook ceased publication the next year, the *Ambrosian* began to publish news about what was happening on campus. The magazine now included accounts of the sports teams, the

First Homecoming Parade Committee, 1922. Rev. Joseph Stahl, vice president; Rev. Jacob Schoenfelder, master of discipline; Ed. J. Dougherty, president of Alumni Association; Rev. William Hannon, president; Dan Hannon, business manager; Tom Coughlin, committee member.

activities of the clubs, and a section of alumni news. In later years it took on some of the other functions of the defunct yearbook and began to publish class photos, pictures of sports teams, and general campus views. As the only St. Ambrose publication during the 1920s, it had a wide readership among students and alumni. It continued to publish through 1936 when the name changed to the *Ambrosian Quarterly*, and it was published under that name until it ceased in World War II.[49]

The K. E. Club was for the college upperclassmen. In 1922, another club, Mu Delta Alpha was organized for the sophomores "to celebrate our happy entrance into the beautiful Davis Hall."[50] Each fall the sophomores gathered the freshmen together to form the Arpas Club and to instill in them the ideals of St. Ambrose. The Arpas elected officers, called the First Verey, Second Verey, Third Verey, and Exclavo, the meanings of which, like the meaning of the name of the group, were obscure even then. It also had a "well-equipped" club room in Davis Hall.[51] As social organizations that closely paralleled college fraternities, the K. E. Club, Mu Delta Alpha, and Arpas indicated the continuing separation of the college from the academy.

The autumnal ritual of the sophomores instructing the freshmen Arpas members about the ideals of St. Ambrose quickly evolved into a formal freshman initiation. This was a far cry from the high-jinks Hauber had

experienced as a student twenty years before. Now it became a ritual which began early in the fall semester when the freshmen were presented with their green beanie caps, each with a different colored button on top: pre-med and pre-dental students had a white button; liberal arts, red; commerce, yellow; engineering, purple; and pre-law, black. Freshmen had to wear the beanies everywhere throughout the fall, and over the years, elaborate rules of behavior were developed. To enforce the rules, upperclassmen carried large paddles. Initiation usually ended on St. Ambrose Day, December 7, with extra humiliating activities for the freshmen which ended when they were allowed to get rid of their beanies.[52] Charles R. Mallary, a student in 1925, characterized the student body: "You can always tell a Senior/By his high and mighty air;/You can always tell a Junior/By the way he combs his hair;/A Sophomore is noted for/The swelling of his bean,/And you can always tell a Freshman/By his wearing of the green."[53]

Organization of freshman initiation would soon become the responsibility of the newly organized student council. Discussions about the formation of a student council had begun with a debate at a Logomachetean Society meeting on November 6, 1923. The issue that was joined that night was: resolved that a student council should be adopted at St. Ambrose College. The debate judges decided in favor of the affirmative.[54] But it would not be

A Great and Lasting Beginning

until the fall of 1925 when students formed a council and wrote a constitution. The purpose of the council was to see to the welfare of the students, offer them opportunities for self-expression, and create a spirit of cooperation between the students and the faculty. Representatives were elected from each of the four college classes.[55] When the faculty was presented with the proposed constitution, they "heartily endorsed" the idea of a student council "in principle," but had some reservations about some of the "details."[56] Nevertheless, the student council began to meet, and over the next few years, it assumed a larger role in campus activities.

Varsity football and basketball returned in 1920 following a two-year period when, because of the war, there were not enough players to field teams. Teams of both sports experienced three lackluster seasons, the worst of which was the 1922-1923 basketball season when the St. Ambrose Saints won one game and lost eleven.

The athletic program began to change in late 1922 when St. Ambrose, and several other members of the old Hawkeye Conference, met to form the new Iowa Conference.[57] St. Ambrose also had a new athletic director, the Reverend James J. Welsh, who is credited with reinvigorating St. Ambrose athletics. One of Welsh's first actions was to hire a new coach, Forrest "Fod" Cotton. Born in Elgin, Illinois, Cotton attended the University of Notre Dame where he played for Knute Rockne. After graduation, Cotton was an assistant coach for Rockne before coming to St. Ambrose.[58] Cotton coached football, basketball, and began a track program which replaced baseball as a varsity sport.

Cotton's teams, called the Cottonpickers by the local newspapers, generated excitement, even though their records were not always stellar. The students formed a cheering section, called the Howlers, and used a special football verse written for Erwin Swindell's song, "The Blue and White," to cheer on the team: "Come on, old team! Up, up, let's go!/Right through the line! Come, hit 'em low!/Hold! Hold 'em boys; don't let 'em gain;/Our colors flying shall remain!/Come on, old team, and let's go through,/To victory for the White and Blue!"[59] The usual opponents were teams from the Iowa Conference: William Penn, Central College, Luther College, and Buena Vista College.

The highlight of the 1925 season was a 16-14 victory against the Notre Dame reserves. But in a return game two years later, the Saints fell to the Fighting Irish 18-0. In 1927, St. Ambrose played Augustana for the first time in several years. Augustana defeated St. Ambrose 12-0. In eight seasons Cotton's football teams compiled a record of 27-29-4. They were never contenders for a title in conference play, in part because they did not play enough games against conference teams.

Under Cotton's coaching, the St. Ambrose basketball teams did better, compiling a record of 73-46. The 1927-1928 team, led by stars Bill O'Connor, Bun Austin, Joe Hratz, and Erwin Math, won the Iowa Conference championship. This team formed the basis for a basketball powerhouse with a three-year record of 42-11.

The track team started by Cotton was slow to develop. In the first years it entered only the Drake Relays. As a team it would not be a contender in Iowa Conference meets, but individual performances stood out. At the 1929 Loyola Relays, the mile medley team, with Cletus Madsen as lead

runner, finished third. Since Madsen won his leg of the race, he received a bronze medal, the first track award ever for an Ambrosian athlete. Norman Snyder was the undoubted track star of the Cotton years. In the 1931 conference meet, he set a conference record in the broad jump and placed third in the high jump. He took first in both events at the Augustana dual meet.

On December 16, 1924, one of the extemporaneous debates in the Logomachetean Society was resolved: St. Ambrose College needs an athletic stadium. The affirmative won the debate.[60] The debaters that night may not have known that physics Professor William Yancy had already drawn plans for a stadium to be located on the property that had been purchased from Frederick Bartemeyer a few years before.[61] The Alumni Association began to raise funds for the stadium by selling a season ticket that would admit a person to all sports of the 1925-1926 athletic season. Income from that source and contributions by clergy raised over $11,000.[62] In 1926, the land was graded and enclosed by a wire fence and included a football field, two baseball diamonds, and a 400 yard track, used for the first time in the fall of 1927. A grandstand seated nearly 2,000 spectators.

Erwin Swindell had contributed the football fight song, "The Blue and White," and he also continued to teach as part of the music program at St. Ambrose. In 1920, the Ambrosian Music Club was organized with members of the orchestra, choir, and glee club to "promote an interest in the different branches of this art, and to advise the public of the important part that it plays in the daily life of St. Ambrose."[63] There had not been a band since 1916, but the orchestra, a choir which provided music for the chapel services, and a glee club remained. The 1920s were the Jazz Age, and for a brief period in 1924-1925, there was a jazz band, Bud's Blue Boys. The band consisted of Leo "Bud" Coleman on violin, and three saxophones, a clarinet, trombone, banjo, flute, piano, and drums.

The musical groups played for events on campus, but now they also had a new venue for performance: the radio. The first commercial radio station in the nation was KDKA in Pittsburgh, which went on the air in 1920. Two years later B. J. Palmer went on the air with radio station WOC, which broadcast from a tower on the roof of the Palmer College of Chiropractic in Davenport. WOC was the first commercial station west of the Mississippi, and Palmer told his listeners he was coming from "Where the West begins . . . in the state where the tall corn grows."[64] Radio quickly became the latest national craze, and Frederick Lewis Allen wrote in *Only Yesterday*, his classic study of the 1920s, that "people wondered what would happen when the edge wore off the novelty of hearing a jazz orchestra in Schenectady or in Davenport, Iowa, play" the latest tune.[65] But the edge did not wear off for the citizens of Davenport or for Ambrosians who were educated in Davenport but now lived elsewhere. By the end of the decade, 40 percent of American households had a radio receiver.

On February 13, 1924, the St. Ambrose orchestra, glee club, and vocal and instrumental soloists appeared on WOC. Hannon joined them and spoke on Christian education. Over the next few days, Hannon heard from alumni in Pennsylvania, New York, Ohio, Wisconsin, Indiana, Texas, Nebraska, Montana, and all around Iowa and Illinois. Ed Henneberry, who had been in the first orchestra in 1900, wrote to say how thrilling it was to hear the St. Ambrose orchestra in his home in Pittsburg, Kansas.[66] The response to the broadcast was astounding, and it illustrated the impact of this new feature of American life. Hannon quickly realized that radio could be a powerful way to show St. Ambrose to the nation, and college groups began to regularly appear on WOC radio.

The radio was another means for Hannon to muster support for the reforms necessary to create his vision of the greater St. Ambrose College. Some progress had been made. The endowment campaign had been a success, but there was still more to be done. In the enthusiasm over the $871,000 pledged at the end of the first drive in the fall of 1920, the original goal of $500,000 had been raised to one million dollars. However, in large measure because of the farm depression of the 1920s, only about 60 percent of the pledges had been paid by 1924. Some of the endowment had been used to build Davis Hall, and more would be needed to finish it. In 1921 tuition was raised to $30 per semester, up from $25 where it had been since 1909, and room and board was raised to $140, up from $125 where it had been since 1914. But that was not enough, and the college continued to operate with an annual deficit, which amounted to $20,000 in 1922-1923 and $22,000 the next year.

In late February 1924, Walsh was made pastor of St. Mary's Parish in Ottumwa, and on June 1, the Reverend Nicholas Peiffer was named chairman of the endowment campaign. Peiffer began a tour of parishes to urge people to pay their pledges to the endowment fund. Economic conditions would not make it possible to ever receive the full amount that had been pledged, but Peiffer did make progress. At the end of 1925, he reported that the endowment amounted to $560,960, most of which was invested in farm mortgages, and that income from the endowment that year was $31,278.[67]

The separation of the academy and the college continued. In 1919, the Iowa State Board of Education (a forerunner of the State Board of Regents) passed a resolution which granted admission without any further examinations to the three state colleges to any high school graduate who presented a transcript showing the courses taken and the credits awarded. To be considered, the student's high school had to show that the "well recognized standards of school administration" regarding "teacher qualifications, equipment, course of study" were met.[68] By 1921, St. Ambrose Academy had met those standards and was accredited by the State University of Iowa as a four-year high school. But the college was still not accredited by the state, much less by the North Central Association.

As an intermediate step, in 1916, the faculty had created a junior college and developed pre-medical, pre-legal, pre-dental, and pre-commerce curricula, as well as a general two-year curriculum that corresponded to the first two years at a standard liberal arts college. Later they added a pre-engineering curriculum to respond to the demands of the business community for "specialists . . . to solve the complex problems of economic output together with the superior quality of their products."[69] In 1921, the junior college program was also accredited by the state schools and St. Ambrose Academy graduates and St. Ambrose Junior College graduates could attend one of them and have all their credits accepted.

On February 22, 1924, the college faculty wrote Bishop Davis to express their frustration at the slow progress on the road to the greater St. Ambrose. The letter was signed by Hannon and all the priest faculty present (two were away in school), two priest members of the academy faculty, and Walsh, still chairman of the endowment. They told the bishop that "we have this record to our discredit, that after forty years of organization we are the smallest college in the State and the only one offering four years of collegiate work that is not recognized by the State Institutions of our own State." They said that the facilities were inadequate to serve the students presently attending, much less the increasing numbers of prospective students in the future. They told the bishop that the solution for this problem was the completion of Davis Hall.[70] This would create more classrooms and provide more boarding space so diocesan high school and St. Ambrose Academy graduates would come to St. Ambrose College rather than go to the state universities.

This letter from the faculty spoke of their growing frustration about the status of St. Ambrose College, and it also spoke to their growing awareness of their status as the faculty. In the nineteenth century, a Catholic college was "an administrator's college." Control was external, and the faculty did not have any part in the important decisions of the college; those would be made from outside, as in the case of St. Ambrose, by the bishop and his councilors.[71] That is not to say that the faculty, individually and as a group, did not have opinions about college policy and curriculum. Most likely the friendly evenings in President Shannahan's rooms years before discussed more than the events of the day.

The faculty was already organized into various committees, the most important being the ones on academic studies, entrance, scholarships and degrees, discipline, the library, and athletics. Now in September 1923, the clerical and lay faculty began to hold formal meetings presided over by Hauber, who had been prefect of studies since 1916 and since 1922, the dean of liberal arts. Regular business consisted of routine announcements from the dean or the registrar, discussions about student absences, and classroom policies. At one meeting they decided to use blue books for examinations and asked Father Edward O'Connor to order some.[72] On a number of occasions, they asked for advance notice if the president intended to declare a free day, spelling an end to the spontaneous student requests that had been the custom for decades. Another common theme of their meetings was expressed on December 2, 1926, that "it was the consensus that there [was] not enough study among the college students."

There is no indication in the minutes of those meetings that Hannon attended, nor is there any indication that the faculty discussed the larger issues that led to their letter to the bishop. But they were now being consulted by the administration and they were making some policy recommendations.[73] The assertion of faculty prerogatives was slow in coming in higher education, but at St. Ambrose, a start in that direction had been made.

In the meantime, the faculty continued to press other issues on the bishop. Bishop Davis was now over seventy and not in good health, so in late December 1923, the Reverend Edward D. Howard, the president of Columbia College (Loras), was named the auxiliary bishop of Davenport. Born in Cresco, Iowa, in the Archdiocese of Dubuque, Howard had been on the Dubuque college's faculty since his ordination in 1906, and had been president since 1921. After his ordination as a bishop on April 8,

A Great and Lasting Beginning

1924, he came to Davenport. Howard would assume many of Bishop Davis' duties throughout the diocese, and would often chair the bishop's council meetings. The faculty of St. Ambrose was delighted with the choice of an educator as auxiliary bishop and sent a message to Howard that extended "the hand of scholastic fellowship" and "bid him a hearty welcome," adding the traditional Roman greeting, "Ad multos annos" (For many years).[74]

Bishop Howard presided over a meeting of the bishop's council in August 1924, where it discussed the financial status of the college. The college debt was mounting because nearly 20 percent of the day students could not afford to pay tuition, or could only pay a part of it, and the policy had been rather than deprive them of an education, the institution should aid them. The council was told that Bishop Davis wanted a finance committee of Bishop Howard and Hannon and Stahl to audit receipts and expenditures and hopefully remove the deficit.[75]

In October 1924, the faculty sent Bishop Davis another letter to urge him to "promote the progress of St. Ambrose College." The letter was signed by twelve of the priest faculty; the only ones who did not sign were the librarian, the Reverend Joseph Code, and Hannon. Calling St. Ambrose a "second-rate institution," they said that the faculty, building, and the library were "clearly inadequate." The lack of accreditation was unfair to the students already there and they believed that it was keeping prospective students away. They thought that with the expenditure of $250,000, St. Ambrose could be a "first-class college" within two years. They pointed out that to serve the college, the priest faculty had given up the "privilege of doing parish work" for which they were ordained, and which they claimed, "would be more congenial and less strenuous" than college work. Finally, they made four recommendations: complete Davis Hall and build a science building by October 1925, appropriate enough money to bring the library up to North Central standards, give a professor in each department the opportunity for graduate study, and install modern kitchen equipment and hire expert supervision to improve the meals.[76]

Bishop Davis called a meeting of his council for November 11, 1924, to respond to the latest faculty letter. In addition to Howard and the councilors, among whom were the three former college presidents, the bishop invited Fathers Hannon, Stahl, Hauber, Lawler from the college faculty, Peiffer, the head of the endowment, and Clark Hall, the diocesan attorney. The bishop read the October 22 letter from the faculty to all present, which led to a lengthy discussion of the endowment and college finances. Shannahan moved: "That the council endorse and approve the programs of improvements as presented by the college faculty." The motion passed.[77]

Next they turned their attention to the means to achieve the goals the faculty had set and the council had just endorsed. They thought that first Davis Hall should be finished. They asked Hannon to talk with Arthur Ebeling, the architect who built the first section of Davis Hall, and ask him for plans to complete the building and to pay him a fee of $3,000. Once they decided to finish Davis Hall, they concluded that there was not enough money to also build the science hall at the present. Davis said he would talk to his long-time friend Frank J. Lewis about it. Lewis had been among the first to donate to the St. Ambrose scholarship fund early in the century, and had already expressed his "willingness" to do something for St. Ambrose.[78] The meeting adjourned without discussion of the other three faculty recommendations: improvement of the library, graduate study for the professors, and upgrading of the kitchen, the first two of which directly related to the continuing efforts to achieve accreditation by the North Central Association.

When Hannon talked with Ebeling a few days later, the architect said that the fee that was offered was a "very considerable reduction" from his usual fee. However, when Hannon told him that the college would require more buildings in the future, Ebeling said he hoped he would be considered for them, and agreed to finish Davis Hall for the $3,000 fee.[79]

One visible indication that St. Ambrose was a college came in April 1925, with the announcement that the college now had an official seal which was "symbolic of the aim and spirit of the institution" and expressed the "spiritual lineage" of her patron, St. Ambrose. The seal was designed by Pierre de Chaignan la Rose of Cambridge, Massachusetts. The central feature was a shield, the upper third of which had a silver background with three black crosses taken from the arms of the Davenport family in England. The lower two-thirds had a red background, representing theology, with a golden beehive and three golden bees. The bees, ancient symbols of "indefatigable labor and industry," had become the symbol of St. Ambrose ever since the legend of the bees swarming around his cradle was published shortly after his death. Three bees were used to represent the Trinity, which Ambrose had defended against the Arians. Surrounding the seal was the name of the school in Latin and at the base was a Greek cross. By choosing these symbolic references to the fourth-century patron of the college, the seal "aptly unites the present with the distant past."[80]

The seal was one symbol of the college and through 1925, the faculty continued to work to make real what the seal symbolized: a college. In early 1926, a symbol of the early years of St. Ambrose passed from the scene with the death at age sixty-six of the second president, Father J. T. A. Flannagan. A student paid tribute to the late president and said that the story of his years at the college was one of "ardent and enduring zeal."[81] As a member of the faculty and then president, Flannagan did shepherd the school through difficult years, but like the proper Victorian clothes he wore while president, Flannagan represented the St. Ambrose of the past. His death in 1926 marked the passing of that era as his successors worked to create a modern St. Ambrose.

Symbols were important, but the North Central Association required actual compliance with the standards it had set for accreditation. In March 1925, the association had revised the list of standards an institution had to meet in order to achieve accreditation: It could only accept students who had graduated from an accredited high school; the college had to require 120 credit hours for graduation; it should have at least eight academic departments, with at least one professor in each with a graduate degree; a department head must have a PhD or equivalent training; faculty should teach no more than sixteen hours per week to classes no larger than thirty students, unless it was a large lecture; the institution had to have at least 100 college students; the library must have at least 8,000 volumes; the school had to have sufficient laboratories for the sciences; and it must generate at least $50,000 income per year, with one-half from sources other than student tuition.[82]

By early 1926, St. Ambrose had met many of those standards but still had work to do. The faculty maintained its pressure on the bishop to bring about real change. On February 15, 1926, Bishop Howard presided over a meeting of the bishop's council. This time the meeting group was enlarged to include diocesan attorney Clark Hall, frequent advisor to the bishop, insurance executive Lee J. Dougherty, and the college and high school faculties. Hannon gave a lengthy presentation of the financial status of the college which projected a deficit of $33,000 for the current year. He said many of the day students could not pay tuition, that income was low in the college because of low enrollment, and that current funds were used to pay interest on the money borrowed to buy more land. As a consequence, the school opened each year already owing bills of $6,000 to $8,000. Next Hannon discussed the salaries of the priests and the lay faculty which led to a discussion about the salary levels necessary to retain the lay faculty. The priests were still on the salary scale established in 1919 that ranged from $300 to $800. The lay faculty was paid $2,000 a year; coach Fod Cotton was paid $3,500 a year. The council listened to eight of the priest faculty members, all of whom called for the completion of Davis Hall, accreditation by North Central, improving the library and laboratories, and generally bringing the college up to a higher standard.[83]

Based on the discussion, the bishop's council formed a finance committee to examine the financial status of the college, to find a way to eliminate the debt, complete Davis Hall, and consider what additional buildings were needed. They were to report their findings to Davis. Howard was appointed to chair the committee which consisted of Schulte, Leonard, Lee J. Dougherty, and Clark Hall. The councilors made it clear that the financial

problems of the college would not be resolved by dismissing the lay faculty with its higher salaries. Before the meeting adjourned, someone suggested that the name of the college be changed to Davenport College, with the names Ambrose Hall and Davis Hall retained. The intention must have been to make the college more acceptable to the larger, non-Catholic community, but the idea failed for lack of support, and the meeting adjourned.[84]

In May the finance committee presented its report to Bishop Davis. It said that the college must be put on a "strict budget basis" where expenditures did not exceed total receipts from a combination of income from students and the endowment. They recommended that the bishop appoint a budget committee made up of the president of the college, a layman or priest appointed by the bishop who would be the bookkeeper, and a priest to act as treasurer. This committee would be responsible for the annual college budget. For the first year the finance committee took that task upon itself and presented a budget for the next academic year. They found that the cost of athletics, mainly the salary of the coach, had "been very large," and was responsible for a "considerable" amount of the annual deficit. This "must be reduced" so that it did not exceed the income from gate receipts plus the $2,500 provided for it in the budget.

They noted the "increasing financial loss" from the day students, and they recommended that each parish pay the difference between what the students from their parish paid and the amount of tuition owed by the students. The committee told the bishop that completing Davis Hall would be of "great benefit" to the college and they recommended that "immediate steps" be taken to complete it. Finally, they noted a "floating indebtedness" which had been accumulating for several years, owed mostly to local merchants, which should not "remain unpaid." They suggested that this debt, and the debt to be incurred by finishing Davis Hall, be combined and refinanced by a ten-year loan from a local bank. Bishop Davis accepted their report and ordered that their recommendations be carried out.[85]

The finance committee's recommendations came in the context of change for the diocese and the college. In late April it was announced that Bishop Howard had been named the archbishop of Oregon City, Oregon. He remained in Davenport through the summer and left for Oregon on August 23. Two weeks later Bishop Davis announced that he had appointed Hannon as pastor of St. Mathias Parish in Muscatine and that he had selected Hauber to replace him as president. These changes would take place on June 10.[86]

Hannon had wanted to give up the presidency for at least a year. He had been at St. Ambrose as student, faculty member, and president for over thirty years, the last ten of which he had led the campaign for the greater St. Ambrose. He had not completed all of the program he had outlined when he became president eleven years earlier, but he had achieved most of it. His main goal, accreditation, had not been achieved, but he could feel confident that under his successor that too would soon be accomplished. Nevertheless, the *Messenger* noted that those years had been the "most fruitful years" of St. Ambrose, and that his work would be a "lasting monument that will endure while the College lasts."[87]

Just before Hannon left Davenport, he was feted at a farewell dinner at the Blackhawk Hotel attended by nearly 250 people. Several speakers, including Archbishop-elect Howard and Hauber, rehearsed his accomplishments. At the end of the evening, Hannon rose to thank those in attendance. He said that "things economic and educational were in a flux during the forepart of his administration," and while he acknowledged the accomplishments of his presidency, he gave most of the credit to the faculty who shared his vision. Hannon singled out for special mention his efforts in "developing and maintaining a fine spirit of helpfulness and understanding between the community and St. Ambrose," especially between the "press and the college."[88]

Hauber had been a disciple of Hannon's during the years he was the chief academic officer, and Hauber's admiration for Hannon did not diminish with time. Writing twenty-seven years later, Hauber said of Hannon, "No one did more for St. Ambrose College than William L. Hannon . . . He trained a faculty, secured a substantial endowment, put the College on the accredited list, built the first gymnasium and a residence building, and steered the old ship through the difficult years of the first world war. And he did it under tremendous handicaps, not the least of which was that the Board of Trustees, including the bishop, were of no help to him whatever. He carried on alone, and succeeded because he had many friends."[89]

Hauber now relied on the faculty and Hannon's many friends to continue to build the greater St. Ambrose. Money was still a problem and on September 1, some of those friends, including the Knights of Columbus, the Daughters of Isabella, and the Catholic Women's League, held a fall festival on campus. The event brought over 1,000 people to the campus to inspect the buildings, watch sporting events, and participate in a card party in the gymnasium. Dinner was served in the refectory, and the day concluded with a dance in the gymnasium. The festival provided an opportunity to show off the college to the community, and it raised over $1,000. It became an annual event for a few years and other groups, including the St. Ambrose Alumni Association, the Tri-City Chapter of the Clarke College Alumnae Association, and the St. Mary's Notre Dame Alumnae Association, joined in sponsoring the event.[90]

The festival-goers who inspected Davis Hall could also look at the construction that had begun on the second, north half of the building. Even as construction proceeded, there was talk about a science building and a new chapel. According to the *Messenger*, such a building program "would enable St. Ambrose to keep its place among up-to-date colleges."[91]

Construction proceeded through the fall and winter. College students from Ambrose Hall and neighborhood houses began to move into the building in April 1927. A chapel was put in the north half of the basement which eased the pressure on the Ambrose Hall chapel, and the library moved into the south half. The upper floors contained more classrooms and residences for students and faculty.[92]

Davis Hall was now complete, but Bishop Davis did not live to see it. Through 1926, his health had been declining, and in July he suffered a heart attack; he had been too ill to attend Archbishop-elect Howard's farewell dinner on August 22. He continued to decline through the fall, and he died on December 2. Tributes to Davis mentioned his support for St. Ambrose, one said that his "most noteworthy achievement" was the growth of the college. Another said that the priests knew that the college was the "apple of his eye."[93] His support for St. Ambrose during its early years was noteworthy. He made trips through the diocese in the 1880s and 1890s to raise funds for the college. He was a frequent and welcome guest and sometimes a speaker at St. Patrick's Day programs and other college activities. As bishop, however, his support for St. Ambrose was more passive: he allowed Hannon and the faculty to make changes but did no more than he had to. When the *Ambrosian* magazine published a laudatory article about him after his death, someone, possibly Hauber, wrote in the margin of a copy of the article, "not really an educational leader, he allowed progress; he didn't understand North Central, the need for an extensive library, [or] the need for continued education for the faculty."[94] Nevertheless, he allowed those things to happen.

In early January 1927, Hauber told the faculty that "little progress had been made" regarding accreditation with North Central. He said that St. Ambrose would qualify as a junior college but not a senior college and he asked the faculty to discuss if that was best.[95] Clearly for Hauber it was not. But Hauber was incorrect when he said little progress had been made. A great deal had been done. The endowment and income from it met the standard; the college now had 143 students; the library had over 10,000 volumes, not counting books in special libraries in chemistry, biology, and physics; there were twenty-one priest faculty and five lay faculty, four of whom had doctorates and most of the rest of whom had Masters Degrees or their equivalent.

In late January, two representatives of the North Central Association, Professor J. D. Ellif of the University of Missouri and Dr. William Cunningham of Notre Dame, came to campus for an inspection visit. They found that St. Ambrose met all of the necessary standards for accreditation but they thought that the faculty lacked preparation in the latest teaching methods. Hauber and the Ambrosians argued that the "personal touch" made possible because of the small classes at St. Ambrose made up for any deficiency. Hauber told them he would hold faculty seminars to study new teaching methods. Based on that promise, Ellif and Cunningham were apparently encouraging enough that Hauber could write in mid-February that membership in North Central could come within a month.[96]

At its annual meeting on March 17, 1927, the North Central Association added St. Ambrose to the list of accredited institutions, subject to a reinspection in 1928.[97] When he announced the news to the faculty, he asked them to read the report from North Central carefully. He singled out recommendations regarding having a faculty seminar to study teaching techniques, which would be the basis for a return visit by the Association the following year.[98]

That was for later. Now Hauber and the faculty could savor the fact that their ten years of work, and the leadership of Hannon, had led to this moment. The editor of the *Messenger* said that the accomplishment was more impressive because not all Iowa colleges which had applied had been granted membership in the North Central Association. The *Davenport Times* said that accreditation was a "recognition of the excellence of the faculty." Accreditation would result in an increased enrollment, and "located as favorably as it is, St. Ambrose college may be expected within a comparatively few years to boast an enrollment which will compare favorably with any Catholic college" in the area.[99]

Housewives of Northwest Davenport were rather astounded these last few days, to have trucks draw up at their doors, young men in green caps leap from them, and request by all manner of pleading, 'brooms, brooms, brooms!' But it was not only housewives who were requested to contribute materials for the greatest bonfire in the history of St. Ambrose. Furniture dealers gave crates of all descriptions, oil and greasing stations gave up large quantities of thick greenish oil, which when applied to such inflammables as those mentioned above, will create much light and not a little heat.[1]

❧ Chapter Seven ❧

The bonfire of oil-soaked brooms and crates was to celebrate homecoming of 1929 and the football game against Luther College. There had been bonfires from the early days on the Locust Street campus, but in 1922, it had become part of the first homecoming celebration, when Father James Welsh, the Alumni Association secretary, suggested that a bonfire would be a "sign for all the old grads to come back, gather around and warm their memories."[2] Signs were posted all around campus to welcome back the alumni. The windows of Davis Hall were painted alternately blue and white. The newly reorganized band wore uniforms of royal blue sweaters with a large white A and a lyre, white duck trousers, and white berets with blue trimming.

But the bonfire and the energy on campus did not help the football team, which lost to Luther College 13-0, on its way to a lackluster 4-4 season. The homecoming revelers did not know that October 24, the day the beanie-clad freshmen were gathering kindling, would be labeled Black Thursday because of the large sell-off of shares on the New York Stock Exchange that day. Nor could they know that five days later, October 29, Black Tuesday, the market would crash, and the resources President Hauber needed to continue to build St. Ambrose, and that the students needed to pay their tuition, would be even harder to get.

Hauber had come to the presidency with reluctance. In April 1926 when it became known that Hannon would leave, Father Schulte, not only the first president but also Hauber's boyhood pastor, had urged him to accept the presidency. But Hauber told Schulte that he "did not want the office of president." He said he was trained as a scientist, and so few priests in the United States were "equipped" to do work in biology, it was not a "good policy" to spend money to train a scientist, and then not use him in that capacity. He told Schulte he would have to learn "new tricks and trades" to be president and that the necessary "executive and administrative work" was "absolutely foreign to him." Hauber had also expressed those views to the priests at the college and made it clear to them he did not want the job. He was so adamant about the presidency that he told Schulte he would be tempted to ask for a transfer to another diocese to avoid it. If the bishop offered him the presidency, he said he would do his best to talk him out of it, and failing that, he would take it only for a year or two. But in spite of

his opposition to the job, he told his old pastor that "in deference" to his request, he would give the "matter more thought and prayers; and for the present, at least, keep my mouth shut about accepting or refusing the presidency."[3]

Hauber had been one of the leaders in the reforms that led to accreditation by the North Central Association, and he told Schulte that more needed to be accomplished if St. Ambrose was "to be what it should be." The challenge was to provide an education for its students that would prepare them to enter the professions, without at the same time abandoning the classical and religious roots of Catholic higher education. The various pre-professional programs at St. Ambrose, the emphasis on labor and business in courses introduced by Father Cone, and the expansion of the sciences were necessary steps to make St. Ambrose into a modern college. But while doing that, Catholic higher education had to avoid what was called the "utilitarian theory of education" that prepared students to make a living but did nothing to teach them how to live.[4] Hauber agreed with that and wrote that the liberal arts college should not make its "primary business to train technical experts," rather, "my conception of the main function of a college . . . is that it should train men to think out the problems that concern the ultimate welfare of human beings, and that means by clear implication, the ultimate welfare of society." Those questions, he said, "lie in the field of religion and ethics, and these subjects have little or no standing in most modern colleges," which are teaching "knowledge, when what the world needs is wisdom."[5]

The conflict between secular education and religion was highlighted by one of the most contentious issues in the United States during the 1920s: the fight by Protestant fundamentalists against the teaching of Darwinian evolution. Fundamentalists believed that the Bible was the only authority about God and the world, and that the creation stories of the Book of Genesis were to be taken literally. Therefore, Darwin, and those scientists who believed and taught his theory, were wrong. This became a national cause celebre in 1925 when John Scopes, a high school biology teacher, was put on trial for violating the Tennessee law against the teaching of evolution. Advocates of science and advocates of religion flocked to Dayton, Tennessee, for the trial. Clarence Darrow, the foremost defense attorney of his day, questioned William Jennings Bryan, a former secretary of state and three-time presidential candidate, who as a witness for the prosecution

A Great and Lasting Beginning

defended the literal scriptural interpretation of creation. Although Scopes was found guilty of breaking the law, Darrow had succeeded in making the fundamentalist position seem illogical.

Hauber had a PhD in biology from the University of Iowa, and as a scientist, he saw no conflict between science and religion. That same year as the Scopes trial, Hauber published a pamphlet, "Creation and Evolution, A Catholic Opinion of the Evolution Theory," where he asserted that "a conflict between true science and genuine religion [was] impossible." Hauber argued that the theologian teaches that God created all life and the scientist "claims to know that [life] developed according to natural law." The religious fundamentalists claimed that evolution was untrue because it was not in the Bible. Hauber replied that the theory of evolution was science and the Bible did not teach science. Those who opposed "sound scientific theories" were doing "harm to the cause of truth. Catholics especially should be ready to

Rev. U.A. Hauber.

accept new findings in the scientific world without losing their grasp on the more fundamental truths of religion . . . Hold fast the old while profiting by the new, that is the course recommended to us by the great Pope Leo XIII." Because they also taught religion in their schools, he said that Catholics should have no fear of also teaching evolution.[6]

If Hauber was ready to profit by the new, not everyone at St. Ambrose was, and he knew that continuing reform there would be met by some resistance. He had already experienced that resistance with the late bishop. In his letter to Schulte, Hauber had complained about Bishop Davis' "conservative attitude toward expansion of the college." Hauber attributed this resistance to the "naturally conservative" nature of Catholicism which believed that the past had "produced much good," and change might "carry us away from the Rock of Ages." Hauber rejected that as "really unCatholic" since it disregarded the "principle of progressive adaptation to circumstances."[7]

Hauber knew that for the college to "be what it should be" would take money. With Davis' death in late 1926, and no successor named by the spring of 1927, Hauber took the initiative and sent a letter to the clergy and laity of the diocese. Dated February 15, one month before the accreditation decision by the North Central Association, Hauber said that the college belonged to the people of the diocese. He described the current situation: the enrollment was good and increasing; housing was currently adequate; with accreditation, the education at St. Ambrose compared favorably with other schools; there were twenty-one priests and five laymen on the faculty, most with advanced degrees; and religion classes and observances were part of the program. He described the work of the special budget committee established by the late bishop and presented the budget for the 1926-1927

year. The largest item in that budget was salaries: an average of $600 for the priests and $2,000 for the laymen. The endowment was now at $577,480, almost all of it invested in farm mortgages which realized about $30,000 per year. Tuition, room, and board was now $189 per semester for college boarders, $174 for high school boarders, $50 per semester for college day students, and $25 for high school day students.

There were 140 college students when Hauber wrote his letter and he was optimistic that enrollment would increase to over 300 college students within two or three years. That would mean an increase in tuition revenues, but that would not be enough revenue to continue to provide the education for the "leaders of thought among Catholic laymen" necessary for the future. He listed some of the things necessary to make St. Ambrose the school it should be. It needed: in the long term, a new science building, a new library, and a separate chapel building; in the short term, money to finish the chapel in the basement of Davis Hall, to furnish the student rooms in the new wing of Davis, to purchase more equipment for the library and Science department, and to make general improvements in Ambrose Hall. Finally, Hauber urged his readers to look again at the advantages offered at St. Ambrose and said, "Every Catholic boy of the diocese who goes to college should be at St. Ambrose for at least two years." Although Hauber said he was not "begging," clearly he was: "Donations will enable us to do better work; they will promote the interests of religion, the welfare of souls, and the honor and glory of God."[8]

Hauber's optimism about increased college enrollment was well-placed. National figures showed 74,849 students in Catholic colleges in 1926, an increase of 14,680 from 1924, the largest two-year increase in the history of Catholic higher education. The enrollment at each college was small: only seventeen men's colleges had over 1,000 students, and only one women's college, St. Mary of the Woods in Indiana, had more than 1,000.[9] Overall, Catholic college enrollment increased by 213 percent in the decade of the 1920s.

This increase in college enrollment was attributable to a growing awareness by Americans that a college education created more opportunities for social and economic advancement. As the quality and number of high schools increased, more students realized that a college education was attainable. To accommodate those new students, college curricula expanded to prepare graduates for a wide range of careers.[10] As Hauber noted in his letter to the diocese, St. Ambrose still educated men for the priesthood, and laymen could still receive degrees in philosophy and the classics. But now they could also receive degrees in the social sciences, English, and commerce, and they could take two year courses in pre-engineering, pre-medicine, and pre-law.

At St. Ambrose the enrollment increase through the late 1920s was

St. Ambrose played Augustana College in LeClaire Gymnasium on February 27, 1929. St. Ambrose won 33-30 on a shot by Bill O'Connor with fifteen seconds left in the game. At halftime, a new college song was introduced to the fans: "Go! St. Ambrose, Go!" with music by Ernst Otto and lyrics by Nic LeGrand.

steady. There were 140 college students in 1926-1927. Enrollment finally reached Hauber's prediction of over 300 students in 1932-1933 when there were 314 college students. The number of students from the Diocese of Davenport decreased during the period from 70 percent in 1927-1928 to 55 percent two years later. During 1927-1928, there were also students from Illinois, New York, Wisconsin, Michigan, South Dakota, Kentucky, Minnesota, and Indiana.

There were also a few students from abroad. In 1920 the first foreign student, Pedro Mendive, had come from Havana, Cuba, where his father was a "wealthy food commissioner."[11] Through the decade there would be students from Uruguay, Mexico, and Puerto Rico. In 1931, Paul Kim arrived from Korea. Kim was a thirty-year-old student with a wife and family in Korea, who came to the United States to learn English. His goal was to receive a college degree and return to Korea to be a catechist. According to the student newspaper, Kim was a "living sermon on the missionary spirit."[12]

There was another factor in the enrollment increase at St. Ambrose. In 1925, an extension division was created for religious sisters who taught in the local Catholic schools. In the 1920s, most grade school teachers in public and private schools still had little more than two years of Normal College preparation; many had only a high school diploma. As states began to require baccalaureate degrees for teacher certification, those sisters had to

find a way to receive more education while continuing to teach their classes. The more progressive religious superiors tried to provide lectures and short courses which were taught in their convents or motherhouses, or they made it possible for their sisters to attend night classes, Saturday classes, or summer school. Since many of those sisters had only a high school diploma, this put them on the so-called twenty-year plan of six hours a summer for twenty summers. Other, less progressive superiors, were concerned that having their sisters take classes would disrupt the routine of the convent, or interfere with the spiritual development of their nuns. Still others forbade their sisters to take any classes from laymen in "any branch of study," and laymen should not be brought in "to teach either Sisters or pupils."[13]

The reluctance to have men and women study together was equally prevalent on male campuses like St. Ambrose. This was in part the opinion among the priests who taught on those campuses that the "best diploma for a woman was a large family and a happy husband."[14] That attitude may have been present at St. Ambrose.

There was another objection to women at St. Ambrose: the seminary. In the 1920s, many educators and bishops still believed that seminaries should be isolated institutions, guided by church law and standards, and free from the secular influences of lay students, whether men or women. Following Bishop McMullen's lead, St. Ambrose had rejected that, and the seminarians took classes alongside lay students. But going to class with women and

A Great and Lasting Beginning

perhaps associating with them socially was a different matter, and even the more progressive educators at St. Ambrose were cautious about crossing that line.

The solution arrived at by male campuses was to teach women off-campus or teach them during the summer when the male students were not present. The desire by these sisters for a college education with access to library and laboratory facilities was obvious to the priests. It was also obvious that if Catholic education was going to be respected by Americans, its teachers had to be as professional as the public school faculties. The extension courses that began in 1925 were one way for St. Ambrose to contribute to the professionalization of the faculties of Catholic schools.

That first year, 1924-1925, there were five sisters enrolled in the extension division. That increased to eight the following year and forty-two the year after that. In 1927-1928, forty-five sisters from five religious communities enrolled. In 1928-1929, for the first time, nineteen laywomen also enrolled. The first two women to receive a degree from St. Ambrose finished in 1931: Sister Mary Aquinas Freehill received a Bachelor of Science and Sister Margaret Mary Dwyer received a Bachelor of Arts, both Sisters of Visitation from the Villa de Chantal in Rock Island.

On May 20, 1927, the Reverend Henry P. Rohlman was named the new bishop of Davenport. Born in 1876 in Germany, Rohlman had studied in the United States and was ordained a priest in 1901. He served in several parishes in the archdiocese of Dubuque, and from 1904 to 1906, he studied sociology at the Catholic University of America. From 1917 to 1924, he served as business manager of Columbia College (Loras) and was in charge of raising an endowment fund of one million dollars. Rohlman was consecrated a bishop on July 25 in Dubuque, and was installed as bishop of Davenport in Sacred Heart Cathedral the next day.

Two days before Rohlman's consecration, Bishop Davis' long-time friend Frank J. Lewis wrote Rohlman to say that at his installation ceremony in Davenport, there would be an "announcement of interest." He told Rohlman that he intended to establish a memorial for his late wife and daughter.[15] The announcement of interest was made by Dubuque Archbishop James J. Keane during the installation Mass, when he told a stunned congregation that Lewis was donating $60,000 to St. Ambrose College to be used to build a new science hall. Lewis' gift was by far the largest in the history of the institution and the latest of his gifts to St. Ambrose that extended back over twenty years. Lewis said later that the gift was an acknowledgment of the "broad development" of the college under the "wise council" of Bishop Davis, and the "energetic leadership of Fathers Schulte, Flannagan, Shannahan, and Father Hannon." With this gift Lewis hoped that this development would continue. Speaking at the luncheon following the installation, the new bishop of Davenport said he could not find the words to adequately express his gratitude to Frank Lewis. In a "glowing tribute," he also acknowledged the work of the St. Ambrose faculty.[16]

That Lewis' gift was designated for a science hall reflected years of preparation by the faculty, especially Hauber. In 1923, the faculty had discussed at length the need for a science building. They pored over some preliminary plans for a building of not less than three floors, one each for physics, chemistry, and biology, and a basement. Anything smaller, they thought, would

be inadequate within a few years. They did not specify a location except to say that it should be far enough from the street so that odors from the chemistry laboratories would not offend passersby.[17] Based on those discussions, architect Arthur Ebeling, who had been promised another building for designing the second half of Davis Hall at a lower fee, began to create plans for the new science hall.

The new bishop's interest in St. Ambrose became clear a week following his installation when he issued his first letter to the people of his diocese. In it he directed that the following Sunday, August 7, be observed as Diocesan College Day. Rohlman noted that most of the priests of the diocese, and a "number . . . but all too few" of the laymen of the diocese had attended the college. He said that he hoped to find in St. Ambrose his "most effective and powerful aid in doing the work Divine Providence" had called him to do. He expected the college to educate all the priests of the diocese and that the "lay alumni of St. Ambrose College be the leaders of a loyal, active, and well-educated body of Catholic laity." To do this required the support of all in the diocese. He reiterated several points from Hauber's February letter and urged the people to send in the names of prospective students.[18]

Four hundred and eighteen future priests and lay leaders entered St. Ambrose in the fall of 1927, 164 in the college and 254 in the academy, each on a separate day. The separation of the college and academy that had begun years before was proceeding. There had been separate athletic programs for over ten years. Beginning with the catalogue of 1921-1922, the college faculty and courses were listed separately from the academy faculty and courses. In May 1928, the college and the academy published separate catalogues. The college students had organized a student council a few years before, and in 1925, the academy students had formed one also. In May 1925, the two schools had separate graduations. Since the founding of St. Ambrose, the president of the college had also been the principal of the academy; in the fall of 1929, the administrations of the two were separated when the Reverend Ambrose Burke became the first principal of St. Ambrose Academy. That year the separation continued when room became available in Ambrose Hall to create a dining room for the academy students. Now college students and academy students each had their own refectory.[19]

Another institutional change that was less obvious to the students occurred when the size of the Board of Trustees was reduced. At the beginning of Hannon's presidency, the size of the board had been increased to include the diocesan deans, other priests, and five prominent Catholic businessmen. There is no indication, however, that this board ever exercised any authority, or even ever met. Important decisions about St. Ambrose continued to be made by the bishop's council. Without explanation in 1927, the laymen and diocesan priests were dropped from the board, which returned to its original three members: the bishop, the vicar general of the diocese, and the president of the college.

Hauber and the faculty had a more serious task that fall. They had to respond to the concerns expressed by the North Central examiners the previous spring about teaching effectiveness. At the first meeting of the faculty in the fall of 1927, Father Patrick J. O'Reilly, the vice president, was

A football game in the late 1920s played on the new field built in 1926. Lee Lohman Arena is now located in the area of the houses in the background of the photograph.

delegated to contact the education department at the University of Iowa to learn what other schools were doing to improve their teaching. Through the fall and winter months, the faculty held seminars to study teaching techniques. Although Hauber later called these seminars "indifferent," they were apparently effective enough that at its meeting in June 1928, the North Central Association continued the membership of St. Ambrose and did not require any further re-visitations.[20]

Homecoming celebrations began that fall with a pep rally and band concert on Thursday evening. Since it was the day before Armistice Day, the music and rally had a patriotic theme. But there was still time for coach Cotton to speak and the cheerleaders to rally the students behind the team for Friday's game against the Notre Dame reserves. Although the Saints lost 18-0 against the Fighting Irish, spirits were still high as 300 alumni gathered for a banquet at the Outing Club. The speakers reflected the growing importance of the newly-accredited St. Ambrose and the presence of a new bishop who intended to play a larger role in the life of the college. Frank D. Throop, publisher of the *Davenport Democrat*, called St. Ambrose a "power of good in the community," and he said it deserved the support of all alum-

ni. The bishop said that the alumni were a "go-between of the school and the outside world," and he reminded them that no school could "progress unless it [had] a vigorous, hearty alumni supporting it." He praised the faculty and promised "great things" for the future of St. Ambrose.[21] For the students the first great thing of the future was that Saturday classes the next day were cancelled.

The bishop's interest in Catholic higher education extended to opportunities for Catholic girls. He wanted a place for girls that would give them the opportunity for a college education equal to that for boys at St. Ambrose. The Sisters of Humility from Ottumwa contacted the bishop in the late winter of 1928 to say they wanted to move their motherhouse and their junior college from Ottumwa to Davenport. Rohlman told them he saw no problem in moving the motherhouse, but that he would not give them a "definite answer" about the junior college. On April 17, Rohlman wrote Mother Mary Isabella, the superior-general of the Sisters of Charity of the Blessed Virgin Mary (BVM) in Dubuque, who had operated the Immaculate Conception Academy (ICA) since 1859. Based on their long record of service to education in Davenport, the bishop said that he

A Great and Lasting Beginning

Lewis Hall on April 26, 1929. View looking northeast toward the current location of Christ the King Chapel, the Rogalski Center, and Lee Lohman Arena.

thought that the BVMs "should have the first chance" to operate a junior college for girls.[22]

In a hastily called meeting, the sisters considered the bishop's request. Within the order there was reluctance to begin the junior college. They were already committing significant resources to build their new Mundelein College in Chicago. Nevertheless, they did not think they could easily turn down Rohlman's request so they reluctantly agreed to open the junior college in 1929. But the Sisters of Humility had said they would open a school in September 1928, so Rohlman pressed the BVMs to open their school then. Once again, with reluctance they acceded to the bishop's wishes.[23]

Rohlman wasted no time in announcing to the newspapers that the junior college would open in September. A story on May 14 told of the proposed college and outlined some of the courses that would be available. The new school was intended for those who had been already taking extension courses from St. Ambrose, but also for the "young women of the tri-cities who desire higher education" but wanted to stay at home.[24]

The new school did not yet have a name, but the newspaper said there had been suggestions that it be called Loras, in honor of Iowa's first bishop. No school had yet been named for him, and it would be an acknowledgment of Bishop Loras' role in bringing the first BVMs to Iowa in 1842. The bishop said that the "christening" of the school was important, and he

noted that the order had just renamed Mt. St. Joseph's College in Dubuque after Mother Mary Francis Clarke, the founder of the order. Rohlman noted that in "these unfortunate days when our Catholic girls are at a disadvantage in the educational field," he said he believed it was "best to have a name" for the junior college that would "not arouse, prima facie, the prejudice of those who are so prone to discriminate," by naming it for a man.[25] However, the order selected the unfortunate name Terelmar, a combination of parts of the names of the founders of the ICA.

With the announcement made, the sisters and Hauber negotiated an agreement to govern the school. Terelmar would become the "women's unit of St. Ambrose," and the faculty, students, and courses of the junior college would be the faculty, students, and courses of St. Ambrose. St. Ambrose would provide most of the faculty, but the sisters had complete control over the finances of the school. An Administrative Board was established to govern the institution consisting of the bishop, the president, vice president, and registrar of St. Ambrose, the mother-general and provincial superior of the Sisters of Charity, and the president and dean of Terelmar.[26] The classes were taught at the ICA, but the St. Ambrose library and to "a limited degree," laboratories were available to the students. Students received credits from St. Ambrose.

The enrollment the first year was small, about twenty freshman students. The sisters at the ICA viewed the junior college as an "unwelcome step-child" taking resources away from the operation of the academy. The expenses had been considerable to the order, some classrooms had been remodeled and a house was purchased north of the ICA campus as a residence hall for the junior college girls. The second year the name was changed to Aquinas Junior College but that did not help enrollment. At the end of that year, the sisters asked the bishop for permission to close the school which he "reluctantly granted."[27]

St. Ambrose took another step in providing education to a broader constituency when it began to offer night and Saturday classes in the fall of 1929. Those classes were intended for school teachers working for a degree and certification, business and professional men "desiring information or skill" in some area, and "adults anxious to complete their education." Over the years courses included accounting, botany, chemistry, economics, education, English, French, history, Latin, mathematics, psychology, philosophy, religion, sociology, and Spanish. Tuition was $5 per semester hour, and unlike the correspondence and extension courses, those were resident courses requiring attendance on campus. The first year one hundred students registered for the classes. Most of the courses were taught by St. Ambrose faculty members, but occasionally a professor would come from the University of Iowa to teach a specialized course.[28]

Through the spring of 1928, the bishop also carried on a correspondence with Frank Lewis. They discussed the purchase of property on which to build the science building. The original idea was to locate the building on the corner of Gaines and Locust Streets. That property was too expensive, so instead the decision was made to locate the building northeast of Davis Hall on property that had been purchased earlier. He also told Lewis that he would begin a fund raising campaign to pay outstanding pledges to the Endowment Fund and to raise money to build the science hall. He said he would ask the priests to match Lewis' $60,000 gift.[29]

That fall Bishop Rohlman formalized the education of seminarians when he created the Ecclesiastical department for third and fourth year students who were studying for the priesthood and appointed the Reverend Leo Kerrigan as the dean. The formal name was the Ecclesiastical department, but most referred to it as the Church department, which gave its members the long-time nickname, the "churchies." The churchies were housed in Ambrose Hall where they could find the "seclusion and quiet so necessary for young men preparing for this sacred calling." They followed a daily schedule of religious exercises, conferences, and devotions. There was a recreation room with Catholic books and magazines.[30] With the creation of the Ecclesiastical department, the Manning Club was revived with Kerrigan as the director. In time, the Manning Club became an all-purpose organization for the activities of the churchies.

When the new school year began, the churchies joined the other members of the campus community at the groundbreaking for the new science hall. This would be the second building, Davis Hall being the first, of the "Greater St. Ambrose College."[31] Work continued through the winter and by spring the superstructure was in place and ready for the cornerstone ceremony on April 28, 1929. The cornerstone contained the names of Frank Lewis, the original donor whose $60,000 gift had started the project, and

136 priest donors who had pledged a total of $122,800 to the building.[32] Davenport banker and Chamber of Commerce president Louis G. Bein spoke for the city. He congratulated St. Ambrose for the building and told his listeners that the future depended on the education of the younger generation and that St. Ambrose was doing "beneficial work" in that field. Father Hannon was the principal speaker and he recalled the words spoken at the laying of the cornerstone of Ambrose Hall forty-four years earlier. On that occasion, the late Father James P. Ryan spoke of the "little seed" they were planting which would "grow and spread until its influence" was felt throughout the region. Hannon said with the new building that "wish and prayer" had come true. The major portion of his speech, however, concerned the relationship of science and religion that had been so controversial throughout the decade. Hannon said that the "deeper we go into science the closer we come to God," and that Lewis Hall would stand as a "silent protest against the teaching of those who say that religion and science are in conflict."[33]

Once more the campus community became sidewalk superintendents as they watched Lewis Hall take shape over the next year. At the same time the routine of campus life continued. Homecoming that fall, with its bonfire of brooms and crates, was celebrated in the context of the financial crisis that would soon lead to the Great Depression. At their meetings the faculty discussed student absences, problems of discipline in the dormitories with the Board of Discipline requesting that the professors on the floors "cooperate in maintaining quiet and order by sending any disorderly student to report to the Dean," and requests from some faculty members that the president speak to the students about studying more. The president asked that there be special meetings of the faculty to discuss "problems of education," which led to a discussion of the "standards and policies in maintaining scholarship." The minutes for the meeting of April 2, 1930, merely noted that "since attendance was light and [there were] no important matters to discuss, the meeting was adjourned early."[34]

With all the changes on campus, one thing had not changed, the students still had a sense of humor:

Professor: Do you know who I am?
Student: No, but if you remember your address, I'll take you home.

Dave: Why are you scratching your head?
Joe: Because I am the only one who knows where it itches.

Bill: What holds a balloon up?
Gus: Hot air.
Bill: What holds you down?

Serious Senior: If those freshies don't stop that infernal racket, they'll drive me out of my mind.
Second Senior: That's not a drive, that's a putt.

As a student at the time said, "It is hard to laugh at the jokes of the age, but the age of the jokes should be worth something."[35]

A Great and Lasting Beginning

Less funny for the students were the rules under which they lived. In 1927, a number of rules that had been part of the General Regulations since 1885 were dropped: discussion of religion, politics, and nationality could now take place; the rule about liquor, tobacco, and firearms was taken out, although apparently smoking was not permitted in the classrooms and corridors; boarders and day students could now talk with one another; and "eatables" could now be sent to the students. The smoking rule was difficult to enforce. At the first faculty meeting of 1927, Hauber asked the faculty not to smoke in the classrooms or corridors since doing so made it harder to enforce the smoking regulations on the students.[36]

Prior to 1926 the rules were enforced by the entire faculty, but that year they delegated the authority to the Faculty Committee on Discipline which would report its actions to the entire faculty. In 1927 Hauber appointed Father Thomas C. Donohoe, professor of philosophy and psychology, to be dean of discipline and chairman of the Board of Discipline. Each year the board discussed the residence hall rules. In January 1929, they adopted rules that included lights out at 10:30, silence at all times in the halls and stairs, smoking permitted only in the students' rooms or in the smoking room, no room visits during study periods, and the day students should not visit the private rooms.[37]

Bishop
Henry P. Rohlman.

Apparently, however, Bishop Rohlman was not satisfied with discipline. On May 10, 1929, he removed Father Donohoe as dean of discipline and appointed Father Martin Cone in his place. Donohoe protested that this was a violation of the agreement he had made with the president about the Board of Discipline when he was appointed as dean. And he said that he had not been consulted about his removal by either the president or the bishop. The bishop tried to reassure Donohoe that he had not intended to "humiliate" him or express displeasure with the conduct of discipline on campus. Nevertheless, Donohoe was humiliated and angry, and he asked the bishop to at least be given an opportunity to resign, an offer the bishop refused.[38]

The same day Donohoe received his letter from the bishop, Rohlman sent a long letter to Hauber and the faculty with recommendations for the 1929-1930 academic year. Rohlman encouraged the faculty to meet at least once a month and to keep him informed of their discussions. He said that the president or vice president had the "privilege" to attend the meetings of all faculty committees and he directed the chairmen of the committees to inform the president of a proposed meeting. All "matters pertaining to the general welfare of the house" must have the approval of the president.

Next the bishop discussed the Board of Studies. He appointed a new board for the college and the academy and he directed them to meet once a month. They were to decide on the textbooks to be used. He noted that

there were $2,000 worth of books in the bookstore and he asked the Board of Studies to decide which could be used in class and therefore sold, and to "destroy those that are obsolete."

The bishop also addressed religious exercises. In addition to what was already in practice, he asked that the students be required to: attend morning and evening prayers, attend daily Mass, receive the sacraments monthly, and listen to the reading of a few verses of the New Testament, or the *Imitation of Christ* before lunch and dinner.

Most of the letter from the bishop concerned the Board of Discipline. He appointed a new board with Cone as the chair and Fathers Donohoe and Edward O'Connor as members and made it clear that the rules and the penalties for nonobservance were to be "determined" by this board. He directed the board to draw up new rules, publish them, and send a copy to the parents of all students. The bishop wanted them to pay particular attention to the granting of permission to leave campus in the evening. He suggested that class standing, student conduct, and the wishes of their parents might be taken into consideration in formulating this rule. He thought that the current rule of dismissal for one violation of this rule was too stringent, and he suggested they develop a "graduated scale of punishment." The Board of Discipline was to meet twice a month and keep minutes. Because the dean would have more responsibility than the faculty priests, the bishop directed that his salary be raised to $1,000. In closing he thanked the faculty for the "excellent work . . . and the good will" they had shown. He urged that he and they "work together, one heart and one soul, for the development of that institution which Divine Providence [had] entrusted" to their care.[39]

For those who might have wanted more involvement in the affairs of the college by Bishops Cosgrove and Davis, this was involvement by the bishop at a high level. There is no record of what the bishop's objections were to the current policies that led him to such radical action. There was no precedent for the bishop to appoint the members of faculty committees, and it seemed to be a return to the style of governance prevalent among nineteenth-century Catholic colleges. Still his involvement was limited to only two committees: the Board of Discipline and the Board of Studies; other committees, like the Library Committee and the Athletic Committee, were not touched, even though they were responsible for the expenditure of a large portion of the budget. In the end, Hauber and the faculty were left to struggle with the bishop's suggestions about the rules and at least in some cases, to try to moderate his views.

The Board of Discipline met in late May to draw up the new rules the bishop had asked for in his letter. Those new rules covered the areas of study and quiet hours, smoking, off-campus permissions, attendance at dances, and reporting of classroom absences. The board decided against another recommendation from the bishop that daily Mass attendance be made mandatory. The dean was directed to present those rules to the bishop for his approval.[40]

The bishop was only partially satisfied because in September, Hauber asked Cone to call the board together to consider further directives from the bishop. Specifically, the bishop asked the Board of Discipline to take action on three matters: compulsory attendance at daily Mass, night prayers in common by all students, and strict regulations concerning permission to leave campus at night. He also asked for recommendations on two other matters: a policy about radios in students' rooms and the hours for opening the gymnasium and swimming pool. Hauber appeared briefly at the meeting, presented the bishop's agenda, and left, but not before he went on record as opposed to compulsory daily Mass attendance.[41]

The board discussed the issues but the members were uncertain about what the bishop wanted, so they adjourned, went to the bishop's house, and reconvened their meeting with the bishop present. Here they agreed that the current permission to leave campus at night would stand; they said that students could have radios, but not with loud speakers and they could not put up an aerial without permission; and the swimming pool hours would be unchanged. However, they continued to disagree on the matter of religious practice. The board reaffirmed its May decision not to require attendance at daily Mass, saying that "full attendance could be effected by education and persuasion." But the bishop insisted on compulsory attendance at Mass, as well as compulsory night prayers.[42]

It seems clear that the bishop thought there was not enough central control at the college. The prodding of Bishop Davis by the faculty a few years before may have given them a sense of independence of action that Bishop Rohlman thought was inappropriate. It may also have been that Hauber's well-known reluctance to be president and his decision to continue to teach while president led him to pay less attention to administrative matters than the bishop thought was necessary. Whatever the reason, the message was clear that this bishop would be watching the actions of the college community more closely than had been the custom in the past. The struggle between the bishop and the faculty did not end with the formation of new rules in 1929.

The following March, Hauber spoke at a meeting of Catholic scientists in Des Moines. He voiced the opinion that it was unfortunate that professors who had been trained for specialized work, like science, were burdened with administrative work. When Bishop Rohlman heard that, he wrote Hauber about it. The bishop reminded him that he knew that Hauber had taken the presidency out of obedience to the bishop and that he had "inti-

Rev. Martin Cone.

mated" more than once that he wanted to "give up the presidency," and return to teaching biology full-time. With the opening of Lewis Hall, Rohlman said that the timing for such a move would be "opportune," and the bishop made it clear he would not "stand in" Hauber's way.[43]

Hauber responded that his remarks in Des Moines should not be taken as "indicating dissatisfaction with my present position or criticism of my bishop." Instead he said he was commenting that Catholics were not doing their share of "first hand work in science," and that because of his administrative duties, he was an example of that. He admitted that he had not done a good job as president in the previous year, and nothing would make him happier if the bishop thought someone else would do a better job. Hauber said that he understood that a college president, "especially under the circumstances that obtain at St. Ambrose now, should be in touch with every department, should know thoroughly what is going on, and should be actively interested in all phases of College life. He should have leisure to study all problems as they come up, and should have the right of initiative and of veto, at his discretion. He should be familiar with the virtues and faults of faculty members, and so on. There is at present no coordination of the several departments of college activities, a situation that will get worse unless the president's office is made a central clearing station for everyone. To do this requires time, and I feel that if I must continue in the president's chair, I shall have to curtail radically my teaching program." Hauber made it clear to the bishop that while he would like to be relieved of the presidency, the larger issue was the welfare of St. Ambrose, and if the bishop thought Hauber should continue, he would do so.[44]

In fact Hauber had given the bishop the opening he wanted. The activities of the year before had made it clear that the bishop was not happy with the situation at St. Ambrose. Moreover, Hauber's job description of a president emphasized the kind of administrative skills Hauber had consistently admitted he did not have; years later he said, "I got tired of going to all those tea-parties."[45] At the same he time his comment about the president's office being a "central clearing station" was an implied criticism of the bishop's actions the year before in appointing committees and their chairs.

Rohlman responded with effusive praise for Hauber's letter where the "spirit of every line is that of a true and noble minded priest who effaces his own self in favor of his holy calling." Rohlman said he had given the matter thought and prayers, and that he had met with the diocesan consultors (a successor group to the bishop's council), and that all agreed that "your services would be of greatest value to St. Ambrose College in the Science Department; in fact they seem to me to be almost indispensable." With the completion of Lewis Hall, science was "launching out on a new era," and since Hauber had been the "inspiration" for the science hall from the

A Great and Lasting Beginning

Four presidents were present for the dedication of Lewis Hall: Rev. Martin Cone, the incoming president; Rev. Msgr. A. J. Schulte, first president; Rev. Msgr. W. P. Shannahan, third president; Rev. U. A. Hauber, incumbent. Rev. J. T. A. Flannagan, the second president, had died a few years before and the Rev. W. L. Hannon was ill and did not attend.

beginning, the bishop said his withdrawal from it would be an "irreparable loss." The bishop told Hauber he had called sixteen senior faculty members individually to his house to ask them the hypothetical question, "If he relieved Hauber of his duties who should replace him?" The bishop said that without exception they all recommended Cone.[46]

That was what the bishop wanted to hear. He had already indicated his confidence in Cone when he had appointed him to chair the Board of Discipline. Now he wrote him on April 9 to appoint him president of St. Ambrose College. He said that Hauber would remain in office through the end of the academic year, but on all matters relating to the following year, Cone had immediate authority. The bishop also told Cone that the responsibilities of the president's office were "so many and varied" that he had to give up teaching so that he could give all his time to "coordinating and directing all the departments and activities of the institution." The *Messenger* said that Cone was a "prudent, capable executive and an organizer of vision and energy."[47]

Cone wasted no time in taking control of the institution. At the request of the bishop, he called a joint meeting of the academy and college faculties for June 12. With the bishop present, Cone presented his administrative program. He warned against too much "decentralization in matters of government," rather that there must be a "balance between decentralization and centralization of powers." He outlined a reorganization of the administration with a committee representing each administrative department. Each committee would have "complete charge in routine affairs," but any policy change would need the approval of the president's office, and presumably, the bishop. He urged them to conduct their affairs with "tolerance, arbitration and friendly discussion of differences, appreciation of our progress, and the discussion of problems of common interest." Following discussion of some routine matters, the bishop made some laudatory

remarks about the schools.[48] With the appointment of Cone, the bishop now had a president with known administrative skills, and one who would gladly devote full-time to the office.

Work progressed rapidly on Lewis Hall through the fall of 1929 and it was completed by early winter. Lewis Hall had fourteen classrooms, three laboratories for chemistry, and one each for biology, geology, and physics. It opened for classes with the beginning of the second semester on February 3, 1930. The science laboratories that had been on the first floor of Davis Hall were moved to Lewis and that space was converted to more student rooms.[49] As the students and faculty settled into the new facility, plans were made for a formal dedication ceremony on May 14.

The archbishop of Dubuque and the bishops of Des Moines and Rockford joined Bishop Rohlman, former presidents Schulte and Shannahan, the outgoing and incoming presidents, the St. Ambrose faculty, some members of the Columbia College (Loras) faculty, and the academy and college students for the dedication. Following the dedication of the building, there was a long, solemn procession to LeClaire Gymnasium for Mass.

Monsignor William Shannahan (he had been created a Monsignor in 1927), the third president, preached the sermon at the Mass. Taking as his text Romans 1:20, "The invisible things of God, from the creation of the world, are clearly seen," Shannahan said it was appropriate to dedicate a science hall where the physical world could be studied and would lead to the invisible things, "the underlying causes." This was especially important since the main area of attack on religion in recent years was in the field of the natural sciences. Shannahan said that a conflict between religion and science was not possible because "truth cannot conflict with truth . . . each

Fr. Hauber with his students in the new Lewis Hall biology laboratory.

has its own proper sphere." Lewis Hall represented "dedication to truth, dedication to the high purpose of imparting the truths of nature to others, dedication to a search after truth that will be thorough and fearless." He singled out Hauber as an exponent of this dedication, and said there needed to be a wider distribution of his pamphlet on religion and evolution.

He also praised the new president, whose work in the social sciences was second in importance only to the field of biology. Under Cone's leadership, St. Ambrose would "rise to higher and higher levels of achievement." Hauber and Cone, both with Doctor of Philosophy Degrees from the University of Iowa, were widely recognized for their "worth as teachers and scholars."

Shannahan also said that Lewis Hall represented a "notable contribution" toward fulfilling the ideal of Catholic education for all young people. Although complete fulfillment was still in the future, he said he looked for the day when Catholic college and university education was within the reach of all young men and women, and none would have a "valid excuse" for "neglecting its opportunities." Shannahan himself was a grandson of immigrants who was given the advantage of a Catholic education by the efforts of the pioneering generation. St. Ambrose College was a product of their work, and now it must dedicate itself to giving to the church in America, the "highest type of Catholic laymen" who would lead lives of "right living and noble purpose." Lewis Hall was an "important means and factor" toward that end. The day concluded with a banquet with toasts and speeches honoring the generosity of the donor, Frank Lewis, and the clergy who had made the building possible.[50]

In Hauber's 1927 letter to the diocese, his long-term priorities had included a new science building, a new library, and a separate chapel. The library was now in the south-half of the Davis Hall basement, and it seemed to be adequate for the moment. The Ambrose Hall chapel was still in use, and the chapel in the basement of Davis Hall was completed and could seat about 250 worshipers. But there was a need for a place where the entire campus community could worship together.

In 1931, Bishop Rohlman saw the possibility of building a chapel when he was promised $200,000 by Mrs. Henry Kahl in memory of her recently deceased husband, who had been a member of the Board of Trustees of the college. But when she died shortly thereafter, Rohlman told Frank Lewis that, unfortunately, she had not put those intentions in her will. Nevertheless, the bishop hoped that her children would honor her commitment. They did not, and any plans Rohlman had to add buildings to the college were stalled because of the Depression.[51]

Bishop Rohlman and the faculty had discussed the frequency of Mass attendance by the students. In 1931, the Reverend Edward Seidel, who taught religion that year, discussed how the community should celebrate Mass. Early in the century Pope Pius X had published a number of directives about the use of Gregorian Chant, frequent Communion, earlier First Communion, and the relaxation of fasting for the infirm. This had given rise to the beginnings of the liturgical renewal movement, first in Europe,

A Great and Lasting Beginning

The band in 1929 with its new uniforms and their leader, Bernard Schultz, on the right.

and in the 1920s among Benedictine monks led by Virgil Michel at St. John's Abbey in Collegeville, Minnesota. The goal of this movement was greater participation in the Mass by the people.

When Seidel came to St. Ambrose in the fall of 1931, he began congregational Gregorian Chant, a practice he had begun in the parishes he had served in the years before he came to the college. He also began a series of articles in the *Ambrosian News* to provide a background so the students could "assist with more intelligence and devotion" at Mass. Citing Pius X, Seidel said the best way to participate was to use the missal and recite the prayers with the priest at the altar, and he devoted one article to explain the use of the missal. People at Mass should not be "passive spectators" but because each one was part of the Mystical Body of Christ, each should be an "active participator," united to each other and the Last Supper and the sacrifice of Christ on the cross. Reflecting on those years, Paul V. Murray, a 1933 graduate, said that Seidel had led a "bit of [a] 'liturgical revolution'. . . He was ahead of his times and we never caught up."[52] Seidel was at St. Ambrose for only one year, but he laid the groundwork for others who would continue liturgical reforms at St. Ambrose in the years ahead.

Meanwhile, the faculty continued to discuss the routine business that made up most of their work. The president asked them to act as advisors to small groups of freshmen and urged that they take an "active interest" in their advisees. The faculty also discussed the advisability of some systemat-

ic form of advising for all students.[53]

The Board of Discipline discussed a pressing issue on campus: student dissatisfaction with the meals. The members noted that the complaints were "quite general" among all the students, and that the students were discussing "organized action." The members of the board felt the student complaints were "well founded," and decided that since such complaints affect discipline, the committee should take the matter to the president for action.[54]

The continuation of boarding facilities for academy students was another issue to come before the faculty. When it was first discussed in June 1930, academy principal Burke urged "cautious consideration" before abandoning the boarding program. The next spring, however, the decision was made to no longer accept boarding students in the academy, and those students already at St. Ambrose would have to find other accommodations. The space in the east wing of Ambrose Hall that had housed the academy boarders was turned over to the seminary, which was quickly filled by the forty-four seminarians at St. Ambrose in 1931.[55]

The students had a new outlet for expressing their ideas when the first issue of the student newspaper, the *Ambrosian News*, appeared on October 9, 1931. For ten years the quarterly the *Ambrosian*, had contained the literary efforts of the students but also reported campus news and alumni activities. Now the newspaper would publish the campus news, and the *Ambrosian* would concentrate on fiction and poetry.

Not surprisingly, a good deal of the space in the new newspaper was devoted to sports activities on campus. Football, basketball, and track remained the three intercollegiate sports, but football and basketball received the most attention. Tennis had been a popular intramural sport and the courts northeast of Davis Hall were usually busy. There had been talk about making it an intercollegiate sport, but that became impossible when Lewis Hall was built in the place the tennis courts had been, and in 1930 there was "agitation" on campus for new tennis courts.[56]

Since 1923, football, basketball, and track had been coached by Fod Cotton. In early 1931, he announced that he would resign in June to take a position as line coach at the Catholic University of America. Cotton was well-liked at St. Ambrose, and the newspaper claimed that under his leadership, the school had risen to be "one of the most feared colleges" in the conference, but his record was mixed.[57] His eight football teams had a record of 27-30-6. His record in basketball was better, 73-46, and his 1928 team won the Conference championship. His track teams had individuals who placed in meets, but the teams had a mediocre record at best. Still one student wrote that Cotton "left behind him a record of victory, character-building, and sportsmanship that no one in the state may hope to equal for a long time to come."[58]

The new football and basketball coach was Wilfred "Dukes" Duford. A 1924 graduate of Marquette University where he was a two-sport star, Duford played professional basketball for the Beloit Wisconsin Fairies and football for the Green Bay Packers. Since 1929, Duford had been the head coach at St. Mary's College in Kansas.[59] The Duford era began with a win in the first football game of the 1931 season, played in the new Municipal Stadium on the riverfront. It was also the first night game in St. Ambrose history. Coming into the homecoming game on November 20 against William Penn College, the team had a 7-1 record.

The students prepared for the returning alumni by erecting a gate at the entrance to campus to welcome them. Signs and streamers bedecked Lewis, Davis, and Ambrose Halls. Nedde Catich and Nick Francisco, both students from Mooseheart, a home west of Chicago for children whose parents were unable to care for them, painted the statue of St. Ambrose green to express the Irish spirit of the school. Floodlights were brought in to illuminate the campus. All was ready for the nearly 3,000 fans who came to campus for the bonfire and pep rally the night before the big game. The crowd was so large that the streets were jammed with cars for several blocks in each direction. The bishop, the president of the college, the vice president of the Alumni Association, and several students spoke to the crowd. But the largest ovation went to Dukes, as everyone now knew him.[60]

The game was played in a constant rain; still 2,500 fans, including the Northwestern University football team which was on its way to play the University of Iowa the next day, watched St. Ambrose win 7-6.[61] The team, which had won two and lost seven in the last year under Cotton, went to a 9-1 season with Duford, scoring 187 points and allowing their opponents only forty-one points, including five games when the opponents were held scoreless. St. Ambrose quarterback Bob Klenck was the all-conference quarterback.

Duford's first basketball team was also successful with a 17-2 record. The most exciting game was against Central College when St. Ambrose broke Central's thirty-five game winning streak, the longest in conference history. The Saint's center, Kenny Austin, was the conference scoring leader and the

center on the all-conference team.

The band played a prominent part of the pep rallies and ball games. Through the later 1920s and into the 1930s, there were several musical groups on campus, including a chapel choir, an orchestra, glee club, and a band. Each of these groups had a series of leaders during these years. The band that played wearing its new uniforms at homecoming of 1929 was led by Bernard Schultz. Born in Buffalo, New York, in 1898, in 1923-1924 Schultz had played trumpet and alto sax in an orchestra on board the ocean liner, *SS Leviathon*, one of the many orchestras in the Paul Whiteman organization. Later he led his own Crescent Orchestra which played and recorded in Chicago. While at St. Ambrose, Schultz and lyricist Frank Sterck composed the "Victory March."

The orchestra, chapel choir, and a new glee club were conducted by Professor Edward Imbus, a new member of the faculty. Imbus stayed only one year and was replaced by Orville Foster who had graduated from St. Ambrose the year before. The band that played for the first Duford teams was led by Nedde Catich.

Catich was born in Montana but, orphaned at age eleven, he was sent to Mooseheart, where he played in the band. Following graduation from high school in 1924, Catich became a sign painter in Chicago, studied at the Art Institute, and played in a jazz band in local clubs. He brought those skills to St. Ambrose where he led the band to help pay his tuition. He led the marching band, and also played the trumpet. Sebastian Menke, then a member of the football team, recalled that those "who played football to his marching band were convinced that his trumpet never gave out an uncertain call for battle."[62]

In addition to the marching band, Catich started a jazz orchestra called the "Ambie Joy Boys," and then later organized the "Royal Ambrosians," which had saxophones, trombone, trumpet, tuba, violins, drums, banjo, and piano, along with vocalist Verdell Williams. The Royal Ambrosians played for "light entertainments," on campus and represented the school when a "lighter vein of music" was asked for outside the college. Catich played trumpet in the Royal Ambrosians, and among the other players was Pasquale Ferrara, another student from Mooseheart, who played the tuba.[63]

There continued to be a greater demand for educational opportunities by school teachers and others who could not take advantage of the traditional day-time academic schedule, so in 1932, St. Ambrose began summer sessions. At least 125 sisters and a number of lay students enrolled in the first summer classes. Tuition was $30 and room and board were available for $40 for the six-week session. Hauber taught two biology classes, and Nedde Catich, who had just finished his freshman year, taught drawing. Other classes included English, education, French, history, mathematics, philosophy, psychology, religion, and sociology. Over the years the number of classes increased and included Gregorian Chant for the seminarians who became regular summer school attendees.

Religious sisters, laywomen, and men continued to attend St. Ambrose by extension courses or at night or Saturday classes. Now in addition to school teachers, nursing students from St. Anthony's Hospital in Rock

Island and Mercy Hospital in Davenport began to attend night classes. In the fall of 1931, nearly 150 students enrolled in night classes at St. Ambrose.[64] A few sisters had already graduated and in July 1933, Sophia Hapke, Vera Johnson Carleton, Katherine Meyers, and Corina Scott became the first laywomen to receive degrees from St. Ambrose.

In 1931 the Diocese of Davenport marked its fiftieth anniversary, and the next year St. Ambrose celebrated its fiftieth anniversary. The growth of the institution over those fifty years was remarkable. From two borrowed rooms in the cathedral grade school, the college now occupied buildings valued at over one million dollars. Thirty-three students entered the first day; in 1931-32, there were 640 students, 218 in the academy, 280 in the college, and 142 in the extension and night courses. Nearly all of the 1882 students were Catholic; in 1933, 65 percent were Catholic.[65] The 1882 curriculum was the classics and elementary commercial courses; now students could receive Bachelor of Arts and Bachelor of Science Degrees in many fields. From a faculty of one priest and one layman and total salaries of $568, the 1932 faculty consisted of twenty-seven priests, four full-time lay professors, two coaches, and three student assistants who were paid salaries of $44,000. Expenses that first year totaled $1,137; in 1931, the total expenses were $116,500.[66]

Bishop Rohlman published a letter to celebrate both anniversaries. Rohlman acknowledged the importance of St. Ambrose for the diocese for the lay leaders and the priests who had been educated there. He noted the generosity of the people, mentioning Frank Lewis specifically, who built the buildings and made the work of the college possible. To continue that work, more buildings would be needed, and he said he knew he could count on their continuing generosity.

Most of the bishop's letter concerned Bishop McMullen. He wrote about his work in Chicago and his work in the new diocese. Rohlman said, "That which particularly stamps Bishop McMullen as a man of discernment and of wide vision was his founding, shortly after his arrival in Davenport, of St. Ambrose College." With a large diocese, a handful of priests, and limited resources, the needs of his people made McMullen, "dare a seminary and a college, 'a garden enclosed,' wherein not only might grow the tree of knowledge but also flow the fountains of everlasting waters; wherein youths might aspire to the highest office possible to mortals, and others might learn to co-ordinate properly the secular and the sacred sciences. An educated priesthood and an educated laity, this was the bishop's paramount aim in the commencing of St. Ambrose. The College stands today [as] the greatest monument to Davenport's great first Bishop."[67]

Rohlman concluded his letter saying that because the laity of the diocese had supported St. Ambrose in "loyalty and self-sacrifice," the institution "believes that its future is bright, stretching out before it with promise." It was a rallying cry for continued support of the college uttered in the midst of the Great Depression. Rohlman must have known that the future of the college was no less certain than it was the day fifty years before when the doors opened to thirty-three boys.

A lack of funds has certainly kept many high school graduates from entering college and has also caused many upperclassmen to drop out. Yet the dearth of employment has opened the eyes of many to the advantages of a college education, and sent them to enroll at the higher institutions in hopes of being in position to get better jobs when they graduate . . . The young people in school now . . . have a seriousness of purpose that was not to be found on our campuses five or so years ago . . . The collegiate 'joy-boy' has practically disappeared from the street corners. Students in college still have a good time, [but]. . . With everyone holding down expenses in this direction and that, it is no disgrace to turn down anything on the score that you are 'broke.' Snobbery, cliques and other manifestations of a 'ritzier than thou' spirit have all melted away into a new fellowship of the poor.

Chapter Eight

Thomas Feeney's editorial appeared in the fall 1932 issue of the *Ambrosian* magazine just before the election where Franklin D. Roosevelt swept Herbert Hoover out of the White House. After four years, the nation was at the lowest point of the Great Depression, and the fellowship of the poor was a very large, nonexclusive group. The Gross National Product had fallen 31 percent since 1929; industrial stocks had lost 80 percent of their value since the crash. Over thirteen million Americans had lost their jobs since 1929, and the current national unemployment rate was nearly 24 percent. Nationally, farm prices had fallen 53 percent since 1929. In Iowa the value of farm land, critical to the mortgages that made up most of the endowment of St. Ambrose, had fallen from a statewide average of $225 an acre in 1920, to $69 an acre in 1932. Nationally, 10,000 banks had failed since 1929 resulting in a loss of $2 billion in deposits. Because of the agricultural depression that had begun in 1921, the bank failures in Iowa were even more startling. There were 1,790 banks in the state in 1921, and by the end of 1932, only 925 of those banks remained; 240 banks closed in 1932 alone. Displaced by the loss of their homes or businesses or farms, hundreds of thousands of Americans became migrants, crisscrossing the country looking for work. And in what some interpreted as a sign, winds blowing down from the Rocky Mountains across the Great Plains made barren by poor farming practices and drought created huge dust storms; black clouds of dust rose up from the land and covered everything, seeping into homes through every crack.

In his editorial, Feeney noted that those conditions had forced colleges to "curtail expenses." Athletic programs, new courses, and programs had been scaled back, and colleges had to call "'time out' in their breathless expansion programs." That was the case at St. Ambrose. Bishop Rohlman was unable to begin a project to build a new chapel because of the Depression, and any other building programs he might have wanted to undertake were abandoned. A notice appeared in the newspaper stating St. Ambrose students would welcome an hour to two of work each day. The extra income would help reduce their college expenses and enable some students to stay in school who might otherwise have to leave. Students found off-campus jobs working at service stations, clerking at drug stores and grocery stores, driving delivery trucks, ushering in theaters, waiting and

bussing tables, anything that could be worked into their academic schedule.[1] They also worked on campus. The most common job was waiting tables in the refectory. One student who worked in the priests' dining room enjoyed getting to know the priests, but he also liked the fact that the waiters could eat what remained after the priests were finished. Another student typed term papers and theses for other students for a "couple extra dollars."[2]

In late January 1933, the bishop sent a letter to the faculty detailing the financial condition of the college. At the end of the first semester, there was still over $7,000 in tuition payments due from students, a figure far greater than usual at that time of the year. It was not likely much of that figure could be paid by the cash-strapped families of students. Income from the endowment was also impacted by the Depression. In 1928, the endowment yielded nearly $30,000; in 1933, that figure had dropped to $3,500. Moreover, the Union Bank which handled most of the St. Ambrose accounts had failed, which tied up all the college deposits, as well as the deposits of supporters of the college.

Those conditions "obliged" the bishop to "consider economies" he had "long resisted." The bishop said that "substantial reductions" were necessary and that effective January 1, all salaries would be reduced. Those making $800 or less would see their salaries reduced by 10 percent. For those salaries over $800, the reduction would be 15 percent. He hoped that no further reductions would be necessary, and given the "gravity of the situation," he hoped they would help in every way possible to keep all expenses to the minimum. He told them he was grateful for the "spirit of harmony and co-operation evidenced by the faculty" and he said there was no reason they all could not "look hopefully into the future."[3]

Other areas of the college operation felt the impact of the bad economic times. In October 1934, the Library Board presented a budget of $2,599, which included a salary of $1,000 for the librarian. There were currently 14,000 volumes in the library, but some departments had not ordered any new books for years and the recent expansion of the curriculum demanded more books. The board wanted at least $800 for the purchase of new books. Monsignor Cone (in 1931 he had been made a Monsignor) responded that he hoped they could appreciate the "difficulty" facing the college. Nearly all of the students were "running accounts" and he could not estimate how

A Great and Lasting Beginning

much of the tuition owed would actually be collected. The previous year had ended with a deficit of nearly $5,000, and he said to go into debt for operating costs was "suicidal." He said the library could have $500 to purchase books in the first semester and another $300 for the second semester, "if warranted." He urged them to look for bargains in lists of marked down books.[4]

If the income from endowment had decreased precipitously and tuition income was incomplete, at least college enrollment increased. In 1929, there had been 207 college students; that increased to 314 in 1932-1933. The number of students coming to St. Ambrose increased in part because local students were unable to go away to school. In August 1933, a *Messenger* editorial noted the increase and said that "during these trying days" many colleges had "suffered a falling off" of enrollment but that St. Ambrose had experienced a "marked influx in the number of students." The editor mentioned the variety of courses and the good faculty as factors in that enrollment increase.[5] Others in the state were also noticing the accomplishment at St. Ambrose. A profile of the college in the *Des Moines Register* said that a "growing student body and a pre-depression budget [made] St. Ambrose . . . unique among Iowa schools in these troublous times." The *Register* article gave the credit to the leadership of Cone.[6]

In spite of the troublous times, Cone was building on the work of his two predecessor presidents to build a greater St. Ambrose. The school was now recognized by the Catholic Educational Association, it was a member of the Association of American Colleges registered by the State Board of Regents of New York, and it was approved by the French Ministry of Education, which made it easier for St. Ambrose graduates to continue their studies at universities in France and Algeria. Following an examination by the Iowa State Board of Educational Examiners, St. Ambrose graduates were eligible for state teaching certificates.

But it was the accreditation by the North Central Association that was the most important. It had been a milestone when it had been achieved in 1927, but Cone now told the faculty they could not rest on that laurel. North Central required that the head of each of the eight academic departments possess a doctorate and St. Ambrose did not yet meet that requirement. So Cone revived the program that had enabled him to receive his degree and began to send two new priest professors away to school each year. Faculty members would be chosen to continue their graduate work based on their seniority, how close they were to finishing a degree, and which departments were without a "properly trained" professor.[7] In the fall of 1934, six priests were away working on doctorates: Raymond Kinnavey was at Catholic University for Latin and Greek; Edward O'Connor was also at Catholic University for philosophy. Ambrose Burke was studying English at Yale. Gerald Lillis was at the University of Iowa working on a degree in chemistry. Albert Goetzman was in Rome working on a doctorate in philosophy, and Joseph Code was in Belgium studying at Louvain. With those new doctorates, and the hiring of laymen and one religious sister with doctorates, the college added nine more professors with terminal degrees over the next few years.

The *Davenport Daily Democrat* noted that with all those professors working on degrees, there were "no better education facilities offered anywhere today than at St. Ambrose." The paper urged that local citizens support its educational facilities just as they support its athletic programs.[8] The

students also noticed a difference. In the October 1934 *Ambrosian News*, published just before homecoming, the editor spoke of the "new St. Ambrose," and the "St. Ambrose of the future." He said the number of students had increased, the athletic schedules were "beginning to sound . . . big time," and the "degrees [were] flying thick and fast among the faculty." He said that the college had "come of age," but, he assured the alumni, it was "still the same college on the hill" they knew, and it was marching on the road they had started, in spite of the "odds of the depression."[9]

Cone also looked to the future of higher education and how St. Ambrose could respond to the challenges presented by the troublous times. Speaking in late 1933, he said that rather than the "doom" of small colleges, the "changing social organization" brought about by the Depression, and the new programs of President Franklin D. Roosevelt's New Deal, would make a "heavy demand upon the genuinely liberal arts college." Traditional-aged college students would need a longer period of education to respond to the new challenges of the period. Cone also predicted that the time might come when working people would retire at age sixty or sixty-five. Those retirees would need adult education to better prepare them for the "enjoyment of their leisure years" and he thought that the liberal arts college was ideally suited to provide that kind of adult education.

St. Ambrose began to accept that challenge when the Reverend Charles Griffith, head of the Social Science department, organized the Social Study Club. Intended for adults who were not in school, the purpose of the club was to discuss the practical problems of the day. At one of its first meetings, fourteen people gathered to discuss old age dependency. Discussions about the problems of families and other current social questions were also scheduled.[10]

The Great Depression was not the only factor in creating the troublous times. World War I had left Europe's political and economic structures in disarray, and liberal democratic leaders were unable to respond effectively to the challenges of the era. Starting with the 1917 Russian Revolution, Europe began to experiment with totalitarian regimes to create order out of chaos. The Italian leader, Benito Mussolini, was rattling his sabers in Africa, and in October 1935, he invaded the independent African country of Ethiopia. In Germany, Adolph Hitler began to look at his neighbors as places for expansion. In Asia, Japan had invaded Manchuria in 1931 and threatened to move south into China. Joseph Stalin had consolidated his power in the new Soviet Union and presented an image of utopian socialism that was attractive to some Americans in the throes of their own economic distress.

Returning home in August 1935, after three years of study in Belgium, Father Joseph Code, the former St. Ambrose librarian, said, "Europe is a volcano. The war threat is more menacing than in 1914. The people are restless and while the man on the street does not want war he expects it within a year. The people have lost confidence in their leaders and are biding their time until they can rise and overthrow the iron hands that now control every action." Code saw the conflict in Ethiopia as the "opening wedge" to another war and he predicted that Germany and Japan would side with Italy in that conflict.[11]

In the United States, the Catholic response to those economic and

St. Ambrose College, 1932.

political upheavals was best represented by the work of Father John A. Ryan who had spoken on the St. Ambrose campus a number of times before World War I. Ryan's understanding of the 1891 encyclical *Rerum Novarum* and the encyclicals that followed it led to his books on distributive justice, a living wage, and his work on the 1919 "Bishop's Program of Social Reconstruction." His work had acclimated the church's traditional theology to the norms of twentieth-century industrial society. At the same time he galvanized "Catholic pressure on the modern state to deal effectively with social problems."[12]

Another response to the challenge presented by the times came from the Sodality which had always advocated prayer and action. In 1925, the Reverend Daniel Lord, SJ, became the national director of the Sodality. Lord found it a "devout and slightly pietistic gathering" that prayed, listened to talks, paid dues, and went home. While the Sodality's purpose was to gather for prayer, it was also "keenly bent in the salvation of souls and intensely alive to the promotion of Catholic truth and defense of the Church."[13] He took what had become a moribund organization and made it a significant force in American Catholic schools, until it became the "most significant movement of American Catholic youth." He understood that the personal piety of Sodalists should lead to "intense Catholic activity," and was a form of "public Catholicism" where students took their faith "out into the world." By 1930, this activity had assumed the name Catholic Action.[14]

If the papal encyclicals, Father John Ryan's work, and the activity of the Sodalists provided the intellectual underpinnings for specialized Catholic Action, the Reverend Joseph Cardijn provided the methodology. Born in Belgium and ordained in 1906, Cardijn taught college for five years and studied working-class conditions in Europe. Concerned that many young workers had abandoned their faith, he urged them to look at life in their workplace and to transform their world by replacing human vision with the vision of God. This developed into his simple methodology of "see, judge, act," which became the operating principle of his groups.[15] Cardijn soon organized the Young Christian Workers (in French, the *Jeunesse Ouvriere Chretienne*, abbreviated as JOC, which gave the groups the popular name of Jocists). Later he formed a similar group for students called the Young Christian Students, or YCS.

Cone had begun to introduce some of these ideas in the courses he developed in the 1920s, and by the middle 1930s, Catholic Action was becoming embedded into the life of St. Ambrose College. An editorial in the *Ambrosian News* of February 7, 1935, discussed the current economic and social problems and said they could not be "shrugged off" by college students. As Catholic college students, it was a "privilege, not just a duty," to apply the teaching of God and the church to the current situation. "There is strong activity against us," it concluded, "it is time for us to unite under a new banner, Catholic Action."[16]

In 1934, the campus paused to remember one of the symbols of its continuity when Joseph Halligan died on April 3 at age seventy-one. After he left St. Ambrose in 1891, Halligan had founded the *Davenport Daily Leader* newspaper, worked for the *Catholic Messenger*, and held the positions of cashier and auditor of the Halligan Coffee Company before he retired in 1912. He was a founder of the Davenport Knights of Columbus and remained active in the local and state KC organizations for the rest of his

A Great and Lasting Beginning

Immaculate Conception Academy.

life. He was a frequent speaker at Catholic events and maintained his interest in the activities of the school he helped to found. His pastor, the Reverend James W. Bulger, preached the funeral sermon. Bulger said that he had been in Halligan's classroom in 1886 and that all the students had "learned to admire his noble Christian manhood." That opinion lasted through the years and Bulger said everyone felt that Halligan was a "real exponent and interpreter of a Christian life."[17] With Halligan's death, only Monsignor A. J. Schulte (he had been made a Monsignor in 1927) and a few of the first thirty-three students remained who remembered that first day.

If Halligan was part of the past, discussions about women on campus were the future. In 1933, a student noted that for several years there had been women in the evening and Saturday classes and he wondered if St. Ambrose could now be considered a coed institution. He answered his own question and said that it was not co-educational since women did not attend the regular day classes. Nevertheless, he concluded that St. Ambrose had tried "to meet the request of local young women, by affording them . . . as large an opportunity for a college education as seemed consistent with its traditional status as a school for boys and young men."[18]

The college had tried to provide educational opportunities for women with the ill-fated junior college experiment a few years before. Cone realized the need for college education for women, and now the larger community had taken up the cause. In the summer of 1933, a petition was circulated in the community asking that St. Ambrose become coed indicating that such a move would have wide-spread support. In response, that fall

semester, additional courses open to women were offered in the late afternoon and evening. At least thirty women enrolled, some as college freshmen intending to work for a degree; others already had some college experience and registered in more advanced courses.[19]

This arrangement was not wholly successful, so in June 1934, Cone convened a meeting to discuss better provisions for female students. Several options were discussed. One was to continue the plan of the previous year. Another was to find accommodations for female students at another location. Still another was to either create a college staffed by sisters from several communities, or to support the establishment of a junior college by a single community of sisters. The discussion soon centered on finding another location and offering a full, day-time curriculum to women.[20]

The next month, Cone announced that St. Ambrose had established a Women's Division of St. Ambrose College.[21] The women who enrolled would be able to pursue a Bachelor's Degree in day classes. As with the junior college six years earlier, all classes except laboratories would be held in space leased from the Immaculate Conception Academy (ICA). Most of the faculty was from St. Ambrose and the college assumed the financial responsibilities. The only additional administrator was Sister Mary Elena Norkett, BVM, who was dean of women.[22]

Twenty-seven girls enrolled in the Women's Division that September. Some of them had been enrolled in the late afternoon and evening courses of the year before, but most were new students. More came in the second semester so that the first year there were thirty-nine students. The academic part of the arrangement went well; other parts of the arrangement took some adjusting, mostly on the part of the men and boys at St. Ambrose.

The first issue of the *Ambrosian News* on October 4 contained a column,

"The Ladies Say," written by Frances Wehman. She talked about other firsts in history and noted that this was "the first time in the history of the college that the fairer sex [had] been able to break out in print." She knew that the column would be "scanned with a keen and critical eye" by the male students. The column was mostly a report on the social activities on campus and rarely strayed into more controversial topics.[23]

One early controversy arose that was discussed when another columnist, Jeanette Datin, objected to a decision by the St. Ambrose student council not to allow the female students to join. Datin said she hoped that the decision would be reversed. There was already a "St. Ambrose Girl's Organization" to promote cooperation among the female students, but they wanted to be part of the college student council where decisions were made about social events on campus.[24]

After six weeks of operation, Cone came to the ICA building to speak to the "girls." He told them that the acceptance of women at St. Ambrose was regarded "entirely as an experiment" to provide an opportunity for local girls who wanted an education but found it financially impossible to go away to school. He asked for their patience while certain "difficulties" were overcome. As for the "misunderstanding" about the student council, he suggested that they form their own student council since they had "no common problems to discuss with the boys." To plan social functions, he suggested that there be a joint meeting of the two councils. That was not what they wanted, but they bowed to reality and the next week elected three women to be their student council.[25]

Cone's comment that the Women's Division was an "experiment" indicated the uncertainty present among the St. Ambrose faculty about the classes. In April 1935, Cone met with the college council consisting of the Reverend Monsignor Martin O'Connell, the vice president; Father Leo Kerrigan, dean of the Ecclesiastical department; the Reverend Edward Butler, registrar; the Reverend Thomas Lew, dean of men; the Reverend Mell Morrin of the English faculty; and Father Hauber. Hauber was credited as being the "postulator" of Terelmar/Aquinas Junior College during his presidency, and now he was the link between St. Ambrose and the BVMs in matters relating to the Women's Division. There were no sisters at the meeting.

Cone opened the meeting by saying that the "problem" of the Women's Division was the "most pressing" issue they faced, namely, should it be continued for another year. The principal problem seemed to be that the enrollment was not as great as they had hoped it would be. Cone said he had visited with recent graduates of the ICA about continuing in the Women's Division, but he was not sure what the outcome of those visits would be. Hauber suggested that the regular two-year college course continue and that permission be given to women to enter upper-division courses. Others objected to St. Ambrose continuing to operate the Women's Division and suggested that they prepare to hand the whole division over to the sisters. Following further discussion, they decided to continue for one more year on the same basis as the current year, offering only the first two years of college. However, they decided that if the enrollment increased "sufficiently," they could change the policy about upper-division students for the 1936-1937 year.[26]

In the meantime, Cone and the faculty discussed the operation of the college. On June 6, 1934, Cone convened a meeting of the College Council that included the bishop. It had been seven years since accreditation by the North Central Association, and Cone said he wanted to be sure that St. Ambrose was in compliance with the current North Central standards. Hauber was blunt in his assessment of the situation. He said that from 1915 to 1927, the goal had been membership in the North Central Association. But now, "We seem to be content to float along somewhat aimlessly. We can't do this . . . The standards of the Association will, and must, vary. We must work out consciously our curriculum and policy. We should put our policy before the public. Boost it! Boast of it!"[27]

The council met again on October 3 in a joint meeting with the faculty. Cone told the group that the current status of the college, along with the changes in the standards for education "prompts us to chart our course anew." He thought St. Ambrose could "fairly measure" up to the North Central standards on the library, laboratories, finances, enrollment numbers, and faculty. With those elements of the college well in place, he said that the college must look to the quality of the product. To assist in this study, he announced the formation of eight standing committees: Educational Policy, Board of Studies, Student Guidance, Ecclesiastical Students, Library, Program, Physical Education, and Business Administration. He appointed chairs and members of each committee and defined the area of responsibility for each. He asked them to begin meeting regularly and to issue reports.[28]

Cone also commissioned four special studies. First, a statement of the objectives of St. Ambrose to be written by Father Henry Takkenberg. Father Mell Morrin was asked to investigate new trends in the revision of standards. Mathematics Professor Cletus Banwarth was to present information on testing of college students. Finally, philosophy professor, the Reverend Joseph Fenton, was asked to present a report on the Catholic ideal of education.[29]

The faculty met on January 18, 1935, to hear and discuss the reports. Morrin's report, "Revision of Standards for Higher Education," outlined new standards that North Central had set in two categories. The first was faculty organization, competence, and service. The second involved instruction and included curricular issues, methods of examination, faculty studies and publications, and the level of student scholarship. In response the president urged his colleagues to give "considerable thought" to Morrin's report. He said the faculty was "very good, and of high caliber" in regard to the first category, but he said in the second, the instruction by the faculty, needed "attention," the same concern expressed by North Central in 1927.

Professor Banwarth's paper, "Some Considerations on College Testing," was directed at the second category. Banwarth reported that in spite of new types of testing, the old procedure of the subjective essay test continued to be used on campus. One suggestion was to switch to objective tests which seemed to be more fair. He also discussed standard testing, the purpose of testing, and suggested they institute comprehensive exams at the end of the semester.[30]

The reports of Takkenberg and Fenton addressed the central identity of St. Ambrose as a Catholic institution. Takkenberg's "Aims and Purposes of St. Ambrose College," said St. Ambrose began as a seminary, then widened its mission to serve those who did not want to be priests but wanted higher education in a Catholic environment. Later as more students entered the professions, the college developed a series of pre-professional courses, evening and Saturday classes, and an as "yet somewhat experimental woman's unit," which indicated that the college responded to the demands of particular circumstances.

Alongside this, the college also had as an objective the "development of Christian culture." Takkenberg argued that the "most important" function for the college was not to teach its students how to make a living, but how to live. To accomplish this, education should be "thoroughly Catholic," which was more than merely teaching religion and ethics. Instead it meant "permeating the entire teaching system with a definite philosophy of life . . . as a unifying principle." Catholic faith must not be seen as a set of classroom theories, but "a life to be lived on campus." It would form the pattern of daily life, determine the policy of student guidance, shape discipline, exclude from the library books "out of harmony" with its principles, and determine the selection of a faculty in "sympathy with the Catholic point of view." Cone commented that North Central wanted to know the objectives of St. Ambrose College and "to what extent" the college approached those objectives. He said that "every faculty member should be in accord" with the objectives Takkenberg had outlined.[31]

Fenton's report, "The Ideal of the Catholic College," picked up on the themes developed by Takkenberg. Fenton argued that a college was based on the idea that humans were "capable of ordered and directive development while a Catholic college raises the awareness of a 'higher destiny.'" The Catholic must have training in the sciences, the arts of expression, Latin and Greek, philosophy, and the fine arts. This training helped a person to recognize the "transcendent beauty of the universe and of nature, but [also] the beauty of the works of man" as they contributed to the welfare of humanity. In words that could have been written by Bishop McMullen, Fenton said that the "ideal of the Catholic college . . . would be a man who is cultured in the strict sense of the word, one who is conversant with the progress and the attainments of the sciences, . . . [and] the literary and the artistic canons of western civilization, one who has attained that cultural appreciation and perspective of the universe which we know as philosophy, and finally one who is intelligently aware of the richness and the power of his own religion." Fenton's final point was that the Catholic college stood as "the citadel of the traditional culture of the west," but it also properly had an interest in the "problems and affairs of the nation."[32]

According to Fenton, those goals could be achieved by the study of philosophy and by the time he presented his report, it had become "commonplace" for Catholic educators to emphasize the role philosophy played as the "unifying core of the curriculum," and the "central formative element in the creation of a Catholic culture."[33] That reflected Cone's own views.[34] He thought that the movement away from the concept of a broad cultural training to more specific vocational training had brought only dissatisfaction. Cone said that St. Ambrose should restate its aims and make it clear that it was part of the intellectual tradition of the church.[35] Those ideas became the foundation of a discussion that continued over the next two years about the organization and future of the college.

To underscore the importance of philosophy to the students, Fenton organized the Thomist seminar which met for two hours every Friday afternoon. In the spring of 1935, the class studied Thomas Aquinas' *Summa*

Contra Gentiles, one of his seminal works. The international philosophy journal, *Angelicum*, noted that the seminar to study Thomism had "happily begun."[36] Two members of the seminar, Francis Marlin and Maurice Dingman edited a journal, *Quodlibet*, which contained student reviews of philosophy articles from other journals and reported on talks given by guest lecturers. The journal was widely circulated and received favorable comments from the chaplain of the Catholic Club at Yale University and the rector of the Theological College at Catholic University. The *Ambrosian News* said that this indicated that St. Ambrose was "moving up," and that the seminar was made up of a "widely appreciated band of young philosophers."[37]

There was already the requirement for all graduates to complete ten hours of philosophy. Now all students were required to complete a twelve-hour minor in philosophy which included a required four-hour course, fundamental philosophy. This course posed basic questions about the nature of man: whether he had a soul, what was his destiny, the basis for right and wrong, whether there was a God, the origin of the universe, the value of human knowledge, and whether human reason could offer answers to those questions.[38]

The continuing discussions about the institution resulted in the creation of two new academic departments. The Department of Fine Arts, made up of music, art, and theater, was created in the summer of 1934 at the same time as the new Women's Division. Although many of the courses for the new department were held in space leased at the ICA, they were open to male and female students.

There had been various bands, glee clubs, choirs, and drama societies since the early years of the college. But their existence often depended on whether there was someone to lead them and in some years, if no one else was available, a student led a musical group. Ned Catich, who had led the band in the previous few years, was just the latest example. During those same years, individual vocal or instrumental music instruction was available, but the student could not receive academic credit. Now with the new department, those activities became a regular part of the college curriculum and students could receive credit.

The chair of the new Fine Arts department was the Reverend Cletus Madsen who took over the chapel choir, orchestra, and the band. Sisters Mary Elena and Mary Franciscus also taught music. Madsen had been a 1924 graduate of the academy and a 1928 graduate of the college where he had played in the orchestra and the band and was star athlete. Following graduation from college, he studied at the North American College in Rome and was ordained a priest in December 1931. He began teaching at St. Ambrose in 1932.

Madsen taught all the music classes, directed the choir for church services, and organized a choral club as the principal vocal music group which soon began to perform on campus and at events in Davenport. In 1936, Madsen began a series of annual performances of the works of Gilbert and Sullivan with singers from the men's and women's divisions of St. Ambrose. In 1937, he organized the first "variety concert of a classical nature" that included 150 male and female students and some members of the faculty as performers. The second year, the "Concert Varieties of 1938" included a forty-piece college orchestra, the combined voices of the Tri-City Oratorio Society (another Madsen group) and the college choral club, and soloists. The program ranged from songs by Victor Herbert to the first American performance of a hymn composed by the director of the seminary choir at Madsen's alma mater, the North American College in Rome.[39]

Art had been part of the St. Ambrose curriculum for several years. In addition to his duties with the band, Ned Catich also taught art. He had been a professional letterer and union sign painter in New York and Chicago, and his skills in calligraphy were already well-established. In 1932, he won the Ramsey Prize at the Tri-City art show and the next year he won the same prize for an abstract watercolor which a Chicago critic said was an "example of what magic can be worked by paint handled in the so-called modern manner."[40] In 1932, he taught painting and lettering and illumination in summer school sessions until he left to do graduate work at the University of Iowa in 1934, so Sister Mary Blanche taught art at the Women's Division. In 1936, the art curriculum expanded to five courses, but Catich was now in the seminary in Rome, so Mr. George Shealy taught art for three years.

The new department also included drama taught by Mrs. Helena Bradford Churchill who had directed plays since 1919 as an activity of the Drama Club.[41] In the tradition of men's schools, all the parts had been played by men. But in 1933, Mrs. Churchill staged a play which featured a mixed cast, the first participation by women in a regular St. Ambrose College activity.[42]

Madsen also was the director of the campus radio station which became a venue for musical and dramatic productions. Lectures and musical performances had been broadcast for a time in the 1920s. In early 1935, the faculty discussed the use of local commercial radio as a means to advertise the college.[43] Later that spring St. Ambrose College of the Air was broadcast on local radio station WOC. Monsignor O'Connell appeared on the first program to talk about the history of the college. In the following weeks, members of the faculty and student music group appeared. Those programs only lasted for a few months, but in 1937, Madsen and Professor of speech Daniel J. Youngerman revived St. Ambrose College of the Air. They took an old store room in the Irish Village and put up some green curtains to make a studio. The programs were broadcast on WOC and became so popular that the next year the college committed more resources to radio. With student labor, they enlarged the studio and created a separate control room. WOC provided broadcast equipment and carried the programs on its frequency.[44]

The new studio was dedicated on November 4, 1938, with the bishop, college officials, Davenport mayor John Jebens, and Moon Reagan, "brother of the famous announcer, Dutch Reagan," in attendance. Madsen spoke with pride about the studio and said that with the modern equipment, he felt sure that it was "comparable to that of any school, and to the studios of many of the medium-sized radio stations."[45]

The other new department was physical education which began offering courses in the fall of 1936 to "improve the health and to build-up the bodies of the students and teach the fundamentals and rules of various sports." All freshmen were required to take the course unless they were out for a varsity sport. A second course was required of all sophomores. The instructor was Robert Klenck, a 1932 graduate of St. Ambrose.

Varsity sports under coach Dukes Duford continued to prosper. Following successful football and basketball seasons in 1931 and 1932, the alumni organized to sell season tickets to the home football and basketball games and track meets. The editor of the *Davenport Daily Democrat* urged his readers to support the season ticket sales because "by boosting athletics, enrollment and educational standards at St. Ambrose College, Davenporters [were] boosting [their] own community."[46]

The fans who bought season tickets were not disappointed. The football team finished near the top of the conference in every Duford season; in 1937, it shared the Iowa Conference championship with Upper Iowa. Following a 12-0 win over Loras College in 1935, St. Ambrose began a streak of 29 wins and 2 ties that extended to the first game of the 1939 season. Nearly every year, at least one St. Ambrose player was on the all-conference team, including notably Joe Gusitius, John Oelerich, Jim Furlong, and Nick Kerasiotis.[47]

The basketball team was equally successful, winning the conference championship in 1933, 1935, 1938, and 1939. In 1932, Kenny Austin was the conference scoring leader and all-conference center. Vic Pahl was all-conference center for two seasons, 1934 and 1935, and led the conference in scoring in 1935. The 1938 team went as far as the quarterfinals in the National Intercollegiate Basketball Tournament in Kansas City. The 1939 team had a perfect 12-0 conference record and placed Francis Tofanelli, Jerry O'Donnell, and Jack Bills on the all-conference team.[48]

In 1934, the athletes organized the Monogram Club, open to all athletic letter winners. The club held picnics, dances, and regularly sponsored benefit games for the mission drive which was still supporting the work of Father Bernard Meyer and his school, St. Ambrose in China. In 1937, it began the tradition of an annual Monogram Madness variety show. The evening featured ushers in circus uniforms, melodrama, a swing orchestra, the St. Ambrose Symphony, and vaudeville acts which included a chorus line of "blonde-wigged brawny athletes."[49]

The old tradition of literary and debating societies continued with the reorganization of the Bronsonian Club and new groups, the Aquin Literary Society and the Chesterbelloc Society, named for Gilbert Keith Chesterton and Hilaire Belloc, "two of the most prominent Catholic laymen of the time, fearless writers and outstanding members of the Church." Like the former literary societies, those new groups were organized to give public speaking and debating opportunities to the residents of Davis Hall.[50]

The church students reorganized the Manning Club as a debating society. The topics of debate were often serious, but not always. One memorable evening, "Neddie Catich, with a denunciation of golf as a menace to modern society, had his audience roaring with laughter. Although the talk he gave was intentionally humorous, it was evidently well-prepared and was delivered in wonderful style."[51]

In 1932, the Reverend Leo Sterck, professor of French, organized *Le Cercle Français*, to complement the classroom work of students studying French. Membership was open to anyone interested in the French language and culture, and when the Women's Division opened, those students were eligible to join. The club met every Monday evening to converse in French and discuss topics of interest. Shortly after organizing, it began to publish

A Great and Lasting Beginning

STUDE of
ST. AMBROSE
DAVENPORT, IA

Students of St. Ambrose College 1939.

L'Ambrosiastre, a "little French newspaper," with campus news and book reviews which was circulated on campus, to every high school in the local area, and to French departments at the University of Iowa and the University of Chicago.

Le Cercle Français also presented evenings of short plays and music. In 1936, Mrs. Churchill and Sterck directed Moliere's *Le Bourgeois Gentilhomme*, which had been previously presented at the first St. Ambrose commencement in 1885. At the end of each year the members gathered for a "soiree" consisting of entertainment and refreshments.[52]

Two other language clubs were organized in the 1930s. In 1933, Sterck organized *El Circulo Español* which met to discuss Spanish literature and to watch movies in Spanish which they bought or rented.[53] The Reverend Paul Laffey, professor of German, organized *Der Deutsche Studenten Verein* in 1938 as a reorganization of the *Bonifacius Verein* that had ceased to exist at the beginning of World War I. Like the others, the German group met regularly to give its members practice in the speaking of conversational German.[54]

In the meantime, the social life of the students continued unabated. Dances were often held after football and basketball games. The homecoming dance, the pre-Lenten dance, CYO dances, and the annual freshman prom held each spring were regular features of the social calendar. Those dances were held at the Blackhawk Hotel or the Outing Club and featured extensive decorations, a grand march, and music provided by one of the many local or regional dance bands.

In February 1935, the Women's Division sponsored its first dance, the February Frolic, at the Blackhawk Hotel. Freshman Madeleine Schmidt was in charge of the ticket sales and more than 150 couples came to dance to the music of the Jack Austin Band. The large turnout was taken as an endorsement by the male student body of the new Women's Division. Each year the Women's Division also sponsored a formal dance at the Blackhawk or the Outing Club. For those dances the female students extended "bids" to the men for dates. Other male students could come by purchasing a ticket for themselves and their dates.[55]

The city of Davenport offered other kinds of entertainment. There were more than a dozen movie theaters showing the latest Hollywood productions. Live entertainment also played in Davenport. One student reported seeing Ted Lewis and his band, Shep Fields, Cab Calloway, Jackie Coogan, and Betty Grable all in the same spring.

Whenever he went out for an evening's entertainment, the Ambrosian still had to return before curfew. Charles Lewis, a freshman from Dallas City, Illinois, wrote his mother that the students had a late permission to be out until 1:00 to attend a CYO dance. He got in at 12:57, but his brother

Tom, a junior, got in a few minutes after 1:00, but that Father Thomas J. Lew, the dean of men, did not say anything. A few weeks later Charles wrote he would like to go to Rock Island to hear Jan Garber and his orchestra. He told his mother it "only cost $2.50 per person to dance. It would be worth it though. I don't suppose T. J. (The Dean) would let a fellow out."[56]

If an Ambrosian had a date, he may have stopped at Steve's Barber Shop on Harrison Street or Ehler's Barber Shop on East Locust for a trim. For those who thought the food served on campus was not adequate, students could go downtown to Mac's Restaurant and Tavern, or the Baltimore Cafeteria, or Koelle's Lunch for tamales, chili, or hamburgers. Closer to campus, there was Gust's Coffee Shop and Bill's Sandwich Shop on Harrison, or the Hawkeye Tavern on East Locust which served butter-fried hamburgers. Tobacco products were available at one of the many Hickey's Cigar Stores downtown or at Geisler's Drug Store at Locust and Harrison.

The activities of the women were a regular feature of the *Ambrosian News*. A column by an anonymous writer known as "The Male Dowager," wrote about the social life of the campus. He reported on who attended a dance with whom, and which couples were seen together at the movies or other social functions. Women's Division student Mary Kathryn Heller's column, "Among the Ladies," concentrated on what the girls were wearing, who made up the latest dating couples, and the various social events.[57]

Ten women who were classified as upperclassmen decided that the first year students of the Women's Division, like their male counterparts, should be initiated. They formulated rules which one student said amounted to the "decemvirate" telling the freshmen, "You're in my power." The freshmen had to wear green ribbons on top of their hair, which had to be worn straight, with no bobby pins. They could not wear make-up, including nail polish. They were to rise and curtsey when an upperclass student entered the room and address the person formally as "Miss" or "Mister." They were to be obedient to all upperclass requests, "within reason."[58] Writing in the "Ladies Say" column, freshman Marguerite Bonte told her readers not to be surprised at what they see. She said the freshmen had "Faith and Hope that the upper class women will have Charity. However, the Golden Rule would hardly be appropriate in this case."[59]

Each fall the male freshmen faced initiation, an ordeal much longer and more complex than that of the women. The green caps remained but other regulations were added year by year. One was the necessity to "button" upon request by an upperclassman. This involved putting one's right hand on the top of the head, the left hand on the belt line, and then executing a deep, profound bow. Charles Lewis told his mother, "Initiation so far isn't half bad. All we have to do is 'button,' run errands for the upperclassmen . . . Last night they made a bunch of us stand on the steps of Davis Hall and sing the school song half a dozen times. While we sang they would throw water out of the windows down on us." He assured his mother that he

A Great and Lasting Beginning

finished his singing before they started throwing water, but that "some guys got soaked."[60]

Initiation ended with "Hell Week" in early December when more rules were added: the freshmen had to carry their books in a fruit basket, they had to wear their shirts backwards, use only the north door of Lewis Hall; the day students had to wear a lady's white stocking pinned to their left shoulder to be visible at all times. As homecoming approached, the principal activity of the freshmen initiates was to gather wood for the bonfire. In time the activities got out of hand and the editor of the newspaper noted that initiation lacked supervision, was detrimental to morale, and only succeeded in "corroborating the oft-suspected judgement that brawn can swing a bludgeon without the assistance of human reasoning." The editorial called on the student council to take over initiation and organize it better.[61]

The student council reformed the tradition by adding more rules. Now only student council members could paddle freshmen; freshmen must report each day to captains for wood gathering; the only menial tasks they could be forced to perform were shining shoes and running errands; freshmen had to show an interest in extracurricular activities and be present at all athletic events prepared to sing the "Victory March" and know the college yells; caps and buttoning were still necessary; and no one could throw a freshman into the pool without the permission of the student council. There were provisions for freshmen to report those who violated the rules and punishments for the offenders were spelled out.[62]

Still objections to freshmen initiation continued. "Initiations are useless . . . outmoded," one *Ambrosian News* editor wrote, but he did think wearing the green cap served a useful purpose. In spite of such objections, the practice continued and the rules got sillier as the years passed: wear one white shoe and one black shoe; shave only one side of the face; carry an open umbrella at all times; wear all clothing inside out; the variety of the rules was limited only by the imaginations of the upperclassmen. Some on campus still objected but most probably agreed with the student who wrote that wearing the green cap was "a striking advertisement that you are going to be a St. Ambrose man . . . it is a credential by which the upperclassman can recognize someone who isn't in a position to claim that he knows what it's all about."[63]

Wearing a green beanie for a few weeks in the fall was just one way in which St. Ambrose men were identified. Ambrosians were also identified by their school songs. There were already at least two fight songs for football and basketball games, the "Victory March" ("Here's to the team and victory"), written by Bernie Schultz when he was leading the St. Ambrose Band a few years before, and "Go! St. Ambrose, Go!" ("Go! St. Ambrose, go! St. Ambrose ever onward.") However, members of the Alumni Association wanted an alma mater, a song that was a hymn of praise to St. Ambrose College, modeled on "Old Gold," the alma mater at the University of Iowa. The Music department had already decided to use the melody, *Finlandia*, by the Finnish composer Jean Sibelius for the song, and in November 1936, it announced a contest for the lyrics to accompany it. The faculty of the English department agreed to serve as judges. In May 1937, William Kerrigan, a senior from Davenport, was declared the winner for his lyrics: "Ambrosian Oaks, what mighty deeds you know;/Our hearts' fair shrine,

ah! Still more dear you grow./What white and blue has wrought all we who know/Shall not forget, nor shall our foe!/When Mississippi's waters cease to flow/Your hearth of glory still shall glow."[64]

A song identified the school and so did a nickname. For the first fifty years, the teams had been called the Saints. By 1936, however, students had come to think that the Saints was neither a "distinctive nor appropriate" name for the Ambrose teams, and the *Ambrosian News* announced a contest to select a new name.[65] There was little interest that year and the matter was dropped.

In announcing a new contest in November 1937, the editor said that the paper had no intention of going "in the face of tradition, as they felt there was none," but that the purpose of the contest was to "establish a cognomen that would remain in the minds of the public, helping pave the way for an advance in St. Ambrose athletic standards." This time suggestions poured in: the Big Oaks; the Ambrosian Oaks; the Buffaloes, the "mightiest of all types of prairie herds"; the SAC (a reference to the initials of the school and to the Indian tribe that once lived in the area); the Blue Tide; and the Fighting Irish were just some of the ideas. Warren Lage, a student from Moline, suggested the Bees, explaining that bees were historically associated with the patron saint of the college, and that "the qualities of a bee, such as its industriousness and its ability to sting might exemplify characteristics that might be associated with our athletic teams. These might include: to strive valiantly, to work hard, to be as troublesome to their opponents as a bee is to his."[66]

The students voted in December, and Bees was "favored heavily in the vote." Monogram Club president Joe McConville, said the club was "heartily in accord with the new name." The newspaper announced it was glad to see a "definite outcome" and pledged its "wholehearted support." True to its word in that same issue, the paper used the new nickname. Almost immediately the nickname got a nickname: the Bees became the "Blue Swarm."[67]

The alma mater and the nickname served as symbols for what St. Ambrose represented. Vic Pahl became another such symbol. Born in Davenport in 1912, Vic was one of 11 children. When he was nine his father died, and his mother sent Pahl and three of his sisters to Mooseheart where he excelled at sports. He was second team all-state in basketball and set a national high school javelin record in track.[68]

He entered St. Ambrose in the fall of 1933 where he was a star in the classroom and a star on the playing field. He was all-Iowa Conference and all-state in football and basketball and he set a school record in the javelin, the high jump, and the pole vault. Coach Duford suggested that he try the decathlon at the 1935 Kansas Relays. Several of the events were new to him; nevertheless, he finished in sixth place which qualified him for the National AAU meet that summer. Duford's ultimate goal for Pahl was the Olympic trials the next year.[69]

After the meet, Pahl, alumnus John Gerwe, and Duford left Kansas in Duford's car to return to Davenport. Early Sunday morning, a few miles east of Muscatine, the left front tire of the car blew out. As they began to replace the tire, an oncoming driver struck them. Pahl and Gerwe were crushed between the cars and Duford was thrown into the ditch. Gerwe had a broken leg, Duford was shaken up, but Pahl had severe bodily injuries and a concussion. He was taken to the Muscatine hospital where he never regained consciousness.[70] All through the week his classmates and friends kept vigil in the chapel, praying for his recovery. But in the early afternoon of April 25, the bell in the Ambrose Hall tower began to toll, and they knew their friend was dead.

The tributes poured in from all over the Midwest. Bert McGrane, long-time *Des Moines Register* sportswriter, called Pahl the "greatest all-around athlete and the finest sportsman I ever encountered." Elmer Layden, athletic director at Notre Dame, said Pahl's "life on and off the field was exemplary." The Davenport papers began to compare him to George Gipp, the legendary Notre Dame player who had died while a student. Coach Duford said he was the "finest boy any coach ever had . . . Anything he attempted he did well. He never gave a moments trouble, either in the classroom or on the field." The editor of the student newspaper said that while he would be missed as an athlete and as a student, the students would miss him most "as Vic Pahl. He was unpretentious, without conceit, friendly, lovable; a clean young man totally unaffected. As will his family, so too shall we miss him as plain Vic."[71]

Vic Pahl who died in 1935.

On Friday afternoon, Pahl's body was brought to the Davis Hall chapel where the students kept vigil all through the night. The next day the entire student body, accompanied by athletes from Augustana College, walked behind the funeral coach to Sacred Heart Cathedral where Bishop Henry Rohlman celebrated the Mass. He was buried at Oakdale Cemetery in Davenport beneath a small stone with just his name, Vic Pahl.[72]

Pahl came to represent the ideal Ambrosian. Two years later his apotheosis was complete when William Kerrigan included a third verse to "Ambrosian Oaks": "Your ivied bell tower with its cross on high,/That one time tolled the death of Vic Pahl,/Still rings our victories, and at its call,/When Ambrose shouts its battle cry,/Vic Pahl in helmet watches from the sky/The men of Ambrose–victors all." When asked about the verse, Kerrigan said that two years after his death, Vic Pahl was "already a tradition," and it was the "single purpose of St. Ambrose to turn out men just like him."[73]

While Vic Pahl lay dying in a Muscatine hospital, his friends and classmates gathered in the chapel to pray for what they hoped would be his recovery. When he died they sat vigil with his body in the chapel. The chapel and the faith it represented continued to be an important part of life at St. Ambrose. The catalogue said St. Ambrose was "primarily" a school for Catholic students which aimed to "give the training in and to encourage the formation of the habits that make for Catholic character."[74] All Catholic students were required to take courses in religion. They were required to attend Sunday and holy day Mass, and they were "urged" to attend weekday Mass at 6:55 in the morning. About one-third to one-half of the boarding students received daily Communion. Each Thursday before First Friday there was a Holy Hour to promote devotion to the Sacred Heart. During Lent there were services on Wednesday and Sunday evenings and the Way of the Cross was celebrated each weekday. Novenas and Marian devotions were also held during the year. All Catholic students were required to make a three day retreat each year; non-Catholic students attended special lectures on those days.

The Sodality remained the principal religious organization on campus and its mission section continued to support the work of Father Meyer in China. Through the years Meyer maintained a regular correspondence with Father Carl Meinberg, the director of the Sodality. When Meyer returned to the United States for visits, he often stopped in Davenport to visit the students at St. Ambrose. In the mid-1930s, the China Meyer served was in the midst of a civil war between nationalist Chinese who espoused democracy and others who advocated communism. Parts of rural China were still under the control of bandits and warlords. As the decade wore on, there was growing danger of invasion of China by Japan. Meyer reported that in the midst of that turmoil, the principles of Catholic Action, based on the Jocist model of "see, act, judge," was the "answer to most of the difficulties connected with spreading the faith."[75]

Like their counterparts in China, students at St. Ambrose who wanted to address the social problems of the day organized the Social Science Club. One year they studied Nazism, communism, fascism, the New Deal, and the Reverend Charles Coughlin and Louisiana Senator Huey Long, both of whom had radical programs for reform in the United States. Another year the club conducted a survey of various issues in the city, including education, unemployment, housing, and delinquency. Calling Davenport a "typical modern American city," president Ray Noonan said the club was neither a reform group nor a Chamber of Commerce, but rather the members hoped to "gain experience with the vital social problems that confront the nation today and in Davenport typical conditions are to be found."[76]

Cone had been instrumental in the formation of the diocesan office of Catholic Charities in the late 1920s. Now in 1937, Bishop Rohlman turned to Cone to organize a Catholic Action week with a conference in October. It brought together speakers from around the country, including Monsignor John A. Ryan, a regular guest speaker over the previous thirty years.

The three-day program began on Sunday with Mass at the cathedral and a large rally on campus. The speaker, the Reverend Norbert C. Hoff, a philosophy professor at the University of Notre Dame, told the crowd which included many students, that modern man was "torn loose from Christ . . . devoid of faith . . . involved in the colossal lie which constitutes irreligion." Leaders had also lost a "sense of direction." Hoff said that Catholic Action could "turn the tide" against this irreligion and be used to "fight for religion

A Great and Lasting Beginning

which is the one thing able to keep men straight."[77]

By 1938, male and female Ambrosians watched events in Asia and Europe with a sense that irreligion was unfolding everywhere. In 1936, Germany had marched into the Rhineland with impunity. That same year civil war erupted in Spain. The next year Japan moved south out of Manchuria into China and would eventually reach the area of St. Ambrose in China at Wuchow in the far south. Then in a 1938 plebiscite, Austrians voted for *anschluss*, or union, with Germany which then turned its attention to Czechoslovakia.

In 1937, Madeleine Schmidt, as the official delegate, and several other students represented St. Ambrose at a Summer School of Catholic Action in Chicago organized by Father Dan Lord and the *Queen's Work*, the journal of the Sodality movement. Over 2,000 delegates from North America and France attended programs to learn to be leaders in Catholic Action.[78]

In November 1938, Monsignor Hauber (he had been made a Monsignor the year before) and students Ray Noonan, Geraldine Beh, and Arnold Meyer attended a peace conference at Clarke College in Dubuque. The conference was sponsored by the Catholic Association for International Peace, created in 1926 by representatives of the Social Action Department of the National Catholic Welfare Conference, the National Council of Catholic Men, and the National Conference of Catholic Women. Its purpose was to promote peace by the study of current issues and to produce pamphlets as a way to educate the public on those issues. The keynote speaker was the Reverend Sylvester Luby, a Loras College faculty member who was vice president of the national association. He introduced the theme of the conference, "Christian Civilization Can Establish and Maintain Peace."[79]

The world situation also became a theme at the football banquet at the end of the 1938 season. The team had just completed a record thirty-one games without a defeat and the Gold Room of the Blackhawk Hotel was overflowing with fans. The Most Reverend Gerald Bergan, bishop of Des Moines, was one of the speakers. He complimented the team on its record and noted that defeat would come someday. The question was would they accept defeat by quitting or with a smile. He said he liked football, especially in the "topsy-turvy world of today where self-sacrifice is not a virtue, and everybody seeks to avoid pain." In America there was too much emphasis on the soft things in life and, "In Europe they have never learned to play . . . We learn to play football in America, but the play the youth of Europe learns is marching with guns." But, the bishop implied, the lessons learned in football would prepare American youth for the challenges the world would present them.[80]

Among the male students there was "controversy over the question of co-education." In early 1938, the "Vox Campus" column of the *Ambrosian News* asked students at random their opinion of co-education. Those in favor said: It should exist in more colleges; it was "fine" since it created academic rivalry between the sexes; it gave a greater appreciation of life and helped to create better social skills; it afforded women an "equal ground for education" and cultivated "an intellectual meeting place"; it added to social

life and "after all social life is part of one's education." Opinions against it included: Uni-sex classrooms were better; both sexes in the classroom distracted students and could be embarrassing; education was best when co-education was "conspicuous by its absence."[81]

The presence of women and laymen on campus also raised concerns about the seminary. Since Bishop Rohlman had established the Ecclesiastical department in 1927, the seminarians had been housed in Ambrose Hall, separated from the other students. To emphasize the fact that the seminarians were a separate group, the catalogue added a note that "to conform adequately with the regulations of the Sacred Congregation of Seminaries," the students were separated from the "general student body." Although they lived separately, seminarians attended classes with women and laymen and participated in other campus activities. This fueled the continuing debate about whether seminarians should study in isolated settings away from the temptations of a secular campus, or as Bishop McMullen thought, should be educated alongside those to whom they would later minister.

By June 1933, the seminary had grown to thirty students from several dioceses, and the *Messenger* said that the "Catholics of the diocese" could take a "just pride in this splendid institution of learning." There was also praise from the Sacred Congregation of Seminaries and Universities in Rome. In late August 1933, the bishop received a letter from the Congregation that commended the seminary and the work of Father Leo Kerrigan as its dean.[82]

The Roman Congregation continued to monitor the activities of all seminarians in the United States and in May 1935, American bishops received a letter from the apostolic delegate, the Most Reverend Amleto Cicognani, about the summertime activities of seminarians. Cicognani said that the best thing for them would be to reside at villas in the summer where they would be "removed from endangering outside influences." Recognizing that would not always be possible, the letter said that seminarians should not take summer jobs in hotels, cafes, theaters, political jobs, driving cabs, or any place where "persons of the opposite sex" were also employed. The letter suggested that they teach in religious vacation schools, attend daily Mass, review their studies from the previous year, and visit their home parishes from time to time. Bishop Rohlman told Cicognani that he would "most cheerfully comply" with the instructions and that his seminarians were all "obliged" to attend summer school at St. Ambrose to study courses in the "methods of teaching religion, in conversational Latin, and in liturgical chant."[83]

Father Kerrigan, the dean of the seminary for nine years, moved to become pastor of St. Mary's Parish in Davenport in October 1936. Father Edward O'Connor became the new dean, beginning a tenure that would last for thirty years. In April 1936, Father William Adrian, who had been on the St. Ambrose faculty since his ordination in 1911, was consecrated as bishop of Nashville, Tennessee. That fall he sent eight seminarians to St. Ambrose.[84] O'Connor now became responsible for thirty seminarians from four dioceses, Davenport, Des Moines, Peoria, and Nashville.

In August 1938, Archbishop Cicognani wrote American bishops again to say that Rome wanted "first hand knowledge" of American seminaries and that he would appoint "visitors" for each seminary. Archbishop Edward A. Mooney of Detroit notified Bishop Rohlman that he had been asked to come to St. Ambrose. Mooney arrived on November 17 for a two-day visit where he met with the bishop and St. Ambrose officials. Rohlman hosted a banquet at the Outing Club whose guests included the clerical and lay faculty of the college, diocesan officials, and the seminarians. Mooney seemed favorably impressed with what he saw, but Madsen said later that Mooney could not understand how St. Ambrose seminarians could be in chorus with girls and participate in sports with lay students.[85]

The response from Rome to Mooney's visit came in December 1940 in a letter from Joseph Cardinal Pizzardo, the prefect of the Sacred Congregation of Seminaries and Universities. Pizzardo called St. Ambrose a "most worthy institution from which proceeded great benefits for the Diocese of Davenport." He was pleased that St. Ambrose had taken the earlier advice of the Congregation and kept the seminarians separated from the other students. But he also had reservations. He said that since St. Ambrose was "not really and properly a Seminary, it is no wonder that there may be something lacking for the proper formation of students for Holy Orders." He recommended monthly days of recollection for the faculty and the students, that "statutes" to govern the "entire life of the College" be drawn up and given to the students, and that the bishop should make sure that Latin was "well fostered and cultivated." He also asked if it was still the custom for seminarians to spend their summer vacation at St. Ambrose.[86]

If Archbishop Mooney and the Roman Congregation were generally satisfied with the St. Ambrose Seminary, nevertheless, its presence on campus colored the discussions about the continuation of the Women's Division. A meeting of the college council in April 1935, however, indicated that the issue was even more complex. Cone called the meeting to discuss St. Ambrose Academy, but it quickly became apparent that the Women's Division, the seminary, and the academy were linked together.

After a lengthy discussion, the group outlined a three-part plan. First, consolidate the ICA and St. Ambrose Academy, presumably at another site. Next, provide a separate place for the Ecclesiastical department, although there was no suggestion as to where that might be. Finally, the Women's Division would be located in the old ICA building. There were several advantages to this program, but the main advantage was that combining the academies was more economical and such a move would give the college more room to expand in Ambrose Hall and at the ICA building. Cone suggested they study the ideas, get the approval of all the parties involved, and then go to the bishop.[87] Discussion about the academies continued for another twenty-five years and came to involve the pastors of the city and the bishop. The Women's Division, however, was a more immediate problem for the college administration and the bishop.

The College Council discussed the issue again in January 1936. Enrollment in the Women's Division was not as great as they had hoped it would be. That meant that tuition income was inadequate to cover the expense incurred by St. Ambrose to continue the program. At the January meeting, the council discussed whether in light of those facts, St. Ambrose should continue to support the Women's Division. Some thought it would be better to concentrate all their resources on the college men. After a long discussion, they deferred any decision on the question.[88]

On August 26, 1936, Sister Mary Evangela, BVM, the new dean of

women, wrote to all recent graduates of the ICA to ask them to consider enrolling in the Women's Division. She assured them that it was an "integral part" of St. Ambrose and that there would be a full slate of courses and extracurricular activities. In a letter written the next day, she explained to Mother Mary Gervase that she had met with Cone the day before to discuss the enrollment. He said he had visited with all the local pastors in both states to ask them to promote the college to their parishioners. Cone admitted that although the college was responsible for advertising the Women's Division, nothing had been done, and that by now it was too late to do anything. Consequently most of the ICA graduates from the previous spring had already made plans to attend other colleges. Sister Evangela said that it would be a "miracle" if they got a "goodly number" of new students that fall, but she said they could begin work for the following year.[89]

The inattention to advertising the Women's Division was indicative of the ambivalence about its continuation on the part of the St. Ambrose administration. However, the bishop was an even larger obstacle to its continuation. Bishop Rohlman had given only passive support to the Women's Division since its inception. He thought it was too great a financial drain on the diocese to support both the men's and women's units of the college. The bishop preferred that a separate college for women be established, supported by a religious community. That had been the subject of a meeting of the St. Ambrose Board of Control and the faculty on December 7, 1936. Cone prepared a report for the meeting where he said that co-education at St. Ambrose was "not generally regarded as possible or desirable." He offered the opinion that in a community of 150,000 people, a junior college for women was feasible and that in his view the "desideratum" was an "affiliate" college run by a community of sisters. Furthermore, he said that the current arrangement of the Women's Division fully supported by St. Ambrose should not be continued beyond the current year. Based on that recommendation, the board appointed a committee of five faculty members to study the issue of Catholic education for women and report back in three months.[90]

The committee met with Bishop Rohlman in early April. They said there was general agreement that it was "desirable and feasible" for a women's college in Davenport; however, St. Ambrose could not obligate itself to fund such a college. They said if the Women's Division was to continue, a community of sisters would have to take the responsibility to promote it, finance it, and provide a building for it. It could continue to affiliate with St. Ambrose and the college would provide faculty and "certain facilities," presumably laboratories.[91]

Following the meeting, Cone wrote Mother Gervase with the details and asked whether the order would agree to the proposal to operate a women's college. She responded a week later to say she had discussed the matter with her council. They agreed that they wanted to continue to provide education in Davenport but they were concerned that supporting a women's college there would compete with Clarke College in Dubuque. The order was also carrying a heavy burden of debt since it had recently opened Mundelein College in Chicago. For those reasons they would not take responsibility for a women's college in Davenport, but they would continue to serve the Women's Division, as long as St. Ambrose provided the buildings and equipment.[92]

The Women's Division located at the ICA continued for another two

A Great and Lasting Beginning

years. St. Ambrose, together with some BVMs, continued to supply the faculty. But that was all the sisters were willing to do. If there was to be a Catholic women's college in Davenport, the bishop would have to look to another religious order to operate it. Rohlman wanted that, but it would not be easy to find the resources and a religious order willing to undertake the project.

One solution would be to separate the seminary from the college so that the college could become co-educational. Kuno Struck told Bishop Rohlman he would donate his own home and property at West Twelfth and Division Streets so a seminary could be built. Rohlman discussed the matter with O'Connor, director of the Ecclesiastical department, and members of the faculty. O'Connor and the others objected to moving the seminary from the college so the bishop turned down Struck's offer.[93]

There was also pressure from the community to establish a women's college. The Reverend Thomas Lawlor, who had become vice president and business manager of St. Ambrose in May 1937, was approached by

Msgr. Carl Meinberg.

members of the Davenport Chamber of Commerce who said that unless St. Ambrose admitted women they would approach education officials in Des Moines to urge that the State of Iowa open a co-educational college in Davenport. They said they preferred not to jeopardize St. Ambrose by such action, but they were convinced that young women of the area should have the opportunity for a college education. Lawlor went to the bishop with that information and Rohlman asked him to take the lead in finding a religious order and the necessary property to start such a school.[94]

As the sisters, the administration, and the bishop discussed the future of the Women's Division, the students prepared for the football season and the homecoming celebration that fall. Madeleine Schmidt, now president of the women's student council, organized their participation in homecoming. They sold homecoming buttons, helped decorate for the banquet, and created a window display honoring the football team at the Adams and Adams Store at the corner of Fourth and Brady Streets.[95]

When the students entered that fall, they were welcomed by Cone. Then in November the announcement came that he would leave St. Ambrose to become the pastor of Sacred Heart Cathedral and vicar general of the diocese, replacing Monsignor William Shannahan who had died in October. The *Ambrosian News* praised Cone's service to the college as a professor of the social sciences. It said he was known for his ability to "interpret, along practical lines, the principles of social justice." He was also a frequent speaker at labor union meetings and other groups, had been the founder of

Catholic Charities in the diocese, and had recently been appointed by Iowa governor Nelson G. Kraschel to a term on the Iowa Board of Social Welfare.[96]

Father Carl Meinberg was named as Cone's successor. A graduate of St. Ambrose, Meinberg was ordained in 1914 and had been at the college since then. He taught church history, Spanish, and religion, had been director of the choir and orchestra, head librarian, and was a longtime spiritual director of the college. As the moderator of the mission unit of the Sodality, Meinberg directed the efforts to support Father Meyer's St. Ambrose in China school. The *Messenger* noted that Meinberg had made a "specialty of spiritual leadership," and that the youth of today needed such leadership.[97]

One of the last changes during the Cone administration came in October 1937 when the college filed a certificate of reorganization with the State of Iowa that extended the life of the corporation for another fifty years.[98] The new articles of incorporation included another change in the membership of the Board of Trustees. Now there were three officers of the corporation: the bishop, the vicar general, and the president of the college. There was also a Board of Control that included the bishop, the vicar general, the president, former presidents Schulte and Hannon, and three laymen: J. Clark Hall, long-time diocesan and college attorney; Lee J. Dougherty, president of Guaranty Life Insurance Company, who had been on the Board of Trustees established in 1915; and Maurice Donegan, a justice and former chief justice of the Iowa Supreme Court.

In the meantime, Lawlor continued his task of securing property for a women's college. In April 1938, he purchased seven-and-one-half acres on West Twelfth Street in Davenport from the J. H. C. Petersen estate for $50,000. At the same time Bishop Rohlman met with Mother Mary Geraldine Upham of the Sisters of the Humility of Mary in Ottumwa about staffing the new college. The sisters agreed to take on the college, and in March 1938, it was announced that Marycrest, a new Catholic college for women, would open in September 1939. Rohlman said the opening of Marycrest was an "event of great importance to the future of Davenport and its surrounding communities . . . Marycrest [would] form a fitting capstone of the educational facilities offered the youth of our fair city."[99]

As it was organized, the new Marycrest College would be a "corporate unit" of St. Ambrose. The Sisters of Humility would have administrative control of Marycrest, be responsible for registration, enrollment, and the academic records of the students. When it opened it would offer only freshmen and sophomore courses and then add upper-division courses in subsequent years. Most of the faculty would be Sisters of Humility, but some members of the St. Ambrose faculty would teach at the new college. Until Marycrest achieved the standards for accreditation by the North Central Association, its students would receive their degrees from St. Ambrose.[100] Mother Mary Geraldine told the bishop she hoped Marycrest would "Measure up fully on our part and that its equipment, organization, and administration be standard from the start . . . With the help and interest you give, the help of affiliation with Saint Ambrose, joined to our own best and most strenuous efforts, it should not be impossible."[101]

With the opening of Marycrest College, the desire of St. Ambrose priests like Hauber, Cone, Meinberg, and Lawlor to provide a college education for Catholic women was now fulfilled. Terelmar/Aquinas Junior College and the Women's Division of St. Ambrose were only stopgap measures that never really fully served the desires of Catholic women who wanted a local college

Msgr. A.J. Schulte, 1938.

education. Because of the financial constraints of the Depression, the luke-warm support by the bishop, the resistance of some St. Ambrose faculty, and the presence of the seminary, St. Ambrose was never really able to support the earlier efforts enough to make them wholly successful. That Marycrest became successful was a tribute to those Ambrosians who continued to support it and the work of the Sisters of Humility who poured their personnel and treasure into it.

When Marycrest opened, the Women's Division of St. Ambrose was eliminated and the remaining students transferred to Marycrest.[102] The women who had been part of St. Ambrose during those years met in the spring of 1939 to form the St. Ambrose Alumnae Association. Their loyalty to St. Ambrose was evident with the stated objective of the Alumnae Association to encourage students to enroll at St. Ambrose and to continue to support it "educationally, socially and financially." At the founding meeting, the members of the new association also passed a resolution to notify the Sisters of Humility that the St. Ambrose alumnae were "backing them in their new college." They also passed a resolution to notify the men's Alumni Association of the support of the alumnae.[103]

On May 19, 1938, the St. Ambrose Board on Educational Policy, consisting of the president and the chairs of the academic departments, met in the president's office with Bishop Henry Rohlman. Rohlman had convened the group to discuss whether St. Ambrose College should award honorary degrees. The discussion was apparently brief and the group concluded that St. Ambrose should grant honorary degrees "within limits, that the policy should be to give few, and only to distinguished individuals." They then voted unanimously to award the first two such degrees to the Reverend Luigi Ligutti, a 1914 graduate, president of the National Catholic Rural Life Conference, and Lee J. Dougherty, a former and current member of the Board of Trustees. Both men received the honorary degree of Doctor of Laws at commencement ceremonies, May 29, 1938.[104]

On December 1, 1938, the *Davenport Democrat and Leader* published a story about the "phenomenal growth" and change at St. Ambrose. Now in its fifty-seventh year, it had become a true college with over 1,000 students and a faculty of forty-six, making it the second largest private college in Iowa. Fifty-two percent of the day students and 70 percent of the entire student body were Catholic and the newspaper noted that while the study of religion was not "obligatory, the necessity for a realization of moral and cultural values" was stressed. The article continued that St. Ambrose was "in the truest sense of the word a 'liberal' college, and the necessity for a broad, liberal knowledge before specialization" was stressed in all its courses. Growth over its fifty-seven years had not "just happened," but was the result of the work of the "efficient faculty" and leadership that began with the presidency of Father William Hannon. It also pointed out that St. Ambrose was a "valuable business asset," spending an estimated $500,000 a year in the community.[105]

Perhaps nothing illustrated the changes that had taken place at the college more than the visit to campus of Monsignor A. J. Schulte who had returned to celebrate Mass for the feast of St. Ambrose on December 8, 1938. As he stood in the Ambrose Hall he had built and looked out a window toward the oak trees, he said with a hint of wistfulness, "Things are different than they were in 1882 when I started" the school. He spoke of Bishop McMullen's hopes for the school. He recalled the "day dodgers," the local boys who came to school every day from their neighborhood homes. He remembered Joseph Halligan and Father J. T. A. Flannagan, the second priest on the faculty, both now dead. And he talked about some of the earliest students who were now pastors of Davenport parishes. When he was asked about something that characterized the first years of the school, he remembered pulling cockleburs, "We spent most of the first few years pulling up cockleburs." The cockleburs his successor presidents dealt with were just as stubborn as those Schulte pulled, but like him, they persisted, and had built the St. Ambrose that McMullen had envisioned when he sent Schulte to the two rooms at St. Marguerite's.

A Great and Lasting Beginning

On October 17, 1940, the new president, Father Ambrose Burke, spoke to the entering class of 1944. He urged them to make the most of their opportunity to go to college. But, he said just going to college did "not guarantee a job, or a successful career, or social position, or abiding happiness." He said that high standards of conduct would help, but that a poor academic record was a handicap. He asked, "May we assume that every green-capped freshman here tonight is properly disposed and mentally equipped for a successful college career?" Burke told them of a professor who asked each student on the first day to look at his neighbor and realize that one of them would not be there the following year. Burke said that was too high a number at St. Ambrose, "yet too large a number of you will not be wearing cap and gown on Commencement Day 1944. Going to college is a great opportunity for service to others as well as to yourself. May I ask you to renew your pledge to the three loyalties that animate every student at this college: For God, for Country, and for St. Ambrose."[1]

❧ Chapter Nine ❧

If the 198 freshmen who heard Burke speak that day were like the 370 students who had participated in a poll the year before, about two-thirds of them expected to be wearing a St. Ambrose cap and gown at commencement 1944. The others were in pre-professional programs who would spend two or three years at St. Ambrose and then finish college somewhere else, or others who were not sure they would finish college at all. Twenty percent of them were undecided about their futures. Of the rest, 14 percent intended to enter some field of business and another 14 percent wanted to be a scientist or engineer. Nine percent were headed for a medical profession and 8 percent for the priesthood. The remainder wanted careers in education, the law, journalism, coaching, radio, aviation, civil service, and miscellaneous others including farming.

One hundred and seventy of those polled, nearly one-half, listed convenience as the primary reason they came to St. Ambrose. The other half of the respondents gave a variety of reasons for coming, including: St. Ambrose had been recommended by someone, the quality of the faculty, it was economical, it had a good curriculum, it was a small college. In the entire pool of respondents, only sixty-eight listed Catholicism as a primary or secondary reason for attending St. Ambrose. Only eight mentioned the influence of sports, and only two mentioned that a father or brother had previously attended St. Ambrose.[2]

For the most part the students at St. Ambrose in the late 1930s were the sons of the middle class. Their fathers were lawyers, doctors, dentists, veterinarians, salesmen or sales executives, small businessmen, bankers, accountants, and engineers. Thirty students were the sons of farmers, and many others had fathers in the building trades, often as supervisors or foremen. Sixteen fathers worked for the government at some level. The experience of the previous ten years had taught them all how difficult it was to remain in the middle class. The parents and students of the late 1930s, like their predecessors in 1882, realized that education would be the key to continuing in the middle class, or perhaps rising higher. They did not realize that none of the freshmen who heard Father Burke that day would be wearing a cap and gown four years hence.[3]

The freshman that fall of 1940 came to campus to find a new library-administration building under construction, the first such project since Lewis Hall was finished ten years earlier. The need for more space had been obvious for years. In his 1927 letter to the diocese shortly after he became president, Father Hauber had said that among the needs of the college were a new classroom and laboratory building, a new library, and a separate chapel building. The classroom and laboratory building was built, but because of the Depression any further building would be out of the question.

Enrollment increased through the decade of the 1930s, but Monsignor Cone said that the college was in "no-wise equipped to accommodate such enrollment." There was a need for more classrooms, laboratories, dormitory space for students, living quarters for priest faculty, and kitchen facilities. If the enrollment continued to increase, the point would soon be reached that a capital expenditure would be necessary. There was discussion about limiting enrollment, but that possibility raised a number of questions about how it could be limited, to whom admission preference would be given, whether the college should concentrate on qualitative development rather than quantitative, and whether St. Ambrose could compete with other, growing institutions. Since St. Ambrose was so dependent on tuition income, it was not likely that the college could afford to limit enrollment. The discussions continued, but no limitation was placed on enrollment.[4]

Discussions also continued about new buildings. Shortly after he became president in late 1937, Father Carl Meinberg expressed his regrets that the chapel was too small to allow day students to join the boarders to celebrate the Mass on St. Ambrose Day. Two years earlier, the chapel in the basement of Davis Hall had been removed to make more space for the library which made the Ambrose Hall chapel even more crowded. Meinberg said he looked "forward to the future when a chapel large enough

A Great and Lasting Beginning

Faculty 1939. Front row: Rev. E. O'Connor, A. Burke, U. Hauber, C. Meinberg. T. Lawlor, R. Kinnavey, C. Griffith, M. Morrin.
Second row: Rev. L. Rohret, L. Mork, J. McAuliffe, L. Sterck, P. Ferrara, S. Menke, E. Butler, W. Lynch, R. Murphy.
Third row: Rev. E. Ruhl, C. McGivern, C. Madsen, F. Williams, CSV, E. Catich, A. Mendez, A. Goetzman, R. Maher.
Fourth row: Dr. J. Goggin, Rev. B Barnes, J. Kennedy, W. Collins, E. Lew, J. Fath, Mr. C. Banwarth.
Top row: Rev. J. McEniry, G. Lillis, Mr. M. Casey, Rev. T. Lew, Coach W. Duford, Rev. F. Kelley, Coach R. Klenck, Dr. B. Miller, Mr. M. St. Angel, Mr. J. Oelerich, Mr. K. DeLene, Mr. J. McCaffrey, Mr. D. Youngerman.
In addition, Rev. W. O'Connor, T. Coonan, R. Welch, J. Surprenant, CSV, Mr. J. Beiser, J. Condon, K. Harman, G. Cummins, G. Hansen, Miss A. Cronin, who taught shorthand and typing, and Miss C. King, assistant librarian, were absent when the photo was taken.

to accommodate the entire student body" could be built.[5] But responding to rumors that there was construction planned at the college, Bishop Rohlman wrote Frank J. Lewis in February 1938 that "the Depression affected us very much during the past five years," and "in spite of its need for more accommodations," there would be no construction on campus at this time.[6]

Within a year, however, Rohlman apparently felt that the time was ripe for a building program. The 1939 summer session had an enrollment of 269 students, ninety more than the previous summer and the largest summer enrollment in history. One hundred and fourteen of those were sisters from nine different religious communities. There were over 200 freshmen in the fall semester, so clearly more room was necessary. Still Rohlman might have hesitated because on September 1, 1939, Germany invaded Poland, beginning World War II and beginning a new period of uncertainty. Nevertheless, two weeks later, the bishop announced a diocesan fund

drive to raise at least $400,000 to be used to achieve several goals. Some of the money would be used to provide additional housing and other services for the orphans and dependent children at St. Vincent's Home. But most of the money would be used at St. Ambrose. Some would go to wiping out the college debt. Some would be used for necessary repairs around the campus. But most would be used for an ambitious project to build a library-administration building and a "much-needed chapel."[7]

In a statement accompanying the announcement, Rohlman said that the clergy of the diocese were "keenly aware" of the need for a new chapel. The seating capacity was too small, and the sanctuary and sacristies were so "cramped," that it no longer served the needs of the campus community. During his recent visit to examine the seminary, Archbishop Edward Mooney had been critical of the chapel facilities for the faculty and the students, and he had urged the bishop to take steps to remedy the situation.[8]

A new library-administration building would make it possible to move the offices and the library out of Davis Hall. The space created could then be used for badly needed student housing.[9]

The "foremost" need for the drive was to put the college in a "sound financial basis through the liquidation of its indebtedness." In the 1920s, the college had borrowed money to finish Davis Hall and to build Lewis Hall. By 1935, the indebtedness had reached $250,000 when it was consolidated into a ten-year first mortgage bond, at 4 percent interest, which would mature in 1945. In five years payments had been made on the mortgage, but $225,000 remained and servicing this debt tied up money that could be used for other purposes. As it stood the debt was nearly half the size of the endowment, estimated at $600,000, mostly in farms and farm land. Although St. Ambrose had the second largest private school enrollment in Iowa, the size of its endowment placed it tenth among nineteen private colleges and far down the list of national colleges for men and Catholic colleges in the nation. There was a concern that a debt of that size compared with the size of the endowment could endanger the standing of the college with the North Central Association. So for the bishop and the administration of the college, the continuing debt was one of the "most pressing problems" facing the college and the diocese.[10]

The bishop named Lee J. Dougherty as general chairman of the drive. The bishop also named Father Walter Cullinan, pastor of St. Mary's Parish in Oskaloosa, to chair the diocesan campaign among the people and priests. The bishop and Dougherty wanted to broaden the base of support for the college beyond the clergy and the Catholics of the diocese. So Dougherty formed the Friends of St. Ambrose, comprised of non-Catholic local business leaders, and he named Cable G. Von Maur, president of Petersen, Harned and Von Maur, as chairman. Von Maur enlisted other Davenport business leaders to serve on his committee, including banker Roscoe O. Byerrum; Ben Comenitz, owner of a news agency; Otto T. Seiffert, president of Seiffert Lumber; publisher Emanuel P. Adler; James U. Nichols, Chamber of Commerce secretary; and John C. Shenk, secretary/treasurer of the First Federal Savings and Loan. In announcing his committee, Von Maur said, "There is no way to estimate the true value of St. Ambrose college to the community . . . [but] the character of St. Ambrose, in its effect spiritually and culturally, makes its value outstanding to the city and community." Von Maur also sounded what would become a familiar theme for the campaign, the economic contribution of the college to the community: "The city of Davenport owes much more to St. Ambrose than it can ever repay," but he said that helping the building project would be a "small token of our debt" to this great community asset.[11] Dougherty and Father Cullinan formed a committee for the diocesan phase of the campaign. This committee included Thomas J. Walsh, a former member of the Board of Trustees as chairman; Homer H. Mueller, a hotel owner from Muscatine; Judge Maurice Donegan, current member of the Board of Trustees; Eugene J. Walsh, a Davenport attorney; and Ralph J. Leysen of the *Davenport Daily Times*.[12] This was a critical part of the campaign because Dougherty said that success among the non-Catholic friends of St. Ambrose would depend on the level of support by the Catholics of the diocese.

This phase of the fund drive included the entire diocese, and each deanery had a campaign committee. Bishop Rohlman attended each of five regional meetings throughout the diocese where he made the case for the campaign. He noted the progress that had been made since he came to the

diocese. He admitted that it had not been "easy sailing" during the Depression: farm values had dropped and income from farms the college owned had fallen from $30,000 a year to practically nothing. He praised the college priests who took "substantial cuts" in their salaries that made it possible to keep the college in the black. Now, however, it was time to make improvements at the college and he was counting on the people of the diocese to make that possible.[13] To keep parishioners informed, a weekly Diocesan Bulletin was provided to every parish for the weekends of October and November that gave an update on the drive and brief endorsements of the effort by Catholics from around the diocese.

Dougherty also sent a letter to the alumni asking for contributions. A follow-up letter in December to those who had not yet pledged pointed out that this was the first time the alumni had been asked to donate to the college. The college had gone into debt to give them an educational opportunity, and now they had an opportunity to say "thank you" to the college.

The kick-off event for the campaign was a dinner on October 31 for fifty community leaders who formed the various special gifts committees for the Friends group. Chairman Emanuel P. Adler announced lead gifts totaling $5,000 toward the Friends goal of $50,000. There were several speakers who emphasized the importance of St. Ambrose to Davenport. John C. Shenk noted that this was the first time in the fifty-seven year history of the college that it had asked for help from the general public. He pointed out that the community would work hard to bring a business that would put $600,000 a year into the local economy as St. Ambrose did, and he said that given that fact he was surprised by the "modesty" of the $50,000 goal for the campaign.

Several speakers noted the tolerance to other faiths shown by St. Ambrose and evidenced by the attendance at the dinner. No one developed that theme more vividly than the Reverend Alfred S. Nickless, pastor of the First Presbyterian Church. Noting that they were meeting on Halloween, Nickless said that through the years St. Ambrose had done much to "save youths from the spooks of ignorance." In the world which was now at war, Nickless noted that there were four philosophies "striving for mastery of the world . . . Communism, the Nazism-Facism doctrine of state supremacy," secularism, and the Kingdom of God. He said if the nation was to "survive as the home of liberty," the Kingdom of God must "have command of our youth." He reported that members of his congregation who had been students there had "only the highest words of praise for St. Ambrose."

With a group made up of leaders from the Protestant and Jewish communities of Davenport, it was not surprising that the emphasis that evening was on raising money for the library-administration building. Attorney Alfred C. Mueller said that supporting the new library-administration building would be evidence of the appreciation of Davenport to the college and as a "symbol of the spirit of Davenport, where we work together regardless of spiritual belief or racial ancestry." In his closing remarks, Bishop Rohlman emphasized the same point and he thanked the leaders for their "willingness to co-operate with us in building a greater St. Ambrose."[14]

Three days after the dinner, the bishop confessed his initial misgivings about the campaign. He knew the need for the buildings and the liquidation of the debt, but he was not sure if the timing was opportune and whether the priests and people would cooperate. He was encouraged by the early reports from the parishes. Then when the first reports of the campaign from among the priests of the diocese indicated that they had pledged more than $91,000, "it dispelled the clouds" and his "misgivings vanished immediately." He said he had been "basking in the sunshine of confidence ever since."[15]

Lee Dougherty was also pleased with the results. At the end of November, he said that the campaign workers were entitled to two Thanksgivings, "first to thank the good Lord that we are American citizens and live in a country far away from war; second to thank the Lord for the fact that we live in Davenport where people actually work and plan together." At the end of the year, Dougherty released the campaign total of $477,511, including $95,200 from the priests, $341,467 from the people of the diocese, and $40,859 from the Friends of St. Ambrose. In early 1940, enough of the pledges had been paid that the college was able to make a $100,000 payment on the debt.[16]

As the campaign continued through the fall of 1939, the *Ambrosian News* reported a conversation allegedly overheard between two students on campus which indicated that little had changed for them: "First student: Let's cut class next period. Second Student: Naw, I can't afford to lose the sleep." The paper also reported that "queer creatures with green-topped heads and grasping hands" were busy gathering wood for the homecoming bonfire. The motto of the beanie-clad freshmen was "If it burns—we need it."[17]

Just before homecoming, it was announced that the college would have the first yearbook since 1923. The editor of that yearbook had been Thomas Lew, and now Father Thomas Lew was named as the advisor for the revived publication. Through the winter and spring, the students held dances to raise money for the yearbook, and in the spring semester there was a subscription campaign. The new publication, the *Oaks*, included St. Ambrose and Marycrest and the yearbook staff had students from both campuses.[18]

Homecoming brought back members of the class of 1919 and other students who were at St. Ambrose during the Great War and the flu epidemic. Their hosts, the current students, were watching another war in Europe with great interest. In early October, Father Thomas Lew, as the college chaplain, led the students in prayers for peace. Later that month the editor of the *Ambrosian News* said that United States' intervention in the war on behalf of England and France would lead to problems not of American concern. If the government proposed to draft American youth it would be a "violation of their Constitutional rights," and he said that the only thing that would prevent the draft would be for "America's youth [to] . . . oppose intervention in Europe and oppose conscription."[19]

On October 25, 1939, six weeks after the beginning of the war in Europe, 205 St. Ambrose students took part in a national poll on the war conducted by *America* magazine. The poll indicated that 95 percent of Ambrosians were opposed to American entry into the war, 51 percent believed the United States would be drawn into the war, 73 percent believed American intervention would not lead to a stable peace, 68 percent said there should be a national referendum before the United States declared war. If war was declared, 14 percent said it would be their duty to volunteer, 41 percent would accept conscription, and 44 percent would consider

conscientious objection. The figures at St. Ambrose generally mirrored the national figures compiled by over 50,000 students from across the country.[20]

The attitude of the students about war reflected the attitude of most Americans in the years leading up to the outbreak of war. By the 1930s, many Americans had become convinced that the United States had been drawn into the Great War in 1917 by British propaganda and Woodrow Wilson's moralism. Rather than make the "world safe for democracy," American participation in the war had only made the world safe for big business which had made enormous profits. In the 1930s, Americans turned inward to isolationism expressed by a series of Neutrality Acts passed by Congress to prevent the United States from supplying nations at war. President Roosevelt did not share those attitudes, and following the invasion of Poland, he said the United States would "remain a neutral nation" but that he could not ask Americans to "remain neutral in thought." As events in Europe unfolded, he was faced with supporting Great Britain while slowly moving Americans away from isolationism.[21]

That fall St. Ambrose took a small step away from the anti-war attitude on campus when it was one of five Iowa colleges selected by the Civil Aeronautics Authority to participate in a civilian pilot training program. The program was to train pilots for civilian aviation and stimulate the growth of private aviation, but many of the students would eventually become military pilots. Twenty students were selected from the fifty who applied. They began their Ground School with Margaret L. Yates and their flight instruction with O. Ray Hansen, the manager of Cram Field in northwest Davenport. Ten of the twenty finished the course and continued for advanced training at flight schools in Oklahoma and Florida, several enlisted in the Army Air Corps, and two enlisted in the Canadian Air Force, which was already in the war.[22]

As the fund drive continued, in December 1939, Monsignor Meinberg called together a group of the college priests to begin discussions about the new chapel. They said the chapel should seat 500 people, have a large sanctuary with a pontifical throne, have ample space for a student choir, and a large sacristy. They wanted a liturgical altar, one that is used solely for the sacrifice of the Mass, rather than an altar where Mass was celebrated and which also held the tabernacle, as was the custom in most churches. Finally, Meinberg said some of the priests were "of the opinion that everything should be on the same level."[23] They decided the chapel would be west of Ambrose Hall (in the current area of the flag pole) and it would face Locust Street.

In January, Casimir I. Krajewski of Dubuque was hired as the chapel architect. Born in Poland, Krajewski had opened an office in Dubuque in 1927. He had previously worked in the Diocese of Davenport when he designed St. Mary's Church in Ottumwa. At the same time the college hired Arthur Ebeling, a local architect, to work with Krajewski on the chapel.[24]

The original intent was to begin the chapel in the spring of 1940 and then "later" begin the library-administration building. Late that spring, it was announced that work would begin that summer and students who returned for the fall semester could expect to see both buildings under construction.[25]

The planning for the two buildings had barely gotten underway when in February 1940, the first of two significant changes at the college was announced. Football coach Dukes Duford, basketball coach Bob Klenck, and track coach Don Geyer were leaving St. Ambrose to coach at St. Louis University. Duford was succeeded as head coach by Larry "Moon" Mullins. A native of California, Mullins had played football at Notre Dame under coach Knute Rockne. Following graduation, Mullins had coached at Kansas University, Loyola of New Orleans, and St. Benedict's in Atchison, Kansas. Jim Dockery, who had played for Mullins at St. Benedict's, was hired as his assistant coach. In addition to his football duties, Dockery also coached basketball and taught physical education.[26]

The week after the announcement that Dukes Duford was leaving, Meinberg was named the pastor of St. Mary's Parish in Iowa City to replace Monsignor A. J. Schulte who had died on January 17. Schulte's life as a priest coincided with that of the diocese; he was the first man Bishop McMullen ordained for the new Diocese of Davenport and his death broke one of the last links with those early days.[27]

As student, professor of history, and president, Meinberg had been at St. Ambrose for thirty-five years. The *Ambrosian News* praised him as "cooperative, assiduous, reserved and resourceful" with a "progressiveness" that would be "a contributing factor to the expansion of an institution which has adopted 'progress' as its watchword." The new buildings would be evidence of this.[28]

In Meinberg's place the bishop named Father Ambrose Burke. Burke was a graduate of St. Ambrose Academy and College. Following his ordination in 1921, he returned to St. Ambrose where he taught and was principal in the Academy, and upon completion of his PhD in English from Yale University, joined the college faculty as a professor of English. Bishop Rohlman wrote Burke on February 14 to make his appointment official, telling him that he was "eminently qualified for this position of responsibility."[29]

The *Messenger* praised Burke as a "leader of extensive experience and high scholastic attainments." Burke said that he was "deeply honored" to become president at a time of such "great prospects." The "current plans for the chapel and administration building . . . [ensured] prosperous times" as he took over the presidency. The student paper said that with Burke's appointment, as well as the new buildings, a "new order" was "manifesting itself at St. Ambrose."[30]

In remarks to the campus community, Burke said he was "somewhat shaken" when he learned that the bishop intended to appoint him as president. With self-deprecation, he said that if the local grade school children were asked who the president of St. Ambrose was they would reply, "Moon Mullins," who had been named the new football coach the same day. He said no president had ever been inaugurated under "more favorable conditions," because with a successful campaign the debt would be eliminated and the building program could begin. He also wondered about the function of a modern college president. Presidents Schulte, Flannagan, and Shannahan "*knew* what their task was. They *ran* the college." They bought groceries, kept the books, selected faculty, were responsible for discipline, and taught a full schedule of classes. But many of those duties were now done by others, so it was difficult to know what he should do. He said a former president told him his "chief problem–and most important duty–[was] to preserve harmony among the faculty." With that he asked for the advice of the faculty, telling them, "St. Ambrose is not the Bishop's college, it is not the President's, it belongs to all of us and all of us should have a voice in determining its policies." Then quoting Polonius' advice to Laertes, "Those friends thou hast, and their adoption tried,/Grapple them to thy soul with hoops of steel," he said he had the courage to become president because he knew he could count on their help and prayers.[31]

In the months ahead the new president would need the support of all his friends on and off campus. First, there was the challenge of planning for the construction of two buildings at the same time. There were also the challenges brought about by the war in Europe. In the months following the fall of Poland in September 1939, there was little fighting in western Europe, leading some in the United States to call what was happening in Europe a "phony war." Like the students polled the previous fall, many Americans thought there was no reason to become involved in the war in Europe. To others it seemed inevitable that eventually American boys would be in uniform on their way to Europe. Among the impacts of that would be a drastic decline in college enrollments.

On March 17, 1940, Burke convened the Committee on National Defense, with Father Gerald Lillis as chair, and nine lay and clerical faculty members. The committee was to "advise in matters pertaining to students" affected by a potential government draft. The committee discussed a policy to enable a student to retain his credit hours if he were to be drafted in the middle of a semester. They agreed that any such policy "must not only be just but also generous." The chair appointed a committee to advise in individual cases, to help students fill out the necessary papers, and to assist the government in gathering information on students. The committee also discussed the possibility of providing on-campus military training for St. Ambrose students, but it did not come to any conclusion.[32]

The appointment of the Committee on National Defense when the war was "phony" was prescient. In April and May 1940, Germany rolled through Denmark, Norway, and the Low Countries. On May 10, Winston Churchill became prime minister of Great Britain proclaiming to the House of Commons that he had "nothing to offer but blood, toil, tears and sweat." Joseph Shekleton, a senior from Peoria and associate editor of the *Ambrosian News* noted Churchill's statement and told his readers, "Students, you are the fodder for our next war . . . You may volunteer . . . this writer doesn't intend to . . . but even if you don't it will be but a matter of months or weeks or even days until you find yourself in a uniform and sitting in front of a plate of beans." He said it would take "a lot of diplomacy to keep America out of this war. That diplomacy doesn't seem to be forthcoming. It looks as if we're stuck, fellow students."[33] At commencement that spring, Irving Berlin's new hymn, "God Bless America," was added to the program.

When Burke spoke to the incoming class in the fall of 1940, the war in Europe was just over one year along. Paris had fallen in June, and the Battle of Britain was raging as he spoke. The Japanese had already swept past Father Meyer's St. Ambrose in China and were beginning the occupation of

A Great and Lasting Beginning

French Indo-China. On September 27, Germany, Italy, and Japan joined together in a three-power pact to "promote the prosperity of their peoples." At home President Franklin D. Roosevelt had signed the Selective Training and Service Act, and the day before Burke spoke over sixteen million American men had registered in preparation for the first draft lottery the next week.

The war was coming to St. Ambrose in other ways. Two new professors who had fled the war came to teach at St. Ambrose. Robert Hernried was a professor of music from Vienna. He was an opera conductor, composer, editor of the letters of Richard Wagner, and in the 1930s, lectured at the University of Heidelberg. At St. Ambrose he taught music and conducted the St. Ambrose-Marycrest Orchestra. Physics Professor Dr. Zaboj V. Harvalik taught and did research in Prague before he left Europe and came to St. Ambrose.

As the alumni returned for homecoming in October 1940, all Ambrosians wondered what role they would play in the widening war in Europe. Two months before, the Reverend Michael J. Martin, the president of Loras College, asked Burke if St. Ambrose was going to do anything about military training on campus. Martin noted that it was under discussion at Loras but the sentiment was "strongly against it." Burke told Martin that if it was necessary, St. Ambrose would cooperate but would not take the initiative in the matter and would simply "await orders." The editor of the *Ambrosian News* took a similar wait-and-see tone when he wrote, "With Rome and Berlin tightening their axis . . . and Washington meeting crisis after crisis, it remains to be seen just what role representatives of this college will be forced to play in the future."[34]

But for now it was homecoming, the students were building another bonfire, and everyone hoped that the activities would divert their attention from the war. Still, the specter of war was present. The paper noted that the bonfire was not the "conflagration of civilization" that many were predicting and that there was no sense that the dancing feet would "soon become marching feet, or the lilting waltz a martial air of battle."

The highlight of the weekend was the football game. The team was undefeated and unscored upon in Moon Mullins' first year as head coach, and that Sunday, hundreds of Ambrosians joined thousands of Americans who gathered to "watch and cheer for their favorites on the gridiron." They relaxed "secure blanketed by the blue skies of freedom and [watched] young men clash in the friendly rivalry which is football. Such is the safety valve of sport; such is Americanism."[35] The Bees' undefeated record remained intact with a 7-0 victory over St. Norbert's. The Bees ended their season two weeks later with a 0-0 game against Loras, running their record to eight wins and one tie, and holding all their opponents scoreless.

Rev. Ambrose Burke.

Planning continued on the library-administration building under the direction of the architectural firm of Kruse and Parish. It was to be built on several pieces of property the college had recently purchased on the corner of Gaines and Locust Streets. Among those properties was a house owned by Frances Armil Wass that was moved to Scott Street, east of Ambrose Hall (known to later generations of students as the Gray House). This Armil house became the first "permanent home" on campus for the Sisters of Humility.

The sisters had staffed the domestic department since St. Ambrose began accepting boarding students in 1887. In the first decades, the sisters did all the work in the kitchen, laundry, and living areas; now they supervised a lay staff. The kitchen supervisor was Sister Mary Carmella, a graduate dietician. Sister Mary Emmanuel supervised the general housekeeping, and Sister Mary of the Cross, who had been at St. Ambrose since 1904, was in charge of the laundry. Another long-serving member of the staff, Sister Mary Bridget, was renowned for her pies.

Through those years they had lived in various places in Ambrose Hall, and for some of those years they also had lived at St. Vincent's Home. Library architect Arthur Ebeling added onto the original house and remodeled it. The second floor had eight bedrooms for the sisters. The first floor contained the chapel with all the furnishings designed and manufactured by Walter Vander Vennet of Moline.[36]

Now that space was opened for construction, contracts for the library-administration building in the amount of $123,747 were let in September 1940. The work began immediately and the campus community quickly became accustomed to the "hubbub of the cement mixer and the clatter of wheelbarrows."[37] The building was designed with a north entrance to the administration section of the first floor which included the president's office and other offices. An east entrance led to several classrooms on the first floor. The campus post office was also located on the first floor. The library on the second floor included a large reading room on the north. The south half contained the stacks and featured narrow windows made of glass blocks. Space was reserved for the future installation of an elevator.[38] Construction continued through the winter and the hope was that it would be finished by June 1941.

On August 20, 1940, the bids for the chapel had been received in the amount of $92,469. The priests had pledged just over $95,000 for the chapel but they were five-year pledges, and there was very little cash available. The decision was made to delay construction of the chapel until more money was available and the students were informed that the chapel would be delayed until the library-administration building was "nearer completion."[39]

As building continued in the spring of 1941, the college community watched as the first of its members received draft notices and left school. Sophomore Andy Lumbrazo, a "hot trumpet player" and the first tenor in the campus quartet, was one of the first to go. He did not know where he would be sent for basic training but said he hoped to be in the Army Air Corps Band. Father Madsen worried about his loss to the music program. Coach Mullins also worried when several of his football players received their notices. As their classmates prepared to leave, twenty-six students were asked by the *Ambrosian News* if they favored the United States entering the war; twenty-five still responded no.[40]

Some Ambrosians were already in the service. The Civilian Pilot Program organized in 1939 was now a regular part of the curriculum. Many of its graduates had entered the armed forces and taken additional training. In January, three Ambrosians had graduated from basic flight training at Randolph Field, Texas, the "West Point of the Air," and were now on active duty. One was a flight instructor, another was with the Army Air Corps at Pearl Harbor, Hawaii. Several more were in the navy, and others had applied to the service and were waiting for orders.[41]

That spring saw the first commencement ceremony held out-of-doors as St. Ambrose, Marycrest, and St. Ambrose Academy graduates gathered on the lawn east of Davis Hall. The speaker was Dr. Franklin Dunham, Director of Education for the National Broadcasting Company. In January President Roosevelt had said that the war in Europe was to preserve the Four Freedoms: the freedom of speech and worship and the freedom from want and fear. Dunham said these were essential to a happy, peaceful, well-ordered life, but he stressed that sacrifice was necessary to live "God's way of life." To the graduates who were facing an uncertain future, he said, "Let nothing disturb you. Let nothing frighten you. All things are passing. God's wants are the only wants."[42]

The radio studio Madsen and the students had built was still in use. In the fall of 1939, the Reverend Francis Williams, a member of the Congregation of St. Viator, joined the faculty and organized the Radio Guild. The Guild included students from St. Ambrose and Marycrest. There were four-and-one-half hours of broadcasting each week over Davenport radio station WOC. The programming was varied and included lectures, interviews with coaches, the broadcast of games, dances, and banquets. Father Madsen had a regular program, "Among the Masters," where he played and discussed music. Sometimes there was special programming; one semester a six-week series of lectures by Monsignor Fulton J. Sheen was aired.[43]

Radio had also become curricular with courses in radio production and radio writing, taught by Father Williams. Harvalik taught a new course in radio and television in the Physics department. In response to a call for more radio operators for defense needs, Williams and Harvalik organized courses to train them. Another war-related course that summer was a twelve-week class in the chemistry of powder and explosives to help individuals obtain jobs in industries with ordnance contracts.[44]

Colleges all through the country were adding courses to train people for defense work. This was a continuation of the trend to provide specialized courses that had begun in the 1920s, and which the St. Ambrose faculty

had discussed in the mid-1930s. Back then Cone had worried that too much emphasis in the curriculum of professional studies would draw St. Ambrose away from its liberal arts core. Now, in the face of those new specialized courses, Hauber expressed a similar concern. In an essay presented to the Contemporary Club in October 1941, Hauber acknowledged the trend to "training experts who will know the answers to technical questions," and said that the war had created a need for more of those experts. But rather than train technical experts, colleges should "train men to think out the problems that concern the ultimate welfare of human beings," they should not concentrate on mankind, as the totalitarian states in Europe had done, and ignore the individual human. The answer, Hauber concluded, was not to teach knowledge, but wisdom.[45]

In the same essay Hauber had also discussed the fact that most economic planners thought that once the war was over, the economic distresses of the Depression would return. A large body of educated people "deprived of the means of a decent livelihood" would be a problem, but Hauber said that economic planning alone was not the solution. Such plans were only "emergency measures, not cures," and they needed to be followed by a "deep-seated moral transformation of the people."

That summer Bishop Rohlman convened a Social Action Conference to address questions of morality and the economic condition of people. The occasion was the fiftieth anniversary of Pope Leo XIII's encyclical *Rerum Novarum*, and the tenth anniversary of Pope Pius XI's, *Quadragesimo Anno*. The conference was organized by a committee of St. Ambrose faculty members, chaired by the Reverend William T. O'Connor. Father Bill, who was the younger brother of Father Ed (as they were known), had graduated from St. Ambrose Academy and College. He studied theology at the Catholic University of America, was ordained in 1933, and was assigned to the faculty of the academy. In 1936, he joined the sociology faculty of the college. After graduate work at Columbia and the Catholic University of America, he had earned his PhD in sociology that spring.

The theme of the conference was to take the principles of social justice in the papal encyclicals, and discuss them in the context of the current economic and social status of Americans. As Father Charles Griffith, one of the conference organizers, noted in a pre-conference article, many American workers were in a "vicious circle" which gave them little chance of improvement. Griffith said the conference would discuss replacing that with a "beneficent circle" based on religious and moral values. The problem was the "low annual income" of Americans. Leo XIII had called for a living wage, and Pius XI expanded that to a living and fully just wage. Griffith said the conference would bring together "competent" people "grown old in study of the Social Question," and "able industrialists, from both capital and labor" to present "proposals for the solution" of the problems.[46]

The list of participants included most of the leaders of Catholic Action in America. Monsignor John A. Ryan spoke about the improvement which had been made in the past fifty years, in large measure because of union activity which had inspired new legislation. Dorothy Day, editor of the *Catholic Worker*, spoke about being on the picket line, where in addition to seeking justice, she spoke of the gospel message to her fellow picketers. Frank Delaney, a wage and hour attorney of the United States Department

A Great and Lasting Beginning

of Labor, discussed the substance of cases which came before his agency. John L. Yancy, an African-American labor leader, spoke about unskilled workers, black and white, who received only about 40 percent of a living wage. Monsignor Luigi Ligutti, the executive secretary of the National Catholic Rural Life Conference, talked about share cropping and tenant farming. Meyer Kestnbaum, president of Hart, Schaffner and Marx said that democracy would work when the "employing and monied class become as anxious to make it work for the many at the bottom as well as for the few at the top."[47]

The 1941 Social Action Conference continued a theme on campus that had begun in the 1920s under the leadership of Cone. Some of the speakers had appeared on campus before, most notably Ryan who first spoke at St. Ambrose before World War I. Day had spoken the previous November, and the year before, her co-founder of the Catholic worker movement, Peter Maurin, had spoken. Baroness Catherine de Heuck, founder of Friendship House in Harlem, spoke in December about bigotry and racial prejudice among Catholics and Christians, and her fight against communism in Harlem.[48] In the years after the war, the O'Connor brothers, Griffith, and others would make those issues an important part of the milieu of St. Ambrose.

In memory of Vic Pahl.

of the new building that included the bishop, St. Ambrose officials, delegates representing thirty-two colleges and educational organizations, the trustees of the college, and guests. Following the invocation by Cone, all sang "America." Honorary degrees were awarded to the Reverend Michael Martin, president of Loras College, the Reverend Monsignor J. J. Boylan, president of Dowling College in Des Moines, and Dr. Virgil Hancher, president of the University of Iowa.

The principal speaker was United States Postmaster general James A. Farley. Farley said they were gathered to dedicate one of "the precious treasures of this world . . . the link which binds the past with the present and the future, the work of the minds of scholars, present, past and future, perfect and imperfect." He told the audience that it was through the contents of the library that we "become a member of the great human family and a citizen of the world." He turned his attention to the war in Europe and said books reveal that those who attempt tyranny "come . . . to desolation . . . Against the dangers that surround us, we must be united in the common cause of country. It is just in defense of such precious things as this library, that we must raise the mighty forces of this nation in defense."[51]

The library-administration building was dedicated in a two-day celebration on October 23-24, 1941. The first event was the dedication of a statue of the Blessed Mother donated by the Alumni Association in memory of Vic Pahl which was placed in the stairway that led to the library. The editor of the *Ambrosian News* said that at the time of Pahl's death, he was remembered as a "gentleman, scholar, and athlete." He asked what more could a "Christian young man strive for" than those ideals?[49]

The next morning Bishop Rohlman celebrated Mass in the reading room of the new library and blessed the building. In his sermon Cone said that the library was the "first of two essential and complementary structures" that would be built on campus. The other was a chapel which Cone said was "the very center of truth on a college campus, the truth reflected in divine revelation. The library, with its volumes, is the repository of the truths which man has learned." In the meantime, the money that had been donated for the chapel remained to serve as the nucleus for a future chapel project.[50]

Following lunch at the Blackhawk Hotel, everyone assembled for the dedication ceremonies. There was an academic procession to the east steps

When Ambrosians awoke the morning of December 7, 1941, they had little reason to suspect that day would be any different than any other Sunday. The newspapers were filled with the dangers of war with Japan. Negotiations were under way to avert war, but the United States' insistence that Japan pull out of China had proved to be a stumbling block. The local newspapers had carried stories all week about the continuing negotiations. That morning a banner headline in the *Davenport Democrat and Leader* announced, "F.D.R. Sends Note to Jap Emperor." But the paper had carried banner headlines about the continuing negotiations all week. Inside the paper, the editor urged that there be no compromise with the Japanese on the issue of China.[52] The other stories on the front page concerned news of the 829th day of the war in Europe.

People who lingered over the paper before church might have looked inside the paper at the ads for holiday gift ideas. There were fourteen shopping days until Christmas. Retail sales were good nation-wide, up about 35 percent from the previous year. In part this was because of a rising industrial payroll and an increase in farm prices due to defense spending. But another reason for the rise in holiday consumer spending was voiced by a New York merchant who said that many people feared 1941 may be the "last chance for a real Christmas for many years."[53] If there was still time before church, the comics provided a momentary diversion, with the adventures of Superman, Popeye, Joe Jinks, Etta Kett, or Brick Bradford, who was engaged in mortal combat with a giant frog. Before the day was over, many may have wished for a man of steel or a spinach-eating sailor-man to set the world aright.

It was the second Sunday of Advent, but Ambrosians celebrated a Solemn High Mass presided over by Bishop Rohlman to celebrate the feast of their patron. The epistle was from Second Timothy where Paul said he had been "poured out like a libation," that he had competed well, finished the race, and "kept the faith." The gospel that morning was from Matthew where Jesus urged his disciples not to hide their light under a bushel basket. Hauber preached and talked about the similarities between Ambrose's world and theirs.[54]

In the refectory for Sunday dinner, the students were most likely not talking about Ambrose's world or how soon many of them would be poured out. Most were probably talking about the studying in store for them that day, or looking forward to the radio broadcast that afternoon of the football game between the Chicago Bears and the Chicago Cardinals, or the talk by Fulton J. Sheen on "The Unity of Mankind," to be broadcast on St. Ambrose College on the Air.

They may have talked about their classmate and friend, Jack Grennan, the center on the football team, who had died the previous week of a brain tumor. An editorial in the *Ambrosian News* entitled, "Death in Our Life," reminded the readers that "time and time again" death had struck quickly in the student body. It mentioned Ed Morrissey, who had died so long ago of a broken leg on the football field; athlete Vic Pahl; Robert Spurling, the editor of the *Ambrosian News* who had died suddenly in 1937; and Louis Machincich, a freshman center on the basketball team who died the next year. The editor said that students could not wait until they were of "advanced age" to prepare themselves for the possibility of death.[55]

Whatever they chose to do, their afternoon was interrupted by the first announcement that American forces at Pearl Harbor had been attacked by

Program for the football dinner, Sunday evening, December 7, 1941.

Japan. The attack began at 7:55 Sunday morning, Hawaii time, when the first of two waves of Japanese carrier-planes attacked naval and air bases. Two hours later it was over–and it had just begun. A total of eighteen American ships were either sunk or disabled, 188 American airplanes were destroyed, and another 159 were damaged. Two thousand four hundred and three Americans were killed, and another 1,178 were wounded. The Japanese also attacked American forces on Guam, Midway, and at Clark Field in the Philippines as well as British colonies on the Malay Peninsula and Hong Kong.

Word quickly spread throughout campus and the students became part of a national community gathered around their radios for the latest news. With so many radios tuned so loud, it was possible to walk across campus that afternoon and not miss anything. Groups of students spontaneously began to sing "Anchors Away," or "We're in the Army Now." One wag said that the St. Ambrose "men with wings," students in the civilian pilot program, did not have a song and he hoped that "some campus Cole Porter would oblige the eagles."[56]

That night 552 people gathered at a banquet to honor the football team which had just finished a 6-2 season under first-year coach Jim Dockery. Moon Mullins, who had led the team to the undefeated, unscored-upon season the year before, had left St. Ambrose to become an assistant coach at the University of Florida.[57]

Notre Dame football coach Frank Leahy was the principal speaker. He said he had looked at the Bees' schedule for the next season and predicted success for the team. Following his talk, Leahy showed films from Notre Dame's undefeated season. Other speakers were also optimistic about the next football season at St. Ambrose. The emotional high point of the evening came when alumnus John Gerwe sang "Ambrosian Oaks." There were tears in the eyes of many listeners when Gerwe, who had been in the car when Vic Pahl was injured, added the rarely sung verse about him, the last two lines of which, "Vic Pahl in helmet watches from the sky/The men of Ambrose, victors all," now took on an added

A Great and Lasting Beginning

meaning. During the program, there was no mention of the events of the day, but after the banquet when coach Dockery was asked about the prospects for the next fall, he replied, "Maybe there won't be any football next fall."[58]

Monday morning was more than the beginning of a new week of school, it was the beginning of a new era. Davenport newspapers reported no "hysteria or false enthusiasm," just a "calm realization that the American people had a new job to do." Still, the editorial in the *Democrat and Leader* began, "Japan Must Suffer." When the navy recruiting office opened that morning, two men were already in line. At the army recruiting office, a man on crutches walked in to enlist. Before the day was over, more than one hundred men had enlisted in Davenport.

Just after noon in Washington, D.C., President Franklin Roosevelt entered the chamber of the House of Representatives and began his war message: "Yesterday, December 7, 1941–a date which will live in infamy–the United States of America was suddenly and deliberately attacked by naval and air forces of the Empire of Japan." Congress quickly voted a declaration of war with only one dissenting vote. Within days Germany and Italy declared war on the United States.

Life in Davenport changed quickly. All private airplanes were grounded and pilots' licenses were suspended. The pilot training program at St. Ambrose was suspended until the citizenship of the students could be determined. Most industrial plants posted extra guards to prevent sabotage. Armed guards were stationed at both ends of the Centennial Bridge.[59]

Later that week Burke met with the students. Like college officials across the country, he urged the students to stay in school. A college education would best prepare them to serve in whatever way the country called them, in war or in the peace that followed. However, he said that if any student wanted to enlist, he would assist him. Then, responding to rumors, Burke declared that St. Ambrose would "be open next semester, next year, and the following year."[60]

As Christmas approached, the students began a novena of prayers at the shrine of the Blessed Mother to ask Mary to help the United States in wartime. They addressed her under the titles Our Lady of the Battlefield, Star of the Sea, and Our Lady of the Airways. They also prayed for the St. Ambrose men already in the service.[61]

The need for prayers as Americans entered the war was great. But two events that weekend that had the most profound consequences for history went unreported. On December 6, Vannevar Bush, head of the federal office of Scientific Research and Development, convened the first meeting of a small group assigned to explore the possible use of uranium-235 as a weapon of war. From this group came the Manhattan Project and the atomic bomb.

On the night of December 7, 700 Jews arrived in the Polish village of Chelmno. The next morning the first groups were loaded into closed trucks and driven to a nearby woods. There the exhaust system was redirected into the back of the trucks, and the Jews were gassed, their bodies dumped into pits. Hitler's SS was beginning to find efficient means for the final solution, the mass extermination of Jews and other "undesirables." The Holocaust had begun.

The second semester began with a decline in enrollment. Some students

had been called into military service, others had taken high-paying defense jobs. For those who did return, ordinary college life continued, but the war was never far from their minds. In late January, the students sponsored a Defense Stamp Ball at the Blackhawk Hotel to promote the purchase of war bonds and stamps. The proceeds from the Loras-St. Ambrose basketball game in March were donated to the Red Cross.[62]

In other ways, little had changed. Residence hall life was still regulated. Students could not leave campus without permission, but they could go to Swan's Drug Store on the corner of Locust and Harrison right after supper. They had to be in their rooms studying from seven- to ten-o'clock. No room visiting was allowed and radios could not be played during that time. However, one student rigged his radio switch to the door so that when the door opened, the radio turned off.[63]

When they did leave campus, they frequented the Airport Inn at Cram Field; the Colonial Fountain at Twelfth and Harrison; one of Heeter's Lunch Tavern Taprooms, usually the one on West Locust; or The Lark out on Brady Street. A group could share a cab for thirty-five cents or ride the ferry between Davenport and Rock Island for a nickel. A favorite downtown hangout was the Walgreen Drug Store, the site of the "Coke League," so called because Marycrest and ICA girls came in for a Coke while waiting to change buses. In the basement of Ambrose Hall was the College Inn, run by William Oberhaus, who dispensed food and advice. Food prices had recently gone up; Oberhaus blamed the war.[64]

The first significant change came in January 1942 with the announcement that in response to a request by the National Committee on Education and Defense, an accelerated program of studies would be offered. Courses normally offered only in the fall semester would now be repeated in the spring so that students could begin a program in January. A new twelve-week summer semester would also be offered. This was especially critical in pre-medical, pre-engineering, and other programs that could directly relate to war-time needs. In addition many new courses would be offered in specialized fields like mapmaking, surveying, navigation, and mathematics courses.[65]

When Burke spoke to the students a few days after Pearl Harbor, some suggested his advice that they stay in school had more to do with their tuition income than their need for a college education. However, Burke was in earnest when he talked about the necessity of a college education to prepare the graduates for war-time or post-war time service to the country. Nevertheless, the potential was there that he could be the president of a college with few or no students. So when the federal government announced that colleges could apply to provide specialized military training programs, like many college presidents, Burke applied.

In April 1942, the Department of the Navy informed Burke that St. Ambrose was an approved college for the V-1 program. Under this plan freshmen or sophomores could enroll in the V-1 program and become enlisted men in the naval reserve. They would take regular college courses and participate in all the usual extracurricular activities. After two years the student could take an exam which would qualify him for the V-5 program for Naval Aviation Cadets or the V-7 program for reserve officers. If accepted into one of those programs, the student would stay at St. Ambrose to earn his college degree.[66] At the same time the Civilian Pilot Training program was accelerated from a sixteen-week program to an eight-week program. In the first year, 1942-1943, over 180 students were in the naval program and the Civilian Pilot Training program.

That fall the college added two one-hour courses in military science and tactics which was compulsory for the college students. The courses were taught by Capt. Clifford J. Dawson, Commander of Company B of the Iowa National Guard headquartered in Davenport. In addition to class work, the courses included regular drill which found the students in formation marching up and down the campus. This contributed to the "prevalence of a war-time spirit" that pervaded the campus and reinforced the "knowledge possessed by each student that only a short time will elapse before he will be in the armed forces." On November 20, those students, along with the V-1 students and the Civilian Pilot Training students, participated in the first military review in the history of the college held on the football field behind Ambrose Hall. The sense that this could be one of their last appearances on campus was heightened by a national news story in the *Ambrosian News* that day with the headline, "College Men Not in Reserves to be Drafted Soon."[67]

In the fall of 1942, American forces were preparing to join British forces in North Africa. In the Pacific, American forces had landed on Guadalcanal and begun the long fight to capture the island and begin the push north through the Solomon Islands. All the while Ambrosians looked over their shoulders wondering when their draft notice would come. While the campus tried to maintain an air of normality, the war had already changed their lives. Homecoming was scaled down. The bonfire was cancelled to conserve war materials; instead the green-capped freshmen collected metal for the scrap drive. The parade was cancelled because rationing regulations had put limits on the availability of gasoline and rubber. Even the game was scaled back as the Bees fought St. Joseph College to a 13-13 tie.[68]

Through the fall rumors floated around campus and in the larger community: St. Ambrose was going to close; the church students were being sent to Peoria; the navy was taking over the college. In mid-January 1943, Burke said that none of those rumors was true. He did say, however, that he had been corresponding with the United States Navy about the use of the campus for more training programs. If St. Ambrose was chosen, the college would remain open to all students. The only significant change would be that quite possibly there would be no boarding facilities for civilian students; day students would not be affected.[69]

There were 400 college students when the second semester began in February 1943. About one hundred were draft eligible, and others had already been drafted. One by one, and in small groups, the notices came and the students left school. One student remembered seeing friends and classmates off at the railroad depot on "cold winter nights." "It was a sad time for us all," he remembered, "their absence was evident everywhere–in the classrooms, the dining room, and in empty rooms in Davis Hall. Those of us still in school waited for the other shoe to drop."[70]

It was not just the students; in January coach Jim Dockery left for the Marine Corps. He had been the football and basketball coach for two seasons. His players admired the "intense fighting spirit of 'Gentleman Jim,'" and they all agreed that "Jim will be right at home with the nation's greatest fighters–the United States Marines." In May the Alumni Association held a

Mass for the parents and members of the families of all the Ambrosians in the service. Hauber preached and said those at home had to help the men in the service with work and prayer.[71]

In early December 1942, the navy department wrote Burke to see if St. Ambrose was still interested in being used as a training center for the navy. Burke replied that the college authorities were "particularly desirous of having the navy take over" St. Ambrose. The college could accommodate 300 men and the entire "physical plant and faculty" would be at the disposal of the navy.[72]

In early April 1943, Burke was informed that St. Ambrose had been selected as a site for the navy's V-12 program and that 300 men would arrive July 1. St. Ambrose agreed to give the navy adequate classrooms and other instructional facilities, the use of all of Davis Hall, and rooms in Ambrose Hall for living quarters, the mess, and sick bay. The navy used four rooms in the library-administration building as offices for the commander and his staff. For this St. Ambrose received $939 per month, $6,000 per month in instructional costs, fifty cents per man per day for medical services, ninety cents per man per day for meals, and $921 per month for maintenance and utilities. Based on 300 men present, this totaled $16,110 for St. Ambrose each month. The college spent about $18,000 in "commissioning expenses," that included electrical and other work to make the spaces ready for the navy. However, Burke said this was work that needed to be done anyway but had not been possible during the meager days of the Depression.[73]

The goal of the program was to "give prospective naval officers the benefits of a college education in those areas most needed by the Navy."[74] The students were ranked as apprentice seamen and wore uniforms while on campus. In addition to classes, their daily schedule included inspection and drill. There were three sixteen-week sessions beginning July 1, November 1, and March 1. The students studied mathematics, English, the historical background of the war, engineering drawing, descriptive geometry, chemistry, psychology, naval organization, and physical training. Except for the explicitly military classes, the St. Ambrose faculty taught all the courses. The V-5 students still at St. Ambrose remained until they finished their program.[75]

The spring commencement on May 23, 1943, was held under the shadow of threatening skies. The rain held off, but the shadow of war was even more pronounced. St. Ambrose naval cadets formed the color guard, and men in uniform were scattered throughout the crowd. The most solemn moment came when Burke read the names of three navy ensigns and three army lieutenants who had died. They were six of the 600 St. Ambrose students who had gone through the Civilian Pilot Training Program and all had died in flying accidents.[76]

The commencement speaker was Rear Admiral John Downes, Commandant of the Ninth Naval District at Great Lakes, Illinois. Downes told the graduates that St. Ambrose had already made a "great contribution to the life of America." He spoke of freedom and said St. Ambrose represented the "right of free minds to continue their long, long search after truth." He mentioned the hundreds of men already trained at St. Ambrose and the 300 V-12 seamen who would arrive shortly and said, "St. Ambrose has

A Great and Lasting Beginning

The first company of naval cadets at St. Ambrose.

fought ignorance and hate and avarice for sixty long years; in her sixty-first she meets them again and through her navy-trained men she will defeat them."[77]

Burke now had to find room to accommodate the navy. He proposed to have 240 seamen in Davis Hall and another sixty in Ambrose Hall. All St. Ambrose boarding students and most of the priest-faculty would have to move off-campus. Current day students at St. Ambrose could remain until they graduated. St. Ambrose continued to accept civilian transfer students, but no new freshmen were admitted.

That summer twenty-six priest-faculty members moved to McAuley Hall at Eighth and Fillmore Streets. Built in the nineteenth century as a school for St. Mary's Parish run by the Sisters of Mercy, in recent years it had been a home for single women. The college purchased the building in May for $10,000 from the sisters and spent another $8,000 to remodel it to accommodate its new residents.[78]

In March 1943, Burke wrote Father Michael J. Martin, president of Loras, that the bishop was thinking of sending the seminarians to Loras if the navy took over St. Ambrose. The bishop wanted to be assured that Loras had been placed on the approved seminaries list by the Selective Service. Martin assured Burke that it was and that if the St. Ambrose seminarians came, their deferred draft status would be protected.[79]

With those assurances, thirty-six Davenport seminarians arrived at Loras College for the 1943 summer session, where they joined over seventy seminarians from the Dioceses of Dubuque, Des Moines, Rockford, and La Crosse. The bishop also asked Father Raymond Kinnavey to be in charge of the Davenport seminarians at Loras. Kinnavey was appointed as professor of Latin and Greek at Loras, the same position he held at St. Ambrose.[80]

The Ambrosians became part of the daily life at Loras. There had been some initial concern about living on the campus of the Bees' chief athletic rival, but they were made to feel welcome. The Ambrosians participated in

Loras clubs, the student newspaper, musical productions, and the freshmen underwent initiation, although minus the Ambrose "green caps." St. Ambrose student Jack Smith sent periodic reports of their activities which were published in the *Catholic Messenger*. Smith reported that at the beginning they were "still singing 'Ambrosian Oaks' in the shower room," but they all thought Loras was a "great place." Although they were students at Loras College, all their classes transferred back to St. Ambrose and when it was time, they returned to campus to graduate.[81]

The lay students and seminarians were not the only ones whose education was impacted by the arrival of the navy. At the time of Pearl Harbor there were about 127,000 people of Japanese ancestry in the United States, most of whom lived on the west coast. Eighty thousand had been born in the United States and were therefore American citizens. In the hysteria following Pearl Harbor, however, a fear arose that those Japanese-Americans could not be loyal to the United States. On February 19, 1942, two months after Pearl Harbor, President Roosevelt signed an executive order that resulted in the internment in desert camps of nearly 110,000 of those people. Sixty percent were American citizens and roughly 2,000 were college students whose education was abruptly interrupted.

In June 1942, a representative of the American Friends Service Committee wrote Burke and said the federal government was anxious to get the college-aged students back into school. He wondered if St. Ambrose would be able to take some of them who "considered themselves to be loyal American citizens" but who had "recognized the exigencies of a war situation and accepted the dislocation of their plans . . . in a spirit of patience and good will." Burke responded that St. Ambrose would take ten or more Catholic Japanese-American students.[82]

In October Burke was notified that St. Ambrose was one of ninety-three colleges that had been approved to receive students. Early the next year, Yonekazu Tanaka entered St. Ambrose. Born in San Francisco, Tanaka had been a student at the University of California at Berkeley before he and his family were sent to a camp at Heart Mountain, Wyoming. The college had also admitted Yonekazu's brother, Yukinori, but he did not come to St. Ambrose. Because the navy came to St. Ambrose that summer, there was concern about his presence on campus, so in the fall of 1943, Yonekazu Tanaka transferred to Columbia University.[83]

The navy came on board the "Good Ship St. Ambrose," on July 1, 1943. Some were already St. Ambrose students, some came from the University of Iowa, Iowa State, William Penn, Simpson, and other Midwestern schools. Others came from ships on duty in the Pacific, including two brothers who had served together on a submarine. Their days began with early morning calisthenics or a brisk, pre-dawn march down Locust Street. There was a formal parade at noon on Saturday, but other than that, their lives were not much different from the civilian students. The people of Davenport opened their homes to the seamen and invited them for meals. In that first summer, there were 296 in the V-12 program, ninety-four in V-5, and sixty-four civilians. It was a big adjustment to an administration which was used to complete control of the campus, but after the navy had been on campus for

six weeks, Burke told a recent graduate, "We are gradually becoming accustomed to the Navy. They are letting up a little on their demands, and we are learning to say, 'No.'"[84]

The demands on the time of the seamen were great, and there was little time left over for the usual collegiate activities. They were not allowed to play football, so for three seasons there was no football at St. Ambrose. The college did find volunteer coaches to put together a navy-St. Ambrose basketball team but it was young: in 1944 four starters were freshmen, and the team lacked height, talent, and wins. Nevertheless, the games were an important part of campus life. At the first home game in December, the massed seamen sang the national anthem and "Anchors Aweigh." During half-time the navy chorus sang songs, and throughout the game the navy band played using instruments loaned by the college. The band was also a regular feature at military parades and at the retiring of the colors each evening.[85]

The seamen published a weekly newspaper, the *Sea Breez*. Publication began in September 1943 and continued for two years when the program was shut down. As the seamen rotated out every few months, a new staff took over the paper, but the content remained the same. There was campus gossip, information about entertainment in town, sports scores, brief introductions of new staff members and seamen, and letters from V-12 graduates now on active duty. In most ways it was no different from the *Ambrosian News* that had chronicled life on campus before ceasing publication when the navy came.

About 20 percent of the V-12 seamen were Catholic, and Burke made sure they did not neglect their religious training. In addition to a daily Mass at 5:30 each morning, on the first Friday of each month, Mass was scheduled at 5:30 in the evening. On Sunday, Communion was distributed at 7:30 in the morning for those who wanted a full breakfast at 8:00. For those who wanted to sleep later, the regular Sunday Mass and Communion was at 9:30.[86]

While the remaining faculty and administration took care of the seamen and the few civilian students on campus, they had not forgotten the Ambrosians in the service. In April 1944, the *Ambrosian Newsletter*, a new publication for the alumni, introduced a columnist, the Reverend Robert J. Welch, who took the name Ambie Al. In the first newsletter, Ambie Al reported that there were about 3,000 alumni serving around the world and Burke assured them, "The Old School survives!" Although affected by the war, the faculty was largely intact, the buildings were in better shape than ever before, and the finances were sound. Burke said he and the faculty wished them "every blessing, protection from all harm and a successful, happy, and useful life in the days after Victory."[87]

When Burke said the faculty was intact, he was not entirely accurate. Several priests enlisted in the army or navy for service as chaplains. Fathers J. Emmet Toomey, Urban Ruhl, and John O. McAuliffe, served in the army, and Edward Lew and Bill O'Connor were in the navy. Their letters home often contained stories of Ambrosians they met. In early January 1944, Ruhl reported that as he was vesting for Christmas Mass on an island in the Pacific, a Marine came up and asked, "How is everything at St. Ambrose?" Ruhl said he turned to find Jim Reed from DeWitt whom he had taught English in college, and said Reed, "served my Mass, went to Holy Communion and helped me pack my Mass kit."[88]

A Great and Lasting Beginning

The newsletter and Ambie Al became very popular. He tried to give them a taste of home, while recognizing their situation. In October 1944, he wrote about the beautiful Indian summer weather and asked forgiveness mentioning it to "you men in the perpetual Turkish bath of the South Pacific, the dull fog of the Aleutians, the hot ovens of Iran and India, the cold and mud of Italy and the German front."[89] They appreciated all the news and they reciprocated: Welch reported receiving 125 letters a month from Ambrosians in the armed forces. As they wrote him, he reported their locations and brief news items about them. That got him into trouble with the military censors who told him he could no longer report where the Ambrosians were serving.

Ambie Al also reported on casualties. By the spring of 1945, at least forty-five Ambrosians had died in the war in places like Okinawa, Iwo Jima, Normandy, Sicily, Anzio, in the Bulge, in air raids over Europe, on unnamed islands in the Pacific, and in training exercises in the United States. Occasionally living and dead Ambrosians met. Father McAuliffe reported from an island in the Pacific that he had come upon the grave of Marine Lt. Joseph La Cesa, who had graduated in 1942. McAuliffe wrote that he had shed tears at the grave, "No more would [La Cesa] wander along the walks of his alma mater, St. Ambrose. The words of the song he loved, 'Ambrosian Oaks,' would now fall on deaf ears. But he had added to the mighty deeds of which that song speaks, which he had often sung." He said that when future Ambrosians "rise to sing that song of deeds well done, they will turn in thought to the South Pacific Isle where one of her most glorious ones lies in honored death."[90]

Andy Adrian, an Ambrosian from 1933 who worked in a shipyard in Texas, reported that he had ridden a new destroyer down the ways at its launching. Later he learned the ship had been named for Ensign Kopl Vesole, also an Ambrosian in 1933 who had been killed in December at Bari, Italy. Adrian had known Vesole at St. Ambrose and he reported, "The war gets plenty close to home in such cases."[91]

The presence of the navy on campus continued to force changes in the customs of the college. The commencement ceremony in June 1944 was held on the Marycrest campus, where forty Marycrest seniors and four Ambrosians received their college degrees. The navy provided a color guard and the band and as in the previous two years, the speaker wore a uniform. This year it was Lt. John Louis Bonn, SJ, a former dean of Boston College.[92]

That same month President Roosevelt signed the Servicemen's Readjustment Act, better known as the GI Bill of Rights. The bill provided short-term unemployment benefits, loan guarantees to purchase homes, businesses, or farms, and preferences in hiring. The most important feature of the bill was the educational benefits. Under the law, the veteran received up to $500 per year for tuition, books, and fees which was paid directly to his college. The veteran himself received $50 a month for expenses, $75 if he was married. Later those amounts were raised. Eventually more than 2.2 million veterans went to college on the GI Bill; even more attended trade schools. Many of those new college students were from working class families and were the first in their family to attend college. Before the war fewer than 10 percent of Americans attended college; by 1948 almost 15 percent did. The educational benefits of the GI Bill propelled "an entire generation along an ascending curve of achievement and affluence that their parents could not have dreamed."[93] For good reason, the bill has been called "the law that changed America."[94] It was also the law that changed American colleges and universities and would prove to be a great challenge to administrators.

As the November 1944 term began, the number of V-12 students had fallen to 217. The V-5 program had been taken over by the navy and its students removed from campus earlier that year. There were also sixty-one civilian students, including five enrolled under the new GI Bill. For the first time since the navy came, there was space available for civilian boarding students in Ambrose Hall. Ambie Al commented, "No one pretends that this is really a 'return to the good old days' but it might be called a little modest beachhead at least."[95]

In March 1945, Ambie Al noted the "quickened tempo" of the war in Europe and the Pacific. There was also a changing tempo on campus. That spring there were only 157 men in the V-12 program at St. Ambrose and 80 civilians. Within two months the war would be over in Europe; in six months it would end in the Pacific. Monsignor Burke was already looking to the end of the war and the future of the college; in February he had spoken about the post-war St. Ambrose. With the prospect of hundreds of new students, those coming for the first time, those returning to finish their interrupted education, and the large numbers of veterans taking advantage of the GI Bill, it would be a new St. Ambrose. Burke was in a position similar to McMullen, Schulte, and Cosgrove over sixty years earlier when they started from nothing and built a school. Burke was not starting from nothing, but he had the opportunity to create a new St. Ambrose. The great and lasting beginning of Bishop McMullen continued.

Ambie Al, drawn by Fr. Catich.

❧ Chapter Ten ❧

The ad spread across the top of a page of the January 4, 1945, edition of the *Messenger* portrayed a hopeful optimism that peace would soon be part of the better tomorrows. The starting date of the spring term indicated that St. Ambrose was still on the accelerated schedule demanded by the navy. In an interview a month later, Monsignor Burke said he hoped that by fall the college could return to the two-semester schedule typical of American colleges. The accelerated three-semester program was unpopular, "Students do not like it, and instructors do not like it." He said veterans would not be treated differently from the regular students and the few veterans already on campus as a result of the GI Bill were doing satisfactory work and were good students. Post-war plans at St. Ambrose included an expansion of facilities: a new field house, a new residence hall, a fine arts building with an auditorium, and a new chapel. Over the next few years these ideas would grow into plans for what Burke began to call the "new college," or the "new St. Ambrose."[1]

Burke had every reason to be optimistic. A year before he had told the far-flung Ambrosians through Ambie Al that he could look forward to the future with "confidence." Many V-12 students had said that after the war they would return to St. Ambrose to finish their education; other servicemen from around the world were writing for information about the college, which Burke said reflected the "influence of Ambrose men scattered" throughout the world, like Lt. Col. Jack Roche.[2] One of the early Civilian Pilot Training students, Roche had flown many missions over Europe in a plane named "Ambrose," with a bee painted on the nose. When he returned home from Europe in June 1945, he said, "Ambrosians overseas back the school one hundred percent. Anytime you find a former student . . . you can be sure that everybody within hearing distance knows all about the school, where it is, and what Lewis Hall is used for."[3]

The inquiries continued to come in, and Burke said this was evidence of the "almost unanimous acceptance" of the desire for higher education by all American youth. They realized that "citizens with a college" degree were more successful than those without one. They also understood that "only a liberal education" of the kind a Catholic college offered, could give them the means to "grapple with the present domestic and international prob-

lems that endanger the security, peace, and happiness of all mankind."[4]

As Burke contemplated the new St. Ambrose, he did so in the context of a significant change. In July 1944, Bishop Rohlman moved to Dubuque to become the archbishop. Unlike his two predecessors, Rohlman had taken a much more active role in the affairs of St. Ambrose. From suggesting changes in the regulations for students early in his tenure, to taking part in discussions about curricular reorganization in the mid-1930s, to his reaching out to the larger Davenport community during the Friends of St. Ambrose campaign just before the war, Rohlman was an enthusiastic participant in the continuing formation of the college.

In October it was announced that the Most Reverend Ralph L. Hayes would be the new bishop of Davenport. Born in Pittsburgh, Hayes had studied in Rome and was ordained there in 1909. Following ordination, Hayes did pastoral work in Pittsburgh, including eight years as diocesan superintendent of schools. In 1933, he became bishop of Helena, Montana, and in 1935, he was appointed the rector of the North American College in Rome. Hayes was installed as bishop of Davenport on January 11, 1945.

Shortly after Hayes arrived in Davenport, he told Burke that he wanted to bring the seminarians back from Loras College. But he was concerned that the navy not "step in again and claim the rooms to be assigned" to the seminarians. He also wanted to be sure that the faculty was able to teach them "adequately," and that proper spiritual direction be provided.[5] Hayes took care of the faculty and spiritual direction when he appointed Father Ed O'Connor as rector, the position he held before the seminarians went to Loras in 1943. He also appointed Father Charles Griffith as spiritual director. Griffith had been on the faculty as a professor of history and campus chaplain until he became pastor of Grand Mound in 1942. Now Hayes told him that while he may not be able to "establish a Minor Seminary in the complete canonical sense of the term," a separate institution for use only as a seminary, he was "determined to approximate that ideal as far as possible."[6] With the addition of the Reverend John Keating as vice rector, Hayes' seminary was now fully staffed.

Perhaps chastened by the reports of the seminary visitations in the 1930s and his own understanding of what a seminary should be, under Hayes the

131

seminary moved away somewhat from the vision represented by Bishop McMullen. In the post-war years the seminarians occupied the east end of Ambrose Hall, an area the lay students called the "Angel Factory." An observer noted that the seminarians "form a world-within-a-world" on the college campus. Their day began with the wake-up bell at 5:45, followed by morning prayer, Mass in the Ambrose Hall chapel, and community breakfast in the seminarian refectory. Prior to the evening meal, the seminarians had a twenty minute conference by the spiritual director, Father Griffith. After the meal there was recreation, study, and night prayers. They participated to some degree in clubs and similar activities, but it was clear they were a more separate group on campus than before.[7]

The bishop also asked Burke to contact Bishop Adrian in Nashville to tell him that the Davenport seminarians would return to campus and that he would be "glad" to have the Nashville seminarians return too. The Nashville connection had become an important source of students for St. Ambrose. By 1946, 20 percent of the priests of the Diocese of Nashville were graduates of St. Ambrose and the two largest high schools in the diocese were staffed almost exclusively by St. Ambrose graduates.[8]

In this 1942 photo, Lt. Col. John R. Roche '41, right, with his co-pilot, Lt. R.L. Brown, are shown next to the first of two planes Roche christened with the Ambrose logo. This one, piloted by another crew, crashed on a mission. The second one also crashed on a mission over North Africa.

groups with the Marycrest students. He reminded Adrian that Hayes was a former seminary rector and had "definite ideas about running a seminary. He knows the mind of Rome."[10] Adrian apparently settled the concerns of his board because within a year, seminarians from Nashville returned to St. Ambrose. With the return of the Nashville seminarians, the Angel Factory now had two species of angels, the northern or "damn Yankee" angels and the southern, or rebel angels. One observer noted that the Tennessee students "added an extra cosmopolitan note to the school at a time when most students came from the Quad-City region," and they added an extra dimension to "previous contentions among the student body . . . concerning the civil war or 'the war between the states.'"[11]

The number of seminarians grew; in 1949 there were eighty-seven in the seminary, twenty-five from Davenport, thirty-two from Nashville, and smaller numbers from the Illinois dioceses of Peoria, Rockford, Springfield, and Joliet.

The Congregation of St. Viator

Burke told Adrian that Hayes had called the fifteen Davenport seminarians home from Loras for the term beginning March 1 and that they would occupy the east wing of Ambrose Hall. Adrian said he would prefer to wait until the navy left St. Ambrose before he sent any seminarians. But more importantly, his Diocesan Board on Seminarians had reservations about the Nashville students returning to St. Ambrose. They felt that church students in contact with lay students in classes and extracurricular activities were "inclined to imbibe too much of a worldly spirit." They wanted stricter discipline than had existed in the pre-war days but he would send seminarians if he could convince the board that St. Ambrose was as "well qualified as most seminaries to train our students."[9]

Burke said he understood the concern of Adrian's board, but he assured the bishop that St. Ambrose seminary was approved as a "minor seminary by the Sacred Congregation of Seminaries and Universities," and he detailed the visitations in recent years, most recently by Archbishop Mooney. He also enclosed copies of their reports. He told Adrian that there would be "stricter discipline" in the seminary than had existed before the war. The students would not be allowed to take part in plays or choral

also sent its seminarians to St. Ambrose in those years. Viatorian priests had worked in the diocese as relief ministers during the summer months. Their students had attended St. Viator College in Bourbonnais, Illinois, but when that closed in 1938, the order made plans to send their students to St. Ambrose. In 1938, the Reverend Eugene J. Surprenant, who joined the St. Ambrose faculty as a professor of philosophy, purchased a house at 2 Temple Lane, a few blocks from campus, to house the Viatorian priests and brothers who would come to teach at St. Ambrose as well as the Viatorian students. That first year sixteen students joined Surprenant at St. Ambrose. Over the next sixteen years (including the war years), an average of fifteen Viatorian students attended St. Ambrose and as many as six Viatorian clerics served on the faculty.[12]

Bishops Hayes and Adrian expressed some concern about the future of the navy on campus but Burke could not give them a definitive answer. In February, the rumor was that the navy would leave the college after July 1 and substitute the V-12 program with a Navy Reserve Officer's Training Program (ROTC). Two months later the rumor was that the navy would stay for the term which would begin on July 1, and then the ROTC program would begin in November. All Burke could say with certainty was that when the term began in early March, there were 157 V-12 students and seventy-seven civilians, including the seminarians.[13]

The answer to the bishops' questions about the future of the navy at St. Ambrose depended on the course of the war. In the Pacific in February and March, there was bitter fighting by U.S. Marines on Iwo Jima, and other American forces prepared to invade Okinawa as they moved closer to Tokyo. In Europe, allied forces were pushing toward Berlin from the west and the east.

After years of fighting in Europe, the end came with the German surrender on May 8, V-E Day. Lt. Arthur K. Burt, the commander of the V-12 program at St. Ambrose wrote in *Sea Breez* that the end of the war in Europe would have little impact on his program. The navy's major effort had been in the Pacific and he guessed that they would have to beat Japan "the hard way," like Germany and that would take "two years or more." One of the student writers for the paper exclaimed, "The lights are on again, the curfew has been lifted."[14]

As Burt predicted, when the new semester began in early July, there were 145 new V-12 students. But Burke continued to prepare for the post-war St. Ambrose. In June the

Rev. Edward M. O'Connor, rector, and Rev. Charles F. Griffith, spiritual director. The two men were appointed to the seminary in 1945 and served until 1967.

navy. St. Ambrose had trained 411 students in the V-5 program and 711 in the V-12 program. Lt. Comm. Arthur E. Jensen presented Burke with a certificate of merit and said that St. Ambrose had done an "outstandingly able job" and had "earned the Navy's richest encomium: 'Well Done.'"

Burke expressed his gratitude to the navy and his pride in the total war effort by Ambrosians. More than 2,000 had served in the armed forces and forty-five had died. Burke also praised the work of the St. Ambrose faculty. With the year-round navy schedule, they had gone without a vacation since September 1941 and they had "faced duty, made adjustments, produced results." While he regretted the departure of the navy, Burke said St. Ambrose faced the future with "confidence" and he hoped the men trained on campus would "never forget their days at St. Ambrose."[16]

Another Ambrosian had a different war-time experience. Father Bernard Meyer had remained in China when the Japanese invaded in 1937. After Pearl Harbor, Meyer and other Maryknoll missionaries in Hong Kong were captured by the Japanese and put into a detention

college published a new advertising folder entitled "Going to College? Meet St. Ambrose" for prospective students. The cover featured the navy trainees assembled in formation on the lawn in front of Lewis Hall, but the rest of the brochure featured pictures of the campus, lists of courses of study, and information about the GI Bill.

The post-war world came more quickly than Burt or any other planners could have imagined. The decision by President Harry Truman to drop an atomic bomb on Hiroshima on August 6 and on Nagasaki three days later brought the surrender of Japan on August 15. V-J Day brought celebrations across the country, but at St. Ambrose it spelled the end of the presence of the navy. On September 21, only three weeks after the formal surrender ceremony on board the *USS Missouri* in Tokyo Harbor, Burke received a letter notifying him that the navy would terminate the V-12 program with "genuine regret."[15]

On October 13, the V-12 seamen assembled for an "impressive military pageant" where St. Ambrose received an "honorable discharge" from the

camp with some 2,500 American and British detainees. The Maryknoll priests were offered their freedom, but Meyer and the others decided to stay to minister to the other prisoners. During his internment, Meyer did what he could for the prisoners, often dealing on the black market for medicines, especially for pregnant women and those with tuberculosis. Calling on his rural Iowa roots, he also planted a garden which enabled him to feed nearly 150 people. With the end of the war, Meyer and the others gained their freedom.[17]

While the V-12 trainees were in the middle of their final semester, sixty freshmen began the first semester of an overlapping peacetime schedule on September 17. This was the largest entering class of civilian students at St. Ambrose since before the war. As a further indication that the campus was returning to normal, it was announced that James W. O'Connor was returning as the basketball coach. O'Connor had coached the last basketball

A Great and Lasting Beginning

team before the navy took over the campus. He had seen service at Bougainville and Leyte in the Pacific theater and was decorated for bravery for going behind enemy lines to rescue a wounded comrade.[18]

That fall peacetime life returned slowly to St. Ambrose, but in January, as the college began the second semester, the campus was filled with students. There were 541 male students, approximately the same number as the last full year before the war. Two-thirds of those were freshmen; there were another seventy-two students in the evening classes; 118 nurses in programs at Mercy Hospital in Davenport, Mercy Hospital in Iowa City, and St. Anthony's Hospital in Rock Island; and 404 students at Marycrest for a total of 1,135 students. The residence halls were full

Following World War II, the college added war-surplus barracks for single and married students and a barracks building for the Music department.

and large numbers of students were forced to live off-campus. The numbers were so great that when Burke received a telegram from the navy in early January 1946 asking to reestablish the V-12 program on campus, he said he regretted that there was no housing available.[19]

That spring Burke was facing what college presidents, Catholic and secular, were facing throughout the United States: an era of tremendous growth. Between 1940 and 1960, enrollment at Catholic colleges increased 164 percent. To serve those new students, the number of faculty grew by 85 percent. Even the number of Catholic colleges grew with thirty-eight new schools opening during those two decades. In large measure, the enrollment growth can be attributed to the GI Bill and other government education programs. To meet the challenge of this growth, in the years ahead college administrators would turn to the federal government for assistance in physical plant expansion, forming an alliance between the government and church-related schools that could not have been imagined before the war.[20]

Moreover, the government would turn to colleges in ways it had not before. During the war colleges like St. Ambrose had served the nation well with various military training programs and research. A 1947 report, *Higher Education for American Democracy*, issued by the President's Commission on Education, noted that "aristocratic" higher education was being replaced with democratic education fueled by the millions of veterans attending college under the GI Bill. Thus higher education would continue to serve the nation by a renewed commitment to national defense. The federal government now came to see colleges as a "source of national strength." Catholic and other religious educators objected to the secular tone of the Commission report. One critic noted that it said youth should be trained for a democratic state which became a "sort of religion, with public education as its church."[21] Nevertheless, in the years ahead, St. Ambrose would be no different from other private institutions that would rely on government funding for classroom and residence buildings, and that would seek to insti-

tute ROTC and other similar training programs to increase student population.

By early May it was clear that enrollment for the fall semester would break all previous records: there were already 350 applications, most of them from veterans. The college learned that the federal government had allocated seventy-five units of emergency housing to hold up to 150 students, but that would not likely be ready for the fall. So later that month Burke announced that on June 1, St. Ambrose would close registration for the fall semester. For now, all former students, current students, all war veterans residing in the communities of eastern Iowa and western Illinois, and "local students with at least average scholarship ratings" were being accepted for the fall. He said that a "limited number of additional boarding students," presumably seminarians, were being accepted on a "highly selective basis" with a preference "extended to students from the Diocese of Davenport."[22]

The first indication of what the next few years would be like came with a summer school enrollment of 627 students, which broke the record for the highest one semester enrollment established in the spring semester that just ended. There had been summer school since 1932 with most of the student body consisting of religious sisters. That summer for the first time, men outnumbered women: there were 347 men, almost all of whom were veterans, and 280 women, half of whom were sisters from sixteen different religious orders.[23]

By mid-summer it was apparent that the numbers for the fall semester would be even greater. Although Burke had announced that registration was closed on June 1, more than 100 applications had arrived since then, for a total of more than 1,400 applications, three times the number who applied before the war. More than 80 percent of the applicants were veterans, and 35 percent of the total applicants were from the Diocese of Davenport. The fear was that because of a lack of space, up to 500 of those applicants would have to be rejected.[24]

To accommodate the larger number of students, the daily schedule was changed. Now classes would be held from 8:00 a.m. to 6:00 p.m., with no pause for a lunch hour. Instead the noon meal would be served over a two hour period of time so that everyone would have a chance to eat.[25]

The housing shortage was not so easily solved. That summer preliminary work was done for the erection of the emergency housing units that the government was donating to the college. Those were war surplus barracks from Fairmont Army Air Base located southwest of Lincoln, Nebraska. The barracks would house 120 single GIs and twelve married veterans and their families. But they were not ready for the beginning of the fall semester. The faculty who had lived in McAuley Hall during the war had returned to campus, so it was remodeled to house up to eighty students. Other students boarded in private homes in the neighborhood of the college. Yet in late August, the college announced that it still needed rooms for an additional 150 students. The editor of the *Ambrosian News* said that St. Ambrose had been a "Big Little College" but would "have to be referred to as the 'Little University' in the future years, as Ambrose will not decrease."[26]

Classes began on September 16 for 1,149 students, most of whom were freshmen and sophomores. Bishop Hayes celebrated the opening Mass and preached. He sounded a theme that made reference to the wartime enemies and one that would become familiar in the Cold War years ahead: the spiritual and moral conflict between "godlessness and godliness–between rampant, active atheism and courageous profession of belief in a personal God." He said that for over sixty years St. Ambrose

St. Ambrose-Loras Victory Bell.

College had "energetically countered that virus of irreligion" and it would continue to do so. It had educated businessmen to understand that "honest dealings are commanded by the law of God"; it taught science graduates that God is the "Alpha and Omega" and that new discoveries were an "additional manifestation of nature's God"; it fashioned educators to understand that they taught "children of God and heirs to the Kingdom of Heaven."

He welcomed especially the veterans who had chosen St. Ambrose, calling their presence a "most felicitous omen" for the college. Following the uncertainty and confusion of the war years, the presence of the veterans and all the new students was a "second spring." He warned them all of the dangers ahead. Family life had been weakened and juvenile delinquency was on the rise, business ethics were so low that the disgrace was in being caught. Ambrosians must be armed to fight those trends. They now faced the "terrible choice between paganism and Christianity," and he prayed that the "men of St. Ambrose be granted the grace and the light and strength to continue, each in his own personal regard, the high destiny of our college of leading men to the knowledge of God, the practice of virtue and the imitation of Jesus Christ."[27]

Everyone had to adjust to the overcrowded campus, an adjustment made easier with the return of many of the usual events of college in the fall. Over sixty men turned out for the football team under new coach Ennio Arboit. According to one reporter, they were a "little weak around the flanks," but

the coach led them to a 5-3 season.[28]

The weekend of November 10, homecoming returned after a four-year absence. Burke and the Reverend Harry Toher took out a full-page ad in the *Ambrosian News* to welcome back the alumni. The weekend began with a dance on Friday night at the Col Ballroom with the Eliot Lawrence Orchestra. The highlight of the dance was the crowning of Rose Mary Lane, a Marycrest junior, as the homecoming queen. Saturday morning began with a pep rally and a parade through the downtown. Sunday morning Mass was celebrated for deceased alumni, especially those lost in the war. The game that afternoon was against St. Norbert's College at Municipal Stadium on the waterfront. Father Cletus Madsen staged a half-time show with the St. Ambrose band and the combined St. Ambrose Choral Club and Marycrest Glee Club. The team lost 19-7, but for most of the fans, the weekend activities represented a return to normal after years of war and uncertainty.[29]

As the second semester began, sixty-four veterans moved into six new barracks on the northwest corner of the campus. Five more barracks were still under construction. That winter the basketball team under coach Pat McCarty completed a 13-11 season that included two losses to long-time rival Loras and one win and one loss to long-time rival Augustana. At the end of the season, coaches Arboit and McCarty resigned, and in March it was announced that they would be replaced by the return of Moon Mullins who brought along a new assistant coach, Leo Deutsch. St. Ambrose fans were thrilled to have Mullins back and welcomed him with a banquet attended by 250 alumni and friends at which the mayor presented Mullins and Deutsch with the keys to the city.[30]

The 1947 football team under Mullins had a 5-3 record. They set an attendance record as 33,500 fans turned out for the five home games. One of those wins, however, marked the end of the longest football rivalry for St. Ambrose. In 1893, St. Ambrose and Augustana played their first football game and the 26-6 St. Ambrose win in 1947 was the last. Augustana president Conrad Bergendoff cited the fact that Augustana had not won against Ambrose in recent years and the difficulty for Augustana to field a winning team under the rules of the Illinois Conference as reasons for the break.[31]

The next season the Bees were 7-3, and the following year, the team was undefeated and untied for the first time since 1937. That season the football Bees had an additional incentive for winning the game against Loras. At the end of the war, St. Ambrose alumnus John de Paul Hansen of

The barracks were located behind Lewis Hall on what is now the lower Galvin parking lot. They housed veterans in the years immediately after the war. Students continued to live in them until East Hall was opened in 1959.

Chicago had been on board a captured Japanese hospital ship, the *Tachibana*, when he took one of its bells. After the war Hansen and the Chicago alumni club presented the bell mounted as a trophy to the two schools as the St. Ambrose-Loras Victory Bell.[32]

Golf became a regular varsity sport after the war. There had been golf teams in the past, usually coached by a member of the team or by a local volunteer. In the mid-1930s, G. Decker French, a veteran Davenport golfer, had coached several strong teams. In 1939, Joe Von Maur, a star on the powerful 1937 and 1938 teams, became the coach. During the war there was no golf team, but in 1947, the Reverend Bernard Kamerick took over as golf coach and led the team to conference titles.

Tennis also emerged as a varsity sport when the Reverend Joseph Hratz became coach. Hratz was a long-time tennis player who had won several local and regional championships. Hratz's teams began slowly, the Bees were 0-7 in their first season, but over the next decades, Hratz would build St. Ambrose into a tennis powerhouse.

Wrestling was another new sport in the post-war years, coached by Matt Starcevich who was also the veteran's administrator on campus and a former college wrestler. Several individual wrestlers won conference championships, and the team took second in the conference in 1948, but the sport lasted only a few years.

In the summer of 1947, St. Ambrose joined four other Catholic colleges: Loras; St. Norbert's, De Pere, Wisconsin; St. Joseph's, Rensselaer, Indiana; and St. Benedict's, Atchison, Kansas, to form the new Midlands Athletic Conference. The *Messenger* noted that the new conference would "stabilize the play of our fine Midwest Catholic teams and give added zest to their competition." Father Toher was one of the founding members and acted as the first president of the conference.[33] At the same time the college remained in the Iowa Conference.

In 1947, Leo Deutsch, the assistant football coach, reintroduced an extensive intramural program so all students would have a "chance to participate in some form of competitive athletics while in school." Within a year, over 700 students took part in basketball, bowling, volleyball, water polo, wrestling, ping-pong, free throw, euchre, pinochle, tennis, horseshoes, boxing, swimming, track, and golf. The students competed under teams named the Klinton Klowns, Umbriagos, Sackhounds, Shot Happy, Gaels, Dirtysocks, Net Busters, and Globetrotters. Deutsch also resurrected the annual Field Day, an all-day event held in the late spring. The day began with a field Mass, then a full day of sports activities, the crowning of the Field Day queen, and ended with a variety show and dance in the evening. The local intramural champions competed in the annual Midlands Conference extra-mural competition among the five conference schools. In 1948, St. Ambrose hosted the event and took first place. St. Ambrose placed second in 1949 and fourth the following year.[34]

The veterans settled into college life. According to one, army jackets were the "clothing of choice," and the GI Bill check was the "currency of choice."[35] Because of their experience in the war, the veterans had a seriousness of purpose that the regular college undergraduate did not. Although the veterans, at least the single ones, took part in most of the college activities, the adjustment was not always smooth. The most common complaint was the rules of dormitory life, especially the enforced study hours and the nightly bed check. The barracks residents remembered that after bed check there was a "stream of students" leaving for the local pubs. But one barracks proctor, the Reverend Ralph Thompson, himself a former army chaplain, apparently "didn't seem to mind the veterans returning late on Saturday night and then playing bridge to sunrise."

Still the rules were a problem for many of them. After one year at St. Ambrose, one McAuley Hall student wrote Burke to complain. He said the forced study hours were "very undesirable" because they deprived the student of free choice. But it was more galling to him that to be excused from study hours, one had to ask for permission, and he told Burke, "As a veteran of three years service, I feel very foolish having to approach Mr. Becker like a secondary school kid with, 'Please Mr. Becker may I leave the building?' With all the abnormalities of army life such conduct was never demanded of a soldier. Military prisoners were required to have permission to leave their barracks, but never free men. Even if permission was required, professors at a college should have foresight enough to allow the spirit of a law to exist. It may be that a veteran having reached manhood is supposed to realize that as a college student he is to be treated as an irresponsible of some sort. I can not help but think that such an attitude toward men breeds irresponsibility. Why are not rules made that will recognize the veteran as though he had the dignity of a man?" He received little sympathy from the president, however, who told him that with so many students living in the dormitories, rules were necessary, and he suggested that he find private accommodations off-campus.[36]

Another area where the culture of the college and the presence of the veterans clashed was the return of freshman initiation. The post-war rules for initiation were set by the student council and were no different from the rules developed in the 1930s, including the green cap, entering and leaving Lewis Hall by the back doors, wood gathering, and paddling. There were some critics of initiation, but the editor of the *Ambrosian News* defended it saying that the so-called "new college student" was no different from the pre-war version. He also noted that the members of the student council were all veterans and that all but one of them had voted for initiation. Their opinion seemed to be that "there is more to be gained out of college than just what a student reads in a text book." It was not "juvenile," and it had "some real value" and the editor said as long as the "proper consideration for the individual" was present, he was for it "100 percent." The proper consideration of which the editor spoke was for the freshmen who were veterans who had "already been initiated by war service." As one veteran recalled, "Who would order a combat marine to put on a beanie and go into Lewis Hall by the back door?"[37]

The concerns of veterans were also reflected in the answers given to a roving reporter's question in the *Ambrosian News*. The reporter asked, "What one important change would you make at St. Ambrose College?" Among the answers were: better transportation from McAuley Hall (where some veterans lived) to campus; "lighter" rules for veterans which were not the same as for seventeen- and eighteen-year-olds; no bed checks for vets. Other answers which may or may not have come from veterans were: "Women are the downfall of man–but man loves it. Let's have a co-ed school"; "I'd institute smoking in my Latin class for 'comfort'"; "Install easy chairs in the classrooms"; "Make the food served in the Bee-Hive cheaper"; "Expand the school's facilities–with permanent structures" (instead of the temporary barracks); "Tear down Ambrose Hall–it disfigures the campus";

Ambrosians gathered to celebrate Mass to open the school year, 1947.

A Great and Lasting Beginning

and not surprisingly, "Build a parking lot. The biggest bottleneck around here now is a lack of parking spaces."[38]

To teach the influx of new students, twenty-seven new faculty members were hired, bringing the number of faculty members, coaching staff, and librarians to eighty-seven. Many of those new faculty members would stay only a few years, but others began careers at St. Ambrose that would stretch into the 1970s. Included in this group were Professors Agnes Renner, history and geography; H. Shannon Boyd, engineering; Prudent Coussens, languages; John McGuire, English; Matthew Hart, business law. They joined other faculty who had come during the war, including Father Bernard Kamerick, religion; the Reverend Francis Marlin, speech; Father Joseph Hratz, mathematics; and the Reverend John Dolan, sociology and psychology.[39]

In 1941-1942 there were thirty-one priests and twenty lay members of the faculty and staff. Now only twenty-eight of the faculty were priests and the large number of lay faculty and staff members led to changes at St. Ambrose. As the number of lay faculty at Catholic colleges grew, concerns about their low salaries increased. In 1934, a writer suggested that salaries were kept low as part of the "living endowment" of Catholic colleges. Those low salaries drove young professors away from Catholic education and the writer concluded, "It would be a happier day for lay leadership in Catholic collegiate education when living endowment is replaced by cash endowment. Its hastening would be an excellent aim for Catholic Action."[40] By the end of the war, lay salaries in Catholic colleges were still behind those of secular colleges.[41]

At St. Ambrose faculty salaries at the end of the war ranged from $2,100 to $4,000 a year, depending on the years of service. But there were no additional benefits. In 1946, the Administrative Council, a committee of faculty and administrators, began a two-year study to develop a pension and life insurance plan which was presented to the Board of Control in May 1948. The insurance and pension plan called for faculty members to contribute 5 percent of their salaries which would be matched by the college. A committee made up of faculty and administrators acted as managing trustees for the plan. The Board of Control approved the proposal, and Burke announced that it would become effective on October 1, 1948. Burke said that with the new plan, along with a cost-of-living increase and a salary scale based on faculty rank and years of service, St. Ambrose now had a "satisfactory program of security for its lay staff members that will compare favorably to similar benefits offered by other colleges."[42]

Another change because of the larger lay faculty came in October 1946, when thirty women met to organize the faculty women's group consisting of female faculty members and faculty wives. Agnes Renner was the chair and the wives of members of the Board of Directors were special guests at the first meeting. Each monthly meeting included a program.[43]

The new members joined a faculty grown stronger as a consequence of the policies begun by Father Hannon in the 1920s to send priests away for graduate studies. Eight of the priest faculty had doctorates and another fourteen had Master's Degrees and some of those were in doctoral programs. Among the lay faculty there were seven PhDs and eight with Master's Degrees. Many of the others were in first-time positions, some of

whom had just graduated from college. In addition to their classroom duties, many of the faculty members were active in research, publication, professional societies, and community service and action.

Burke noted that the faculty was strongest in the study of the sciences and in the study of social and economic problems.[44] The study of science had been one of Schulte's goals back in the 1880s and it was fitting that Burke cited its strength. The leading chemist was Dr. Jeremiah Goggin (known to all as Doc Goggin) who had been on the faculty since 1928. Goggin was an inspired teacher who was also a gifted researcher. In the middle 1930s, Goggin and a local man, Reinhold Schultz, experimented with luminous materials and developed a luminous paint. With money from Harold Bechtel, a local banker, they formed the Lunex Company to manufacture it. During the war the entire output of the company went to the government.[45]

The Reverend William Lynch, a biologist, published articles on his research specialty, changing life forms in the bugula larvae, a small animal that lives in colonies on underwater structures. A member of a number of national and international professional societies, Lynch was elected to membership in the Marine Biological Laboratory at Wood's Hole, Massachusetts, an honor limited to only 400 biologists at one time.

The leading scientist was Hauber whose field was also biology. Hauber's specialization was the study of midges where he discovered several new species and published a number of articles. In the 1920s he had published a pamphlet about science and religion, and in the years since he had revised it. Hauber insisted that science was more than "mere profane learning," it fulfilled "an almost sacred duty of ours to try to know something about the things that God made and called good." It also helped to make proper use of the "forces of nature over which he has dominion." Hauber said that when science was used to "further divinely instituted ends of man, there is no quarrel between science and religion."[46]

Hauber published two textbooks, the second one of which, *Essentials of Zoology* (1949), included illustrations by the Reverend Edward Catich, who had been ordained in 1938 and had returned to the art faculty at St. Ambrose. Hauber dedicated the book to "The Youth of America who eager and alert but bewildered are searching for truth." In the preface he expressed his view of the study of biology, and by extension all of the liberal arts: "Biology can be more than just a field of study. It should be a civilizing influence that will help men and women to live more abundantly; it can and should be a leaven that will permeate society and elevate its standards."[47]

The Administrative Council was also a change at St. Ambrose. In 1930, the president, vice president, academic dean, seminary rector, business manager, and sometimes other college officers formed the College Council that served as a governing body for the ordinary decisions of the college. In 1946 this became the Administrative Council with the same officers as members ex officio and three elected faculty members. This group met once a month to consider college policy. Burke said although the bishop had the "last word," Hayes was "ordinarily . . . satisfied to let us run the college."[48]

The fact that the retirement plan was taken to the Board of Directors indicates that under Bishop Hayes and Burke that board would become increasingly important. It would decide issues that formerly would have been dealt with by the Bishop's Council and later the Consultors. The Board of Directors (or as it was also called the Board of Control) had been reorganized in 1937 with the addition of several priests and three laymen. Now in the fall of 1946, prompted by Burke, Hayes wrote the Reverend Monsignor Thomas Galligan, pastor of St. Mary's Parish in Clinton; Father Thomas Lawlor, former business manager of the college and now the pastor of Holy Family Parish in Davenport; Thomas Walsh, head of Walsh Construction and a former member of the Board; and Bernard A. Spaeth, a manufacturer's agent and director of Pabst Brewing Company, to ask them to join the board. Hayes told them that with enrollment now over the 1,100 mark, it would result in "many problems which require consultation and advice." Although the meetings would be called at "irregular intervals," Burke and the bishop would use the board.[49]

Hauber's wide-ranging interests led to a new agriculture program at St. Ambrose. Hauber had not been involved in teaching the V-12 students and with few non-navy students on campus, he took a sabbatical. He had observed that St. Ambrose sat in the middle of a rapidly changing farm belt. With the mechanization of agriculture, fewer workers were needed on the farm and eleven of the twenty-two counties in the Diocese of Davenport lost population in the decade of the 1940s. Hauber saw this as an "ominous trend" to which St. Ambrose had paid little attention.[50] For four months he traveled and visited colleges in the eastern and southern parts of the country to learn about their programs for farmers. His visits led him to conclude that St. Ambrose needed to create a program that would help farmers.

When he returned he formed a committee with himself as chair and included the Reverend William Collins, and Fathers Charles Griffith, John Dolan, and Francis Marlin. They gathered information from Midwestern Catholic colleges with agricultural programs. They also brought in the Reverend Monsignor Luigi Ligutti to consult with them.

Born in Italy, Ligutti had come the United States at age 17 and settled with family in Des Moines. He came to St. Ambrose and graduated in 1914. Ordained in 1917, Ligutti was on the first faculty of what became Dowling High School in Des Moines. In 1926, he was appointed as pastor in Granger, Iowa, a coal mining community with many Italian immigrants; Ligutti worked to improve their living situation.[51]

Ligutti's solution had its roots in Pope Leo XIII's *Rerum Novarum* which declared that people should own not just the "fruits of the earth, but also the very soil." It is a "most sacred law of nature that a father should provide food and all necessaries for those whom he has begotten." Land ownership would provide that and also it would bridge the gap between wealth and poverty, and provide more abundance from the earth. The opportunity to make this possible for the miners of Granger came in the mid-1930s with a New Deal program when he applied for and received money to build the Granger Homesteads. Those homes gave the coal miners and their families decent housing and land upon which to grow food. The project received national attention, especially when Mrs. Eleanor Roosevelt came to visit.

Although Ligutti was willing to rely on the state for help, he said that families "precede the state" and are the "fundamental units of actions . . . A wholesome society will be characterized by the responsible activity of local

groups."[52] In 1941, he became executive director of the National Catholic Rural Life Conference where he had a national platform to put his ideas in action. In 1948, he was named the Vatican's observer to the United Nations Food and Agriculture Organization.

Based on their discussions with Ligutti, Hauber's committee issued a report on September 4, 1945, that said the objective of St. Ambrose should be to give a "suitable education" to boys who would stay on the farm. With that objective, the report outlined what the college should not do. The college did not have the faculty or the equipment for a specialized agricultural program. In addition such a program would be inconsistent with the liberal arts objectives of the college and the objective to educate "boys for life on the family farm." In fact, Hauber wrote that boys who came to a city campus were often "alienated from the ideals of farm life."

The committee identified two groups interested in some form of agricultural education. First, non-farmers who had an acreage and commuted to jobs in the city. They thought there would be a post-war increase in the number of those and that "many GI boys" had expressed interest and were looking for education to help them. The second group were boys raised on a farm who wanted to remain on the farm. They wanted education to help them to become more efficient farmers, but also to learn to appreciate literature and music and to become more solidly grounded in their faith. Hauber thought that this group would form an educated Catholic foundation for a stable middle class.

Those objectives could be realized by providing courses for non-farmers in rural sociology, farm economics, and science courses that would focus on farm issues. For those who were from farms and wanted to remain, the committee recommended that the college or the diocese acquire a farm to serve as a demonstration farm, with a residence building where the students could stay during the courses. None of those courses would lead to a college degree, but they recommended that a diploma or certificate be awarded upon completion.[53]

In the following weeks, members of the committee contacted a number of rural pastors and received their support for a "short course" whose aim would be to give a better appreciation of Catholic rural philosophy, teach skills to make the participants better farmers, and create a network among southeast Iowa farmers. It would also be good advertising for the college, put it in touch with rural youth, secure the good will of farmers, and improve contacts between rural pastors and the college. The committee recommended that for the short course to be successful, a "competent director" should be hired.[54]

Bishop Hayes lent his enthusiastic support to the project. Writing Hauber in late November 1945, Hayes said that the proposed institute was "welcome" news. Rural problems were both economic and religious and Hayes said the church was concerned with both aspects. During his confirmation tours through the diocese, Hayes said he was "edified by the spectacle of the deeply religious and thoroughly Catholic family life" in the rural parishes which could be "enlarged by competent study and direction" of such a rural institute. Hayes assured Hauber that the rural pastors would be "eager" to participate and they would be pleased "to select from their parishes boys and men who will profit by attendance at the Institute."[55]

On December 10, Burke wrote the priests of the diocese to announce that there would be a two-week agricultural institute at St. Ambrose beginning February 10, 1946. Burke said the faculty had felt for "some time" that such an institute was needed "to foster interest in Catholic rural life; to bring to our Catholic rural youth information on better farming; and to give these youths opportunity to show that they can be leaders in Catholic action." He also announced that the leader in this "pioneer venture" would be Dr. Paul Sacco.[56]

Sacco had been on the faculty at Penn State University and had developed agricultural programs for the Archdiocese of Philadelphia. Sacco said the greatest need for programs like that proposed at St. Ambrose was to train a generation of farmers to not look upon agriculture as a business, but as a "way of life: men who appreciate fully their responsibility to their family, church and nation; men who will till the soil with reverence and safeguard its riches for their children; men who will have sound agricultural fundamentals without the ambition to be one-crop specialists; men enjoying and realizing the wonders of ownership yet devoid of the overpowering desire to accumulate more and more land, or even a white collar."[57] Sacco warned, "If a farmer is not making a living on the land we can preach to him forever about the advantages of staying on the land–but we will not keep him there."[58]

Nearly fifty young farmers from counties throughout the diocese and some from Illinois attended the institute. As part of the program, they visited farms, a packing plant, and local farm implement companies. A number of speakers were from the St. Ambrose faculty: Hauber and Sacco spoke on the anatomy and physiology of crop plants; Father John Dolan discussed rural sociology; Father William Collins talked on farm economics. Experts from outside the campus spoke on farm management, economics, plant pests, and a variety of other topics. In their spare time the participants took advantage of the campus swimming pool and athletic facilities. The institute was pronounced a success by the farmers in attendance and the speakers alike. The Reverend George Hildner, a rural pastor from Missouri who was one of the speakers, said that St. Ambrose could be proud of its leadership by which it had shown "the way to the Catholic colleges of the nation."[59] Within weeks Hauber began planning for the next institute to be held the following February. Over the next few years, nearly twenty such institutes and short courses would be held on campus as well as in rural parishes throughout the diocese.

A second phase of Hauber's program dealt with the perception that teachers in Catholic high schools, mostly priests and nuns, were unwittingly preparing their students for city life. The solution to this came from the Reverend Joseph Wagner, the pastor of St. Mary's Parish, West Point. Wagner's solution was the "infiltration of agricultural subject matter" into the courses already in the curriculum. To facilitate that, Hauber, Sacco, and others created a summer school curriculum at St. Ambrose for high school teachers. The curriculum included regular science classes, but also courses in general agriculture, soils, botany, geology, horticulture, and rural sociology.[60] Wagner would later be named rural life director for the diocese.

Burke had also said the faculty was strong in the study of social and economic problems, a continuation of an emphasis stretching back for over forty years. Based on the encyclicals of Popes Leo XIII and Pius XI, and the work of Monsignor John A. Ryan, this had taken root through the efforts of Cone in the 1920s and the O'Connor brothers and Griffith, among others in the 1930s and 1940s. Those earlier efforts were reinforced by new papal encyclicals. In 1943, Pope Pius XII published *Mystici Corporis* (the Mystical Body) which argued that the church was the body of Christ and each member was graced with particular gifts that should be used for the improvement of the whole body. Four years later Pius issued *Mediator Dei* (Mediator Between God and Man), usually referred to as "On the Sacred Liturgy." Here Pius connected the way people worshiped and the way they lived their lives in society. Taken together, the documents said that lay Catholics must work together with the clergy and the hierarchy to promote social justice.

By the mid-1940s, those ideas were a part of the fabric of life at St. Ambrose College. Father Cletus Madsen was one of the founding group of the National Liturgical Conference and was engaged in liturgical reforms that would come to fruition during the Second Vatican Council. Father Edward Catich was beginning his revolutionary and often controversial liturgical art that asked people to view representations of Jesus Christ and the saints as representative of their own time, speaking to them in a visual vocabulary that would be familiar. Together their work suggested a link between the liturgy and social justice.

The issues that received the most publicity, however, were the issues of race and labor. Here the guiding forces were the O'Connor brothers, Griffith, and Father Urban "Penny" Ruhl. Those priests used their classes in sociology, philosophy, English, and history to teach about the social encyclicals and the issues of the day. Moreover, in good Jocist fashion, they urged their students to get involved, to study a situation, and take action.

Ed O'Connor taught at St. Ambrose and Marycrest and regularly lectured about civil rights and race discrimination in Davenport. He sent his classes into the community with a questionnaire to survey attitudes about race. One student said she had lived in Davenport all her life but had never known a "single Negro." Unaware that there was so much "infringement" on the rights of blacks, she said this was her "own personal awakening to the situation."[61]

O'Connor was also responsible for the formation of a campus chapter of the National Association for the Advancement of Colored People (NAACP). In early 1947, Richard Kendall, a junior from Silvis, Illinois, wrote the NAACP to inquire about organizing a chapter at St. Ambrose. Ruby Hurley, the Youth Secretary, sent information and in April Kendall reported there were twenty-five members to "start the ball rolling." Kendall had sent Hurley the results of the survey the students had done in Ed O'Connor's class. She congratulated the students and said she had shown it to a number of people who were interested in undertaking a similar survey. Kendall reported that some members had visited with Iowa legislators about a Fair Employment Practices Committee for Iowa. They were unsuccessful with the legislature but were going to try to organize Iowa colleges to jointly press the issue in the next session of the Iowa legislature. When the charter for the St. Ambrose chapter arrived in May, Hurley commended the group for the "manner in which you are conducting" the program and told them the St. Ambrose group was the first NAACP chapter on a Catholic college campus, which was "really an advancement."[62]

Like his brother, Father Bill O'Connor also created opportunities for his students to apply what they learned in class. In 1948, he formed the

Inter-Racial Club and had the members take a Quad-City Personal Poll to learn the economic status of African-Americans in the community. The poll sought to learn about living conditions, education levels, job status, and salary. The results indicated that there was a high level of discrimination in Davenport that was "strictly, if not officially enforced" as blacks were barred from restaurants, hotels, and barber shops. Most blacks were unable to buy a home except in a few specified areas of town. Most had unskilled jobs that did not allow them to provide for more than the bare necessities for their families.[63]

The group took a similar poll of students at St. Ambrose which indicated that the students generally thought that blacks should have opportunities at jobs and access to public accommodations. Seventy-two percent said that they would not object to a black living on their block and 81 percent said they would not object to a black's application for membership in their church. Sixty percent said they would not object to working under the supervision of a black, but 51 percent said they did not favor a law forbidding an employer to discriminate against race or creed.[64]

In 1949, Bill O'Connor organized the Industrial and Human Relations Council which was divided into a labor study group, an interracial group, and an economic survey group. That spring the interracial and economic survey groups did an extensive survey of Mexican-Americans who lived at Cook's Point, located in west Davenport at the end of Howell Street, between the railroad tracks, the entrance to Credit Island, and the river. Two hundred and seventy people lived in fifty-six homes on a U-shaped, unpaved street with no running water, one pump which served all the residents, and no sanitary sewer. The survey found that one family of thirteen lived in three rooms, another family of thirteen lived in four rooms, and eight homes had two families each. Sixty-eight people had full-time employment with an average weekly wage of $48.92. Most of the children attended school, but for recreation, they played either in the mud street or in the nearby city dump. The lack of sanitation and the proximity to the dump resulted in a high incidence of disease, including tuberculosis.[65] That same spring the labor study group polled St. Ambrose students to determine their attitude about organized labor.

In the years following World War II, students took advantage of the many speakers who came to Davenport under the auspices of Te Deum, a speaker's bureau operating in the Midwest. Charles Costello, who taught speech and drama at St. Ambrose, was the local chairman of Te Deum. Speakers included the poet Robert Lowell, Catholic publisher Frank Sheed, his wife, Masie Sheed, George Shuster, the former editor of Commonweal, labor priests, and a former chancellor of Austria. Topics included labor issues, the Soviet Union, international politics, and scientific subjects.

Various student organizations carried on the ideas of Catholic Action, social involvement, and issues of economic and social injustice. The Legion of Mary, an association of lay men and women, emphasized spiritual advancement and at least two hours of apostolic work each week. The moderator, Father Bernard Kamerick, believed that Catholic Action was an integral part of the educational process. "Spirituality is something you can't absorb in the classroom," he said, "you've got to learn it the hard way: by doing."[66]

There was a chapter of Father Cardijn's Young Christian Students (YCS) on campus. In 1947, they undertook a campaign against indecency in Davenport when they demonstrated against a controversial motion picture, "Forever Amber." The next spring they began a campaign for decent talk on campus. The editor of the Ambrosian News urged the full cooperation of the students, stating "filthy language doesn't prove you are a he-man."[67]

Eventually most of the Catholic Action activities at St. Ambrose fell under the aegis of the National Federation of Catholic College Students (NFCCS). Founded in 1937, its purpose was to stimulate thought and action on current issues and to encourage personal commitment by the students in the work of the church.

Working through the student council, the NFCCS coordinated a wide variety of social action activities on campus. The students held a forum on recent laws passed by Congress and the state legislature. They sponsored a short story contest on the theme of minority groups. To help contestants with their stories, it was suggested they read the Papal encyclicals, and recent works by Jacques Maritain, John LaFarge, Gunnar Myrdal, and the President's Committee on Civil Rights. The college students sponsored a Catholic Action school for high school students. They presented talks on various aspects of Catholic Action to illustrate the opportunities for the younger students to form their own Catholic Action groups.[68] At a convention of the NFCCS, the St. Ambrose representative had been successful in getting the group to pass a resolution about equal admission of African-American students to Catholic colleges.

One of the largest student efforts was to raise funds to purchase food to send to post-war Europe. In November 1947, a food committee formed with Lawrence McCaffrey, a junior from Dolton, Illinois, as chair. The situation was desperate in Europe. One German worker wrote, "For months we have had no meat, no fat of any kind, no milk, no potatoes." In the context of the Cold War, the fear in the West was that communists would take advantage of the dire situation and increase their hold on Europe. The drive continued through the winter and spring with the result that the students donated $1,000 to the European Student Relief campaign and another $250 to the Bishops' Relief Fund. With that money more than 1,500 pounds of food was shipped to Europe.[69]

In Italy that spring, elections were approaching and the fear was that the communists would take control. In Milan, a church leader rallied Catholics against the communists by appealing to their patron, "May St. Ambrose protect Milan." Father Kamerick read about that in Time magazine, and organized the students who took that as their battle cry and raised $1,700, one-third of which went for food in Milan and the rest to the Bishops' Relief fund. Months later Burke received an album of over 100 drawings and autographs of the citizens of Milan in gratitude for the food packages.[70]

In November 1949, St. Ambrose hosted a regional workshop for NFCCS members. There were panel discussions on Catholic Action, Mariology, student government, international issues, and press and publicity issues. In introductory remarks, Bishop Hayes said that "secularism [was] the challenge of youth. Over the years, youth have done great things for the church, and the future belongs to youth." He called for personal piety and participation in "worthy student organizations," and he urged the students to "pool ideas" and "promote Catholic Action."

The Reverend Joseph Schneider, the national promoter of Catholic Action for the NFCCS, was the principal speaker. Schneider said that organizations like the NFCCS could be "instrumental in re-christianizing the youth of the world to aid in preventing the further growth of secularism, materialism, and godlessness."[71]

Apparently, however, not all Ambrosians thought that those activities were worthwhile. One student who signed himself "Agitated Ambrosian," wrote that the merits of the NFCCS did not equal its demerits. He said its delegates attended conventions and learned nothing and "as far as myself and a lot of other boys around campus can see, nothing is ever derived from these get-togethers except some vocal experience for a small minority of 'Ambrosians' and some more money for the restaurants, hotels and public transportation companies." Ambrose student Tony Kuchan, vice president of the Iowa region of the NFCCS, defended the organization. He said the spiritual benefits were "immeasurable," and it provided an opportunity for the St. Ambrose students to get into Catholic Action. Without it, Kuchan concluded, St. Ambrose would be "stagnant."[72]

Of all the priests involved in Catholic Action at St. Ambrose by the late 1940s, the most visible and vocal was Bill O'Connor. As it developed in the twentieth century, Catholic Action was a multifaceted effort to address injustice in racial, housing, economic, and social issues, but O'Connor concentrated on the rights of labor to organize and strike to achieve economic justice. He used his classes as a forum for the Church's social teachings; some students said later that no matter what the course syllabus said, the course content was the social encyclicals as they applied to labor. As one student later remembered, O'Connor was "ringing our ears for *Rerum Novarum*."[73]

Bill O'Connor and other Ambrose faculty also began to have "labor schools" on campus and in local labor halls. They were usually held one night a week for a period of six weeks and the topics included labor history, ethics, negotiations, and parliamentary procedure. With little variation, those schools continued into the 1950s. When C. W. Anderson, the vice president of the Associated Industries of the Quad-Cities, wrote Burke to object to O'Connor's activities, Burke defended him and suggested that Anderson's group support O'Connor in his efforts to put on "Employer Schools, like the widely-supported labor schools."[74]

O'Connor was a frequent participant in local labor disputes, often with a rhetoric borne of his passion for the issue. His public stance for labor brought criticism of him, and through him, of the college. In early 1946, he supported approximately 5,500 workers who were on strike against International Harvester and J. I. Case. O'Connor spoke to the strikers and was one of several Protestant and Jewish clergymen who signed an advertisement in the local newspapers in support of the workers. Proclaiming that labor deserved a living wage, the group said that the condemnation of strikers was "unjust" and without "purchasing power in the country there can be nothing but unemployment, depression and human degradation."[75]

O'Connor's stance was complicated because the Congress of Industrial Organizations (CIO), the more radical of the national labor groups, was involved in the strike. One man wrote O'Connor suggesting that his efforts were not in the best interest of labor because the CIO used methods that were "questionable," and were "tainted with the same foreign element . . . that the Roman Catholic Church condemns."[76] Letters also came to Burke. One businessman said Burke should know of the "resentment and unfavorable comment" among businessmen regarding O'Connor's actions and the advertisement. O'Connor and the others were playing into the hands of the

CIO "who represent so many of the radical element of the working men," and he hoped that O'Connor's views did not reflect the thinking of all the Catholic clergy.[77]

Over the years Burke and Bishop Hayes received many similar letters, which often included the sometimes not very veiled suggestion that the writer would withdraw support from the college because of O'Connor's activities. The bishop and Burke did their best to distance the college from O'Connor's actions, saying he acted as an individual and a citizen, but it is clear that his actions created a rift between some members of the local business community, harming the relationship the college had been building since the Friends Campaign of 1939. As for Bill O'Connor, his standard answer for his critics was to place himself in the mainstream of Catholic social philosophy. In 1956, he responded to a later president of St. Ambrose that he had learned this philosophy "under the greatest men in the field, the late Bishop [Francis] Haas and the late Monsignor John A. Ryan. Loyalty to the cause of Christ prompts me to stress that area of Catholic teaching for which I am well trained. Certainly it would be much easier for me to abandon my efforts, but genuine concern for Catholic Social teaching prompts me to urge you to encourage rather than discourage such work . . . I am convinced that my teaching and behavior are solidly grounded in the papal encyclicals and the interpretations of outstanding authorities."[78]

The largest Catholic Action activity in those years was a four-day Conference on Social Responsibility held in March 1949. Bill O'Connor was one of those who suggested St. Ambrose host the conference and that the college involve the National Catholic Welfare Conference. Linna Bresette, a staff member of the national group, wrote Burke that Hayes had agreed to be the official host, but that it would be better if the bishop appointed Burke rather than O'Connor as chair. O'Connor was identified with labor and Bresette said "we should avoid giving the impression that this is a labor conference." In reply Burke said that she was "quite right in thinking that Father O'Connor [was] identified in the local public mind as being a labor man, if not a Communist." Burke said he would serve as chair but would call on O'Connor "to do a great deal of the work."[79]

On the eve of the conference, the *Ambrosian News* noted that "post-war interest in social problems among St. Ambrose students will reach a climax" when the four-day conference began on March 21. Bishop Hayes was the host, along with the archbishop of Dubuque and the bishops of Des Moines, Sioux City, and Peoria. Attendees included clergy, religious, and lay people from all over the Midwest.[80] Classes were canceled at St. Ambrose to allow the students to participate in all four days of the conference.

The theme was "Christian Social Responsibilities" and speakers came from national organizations such as the National Catholic Welfare Conference, the National Catholic Family Life and Rural Life Conference, the Catholic Conference on Industrial Problems, and the Catholic Association for International Peace. Representatives also came from colleges such as Loyola, Loras, Notre Dame, Catholic University, St. Louis University, DePaul, and St. Ambrose, and from local and national labor groups. They included notable names such as Lugitti, the Reverend Daniel Cantwell of the Catholic Labor Alliance in Chicago, the Reverend William Gibbons, SJ, former editor of *America* magazine, David J. McDonald, secretary-treasurer of the United Steel Workers of America, and Edward Marciniak, editor of *Work* and professor of sociology at Loyola in Chicago.

The keynote address was delivered by Bishop Hayes who told the participants that "these are not times for colorless neutrality. The duty of the Christian is to share generously and courageously in the effort to solve these problems of social justice." There were sessions on teaching social justice in the schools, employer-labor relations, agriculture, labor schools, health care and hospitals, family life, and economics. One session for the clergy concerned ministry to Spanish-speaking immigrants. The implications of the papal encyclicals were woven through most of the sessions. Hundreds of people came to campus for the conference and several of the major sessions were filled to overflowing. The conference was a great success; the Reverend B. L. Masse, SJ, from *America* magazine said it was "one of the greatest things the Church has done in this country." The *Ambrosian News* said it illustrated well that "there was never in the past so great an interest on the campus in social problems" as now.[81]

In 1951, Mike Lawrence, a St. Ambrose student of Bill O'Connor, and other St. Ambrose and Marycrest students who had been involved in those Catholic Action groups, formed the League for Social Justice. Among its purposes was to promote the principles of the papal encyclicals on labor and the social order; to promote trade unionism and labor and management cooperation; and to "work toward the complete integration of the Negro, Mexican and other minority groups into American society."[82] The League was a lay group, and although Bill O'Connor or another priest occasionally met with them, they did not want to have to check with "Father" before they took any action.

The group met twice a month where they conducted business. They also discussed the encyclicals, especially the two of Pius XII on the Mystical Body and the liturgy. The concept of the Mystical Body became the organizing principle of the League and understanding and living the liturgy formed an "indispensable basis for Christian social action."[83]

The group put their discussions into action in three areas. First was wartime rent controls that were still in place. The city of Davenport, however, was about to remove controls, a move League members said would raise rents and make it difficult for people to find adequate housing. The city reimposed rent controls, but League members found it was easy for landlords to receive an exemption and raise rents anyway.

The second area of action was to follow up on the survey done a few years before by Father Ed O'Connor's students and investigate racial discrimination in Davenport. Their methodology was to identify seven general areas of life: employment, housing, health, education, public places, organizations, and recreation. Some members called barbershops, funeral homes, hospitals, doctors, dentists, and schools to ask whether they would accept Negro customers or patients. A white couple and a black couple went together to restaurants to find out if they could get served.

The League compiled the information and in November 1951 published it in a booklet titled, *Citizen 2nd Class, Negro Segregation and Discrimination in Davenport*. It pointed out that all citizens voted, paid taxes, sent their sons to war, and obeyed the law, but because of the color of their skin, "second-class citizens" were denied the wide range of economic and social opportunities the city offered. The report then gave the details of each general area that had been surveyed and concluded in a note to "Mr. and Mrs. Davenport," that discrimination existed because of ignorance and fear that if a white businessman tried to serve Negroes he would lose his white customers or his white employees would object. It urged white Davenport to open its mind, study the facts, and then summon the courage to change.

Within weeks of the publication of *Citizen 2nd Class*, the League became involved with discrimination against the Mexican-Americans at Cook's Point which the Industrial and Human Relations Council had surveyed a few years before. They were now being forced to move so the owner of the land could build a factory. But a survey by League members indicated that because of discrimination against them, there was no place for the residents to move. The League members appeared at city council meetings and helped in the formation of a special committee to try to find housing. Slowly the families on Cook's Point were able to find homes. One family owned land on old Highway 22, west of Davenport on which they hoped to build houses. League members agreed to help and Bishop Hayes agreed to enlist the help of the seminarians at St. Ambrose. On a Saturday in April, twenty-four St. Ambrose students were trucked out to the site for a full day's work. With their help over the next few weeks, the houses were completed and the families moved from Cook's Point.

The League continued for another year but some members had moved away and others had growing families which put different demands on their time. For many of them, their time at St. Ambrose and Marycrest and their involvement with the League prepared them for future battles against injustice and discrimination. The study of the social encyclicals, their discussions of the place of the liturgy and worship in their lives, their contacts with the Jocist methodology, and their education at St. Ambrose or contact with

A Great and Lasting Beginning

members of its faculty were the keys to their activism. Their education had combined the theoretical with the practical, and it had changed them. Mike Lawrence remembered that his work with the League was a "sensational experience," adding, "We thought we were going to make a difference."[84]

As the letter to the *Ambrosian News* which had objected to the NFCCS indicated, not everyone at St. Ambrose was impacted by the social activism of the

Married barracks along Gaines Street.

late 1940s, but some were. Looking back on those years, one Marycrest student said, "I don't think we realized . . . at the time that there was something different at St. Ambrose."[85] Another said that there was a "ferment on or near Locust St. that made . . . the College something special."[86] The Reverend Marvin Mottet remembered vividly the effect of the social justice message while he was a student in those years. "It hit me like a ton of bricks," he said. "Everywhere you turned you got it from the O'Connors, you got it from Grif, you got it from Ruhl . . . [and you] wanted . . . to go out of there and knock down walls."[87]

College officials were not knocking down walls, but they were knocking on doors to find places for students to room. In September 1948, the Reverend Bernard Brugman, the dean of men, said the housing situation was "more acute" than the previous year since the entering class was larger. At the time he needed thirty-five apartments for married students and faculty members, and he said he could use one hundred sleeping rooms for single students. Two women who had rented rooms to St. Ambrose students before said it had been a good experience. "I'm very happy with the boys they send me," one said. The other remarked, "I've had none but the finest gentlemen. I think they send me the choice of the college."[88]

The post-war housing shortage in Davenport was also illustrated when Dan McKinnon, who had been hired as the basketball coach for 1947-1948, resigned in March 1948. He could not find suitable housing so his family was living in a "cabin on the edge of Davenport." He regretted resigning but said he had to consider the welfare of his family.[89]

One group who did find housing on campus was the twelve married couples and their children who lived in the married barracks in the area called, "the Valley." In the spring of 1948, there were eight children among the twelve families with another on the way, and the sight of young mothers pushing baby carriages across campus or taking diapers down from the clothesline became commonplace. The three-room apartments were hardly luxurious, but the families developed a community based on their common experience as young married couples living in less than adequate facilities.

A reporter of the time wrote that theirs was a story of "hardships and laughter, broken water pipes and 'sweater dances,' stretching the GI check till the end of the month and rooting at football games, doing the washing and ironing while hubby does his accounting, typing out his assignments while he does the dishes. . . .[It was the] story of a young couple making a home out of three rooms and a shower, complete with hot and cold running water."[90] One wife recalled, "Living in the barracks is cheap, but there's more to it than that. You get to know everybody so well, and they're all so friendly."[91]

Much of their social life revolved around campus events. A common activity was a dance in the gymnasium held after a basketball game, "much to the chagrin of some sleepy-eyed profs in Ambrose Hall who cannot be lulled to sleep by such tunes as the 'Woodchopper's Ball' or the 'Sabre Dance.'" There were Sunday afternoon Matinee Mixers, the Junior-Senior prom at St. Ambrose, the prom at Marycrest, band and choral concerts, on-campus speakers, clubs, and home games.[92] When the students, married and single, could get off-campus, they went to the Arrow Club or Marie's Lunch or the Tiptopper on Harrison Street, Mac's Tavern, Heeter's, the Maid-Rite, or Sturtevant's Ice Cream. The veterans regularly went to Snug Harbor at the American Legion Post down on the river.

The Bee Hive, a new on-campus hangout in the basement of the library-administration building, opened on February 8, 1948. The Reverend Fred Verbeckmoes, who had opened a new bookstore in the basement of Davis Hall the year before, was the manager. The space that had been used for storage was redecorated with green and red block floor tiles and a yellow ceiling with red and green stripes on the beams. There were booths and a bar that could accommodate up to ninety patrons. On opening day, Bishop Hayes, Burke, a group of sisters from Marycrest, and St. Ambrose and Marycrest students "flocked" to see it.[93]

Clubs continued to play an important role. The old literary and debating societies were long gone and only a few of the pre-war groups continued to meet: the Manning Club, the Monogram Club, and the French Club (formerly *Le Cercle Français*). A number of new clubs were organized by academic discipline: the Commerce Club, Fine Arts Club, the Choral Club, the Education Club, Pre-Legal Club, History Club, the Forensic Society. However, many of the new clubs were social. The Chicago Club, the Central Illinois Club, the Ottumwa Deanery Club, and the Quad-City Club brought together students from a particular region. In 1948, a Rocket Club organized as a chapter of the American Rocket Society. In 1950, the Rifle Club was formed with the Reverend J. Ryan Beiser, a history professor, as the advisor. The club received a charter from the National Rifle

Association and used the police department range for shooting practice. In 1952 the students organized the Film Society of St. Ambrose and regularly screened motion pictures, including one semester, *Of Mice and Men, The Bank Dick, Stagecoach*, and *Pygmalion*. Following the Korean War, the Veteran's Club reorganized and included among its membership the men who had done six months of active duty training and were serving in the reserves. The waiters in the student dining rooms organized the Royal Order of Greasy Spoons (R.O.G.S.). The married students regularly took part in club activities, and in 1949 the wives of science majors formed their own social club with the help of the wives of two science professors. To coordinate the activities of all the clubs, in 1949 the Inter-Club Council was formed. A member from each club served on the Council which coordinated the annual Field Day and the Christmas party.[94]

In February 1945, just as the war was ending, Burke had spoken of his post-war plans for the college, including the chapel that had been planned in 1940, but which had been postponed because of the war. Now with enrollment at 1,311 students in 1948-1949, Burke thought that the time was ripe to begin the chapel project. In January 1949, Hayes wrote to the priests of the diocese to report on the status of the chapel fund. As a result of the earlier campaign among the priests, as well as subsequent fund raising from priests ordained since then, he said that there was $106,277 in the fund. Hayes said, however, that the amount on hand was not sufficient to justify building the chapel at that time. Nevertheless, he asked the priests of the diocese for comments about the possibility of a new chapel.[95]

If Burke was disappointed in Hayes' decision not to begin the chapel project immediately, he did not indicate it. Instead he took it upon himself to rally the priests of the diocese to support it. He followed the bishop's letter with one of his own. He said that it had been ten years since the last drive "among the priests of the diocese for a new chapel," and asked them if another ten years should pass. He said, "Let's provide a worthy place at our Diocesan college to house Him whom we all serve and love." He also urged them to write the bishop if they wanted a new chapel.[96]

Burke also began to build a case for the new chapel. The present chapel had been built in 1901 for 102 students but currently there were nearly 1,300 students in the college and another 370 in the academy. Therefore, to accommodate all the students for the various religious services, other parts of the campus had to be used. Daily and Sunday Masses were celebrated in the Ambrose Hall chapel, the Davis Hall chapel, and at McAuley Hall. For their annual retreat, the students were divided into two groups and each group met in the gymnasium at different times of the day. Because the chapel was small, Burke said that "the full beauty of liturgical worship" was unknown to the lay students and the eighty seminarians. Finally the Ambrose Hall chapel was inadequate for the annual diocesan priests' retreat. He said that the steps were difficult for the priests with heart conditions, there was inadequate ventilation, and the pews were uncomfortable and creaky. In sum he said that St. Ambrose had the "poorest chapel accommodations of any Catholic college in the United States."[97]

Next, Burke visited the diocesan deans who told him that since receiving the bishop's letter in January, the priests around the diocese had been talking about the proposed chapel and they were unanimous in their opinion, albeit "expressed with various degrees of enthusiasm," that the priests would respond favorably to a fund drive. But they also wanted to know the level of support from the bishop for the project and whether he was merely giving "hesitant approval" to the plans of the college. If he wanted a chapel they said he should say so definitively. Moreover, he should "command" subscriptions to the drive. The deans said that the "priests expect this leadership from the Bishop and not from anyone else."[98]

Burke knew that the bishop would be swayed if he could be shown that the money could be raised. So his plan was to enlist the priests on campus and get them to make financial commitments. He thought that if the forty-five college and academy priests, which were "a considerable segment of all the priests of the Diocese," could pledge $45,000, the bishop would "have to act."[99] In mid-March Burke reported that the fund drive among the college priests had been successful; they had pledged a total of $45,177, just slightly over Burke's goal.[100]

Hayes was convinced. On April 9, 1949, he wrote a letter to the priests of the diocese and thanked them for their "encouraging" response to his January letter. He told them that St. Ambrose had been "a large part of the history and traditions of our Diocese. We have every reason to be proud of its contribution to the good name of the Diocese of Davenport." For many years "a new, a worthy, and a beautiful Chapel has been the dream and ambition of Bishops and priests. Now we have a favorable opportunity to realize that ambition and to make that dream come true." He said that they could make a pledge payable over five years, and he enclosed a pledge card and told them to return it directly to him. If the campaign was successful, he told them that ground could be broken in the spring of 1950.[101]

Now that he had the fund raising underway, Burke next began to consider an architect who could build the chapel. The faculty priests had been looking through church architecture magazines for ideas about design and architects. A photo of St. Stephen's church in Newport, Kentucky, "caught the eye of many" of them. It had been designed by Edward J. Schulte of Cincinnati, Ohio. Schulte was a well-established architect whose work included office buildings and a theatre in Pittsburgh, the Wurlitzer building in Cincinnati, and cathedrals in Cincinnati, LaCrosse, Wisconsin, and Salina, Kansas. At the time he was working on buildings at Holy Cross Seminary in LaCrosse, and a complex of buildings for the Benedictine sisters of Yankton, South Dakota.[102]

Burke made inquiries about Schulte and when he received good recommendations, he invited Schulte to a dinner with the faculty, the diocesan deans, and the vicar general on May 16, 1949.

Burke told the priests that Schulte understood that the college and any "future building committee" were under no obligation to him and that other architects would be given the same opportunity. But Burke said that the visit would be worthwhile because it would help them to "crystalize [their] thinking on what kind of chapel" they wanted for St. Ambrose.[103]

At dinner that night Burke introduced Schulte who talked about his career and his ideas for a chapel. One of his listeners, the Reverend Charles Shepler, a professor of speech, analyzed Schulte's presentation and when he was finished, Shepler thought, "He's got these guys." At least he had Burke, who told the priests, "Gentlemen, as you know we had planned to have various nationally known architects come and present their views, but after listening to Mr. Schulte I don't think we need to look any further."[104] But

A Great and Lasting Beginning

there was still a great deal to be done before a contract could be offered and signed.

On October 1, Hayes wrote the priests to report on the progress of the fund raising. He said that including the money that had been raised in the earlier campaign, new cash and pledges brought the total to $249,014. He assured the priests that work on the chapel would begin "just as soon as our financial situation justifies that step." Hayes also promised that he would appoint a building committee by November 1, but he appeared to be dragging

The building committee for the new chapel. Seated: Rev. Harry Toher, Bishop Ralph Hayes, Msgr. Ambrose Burke. Standing: Rev. Thomas Coleman, Rev. Louis Rohret, Msgr. William Schmidt, Msgr. Martin Cone, Msgr. Carl Meinberg, Rev. Paul Albers.

his feet. Frustrated by Hayes' reluctance to move forward, Burke told Schulte he would call the bishop the next day and "suggest that we get going again."[105]

Burke's "suggestion" must have been effective, because within a few days, the bishop appointed a building committee. The committee would select an architect, develop the plans and specifications of the building, and locate it on campus. The committee included the bishop, the president, Toher, Cone, now the vicar general, and five pastors, Meinberg, the Reverend Thomas P. Coleman, the Reverend Louis A. Rohret, the Reverend William B. Schmidt, and the Reverend Paul C. Albers.[106]

Hayes called the first meeting for December 6 in the priests' refectory at the college where discussion centered on the choice of an architect. It was reported that eight firms, including Schulte's, had already asked to be considered and the committee added seven more names. Following a "lengthy discussion" about their qualifications, they decided to invite Schulte to meet with them in January. Next Meinberg said that faculty involvement in the project was important, and the committee passed his motion that the priest faculty elect a committee of six to help with the planning.[107]

The building committee met with Schulte on January 13, 1950. He was introduced as a "Catholic architect" who had engaged "almost exclusively in Catholic Church architecture" since 1921. Schulte listed his projects and said he could build a "very fine, sturdy, lasting chapel" for about $350,000. The committee questioned him for an hour and a half and then asked Schulte to leave the room. After further discussion, the committee voted unanimously to hire Schulte.[108]

In the meantime, the St. Ambrose priest faculty had elected Ed O'Connor, Griffith, Kamerick, Sterck, now the dean of studies and registrar, Emmet Toomey of the academy faculty, and Hauber to the faculty committee.[109] As the committee met, the scope of their discussions broadened to the need for a campus master plan that would include a number of new buildings. The question of a master plan had apparently been a matter of discussion among the faculty for some time. In their responses to Bishop

Hayes the previous January, some of the faculty priests had raised the issue. One had said that the location of the new chapel was critical and that in the past, the college had been "too short sighted in planning" for new buildings. Another said the bishop should give "serious consideration to future locations of other buildings" and asked for a "comprehensive and definitive plan" for the campus. Burke himself had said that "we have quite a problem . . . of planning for future building. Our campus with its buildings has grown like Topsy."[110]

The faculty committee agreed that Ambrose, Davis, and Lewis Halls, the library-administration building, and LeClaire Gymnasium had "permanent value." With those buildings as a base, the committee made five recommendations. First, work should begin immediately on a master plan for the campus. Second, priority should be given to solving current physical plant problems. Third, the college should acquire all the remaining property between Locust and Lombard, and Gaines and Scott Streets. Fourth, a master plan should be developed that included "at least four more buildings, in addition to the chapel," including a classroom building, more dormitory space, a fine arts building with an auditorium that would seat 1,000 people, a faculty residence hall for at least twenty priests, a seminary building, a field house to seat 5,000 spectators, and increased dining facilities.[111]

Their first priority was a seminary attached to the new chapel, to be built simultaneously with it. They pointed out that the current seminary on the second, third, and fourth floors of the east end of Ambrose Hall was overcrowded and that some students had to be housed in another part of the building outside the supervision of the seminary faculty. Moreover, according to the Davenport fire department, the Ambrose Hall rooms were "unsafe," and the priests warned that the recent tragic fire at St. Elizabeth's Hospital that had resulted in forty-one deaths could be repeated in Ambrose Hall. Burke presented the plan, along with a drawing of a chapel-seminary complex to the bishop in the hope that he would "come to the conclusion by himself that the two buildings should be erected simultaneously." However, while Hayes said that a new seminary should "rank high" on a list of projects, he felt there should be a greater study of building priorities before a decision was made to build the seminary. Nevertheless, Burke and Hayes agreed that Schulte should be hired to integrate the chapel into a campus master plan that would include most of the suggestions from the faculty priests' committee.[112]

With the bishop's agreement to at least have Schulte begin to develop a master plan, Burke had taken a major step toward realizing the goal he spoke about in February 1945 for a new St. Ambrose. However, as Schulte worked on the plan, the Korean War began, bringing uncertainty to any planning for the future.

What the Korean situation will do to our enrollment and to our lay faculty I don't know. It looks as though the college will have hard sledding for the next ten years. We will have 1,000 students when school opens, but how long we'll have them is anybody's guess. I have already written a great many letters on behalf of students to draft boards.[1]

Chapter Eleven

Monsignor Burke's plans for the "new St. Ambrose" were ambitious in the best of times. When he announced them just before the end of World War II, he hoped he could begin to put them in place quickly. What he could not have anticipated were delays because of the post-war adjustments needed to accommodate the rapid increase in the size of the student body and faculty. Now that the plans for a new chapel were folded into a campus master plan of several new buildings, Burke thought he could once again dream of the new St. Ambrose. But the war that began in Korea in June 1950 threatened to delay his plans once again. As he wrote a friend that September, what the new war in Korea meant was "anybody's guess." Still he pressed on in spite of the uncertainty.

Burke was happy to have Bishop Hayes' agreement that work should begin on the master plan. But it slowed the planning of the chapel and Hayes was not happy with that. In June 1950, just as the Korean War began, he told Burke that he wanted to speak with the priests when they were on campus for their annual retreat. He said the "priests were tired of hearing him talk in generalities about the chapel" and they would come "expecting to hear something definite." He asked Burke to write Edward Schulte for information and to tell him again that the bishop wanted to "start digging before the end of the year." Schulte said he would "bend every effort" to start building before the end of the year, but that Burke and the bishop must understand that the master plan would "take some time."[2]

In August Hayes wrote Schulte, "Summer has passed almost entirely and, as far as I can see, we have made no progress." Hayes said the priests were asking him questions he could not answer. Moreover, the delay had had a "bad effect" on fund raising and he said he was "most anxious" to have "something concrete to show before the winter sets in." Schulte replied that he was sorry he was causing Hayes "some concern" but that he had been "deeply engaged in the very difficult task of the master plan," but he hoped that in the "not too distant future" he would have some plans to show the bishop.[3]

The not too distant future proved to be eight months. In January 1951, Schulte presented a sketch of the chapel and seminary which was published in the *Ambrosian News* and the *Ambrosian Alumnus*. Schulte described the building as "contemporary ecclesiastical architecture" which would "occupy the dominant position of the contemplated quadrangle." The tower would become the "main axis" of the campus and reflect the theme of the cross and the crown emblematic of Christ the King. The chapel would seat a total of 519 people in the nave, side chapel, choir loft, and vested choir stalls. On the lower level, there would be fifteen chapels for the daily use of the priest faculty. The planned adjoining seminary would have room for 100 students

and suites for three faculty members.[4]

Hayes wrote to all the priests of the diocese in April 1951 to bring them up-to-date and to describe the master plan for the "new St. Ambrose College." The seminary would be added to the east side of the chapel and to the east of that would be a dormitory. There was to be a faculty residence north of Davis Hall and a field house north of that. Just to the east of the library-administration building on Locust Street would be a fine arts building with an auditorium behind it. To the east of Ambrose Hall along Scott Street would be a liberal arts building with an adjoining student union. Those new buildings would be in a U-shaped group with the chapel at the center so it became the "focal point of the completed plan" with the tower dominating the "entire campus." To accomplish that meant the "ultimate removal of the old St. Ambrose Hall."

Hayes reported that there was $263,700 in cash and pledges for the chapel and he said that if the priests had not yet made a pledge, he would "be very happy to hear from" them. The chapel, he reminded them, was "the exclusive project of the priests of the Diocese."[5]

Since at least 1945, Burke had been referring to a "new campus," a "new college," but this was the first time the bishop had used the term. Burke's plan was to create a modern campus that would have made it "Burke's" college and apparently erase the nineteenth century roots of the campus. It is very clear that he had led the bishop and the faculty to this point, and that he had a willing ally in Edward Schulte. The first priority of the plan was to build the chapel.

Schulte met with the bishop's committee on April 13, 1951, and presented drawings for the chapel. He told them that working plans could be completed and construction contracts awarded by July 1. But by mid-July he had not completed the plans and Burke was growing frustrated by the lack of progress. He told one correspondent in early July that he "never knew the preliminary steps to building were such a slow process."[6] A month later he wrote Schulte that he was being asked daily, "What about the new chapel? When are you going to start building?" Burke said that the bishop and the committee were wondering the same thing and he pressed Schulte for "definite information." And to another correspondent, he confessed his impatience with Schulte, and added, "Please God, we'll get started this fall."[7]

The proposed new fine arts building would replace the "new" music building which had been erected in 1948. Since the 1930s, the Music department had used space in the Irish Village on the fourth floor of Ambrose Hall.[8] But

A Great and Lasting Beginning

the music program was expanding; in 1947 Clarence Kriesa was hired as the first full-time band instructor. Within a year the band had sixty members who played a regular series of concerts on campus, toured area high schools, and served as a marching band at football games under the leadership of drum major, Don Wooten, a student from Memphis, Tennessee.[9]

The Music building.

Father Madsen continued to lead the vocal music program. In addition to concerts with the band, one of the highlights of the vocal music season was the annual Christmas concert at the Masonic Temple where the St. Ambrose Choral Club was joined by vocal groups from Marycrest, the Tri-City Oratorio Society, and the boys' choir from Sacred Heart Cathedral. During Lent the vocal group presented the classic, "Seven Last Words." Smaller music groups also provided entertainment on campus, the most popular of which was the "Bee Flats," a quartet of Don Wooten, Wayne Loui, Bernard Vogel, and Tom Fitzpatrick.[10]

To accommodate the growing department, in 1948 the college obtained a war-surplus building which had been the Bachelor Officers' Quarters at the Ottumwa Naval Air Station. The two-story building was located north of Davis Hall and had room for two rehearsal halls, twelve practice rooms, six studios, a student lounge, an instrument storage room, and a wardrobe room. The hope was that the building would serve the needs of the department for up to five years until the new fine arts building was erected. The space vacated by the Music department in the Irish Village was turned over to the seminary.[11]

The Drama department had also expanded. Through the 1920s and 1930s, plays had been directed by Mrs. Helena Bradford Churchill. When she died in 1939, one of her students, Charles Costello, was hired as professor of speech and dramatics. Costello graduated from St. Ambrose Academy and Junior College in the early 1920s. He had appeared in the first play

Churchill directed at St. Ambrose, and she pronounced his performance as Shylock during those years as the best she had ever seen. He had a Master's Degree from Loyola of Chicago and was a member of Actor's Equity and the Screen Actor's Guild.[12]

At St. Ambrose he taught speech classes and was involved in radio. During the war years, he produced radio dramas adapted from literary classics starring St. Ambrose students. He coordinated the Te Deum program, and directed plays at St. Ambrose and Marycrest. Because the third floor auditorium in Ambrose Hall was small, most of the St. Ambrose productions were at Marycrest. The hope was that this arrangement would change within a few years when the new fine arts building in the master plan became a reality.[13]

Madsen continued his work with liturgical renewal. Speaking in 1949 to the Catholic Music Educators Association where he was chair of the Gregorian Chant committee, he said, "Singing of Church music must become a prayer of vital interest to the students if the desired end [of renewal] is to be obtained." Madsen observed that in higher education, students were taught the laws of grammar and how to seek knowledge by scientific experimentation, and he asked if "equal care" should not be taken "in the matter of how we adore God?"[14]

Madsen began to talk to religion classes about more active participation in the Mass. He emphasized the role each individual played in the celebration of the liturgy. To help the students understand their role, the Religion and Music departments combined to provide instruction in congregational singing. In the fall of 1951, Father Kamerick, the college chaplain, announced there would be a new class in the Religion department to study the liturgy. Enrollment would be limited to twenty-five

Liturgy Commission, 1955. Seated: Fred Lorenz, Ed Fitzgerald, Jim Brennan, Dick Hahn, Rev. Cletus Madsen. Standing: Dick Wood, Norbert Siegel, Dick Eversman, Eddie Dunn, Dean Walling, Gene Lamoureax.

students who would then attend the 8:30 Sunday morning Mass to support the congregational singing.[15]

In 1952, the NFCCS formed a Liturgy Committee to foster the study of the Mass. Over the next few years, the committee sponsored panel discussions on the Mass and the sacraments, and held demonstration Masses as ways to encourage greater participation by the students. Kamerick, the NFCCS moderator, said those panels marked a "milestone in the journey of the lay apostolate at St. Ambrose. In our interest in laymen, lies the hope of training an army for the cause of our Redeemer."[16]

The *Ambrosian News* was also used to further liturgical education. Sometimes Madsen wrote a column, but most often there were articles written by interested students. One year Xavier Mankel, a seminarian from Nashville, wrote a series of articles about the liturgical symbols in the newly constructed chapel, and another series about the recently revised Holy Week liturgy. The student newspaper also regularly featured a liturgical question of the week. One week it asked about the idea of active participation (a fine thing to do); another week it asked whether the students would still go to Mass even if the pope said they did not have to (most said they would); still another question asked the students' opinions about the Latin to English translation used at the weekly dialogue Mass (a good idea if it helps participation). After the new chapel was built, the question concerned whether St. Ambrose should adopt a new practice and have an offertory procession (yes).[17]

A good deal of the discussion centered on congregational singing, a priority for Madsen and the liturgical reformers. In 1957, while serving as president of the National Catholic Music Educator's Association, he published *Propers of the Mass*, intended for parish congregational singing, which included organ parts by Professor Howard Snyder, a member of the Music department since 1949. He was a contributor to *Our Parish Prays and Sings* (1959), one of the first hymn books in English for use by people at Mass. If not everyone liked the idea of singing in public, at least one student caught the spirit when he said he realized that Mass was "fundamentally a social prayer in which everyone has a part," and that the best way to make that a reality was to sing.[18]

Mankel and others complained that so few students participated in the NFCCS liturgy panels; most of the time there were fewer than ten students present. In 1955, Madsen noted that there was a Solemn High Mass every Sunday at 9:00, yet "less than a fourth" of the boarding students attended. Edmund Fitzgerald, a biology major from Knoxville, Tennessee, noted in the *Ambrosian News*, however, that "St. Ambrose leads the pack in giving to the students sound ideas in the fields of liturgy and sociology," topics of several of the papal encyclicals of the previous seventy years. He urged his readers to "Take the training that St. Ambrose has given you; apply it to your

Rev. Edward Catich, Theophora, *1950.*

daily lives–from the manner in which you participate in the parish mass where you live to the way in which you treat your fellow members of society. No fuller life could be had than the one lived along these principles."[19]

Madsen was asking the students to think differently about their role as members of the Christian community and their place in its worship life. Father Catich was also challenging people to look at religious art in new ways. Catich believed that religious art should "express religious truths in contemporary terms" and so the artist must use images "proper" to his own age. Thus for the people of each age, Christ should be portrayed as the "ideal man of their culture."[20] This was accomplished by the use of clothing that would be contemporary, but which did not call attention to itself and distract from the religious message, so the viewers could understand that the religious message applied to them.[21]

Catich's contemporary images of familiar religious themes generated controversy far beyond the campus. In 1950 one of his works, a contemporary icon, "Theophora," was accepted for a show at the Metropolitan Museum of Art in New York. It portrayed a white Madonna holding a black Jesus that also contained various images, including a mouse trap, an apple, a beaker of water, a snake, and sharks. Catich reportedly received a letter from the apostolic delegate telling him to withdraw the painting from exhibition.[22]

Judgments about Catich's early work was done in the context of a 1952 document on sacred art from the Congregation of the Holy Office in Rome. It cited earlier church pronouncements that bishops should be vigilant that art not be "foreign to the faith" or not in "harmony" with tradition. It noted that in *Mediator Dei*, the 1947 encyclical on liturgy, Pope Pius XII had said, "We cannot but deplore and reprove those images and forms recently introduced by some, which seem to be deformations and debasements of sane art" and which sometimes "offend true religious sentiment."[23]

The 1952 statement made it very clear that the church, through the local bishop, would be the arbiter of sacred art. Bishop Hayes was generally supportive of Catich's work, at least to the Roman authorities. In 1955, when Hayes received his copy of a letter from the apostolic delegate regarding "aberrations in vogue today" in sacred art, the bishop quickly replied that his diocese would "cooperate in fulfilling the desires of the Holy See on the subject of Sacred Art. So far, no problems have arisen in the Diocese of Davenport in the matter of distortions which offend against the mind of the Church in this field, nor do I anticipate any problems in the future."[24] Later, however, when it came to Catich's art in the proposed new chapel, the bishop would not be nearly so supportive.

Burke's ambitious plans for a new St. Ambrose faced significant obstacles. As he had predicted, enrollment began to decline. From a high of 1,257 men in the fall of 1948, over the next five years it had steadily fallen to 588 men in the fall of 1953. There were additional evening class students and nursing students, but overall the enrollment decline was a matter of concern. One reason Burke gave for the lower enrollment was that because of a lower birthrate during

Freshmen nurses confer about their schedules with Sister Mary Brigid, RSM.

the Depression, there were now fewer eighteen- and nineteen-year-old males. Another was the Korean War and the number of men in the service. In the fall and winter of 1950-1951, Burke watched as students and faculty left school for the military. The January 12, 1951, *Ambrosian News* reported that forty-three students had left; the next week it told of twenty-six more. That month he issued a statement about whether to enlist or wait for the draft. As he had at the beginning of World War II, he advised them not to enlist "now," but that it was an individual decision, and he urged them to "proceed slowly." Burke gave as a third reason for the enrollment decline that because of the war, there were many well-paying jobs in defense industries.[25]

What he did not mention was the graduation rate of the large number of GIs who had come to college in the first years after World War II. Those students, many of whom would not have come to St. Ambrose under other circumstances, had created a bubble in the long-term enrollment figures. By the early 1950s, the enrollment of around 600 students was closer to the pre-World War II enrollment levels. Nevertheless, the enrollment decline meant lower tuition revenues. Tuition had risen from $125 per semester in 1946 to $180 in 1951, but the decline in enrollment meant less money was coming in even with the higher tuition rate. Burke tried to remain optimistic and he predicted that by 1956, the enrollment would be on an "upswing," and that it would "reach an all-time peak" by 1965. He said the college should be preparing for that now, but "instead we are hampered by building restrictions and insufficient financial help." The enrollment decline had other consequences as well. Writing to a friend in October 1952, Burke said that the football team, "riddled by the draft [and] injuries," was not "doing too well."[26]

In wartime and peacetime, the fortunes of the various athletic teams was a subject of interest to presidents, faculty, and students alike. A poll of the students in October 1951 asked what they thought was the "proper place"

of intercollegiate athletics in college life. The respondents all agreed that sports contributed to college life, but they should not be stressed to the detriment of education. Student council president George Fuller said that "no college should be a complete 'brick-brain' factory, but should maintain a balance between education and athletics."[27]

Throughout the decade of the 1950s, St. Ambrose continued to compete in tennis, golf, and track. Wrestling, which had become a sport in the late 1940s, was dropped in 1954. The two major sports of football and basketball received the most attention and football became the most controversial.

The spring of 1951 saw the resignation of Moon Mullins as football coach to take a position at Kansas State. Mullins' teams compiled a four season 32-7 record. Frank Brogger, an assistant coach at Michigan State, was chosen as Mullins' successor. Brogger said he was impressed with the "spirit" and the "willingness to learn" exhibited by the team. He said the team would use his own "V" formation, which had "all the deception of the 'T' and all the power of the single-wing."[28] After four years at St. Ambrose, and a 19-17 record, Brogger resigned and was replaced by Louis Friedrichs.

For two seasons, 1950 and 1951, the St. Ambrose football team had dominated Iowa Conference play. Each season they were 5-0 in their division, and in each they defeated the other division champion, Loras College, for the Conference title. Because of this dominance, following the 1951 season, the other conference teams dropped St. Ambrose and Loras from football competition.[29]

Jim O'Connor had been the basketball coach since 1947 and his teams had a five season record of 59-41. In 1951, he resigned as coach and was replaced by Robert Duax, who began his long career at St. Ambrose as a coach and teacher. In 1953, the Bees defeated Loras for the Iowa Conference championship. The next year they lost the championship in the playoff game, but they set a conference scoring record, averaging 94.8 points in eleven conference games.[30]

In 1955, the Iowa Conference reorganized. St. Ambrose and Loras were dropped from the league because they were too strong, two other teams were dropped because they were too weak. St. Ambrose had made its mark in the Conference. From the formation of the Conference in 1923 until 1960 (five years after St. Ambrose left the Conference), the Bees had the highest win percentage in football of all members (nearly 73 percent), and the highest win percentage in basketball (nearly 72 percent).[31] But without the Conference structure, in the years ahead the college would find it more difficult to schedule games.

Burke continued to look for ways to increase the enrollment. One possibility was another partnership with the government to provide military training on campus. In early September 1950, just three months after the beginning of the Korean War, there was the possibility that St. Ambrose would host a program similar to the World War II V-12 program. But St. Ambrose was not selected.[32]

Early the next year, Burke tried to secure an Air Force ROTC unit. A poll among students and faculty revealed that the majority were "strongly in favor" of ROTC. Burke solicited letters from the mayor, the president of the Chamber of Commerce, and other prominent Davenport leaders. He visited Iowa's senators and members of Congress to enlist their support. In mid-February, air force officers visited campus to inspect the facilities and gave a favorable report, but once again St. Ambrose was not selected.[33]

One successful addition to the school came with the affiliation of the Mercy Hospital Nursing program with St. Ambrose in 1951. Since 1929, members of the St. Ambrose faculty had taught religion, sociology, philosophy, and the basic sciences at Mercy Hospital in Davenport. In the years after that, some of those same classes were taught at St. Anthony's Hospital in Rock Island and Mercy Hospital, Iowa City. In 1949, the Mercy Sisters in Iowa City and Davenport asked St. Ambrose to offer more courses that could lead to a Bachelor of Science in Nursing.[34]

The two groups renewed their request the next year and a series of meetings with the Sisters of Mercy in Davenport led to the creation of a Nursing Division of St. Ambrose College. Nurses in the program could earn a three-year diploma, or remain for a fourth year and earn the Bachelor of Science in Nursing, an option about one-half of the nurses took. Sister Mary Annetta Moloney, RSM, was named the head of the Nursing Division and St. Ambrose granted faculty status to the fifteen nursing faculty at Mercy Hospital.[35]

Sister Annetta noted that nursing was going through a time of transition and nurses no longer did things they used to. Instead, other hospital employees and volunteers now performed the more routine tasks. Thus she said it was "quite important" that nurses have a well-rounded education, not only in their profession but in the humanities and liberal arts so they would be prepared to enter supervisory and administrative positions. "This," she said, "they can now get at St. Ambrose College."[36]

The agreement was announced in late May 1951 and the first classes began in September. There were seventy-eight nursing students the first fall, and that number rose to 198 the following year. The first nurses graduated in 1952 when nineteen received the nursing diploma and six received the Bachelor of Science Degree in Nursing. That year the division was granted full accreditation by the national Nursing Accrediting Service of New York.

The *Ambrosian News* hailed the announcement with a headline, "A New Era—We're Co-Educational." It said that nurses were no longer "guests" taking courses, they were now St. Ambrose students taking classes. That would require some "necessary changes in the thinking of the students," but the nurses were students and they deserved the "rights of students."[37] The student nurses lived at Marian Hall on the grounds of Mercy Hospital. They participated in campus activities, formed their own student council, had their own section in the yearbook, a column in the student newspaper, and became part of the life on campus. It did not take long for the nurses and the male students to get "used to having each other around." They were in the Bee Hive, walking around campus, and the male students seized the opportunities to walk them the few blocks back to Mercy Hospital. Soon engagements were announced, and when the first couples were married, the "students realized that Ambrosians were . . . marrying Ambrosians."[38]

The possibility of a new navy program or ROTC would have had an impact on the enrollment which also meant more income from tuition. The Nursing program helped, but if Burke was going to operate the college without going into serious debt, much less begin to build his new St. Ambrose, he had to reverse the enrollment trend. To make his case for the new buildings, Burke had to show that a growing student body required more classrooms, laboratories, and dormitory space. As long as the war in Korea continued, however, it was not likely that the enrollment would increase significantly.

In the fall of 1951, Bishop Hayes wrote the pastors of the diocese to ask them to talk about St. Ambrose and urge their parishioners to send their sons to the college. Burke wrote a similar letter to the bishops of Peoria and Rockford. Burke also emphasized the scholarships available to students attending St. Ambrose, while also noting that many were inadequately funded.[39]

Burke formed a Committee on Recruitment which reported that the college had not done a good job of recruiting new students and it could no longer rely solely on the good will of pastors to urge their parishioners to consider St. Ambrose, or parent alumni who would send their sons. The committee developed a recruitment program. Clarence Kriesa, who had been on the music faculty since 1947, was named to the newly created position of coordinator of recruiting. Kriesa would answer correspondence, arrange recruiting visits to high schools, enlist faculty and alumni to volunteer as recruiters, and follow up on contacts. The committee also recommended that a recruiter's handbook be prepared, that better coordination between campus offices be developed to assist in the recruitment and enrollment of new students, that teams of students be enlisted to act as recruiters in the own high schools, and that alumni be used as recruiters.[40]

The endowment was another financial concern. At the end of the war, it had totaled $526,499 in fifteen farms, farm mortgages, and stocks and bonds. In the following years, the college sold most of the farms and reinvested that money in other places so that by April 1951 the endowment was $587,020. Tuition income and income from room and board were down, but expenses were up. In 1941 faculty salaries totaled $61,330; ten years later that figure was $214,335. That year the college had to borrow $69,000 to break even.[41]

Burke saw the alumni as a key component of any plan to increase the enrollment and raise money for the endowment, as well as any capital

A Great and Lasting Beginning

projects the college might undertake. Prior to this, the Alumni Association met at homecoming when it elected officers, but rarely at other times. In 1949, the constitution was revised to provide for an executive committee that would meet six times a year to deal with homecoming, local reunions, the alumni's role in recruitment and fund raising, ticket sales for athletic events, and any other business that might involve the alumni.

To strengthen the alumni organization in May 1952, the executive committee began to form local alumni associations. The objective of each local group would be social, but there was also a more serious purpose. Through its regular meetings the local association would look for ways to support the college, especially helping with fund raising. Within a few years there were local clubs in Peoria, Chicago, Alton, St. Louis, Kansas City, Omaha, New York City, Washington, D.C., Clinton, Des Moines, Ottumwa, Milwaukee, Los Angeles, San Francisco, and Denver, with plans to organize in more cities.[42]

To keep the alumni informed of events on campus, in 1949 a new magazine, the *Ambrosian Alumnus*, began publication. There had been previous attempts at an alumni newsletter. In November 1942, John Kamerick, a student from Ottumwa, had suggested that the student newspaper publish the *Alumnus* for alumni who were spread throughout the world as a result of the war. Only a few issues appeared before Kamerick and the other student publishers found themselves in the service.[43] It was taken over by Father Robert Welch, who wrote the issues sent to the alumni during the war that featured Ambie Al. But after the war it ceased publication. The new *Ambrosian Alumnus* was published nine times a year and contained news from the campus including sports reports, pictures, and Ambie Al continued to report on the activities of the alumni. Burke used it effectively with his periodic "State of the College" reports. The most popular feature for the first seven years was a historical column written by Monsignor Hauber, called "In Retrospect."

In April 1950, the Alumni Association announced that it had established a Living Endowment Fund which would become an annual drive to raise funds for the college. The drive kicked off with a dinner and dance at the Blackhawk Hotel. This was the first drive explicitly for an endowment since the 1920 campaign. Alumni Association president David Klise said that in the past, "undoubtedly" many alumni had wanted to do something for St. Ambrose and now was the chance. "The phenomenal growth of St. Ambrose College in recent years thrills and amazes every alumnus," Klise wrote, "but St. Ambrose is still growing and will continue to grow through the years ahead. Growth requires expansion of facilities, means more buildings and equipment, which are needed–needed now."[44] The goal of the first drive was to raise $5,000. As it turned out, 338 alumni in twenty-two states contributed $5,007. The campaign became more successful each year so that after six years it had raised a total of $90,506.[45]

Another source of annual revenue came from the new Iowa College Foundation. In September 1952, Burke was among eighteen Iowa private college presidents who met with representatives of the Iowa Manufacturers Association to form the new group. The foundation was a means to solicit funds from Iowa businesses which would then be divided among the member schools. Burke was appointed to an interim committee to draw up a constitution and when that was ratified, he became vice president of the foundation. The first year the Iowa College Foundation received $53,520

from forty corporate donors. St. Ambrose's share was $2,455.[46] Within two years the number of contributors grew to 116 Iowa firms who donated $90,691.

All of that helped, but to keep the college budget in the black and find the resources to build the new St. Ambrose, Burke also turned to the local business community. A good relationship with local businessmen had been built through the Hannon and Cone years as evidenced by the 1939 Friends of St. Ambrose campaign. Overall there was still a good feeling for the college locally. In 1949, Mayor Arthur Kropach proclaimed homecoming week, October 17-23, as St. Ambrose College Appreciation Week. The proclamation noted the service the college provided to the city, its high standards in education and athletics which brought national recognition to Davenport, and the students from outside the city who contributed to the local economy. To celebrate the event, the college flag flew from city hall, downtown stores decorated their windows, and city officials appeared at homecoming events. In return, at homecoming Burke presented the mayor with a freshman beanie and immediately declared him an alumnus of the college.[47]

But that good will was strained in the post-war years, in part due to the pro-labor activities of Father Bill O'Connor. In 1951 Burke had to allay the concerns of some in the business community about a survey underway by the Human Resources Club. Writing John Dauner, executive secretary of the Davenport Chamber of Commerce, Burke said the survey was "strictly a student club project and not an activity of St. Ambrose College" to survey "employment practices in the Davenport area with particular reference to colored employees." Burke told Dauner such projects were valuable because they made more meaningful what the students read in textbooks and he said such activities "should be encouraged."[48]

Meanwhile the economic situation at St. Ambrose was getting worse. The 1949-1950 year ended with a deficit of $33,000 and Burke predicted that in 1950-1951, with decreasing enrollments because of the war, it would be even worse, perhaps as high as a $70,000 deficit. He said the explanation was simple: "mounting costs and decreased revenue." The institution had tried to economize, had raised tuition, had begun the Living Endowment annual gifts program, but still the debt remained.[49]

An article in *Time* magazine indicated that St. Ambrose was not alone. Many of the 900 private colleges and universities were "shaking in their boots" for the same reasons Burke cited. Many of them, like St. Ambrose, had reached out to the government for military programs. Many had begun new recruitment programs, a step St. Ambrose was about to take. Still others with traditional male campuses had made the decision to become coed, a step St. Ambrose would not fully take for another seventeen years. The article wondered when the new crop of GIs came home from the Korean War, how many of the 900 colleges would still be there to take them.[50]

To ensure that St. Ambrose would be around, Burke invited a group of Catholic business leaders to a dinner held at the Blackhawk Hotel on June 5, 1951. The nineteen who attended the meeting included bankers, industrialists, doctors, lawyers, and brokers, some of whom had already expressed some reservations about the activities of Bill O'Connor and other members of the faculty. After dinner Burke presented the economic situation of St. Ambrose, the attempts already made to remedy it, and the importance of St. Ambrose to the community. He reminded them of the Friends of St.

Ambrose Campaign of 1939 and ended by asking them for their suggestions. The group formed an advisory committee which recommended an annual appeal to local industrial and business firms with a goal of $25,000 raised by January 1952.[51]

The meeting went well and Burke was pleased with the result. But his spirits were dampened a few days later when he received a letter from one of the participants, Bernard L. Spaeth. Spaeth said he had enjoyed the dinner, but the table conversation alarmed him. He said he was aware of the feeling among some Catholic businessmen

Groundbreaking ceremony for the chapel, April 24, 1952. Left to right: Bishop Ralph Hayes, Msgr. Ambrose Burke, president, John Tunnicliff, contractor, Rev. Harry Toher, vice president, George Fuller, student council president.

"which one might conservatively call conservative," but he was not prepared for the "universality of opinion expressed after the dinner" about Bill O'Connor. Spaeth said he was "afraid that a majority of that group would find *Rerum Novarum* and *Quadragesimo Anno* as objectionable as Marx–if they ever troubled to read them." He said their objection was not just to O'Connor's "approach but to the tenets of this teaching." Spaeth admitted that he agreed with them about his approach, but to criticize the teaching "comes pretty close to violating an article of faith." He said the group was "as radical as the people to whom they object and much more out of step with the times."[52]

Burke had to begin to show that St. Ambrose as an institution was not just pro-labor and convince local management that the college was not, "as [had] been charged, 'communistic' but [was] working for the best interests of industry as well." In early 1952, the college sponsored a two-day conference on industrial cooperation which he hoped would "remove misunderstanding and suspicion." Representatives of labor unions and representatives of local businesses, including Red Jacket Manufacturing, American Machine and Metal, Deere and Company, Eagle Signal, Dewey Portland Cement, and International Harvester were invited. Some 250 students turned out to hear panel discussions on labor-management cooperation, the threat of inflation, and the problems of discrimination in the work place. One student said that the sessions had "Created more thought and discussion among the students . . . since the Social Responsibility Conference" a few years before. He added that a "large segment" of the student body thought that more such discussions "should be encouraged." The editor of the *Messenger* congratulated St. Ambrose for its "great service" in holding the conference. It was especially commendable because it brought both sides of the issues together at the same time and while it vindicated the rights of labor, it also taught the duties of labor and the rights of management.[53]

Burke's efforts with the business community began to turn the situation around. Although the $25,000 goal set by the advisory committee following the June 1951 dinner meeting was not met, over $7,000 was raised from the local business community in 1952. Reporting to the alumni in January 1953, Burke called this a "very significant development," and he found it "gratifying to know that we have genuine friends among industrial leaders in Davenport. . . . [and] to know that St. Ambrose College is at long last regarded as an asset to this community and that local executives want to see the College maintained and flourishing."[54]

In early 1952, another of Burke's long-time projects took an important step when Bishop Hayes called a meeting of the chapel building committee for January 24 to consider a lengthy list of contractors who had asked to submit bids. The committee asked Schulte to review the firms and decide which should be asked to bid.[55] Schulte managed the bidding process and selected March 17 for the meeting to open the bids. Hayes considered St. Patrick's Day as a "good omen," but because of more delays, the bids were not opened until April 7, Monday of Holy Week.[56] For as long as it took to arrive at this point the bid opening seemed almost anticlimactic. Tunnicliff Construction was chosen as the general contractor, Ryan Plumbing and Heating was awarded the heating and plumbing contract, and the electrical contract went to Tri-City Electric. The total construction project was $450,768.[57]

Bishop Hayes turned the first spade of dirt on April 24 and construction began immediately. The first task was to remove twenty-seven oak trees from the site. Writing in the *Ambrosian Alumnus*, Hauber noted the sadness Ambrosians felt at losing the trees, some of which had stood since the 1830s. He reassured his readers, however, that there were still 155 oaks on campus, and that new trees would take the place of those cut down. But, he said, the important thing was that "on this campus, where once the native trees, in their own unconscious way, blindly worshiped the God who made them, there is to be a House for God Himself, built in His honor by those who know and love Him."[58] With the trees down, the stone grotto was razed and the statue was moved behind Ambrose Hall where a small wooden shrine was built for it.

Construction had barely begun, however, when the iron workers and carpenters went on strike and work stopped for three weeks. Once the strike

A Great and Lasting Beginning

was settled, work proceeded through the summer. When the students returned for the fall semester in mid-September, the building was above ground level. Bishop Hayes laid the chapel cornerstone on September 23, 1952, which contained a box with campus publications and handbooks; Davenport newspapers of that day; some Vatican coins from the 1950 Holy Year; a pamphlet written by Burke, *Sainthood, the Universal Vocation*; two pamphlets by Catich on chalice design and the Stations of the Cross; and

The opening of school Mass in the unfinished Christ the King Chapel, September 24, 1953.

a copper medallion by Catich of the Madonna and Child. The bishop used a silver trowel that Bishop Cosgrove had used in 1890 to lay the cornerstone for Sacred Heart Cathedral.[59]

If earlier financial concerns had made Hayes a reluctant builder, once the money was in and the building was underway, he became an enthusiastic participant. He was involved in small and large decisions about the interior design and furnishing of the chapel. He questioned whether there should be two or four candlesticks on each of the private altars in the basement; he decided there should not be book racks attached to the pews; he said the architect wanted too much money for a plaster of Paris model of a crucifix for the carver; when a painting firm from Cincinnati wanted over $14,000 to paint the interior and decorate the ceiling with "ornament, symbolism, and embellished in gold or silver leaf," he said that was too much, left the ceiling unpainted, and hired a local firm to do most of the work.[60] Throughout the project, Burke rarely did anything without first checking with the bishop and it was the bishop who authorized the payment of all the bills.

The question about whether to decorate the ceiling was based largely on financial considerations. The question of the Stations of the Cross, however, put Hayes, Burke, and Schulte in the center of the dispute about the art of Father Catich. Catich had not been elected by his faculty colleagues to the faculty chapel committee, but he let it be known that he had designs in mind for the windows and the Stations. The recent controversy about the Madonna with the black Christ child was still fresh; nevertheless, late in 1952, Hayes told Burke that he wanted Catich to be given the chance to design such items as "candle sticks, crucifixes, stations of the cross, [and a] processional cross."[61]

By early 1953, Catich had not submitted any designs and Burke wondered what to do. Hayes said that "regarding Father Catich, direct action is always best" and that Burke should "put the matter" to Catich. When he

did so, Catich quickly produced images for the Stations. But Burke did not want to be "solely responsible" for the decision about the Catich Stations, so he urged the bishop to call a meeting of the building committee to decide the matter. The committee met on April 16 and Catich showed them thirteen pencil drawings of his proposed Stations. After Catich left the room, the committee discussed his proposal and voted unanimously to reject Catich's Stations. The next day Burke told him the committee had voted to postpone ordering and erecting any Stations "for the present."[62]

Burke still had to find an artist to design the Stations. Late in the fall of 1953, Schulte sent Burke samples of the work of Carl Zimmerman, a professor at the Art Institute of Cincinnati. Burke and Hayes liked what they saw, and in November, Zimmerman was hired to paint the Stations. Clearly the Stations would not be ready for the dedication of the chapel, now scheduled for December 2, but Burke hoped they could be in place by Ash Wednesday. But that date was too ambitious and they were not erected until July 1954. Burke said that "all the priests who have seen the Stations like them very much . . . [and] that besides prompting devotion they will serve to give color to the interior."[63]

The last major design decision concerned the stained glass windows. Catich had also hoped to design them, but he did not even get a hearing on his proposal. Instead, at Schulte's recommendation, the T. C. Esser Company of Milwaukee was contracted to construct the windows based on designs by Anton Wendling, a professor at the University of Aachen.[64] The first two windows, which had symbols representing the Eucharist, were installed on the west wall of the sanctuary in time for the dedication in December. Later windows would honor Mary, the priesthood, the college patron St. Ambrose, Pope St. Pius X, and symbols depicting the various professions St. Ambrose graduates entered. The last of the windows were installed in 1959.

Following the cornerstone ceremony in September 1952, construction continued and once again Ambrosians engaged in a favorite activity, sidewalk superintending. Each day Burke's excitement grew but his correspondence indicates some opposition to the project among some members of the campus community. The question of the Catich Stations was played out over those months. In addition, Madsen was unhappy with the placement of the organ pipes and other music-related issues. And there may have been other critics on campus. Nevertheless, Burke tried to remain upbeat. Shortly before the cornerstone ceremony, Burke wrote a friend that "even those who were somewhat critical of the chapel plans are beginning to show some enthusiasm."[65] A few months later he told another correspondent that the "critics may not be entirely appeased" but that he was "confident that everyone will admit that the chapel will be a credit to the campus when finished."[66] Still the strain was beginning to show; in January 1953, Burke was hospitalized for the treatment of an ulcer.[67] It probably did not help his ulcer when the construction workers went on strike for the entire month of June.

As the building progressed, Burke had to find donors for the furnishings to go in the interior: the pews, cabinets, chairs, tables, benches, and enough supplies to service the main chapel and the sixteen chapels in the basement. The bishop made it clear that while the priests built the chapel, he expected the laity of the diocese to furnish it. Burke published a brochure which listed the memorial possibilities for donors which ranged from $3 for a set of cruets, to $4,700 for the large crucifix and tester over the main altar, to $8,780 for the choir screen. One special gift came from the B. A. Spaeth family who donated $20,000 for a Kilgen pipe organ. Donations flowed in, including over $2,000 from a campaign organized by the student council to raise money from the current students and their parents. The editor of the *Ambrosian News* wrote that students "should take pride in being able to have a part in the erection of the Chapel . . . for this Chapel will serve our school far greater than anything else on this campus."[68]

The chapel was used for the first time for the opening of school Mass on September 24, 1953. It was not finished: the main altar and its screen were not in place, the windows were still clear glass, and there were no pews, so chairs were set up for the faculty and the students stood behind them. Still it must have been a glorious day for Burke as he celebrated the Solemn High Mass. The Reverend Maurice Dingman, the diocesan chancellor, preached and urged his listeners to "be worthy of the vocation [of student] to which God" had called them. This vocation was a "pattern of life" which required the virtues of docility, an openness to the truth, and industriousness, or the "willingness to make the effort to learn" the truth. He said that the social aspect of college was important, but it was more important that they live a life of service as members of the Mystical Body of Christ.[69]

On dedication day, December 2, the weather was not good, but the rain held off until after Samuel Cardinal Stritch, the archbishop of Chicago, had blessed the outside of the building. Bishop Hayes celebrated the Mass which was attended by twenty bishops, three abbots, and the priests of the diocese, prompting one student to remark that it was the "first time that birettas ever outnumbered oak trees" on campus.[70] In his sermon for the dedication Mass, Cardinal Stritch noted that St. Ambrose College had been founded to train men for the priesthood and for lay leadership and that "for many years," there had been a "desire to crown this work with the building of a beautiful college church." He said that Christ the King Chapel stood "as the very center of this educational institution, proclaiming to all that truth is one and that you cannot separate truth attained by mere reason from the truths of divine revelation." He continued, "this beautiful chapel proclaims the whole reason for the existence of this institution."[71]

The next day Burke celebrated Mass for the students. He said later that it was hard for him to "realize when I step into the building that I am at St. Ambrose. The contrast from having so little in the past to having so much is too new and sudden to be grasped all at once." The Quad-City community observed the change as well. An editorial in the *Morning Democrat* noted the "important milestone" marked by the dedication of the chapel. It said that St. Ambrose College had grown from a "small preparatory seminary" to "one of the leading private colleges in Iowa," a growth it called "phenomenal." Moreover, St. Ambrose was no longer just a Catholic institution but it was a "community institution," and the chapel provided the opportunity of "intensifying and increasing its service" to its students.[72]

It remained for David Klise, who had been a student with Burke forty years earlier and was now the president of the Alumni Association, to have the last word. In a letter to the alumni he wrote, "For a thousand years, day and night, the Chapel of Christ, the King, will sing praises to God. It will live intimately with you. I like to think of its tabernacle enshrining the youthful Christ, the Christ of the Campus. To young men through the ages it will impart virtue and strength and love and goodness that will beget leaders in character, leaders in faith and truth. I hope it will see only good days–days good to God, free and unoppressed."[73]

By the time the chapel was dedicated, the Korean War was over, but the Cold War was still in its early stages. David Klise's hope that Ambrosians see days "free and unoppressed," was a reference to the political division of the Cold War world commonly expressed as a contest between free peoples and enslaved peoples, between godliness and godless communism. Hayes had sounded the theme when he spoke to the students in September 1946. Archbishop Rohlman had echoed the theme when he returned to campus to celebrate the baccalaureate Mass of 1948 where he noted that secularism was the "root of evil in society today . . . [the] practical exclusion of God from human thinking and living." He offered Ambrose of Milan as an example of one who spoke the truth and urged the graduates to emulate their patron in a world where the state claimed to hold the truth.[74]

As the Cold War deepened in Europe, Ambrosians joined other Iowa colleges in the Crusade for Freedom, which raised money to support the government-sponsored Radio Free Europe. But when it came to fighting communism at home, some Ambrosians were not so supportive. When asked their opinions about Wisconsin Senator Joseph McCarthy's anti-communism campaign, one student said the senator's tactics were for "personal gain. We cannot allow his theory of 'guilt by association' to continue." Another student said that an "accusation without some foundation was idiotic," and that McCarthy did not realize the harm he was doing.[75]

When Pope Pius XII declared May 1 the Feast of St. Joseph the Worker to counteract the annual communist May Day celebrations, Ambrosians celebrated with Loyalty Day ceremonies to rally the "forces of Christ." In 1956, the celebration included recitation of the rosary and Benediction of the Blessed Sacrament. Father Edward Lew preached a sermon saying the day was a rededication to the principles laid down in the labor encyclicals of Popes Leo XIII and Pius XI.[76]

In 1953, St. Ambrose was chosen by the Federal Mutual Security Agency to participate in a foreign student-worker program. Forty skilled workers from France, Switzerland, Belgium, Norway, Greece, Austria, and West

A Great and Lasting Beginning

St. Ambrose College faculty and students October 5, 1951.

Germany came for a one-year program to learn about American labor practices and American life. They took courses and joined local unions to receive first-hand experience in labor activities. Burke said this effort would "strengthen our own defense against communistic Russia," and also give St. Ambrose students a "first hand . . . lesson in international relations." Burke also pointed out that it would help the relations between the college and local management which had not been good lately.[77]

St. Ambrose graduates also went to study in Europe. In May 1953, Thomas Fitzpatrick, a 1951 graduate who had gone on to study music at the Julliard School and at the Aspen Music Festival, received a Fulbright Scholarship to study music at the Universita per Strainieri in Siena, Italy. In 1954, Donald Braddock, an art student of Catich's who graduated that spring, became the first to receive a Fulbright Scholarship while still at St. Ambrose. Braddock spent a year at the Academy of Art in Dusseldorf.[78]

If worries about world events drew the attention of the campus outward, Burke had worries enough on campus to keep him occupied. Enrollment was down, and although endowment income was up somewhat, there was still a deficit of over $50,000 in the previous year. He continued to court the local business community and when the federal government's Small Business Administration asked St. Ambrose and Drake to be the only two colleges in Iowa to sponsor an institute on small business, Burke leapt at the chance. He formed an advisory committee of local business leaders, and in October 1955 the series began. Over a period of eight weeks, speakers came to campus to teach a select group of thirty local small businessmen. Burke

noted this was another attempt to "establish friendlier relations with industrial leaders, for we have much to give one another."[79]

Creating good will among local businessmen was a long-term solution to the financial problems of the college; a more immediate problem was the drain on college resources by the continuing presence of St. Ambrose Academy on campus. The academy had continued to operate alongside the college, and according to one estimate, it used about 40 percent of Ambrose Hall. As early as 1947, the bishop had indicated his support of the idea to separate the college and the academy and at that time he had given Father John McEniry, the principal of the academy since 1935, permission to discuss building a central high school. But discussions moved slowly, and it was not until 1952 that McEniry and a group of laymen recommended that the two Ambrose institutions be operated separately. Burke and Father Toher told the bishop they "heartily" concurred in that recommendation.[80]

Hayes called a meeting of the pastors of the city in early August where they discussed the separation. Burke explained the difficulty of meeting current expenses and that the academy was part of the reason. He suggested that the two schools be separated and that the pastors assume the financial responsibility of the academy. Over the next year, discussions continued while the pastors worked out just how to apportion the academy expenses over the several parishes. Finally in 1953, the Davenport and Bettendorf parishes gave $13,000 to St. Ambrose College to "offset the loss incurred maintaining the Academy." While that did not cover all the expenses, Burke admitted that it helped.[81]

The physical separation of the academy and the college began slowly. With the decline in college enrollment, McAuley Hall was no longer needed

for college students, so in 1955 the academy priests moved out of their rooms on campus to McAuley Hall. This opened space for forty more college students to live on campus.[82]

In the meantime, the pastors continued discussions about building a central high school to include St. Ambrose Academy and Immaculate Conception Academy. Both were in aging buildings and according to baptismal records and birth rates, the enrollment of both academies could expect to double in seven years. So in the fall of 1955, the announcement came that a new Assumption Catholic High School would be built on property that had been purchased on West Central Park, just west of the St. Vincent's Home.

Assumption High School opened in the fall of 1958. The space it had occupied in Ambrose Hall was remodeled, creating more college residence space and several more college classrooms. The separation of the two parts of the institution was the last step in a long process and a final break with the beginning of the institution. Although Bishop McMullen had hoped for a great university, St. Ambrose had begun as a school for high school-aged boys. Leaders from the earliest part of the twentieth century had realized that it would never be a real college until the high school and college students were separated. They began the slow process of separating the two, first with athletics, then curricula, faculties, catalogues, and by 1929, there were separate administrations. Now with the physical move to the new institution, the separation was complete.

Another separation came when Marycrest College became independent. Since its opening in 1939, Marycrest had operated as a part of St. Ambrose.

It was accredited through St. Ambrose and its graduates received St. Ambrose degrees. On June 30, 1954, St. Ambrose and Marycrest separated into two colleges, and Marycrest sought it own accreditation from North Central. The last St. Ambrose degrees granted to Marycrest students occurred at the commencements of May and July 1954.

Students from the two colleges continued to participate in some joint activities, especially in music and the theatre, and each was part of the social life of the other. As a remembrance of the relationship of the two schools, in 1957, Mother Geraldine Upham, CHM, the president of Marycrest, presented a wooden statue of St. Ambrose created by Sister Mary Clarice Eberdt, CHM, professor of art, and Miss Donna Meyer to St. Ambrose.[83]

Through those years, Burke worked to improve the quality of the academic core of St. Ambrose College at a time when some were questioning whether academic quality was possible at a Catholic institution. In 1955, Monsignor John Tracy Ellis published a controversial article that said the failure to develop a strong intellectual tradition had become the "great scandal" of American Catholicism. Ellis cited studies that indicated the abandonment by Catholic colleges of the humanities and liberal arts tradition that was their unique heritage. They were also weak in the natural sciences. American Catholics were under-represented in American graduate schools and by scholarly activities by its professors. Ellis cited a number of reasons for this but said the "chief blame" lay with the self-imposed "ghetto mentality which prevents them from mingling as they should with their non-Catholic colleagues, and in their lack of industry and habits of work."[84]

Speaking at a conference later that year, the Reverend John Courtney

A Great and Lasting Beginning

McAuley Hall was purchased during the war to house faculty who moved out of their campus rooms to make room for the navy. In the years after the war, it housed students.

Murray, a leading Jesuit intellectual, said the "responsibility of the university is a responsibility for intellectual order, for the order of truth–or more exactly, for the unity of truth." Murray spoke about the "gigantic divorce operation" when the truths of faith and theology were divorced "from all the things that men think about and do–from morality, philosophy, politics, law, economics, science, technology, medicine, psychiatry, art and the creative imagination, poetry, drama and even sport." But speaking at the same conference, the Most Reverend John Wright, bishop of Worcester, Massachusetts, noted the "nervous spirit of impatient and sullen anti-intellectualism" that was "sometimes evident among Catholics."[85]

The core of the Catholic college was a respect for the intellectual inquiry in the context of the Catholic tradition, but there was a strong anti-intellectualism in American Catholicism. Historian Richard Hofstadter had noted the nineteenth-century roots of this Catholic anti-intellectualism, and said that in the 1950s it was reinforced by the alliance of Catholics with Protestant fundamentalists in their support of the anti-communist campaign of Senator Joseph McCarthy.[86]

Bishop McMullen had not been fearful of intellectual inquiry and in Chicago he had tried to build a university where it was encouraged. That was what he wanted for St. Ambrose. The efforts of Presidents Hannon and Hauber to achieve accreditation in the 1920s, and Cone who led the discussions about the liberal arts and humanities at St. Ambrose in the 1930s,

were steps to achieve that goal at a time when higher education was becoming more complex. Burke understood that a successful college, one where the students were not just marking time in a classroom, was a complex organization that included an adequate laboratory and library resources, a growing endowment with an annual income that led to a balanced budget, an active alumni, and a supportive community.

Those features were important, but according to Burke, they were all in support of a faculty which was the "strength of a college." In 1953, he reported to the alumni that there were twenty-one priests and thirty-four lay persons on the faculty. Forty-three of those had advanced degrees, seventeen PhDs, two JDs, and twenty-six MAs, several of whom were in doctoral programs. Burke cited the work of Father Lynch who continued to publish on bugula larvae; the papers presented by several faculty at professional conferences; Professor Howard Snyder's recent composition *Poeme*, which he had performed at the Iowa Music Teachers' Association meeting; exhibitions of Catich's works; a new translation of a French work by the Reverend John Otto of the philosophy faculty; and Dr. Paul Sacco who was the current vice president of the National Catholic Rural Life Conference.

All faculty members had to belong to a learned society. To encourage this, the college paid half of the expenses to attend meetings, the full expenses if the person was an officer or was to present a paper. Sounding like Bishop McMullen who had decried intellectual torpidity nearly a century before, Burke said the publication of research and discussions at a bi-weekly faculty forum continued "true liberal higher education and eliminated [the] mental stagnation and fixed opinion that often beset faculty members."[87]

The college was affiliated with a number of national agencies: the National Catholic Educational Association, the Association of American Colleges, the Catholic Commission on Intellectual and Cultural Affairs, the National Conference of Church-Related Colleges, and the two most important, the American Council on Education and the North Central Association of Colleges and Secondary Schools.[88] To continue as a member of those organizations meant a periodic review that would show the college was not just maintaining the status quo, but making progress in weaker areas of operation.

Shortly after he became president, Burke had invited Dr. J. M. Campbell, dean of the College of Arts and Sciences at the Catholic University of America, to visit St. Ambrose to assess the various aspects of college operation. In 1954, Burke reported on Campbell's fifth visit to campus. Campbell noted the improvement in the faculty, the alumni and recruiting efforts, the publication of the *Ambrosian Alumnus*, and improvements in most other areas of the college. He expressed concern about the budget process and said that an annual budget was one of the "most pressing needs." Overall, he was pleased with the progress, and he had a special word of praise for the administration who, in spite of a decline in enrollment and a continuing debt, had "refused to yield to mere expediency and [had] maintained a patient, statesmanlike effort to improve things as opportunity [had] been offered." Following a sixth visit in 1958, Campbell noted improvements in twenty-two specific areas which suggested "something of the energy and courage and flexibility with which the college continues to face problems common to all American colleges today."[89]

Hauber now spent all of his time promoting the agriculture program at St. Ambrose. He wrote articles and gave speeches and soon the agriculture program was receiving wide notice. A 1950 article about it in the *Commonweal* was reprinted in the September 2, 1950, issue of *L'Osservatore Romano*, the official Vatican newspaper.[90]

In 1951, Hauber organized the Rural Life Club among the seminarians, about three-fourths of whom were from cities, "to prepare the future priests of the diocese to work efficiently in rural parishes." The club held regular discussion meetings on the National Catholic Rural Life Conference's 1939 "Manifesto on Rural Life," and a 1946 address by Pope Pius XII on agricul-

Inauguration of Rev. William Collins as the ninth president of St. Ambrose, May 22, 1956. Msgr. U.A. Hauber is seated between Collins and Bishop Hayes.

rural issues. In time a regular feature in the spring was a visit to a farm area to learn first hand about farming and rural parish life.[91]

Sacco and Hauber continued to sponsor the rural life institutes around the diocese and the annual forum on campus. A theme at the sixth annual forum in 1951 was the preparation of teachers for rural schools. Father Joseph Wagner, who had developed the idea of "infiltration" of agriculture into regular courses, called this the work of "saints and scholars," especially now in the context of the world-wide struggle against communism. He said the church was "losing out badly" in that battle and noted the work of communists with rural peasants in Russia and China. To safeguard rural Catholics in America against communism, Wagner said the idea that there were dual standards of living, one urban, one rural, must be abolished; the rural populace must be aroused to demand social justice through legal means; and the church must develop rural leaders.[92]

To assist in those goals, in 1952, Hauber and Sacco organized a Department of Agriculture with Sacco as chairman. In the first year seven courses were offered for: farm boys who wanted one or two years of college before returning to the farm; those who wanted general courses before transferring to a university in agriculture or forestry; the general student interested in gardening or homesteading; or students who wanted a career teaching high school science in rural areas. Hauber reported that only two other Catholic colleges in the nation offered agriculture courses.[93]

Paul Sacco had made a great contribution to St. Ambrose and the diocese, but in April 1955, he resigned to take a new position in South Carolina. In his nine years he had conducted 110 parish farm institutes, established experimental farms for use by the students, organized two major agricultural institutes, and helped develop the summer school classes and the Agriculture department. He also was the diocesan rural life director and worked with the Displaced Persons program in the diocese which resettled European immigrants uprooted by the war. But he had a growing family, and in nine years had received only one salary adjustment. He told the bishop and his colleagues at St. Ambrose that his years in Davenport were "the most cherished" and that he left with sadness. With the same spirit of sadness and loss, Hayes accepted his resignation.[94]

In the fall of 1955, most of the numbers looked better than they had in several years. Total enrollment, including male students, nurses, and the evening division was 1,380, an increase of 200 from the year before. The Living Endowment was steadily increasing each year, from $5,007 in 1950,

A Great and Lasting Beginning

to $30,307 in 1955.[95] There was still a debt, but the bishop lent his assistance in 1955 with a $30,000 loan at 3 percent interest. Hayes later cancelled the note and the accrued interest, and by November 1955, Burke reported that the financial condition was "much improved." With a rising enrollment and larger contributions, he hoped to reduce the remaining debt considerably.[96]

The improving situation may have been the reason Burke asked to leave St. Ambrose. Hayes made it official in a January 15, 1956, letter to Burke relieving him of the presidency and assigning him to the pastorate of St. Mary's Parish in Clinton. Hayes said the college was "one of the glories of the Diocese of Davenport," and that Burke's "personal contribution [had] been outstanding and unexcelled."[97]

Burke had been president for sixteen years, the longest presidency to that time. He saw the college through World War II and the navy. He began the planning for the post-war St. Ambrose, a plan stalled by the Korean War and the impact of declining enrollments in the early- and mid-1950s. He marshaled the alumni, established an alumni office, and began the publication of an alumni magazine. He established the Living Endowment which became an annual fund to support the college. He made the college co-educational with the addition of the Nursing Division. Under his leadership, the faculty received a benefit package and he encouraged their scholarship. He worked to bring the college up to national standards for higher education. But his crowning achievement was the chapel. It was Burke's chapel. He had the vision to build it, he hired the architect, he convinced a reluctant bishop that it could be built, he raised the money, and he overcame the opposition of his faculty. And Burke was involved in every decision, major and minor. If his entire master plan of buildings was not realized during his presidency, the groundwork was laid for others.

In his final message to the alumni, he rejoiced that "at long last I am to become an ALUMNUS of St. Ambrose." He recalled that he had arrived in September 1911 and that except for his years in the seminary and graduate school and a brief work experience, he had been at St. Ambrose ever since. But he said he had been president "too long" and it was time for a new president with "new enthusiasm, [and] a new approach to old and current problems."[98]

That new president was Father William Collins. Collins had attended St. Ambrose Academy and graduated from the college in 1925. Following seminary studies, he was ordained in 1929 and came to St. Ambrose where he taught economics and political science. In recent years he had been active in the Alumni Association and had been the priest-alumni chair of the Living Endowment. In his letter of appointment, Hayes praised the role Collins had played in the "progress and success" of St. Ambrose and that under his leadership he could look forward "with confidence" to the future.[99]

Some in the faculty were surprised at the choice of Collins; they thought that the Reverend Sebastian Menke, professor of Latin and Greek, was the "logical choice." But Collins apparently wanted the presidency, was therefore "available," so the bishop appointed him. A friend who had known Collins since high school described him as "shy and reserved," not a scholar, "just a stubborn plodder," whose "devotion to duty could never be questioned."[100] Those characteristics, however, would not serve him well in the years ahead. He relied too much on himself and adamantly stuck to a deci-

sion once he had arrived at it, even in the face of opposition.

An early indication of something new came when Collins announced that he would be formally installed on May 22. Since Bishop McMullen had appointed Father Schulte president in 1882, all presidents, including Collins, were appointed by the bishop. But all of his predecessors had simply walked into the office on the first day and begun work. While Collins did that too, he wanted his presidency to be celebrated by the campus and Quad-City community.

The ceremony took place under the oaks in front of Ambrose Hall in the presence of the students, faculty, alumni, civic officials, and delegates from neighboring colleges and universities in full academic dress. The bishop praised Collins' accomplishments as a professor and said his opportunity to serve had now been enlarged. Collins spoke of his new position and said in words that were more prophetic than anyone could have realized, that the "succeeding months and years may bring disillusionment but today I am confident that the work can be done, the problems solved and progress made."[101]

Monsignor Hauber rose to speak and referred to the oak trees which had been "planted by the ancestors many generations removed, of the squirrels which [are] at the moment frisking about the grounds." He reminded his listeners of the group that had gathered seventy-one years earlier to lay the cornerstone of the building behind him. Like their successors, now to be led by Collins, they were looking to the future. Hauber issued a gentle warning that the "better St. Ambrose" did not necessarily mean "constant expansion, more teachers, more buildings, more students." He admitted that the college "must grow, or like all living things it will die." But in that growth to meet the "requirements of the changing times," it must not forget to "grow in the discharge of its duty to educate the whole man."[102] This would be his valedictory; Hauber would be dead in five weeks.

Monsignor Ulrich A. Hauber died peacefully on July 1 in his room on campus having just returned from celebrating the Sunday afternoon Benediction of the Blessed Sacrament. Bishop Hayes celebrated the funeral Mass in Christ the King Chapel. Monsignor Carl Meinberg preached the funeral sermon. He reminded the congregation of Hauber's words five weeks earlier and said that the institution St. Ambrose had become was in large measure due to the work of Hauber. Even in his later years, Hauber retained his interest in the students. If there were aspects of the college of the 1950s that he did not like, "He tolerated what he could not change, was silent when words were futile." Meinberg concluded that Hauber's work would continue in the priests, sisters, and lay men and women he taught.[103]

Hauber died at the end of the seventy-fourth year of St. Ambrose College, having been a part of it for fifty-five of those years. In a profile in the *Messenger* the year before, Father Maurice Dingman had said, "When the historian writes the history of St. Ambrose College, the thread that will bind together the past fifty years will be Monsignor Hauber. . . . For these past fifty years we can say of St. Ambrose College that St. Ambrose was Monsignor Hauber and Monsignor Hauber was St. Ambrose." Following his death, Nashville Bishop William Adrian said simply, "St. Ambrose college without Monsignor Hauber is difficult to imagine."[104]

In January 1957, the *Ambrosian News* asked, "What do you think about Elvis Presley?" A freshman admitted he enjoyed "some" of his records but because of his "licentious actions, perverse appeal, shameful statements and repulsive appearance" he deserved no support. Another freshman said that underneath all of that Elvis was a "normal, twenty-one year old boy" and charges that he was "vulgar" were a "lot of nonsense." Other students said that a "trained chimpanzee" could perform just as well; he had very little talent but was "interesting because he [was] so different"; he was "disgusting, suggestive, immoral and entirely without talent." Another freshman asked, "I don't know. What class does he teach?"

❧ Chapter Twelve ❧

The paper asked the question in the wake of Elvis' third appearance on the *Ed Sullivan Show*, where because of the kinds of charges made by the Ambrosians, Sullivan had decreed that Elvis was to be shown only from the waist up. In the following issue of the *Ambrosian News*, a letter to the editor appeared from a Carl Presley that took to task "those cats up there at Ambrose" for their generally negative comments about Elvis. The writer defended Elvis and said, "Anyone who cannot recognize in Elvis the seeds of genius, the sensitivity of creative awareness, and the attunement to musical beauty, is really out to lunch."[1] The "cats" at St. Ambrose may have missed the point of Elvis Presley, but millions of American teenagers had not. Sensitive observers of the American cultural scene realized that even if Elvis did not have the seeds of "genius," he was sowing the seeds of change.

The 1950s are often referred to as a decade of conformity. Prosperity, the greater availability of consumer goods, higher wages, better educational systems, combined with Cold War "successes" and the fear of being different instilled by the Red Scare and Senator Joseph McCarthy had created an "ideal" American. The husband left his home in the suburbs to go off to work for an organization to which he was expected to give his full devotion. His wife stayed home to tend the children and the house. Evenings after dinner, they gathered around the family television set. On weekends in the morning, it was golf, and in the evening, they joined with friends on the patio for a barbecue. On Sunday the whole family attended church. The goal in life was to have at least what other people had, if not a bit more: a *two* car garage, a *bigger* patio, a *larger* house in a *more exclusive* suburb. And they hoped their sons and daughters would follow in their footsteps.

Even religion fell to the sin of conformity. Will Herberg's *Protestant, Catholic, Jew* (1955) pointed out that while there was an increased zeal for religion, there was a decline in piety; church attendance was up, but religious commitment was down. Denominational differences were glossed over in favor of a "faith in faith." Religious figures like Billy Graham, Norman Vincent Peale, and Bishop Fulton J. Sheen made use of modern organizational techniques and the medium of television to carry the message to countless millions of people. In 1952, Sheen had the number one show on prime time television, appeared on the cover of *Time* magazine, and won an Emmy. American children prayed in the classroom, Congress added "under God" to the Pledge of Allegiance, and President Dwight D. Eisenhower solemnly proclaimed, "Our government makes no sense unless it is founded on a deeply felt religious faith–and I don't care what it is."

There were dissenters. Periodically throughout the decade, books were published challenging the conforming norm, but few paid attention. The Beats tried to establish a non-conforming way of life, but most Americans laughed at them. On campus, Madsen and Catich challenged the way people worshiped. Bill O'Connor questioned whether conformity to the corporate ideal was just. Ed O'Connor asked whether all Americans were sharing equally in the prosperity. But most people, on-campus and off, were glad to share in what one historian has called the "Eisenhower equilibrium": peace abroad enforced by American military might, and prosperity at home created by massive government spending for defense, public schools, veterans benefits, and infrastructure projects like the interstate highway system.[2]

Composer Malvina Reynolds satirized this when she sang about "Little boxes on the hillside/Little boxes made of ticky tacky/Little boxes on the hillside,/Little boxes all the same," in which lived people who "All went to the university/Where they were put in boxes/And they came out all the same/And there's doctors and lawyers/And business executives/And they're all made out of ticky tacky/And they all look just the same."

But the seeds of change had already been sown. The 1954 Supreme Court decision, *Brown v. Board of Education of Topeka*, crystallized the decades-long struggle for civil rights into a national movement. Some people began to ask questions about poverty, the place of women in society, and the ecological dangers of uncontrolled industrialization and large-scale agricultural growth. The imperatives of Cold War defense had led to a nuclear arms race marked by frightening terms like massive deterrence. And by the middle of the decade, American leaders were making decisions about a far-off place called Vietnam. Elvis Presley was just the most visible sign of the changes, some would say the revolution, that was ahead.

It is not certain whether the new president of St. Ambrose was aware of the changes that were abroad in American society; he was in the midst of planning for changes at St. Ambrose. In the weeks following his installation, Collins made a number of administrative changes. Father Harry Toher, who had been vice president since 1943, was replaced by the Reverend Carl Rice. Rice had been a biology student of Hauber's and had joined the

A Great and Lasting Beginning

college faculty in 1954 in the Biology department. Father John Dolan, who had been dean of the college, stepped down and was replaced by the Reverend Thomas Taylor, a member of the Mathematics department. Father Charles Shepler was named athletic director replacing Leo Deutsch. The Reverend Sebastian Menke became the student chaplain, a position held by Father Kamerick, who now became the director of Catholic Action. Juanita Monholland, who had been named registrar in 1952, remained in her post.

Collins added two alumni to the public relations staff. There had been a director of Public Relations since the end of the war and since 1949, Charles Daugherty had held the post. In 1952, his title was changed to director of Public and Alumni Relations. Now Thomas J. Mulligan, a 1953 graduate, became Daugherty's assistant, and Arthur K. Serbo, also a 1953 graduate, became sports secretary and sports publicity director.[3]

Msgr. Collins viewing a drawing of one of the buildings in his development program.

Collins' appointments reflected his ideas about what was necessary for the survival of private liberal arts colleges and his background as a professor of economics and business. The first priority was to do a better job of public relations, relating what St. Ambrose was doing and why it was important. He also had to cultivate sources of income. Tied to those was the necessity to use sound business practices in running the operations of the school. In an interview after he became president, Collins stressed the imperative to do those things: by 1975, St. Ambrose had to be ready to educate twice as many students as it was currently doing. He said he was optimistic that those things could be done at St. Ambrose, but that it would take a "lot of work."[4]

The work began immediately. In 1957, the college would observe its seventy-fifth anniversary and Collins planned a year-long celebration. It began with a "Jubilee Fair" in November 1956. The theme was the Gay Nineties and the Roaring Twenties, and fair-goers were to dress appropriately. Apparently, the most common male appurtenance was a fake handlebar mustache. LeClaire Gymnasium was filled with booths for food and games, and the evening ended with a stage show.[5]

Through the spring of 1957, the Diamond Jubilee Year was marked by faculty lectures, concerts, an alumni reunion, and in May, a dinner for the Quad-City radio and television press. At the end of May, Bishop Hayes declared a St. Ambrose College Day throughout the diocese. When the priests of the diocese were on campus for their annual retreat that summer, Collins hosted a Priests' Day with a banquet. The bishop told the assembled priests that the college stood as a "monument to the zeal of the diocesan priests," since it would not have come into existence without them, and

it would not have "survived difficult years if it were not for their self-sacrificing labors." Later that summer, Collins hosted an alumnae reunion for the sisters who had received their degrees from St. Ambrose.[6]

This was all a build-up to the announcement in December of a $6 million expansion plan for the college. To prepare for the announcement, on November 5-7, Collins held Campus and Community Days to bring members of the public to campus. On the first night they heard a lecture on industrial-educational cooperation delivered by a professor of physics from the University of Iowa. The second night the lecture asked, "Are the Liberal Arts Passé?" delivered by the chairman of the Board of Education of the Diocese of Pittsburgh. This included a presentation of the functions of the six divisions of St. Ambrose College. The third night there was an open house around campus so each department could explain its function. Each night there were exhibits by the leading Quad-City industries. The editor of the *Daily Times* said the Community Days were another example of the "benevolent influence" of the college on the community, and a sign of the "readiness of the administration to assume an increasing responsibility to the people of this area."[7]

The next week Collins held a series of luncheons for the Friends of St. Ambrose. Frank Schierbrock, the president of the Friends Executive Committee, told the group that too many people failed to consider St. Ambrose as a "community college." He pointed out that the college was open to all who could qualify and that nearly 20 percent of the students were not Catholic. In addition to the money spent by the college to operate the school and money spent by the faculty, the students spent nearly $450,000 each year in the community.

William Howes, business manager of the college, said that for the current academic year the college had a budget of $944,000, with a monthly payroll of nearly $37,000. He explained the sources of income for the college: $459,000 from student fees, $39,000 from endowment income, $91,000 from contributed services by the priests, $36,000 from gifts, and $8,900 from other sources. Moreover, he said that at the end of the previous academic year the college became debt free. Father Taylor explained the planned expansion of the facilities and Collins told the groups that the college needed the "friendship and good will of the community" to accomplish its goals.[8]

Collins unveiled the $6 million development program on December 4. The central purpose of the program was to improve the quality of education at St. Ambrose, an essential element of which was to improve the quality of teaching. Two years before the college had received a grant of nearly $135,000 from the Ford Foundation, the income from which was to be used for faculty salaries.[9] Now $1 million from the new development

As part of the 75th anniversary celebration, Msgr. Collins held a Sister's Alumnae Day with a luncheon in the refectory.

campaign would go to a "supplementary endowment" to underwrite a Great Teaching Program. Another $300,000 was designated to increase the money available to underwrite student scholarships so that no one would be denied an education because of an inability to pay.

The centerpiece of the program was the construction of eight new buildings. Moline architect William Bernbrock took the master plan created by Edward Schulte when he designed the chapel in 1950, and used it to create drawings for the proposed buildings: a dormitory for 250 men on Scott Street; a liberal arts building on the corner of Scott and Locust Streets; a student union along Locust Street attached to the liberal arts building; a fine arts building on Locust Street on the west side of the campus (in the area of the flag pole on the current campus); an 800-seat auditorium behind the fine arts building; a residence building of thirty apartments for the priest faculty to be located north of Davis Hall; a field house with a seating capacity of 4,000 to be built on the corner of Gaines and Lombard Streets; and a new seminary building attached to the east side of Christ the King Chapel. The estimated cost of the eight buildings was $4 million, plus another $600,000 for furnishings.

Like the Schulte plan of a few years before, this plan envisioned the demolition of Ambrose Hall. But since that would be the last step in the project, $200,000 was included in the development plan to remodel the building when the academy moved out. It was hoped that this would breathe another twenty years of life into the old building before it would be torn down.[10]

Collins said this plan was the "essence of 75 years of thought and hope," to "continuously and properly" improve the quality of education at the college, which was the "primary and essential reason for the existence of St. Ambrose." As he told the priests of the diocese, "Unless St. Ambrose is continuously able to present for graduation . . . educated men, possessing an integrated body of knowledge and prepared basically to live up to the level of their time, Commencement Day in the true sense will be impossible."[11]

Local reaction to the program was positive. The *Daily Times* editorialized that the college plan deserved the "careful attention and support" of the entire community, and it praised the fact that it was more than just buildings but included increasing the endowment and raising faculty salaries.[12] The *Morning Democrat* called St. Ambrose Davenport's "own college" which had served thousands of local young men who could not have afforded to leave town for their education. It said that while there were no plans for financing the projects in the announcement, nevertheless, it praised Collins' "bold, specific plans" to build a larger college to meet the needs of a growing community.[13]

Another consequence of the Diamond Jubilee celebration and the new development program was to increase the size of the Board of Trustees. The bishop, vicar general, and the president of the college continued to be the Board of Control, responsible for formulating policy and voting to make decisions. Since early in the decade, twelve priests and laymen had served in an advisory capacity on the board. In May 1957, they voted to increase its size and that August, the bishop named twelve more men to the board.

A Great and Lasting Beginning

Hayes told them their "acceptance in this Diamond Jubilee Year . . . would give substantial and generous encouragement to our planning as the College moves forward into the next 25 years." In addition to the members from the Quad-Cities area, the board now had members from Colfax, Des Moines, Ft. Madison, Clinton, Iowa City in Iowa, and Joliet and Peoria in Illinois. The next year the bishop added seven more men. In 1959, Mrs. B. A. Spaeth, the widow of Bernard Spaeth who had himself served on the board, Mrs. Phillip Rogge, a nurse who had served on various nursing and community service boards, and Miss Gertrude Kelly, the director of nursing at the Davenport Osteopathic Hospital, were named to the board. Hayes told them that while St. Ambrose was not, "according to the usual meaning of the term, coeducational," it did have a Nursing Division, had many alumnae from the Women's Division and summer schools, and a number of female faculty members. Therefore, he said he needed women on the board to help discuss the issues of the college.[14] Discuss the issues was all they could do. The enlarged board remained an advisory, not a legislative, body.

Hayes created five board committees: Educational Policies, Finance, Development, Rural Service, and Associates.[15] The last committee formed a new Quad-City group, the St. Ambrose Associates made up of local "influential and representative citizens," who were interested in the work of St. Ambrose. The committee said the Associates would "serve as a 'friend-raising' organization rather than a 'fund-raising'" group. The group would meet several times a year to hear reports from college officials and to listen to a speaker.[16] In February 1959, for example, Oscar Mayer spoke to the group on "Certain Phases of the Meat Packing Industry, With Emphasis on Recent Developments in Pork Processing."

As consumers of Oscar Mayer's meat products, the students took a special interest in the news that the college had contracted with the SAGA food service to take over the kitchens and the Bee Hive in February 1957. SAGA had been formed in 1948 and St. Ambrose was the sixteenth school to contract with the company. Manager Richard Vanek said he would try to "give the students the kind of food they liked and in sufficient quantities." This included steak night on Saturday which featured steak, french fries, salad, and all the milk they wanted to drink. After the first semester, college business manager William Howes said that St. Ambrose now had the "best food of any college in the Middle West," even the faculty were "raving" about it so you knew "it had to be good."[17]

The next year the college added another new service for the students when an IBM computer system was installed. The registrar's office was the primary user, but the alumni office also made use of it. Now the permanent record of each student and alumnus could be stored on an IBM card for quick retrieval of the information. Students and alumni were sent a card to fill out with their vital information so it could be entered into the system.[18]

A few years earlier a student poll asked the question, "Why are you going to college?" Forty percent stressed job training as the most important thing about college; one could no longer practice law or teach school without a college degree. Fifty percent of the respondents said job training was important, but also said training in moral and social perfection was equally important.[19]

For whatever reason Ambrosians had enrolled in college, those who attended college were still a small percentage of Americans. In 1957, for example, there were 3.3 million students registered in institutions of higher education in the United States, one million more than ten years previously. The freshmen that year had been born as the Great Depression came to an end in the United States and World War II began in Europe. Most of them were sons of the middle class whose college education was made possible, in part, by post-war prosperity. They and their parents had already learned the lesson expressed by the students who had been polled a few years before: a college education was necessary for success.

In the fall of 1957, total enrollment at St. Ambrose was 1,417 students, 1,021 male day students and nurses. There were another 120 nurses in Rock Island and Iowa City, 123 religious sisters, and 153 students in the evening division. Most of them were from Iowa or Illinois, including 194 from the immediate Quad-City area. Seventy-three percent identified themselves as Catholic.[20]

Freshmen initiation had returned after the war but the presence of so many veterans had made it less popular than before. The student council had tried to scale back the activities, a fact noted by a correspondent to the *Ambrosian News* congratulating the students who had "partly succeeded in ending one of our silliest educational sideshows. Education is at best a difficult and uncertain process," and freshmen should not have to put up with "nonsense."[21] By 1955 it had been "cut to the bone." The freshmen still wore beanies and they had to be sure they were "squared," the brim resting two finger widths above the eyebrow; beanie patrols were created to make sure. They had to be able to sing the school song at a moment's notice and perform menial tasks upon request. The Cold War injected itself even here with the introduction of a new initiation activity, fake air raids when freshmen were made to duck and cover at a moment's notice. During the final week of initiation, they were compelled to follow the old rules of wearing their clothes backward, using only certain sidewalks, and serving the upperclassmen.

In 1958, a faculty committee chaired by Agnes Renner discussed the issue and recommended to the president that the practice of freshmen beanies continue. The time of initiation was shortened to only a few weeks and it ended in early October with the Beanie Burning Dance. The Beanie king and queen lit the bonfire, beanies were tossed on, and then as they burned, the students roasted marshmallows. This was followed by a Grand March around campus to the dance in LeClaire Gymnasium. One student commented, "With their beanies gone, the freshmen can finally settle down to the normal life of a college student." When they were polled, some of the freshmen thought it was fun, others thought it should be eliminated, and one said that the freshmen had it over the seniors, since at least the freshmen knew the school song.[22]

The normal life of a college student included a social life in the late 1950s not that much different from the decade before. Elvis Presley may have been a hit on Ed Sullivan, but his music appeared to make little impression on campus. There was a regular music column in the *Ambrosian News* but it usually discussed the latest in jazz recordings. Music for the formal dances at homecoming or the spring cotillion was provided by bands like Les Elgart, "the band with the dancing sound"; or Tex Beneke, who had taken over the old Glenn Miller Orchestra; or Russ Carlyle; or Harry Wolfe and his Rhythm Kings.

Those were formal events with the ladies in prom dresses and the gentlemen in coats and ties. They danced at the Coliseum or the Starlight Ballroom or in the highly decorated LeClaire Gymnasium. Preparing for those dances might have meant a visit to the Syndicate Hub or Simon and Landauer or Britt's Men's Wear for a new suit. A formal dance also meant a stop at Don's Barber Shop on Harrison Street, where "U-R Next." Less formal dances included the Tri-School dance at the beginning of the year, dances sponsored by the Chicago Club, the Vet's Club, the Ottumwa Club, or the Monogram Club.

On Friday or Saturday nights, students traveled west on Locust Street to gather at Riefe's or Heeters, "the half way mark for Ambrosians and Cresters"; or to Harrison Street at the Maid Rite or Dick and Don's Tiptopper, or the Arrow Club, the "popular meeting place for Ambrosians"; or for a malted at Swan's Drug at Harrison and Locust. Or they might have ventured across the river to the Zebra or the Panther cocktail lounges in Rock Island.

The dean of men kept a close watch on the on-campus lives of the students. In 1958, Father Charles Shepler became dean. He had been the assistant dean to Father Hratz for several years and one incident during that time became legendary. One night Shepler had to deal with a student in the barracks who had been a problem, and that night under the influence of too much alcohol, the student got a gun and made threats against him. When Shepler called Father Hratz to tell him of the threat, Hratz paused for a moment, then said, "That man bears watching," and hung up.

As dean, Shepler was a stickler for the rules and reportedly regularly patrolled the hallways of the dormitories late at night to make sure they were observed. Students caught in bed at the rising hour paid Shepler's "sleeping beauty" fine, the proceeds from which bought much-needed equipment for the office. But he also took extra effort when a student was in need, including purchasing an airplane ticket or giving the student his own car if he needed to get home because of a family emergency.

Shepler was dean for only five years, but one of his actions contributed to the quality of student life for many years after that. In 1960, he hired Mrs. Kathleen Spencer as his secretary. Mrs. Spencer, as the students invariably called her, quickly became an intermediary between the students and the dean, providing information for both and serving as an advocate for both. Students soon learned that if they needed something, including a friendly ear or a shoulder to cry on, they went first to Mrs. Spencer. She said, "You have to like young people and you have to learn to never be shocked."[23]

Meanwhile, discussion continued about which building in the development

A Great and Lasting Beginning

plan would be built first. The church students in Ambrose Hall were housed "inadequately and unsafely." The Administrative Council suggested that for the seventy-fifth anniversary, the college complete the original chapel plan by building a new seminary, and build a new dormitory for lay students which would include a dining room on the first floor. Over the next eighteen months, Burke reiterated the same point, asking whether St. Ambrose could "afford NOT to build?" He said the facilities were

Following the dedication of East Hall, the official party and the graduates processed to the graduation ceremonies.

"woefully insufficient for the immediate future," and St. Ambrose could not "long continue to ignore future demands."[24] But once again, a new seminary building would have to wait.

The Administrative Council had also discussed the condition of the barracks. They noted that in 1946 the Davenport City Council had granted a permit for them as a "temporary measure," but that now they could be condemned at any time. In 1958, the barracks still housed 120 men and twelve couples and their families. The walls and ceilings were plasterboard, the walls so thin a neighbor's conversations and television could be heard, the screens and storm windows did not fit properly; nevertheless, they were still seen as congenial places to live, especially for the couples.

In early December 1957, just as Collins announced the development plan, the college applied for a $920,000 loan from the Federal Housing and Home Finance Agency to build the new dormitory to be named East Hall (later renamed Rohlman Hall). Preliminary approval of the loan came in late January, but for final approval, the college had to submit preliminary designs. Collins appointed a faculty committee of Fathers Catich, Menke, and Shepler, and H. Shannon Boyd, professor of engineering and Wallace M. Evans, professor of accounting. He also created a sixteen member Student Building Advisory Committee to collect opinions from the students about what the building should contain. A third committee was formed to raise $148,000 for the furnishings. Those committees would advise William Bernbrock who was hired as the architect.[25]

Final approval for the government loan came in August, contracts were awarded in mid-October, and on October 22, 1958, Bishop Hayes presided at the groundbreaking ceremony. The four-story building would have rooms to house 248 students in double rooms, and one two-room suite for a priest on each floor. Sidewalk superintending once again became a popular occupation as the building went up through the winter and spring. The hope was that it would be ready for occupancy in September 1959.[26] But the September date was not met, and the first students did not move into the building until November when the first floor was ready for occupancy.

The first residents were impressed with the accommodations. They found it to be quiet, good for studying and sleeping. The *Ambrosian News* noted that "Few had expected to be surrounded by such luxury after having resided in the barracks." In early January, Collins hosted an open house so the community could see the building. It was completed by the end of the month and fully occupied with the beginning of the second semester.[27]

East Hall was dedicated at commencement May 29, 1960. The faculty, graduates, and the official party gathered in front of the new building for a blessing by the bishop and a speech by Charles H. Whitmore, president of the Iowa-Illinois Gas and Electric Company and a member of the Board of Trustees. Whitmore hailed Bishop McMullen's vision in founding St. Ambrose seventy-eight years before. He praised the college "as an active and constructive influence in the community life of the Quad-Cities. The future of the college and that of the community are closely interwoven. As one progresses, so will the other." Following the dedication ceremony, the group processed across campus to assemble under the oaks for commencement.[28] That summer, the barracks were torn down and the space they had occupied since 1946 became a parking lot.[29]

While planning proceeded for East Hall, Collins also worked on another of the goals of the development program, the Great Teaching Program. He saw it as an "essential goal," and one way to achieve that was to increase the salaries of teachers. This would encourage good ones to come to St. Ambrose and provide an incentive for faculty already on the staff to stay.

To accomplish all that he hoped, Collins had to find funds. Part of the funds came from the government loan to build East Hall which would be repaid by room fees. Part would come from various fund-raising efforts, including the Living Endowment. Another source of funds would come from the new Parent's Council, organized in the summer of 1957 by Clarence Kriesa, the coordinator of recruiting. Fourteen sets of parents became the nucleus for the organization which would be involved in student recruitment and fund raising. At the first annual Parent's Day on November 17, 250 people gathered for Mass followed by lunch and a program. Father Taylor told them that the college supplied the "environment, the climate, the desire to satisfy the curiosity of the student." The goal was to teach their sons to know themselves and the world they lived in so they could continue to learn for the rest of their lives. Father Menke continued that theme when he discussed the trivium and quadrivium, the liberal arts which were "designed to prepare the student . . . to think."[30]

The final speaker was John F. McGuire, director of the college placement bureau. The placement bureau had been organized in September 1948 to help students find permanent and part-time jobs. In its first year of operation, it had found jobs for 442 students and alumni. By the time McGuire spoke to the parents, the bureau had found over 7,000 part-time jobs for

A freshman ritual, being fitted with a new beanie.

students while they were in school. The previous year it had facilitated 380 interviews with forty-one firms for graduating seniors and had placed thirty-three graduates in accounting, teaching, sales, industry, and office management positions, and placed another ten graduates in the military. Those were the kinds of statistics parents wanted to hear and McGuire explained the criteria a prospective employer used when looking at St. Ambrose graduates: the student's mastery of his subject, the ability to continue learning after graduation, the ability to adapt to new situations, and the ability to think and express himself clearly orally and in writing.[31] Within two years the Parent's Day became the Parent's Weekend and in addition to the Mass and lunch, it now included a football game and a play.

One reason for involving the parents was to raise funds for the school, but the amount of money they could raise was modest; in 1958 the hope was to raise $5,000. But the Great Teaching Program needed much more support than that. Faculty salaries had not kept up with inflation. In 1956-1957, salaries ranged from $3,500 for instructors to $5,700 for professors. The next year it ranged from $4,000 to $6,200. Now in March 1958, Collins said it would be raised to $4,200 for instructors and up to $12,000 for professors.[32] In 1957, the priest faculty had seen their salaries increased from $600 to $720 for those ordained up to twenty years (fifteen of the priest faculty that year), and from $960 to $1,440 for those ordained more than twenty years (thirteen priest faculty members).[33]

The college also established a faculty loan program that provided loans at no interest to study for an advanced degree. The loan would be cancelled if once the degree was received, the faculty member remained at St.

Ambrose for three years. Within weeks of the announcement, ten faculty members applied for the loan. The loans were a helpful benefit, but Father Taylor, the academic dean, hoped for more and said he looked forward to the day when faculty members could take sabbaticals.[34]

Tuition was another source of revenue for the college. In 1958, tuition income paid for about 60 percent of the cost of providing an education. Tuition had steadily increased through the decade from $150 a semester in 1950 to $250 in 1957. To support the Great Teaching Program, in February 1958, Collins announced that tuition would be raised to $275 for the upcoming fall semester.[35]

In 1958 there were thirty-five full-time lay professors and twenty-seven priests. There were another sixteen part-time faculty members. Late that year, twenty-nine members of the faculty formed a chapter of the American Association of University Professors (AAUP). Organized in 1915, the AAUP sought to ensure that faculty members taught in a climate of academic freedom and it acted as an advocate for faculty issues. At St. Ambrose, the charter members elected Professor of philosophy Hellmuth J. Kornmueller as president; Father Sebastian Menke, student chaplain and professor of Latin and Greek, vice president; Father Patrick McCoy, associate professor of English, secretary; and Bernard Bornong, assistant professor of chemistry, treasurer. Father William Lynch and Prudent Coussens, associate professor of German and Latin, served as members of the executive committee.

A Great and Lasting Beginning

The economic situation of the faculty and the students found its way into campus humor:

One Ambrosian said to another, "I don't see where I'm going to get money for the prom."

"What did you do with the money you made last summer, with the money you've been making in the Bee Hive, with the money your folks have been sending you?"

The no-longer-wealthy Ambrosian shook his head and said, "Part of it I spent at Heeters, part of it on my car, and part of it on girls from Marycrest and Marian Hall. The rest I spent foolishly."

"Someone has said that the only difference between a college professor and a student is a new car. The college professor doesn't have one."[36]

All of those student and faculty cars contributed to one of the most intractable campus problems: parking. A 1959 poll in the *Ambrosian News* asked what could be done to "ease the parking problem at St. Ambrose?" One respondent said the problem was not "too bad now" if you did not mind a short walk, but that it was getting worse every semester. He suggested that the area to be vacated by the barracks could become a parking lot, or that the college build a multi-level parking garage where students and faculty could pay to rent a space. Another student said parking was "quite a problem" and suggested that Locust and Gaines Streets be widened to accommodate more parking or that the college cut down some of the trees in front of Ambrose Hall and put a parking lot there. A third respondent said he had talked with the Davenport Police Department who told him that parking was going to be eliminated on Locust Street and the east side of Gaines Street, and that therefore the only solution was a parking lot in front of Ambrose Hall.[37]

On October 4, 1957, the Soviet Union launched *Sputnik,* the first man-made object to orbit the earth. In the late summer, the Soviets had successfully tested an intercontinental ballistic missile which sent a dummy warhead a distance of 4,000 miles, heightening fears that the Soviets now had a greater ability to wage nuclear war with weapons that could reach American soil. Now with *Sputnik,* Americans had only to look up into the October night sky and see a Soviet-made object soar over their homes. President Eisenhower responded with an order that American scientists should give "top priority" to the development of ballistic missiles at the "earliest possible date."[38] Americans asked why "Ivan and Ivana could do things that Johnnie and Jeannie could not." The Soviets seemed so "purposeful; the Americans, awash in Eisenhower-era prosperity and its challenges, seemed so aimless and slothful."[39] Many of those Americans blamed the education system, and called for a greater emphasis on teaching science and mathematics.

St. Ambrose joined colleges across the country to find ways to aid the American effort in the Cold War. In April 1957, even before *Sputnik*, the college announced a new engineering physics major. This was a two-year program for students interested in physics, atomic energy, and allied subjects. Collins said the college was "proud to be able to take this important step toward educating young men in a profession which is of such great importance in this atomic age." The next summer John A. Heider of Milan became the first graduate from the program.[40]

In 1951, President Harry Truman had created the Federal Civil Defense Administration to coordinate ways for the American people to protect themselves in the event of nuclear attack. Over the years debate raged about whether any protective measure would be successful in the event of an all-out nuclear attack; nevertheless, American school children practiced "duck and cover" drills in their schoolrooms, Americans built backyard fallout shelters, and designated public buildings as shelters stocked with supplies it was thought would allow Americans to survive an attack. At the heart of the Civil Defense program was the idea that citizens would take protection into their own hands and so training programs were developed to help them do that. In 1958, St. Ambrose physics Professor Edwin M. Vaughan, in cooperation with the Iowa Office of Civil Defense, developed a course to train people to operate instruments that could detect radiation if an attack came.[41]

One of the national debates concerned the efficacy of fallout shelters. A poll in the *Ambrosian News* found that most respondents thought fallout shelters here were not necessary, a useless expense, and inadequate to offer real protection. Vaughan agreed and said that because of the Rock Island Arsenal, the Quad-Cities were probably a target area for attack, in which case they were defenseless, and "as good as dead." He thought that if the country was attacked elsewhere, the wind patterns would not bring significant fallout to the area and that a good basement, such as that in Lewis Hall, would be protection enough. In the larger picture, Vaughan believed that war could be avoided if people stopped thinking only of themselves and pondered the "grave problems" facing "humanity as a whole and our civilization in particular." He said that people had to overcome the hatred in their hearts.[42]

One group dedicated to better understanding was the International Relations Club, organized as an NFCCS commission in February 1959. Its first president, Patrick Guinan, a student from Ireland, said the goal was "to foster a better understanding of international relations among the students." The members made it clear that this was not a social club but a study club. Political science professor Matthew McMahon was the moderator. Language Professor Gregory Lensing urged the students to study Russian. That country held an important position in the world, Lensing said, and it was necessary to learn about the country and the people if the United States was to deal with the Soviets.[43]

The students may have been looking to the sky for *Sputnik* and its successor satellites or looking over their shoulder for communists at home, but most of their attention was focused on their lives on campus. In 1957, nine out of ten students participated in intramurals. Intramurals had been part of campus life for years, but in 1953 they received a renewed emphasis when Leo Deutsch returned to campus as athletic director and director of intramurals. Deutsch developed a program that included tennis, volleyball, basketball, swimming, bowling, ping pong, golf, and softball. The next year Leo Kilfoy joined the faculty as a physical education instructor, track coach, assistant football coach, and assistant intramural director. A native of Chicago and a 1951 graduate of St. Ambrose, Kilfoy had been teaching and coaching at the Cathedral school in Springfield, Illinois.[44]

Under Deutsch and Kilfoy, Field Day returned as a major spring event. The day began with Mass, a flag raising, and the crowning of the Field Day queen. The track and field events were held in the morning, and after lunch the students competed in softball and tennis. The day was capped off by a dance in the evening. In 1956, Kilfoy became director of the intramural program and two years later, Roy Owen, a star athlete at St. Ambrose and a 1958 graduate, became Kilfoy's assistant.[45]

Through most of the decade, there were five varsity sports. The track team, coached by Kilfoy, had a series of losing seasons. Golf, coached by Bob Duax, was not much better. Father Hratz' tennis teams were very successful, winning several conference championships. Duax' basketball teams did much better. After seven seasons his teams had a 90-73 record, and had won two Midland Conference titles, two Iowa Conference divisional titles, and one Iowa Conference title.[46]

There was still the football team but there were discussions about its future. Some Catholic colleges dropped football because it had become expensive or they thought that a big football program was not consistent with the academic mission of their school. Georgetown University had done so in 1951 and although 84 percent of the Georgetown alumni favored the return of football, the president said they usually qualified that statement by saying only if it did not "interfere with financial or academic standing." He said that the question could be reopened if football could be made economically feasible, but it was a "luxury" and Georgetown had to put education first.

At the beginning of the 1952 football season, the first since St. Ambrose had been dropped from the Iowa Conference, Burke told the ticket drive committee that it would be a "test year" for football. Mounting costs and decreasing attendance were a concern at a time when overall enrollment was declining and the annual debt was mounting. At the end of that season, the team had a 4-5 record, one of the poorest in years. Two days after the last game, which the Bees lost to Loras 34-6, the Athletic Board met to discuss the future of football. Burke came out of the meeting and announced that although attendance had not increased as everyone had hoped, nevertheless, football would remain at St. Ambrose. Burke said, "There was football at St. Ambrose before and I don't want to be the first president to drop the sport."[47]

In 1953, St. Ambrose left the Midlands Conference which it had helped to form in 1947. It continued to play many of the same teams, but without the conference structure, the scheduling of games became a greater problem. In addition, attendance at football games was declining, cutting down the gate receipts. With the growing popularity of television, football fans could stay home to see major college football games, which often provided a level of play much higher than they could see from their local college team. In 1955, most of the remaining Iowa Conference schools cited the competition from television and reported they were losing money on football. A similar debate was occurring at St. Ambrose, but when business manager William Howes was asked in 1957 if football would be dropped, he said it would not.[48]

In late 1959, Loras College announced that it was dropping football due to "increasing costs and decreasing gate receipts" and scheduling problems created by not being in a conference. Loras College president, the Reverend Monsignor Dorance Foley, said Loras faced two alternatives: continue to lose larger amounts of money on football and make up the loss by raising tuition or cancel football.[49]

The action by Loras renewed the debate about football at St. Ambrose. The February 5, 1960, *Ambrosian News* ran columns with opposing views on the issue. Arguing for keeping football, John Coffey said if it was cancelled, enrollment would decline; homecoming, which had been built around the football game, would "no longer exist"; the coach would be out of a job; and students already at St. Ambrose would transfer to a school with a program. If football were dropped, morale would also drop; it was an "important factor in the makeup of any school," and to take it away would be like "taking the yoke out of the egg; all that is left is the shell."

Dave Kelly argued for dropping football. He cited declining attendance: several years before, home games drew 4,000 to 5,000 fans, but in recent years 1,000 fans at a game was considered good. Even the students had not been supporting the team, they did not seem to "have enough interest in the team to attend the games and [were] content on getting a play-by-play from somebody who did." The biggest factor, however, was that the college was losing money each year. Kelly claimed that the college had a total deficit in all sports of nearly $60,000, money that could have been better used on academic programs. Kelly observed that only four Catholic colleges west of the Mississippi still played football, and that St. Ambrose should follow the trend of those colleges who had already dropped it.[50]

Neither the president nor the athletic director would comment for the paper. Father Taylor, however, did comment and pointed out that no one was sure how much money would be saved if football were dropped. The question the administration had to answer before any decision could be made was whether the college was "getting out of football" what it was "putting into it." Taylor acknowledged that a decision to drop football would be controversial and that the "biggest 'squawk' would come from the Alumni."[51]

Letters to the editor argued for both positions. One asked why so much money was lost on football when one considered the low salaries of campus maids and maintenance men, the needs of the physical plant, and the requirements of the educational program. Another said that football could continue if it were "handled properly." He ended his letter with a romantic vision of a "sunny October Saturday afternoon [which] would be lost without the sound of young howling voices, the thud of a football, and a pretty little cheerleader bounding around–yes, even here at St. Ambrose. God Bless Football."[52]

In 1959-1960, total expenses including scholarships for the entire athletic program was about $100,000, and income from all sports was about $17,000. It is difficult to know just how much of those expenses and income can be attributed to the football program, but a reasonable estimate is that at least half of it was. With income declining from gate receipts and ticket sales, the cost of football was mounting. With those figures at hand, Collins and his advisors came to the conclusion that football should not be continued after the end of the fall 1960 season. Then on March 3, 1960, coach Lou Friedrichs suddenly resigned. Collins called an emergency meeting of the Administrative Council which discussed two options: find someone to coach the team for what would most likely be its last season or drop football immediately. The Council quickly decided that it did not make

A Great and Lasting Beginning

sense to hire a coach for only one season, so they voted to drop the football program.[53]

Collins announced the decision the next day. He explained that this was the result of a four-year study of the "specific role of athletics in an integrated academic program," in the context of increasing costs, declining attendance, and the difficulty of scheduling without a conference affiliation. He said it would be unfair to recruit football players knowing they could not play for four years and he wondered what the impact would be on a "lame duck" team in the fall of 1960. The school would honor the commitment it had made to student athletes on scholarships. St. Ambrose would continue to compete in the intercollegiate sports of basketball, track, tennis, and golf. It would also increase the intramural program, especially in the fall season.[54]

If the faculty, students, and the community were not entirely surprised at the decision, they were stunned by its suddenness. The editor of the *Davenport Times* said the decision brought "echoes of regret" but noted that St. Ambrose had continued football long after other Catholic colleges had dropped it. Collins reported that comments from the community and the alumni were "virtually all favorable."[55] But some alumni expressed regret and sorrow. Football had been the "king of sports" at St. Ambrose, one wrote, and the background for many alumni activities. The writer thought that the action would "reduce the esteem" of the college in the eyes of the alumni and the public and be a setback to student recruitment.[56]

The controversy about football subsided through the spring as the Ambrose community focused its attention on the spring social calendar, the spring sports schedule, and the approaching final examinations. Collins prepared for the dedication of East Hall and commencement. The commencement speaker was Dr. Paul T. Harkins, professor of classical languages at Xavier University in Cincinnati. He told the graduates, "Make sure that your development continues to be liberal as your education was liberal." Sounding a theme that would become familiar on campuses and in homes in the following decade, he said the graduates owed it to society "to transfuse your elders with blood that is young, vigorous, and a bit rebellious. Do not conform for the mere sake of conforming. Do not conform until you are convinced conformity is correct . . . Be a little bit angry, not with your heritage, but with yourselves. We need some genuinely angry young people."[57]

Ambrosians were not angry young men in the early 1960s, but they were willing to challenge the accepted way of doing things at the college. One venue for the discussion about football was the *St. Ambrose Free Press*, a mimeographed publication that challenged the policies of the *Ambrosian News*. The first issue of the *Free Press* on January 15, 1960, alleged that the *News* was "an administrative publicity release," which merely published news releases from the college publicity department. The charge was reinforced by the fact that the director of the News Bureau was also the advisor to the newspaper. The *Free Press* called for the separation of the *News* from any administrative official: it should have its own office and there should be a publications board of faculty and students to oversee the operations of the newspaper. The editor of the *Ambrosian News* admitted that there was little student interest in the newspaper and that repeated pleas for more student

involvement had been unsuccessful. But the *Free Press* was also unsuccessful in raising interest in its cause. In its last issue, it admitted that the students and faculty were "entertained" by it, but that the ideas it contained were not taken seriously by the readers, who it alleged "apparently [felt] that [they] had been daring enough just to read it–and it [had] little effect on them beyond that."[58]

In mid-February a group of students and faculty petitioned the student council to investigate the *Ambrosian News* and its policies, but the council rejected the petition; instead it formed a committee to investigate what policies other colleges had with regard to their newspapers. But little was done and two years later, another editor of the *Ambrosian News* complained about the lack of interest on the part of students in the newspaper, and the "know-it-all critics" who complained about it.[59]

That fall there was another controversy about whether the student council was acting within the limits of its constitution. Articles and letters to the editor appeared in the student newspaper, but like the controversy about the paper the previous spring, there was no real resolution to the dispute. Most students that fall were more interested in the presidential election between Senators John F. Kennedy and Richard M. Nixon. When Kennedy flew into the Quad-Cities late in the campaign, the St. Ambrose Young Democrats were in the line to greet him at the airport, and Ambrosians lined the streets of downtown Davenport to watch his motorcade. The editors of the *Ambrosian News* were able to interview the candidate's mother, who was careful not to express a political opinion, except to say she thought "Jack would win." A few days later when Nixon made a similar appearance, the St. Ambrose Young Republicans turned out to see him. But the *Ambrosian News* did not comment on Kennedy's narrow victory nor his call to see what they could do for their country in his inaugural address.[60]

The social changes in the broader society and the challenges to its norms symbolized by Elvis Presley came gently to St. Ambrose. When the students were polled about whether the Twist, the latest dance craze, was too wild, one said it was not, that it was only a fad and would go away; another said it followed the "modern trend of music which was fast"; and another protested that it was "not as wild as it seems. In this Atomic Age of unceasing motion, the Twist fits in perfectly." In October 1961, the student council sponsored a concert by the Chad Mitchell Trio, who sang their signature "Mighty Day," and the anti-war, "When Johnny Comes Marching Home." The second half of the concert featured Miriam Makeba. Those artists were part of the growing folk revival movement that was part of an emerging protest movement in the country. For the students, it was a night many would "never forget."[61]

Bishop McMullen wanted to educate laity to take their place in society, not just as businessmen and professionals, but also to create a better society. His own work with the Good Shepherd Home, his efforts for delinquent boys, and his ministry to prisoners became examples for his students to emulate. By the 1920s, Cone had begun to bring the Catholic Action message of Popes Leo XIII and Pius XI to campus, which was carried on through the 1930s and 1940s by the O'Connor brothers and others. Like his predecessors, Pope Pius XII emphasized the importance of lay involvement in the betterment of society. As members of the Mystical Body, Pius said lay people were an "indispensable necessity" to carrying out the work of the apostolate. Those themes were the formative influence of the League for Social Justice in the early 1950s.

The issues the League fought then became more urgent after the *Brown* decision and the peaceful civil rights protests in the south. In 1956, Pope Pius XII wrote that "God did not create a human family made up of segregated, dissociated, mutually independent members." Two

Donald Miller, president of the Young Democrats, and Charles Bubany, secretary-treasurer of the Young Republicans, shake hands before the St. Ambrose version of the presidential debates of 1960.

missions. In March 1962, St. Ambrose hosted the regional NFCCS seminar. Students from schools including St. Ambrose, Marycrest, Loras, Clarke, Mt. St. Clare, Mt. Mercy, and Briar Cliff in Iowa, and Mt. Marty College in Yankton, South Dakota, attended. The featured speaker of the seminar came from the President's Commission on Migratory Labor and discussed that issue. There was a panel discussion featuring John Kamerick, a St. Ambrose graduate

years later the American bishops issued a statement, "Discrimination and Christian Conscience," that quoted Pius and said the "heart of the race question is moral and religious," and that they hoped all "soberminded Americans of all religious faiths," would "seize the mantle of leadership from the agitator and the racist." They urged action now, "before it is too late."

In that spirit, in 1958 some of the former members of the League for Social Justice joined others, including a large number of students, to form the Catholic Interracial Council. Its goal was to support in any way possible the "full realization of human rights and interracial justice in our area." According to the Reverend Francis Duncan, this was a "true Catholic action movement–lay participation in the work of the hierarchy." Duncan said it provided "all students with the opportunity to stand up and be counted on the question of racial discrimination." St. Ambrose students remained active in the Catholic Interracial Council; by 1963, all the seminarians were members as were forty-one other students and thirteen faculty members.[62]

Other students belonged to the Young Christian Students (YCS) which raised similar questions. Through scripture and liturgy study groups, they hoped to establish a pattern of campus activity to advance social justice issues in the minds of students. To emphasize the importance of lay activity, YCS was one of the hosts of several study weeks on the lay apostolate held on campus. At the second of those held in August 1961, Bishop Hayes told the more than 550 students, religious, and lay adults present that they were not "trying to invade a domain special to the hierarchy and the clergy, you are trying to form yourselves as leaders, and that is what the Church has always wanted you to be." At the third study week the next year, there were over 800 participants.[63]

Another venue for those issues on campus was the various NFCCS com-

and current dean of the College of Fine and Professional Arts at Kent State University and Joseph Kimmel, head of Republic Electric in Davenport, who debated "The New Conservatism: Promise, Menace." A panel that included Professor Matt McMahon, Charles Toney, the president of the Catholic Interracial Council, and Mel Pettis from the Quad-City Federation of Labor, discussed the problems of Midwest interracial justice. Another panel discussed the role of the government in labor relations, and the Reverend Edmund Kurth from Loras College spoke about the future of farming. Father Bernard Kamerick, the long-time regional director of the NFCCS, said the seminar was "very successful," and was "indicative" of what could be done by an active organization.[64]

The NFCCS liturgy commission also brought together the themes of active participation by the laity and social involvement. With the leadership of Father Madsen, it continued to study the renewal of the liturgy. During Lent 1962, Madsen celebrated a "dry Mass," with many of the parts taken from Mass in the sixth century, with the altar facing the people and four processions. Madsen explained, "We are presenting this as an approach to the climax of Lent since a better understanding of the Mass is a better understanding of our whole religion."[65]

The Reverend John Burns, college chaplain, began to write a regular column in the *Ambrosian News*. Introducing the articles, the *News* noted that no one was late for an athletic event, but that many were regularly late for Mass. Burns noted that about 40 percent of the 500 resident students attended daily Mass during Lent. He noted that it was the "age of the laity," and that the liturgy was the "integral public worship" of the Mystical Body of Christ, of which all were members. He urged the students to participate in Mass by answering prayers and singing hymns. This would be easier when in a day not "too far off," the Mass would be in English. The regular

A Great and Lasting Beginning

schedule included a weekday Dialogue Mass and three Masses on Sunday, including a Solemn High Mass at 11:15.[66]

Those themes of Catholic Action, liturgical renewal, economic justice, the role of the laity, and the role of the church in the modern world were taken up by the Second Vatican Council, called by Pope John XXIII, which opened in October 1962. Mike Van de Kerckhove, the editor of the *Ambrosian News*, said the Council had two purposes: reforma-

In the fall of 1960, Tillie Sobek left the post office long enough to serve at a reception for new students.

The biggest football game of the fall, however, was the second annual Mud Bowl, a competition between the students of Davis Hall and East Hall. The first Mud Bowl had been January 16, 1960, so named because it had rained for several days, and the field was "thick with mud." A participant in that first game recalled, "It was fun to play then and there weren't many injuries either." For the third Mud Bowl in 1961, a committee organized a dance for that evening and a Mud Bowl queen

tion or renovation of the Church and Christian unity. He noted that the first document to be considered was on the liturgy and that the expected shift to the vernacular should make unity easier, and he concluded that with the Council, "the Church is now coming out of its own world into the world surrounding it."[67] Ambrosians, like Catholics everywhere, watched the Council through its four sessions. Upon his return from each session, Bishop Hayes came to campus to report on the activities of the Council and explain its actions. But no one, Hayes included, would fully understand the impact of the Council on the Church, their lives, and Catholic education.

When school began in the fall of 1960, enrollment was down by forty-eight students, not nearly as great a drop as some had predicted if football were dropped. At homecoming, each class and student organization was given a place on campus to decorate. Most chose a historical theme, but others chose themes appropriate to their discipline; the Math-Engineering-Physics Club did a display on computers and rockets. The theme of the homecoming dance on Friday night was "Remember When," and the attendees danced to the music of the Jimmy Dorsey Orchestra, one of the groups from the big band era of a generation before. That fall, over 200 students participated in a new, intramural touch football league, and on Saturday afternoon, the championship game was played, with the players dressed in 1910 vintage football attire. At half-time, the homecoming queen was crowned. That evening the traditional bonfire was lit, followed by a dance in LeClaire Gymnasium. Those who had predicted that a homecoming without football would lack unity were shown to be wrong, as students and alumni unified around the common bond of being Ambrosians.[68]

was selected. By 1963, students sought ways to liven up the event even more. Some suggested that the Mud Bowl become the homecoming game or be played as part of Parent's Weekend. But little was done and the Mud Bowl gave way to other activities.[69]

With East Hall completed, Collins could now turn his attention to other building projects. When the academy had moved out of Ambrose Hall two years before, the building was rewired, new fire escapes were installed, eleven classrooms were remodeled, parts of the dining rooms and kitchen were remodeled, and some faculty offices were reconfigured. Later new dormitory rooms were created in the old Irish Village, the rooms on the fourth floor and the east end of Ambrose Hall occupied by the seminary were renovated, and a sprinkler system was installed in the building. On the outside, the mansard roof with its slate shingles and dormers on the original building and the 1893 addition and the ornate features of the tower designed by Victor Huot were removed. It was replaced by a vertical roof line with asphalt shingles trimmed with sleek, stainless steel giving the front "modern lines across the top."[70]

This work was done by John J. Morrissey, a local independent contractor. Then in November 1959, he was hired as superintendent of buildings and grounds for the college. He was later succeeded by his son, John Jr., and together they oversaw the physical plant for forty-two years.[71]

In the fall of 1960, the ground floor on the west end was remodeled and the post office moved in. Tillie Sobek continued as postmistress, a job she had held since 1937. When she began, mail was simply laid out on a table for the students to pick up. In addition to her duties in the post office, in the early years she served as a secretary to the president. She also served as a typist for the faculty and ran the ticket booth at basketball games.[72]

The next spring work began on a $100,000 project to create a new college center in the northeast corner of Ambrose Hall. When it was built in 1908, the area had served as the gymnasium. After LeClaire Gymnasium was built, a second floor was added to the high-ceilinged room, and it became the manual training area for the academy. John Morrissey, Sr., and his crew took out the second floor to create a balcony that was connected by a circular staircase to the lounge area and a conversation pit below. They dug out the space behind this to create a game room, a quiet room, and a snack bar area.[73] When it was finished, the Bee Hive moved from the basement of the library-administration building to the new space. To carry out the Bee Hive theme, a two-story wall was constructed outside using open cement blocks in a pattern that was meant to resemble a beehive.

The new Bee Hive opened as part of the homecoming celebration of 1961. There to greet the students was Mrs. Loretta Salsbury, director of the college center, and Mrs. Edna Deardoff, her assistant. Their duties included scheduling meetings; making announcements on the public address system, usually because someone had a phone call; picking up after the not-always-so-neat students; and providing a "fourth for a game of cards." After a few years in the position, she said, "I keep things halfway under control . . . Without a woman, this place would be terribly wild . . . You need patience, a sense of humor and stamina to deal with students, especially boys, but I love it." Over the years, Mrs. Salsbury, and the other women who served with her, also became confidants of generations of students away from home.[74]

Collins also turned his attention to other buildings. After East Hall opened, Davis Hall was rewired, the rooms were renovated, and new furniture like that used in East Hall was installed. To accommodate the new furniture, the doors in each room had to be moved a few inches. In the library, the stack area was expanded, a balcony was installed on the south wall of the reading room, and the basement area where the Bee Hive had been became the journal browsing area and reading room.

The strain all this placed on Collins was beginning to tell; in August 1961, he suffered a breakdown and was hospitalized. There had been growing concern about Collins among the faculty. He had begun his presidency well: he appointed committees, listened to their recommendations, and the faculty responded to his initiatives. But in time, he began to ignore the committee structure and took actions without consultation. As one member of the faculty observed, Collins felt "personally responsible for everything, and perfectly capable of doing everything."[75]

With Collins away, the bishop appointed the Reverend Frederick McMahan, who had been vice president since 1960, as acting president. You are in "complete charge of St. Ambrose College," Hayes told McMahan, with all the powers and duties which were vested in the presidency. Aware that in the community Collins was closely identified with the development program, McMahan issued a statement to "assure all the many friends of the College that the fine programs . . . instituted by Msgr. Collins [would] continue" and with the help of those friends, "be improved."[76] Collins returned to his duties at the beginning of December.

When he was named acting president, McMahan was already in negotiations with the Sisters of Mercy about the Nursing Division at St. Ambrose. Nursing education was changing, and the Registered Nurse diploma was replaced by a four-year degree program in professional nursing. In March 1961, McMahan informed the division chairs at St. Ambrose that the college and the sisters were investigating the possibility of offering a degree-level Nursing program to replace the RN and BS programs the college offered since 1952. McMahan said it was his "firm conviction" that if St. Ambrose did this it should be a "sound degree program," otherwise the college would "invite disaster." McMahan asked the chairs to work with Sister Mary Brigid Condon, RSM, director of nursing, to have a program ready for the fall of 1962, and he said he felt this was "an extremely important step on the part of the College."[77]

Sister Brigid told McMahan that for the program to begin in the fall of 1962, approval from the Iowa Board of Nurse Examiners was needed prior to recruiting students. Also the Mother Provincial wanted a letter from St. Ambrose that said the college would assume full responsibility for the program, including curriculum, faculty, administration, and finances. She also insisted that a Sister of Mercy be named the chair of the Nursing Division with equal status of the other college divisional chairs. If that occurred, she said the sisters would relinquish the three-year diploma program and provide clinical practice for the St. Ambrose students. But the Sisters of Mercy also made it clear that if the change were made, they could not guarantee that they could provide sisters to both the St. Ambrose program and to Mercy Hospital.[78]

Those terms became the basis of a contract that established the four-year program.[79] The next spring St. Ambrose recommended that tuition for the nursing students be raised from $15 to $33.50 per semester hour. When the Nursing Division began in 1952, the tuition for all St. Ambrose students was $15 per semester hour. Over the ten-year period, however, while the

Mrs. Salsbury controlled the ebb and flow of events in the Bee Hive.

A Great and Lasting Beginning

tuition for nurses remained at $15, for all other students, it was increased to $33.50. Thus the proposed tuition for the new nursing program created tuition parity for all students. Sister Brigid objected to the proposed tuition. Writing McMahan on April 9, 1962, she said this was an increase of 121 percent, and although she acknowledged the right of St. Ambrose to determine tuition rates, she said such an increase was unfair. Students had been recruited and a commitment had been made at the lower figure. This

Professors Wayne Loui and Thomas Chouteau and Rev. James Greene prepare for the 1961 St. Ambrose-Marycrest production of Carousel.

was a "gross injustice" to the students and their families, as well as a public relations problem for St. Ambrose. Moreover, it would not be possible for the students to find another school at that late date. She asked McMahan to allow the nurses to attend St. Ambrose for one more year at the lower tuition rate, which would give the sisters an "opportunity to make other plans for the nursing program."[80]

In June Sister Brigid informed Collins that the sisters realized the proposed program would "present many difficulties" for St. Ambrose and that they had approached Marycrest College, which was willing to establish a Nursing program and would admit the first students in the fall of 1963. Therefore, Mercy School of Nursing would not contract for any academic courses after June 1, 1963. In mid-July an announcement about the change was made.[81]

The summer of 1962 also saw the completion of work by the AAUP chapter, the administration, and the Board of Trustees on the question of tenure for the faculty. A set of criteria for the promotion in rank of the faculty was already in place. Those included effectiveness of teaching, membership in learned societies, scholarship, attendance at professional meetings, and recommendations from the department or division head and five faculty members from the rank to which the person sought to be promoted. A Master's Degree was required for promotion to assistant professor; a PhD and seven years of teaching at St. Ambrose for promotion to associate professor; and a PhD and five more years of teaching at St. Ambrose for

professor.

The AAUP recommended that the administration require an annual progress report from faculty members, establish a Committee on Procurement, Tenure, and Rank, and outline how to apply for promotion. Tenure in the form of a permanent contract would be granted after seven years of college teaching, at least three of which had to be at St. Ambrose. Procedures were outlined for the removal of tenure. It also said that there would be automatic termination of tenure when the faculty member reached sixty-five years of age. The program was approved by the faculty on May 17, 1962, and approved by the Board of Trustees on August 7.[82]

Shortly after Pope John XXIII and 2,500 bishops from around the world opened Vatican Council II on October 11, 1962, President John F. Kennedy received evidence that the Soviet Union was placing medium-range missiles in Cuba. Ambrosians already knew something of life in that country from Jose Llana, a refugee from Cuba. Llana had been at Havana University but found life in Cuba oppressive; there was a lack of food, no real education, and official atheism, so he fled in December 1961. Llana hoped to become an American citizen and said, "Cubans get up every day with only one hope—that the United States will help them to be free again."[83]

For Kennedy and his advisors, the question was not just how to help Cuba be free, but in the face of missiles so close, how to keep the United States free and safe. For nearly two weeks, Kennedy and his advisors struggled to find a way to get the missiles out of Cuba without starting a nuclear war. On October 22, he told a world-wide television audience about the missiles and demanded that the Soviets retreat. Across the campus and across the nation, draft-age students wondered if they would be able to finish the semester. In an article written before the crisis was over, an Ambrosian said there was no purpose in continuing college if passive acceptance of the Soviets' actions allowed the "free world to be overtaken by an atheistic power." A compromise was reached and the Soviet missiles were withdrawn, but the point was driven home to Ambrosians about how dire the situation had been when, in the midst of the crisis, fallout shelters with their familiar yellow and black signs were established in campus buildings.[84]

The spring musical in 1963 was Meredith Willson's *The Music Man*, a piece of Americana that allowed Iowans to laugh at themselves, but whose values of small-town security were somehow reassuring while world tensions increased. The musical was a combined production of the Theatre and Music departments. In 1957, Wayne Loui, a 1952 graduate, had returned as assistant professor of speech and drama. Loui believed that theatre encompassed all branches of the liberal arts, and that college productions should be taken seriously and "evaluated on the same grounds as a professional theatre."[85] To accomplish that, Loui founded Theatre III, which used the lecture hall, Lewis 111, as a theatre. There a remarkable group of student actors, including Michael Kennedy and James Willaert, both of whom would later join the speech and drama faculty, presented plays from the classical and modern theatre.

The same year Loui joined the faculty, the Reverend James Greene returned following study in Paris. Greene taught the organ, played for Sunday Mass, and directed the chorus made up of St. Ambrose and Marycrest students. Under Greene the mixed choral group performed works ranging from Mozart's eighteenth-century *Coronation Mass* to Carl Orff's 1937 work, *Carmina Burana*. In 1959, Greene and Loui joined forces to produce the first musical, *Kismet*, followed in the next years by *Brigadoon, Carousel*, and *Oklahoma*. Because there was no stage on campus large enough to accommodate a musical production, the combined St. Ambrose-Marycrest cast used the auditorium at the new Assumption High School. Greene said that the productions gave the music students a "diversity of work" and a "chance to apply what they have learned in their fine arts courses," which was especially good for those who intended to teach music.[86]

The prospective music teachers were part of a growing group of students on campus. St. Ambrose had been preparing teachers since 1924. One of the consequences of the national self-doubt created by the launch of *Sputnik* in 1957 was a call for more elementary and secondary school teachers. In 1958, Congress passed the National Defense Education Act to support the advancement of education in mathematics, the sciences, and foreign languages. It also provided funds for students who planned to teach in elementary or secondary schools. In 1958, St. Ambrose received $1,497 from this fund. In the next three years, the amount increased and the college received $34,800 for the 1961-1962 year. By 1963, nearly one-third of all students were involved in the teacher education program; about 22 percent of recent graduates became teachers.[87]

To meet the need for more teachers, in 1963 the Education department added elementary education to its curriculum. According to Professor Donald Critchlow, area school officials had urged that St. Ambrose make this move for some time and following a two-year study by the college, the State Board of Public Instruction approved the program. Students included those who entered St. Ambrose as freshmen and area teachers already in the classroom who were working on a Bachelor's Degree.[88]

While the college was doing well, its president was not. Through the spring and summer of 1963, Collins became more unstable and alone. Finally, in early September, he suffered another breakdown and this time the bishop relieved him of the presidency. Faculty members noted his contribution to the building and remodeling of the campus and his work in raising faculty salaries and faculty organization. An old friend said Collins was "sadly miscast" as an administrator and he suspected Collins knew it. To overcompensate, he tried to do it all; and his refusal to seek help, or accept it when it was offered, led to his breakdown.[89] The bishop appointed Collins as the chaplain at the Kahl Home for the Aged and Infirm where he resided until his death in 1981.[90] McMahan was appointed acting president.

At noontime, November 22, 1963, Ambrosians rushed to their radios or to the few television sets on campus to follow the news from Dallas about the shooting of President John F. Kennedy. Not since the Sunday afternoon of Pearl Harbor nearly twenty-two years before had the attention of Ambrosians and the nation been so focused on the same event. When the news came that Kennedy had died, they gathered in the chapel for prayers. Memorial Masses were celebrated and the community settled in to watch the events unfold that led to the funeral on Monday.

As they struggled to cope with the shock of the death of the young, popular president, some Ambrosians tried to assess the man. Greg Cusack compared Kennedy to Pope John XXIII who had died the previous June. Both had opened windows and left work to be completed by their successors, both were concerned with peace, and both were known for their outgoing personalities. Echoing the words Kennedy had used at his inauguration, Ken Wolf said, "The death of John Kennedy has emphatically reaffirmed the awesome responsibility facing today's student leaders . . . of bringing the Kennedy program to fruition . . . The life of John Kennedy can provide us with untold inspiration and challenge."[91] To meet that challenge, some students wanted to establish the JFK Social Action seminar. Others wanted to remember the dead president by renaming East Hall for him.[92]

Kennedy's legacy has been a subject of assessment by Americans ever since. His death ended the sense of American invincibility that had marked the 1950s with its economic prosperity, build-up of military and political power, and general agreement about America's place in the world. What followed was the 1960s, a time when those assumptions were questioned, and often it was the students of the nation who led the questioning. Ambrosians were among those who looked again at equality and justice in this country and questioned the wisdom of the extension of American power abroad. Some would be engaged in those questions, while others dropped out and turned inward, demanding to be allowed the freedom to follow their own paths. The seeds of change that Elvis represented when he burst into peoples' living rooms on the *Ed Sullivan Show* would now blossom, and Collins' successors would deal with a student body unlike anything he or his predecessors could have imagined.

A Great and Lasting Beginning

We are in the midst of a developing revolution. But lest we fear too much, let us remember the revolutionary nature of the Gospel, the radicalism of Christ, the terribleness of human freedom (yet to be achieved), the change and even the suffering necessary for any blessedness, here and hereafter. When man, or society, or the Church ceases to be revolutionary, growth stops . . . It seems fairly certain that we who call ourselves Christians will never be able to rest perfectly content with life as we find it. Our loving of the world is always a conditioned relationship. Our living in it, a thrilling dissatisfaction . . . Colleges are the intellectual disturbers of status and apathy in the communities where they are, the moral consciences of their communities.

– The Reverend John S. Smith

❧ Chapter Thirteen ❧

Father Jack Smith's guest editorial about revolution appeared in the October 11, 1963, edition of the *Ambrosian News* under the headline, "Collegians Should Lead in 'Revolution of 1963.'" He was referring to the fight for civil rights which that summer had seen a series of events that intensified the struggle: at the order of the chief of police, dogs had attacked young, peaceful demonstrators in Birmingham, Alabama; with the intervention of the federal government, two African-American students had integrated the University of Alabama; President Kennedy had spoken on national television and called civil rights a "moral issue . . . as old as the scriptures and . . . as clear as the American Constitution," and he called for action by Congress; that same night civil rights worker Medgar Evers was shot down in his driveway in Mississippi; and in August, Martin Luther King, Jr., told the 200,000 people gathered in front of the Lincoln Memorial and the millions watching on television that he had a dream where he and all God's children would be "free at last."

Smith was a Davenport native and a graduate of St. Ambrose. Following his ordination in 1949, he had joined the history faculty. He was a member of the board of the Catholic Interracial Council (CIC) and was among those who established the Pacem in Terris Peace and Freedom Award, named for Pope John XXIII's encyclical and given to those who exemplified its principles. That summer he had helped organize a civil rights demonstration in Davenport. A gifted teacher with a hypnotic voice and a touch of the prophet, Smith was among the St. Ambrose faculty who continued the earlier work of Ambrosians to challenge the status quo.

The students to whom Smith was speaking were profiled by the Reverend Andrew Greeley in a 1964 article in *America* magazine. Greeley said the "cool and apathetic" student of the 1950s had not "vanished," but alongside him a new breed arose. Greeley said this new breed was "greatly concerned about things like honesty, integrity and authenticity," and they needed to know the reason why before they obeyed. They had an "inability to be devious or opportunistic – or even diplomatic," and they wanted to discuss all issues large and small. In those discussions the "truth must be spoken even if speaking it does no good and may even cause harm." They could not understand when that honesty was taken as disrespect and their "desire to discuss is understood as disobedience." They thought those in charge were "better off with the consent of free men than the compliance

of automatons." They exhibited a "fierce personalism" that demanded fulfillment in every relationship. They were activists who tried to do more than merely talk about human suffering; they volunteered in a variety of humanitarian causes. In all of this Greeley said they were not "easy to deal with," yet, "we may be witnessing a major social change," as a result of their actions. They lived in a world of "expanding expectations," and since they had seen change already, they wanted more, and "they will live to bury those who stand in their way." Their patron saint was John F. Kennedy, who, "with his youthfulness, his pragmatism, his restlessness, his desire for challenge and service, his vision of a new freedom, reflected in so many ways what the New Breed wants to be." Greeley expressed ambivalence about this new breed, but he said that everything was "on their side–their youth, time, the wave of history, and, one suspects, the Holy Spirit."[1]

Later historical assessment has painted a less positive picture of John Kennedy and his presidency, but while he was alive and in the time following his assassination, he inspired a generation of students to action. Nothing exemplified the spirit of service more than the Peace Corps. In his inaugural address, Kennedy had spoken of the torch being passed to a new generation. Now he wanted to appeal to the idealism of that generation to "serve the cause of freedom as servants of peace."[2] He created the Peace Corps which sent young Americans throughout the world to provide educational, agricultural, and health care aid in developing countries. Ambrosians responded to this opportunity for service, and by 1966, twelve of them were engaged in agricultural work in Pakistan and Nigeria; secondary education in Sierra Leone, Nigeria, and the Philippines; physical education in Venezuela; and rural cooperatives in Panama and Brazil. Later Ambrosians would serve in Ethiopia, India, and Liberia.[3]

Another outlet for service was student involvement in the Papal Volunteers for Latin America (PAVLA). Formed in response to a call from Pope John XXIII for volunteers to serve in Latin America and approved by the Pontifical Commission for Latin America in April 1960, soon dozens of American bishops had named diocesan directors for PAVLA. In February 1961, Bishop Hayes named the Reverend Louis M. Colonnese, a 1953 graduate of St. Ambrose and the current diocesan director of YCS, director of PAVLA in the Diocese of Davenport. Soon Colonnese became a familiar figure on campus as he sought volunteers for the program. That fall the

A Great and Lasting Beginning

bishop named Professor Donald Critchlow the faculty representative for PAVLA and Bill O'Keefe as the student representative. Critchlow and O'Keefe formed a student group who raised money for the effort. *Ambrosian News* editor Ken Wolf said this would "stimulate student interest in the responsibility of laymen" for the work of the church. In addition to support by students through fund raising, in 1964, four Ambrose students spent the summer in Mexico working on a school staffed by PAVLA volunteers, and in 1967, Edmond Dunn, a 1958 graduate, spent two years in Peru as a teacher and choral direc-

John Jablkowski, John Crocitto, and Fr. Duncan returned from Selma and formed a chapter of the NAACP. They received the charter from William Cribbs, local NAACP chairman.

tor.[4] Other students served as volunteers in the United States through the Catholic Extension Society.

Ambrosians also enlisted in the moral issue of civil rights Kennedy described. Some were already involved in the activities of the Catholic Interracial Council. In 1964, Father Duncan, one of the founders of the CIC, spent two weeks in Mississippi helping with voter registration, and he returned more committed than ever in the cause of civil rights. He urged Ambrosians to inform themselves about the situation in the United States and then volunteer if possible, telling them, "Remember this is the chance for Christianity in action, and that Christ said, 'How can you say you love God, whom you don't see, when you can't love your neighbor whom you can see?'"[5]

The opportunity for action came the next month in Selma, Alabama, where African-Americans were trying to register to vote. On March 7, 1965, about 600 marchers set out from Selma to the capitol in Montgomery. They were stopped at the Edmund Pettis Bridge where they were violently attacked by state troopers. Dr. Martin Luther King, Jr., organized a second march two days later and called for people from across the country to join him. The group marched to the same bridge, held a prayer service, and returned to town. That night the Reverend James Reeb, a white minister from Boston, was attacked and beaten. He died two days later.

At St. Ambrose Duncan enlisted four students, John Jablkowski, John Crocitto, Larry Kamin, and Don Knapp to go to Selma with him to march with King. The group left Davenport on Friday, March 12, and arrived in Jackson, Mississippi, the next afternoon where they stayed the night. On Sunday they went to Selma, attended meetings, and participated in a demonstration where they were assaulted with epithets from onlookers. On Monday they marched with others to a barricade the police had set up in front of the courthouse. That afternoon they attended a memorial service

for Reeb where King asked Duncan to say a prayer. They left Selma late that night to return to campus.

When they were asked why they went, Knapp said to "see if conditions in the South were really as bad" as they had heard. Knapp said they were and that it would be a long time before they were better. Crocitto was appalled with the living conditions for blacks in the south. All said they would return if the opportunity arose.[6]

Shortly after they came back from Selma, the students were among those who met to form a new chapter of the NAACP on campus. They planned activities for the rest of the semester and applied for a charter from the national organization. When that was received the next October, the chapter elected Crocitto president and Duncan served as advisor. The NAACP became active on campus and in the Davenport community where they tutored students and collected food for families. On campus they provided information and sponsored programs to discuss the issues of discrimination and segregation.[7]

While some St. Ambrose students and faculty were watching events unfold in Selma and elsewhere in the American south, others watched events unfold half-way around the world in Vietnam. The United States had been involved there since the late 1940s when it supported France in a war to prevent the takeover of Vietnam by communist forces. When that failed, through the 1950s and early 1960s, the United States supported a non-communist regime in South Vietnam with economic and military aid, as well as American troops and advisors. But those efforts were also less than successful and the American presence in Vietnam grew. By March 1965, there were some 27,000 American forces in the country and President Lyndon B. Johnson was urged by his advisors to escalate the American presence. When American forces were attacked in early February, Johnson ordered a series of air attacks, named Rolling Thunder, and sent in more ground troops. By the end of 1965, there were 185,000 American troops in Vietnam.

For most Americans and Ambrosians, Vietnam was a long way away and their understanding of the issues was limited. But the escalation of the American presence led many to begin to learn. On American campuses, professors began "teach-ins," and made the events in Southeast Asia a part of their classes. Not everyone was convinced that the teach-ins and class lectures were helpful. One commented that "too often intellectuals ignore grim and unpleasant realities of world power politics." Another said flatly that the professors leading the protests were "not qualified." The common reaction on campus in the spring of 1965 was that everyone needed a "true understanding of the complex issues" of the day.[8]

In the fall, the student council discussed whether it should follow the action of councils on many campuses, and take a stand on American involvement in Vietnam. Don Miller, the editor of the *Ambrosian News*, said the first responsibility of Ambrosians was to be informed and he urged the various campus organizations to sponsor a "St. Ambrose Debate-In" to encourage dialogue. Another student leader, Tom Higgins, noted the protest on other campuses but said they were no cause for alarm. Discussion should be encouraged, "free and unhampered debate" might provide the solution for a just settlement of the war. "This is one occasion where we must be right before we go ahead," Higgins wrote.[9]

For the students involved in civil rights or PAVLA or the Big Brothers program or NFCCS or other service groups, those groups were part of their college lives. Other students had sports, or the Chicago Club or one of the other regional clubs, or the student council, or theater, or music to fill out their time at St. Ambrose. Still other students simply wanted to go to class, earn a degree, and get a job. One new activity for the students was the new radio station. Radio came to St. Ambrose early in the century when the antenna was erected on the roof of Ambrose Hall. Over the years, Ambrosians broadcast programs on local radio stations from the studios in the Irish Village. In 1962, a radio station began to broadcast on the third floor of East Hall when Bernie Miraglia turned up his stereo to awaken his floor mates. He purchased a low power transmitter to broadcast from 6:40 to 6:55 each weekday morning. The program content began with a song, the news and weath-er, and a constant reminder of how much time remained before the rising hour check by the proc-tors.[10]

While Miraglia broadcast on the third floor, others were plan-ning a new radio sta-tion to broadcast to the entire campus. Station manager Ken O'Brien and technical director John Mikesch, put the studio together with old equipment that had been used in earli-er broadcasting efforts. In November 1963, the student council endorsed the proposed

station and wrote Father McMahan that it would provide "better student communications." They urged him to approve it as soon as possible.[11]

McMahan replied in early January 1964 that the station was given "operational approval" but he warned that it "must prove itself by successful operation in order to continue in the future." KSAR (St. Ambrose Radio) went on the air February 16. It broadcast popular music through the electric power lines in the campus buildings from 4:00 to 10:30 p.m. Two years later Marycrest added equipment so KSAR could broadcast on that campus. In November 1967, KALA (Ambrose Liberal Arts), an FM station, began to broadcast.[12]

As acting president, McMahan faced the first real confrontation between the students and the administration because of the activities of the National Student Association (NSA). Founded in Europe in 1946 as a confederation of student organizations, representatives of 350 American colleges, about one-fourth of which were Catholic, met the next summer in Madison, Wisconsin, and formed the United States National Student Association. Intended as a forum to keep students aware of international issues, it also sought to strengthen student governments and was responsible for the first student bill of rights. Although it was not intended to be a political organization, in time it came to reflect "Cold War liberalism: consistently anti-Communist, but also opposed to McCarthyism and left of center on domestic issues." Unknown to most of its members in the 1950s and early 1960s, it was partially funded by the CIA.[13]

The St. Ambrose student council affiliated with the NSA in the spring of 1962 and in December, four students attended the regional convention in Des Moines. There they heard a discussion of student rights given by the dean of students at the University of Minnesota. His talk centered on *in loco parentis* where he pointed out that students had only that power the college gave them, but that with reasonable discussion with the authorities, they could win more power. He urged the students to use good tactics in seeking change because, "some tactics create resistance to change" by college administrations and faculty. He said a revision of college discipline should be forthcoming and concluded with the prescient remark that "within the next decade, the revolution on college campuses will be a long

Through his classes, Professor Matt McMahon urged his students to leave the classroom and challenge the status quo.

overdue enactment of student rights."[14]

In the spring of 1963, the St. Ambrose NSA sponsored several speakers. One was John Howard Griffin, a white man who had his skin dyed black so he could live in the south to experience racism. Griffin had written about his experience in a memoir, *Black Like Me* (1962).[15] They also invited Richard Criley, a long-time political activist who in 1960 had co-founded the National Committee to Abolish the House Un-American Activities

Suitors played by Jerry Bauer and Tom Mooney vie for the affections of the Merry Widow, *played by Susan Ryan in this scene from the 1964 musical.*

Committee (HUAC), which held hearings to uncover communists in the State Department and the motion picture industry. Criley's opponents accused him of being a communist, but when asked, he refused to answer. Criley spoke about HUAC and said it had acted as "prosecutor, judge and jury all wrapped into one," and that its activities were an "invasion of the sovereign rights" of the American people. Mark Vovos, the student NSA coordinator on campus, said his appearance did not imply approval or disapproval of Criley by the students or the administration of St. Ambrose. Nevertheless, many in both groups objected to Criley's appearance and debate about him and the NSA continued for the rest of the semester.[16]

The next fall *Ambrosian News* editor Ken Wolf noted that the controversies of the previous year over the NSA, the "Criley affair, the discussions of HUAC, race relations and academic freedom" were not just isolated "trouble spots." But Wolf said the positions taken by segments of the college community were not as important as the fact that "students were arguing, emoting, discussing, intellectualizing, growing, and *thinking*." He noted that St. Ambrose, like the Catholic Church with Vatican II, was opening windows, and "experiencing a campus wide change in climate . . . Apathy, we predict, will never return."[17]

When the NSA proposed to invite other controversial speakers to campus some in the administration became alarmed. Col. Carroll J. Williams, the director of placement, wrote McMahan to warn about the possibility that the college could be held liable for the remarks made by speakers on campus.[18] McMahan issued a directive that in the future, the sponsoring organization had to supply the religious, political, professional, and social affiliations of a proposed speaker fifteen days in advance and that no speaker could come without the approval of the president. When asked for a

clarification about his directive, McMahan merely said, "The ruling is very clear as stated."[19]

At the first meeting of the group in January 1964, they were stunned when Father Menke, the faculty advisor, read a letter from McMahan. The acting president said the "continued existence" of the NSA was "no longer in the best interests of the college" and that the organization was "terminated by this directive." In an interview, McMahan said it was a "disappointing step to take. It is an admission that we were unsuccessful in our attempts to establish student freedom with responsibility."[20]

Not surprisingly, there was a wide range of opinion from the students and faculty. Some blamed the leadership of the NSA for acting irresponsibly in bringing Criley to campus. Others admitted that the NSA was "susceptible to left-wing influences" at the national level, but that locally the students had a responsibility to learn about all sides of the issues. Still others attacked McMahan for his "direct insult to the basic integrity of the . . . student body." The senior class voted to not consider a gift to the Endowment Fund until the matter was settled. The students demanded a vote on whether to reinstate NSA.

Some faculty were publicly opposed to McMahan's action. Smith said it was evidence that one could tell if an administration was "too embedded" in its own institution when it could not accept criticism. But privately McMahan heard from supporters of his decision. Duncan called it "courageous and convincing" and said many students had told him they agreed with it. Agnes Renner said his action was "superb." Dennis Hayes from the speech faculty said he was concerned about the "abrupt announcement," but when he heard McMahan's explanation, he said McMahan was a "just and considerate man" and he supported the decision. McMahan also heard from alumni who expressed many of the same opinions.[21]

The Physical Education department circulated a petition which received 230 signatures indicating their "unqualified vote of confidence" in McMahan, who had been "consistent, diligent, and honest" in defending the rights of students. It was bad policy for people who did not "understand all the issues involved" to turn on the president. Of the 39 percent of the students who voted in a referendum, 77 percent disapproved of McMahan's actions; 44 percent said NSA was beneficial to the students, 56 percent said it was not. A faculty vote was 16-6 in support of McMahan and 18-4 against having NSA on campus. In spite of the efforts of its proponents, NSA was, for the time being, not a part of campus life. Ken Wolf said in the *Ambrosian News*, "Banning NSA reveals that the college administration has lost faith in the validity of student freedom. This is unfortunate, especially in this age when Pope John XXIII asked us to 'open a few windows.'"[22]

By mid-March the controversy had died down and a *News* columnist noted, "Relative tranquility settles quietly on this campus, and factional frowns melt into spring smiles . . . But, as the March lion somehow comes out a lamb, Ambrosians' thoughts seem to thaw into equally different and much warmer thoughts of Easter vacation." But he wondered if the same thing would happen again the next year.

In the meantime, the cast of the spring musical, *The Merry Widow* prepared for its opening night; the history club was organizing a forum on the encyclical *Pacem in Terris*; two students were going to attend a model United Nations at the University of Minnesota; the Huns defended their intramural basketball title; and the neighbors around Marycrest complained of the noise created by the girls' boyfriends honking their horns on the streets. The paper noted, "It is spring indeed!"[23]

As the controversy about NSA played out, Ambrosians waited for news about who would be the new college president. At the time Bishop Hayes removed Collins as president and appointed McMahan as acting president, Monsignor Dingman, the diocesan chancellor, told Hayes that before the bishop left for the second session of the Vatican Council scheduled to open on September 29, 1963, he should consider appointing a new president for the college. Dingman urged him to consult with the faculty, telling the bishop that he was "very worried about what might happen and the problems that would arise if the faculty [was] not consulted."[24] But Hayes left for Rome without taking any action.

When Hayes returned from the Council in December, a letter was waiting for him from the St. Ambrose student council regarding a "permanent president" for the college. Written before McMahan's actions on the NSA, the students said the college needed a "progressive leader who realizes the great need for good public relations with the faculty, the students and the community." They said that McMahan did not fill that role as president, he did not "seek the cooperation of faculty and students and . . . does not command the respect so necessary for a leader." They suggested several other campus priests, including Madsen, Menke, Smith, and Taylor, but they realized the decision was the bishop's "alone." Nevertheless, they hoped "that in the new ecumenical spirit of closer cooperation between clergy and laity that this letter, representing a segment vitally concerned in your decision–the students–will aid in that decision."[25]

Meanwhile, Dingman continued to press the bishop for a decision. He recommended Menke who he said had the good will of the various constituent groups on campus. Menke knew the diocese and the college and had "well-defined goals in mind" for it. St. Ambrose had "many problems" and Menke would attack them with a "real seriousness of purpose." Dingman described Menke as frugal, exacting, possessing youth and experience, and with a sense of humor.[26]

In early June, Hayes appointed Menke as the tenth president of St.

Ambrose. Menke was a graduate of the academy and the college where he was a football star. Following ordination in 1938, he had been on the faculty where he taught Latin and Greek. But he also taught astronomy and through his efforts, an observatory was built on campus in 1962. The *Messenger* said the appointment continued a "distinguished line of educators" who had served the college well. When the students returned in the fall, the *Ambrosian News* said the reflection of the college to the community lay with the president and that Menke was a "luminous" reflection and predicted a "great" tenure for him. The *Davenport Times-Democrat* noted that he was a teacher "liked for his patience, good humor and willingness to counsel students on matters not directly related to his teaching subject."[27]

The first semester of Menke's presidency began in the context of continuing strife in the American south and a growing restiveness among younger blacks impatient with the slow progress of King's non-violent approach. Just weeks before classes began, Congress passed the Gulf of Tonkin Resolution in response to a request from President Johnson for authority to protect American lives in Vietnam. Johnson would use that as the basis for rapidly increasing the American commitment in Vietnam, but not before the presidential election that fall. Those events in other parts of the country and the world would be brought home to St. Ambrose and would challenge Menke in the years ahead.

When he met with the students and faculty that fall, Menke stressed that his immediate goal was to get the faculty, students, and administration to "operate as a community." He was not afraid of differences of opinion; they were "important in learning. Only when challenged do we tend to reflect upon and rethink our own position." Menke told the college community that he wanted to see the responsible freedom of expression continue on campus which should be a "forum," and he warned that the "days of the docile, passive student" were long past.[28]

On one issue, however, there would apparently be no room for discussion. Menke said he would not "consider restoring football" at the college. He reminded the community that in spite of "splendid" teams in the 1950s, people did not attend the games, preferring to travel to Iowa City or South Bend for college football.[29]

If there was no football, there was still basketball, track, tennis, golf, and cross country as intercollegiate sports at St. Ambrose during the 1960s. Since 1951, Bob Duax had been basketball coach, but ill health forced him to step down in 1966. He was replaced by Leo Kilfoy, the assistant coach for the previous eight years. Another coaching change occurred in 1962 when long-time tennis coach, Father Joseph Hratz gave up coaching and was replaced by first Kilfoy, then Ed Scheck.

All of the St. Ambrose teams benefitted when the school joined with Dominican College, Lewis, Loras, Quincy, and St. Norbert's to form a new Midlands Conference in the spring of 1965. Kilfoy said they hoped to add more teams in the fall.[30] That same spring St. Ambrose and Augustana Colleges renewed the athletic competition that had been suspended in 1948. The first meeting of the two schools occurred that spring when coach Roy Owen's track team defeated Augustana.[31]

A Great and Lasting Beginning

Ambrosians take a break from sandbagging during the flood of 1965.

Menke may have thought there was a climate of freedom on campus, but many of the resident students did not. Some of the rules in 1964 were not much different from the *in loco parentis* rules written by Father Flannagan in 1885. Dormitory residents still had to be in their rooms by 10:30 on Sunday through Thursday nights unless they had special permission to be out later. Friday night they could stay out until 1:00 a.m. and Saturday night until midnight, and proctors would enter the rooms without knocking to check. All students had to be out of the dormitory by the 6:50 a.m. rising hour, Monday through Friday. Once again proctors would check and assess a fine of $1 if the student was still in bed and fifty cents if the student was up but still in the room. Freshmen could leave for one weekend a month, sophomores twice a month, and there were no limitations for juniors or seniors. Suspension or expulsion could occur for leaving campus without permission after night check, possession of intoxicants, habitual disregard for ordinary regulations, intoxication, or immorality. Other forbidden things included gambling on campus, frequenting hotels or motels, inviting women into the dormitory without permission, possession of firearms or explosives, and throwing snowballs on campus. Television sets were not permitted in student rooms, and during study hours from 7:00 to 9:00 p.m., radios and phonographs had to be turned off. No room visitation was allowed during study hours and from 8:00 to 11:00 a.m. and 1:00 to 4:00 p.m. Dormitory students had to attend Sunday Mass dressed in suit and tie. At noon and evening meals on Sunday and holy days, a necktie with a sweater or jacket was required. All the rules were contained in "The Bee-Line," the handbook the students received each year.

Even the "apathetic" students of those years did not like the rules, but the one that was disliked the most was the rising hour. An opinion poll taken by the *Ambrosian News* in February 1962 found respondents felt there should be no regulations; in college the students were "on their own" and they should regulate themselves. The rising hour, one said, was a form of "enforced virtue."[32] In Menke's first year there was a loosening of this rule: now only freshmen and some sophomores were obliged to observe it. But this small change in the rules was not enough for a student population

with, in Andrew Greeley's phrase, "rising expectations" about their personal freedom.

Just how much freedom the students should expect, and whether *in loco parentis* was still an appropriate policy for a college to espouse, were matters of great debate in the middle of the decade. No one, except the most radical students and faculty, advocated a campus with no rules or structure at all. College was a community of scholars with its own laws of life and when students enrolled, they entered into that life.

The search for freedom was a part of those times, not freedom which said anything was allowed which was not specifically forbidden, but a freedom that allowed the individual "to achieve personal fulfillment . . . the freedom to create–to create, most of all, himself." But that meant the students be allowed to find their "own intrinsic limits" within the laws of life of the college community.[33] For the students that freedom was a fundamental right, and it served as a fountain from which all other rights, real and imagined, flowed.

Menke told the faculty that the students would make mistakes, and it was a wise leader who realized that and who lived in the hope that they could learn from those mistakes. And it was a patient leader who could balance the demands of students with a wide variety of disciplined and undisciplined ideas, and a faculty which was equally divided on the questions of academic life and student behavior.

Those ideas were the theme of the keynote address by Kenneth Woodward, associate religion editor of *Newsweek* magazine, at the NFCCS convention hosted by St. Ambrose in February 1965. Woodward's address was an attack on *in loco parentis* which he said made "cripples out of our students, it seems as though the small Catholic colleges . . . don't feel it necessary to open their students to any unnecessary risks." He said, "College ought to be a place where a student can discover and form his own values . . . Universities which try to 'preserve' their students and do not allow moral and spiritual risks are dead." He said that in spite of rules, morality did not come through and he cited recent cheating scandals and drug use on some campuses. Rather he said it would be better to allow the students to "think

out" for themselves how they will behave based on what they observe: "Students want to see a Christian commitment acted out in people they meet thus finding their own values, then living them."[34]

As the higher education community questioned the relevancy of rules based on *in loco parentis* in a rapidly changing climate, the enforcer of the rules at St. Ambrose also changed rapidly. In 1962, Father Shepler, who had exemplified the now discredited philosophy, left the dean's position. He was replaced for one year by Father Taylor. The next year the Reverend Ronald Schmitz, a newly ordained priest who noted his inexperience for the position, became dean of men. The year after that, Schmitz was replaced by the Reverend Thomas Dinges, who came to St. Ambrose from St. Mary's Parish in Davenport. He was succeeded in 1966 by Clifford Rogers, the first layman to assume to role of dean. With a background in psychology, Rogers rejected the *in loco parentis* philosophy and he told the students he would not act as a replacement for their parents. But in return he said he expected "individual responsibility" and cooperation from them. Appearing at his first student council meeting in September 1966, he announced the rising hour rule was eliminated, other restrictions would be eliminated on juniors and seniors and they could expect other "substantial changes" throughout the year. Finally, he announced that his title had changed to dean of students, adding that dean of men was "archaic when you consider that college living has changed so greatly."[35]

When Rogers came, the students already had a head start in asserting their rights and trying to assume responsibility for their lives on campus. The first formal statement of the rights of students came with a revision of the student government constitution in the spring of 1964. There were several changes from the previous constitution, including increased representation of groups of students, the right of recall of a member, the right to petition, and the creation of a standing committee for the NFCCS. But the most significant change was the addition of a Bill of Rights. Those included equal suffrage of all students, the freedom of association and peaceable assembly, the right of all student organizations to conduct programs, the right to attend all student council meetings and speak, the right of a student to be "secure in his room, person, and possessions against unreasonable search and seizure, and the right to freedom of speech and the press." Those changes to the constitution all pointed to an "increased student power."[36]

The election for the president of the student council in the spring of 1964 gave evidence of some of those themes. There were three candidates, two of whom, Dick Aubry and Ken Wolf, ran on platforms that emphasized revising the social calendar, homecoming activities, freshmen orientation, better attendance at basketball games, working more closely with Marycrest, and more campus speakers, all of which were typical student council responsibilities. Art Moore, the third candidate and eventual winner, listed some of those same issues, but he also called for a better awareness by students of campus issues and better cooperation by students, faculty, and the administration.

Over the next year, the student council still emphasized social activities. It planned homecoming weekend and Field Day and sponsored a concert by the Chad Mitchell Trio. But the most significant thing it did came in May 1965 when it approved the formation of the student judiciary committee. The intent was to replace the faculty board of discipline in matters of conduct and discipline and to assist the dean of students in the "modification or formulation of campus rules." This five-man committee consisted of the president of the student council, two members appointed by the council, and two elected at large by the students. The dean of students and the faculty moderator of the council served as advisors without a vote. There was initial suspicion by some students that this would be a "kangaroo court," or a way for one student to "get another." But once details about the operation of the board and the relationship of it to the dean's office and the college were worked out, most of the suspicions were allayed and it was hailed as the "most significant step forward the students have taken . . . toward a more responsible exercise of their freedom." The constitution of the judiciary board was presented to Menke, who approved it and said he

A Great and Lasting Beginning

hoped the "students could join the college community in a more mature role by means of this committee."[37]

Ken Wolf, one of the leaders of the council, said this was the realization of four years of work. Greg Cusack, another of the leaders, gave the credit for the board to student council president Art Moore. In a column in the *Ambrosian News*, Cusack quoted an "erstwhile Ambrosian . . . 'By golly,' he mumbled while deftly quaffing his beer, 'things sure have changed.'" In his own voice Cusack added, "Things have indeed changed at St. Ambrose. Tremendous opportunities now lie ahead for those who are willing enough to risk momentary censure for enduring gains." After one year, 40 percent of 609 students polled agreed or agreed strongly that the board was doing a good job; 25 percent disagreed or disagreed strongly; the remainder had no opinion.[38]

Rev. Sebastian Menke.

The winter of 1964-1965 had seen heavy snowfalls in the upper Mississippi valley. In mid-March that snow began to melt and by mid-April, Quad-Citians expected the highest flood crest in years. Preparations began to build sandbag dikes at critical points along the river, but it kept rising, and the estimate of the height of the crest kept rising along with it. When a record-breaking crest was predicted for Wednesday, April 28, a call went out for more help.[39]

On Monday morning, April 26, Menke cancelled classes at noon and Ambrosians joined students from local high schools and area colleges and reported for duty. About 250 Ambrosians reported to a sandbag filling station at Third and Scott Streets. Another 250 were sent to the Davenport Waterworks on East River Drive. Classes were cancelled on Tuesday and about 700 students responded to the call, many of whom built dikes at Point Mississippi in Bettendorf, an area with large gasoline storage tanks. On Wednesday, the day of the 22.5 foot crest, classes were again cancelled and students were trucked to Milan where they worked until 3:00 a.m. to reinforce the dikes. SAGA food service carried food to the student workers. LeClaire Gymnasium became the Red Cross administrative center where area flood victims could come and register for assistance.

After working on the dikes, the students returned to their dormitory, stripped off their sandy, smelly, wet clothes, left them in piles in the hallway, showered, and went to bed. After a sleep of a few hours, they put those same clothes on again to return to fill more sandbags. Although classes resumed on Thursday, some students continued on flood duty. When the waters had subsided and the crisis was over, Davenport Mayor Ray T. O'Brien spoke about the important work the Ambrosians had done, especially at the Davenport Waterworks, "Officials at the plant told me that once the boys took a fifteen minute break, and they were beginning to get concerned about the rising waters as the boys rested, but when they were

rested a bit, a mighty cheer was raised for Ambrose and then, my god, you should have seen the sandbags flying."[40]

In the fall of 1965, the rules still demanded a coat and tie for Sunday Mass and a tie with a jacket or sweater for the noon meal on Sunday. Many professors had dress codes for the classroom that included shirts with a collar, long pants, shoes, and socks. Moreover, there was still a steady stream of Ambrosians going down Harrison Street to Don's Barber Shop for a crew cut. But slowly those norms were changing. That fall the *Ambrosian News* noted a "persistent drop in the quality of campus dress," as "Beatle-mania" had arrived, and there was a growing number of "mop-topped, sockless, sweatshirted collegians." The editor noted that college was a "semi-formal institution," which called for a certain amount of dignity and decorum. Gym shorts and tops, shorts of any kind, sweat clothes, t-shirts worn as an outer garment, and shoes without socks were considered inappropriate in both the classroom and cafeteria. The student council enacted a dress code for its meetings but at its next gathering, it was noted that some members put "their own comfort above responsibility" and violated their own code.[41]

As some members of the student council and most of the faculty worried about the dress of the students, for the most part the student council was slow to join the kinds of protests and challenges to the administration that was present on other campuses. That however, was beginning to change. In December 1965, the council announced it would begin an evaluation of the academic departments. The Sacred Doctrine department was chosen the first to be evaluated because, according to a member, it "should be the backbone of the rest of the curriculum."[42]

Thirty years before when Fathers Takkenberg and Fenton presented their papers to the faculty, they reflected the prevailing thought in Catholic higher education that philosophy was the integrating discipline in a Catholic curriculum. It was the necessary first course that made all other disciplines intelligible. But in the years after Takkenberg and Fenton wrote, other ideas about the integration of thought emerged. Spurred by the 1945 centenary of John Henry Newman's *The Idea of a University*, which held that theology was essential to the "integrity of a Catholic university," and the work of Christopher Dawson, who held that religion was central to understanding all world cultures, some suggested that theology should supplant philosophy as the integrating discipline.[43]

Within that discipline there was a debate between those who said that theology for the undergraduate should essentially be taught as catechism, the mastery of which would prepare the Catholic to face the world armed with the truth, and others who said that undergraduate religion should aim at "deepening the students' existential grasp of their faith and quickening their sense of its relation to daily life." Theologians said this "religious education" emphasized the experiential and ignored theological content. In an attempt to bring the two views together, in the mid-1950s, teachers of religion adopted the name Sacred Doctrine for their discipline as a way to integrate religion and theology.[44]

There had been a Department of Religion at St. Ambrose since the curriculum revisions of the 1920s. Each Catholic student was required to take a one-hour course each semester with such titles as: the Eucharist, the Sacraments, Christian Morals, the Life of Christ, the Liturgy, Christian Marriage, and in more recent years, Catholic Action, the Lay Apostolate, and the Bible. There were also courses open only to the church students: Catholic Rural Life, Audio-Visual Aids in Religious Education, the Old Testament, and Recent Trends in Catholic Apologetics. Although the student only earned one hour of credit, each course met two hours each week. In 1965, following the national

Leaders of the 1966-1967 student council, left to right: Tom Higgins, president, Bob Wagner, Mark Ohlendorf, vice president, Tom Rochford, Steve Miclot, treasurer, Mike Casey, parliamentarian, Art DeVooght, secretary.

trend, the department changed its name to the Department of Sacred Doctrine, but it was only a change in name, the courses remained the same.

One student commented of those courses, "Why do I have to take religion here? It's dry and just a plain waste of time. Even the profs don't know what they're talking about most of the time." This attitude was reinforced by a poll taken during the annual retreat in February 1966. The students were asked to respond to the statement, "The theology courses at St. Ambrose are adequate." Of the 628 students who answered, 32 percent strongly agreed or agreed; 47 percent strongly disagreed or disagreed; 21 percent had no opinion.[45]

The students clearly wanted change in the Religion department, but the change came slowly. The next fall the student council recommended that some of the religion courses be transferred to other departments and a few eventually were. Some of the courses were raised to two credit hours. But it would be another two years before significant change took place. Beginning in 1969, with the leadership of the Reverend Anthony G. Farrell, who had taught Latin and Greek and had just returned to St. Ambrose following graduate study in theology, the name was changed to the Department of Theology. The classes were revised and made into three-hour courses, and the graduation requirement was amended to require of all Catholic students eight hours of theology, including Theology 101, Contemporary Theological Issues, Theology 102, the Old and New testaments, and one other course.[46]

Bob Boyd and Tom Higgins, the candidates for student council president in the spring of 1966, ran on similar platforms which called for the abolition of sophomore hours in the dormitories and the modification of the class cut system. Higgins also supported putting students on all administrative committees. Neither candidate mentioned social activities in their platform. Higgins won the election and the *Ambrosian News* commented that his victory said that St. Ambrose was a "college with a future, a college without the tacky complacency of many other institutions its size. 'Tommy on the spot' won because of the newly emerging student interest." The paper said Higgins' ideas would have a profound impact on campus, "if he is allowed to move unencumbered by our present council machinery."[47]

At his first meeting as president, Higgins announced the formation of a committee to investigate the class cut system. The current policy said that when the number of unexcused absences exceeded the number of classes per week, all credit for the course would be lost. One student said that such a system had "no place in a college community of mature individuals." A survey indicated that 62 percent of the faculty thought the system should be changed. Dean of students Rogers agreed the system was "absurd," but told the council they would have to be patient with change. In spite of several proposals by the student council, the policy did not change until the fall of 1968, when the number of cuts allowable in a class was to be determined by the professor.[48]

The student council also pushed for a change in the academic calendar. Typical of American colleges, at St. Ambrose the fall semester began in late September and ended in late January. That meant the last weeks of the semester were interrupted by Christmas vacation. The second semester began in early February and ended in late May or early June. The students wanted to begin the fall semester in early September so that it ended before Christmas. The second semester would begin in mid-January and end in mid-May. The Educational Policy Committee had voted in favor of such a change, and it was apparently supported by most of the faculty. But the requested change was turned down by the administration. Menke said Marycrest had the same calendar as St. Ambrose and he thought the two should maintain the same schedule to facilitate better coordination of programs. Once again the patience urged by the dean was needed since the proposed calendar change did not begin until the fall of 1971.[49]

An article assessing Higgins' leadership after a few months noted that he was batting .450 and that "the world seems suddenly brighter." The

185

A Great and Lasting Beginning

Reverend William "Digger" Dawson, the student council advisor, said there had been a "healthy kind of restlessness present in this council, and this can only mean a healthier St. Ambrose College." But Lawrence Tiernan, editor of the *Ambrosian News*, said that "liberality in Student Affairs" did not exist. The council was operating in a "web of old business and [was] acting slowly." The administration had ruled against most of the council issues so Tiernan said the students needed an identity, and he suggested that they take the "concept of *student power* to heart; use it, don't abuse it unless there is just provocation to do so." He urged collective action by the students and said their "power to do good" would "overcome the apathy apparent in many things." As editor, Tiernan had added the slogan "perfect the establishment" to the paper's masthead. Now he added another slogan: "The student press for student power."[50]

In March 1968, the student council ratified a new constitution. Perhaps the most significant change in the new document was the body now had a new name: the Student Government Association (SGA).[51] The name change indicated that hereafter students wanted to be a governing body and that included at least a share in the governance of the college.

Another change advocated by the students was to place them on administrative committees. They argued that those committees impacted both faculty and students, so both groups should have impact upon the committees' discussions. They suggested five committees on which students should sit: Educational Policy, the Athletic Committee, the Space Utilization Committee, the Alumni Committee, and the Library Committee. Through the winter and spring, the *Ambrosian News* ran articles about other campuses where this had already taken place: at New Hampshire, where there was reportedly a "true partnership" between the students, faculty, trustees, and administration; at Tarkio College where the students were voting members of every committee; at Northwestern where students sat on the board of the College of Medicine. In May 1967, Menke announced that students chosen by the student council and the administration would sit as non-voting members of the Athletics, Library, Alumni Relations, Student Personnel, and Space Utilization Committees. However, they would not sit on the other committees, including Faculty Procurement Tenure and Advancement and the Budget Committee.[52]

The next fall Menke announced the formation of a new Academic Senate with representatives of the students, administration, and the faculty. Senate agreement would be necessary for all decisions on curriculum, subject matter, methods of instruction, general faculty status, and the areas of student life that related to academics. The *News* said this was "one of the most significant steps" and that now students would finally have a voice in the "molding of policy."[53]

At the first meeting of the Senate in January 1968, Menke asked the members to consider the status of St. Ambrose as a Catholic/Christian institution. Menke's request spoke to a debate underway in Catholic higher education. At the 1965 National Catholic Education Association convention, there were several presentations about the future of Catholic colleges. There was consensus that while there were serious problems, the system was not on the verge of collapse. Rather the problem was one of identity and purpose. Speakers said that for decades in their attempts for accreditation and acceptance by the American higher education community, Catholic colleges had stressed how similar they were to higher education in general. Now,

speakers said they should "seize upon and emphasize those elements that make them different from other institutions." Other speakers noted that in the current spirit of ecumenism, the earlier justification for Catholic education as a bulwark against the Protestant influence on American secular education no longer was necessary. In fact, many secular institutions had added religious courses to their curricula. Another speaker asked the blunt question of whether there was "room for any kind of belief as a precondition for learning?" Society had changed and would continue to change rapidly, and colleges could not shield their students from the "true picture of current society."[54]

Those discussions touched on other areas of Catholic higher education in addition to the place of religion. There was growing concern about the implications of various government funding programs. There were also questions about corporate control of institutions by their founding religious orders, or in the case of diocesan schools like St. Ambrose, by the diocesan bishop.

Menke's directive to the Academic Senate about Catholic/Christian status went directly to the role of religion as a guiding principle of the institution. Menke had set the theme for the discussions a year before when he spoke at the opening of the retreat in February 1967. He said that Christianity acknowledged a "whole realm of truth beyond human reasoning" which was known through revelation. It was the task of the Catholic university to teach reasoning and revelation. He said at St. Ambrose this was done in three ways. First, in religion classes where the student learned the basic truths and examined them, a task made more difficult "while indifference reigned in much of our society." The second area was action and at St. Ambrose there was an "environment of action in which the students may participate, and thus gain more meaning from those actions." A third way for the students to be led to faith was through counseling. Faith would lead the student to an understanding of himself and the world. Menke told them they must make a "commitment in campus, community, and world problems."[55]

The amount of government funds received by higher education, including church-related schools, had become a significant part of college budgets. The GI Bill after World War II had provided direct aid to veterans; various government programs enabled schools to build more facilities to accommodate a growing student population; colleges undertook research and development to aid the United State's defense efforts during the Cold War; as part of President Johnson's Great Society, Congress had created loan programs and direct aid to students through work-study programs. By 1967, St. Ambrose was participating in at least twenty-three government programs ranging from small amounts of money to purchase equipment for the science laboratories, to a long-term government loan that had helped build East Hall, to $26,000 from the work-study program for students from low-income families, to over $350,000 in loans to 409 students. Some said this was a sign that "big government" was "drawing the financial noose around education each year," but the reality was that no school could afford to ignore government funding.[56]

It was not just federal funding. Menke was among the private college presidents who worked to seek ways to get state funding for Iowa students who attended private colleges. The public universities opposed the plan and some of the private college leaders had to be convinced that "the government would not impinge on their freedom or try to control their programs." But Menke and the other supporters of the idea convinced their presidential colleagues and successfully lobbied the Iowa General Assembly to enact the Iowa Tuition Grant Program for students from Iowa who attended private schools. The grants began in 1969 by giving a "modest amount of support" to students, but over the years the amount had "steadily increased" and had "become a considerable benefit to private institutions."[57]

The question of the relationship between the colleges and their religious governing structures was addressed in 1967 when a number of Catholic college administrators gathered and produced, "The Nature of the Contemporary Catholic University," known familiarly as the Land O' Lakes statement, because it was written at a lodge in northern Wisconsin. The document affirmed the importance of theology and religion to a Catholic institution. But the most far-reaching statement came from the beginning of the document which said, "To perform its teaching and research function effectively the Catholic university must have a true autonomy and academic freedom in the face of authority of whatever kind, lay or clerical, external to the academic community itself." According to historian Philip Gleason, this was a "symbolic manifesto that marked the opening of a new era in American Catholic higher education . . . a declaration of independence from the hierarchy."[58] Another commentator said the relationship between the church and the university was "asymmetrical: *to* the church the university offers the 'benefit of continual counsel'; *from* the church the university asks only to be left alone."[59]

One way to ensure independent control of the colleges and universities was to laicize the governing boards. At St. Ambrose lay people had sat on the Board of Trustees in advisory capacities since World War I, but as in most colleges they did not "substantially participate" until after Vatican II.[60] The Council had recognized the "specific skills and perspectives" of the laity, and college presidents realized that lay people could help them run increasingly complex institutions. There was also a concern that Catholic colleges would lose government funds if they were under religious control.[61]

In the mid-1960s, the St. Ambrose board included diocesan priests and lay men and women but since 1885 the bishop, vicar general, and president of the college served as the corporate board of control, now called the Board of Managers, and that had not changed. The Board of Managers met regularly, most of the time to deal with financial or contractual issues. The entire board voted on other issues, but the Board of Mangers could override any of those votes. In 1965, Menke had asked the Board of Trustees to discuss possible ways for them to "assume greater responsibility for policies, financing, and development" of the college. But little more than discussion took place.[62]

At St. Ambrose those discussions took place under the chairmanship of a new bishop. On October 20, 1966, eighty-two-year-old Bishop Ralph L.

Bishop Gerald O'Keefe.

Hayes retired. Hayes had supported St. Ambrose, but unlike his predecessor Bishop Rohlman, he did not try to direct policy and programs at the college. He took an active interest in the decisions about building the chapel because he thought that as bishop he had a special responsibility to the religious center of the campus. For the most part, however, he was happy to allow the administration of the college to do its job.

Hayes was succeeded by the forty-eight-year-old Most Reverend Gerald F. O'Keefe. Born and educated in St. Paul, Minnesota, O'Keefe had been ordained in 1944. Where Hayes had spent time as a parish priest and diocesan superintendent of schools, O'Keefe spent most of the years before he came to Davenport in various offices in the chancery of the Archdiocese of St. Paul. He had gone to the Vatican Council unconvinced that the kinds of changes proposed there were necessary, but he came to see that the church needed to open the windows and adapt where it could to the modern world. Still he was a man of the institutional church and, especially in his relationship to the college in his early years in Davenport, the struggle between change and respecting the institutional church was evident.

As Menke indicated, the classroom was not the only place religion was taught. Through 1965, the proceedings of the Vatican Council remained a topic under discussion on campus. The Constitution on the Sacred Liturgy, the first one promulgated by the Council in December 1963, declared that the liturgy was "the outstanding means by which the faithful can express in their lives, and manifest to others, the mystery of Christ and the real nature of the true Church." That was a message Father Seidel had discussed in the early 1930s and which was carried on by Madsen. Madsen continued to teach about the theology of liturgy and said that Vatican II was "trying to put our whole religion into the orbit of our relationship to God" and was laying the groundwork for continuing renewal.[63]

Madsen left St. Ambrose in the summer of 1965 to become the pastor of St. Mary's Parish in Fairfield. The continuing renewal at the college was now in the hands of the new chaplain, Father Jack Smith. Smith wrote a regular religion column for the *Ambrosian News* called "Amen-65," where he commented on religious matters, but he also brought a political message as well. In November 1965, for example, he wrote about draft card burning, an anti-war protest that was appearing on some campuses around the country. He told Ambrosians not to "rule out the possibility that here we may have some sincere protest against the obvious inadequacies of our modern American culture. It is not un-American to note that a society which attaches so much prestige to clean teeth, Cadillac cars and charcoal burners falls somewhat short of a committed Christian awareness."[64] Such an overt political message from the chaplain made some Ambrosians, and many Catholics, uncomfortable, but St. Ambrose priests had a long record

A Great and Lasting Beginning

of challenging the status quo regarding labor unions, corporate greed, racial discrimination, and other social issues. Smith's comments were an early indication that some of the priests at St. Ambrose would continue those challenges in the area of war and peace.

With Smith as chaplain, and the next year with Father Farrell who replaced him, the liturgical changes so long advocated by Madsen and made possible by Vatican II were put into practice. Smith began a daily 5:00 p.m. Mass which he called a "very gratifying innovation." Concelebration by several priests became the norm, offertory processions appeared, and lay people served as lectors and commentators at Mass. On December 8, 1965, the college celebrated a special 5:00 p.m. Mass to mark the closing of the Vatican Council. In his homily, Smith said that most Catholics were "just beginning to appreciate what a tremendous thing" the Council had been, "not only for the Pope and bishops, but for priests and people alike."[65]

Another innovation while Smith was chaplain was a change in the format of the annual retreat. Instead of two days of conferences by a priest, in February 1966, a series of evening lectures were scheduled on a variety of topics, and class time was used by the professors for reflection on what the students had heard the night before. The intention was to integrate the religious exercise more closely with the academic life of the campus.[66]

The place where religious exercises and academic life intersected most closely was the seminary. A seminary building attached to Christ the King Chapel had been part of Edward Schulte's design fifteen years before and was made part of the development plan Collins had announced in 1957. Now Menke brought the proposal for a seminary building to the Trustees at a meeting on January 27, 1965. He said if a new seminary were built, it would free up needed space in Ambrose Hall for student housing, classrooms, and faculty offices.[67]

As planning proceeded over the next eighteen months, a new seminary became part of a larger building program that included a dormitory-cafeteria building, a fine arts complex, and a new field house. The goal was that those four buildings would be finished by 1971. Menke was not pleased with the chapel and East Hall architects, so he hired the East Moline firm of Bracke, Hayes, and Miller to design the buildings. Additional buildings, including a classroom building east of Davis Hall, a library between the library-administration building and Ambrose Hall, and two wings stretching west toward Gaines Street from Davis Hall would be completed by the time of the centennial of the college in 1982. Menke noted that the "primary purpose" of the college was the intellectual development of the student, but there was also an obligation to his "physical, social, cultural and spiritual growth" which those new buildings would enhance.[68]

When Menke outlined the project to Hayes, the bishop was reluctant. But when Menke told him that the success or failure of the building project would reflect on his leadership of the college, Hayes agreed to proceed. The $6 million plan for the first phase was announced in September 1966. V. O. Figge, president of Davenport Bank and Trust, and Bishop Hayes served as honorary co-chairmen, John Quail, president of Quail and Company, an investment firm, was the general campaign manager, and Robert Motto served as campaign coordinator. Together, they planned a fund campaign to raise $3 million in the city of Davenport, the parishes of

the diocese, and gifts from individual donors. The other $3 million would come from federal government grants and loans.[69]

When the campaign began, the seminary was already under construction with the hope that it would be ready for occupancy in September 1967. It would have two floors of rooms for seminarians, an apartment for the seminary rector and another for the spiritual director, and six apartments for other priest faculty. The ground floor would have classrooms. The *Messenger* reminded its readers of the importance of the seminary to the diocese. Since Bishop McMullen had founded St. Ambrose in 1882, the training of "young men in the liberal arts studies in preparation for the priesthood" had remained "an important part of St. Ambrose's contribution to the life of the Diocese." Four hundred and nineteen priests of the diocese had studied at St. Ambrose, including 185 of the 220 priests currently serving. In another part of McMullen's vision, the opportunities for seminarians to have "contact with young laymen pursuing a variety of careers . . . [had] helped St. Ambrose to train priests unusually well prepared for their various pastoral duties."[70] Because of that, the funds raised from the priests and in the parishes of the diocese would be applied to the seminary.

The campaign was set for Sunday, December 4, when some 5,000 volunteers would visit every Catholic household in the diocese. To prepare for this, Menke scheduled meetings in every deanery of the diocese. Now Hayes was an active participant. He attended every meeting and "spoke eloquently" about the needs of the college and the success of the building program. He ended every meeting with the statement, "I have never asked you [the people of the diocese] for anything during my entire stay in Davenport and I am asking you to really support this program. Please don't let me down." Menke was pleased with the bishop's participation and later commented that he "did a great job on the campaign."[71]

The campaign received an endorsement from the new bishop of Davenport. Writing from St. Paul, O'Keefe said his first letter to the diocese concerned St. Ambrose, which was at the "heart of our Catholic educational system" in the diocese. In the years ahead, "far from diminishing in importance in this new age, education, and Catholic education in particular, has assumed an even more essential purpose to our people and the Church of God." In that role, the seminary had the "greatest importance," and he said the "success" of his "future apostolate" was dependent on the successful outcome of the campaign.[72]

The priests had already pledged $204,120 to the campaign, and on December 4, the people of the diocese added nearly $1.8 million, $500,000 more than the goal. Robert Motto pronounced the campaign an "unqualified success" and began planning for the next phase of fund raising from local businesses and industry.[73] The campaign eventually raised $2.9 million from the priests, parishes, business and industry, friends, parents, and alumni.

Construction of the seminary building continued through 1967. It was not finished in September when the seminarians returned for the fall semester, so they lived at Marian Hall, the former nurses' dormitory at Mercy Hospital. There was also a new seminary staff. Long-time rector Father Edward O'Connor, and spiritual director Father Charles Griffith, retired, replaced by the Reverend Lawrence Soens as rector and the Reverend Paul Coleman as spiritual director. When they all finally moved into the building in January 1968, it was announced that it had been named

Hayes Hall.[74]

When Bishop O'Keefe arrived in Davenport in January 1967, the relationship between St. Ambrose and Marycrest was under discussion. The previous fall the two colleges began a co-curricular program which gave the students the opportunity to register for some classes on either campus. Each school maintained its individual identity while strengthening the curricula of both. This gave the students the "advantages of a large university's curriculum with the time-proven advantages of a small college campus."[75]

In early 1968, the Administrative Councils of both schools met to discuss their relationship. Marycrest wanted to continue the cooperative curricular arrangement that had begun the previous fall. Menke, however, did not see it provided any real value to St. Ambrose; instead he recommended that both schools become co-educational, a move Marycrest rejected. Some on campus and in the community, however, thought that the two

Fr. Catich's contemporary images of religious figures created controversy, but he believed that people should relate to images from their own time.

schools should merge. When he was asked about a possible merger at a forum in mid-February, Menke said it was a "good idea," but he said the difficulties of such a move included getting both faculties to work together, the distance between the two schools, and concern by alumni of the school losing its identity. An *Ambrosian News* editorial noted that high costs meant that neither school could continue as a separate institution. The best solution was merger, a position favored by the "majority of students." The paper asked, "What's being done?"[76]

Religious and lay women had been students at St. Ambrose since 1925, and the junior college, the evening and Saturday classes, the Women's Division of the 1930s, and the Nursing Division of the 1950s and early 1960s were all attempts to provide a college education to women. Over the years the largest number of female students were the sisters from various religious communities who attended summer school on the twenty-year plan. It was estimated that by the mid-1960s, more than 500 women had received degrees from St. Ambrose.[77]

Women had also been a part of the faculty since Mrs. Helena Bradford Churchill began directing plays after World War I. The number of lay women on the faculty increased after World War II. In 1965, Sister Ritamary Bradley, CHM, joined the English faculty. The next year Sister Annette Walters, CSJ, joined the faculty as head of the new Department of Psychology. In 1968, three more sisters joined the faculty: Sister Anne Claire Coleman, a Sister of Loretto, taught French; Sister Catherine Fay, BVM, taught theology; and Sister Patricia Kennedy, OSB, taught English. The sisters lived on campus and they "integrated" the priests' dining room. Consistent with many religious sisters of the 1960s, four of them no longer wore the traditional habit of their communities.[78]

For Menke and others, the issue was not women on campus, but whether St. Ambrose should become fully co-educational. Following a decline in the mid-1950s, enrollment had slowly increased so that in the fall of 1965, 1,292 day and evening students was the highest number since the years immediately after World War II. But in the years since, enrollment had increased only slightly, and the possibility that the manpower needs of the Vietnam War would lead Congress to eliminate the student deferment from the draft meant that the enrollment could decline in the years ahead.

So there was a special urgency when Menke put the issue of co-education on the agenda of the March 18, 1968, meeting of the Board of Trustees. He outlined the recent discussions with Marycrest and noted that the college regularly received applications from girls, and that 82 percent of male applicants from the Chicago area, a major source of students, said they preferred co-education. A recent survey among Assumption High School students indicated the same thing. To those who suggested that unilateral action by St. Ambrose would upset the Catholic women's colleges, Menke pointed out that Ottumwa Heights Junior College, operated by the Sisters of Humility, became co-educational without consulting St. Ambrose, as did the Franciscan Mt. St. Clare in Clinton. One trustee suggested that a merger "might be necessary," and asked about hiring a consultant to advise them on the issue. Menke argued against a merger, saying it would take at least five years to effect and would not solve the short-term problem of enrollment. Nevertheless, Menke said he was amenable to having a consultant study the problem.

Bishop O'Keefe argued against co-education, saying that the Catholic tradition of separate education for men and women would be "nullified." He noted that the Sisters of Humility had made a "huge investment" in the physical plant at Marycrest which had performed a valuable service for the community and the diocese. He feared that the goodwill St. Ambrose had built in the community would be lost and said that "several . . . prominent people" had indicated to him that they would no longer support the college if it became coed. Finally, he worried about the presence of the seminary and said that although several other seminaries had moved to co-educational campuses, "he had his doubts as to the propriety of this action."

At the end of the discussion, trustee Robert Motto moved "That St. Ambrose College allow daytime commuter women students to register and graduate but to exclude present enrollees at Marycrest." The motion was seconded by Mrs. Margaret Tiedemann. Ten trustees voted in favor of the motion, including Menke and four priests of the diocese. One trustee, James M. Hutchinson who had advocated merger, abstained. Only O'Keefe and the Reverend Monsignor Paul D. Moore, the vicar general, voted no.[79]

The next day O'Keefe pointed out to Menke that two of the three members of the Board of Managers, himself and Moore, had voted against coeducation, and therefore, St. Ambrose would remain a male school. Menke reminded the bishop that most of the trustees had voted in favor of coeducation, but the bishop replied that the trustees votes did not count. Menke convinced O'Keefe to call a meeting of the Board of Managers for March 29. The three managers discussed the issue again, Moore changed his vote, and a resolution to admit non-boarding women students in the fall of 1968 passed.[80]

Before the public announcement, Father Soens, the rector of the seminary, wrote Peoria Bishop John Franz and Rockford Bishop Loras Lane, both of whom had seminarians at St. Ambrose, to tell them of the change. He said the decision was made only after "careful and long consideration." He assured them there would be no change in the seminary program which would continue with its own residence hall, rector, and spiritual director. The women would live in their own residence hall, already in the planning stages. He admitted that there would be a "co-ed atmosphere in some of the college classes" but that most of the activities in which the seminarians took part were by nature not coed.[81]

American Catholic higher education had been slow in the movement to co-education and St. Ambrose was no exception. By 1950, about one in five Catholic colleges were coed. Spurred largely by economic necessity in the next two decades, many Catholic men's schools made the move to co-education, so that by 1970 almost all men's schools had become coed. Similar economic necessity spurred many women's campuses to begin to admit men.[82] Although St. Ambrose was now part of a national trend, it was still a major change for the college, but one that reflected "the change in the attitude of the college generation." Menke said it indicated "that more and more young women were interested in academic programs that were formerly considered appropriate only to men." He added that in recent months the college had received over forty applications from girls outside the Quad-Cities.[83] That fall 166 women enrolled as commuter students at St. Ambrose.

Throughout 1966 and 1967, debate continued about the growing American presence in Vietnam. In April 1966, the St. Ambrose YCS group and the Lutheran Student Organization from Augustana College held a discussion in the Bee Hive on the "expanding problem of Vietnam." The discussion centered on the continuing American role in that country and whether the United States had a moral right to control the government of Vietnam or any foreign government. In the fall there were town meetings featuring speakers representing a variety of perspectives on the issue. Mike Fitzsimmons, a senior in political science, wrote articles for the *Ambrosian News* tracing the history of Vietnam.[84]

The next spring the first anti-war demonstrations were held in front of the Federal Building in downtown Davenport, led by history Professor Wayne DeJohn and his wife, Nora. A letter to the *Ambrosian News* noted the demonstration with the comment that many people at St. Ambrose had a lot to say but "rarely does action ensue." The writer said that it took courage to stand up and be counted, and "if only for this, the DeJohns deserve our admiration and support."[85]

In May 1967, DeJohn, Father Jack Smith, and history Professor Richard Geiger planned the celebration of a Mass for peace on May 22. DeJohn said, "We feel very much the need for some further public expression of our desire that peace be restored in Vietnam, that there be a disengagement of military forces in that tragic land." The Mass was to begin with a procession from the west end of Ambrose Hall to the chapel, with student leaders and some members of the faculty carrying placards with messages from papal encyclicals and scripture about peace, but with no specific mention of Vietnam. The week before the Mass, four students objected to the procession and raised the possibility of a "counter-demonstration" to the dean of students, Cliff Rogers. Rogers said their objection was not with the Mass, "which they thought was great," but with the procession because they feared it would say to the community that the "majority opinion at the school dissented from the war," and that the procession would "reflect badly on the school."[86]

On the day of the Mass, a group of twenty-five processed with their banners and singing "Kumbaya." When they arrived in the chapel, they found copies of a letter in the pews from Father Bernard Kamerick. Kamerick said that no Catholic can be opposed to praying for peace but that to join the Mass with a "particular political outlook cannot be condemned in too strong terms." He said the Mass and the procession that day were "nonsense and a disgrace to the Catholic Church. Father Smith and Mr. DeJohn know better, or ought to." Kamerick claimed his letter was supported by a "considerable portion" of the students and faculty.[87]

About 175 people joined several campus priests who concelebrated the Mass. In his sermon, Father Smith said it was the "genius of Pope John to have discovered the common denominator of unity and peace and brotherhood . . . [in the] dignity of the human person." Therefore, he said that peace in Vietnam, equality at home, and the attempts to ease poverty were "facets of the same great thrust to uplift humanity." He said peace must be "willed, it must be seized," and it was up to each individual to take the responsibility for it. Smith concluded with a peroration: "If we can start by dissipating the undue fears in our lives, the other person may quickly cease to be the scapegoat for our hostilities. If we can summon the energy to trust

A neighborhood boy watches as Sister Ritamary Bradley, Sister Annette Walters, Professor Wayne DeJohn, Nora DeJohn, and Professor Matt McMahon (holding "Blessed" sign) march to the chapel for a Mass on May 22, 1967.

even when sufficient reason is absent, we will be gratified to discover how other persons blossom under the sun of our humanity. If we can eliminate suspicion, avoid accusation, free ourselves from the tyranny of success, cast out the devils of image-making and type-casting, reject anti-intellectualism, exorcize false mystiques and superstition, peace will begin where it must commence, in ourselves."[88]

Smith made only two direct references to Vietnam in his sermon, but it was clear that the war was the focus of the liturgy; as one participant said, "There is only one war going on." DeJohn admitted that "you could read political overtones into it." When asked about that, Smith said that all they wanted was peace and if the procession and Mass "gets us involved in recommendations of a political nature, then we will not abdicate our responsibility."[89]

For some on the St. Ambrose campus the issue of Vietnam was clear, but many others continued to express ambivalence about the war and American policy. In late September 1967, 172 Ambrose students and faculty participated in a poll about the war. Fifty-four percent favored one of the three "dove-like" options, the largest group of which, 34 percent, opted for "stop bombing and negotiate." Forty-six percent of the respondents favored a "hawkish, pro-war position," including the invasion of North Vietnam.

Significantly, of the hawkish group, only 3 percent favored continuing the current policy. When they were asked about the progress of the war, 64 percent said the United States was making "no progress"; 21 percent said the United States was "realizing" its objective; 12 percent said the country was "losing ground" in Vietnam; and another 5 percent had no opinion.[90]

For the eighteen- to twenty-two-year-old male students at St. Ambrose, their draft eligibility was more real than the various political opinions about the war being expressed on campus. In 1962, sophomore Greg Cusack wrote that a then current campaign to repeal the draft was a "cry without responsibility." He said that to abandon the draft without an "adequate alternative" would be foolish; even with its shortcomings, the draft was "still the most effective answer . . . to the challenge of manpower imposed upon us by our world leadership."[91]

In 1962, it was accepted that eighteen-year-olds register for the draft and if they were in college, they received a student deferment. But when Cusack wrote that year, there were only about 10,000 Americans in Vietnam, with only forty-two American deaths since 1960. For most Americans, the Vietnam war was a little-known conflict in a distant land. By the beginning of 1966, however, there were some 184,000 Americans serving in Vietnam, and there had been 1,636 American deaths. The war was now well-known,

A Great and Lasting Beginning

and college students were well aware that upon graduation, their deferments would be up and they would have to serve. Thus the draft system itself became another target of protest.

At the end of January 1968, a major attack by the forces of North Vietnam during the Tet holiday was an American military victory but a public relations defeat. As the war in Vietnam intensified, the debate about the draft became more contentious. In February, just after the Tet offensive, the NFCCS and the Manning Club sponsored a teach-in on the draft. Two speakers came from the Chicago Area Draft Resisters (CADRE) to speak against it. They urged men to burn their draft cards and discouraged eighteen-year-olds from registering in the first place. They said they were not avoiding the draft, but confronting it. Two members of the St. Ambrose political science faculty, Professors John Norton and Robert Newton, agreed with CADRE's position on the draft but did not think that the resistence they advocated was an effective response. When the discussion was opened to those in the audience, Father Charles Shepler, in an "angry address," spoke against the anti-war movement. He said that the United States was fighting the communists by proxy in Vietnam and that all Americans should support that effort.[92]

Shepler's remarks illustrated the complexity of the issue of the Vietnam War. Some opposed the draft as a less-than-perfect system that seemed to reward middle-class Americans who could afford to attend college but were uncertain about the war. Others thought that the elimination of the draft would also end the war which they viewed as evil. Some saw the Vietnam War as a local conflict concerning the governance of that country. Others, like Shepler, saw it as part of the larger, Cold War dynamic to contain communism, Vietnam merely being the latest front in that larger war.

Another position on the war supported the American soldiers while admitting an ambivalence about the morality of the war. That was the position of the Americans in Support of America Committee, formed on campus in early 1968. T. Walter Newmaster, a junior at St. Ambrose, wrote that regardless of one's political or moral beliefs, one could still support the fighting man in Vietnam who had "unjustly borne the brunt of what is a 'political' battle concerning the administration's policy of military commitment in Vietnam." In response, Father Smith said that all people would like the kind of "a-political" world of which Newmaster wrote, but the real world was not like that, it was a place where people daily wrestled with gray issues and the American presence in Vietnam was a "very sad, very gray issue." Smith said that the servicemen were instruments of the American policy and "parades in support of the boys in Vietnam become mass demonstrations of the policy they implement." Smith continued, "All human realities have moral implications. War does not change this. In this case, consistency might well require that we express equal, or even more loyalty to those young men who have refused service because in conscience

The incomparable Mrs. Spencer, secretary for the dean of students for twenty-two years.

they believe this to be a wrong policy, a wrong war."[93]

As the debate continued through the spring of 1968, the campus community watched a continuing series of events that added new uncertainties to their world: the withdrawal from the presidential race by President Johnson at the end of March and the assassination of Martin Luther King, Jr., in early April.

Meanwhile the students went to class, prepared for exams, and wrote papers. They again became sidewalk superintendents as work began on the new dormitory-food service facility. Director James Willaert was in final rehearsals with the Theatre III actors for their presentation of *Gideon*, starring Frank Schneeberger as Gideon and David McDaniel as God. Rehearsals were underway for the spring musical, *Carnival*, with Christine Bender as Lilli. Ambrosians celebrated at the annual Marycrest Mardi Gras, which had a "South of the Border" theme. The senior class sponsored a perennially popular group, "Your Father's Mustache," at Danceland. The spring cotillion featured a dance on Friday night and a picnic at Emeis Park on Saturday afternoon. The spring sports were beginning their seasons that would see the tennis and track teams win the Midlands Conference championship and the golf team finished second in the conference. In May the St. Ambrose and Marycrest musicians performed Gabriel Faure's *Requiem* in memory of Mr. Arthur Petersen, a long-time music teacher at St. Ambrose who had recently died.

For two years Dan Doran had written a column for the *Ambrosian News* entitled, "The Wingtipped Warrior." In May 1968, just weeks before he graduated, he wrote his last column about his experience at St. Ambrose which he called "the most truly enlightening portion of my life. For here, under the Oaks . . . I was able to grow." He said he saw students struggle to achieve in the classroom, in their social lives, in their religious lives. He served as a proctor and he saw them get into and out of trouble, and "laugh, cry, shout, whisper . . . live." He realized that it was the people who made St. Ambrose worth whatever it cost to attend, "People who have trouble getting papers in on time, people who don't have trouble; people who get into trouble, people who never get into trouble; people who frequent the Tiptopper, people who never go into the Tiptopper; people who sit in the student center and who solve the problems of the day, people who never go into the student center. The people who are not in the categories above [are] people like Margarette behind the counter; Mrs. Salsbury on the PA; and surely the most underrated woman on the campus, the incomparable Mrs. Spencer in the Dean's office. This is Ambrose. Ambrose is essentially people, the ones you know and the ones you don't know." This last column was his attempt to express his thanks to the institution, its people, and "even to the oaks . . . Ambrose has been good to the Warrior and quite simply, I came . . . I saw . . . I loved . . . I lived. Thank you."[94]

The most obvious alteration is the change in the attitude and role of the student. We all are aware of student unrest, aware that at least a number of students are dissatisfied with the educational program and with the condition of our society. They register this discontent in a variety of ways . . . We need to understand more fully the reasons for student discontent and adapt our program to serve the needs of the student. It is my conviction that students are willing to assume responsibility if they are given the opportunity . . . We need to expand the areas in which students can contribute to the College program.[1]

– Monsignor Sebastian Menke

Chapter Fourteen

Nineteen sixty-eight was not yet over. In June Senator Robert Kennedy was assassinated. In August the pent-up social and political conflict as a result of the war and the growing counterculture exploded at the Democratic national convention in Chicago. The war continued to escalate; there were now over 500,000 American troops in Vietnam and 1968 would see 14,589 of them killed. When the students returned that fall, controversy about the war and debates about the question of student power continued.

Reflecting on his first years as president, Menke noted the dissatisfaction of the students with the educational program and the condition of society. He understood they were impatient and he understood that he would need continuing patience to listen to them. He had to try to move the institution fast enough to satisfy them, but not so fast that other, more traditional groups on campus would be disturbed.

The campus was already divided into two camps about the war and both sides used the student newspaper, renamed the *Paper SAC* that fall, to press their views.[2] Various groups sponsored speakers and panel discussions to air the issues. And there were frequent demonstrations, some large and planned, others small, seemingly unplanned operations. Those who were opposed to American involvement were often called "appeasers" or "non-patriots" by those who supported American policy and who wondered what there was to discuss. But the opponents of the war argued that where dissent was discouraged, "intelligent opposition" diminished. A student from that time remembered, "There certainly was an electricity in the air during that period and a lot of conflict on campus, the hawks and doves, the pros and cons, the conservatives and the liberals and even a few hippies thrown into the mix."[3]

Menke was charged with trying to harness that electricity and turn it into a creative force for change. In 1968 he was assisted in that task by a new dean of students, Edward Rogalski. Born in Manville, New Jersey, Rogalski studied at Wilkes College in Wilkes-Barre, Pennsylvania, and Rutgers University, and received his Bachelor of Arts Degree from Parsons College in Fairfield, Iowa. As a student at Parsons, he was a head resident and after graduation, he served as assistant to the dean of admissions and records, assistant dean of students, and acting dean of men. He left Parsons to pursue a Master's Degree in college student personnel administration at the University of Iowa. In 1968, when Menke was searching for a new dean

of students, Father Cletus Madsen, now the pastor of St. Mary's Parish in Fairfield, recommended Rogalski to him. Menke made several trips to Iowa City to convince Rogalski to take the job. He was successful, and that summer Rogalski and his new wife, Bobbi, moved to St. Ambrose.[4]

Rogalski came to St. Ambrose because he found it a "good campus community of scholars," and for the challenge of working closely with the three elements of the campus community: the students, faculty, and administration. As dean, his task was to enforce the traditional policies of the college. Rather than a strict disciplinarian, Rogalski preferred the model of the dean as an educator who could lead the students to assume greater responsibility.

Rogalski began as dean with a valuable asset, the incomparable Mrs. Spencer. Rogalski was her sixth dean and no one knew the campus and students better than she. She had seen many changes on campus since Father Shepler had hired her, and she thought much of it was good. But Mrs. Spencer and her new dean had no idea what changes were in store for the campus in the next few years.

Rogalski became dean at a time when the rules were changing; Menke had already modified or eliminated some of the long-time rules, but Rogalski wanted to go even farther. For decades, a priest lived on each dormitory floor to watch over the students. There were also students on each floor, in the early years called prefects, later called proctors, who were charged with enforcing the rules. But in the mid-1960s, the priests began to move off the floors, leaving only the proctors to enforce the old rules. Rogalski wanted to create a system of "para-professional" resident advisors who would be more than just enforcers of the rules. He went to Menke and told him in order to make the kinds of changes necessary he would need additional resources. Menke told the new dean that he knew more about it than he did, so he should "go ahead."[5]

The Student Government Association remained the principal catalyst for activity on campus, but there were other groups that added to the debates. In the fall of 1966, the National Student Association (NSA) was reinstated as a committee of the student council. Ken Brune, its primary advocate, said this was a "trial stage . . . to see if it can again become a vital part of student life." Critics of the NSA said it was merely a forum for liberal political views. Brune defended the group, contending that perhaps only 20 percent of its activities were political. Nevertheless, one of its first

A Great and Lasting Beginning

The flag pole became a familiar place for campus protests. Here Rev. Jack Smith and students register their support of the Catonsville Nine.

actions was to introduce a series of resolutions to send letters of protest to President Johnson about alleged CIA involvement in student groups and activities.[6]

The NFCCS continued to hold its annual regional seminar. The seventh annual seminar in March 1968 featured a debate on political conservatism, a lecture on the social context of sex, another on psychedelic drugs, a debate on civil rights, and after Mass on Sunday morning, a lecture by Wayne DeJohn on "The Future of Dissent." The *Ambrosian News* noted that the academic curriculum was too slow to incorporate those "relevant themes" which made the NFCCS seminar a "basic supplement to a college education." And more important, the seminar represented "student power and responsibility." But it was the last of those seminars. In May the national offices closed, putting the NFCCS out of business. The Midwest region in which St. Ambrose had been so active, reorganized as GOYA, which according to St. Ambrose representative Bill Assell, was a "nonsense" word. The group hoped to "promote the idea of action" on campus and in 1969, it continued the NFCCS tradition of a regional conference.[7]

A new group was organized in early 1969 when a St. Ambrose chapter of the Students for a Democratic Society (SDS) formed. SDS had been founded in 1960 and was a vehicle for liberal causes on campuses across the country. In 1965, it turned to antiwar activism and for the next few years was involved in large anti-war demonstrations, most notably the 1968 protests at Columbia University. By the time it organized at St. Ambrose, the national group had collapsed. The Ambrose group hoped to be a "democratic autonomous" unit for the students, and press for student-centered

issues. It also was involved in anti-war demonstrations, most notably when members hung a large sheet painted to resemble the American flag on the wall in front of the Bee Hive. The flag had holes to represent bullet holes with red paint to resemble blood dripping down from them. Pro-war Ambrosians tore the banner down and as one student remembered, there was a "lot of angry rhetoric," but anything more serious was averted.[8]

The first demonstration in the fall of 1968 occurred when about thirty students and faculty held a prayer meeting in the chapel on Sunday evening October 6, in support of the Catonsville Nine. This was a group of protesters led by two priest brothers, Philip and Daniel Berrigan, who had broken into a draft board office in Catonsville, Maryland, removed records, and burned them. They were arrested and their trial was to begin the day after the St. Ambrose demonstration. At the Ambrose chapel meeting, a statement was read that said the Catonsville Nine had "seriously challenged" the war policy of the United States, which it said was "immoral." For the next three days the group met at noon at the flagpole on campus for discussions and readings. Father Jack Smith said those St. Ambrose demonstrations were "an act of conscience by which we seek to identify with the Catonsville Nine in their present trial."[9] In Baltimore, the Catonsville Nine were convicted and sent to prison.

Student opinion on the war and on anti-war demonstrations reflected a wide range of opinions. Senior Mike Walsh wrote he thought the United States should take steps to "end the disaster which . . . is Vietnam" and withdraw as soon as possible. He also thought the draft was unfair and should be changed. But he said he could not "buy the idea of the Catonsville Nine," a violent act did not stop violence, and he said those who preached peace should practice it. Other students complained that the speakers brought to campus represented only the "liberal" side of issues. Writing in the *Paper SAC*, Gene Conrad said that students were "tired' of such a "limited presentation," and urged sponsoring groups to let the students decide for themselves. Conrad said it seemed the groups who sponsored speakers felt that "the admission to the campus of conservatism [brought] about a corresponding decline in intellectualism."[10]

On Armistice Day 1968, the Quad-Citians for Peace, a new group founded by Father Smith and DeJohn, gathered for a "peace service." Forty-nine years earlier, Father Hannon had led the students in the first Armistice Day celebration at St. Ambrose. That day, Hannon had said that the sacrifice of lives made during World War I had created a debt the students would have to repay, and he asked those students what they were going to do to repay it. Now this new group of Ambrosians gathered to mark the anniversary of the end of one war in the midst of another. Drake Shafer, a senior seminarian, spoke of the hope that with the peace of Versailles which had ended World War I, real peace would come. Instead there had been more wars, and now they were gathered not to celebrate war, but to work for peace.[11]

The Quad-Citians for Peace opened an office in downtown Davenport to make draft counseling available. Draft-aged students came with questions about student, occupational, and hardship deferments. Others came to discuss leaving the country rather than face the draft. The counselors also helped a number of St. Ambrose students file for conscientious objector status. Smith said later that in all the draft counseling he did, he never found anyone "selfishly avoiding the army." Rather most expressed an aversion to violence, or an opposition to participating in a government policy they felt was wrong, or a belief in the futility of war. Smith said patriotism was loyalty to a country that must leave room for dissent.[12]

So far the anti-war demonstrations at St. Ambrose had been relatively peaceful. To ensure that continued, in November, Rogalski presented the SGA with a new policy regarding demonstrations. Penalties would be levied for the unauthorized entry or occupation of campus rooms or buildings or for demonstrations that purposefully disrupted the order of the college, obstructed access to buildings, took place inside buildings except with the permission of the dean, interfered with the rights of others on campus, created a risk of injury.[13]

Menke had written of the need to understand the reasons for student discontent and that meant listening to them. On December 11, 1968, he held an open forum with about sixty students. He complimented them on the recent homecoming celebration which he said was the best in at least ten years. He said the new residence hall was progressing, and he proposed to use the space in Ambrose Hall that would be abandoned when the dining hall moved, for offices for student organizations. Menke then answered questions about the academic calender; allowing seniors to live off-campus (he had no objection if the dormitories were full); the reinstatement of football (he was opposed); the proposed change in the Department of Sacred Doctrine; the quality of the food (he said the head of the food service should hold a similar open forum); whether students should sit on the board of studies (no); and was asked if military recruiters would be allowed on campus, a resolution the SGA had just defeated that would have barred them (he said yes, but only in the faculty lounge, not in the student union).[14]

The next February, Rogalski held a "Gripe Session" attended by about 200 students. In addition to Rogalski, other administration officials were present. Many of the questions were directed to Thomas Grady, the college business manager, about the food service contract, student parking, and fire alarms in the residence halls. John Gavrilla, the SAGA food service manager, fielded questions about the cost of meals and the requirement that students wear a jacket and tie to Sunday dinner (Gavrilla said he only enforced a rule passed by the Student Government Association). Rogalski was asked about a picnic that spring and he responded there would be one, but that alcohol could not be served.[15]

That month Rogalski also formed the Dorm Council as a governing body for on-campus students. He hoped the Dorm Council would relieve the resident advisors of their "police-like duties" so they could concentrate on their duties as an "advisor." One issue under discussion on campus was the dress policy in the refectory. A letter to the editor of the *Paper SAC* the month before complained that students still had to wear a tie and jacket to Sunday dinner. The writer pointed out that he could get into most eating establishments in the Quad-Cities with a turtle neck, but not in the St. Ambrose refectory. When the SDS formed that spring, they also discussed the issue of dress in the refectory. Rogalski said the new Dorm Council should address that issue and others such as providing a canteen service in the dormitories and promoting cultural activity on campus.[16]

Rogalski's efforts at a more open exchange of ideas and his willingness to look at long-standing rules received a positive response. After his first year, Rick Moskowitz, editor of the *Paper SAC*, noted the sense of change on campus, which he said was due to a "forward-looking president, and moreover, the campus life is succeeding as a result of Dean Rogalski." The dean had brought the campus a "long way on the right path in a short time" and he deserved a "respectable 'tip of the hat.'" Another student said he had been at St. Ambrose for six years and was finally graduating. During that time he said the management of the Tiptopper had changed hands four times and there had been four deans of students who had become "more progressive, more lenient, and understanding over the six years."[17]

Menke and Rogalski were dealing with issues that swept across higher education in the decade of the sixties that led to changes in the relationship of the various segments of the campus community. Historian Philip Gleason noted that "freedom" was the "central theme in American Catholic higher education" during those years. One component of that was the participation of students in campus upheavals which included a "discrediting of authority, questioning of doctrine, and often contemptuous rejection of the past."[18] By the late 1960s, students at St. Ambrose had already challenged *in loco parentis*, had asked for representation on campus committees, and had challenged the religious curriculum.

Through 1969, the students continued to press the issue of student freedom and student power. Menke convened a meeting on April 17 of the SGA, the faculty, and representatives of the administration to discuss those issues. SGA president Michael Walsh presented a plan for the formation of an all-college senate composed of equal numbers of students, faculty, and administrators. There was a general consensus that such a plan was a good idea. Professor Prudent Coussens spoke strongly in favor of it while Menke expressed reservations about the competence of the students to make decisions in specifically academic areas. The meeting adjourned with a committee appointed to draw a plan for better communication among the three components of the college community.[19]

Over the next three years, the most consistent voice advocating student power came from Joe Smith,

Melodee Grimshaw, a freshman from Bettendorf, helps a custodian convert the campus to co-education.

Hall (later named Cosgrove Hall), the second part of Menke's building program. South Hall had four floors of student rooms arranged in a pair of double rooms separated by a common bathroom. This room arrangement gave rise to a new term on campus: suite-mates. The main floor was the new student dining room, a dining room for the priests and another one for the seminarians. On the ground floor there was a large lounge, the offices of the dean

a sophomore English major from Rock Island. Commenting in the *Paper SAC* on the April meeting, Smith said STUDENT POWER (he emphasized it with capital letters) were frightening words to some college administrators and asked what "STUDENT POWER meant to St. Ambrose College?" For Smith it was a "logical extension of the democratic principle that people should control their own lives." He said "some students" would like to be more than "advisors who are listened to or ignored depending on which is more convenient for the real decision-makers." Smith said students were "mature adults capable of controlling their own lives," and they did not want a faculty-administration committee telling them who their teachers would be, and they questioned "the necessity of a Dean of Students, a Big Brother."[20]

Smith said the administration had to "relinquish its strangle hold" on St. Ambrose and he wanted the students to have an elected majority on the Academic Senate and students on the Procurement, Tenure, and Advancement Committee. Then they could address the issue of the evaluation of faculty and discuss the "necessity and function of the Dean of Students." He said members of the St. Ambrose community who believed the college could avoid the kinds of reforms happening on other campuses "are fools." He ended by quoting Bob Dylan: "Don't stand in the doorway/Don't block up the hall./For he that gets hurt/Will be he who has stalled./There's a battle outside/And it's ragin'/It'll soon shake your windows/And rattle your walls/For the times they are a changin'."[21] The times were "a changin'" at St. Ambrose, but for Smith and some others, the change was not happening fast enough or completely enough.

One of the most noticeable changes in the fall of 1969 was the presence of women living on campus. Forty-six women moved into the new South

of students, student health, the bookstore, and Tillie Sobek's post office.

That fall Rogalski was asked if he expected more student unrest in the coming year. He said he did not, but if dissent arose, he thought it could be "settled peacefully." But not everyone was so sure and at a meeting of the Board of Trustees in mid-September, Robert Motto asked about regulations for "violations and lawlessness" on campus. Menke said regulations were in place: peaceful demonstrations were permitted "within the freedoms for students and faculty"; obstruction of access to campus property or other violations would bring a warning to "terminate such action"; "take-overs, sit-ins" would be handled by "police action" if warnings were "unheeded." Menke said in all cases due process must be observed and any actions must "proceed with prudence."[22] With that explanation, the board seemed satisfied that an adequate policy was in place.

Regulations would be necessary. On October 15, Ambrosians participated in the National War Moratorium. The SGA passed an anti-war resolution and called for all students to participate in the day's demonstrations. The Academic Senate left it up to individual instructors whether to cancel classes that day, and in the end about one-fourth did. The day began with a prayer service in the chapel and a march to LeClaire Park where there were bands and a Festival of Life. Later, the students began an all-night-long reading of the names of all the American dead in Vietnam.[23]

Homecoming that fall gave little indication of the campus turmoil. Held the week after the moratorium demonstrations, the five-day celebration began on Wednesday with the election of Diana Driscoll, a junior, as the first St. Ambrose woman to be named homecoming queen. That night there was a variety show in the Marycrest auditorium. Thursday featured the Queen's Tea and the float rally at the Mississippi Valley Fairgrounds. The homecoming dance was Friday night at the Col Ballroom with music by Meen. The parade began at 1:00 Saturday afternoon at Municipal

Stadium on the riverfront and wound its way through downtown and back to the stadium for the 3:00 rugby game against Northern Illinois.[24]

For several years there had been interest in establishing a fall sport, and most students preferred soccer. The school was not willing to sponsor it, so the student council had offered to sponsor it as a club sport, but interest waned. Then in the spring of 1969, enthusiasts from the Palmer College of Chiropractic helped St. Ambrose form a rugby team.[25]

The team lost to Northern Illinois 9-0 in the homecoming game, but the loss did not dampen the enthusiasm of the students who ended the day with a concert performed by the groups Brooklyn Bridge and Maffitt and Davies held at Centennial Hall at Augustana. The weekend concluded with a Mass for Ambrosians and Cresters in Christ the King Chapel.

One of the focuses of the war protests was the draft and its system of deferments which many said favored middle-class males who could afford to go to college. To address that, the Selective Service System created a lottery where numbers would be drawn corresponding to the day of birth for males born between 1944 and 1950. President Richard Nixon had supported the lottery in the hope that its seeming randomness would quiet the protesters.

The first drawing was December 1, 1969, and Ambrosians joined their counterparts across the country to sit in front of television sets to watch what the Ambrosians were calling "Mr. Nixon's Bingo." They knew that the military would not need all of them, so they rooted for a high number which they thought would keep them from being called into service. Mike Maury, an accounting major from Park Ridge, Illinois, got number thirteen. He said his future plans were now "pretty well decided. The drawing made that definite." Gil Cervelli, a business administration major from Prospect Heights, Illinois, drew number 106. He had hoped that the lottery would keep him out of the service, but "it's over and there's no more hope. At least we know where we stand." Kevin McEneely, a business education major from Mount Prospect, Illinois, drew 350. "If they get around to drafting me with No. 350," he said," we'll all have to go anyhow." Many, however, were like Dick Brice, also from Mount Prospect, who got number 139. I'm "still in the middle, not knowing for sure whether I'll be drafted or not."[26] In the end those who received numbers lower than 196 were called into service. At the

time the lottery was perceived to be fair and it did fulfill the president's hope that it would quiet the war protesters. But the hope that it would democratize the process of calling men into service was not realized because deferments for students who already had them were continued for another two years, lower troop levels in Vietnam late in the war decreased the need for more recruits, and physical exemptions were "relatively easy for the privileged to attain."[27]

On September 15, 1969, Menke presented the board with revised articles of incorporation. Since the college was incorporated in 1885, the bishop, vicar general, and president had served as the Board of Managers, exercising the corporate power of the college. The proposed new structure eliminated the Board of Managers and created a seven-person Board of Directors by adding four laymen. Privately, Bishop O'Keefe questioned the impact of such a move. Although he still remained the chairman of the board, and the vicar general and the president both of whom for the moment were priests, still served as vice president and secretary-treasurer, adding laymen dramatically changed the identity and center of power of the board. Now it could be possible for the bishop's wishes to be outvoted by the expanded board. O'Keefe also worried about what such a move would mean to the identity of St. Ambrose as a diocesan, Catholic college; what impact it would have on fund raising; and whether the priests of the diocese would continue to support the college to the degree they had in the past.

When the Board of Trustees discussed the issue at the September 15 meeting, O'Keefe explained that the change was a departure from the "light control presently in effect" with the three-member board. He explained that this move separated the college from the diocese, breaking the custom in effect since the founding of the college by Bishop McMullen. However, that separation would put the college in a better position to apply for government funds and it would bring to the board the wisdom and experience of the new lay members.

Discussion among the trustees indicated support for the change, but one asked what would happen to the current Board of Trustees. Menke replied that there would be no change in that board, it would remain as an advisory group to the new Board of Directors. Upon motion, the board voted to revise the articles of incorporation to create a

Gil Cervelli, Mike Maury, Dick Brice, Kevin McEneely, and Phil LaMonaco came to St. Ambrose from St. Viator High School in Arlington Heights, Illinois. They display the numbers they drew in "Mr. Nixon's Bingo."

A Great and Lasting Beginning

new Board of Directors, which would "bear the full responsibility for the college as a corporate entity. The property affairs, business and concerns shall be vested in the Board subject to the law and the articles of Incorporation of the College." The new board was authorized to appoint up to six new members, "all younger men." The motion passed and the revised articles of incorporation were filed with the State of Iowa on September 23, 1969.[28]

Four new members were appointed to the Board of Directors: John Figge, vice president and director of Davenport Bank and Trust; Dr. Philip G. Hubbard, vice provost and dean of academic affairs at the University of Iowa; James McLaughlin, an academy and college graduate and president of McLaughlin Body Company in Moline; and Robert S. Motto, a graduate of the college and president of Midwest Timmermann Company in Davenport. The remaining members of the former board were appointed to a new Board of Trustees. Two years later the articles of incorporation were amended to add more members and Mrs. Margaret Tiedemann was appointed as the first woman on the Board of Directors. At the same time it granted non-voting membership to the president of the faculty assembly and the president of the Student Government Association.[29] With those changes, St. Ambrose joined the trend present in Catholic higher education. By 1970, just over 68 percent of Catholic colleges had added laypersons to their corporate structures, the highest percentage of those colleges being in the Midwest.[30]

In December 1969, the new Board of Directors met with the Board of Control of Marycrest to discuss "possibilities of cooperation between the two institutions." Students from both schools had participated in music and drama activities since Marycrest was founded in 1939. In recent years the two colleges had broadened the opportunities for students at one college to take classes at the other institution. Still, in 1968, one student noted an "undercurrent of un-cooperation between the two schools."[31] Those joint board discussions about cooperation, however, had a sub-text: the merger of the two schools.

During the discussions about co-education at St. Ambrose, an alternative proposal had been to merge the two schools. In November 1968, St. Ambrose student Gene Conrad wrote in the *Paper SAC* that with rising tuition costs St. Ambrose should look at its future. It had embarked on an "aggressive expansion program" including co-education to increase enroll-

Director James Willaert, left, giving notes to the cast of The Odd Couple, *May 1969. Willaert joined the faculty in 1962 and through the 1960s directed a series of remarkable productions in the limited space of Theatre III.*

ment, but he said the best answer was to merge with Marycrest. Conrad said it was absurd to have two administrations and faculties for a student body which was "spiritually one." Rather, they should operate as one school on two campuses, and perhaps in the future, add Assumption High School. He said the bishop should "order" the merger of the two schools and that the building program at St. Ambrose should be "reevaluated" because in the future "the Assumption campus may be the answer to our needs."[32]

At his open forum in December 1968, Menke had been asked about the possibility of a merger with Marycrest. He said St. Ambrose would continue to cooperate with Marycrest and that progress was being made on more cooperation, but that the question of merger was legally and academically complex. The next month, Sister Mary Helen Rappenecker, CHM, the president of Marycrest, agreed with Menke that progress was being made. But St. Ambrose's decision to become coed had increased competition between the two schools and made cooperation more difficult. She did not rule out merger, but said she did not think it was possible in under five years.[33] So when the two boards met in December 1969, the talk was about cooperation, not merger.

While the Board of Trustees reorganized in the fall of 1969, the St. Ambrose faculty took steps to create a Faculty Association. Currently the faculty was represented on the Academic Senate which had been organized in 1967 to determine academic policy at St. Ambrose. In 1969, the faculty members of that body called for a meeting of the entire faculty to discuss the formation of an association. The suggestion had originally come from the Reverend James McGinley of the Center for Social Studies at Cambridge, Massachusetts, who had been on campus helping in preparations for a visit of the North Central Association.

At a meeting on October 9, 1969, the faculty made three decisions: an association was needed; it would be composed of the teaching faculty only; and Agnes Renner was elected as temporary chair. Over the next few weeks, a committee drew up a constitution which was adopted on November 20. The Association would "provide a forum for substantive discussion and recommendation relating to the interests and concerns" of the faculty. At the first formal meeting of the new association on January 15, 1970, Renner was elected chairman. In its first semester of operation, the Faculty Association discussed salaries, supported the revision of the academic calendar, and established a format for naming faculty members to college committees. At the end of the first year, Renner reminded the faculty that Father McGinley had said an "exclusively faculty organization" served as a "counterpart to the exclusively student organization" already on campus. He had told them that the task ahead provided "good group therapy for acquiring patience with human nature," but that "going through the maelstrom of forming a faculty organization whose voice will be accepted as that of *The Faculty*, is a fine experience."[34]

When school resumed on April 2, 1970, following the week-long Easter recess, no one could have predicted the maelstrom in which all Ambrosians would soon find themselves. The war continued in Vietnam but in late 1969, President Richard Nixon announced the beginning of the withdrawal of American troops in support of his policy of Vietnamization, the training and equipping of the South Vietnamese Army to fight its own war. He also supported the end of the draft and the creation of the draft lottery. Since those had been the major issues of the anti-war protesters, there was a marked diminishment of protest in the first months of 1970. The irenic atmosphere of the spring was reinforced by the first Earth Day celebration on April 22. The college allowed the use of classrooms for films and lectures about ecological issues.[35]

Then on April 30, the president announced that he was sending American troops into Cambodia in an attempt to attack enemy bases in that country which bordered Vietnam. Anti-war protesters who thought Nixon's actions of the previous months represented a narrowing of American involvement saw the move into Cambodia as just the opposite, a widening of the war.

On campuses across the country, the anti-war movement was reinvigorated by Nixon's action and protests erupted. On Monday, May 4, at Kent State University in Ohio, those protests became tragically violent when four students were shot and killed by members of the Ohio National Guard. That night SGA president Bill O'Connor and Joe Smith met with Monsignor Menke to discuss the possibility of closing the school on Thursday, May 7, which had already been designated National Strike Day. That night, and at a meeting with 300 students the next day, Menke said he would not close the school.

On Wednesday, May 6, students began to wear black and white arm bands and carry signs with a red fist and the word "strike." That morning saw more meetings of the SGA, an all-school meeting regarding a strike, and a peace vigil at the flag pole at 11:00. In the afternoon, by a vote of 7-6, the Academic Senate passed a motion made by Father Dawson that May 6, 7, and 8 be "open days": regular classes would be held, but there would be no penalty for nonattendance. But that action did not go as far as student leaders wanted, so at a meeting of the SGA that night, president Bill O'Connor called for a general strike on those days.

On Thursday, May 7, the day designated as National Strike Day, Father Dawson celebrated Mass at the flag pole and then led a march of some 500 students to the Federal Building in downtown Davenport. For the rest of the week, speakers came from off-campus, faculty members held forums and teach-ins, and student leaders made contacts with their counterparts on other Iowa campuses to plan a state-wide protest effort. On Sunday, May 10, St. Ambrose students stood outside local churches with leaflets about the war.

The turmoil of that week took the focus off the usual academic pursuits in the last few weeks of the semester. At an SGA meeting on Sunday night, May 10, a resolution was passed that said the college should remain open for those students who wanted to finish the last three weeks of the semester. But those who wanted to leave school early should have the option of taking their grades based on work completed on May 5. The next day the Academic Senate took up the SGA motion and passed it on a vote of 12-0, with one abstention. The Academic Senate added that students who no longer wanted to go to class but remain on campus for further protest activities or public service activities, could continue with their regular room and board accommodations. The next day the Faculty Association endorsed the action of the Academic Senate.

In a letter to parents two days later, Menke acknowledged that they had by now "undoubtedly heard" about the options given the students. He said it was difficult for "us and the general public to appreciate the depth of concern expressed by the students" as a result of the widening of the war and the deaths at Kent State. He explained the motion the Academic Senate had passed and told the parents he thought it was a "sound" decision. It would be difficult to continue classes under those conditions, Menke said, "and perhaps the activity they engage in will be of some educational value to them. At least I hope so." He assured them that the faculty would help those students who decided to leave early so no "damage" would result from their decision.

Student reaction to the strike reflected the divisions in the larger American society about the war and the protests. Writing a week after the deaths at Kent State, Rick Moskowitz, the editor of the *Paper SAC*, said the good things of the past week had outweighed the "not-so-good." It was not-so-good that the administration had been reluctant to take a stronger stand from the beginning regarding granting days off from regular classes. But it was good to observe freedom in action as students marched and spoke out. It was also good to see groups who had formerly opposed one another on issues unite in common cause.[36]

The most ardent of the strikers and protesters continued their activities for the rest of May and into the summer. The students who remained in school finished the semester and the seniors prepared for the May 31 commencement ceremony under the oaks. The strike was still on their minds, however, as a number of graduates had the red fist of the strike posters pinned to the back of their graduation gown. Iowa Congressman John Culver delivered the commencement address. He commented on how all colleges had been "deeply affected" by the recent escalation of the war which had resulted in the questioning of the "inherited assumptions of our national purposes." He praised the student critics of the war and said they could be opening doors to solve other problems, "Surely you graduates are well-prepared to affirm your idealism in a life of serious action and individual service."[37]

In July, the Faculty Association met and passed three motions. First, a

A Great and Lasting Beginning

Revs. Joseph Braig, Dawson and John Bonn celebrate liturgy before leading a march to the Federal Building in downtown Davenport.

motion was made to rule out violence or its threat as instruments of change. A second motion said the academic schedule must be maintained. Some colleges had already announced that they would call off classes two weeks before the upcoming fall election so the students could campaign. The Faculty Assembly had defeated such a motion by a vote of 33-12 in May, and Menke was certain such a request would come from the student government in the fall, and he was anxious to have a position in place when that request came. A third motion called for the reconstitution of the Board of Discipline to review the decisions of the Student Judiciary committee.[38]

The three actions by the Faculty Association were clearly prompted by the events of the previous May. They suggested that not all of the faculty supported the decisions made in May and they were laying the groundwork for administration policy in the event of further protests. The students perceived them as a step backward in the movement for students rights that had been a theme in recent years. When the students returned in September, the *Paper SAC* ran a story on the resolutions under the headline, "Faculty Acts in Haste to Block Student Rights."[39]

The Board of Directors affirmed the first two faculty resolutions and

established a committee to investigate the third to reestablish the Board of Discipline. Menke sent copies to the parents of St. Ambrose students in a letter on July 17, 1970. He told the parents that due to the "good sense and maturity of the overwhelming majority of the students," the college had not experienced any violence in the past year and that it held "firmly to the right of the students to express their views freely and to dissent in a peaceful way." He said "intellectual inquiry and reasoned discussion" were the proper instruments for change when it was needed, but that those were "imperilled by violence" or its threat. The faculty reaffirmed its belief that the "central functions of the College are learning, teaching, research and scholarship." He explained the potential for a request by students for time-off before the fall elections and said that St. Ambrose would maintain its published academic schedule for the next year.[40]

When school began in the fall, two-thirds of students who responded to a survey indicated that they had participated in the strike in some way. But they were no longer sure it had accomplished anything. Those who administered the survey commented, "Most of those who participated in the strike seemed happy that they had made a decision and stuck with it, but were becoming disillusioned with the way everything [was] going" by the fall.[41]

Not everything on campus was as serious as war and peace and the push for student rights. In 1969, the Polish-American Club was organized by John Dulin with the promise of "fun through creativity." Its constitution proclaimed it was organized by "Those of us who feel the ephemeral and aesthetic intricacies and simplicities of Polish life, customs and arts are worth parading before those who don't." The president was given broad powers, including laying taxes and declaring war. Among the duties of each member was to "worship something in his own way." Its activities included a homecoming float and a pig roast late in the second semester. Through its publication, "The Po-Am News," the group added levity to a sometimes grim campus.[42]

Another new organization had noted that the right hand was missing from the statue of St. Ambrose. The hand had been missing since the 1930s and periodically someone claimed to know what happened or to have the missing hand in his possession. Now some students formed the Committee for the Restoration and Preservation of the Right Hand of St. Ambrose. They called for a number of actions including asking Menke to "lend a hand" to their cause; that the chaplain "rightfully" take a stand on this sign of disrespect; that the faculty make "offhand" remarks to stimulate interest in their cause; and that the SGA allocate funds for the restoration of the hand and to adopt a "hands-off policy" in the future.

Their tongue-in-cheek agenda had a sly political agenda as well; they noted that the missing hand was the right hand and they called for more right-handedness on a campus with a strong left-hand presence.[43]

In the spring of 1970, just before the Kent State incident and the controversy over the strike at St. Ambrose, the college was visited by a team from the North Central Association. In July, Menke received word that accreditation of the college was continued, but because of a number of concerns, it was placed on "private probation." The report cited several areas of special concern: the curriculum, the qualifications of the faculty, faculty governance, the library, and the financial situation which it called "uncertain."[44]

One area the examiners addressed was student affairs. The 1960 report of the North Central Association had suggested that St. Ambrose appoint a dean of student affairs, which had been done with the hiring of Rogalski in 1968. They noted that in his first two years Rogalski had "worked to relax the high disciplinary nature of the program that had existed before he came." He also was working for more "effective" student representation on the committees involved in "the running of the college." They said, however, that "many" students saw his efforts as "tokenism," and that they did not want to "make the decisions" but they did want to be included in the process. The students expressed concern in several areas: class attendance rules; theology and philosophy course requirements; the dean's right of search and seizure; and college disciplinary procedures that the students thought violated due process and students' rights. Overall, the examiners said Rogalski was "well liked and respected by the student body as a whole." However, they noted the "special problems" of the forty black students on campus who expressed a "general feeling of alienation," and who "mistrusted" the dean.[45]

There was a long-time involvement by Ambrosians in the issue of civil rights and racial discrimination. But before the mid-1960s, activity by the students of the O'Connors, the League for Social Justice, the two NAACP chapters at St. Ambrose, and the students who traveled to Selma with Father Duncan, focused on the larger community. Now the focus was turned inward to racial issues on campus.

There had been black students at St. Ambrose since at least the 1930s, the first probably being Charles Toney who came to school in 1932, but left after one year to find work. That there were so few blacks at St. Ambrose was probably because the number of blacks in Davenport was small and most of those were not Catholic. When James Collins, an African-American from Rock Island entered in 1964, he was one of only three black students.[46] The next year, James Grayson, an African-American from Washington, D.C., which was a predominantly black community, confessed nervousness at coming to the nearly all-white St. Ambrose. By 1970, the number of black students had risen to about forty.

In the same half-decade, American blacks had moved from the peaceful

A Great and Lasting Beginning

confrontation with legal and social segregation exemplified by Dr. Martin Luther King, Jr., to a more aggressive, black power approach. One consequence of this was a different kind of segregation at St. Ambrose where black students accused whites of claiming "squatter's rights" on parts of the union and whites said blacks were a "tightly organized clique" in their own corner of the union. In the fall of 1969, the situation had grown so tense that there was a call for a forum on black/white issues.[47]

At the same time black students made demands on the institution that included more scholarships for African-American students, a committee to investigate racism on campus, recruitment of black professors and staff, and an "Afro-House" on campus. In response, the SGA appropriated $1,000 to support some black programing, but the African-American students wanted more. The college gave the students a house on Scott Street for use as a Black Student Union but this did little to ease the tensions. The next fall, Mike Grant, a leader of the African-American group on campus said at St. Ambrose there must be "fair play and respect for other students." He said whites had to face the "absurdity of white supremacy." Being black or white did not make one good, instead goodness came when an individual could "face his situation realistically, face his fellow man with a spirit of equality, and face himself honestly."[48]

While Ambrosians discussed how to bring white and black students together, the Board of Directors discussed a report by Dr. Charles E. Ford of the Center for Christian Education in St. Louis, concerning cooperation between St. Ambrose and Marycrest. Ford had investigated the possibilities for coordinating instruction, the libraries, registration procedures, and business services. He suggested immediate short-term planning for the 1970-1971 year and long-term planning for the year beginning in September 1971. Ford urged both schools to determine how "strengths and competencies of the faculty members could be more fully realized with a more unified approach to academic planning." The St. Ambrose Board approved the report and urged that each department of both colleges "implement their activities toward cooperation."[49]

The Ford report recommended more cooperation and the St. Ambrose Board urged cooperation, a position they had held for several years. But at Marycrest, a new president wanted more than cooperation. On June 18, 1970, Dr. Louis C. Vaccaro was named the president of Marycrest College. Vaccaro praised Marycrest as a "fine women's college" and said he was pleased that it had recently become co-educational. He also said he was "excited" by the possibilities for cooperation between Marycrest, St. Ambrose, and Augustana Colleges and area junior colleges.[50]

Through the summer and fall, Menke and Vaccaro met to discuss cooperation, and some of the academic departments of the two schools met to try to develop cooperative curricula. But from the standpoint of Marycrest, the Ambrosians were moving too slowly. In a November 1 memo, Sister Elizabeth Anne Schneider, CHM, the vice president of academic affairs at Marycrest, told Vaccaro that all contacts with St. Ambrose were initiated by Marycrest and a large number of the faculty were "beginning to question the need and the desirability of further insistence on cooperation when it seems one-sided and really not to our advantage." She added that the process was damaging Marycrest by "seeking cooperation where we are not

wanted." To remedy that, she said "some definite statement by the St. Ambrose administration should be made to St. Ambrose chairmen and publicized on the Marycrest campus."[51]

Vaccaro agreed and wrote the boards of both colleges to state that the "grass roots" method of cooperation recommended by the Ford report was "too slow" and the project was "too important to rely on this approach." He cited the "fear, suspicion, uncertainty, and mistrust among faculties, departments and administrators" that made cooperation difficult, "if not impossible to achieve." Vaccaro recommended a single Board of Trustees and some sort of confederation of the two schools with a central administration, amalgamation of support services, and the development of a single faculty. He also recommended a sub-committee made up of members of both boards to work out a merger of the two schools.[52]

The two boards met in a joint meeting on December 7, 1970, the feast of St. Ambrose, where Vaccaro presented the proposals from his earlier memo. He said his proposed "umbrella university" would save money, attract students, and be supported by the Quad-City community. He believed such a plan could be in effect by September 1, 1971, just ten months away. The meeting recessed while each board met separately to discuss the proposal. When they reconvened, Sister Bernadine Pieper, CHM, moved to form a sub-committee consisting of the presidents, academic deans, and financial officers from each school to study the feasability of a merger; Menke seconded the motion and it was unanimously approved. The boards also agreed to a common calender where the first semester ended before Christmas, the continuation of the ability of students from one campus to enroll on the other, the continued discussions between academic departments, and to work to provide a shuttle service between the campuses.[53]

When the students returned in September 1970, Menke welcomed them to campus and told them that a college education was not essential to a good life but it could "contribute a great deal to make life more interesting and give you a much greater capacity for good if it is properly pursued." He noted the student concern for "human freedom," and he addressed the issue of drugs and alcohol. While human slavery had been abolished a century before, the student who did not have the courage to face life and resorted to drugs or alcohol and became a slave to them was not free. The student who did not have the courage to follow his own convictions for fear of what others would say was not free: "genuine freedom involved a great sense of responsibility and courage." Menke said St. Ambrose wanted them to be concerned about the problems of society and to become interested citizens, but to do that they must have the capacity to work with others.[54]

In the same issue of the *Paper SAC* that Menke published his welcome, the new editor, Joe Smith, also welcomed the new students to St. Ambrose, "Home of the bees, the oaks, and other such traditions, questionable and otherwise." The students were "slowly" discarding some of those traditions: the "parental attitude of the administration toward the student body and the related police powers of the Dean of Students, the traditionally passive role of the student, the place of intercollegiate athletics at St. Ambrose, and finally, the raa-raa-sis-boom-baa beer-chugging stereotype of student that is a carry over from the Ambrose of the fifties." Smith mentioned one other tradition he hoped the college would never lose: its friendliness. As a mark of that he pointed out that there would no longer be freshman initiation, so the freshmen were welcome, "no strings attached."[55]

Menke had eliminated initiation in part because of the presence of women on campus. Its elimination was one of the few things upon which the president and the editor of the student newspaper agreed. In their messages of welcome, Menke and Smith had both mentioned the necessity of working together for the benefit of the college, but each had a different understanding of what that meant. Smith meant that the students should work together to challenge the administration and its policies and hopefully bend the school to a form designed by the students. Menke meant that all segments of the college community should work together to effect change where it was appropriate, but to do so in ways that would not destroy the basic fabric of the institution and its heritage. In his position as editor, Smith, and his associate editor Randy Richards, used the *Paper SAC* to continue to push for student rights, a position both had advocated for the previous two years. But now the editorials and articles were increasingly more strident and the characterization of the people and situations on campus grew more acerbic.

The strike the previous May had created tensions between the administration and the students which were exacerbated on May 26, 1970, when two students on campus and two off-campus students were arrested by the Scott County Sheriff for the possession and sale of drugs. St. Ambrose had promulgated a drug policy in May 1968 which said that the student use, distribution, or sale of drugs was a matter of concern to the college, whether it occurred on or off campus. Any such involvement, "especially distribution or sale" could result in suspension or expulsion from the college. Thus whatever civil laws they may have broken, they were clearly in violation of campus policy. During the summer, civil charges against two of them were reduced, but Carmichael Peters and Vincent Tokatlian were convicted and sentenced to two years in prison. Both appealed their convictions to the Iowa Supreme Court.[56]

In the fall of 1970, Peters petitioned the Student Judiciary Board (J-Board) to be readmitted to school that semester so he could complete his course work and graduate. Peters denied the charges against him and presented a number of character witnesses, including several members of the faculty. All argued that it would benefit Peters and the school to allow him to finish and graduate. Witnesses also warned that refusing to admit Peters, who was black, would "anger the black communities of St. Ambrose and Davenport." After a hearing on October 12, the J-Board voted to readmit Peters. The situation became more contentious when Menke asked the J-Board to reconsider its decision and to rule on whether Peters had violated the college rules regarding drugs. At this meeting the J-Board found him guilty of violating the rules, but refused to invoke the penalty and stated again that he be readmitted.[57] Menke took the case to the Administrative Council which passed a motion by Rogalski that Peters be readmitted for the current semester to complete his graduation requirements, that he be under the "strictest form of disciplinary probation" under the "jurisdiction of the Dean of Students."[58]

The J-Board operated as a panel of judges among whose powers was the ability to issue search warrants for rooms on campus. At a meeting in late fall, Rogalski removed the power to issue search warrants from the J-Board and reserved it to himself. In an editorial headlined, "Dean's Hand Quicker Than Your Eye," Joe Smith asked why it had been done. He said the move seemed to say that the students were incapable of handling responsibility. And he asked why the dean, who had been trying to rid himself of police powers, had taken this one onto himself.[59]

In January, the J-Board used the precedent of having admitted Peters and voted to readmit Tokatlian. In response Menke overruled the board, denied admission to Tokatlian, and directed Rogalski to dissolve the all-student judiciary board and reconstitute it with students, faculty, and administrators. Two days later, Menke announced he still would not allow Tokatlian to register, but that he would not dissolve the J-Board.[60]

Menke attended an SGA meeting where he defended his recent decisions. He said he had acted in the best interests of the college and that he had a responsibility to keep a student out who had been convicted of a criminal act. He urged the students to "condemn the use of drugs as a cop out," uphold state liquor laws, and avoid vulgarity in their dealings with one another. After Menke's presentation, students who felt that student justice was "at best an illusion" created by Menke's office, failed by a vote of 9-7 in their effort to pass a motion to censure Menke.[61]

In the *Paper SAC*, Randy Richards called Menke's actions "dangerous" and said they could "prove destructive unless students get tough about their rights." Richards contended that Menke dismissed Tokatlian because he did not like him. The next week the SGA voted 12-8 to censure Menke, but a motion calling for his resignation failed.[62]

Smith and Richards had gone too far and the Publications Board ordered Smith to print a retraction. Smith conceded that he had intended to be "nasty but not false." Regarding the search warrants, he now knew that the dean did not take them for himself, he already had the power but had delegated it to the J-Board that year on an experimental basis. He said that neither Rogalski nor the resident advisors in the dormitories had violated the SGA constitution or the by-laws of the J-Board. Smith's retraction, however, still took a swipe at Rogalski who he said was a "bad dean" because he was a "big brother," doing things for the students that they could do for themselves.[63]

The recent events brought the issue of drug abuse on campus into the open. Rogalski discussed the drug problem at a February 1971 meeting of the SGA where he characterized the situation as "close to desperate." He warned that the school was "possibly open to more busts" by the local police. He outlined a program that he hoped would prevent such action. First he established a drug information center in the library containing reports about drugs and their abuse. Second, he offered a period of amnesty for students who used drugs during which time they could seek help with no punitive consequences by the school. Third was a series of "stringent penalties" for students who continued to use drugs.[64]

At the same meeting, Rogalski and the students discussed the "experimental" open dorm policy that had been in place. In January 1970, he had suggested that dorm hours be eliminated. In the fall the SGA and the Dorm Council discussed the issue and the development of procedures for room visitations. At a meeting in October, the SGA passed a number of bills, including one that called for the elimination of freshmen hours. Now Rogalski said the "experiment" was being evaluated to determine if it was feasible to continue.[65] Over the next few years, the issue of dormitory

Dean Rogalski and Mark Yanello, '72.

visitation policies would occupy the dean, the students, the president, and the Board of Directors.

After ten years as hostess in the Bee Hive, Mrs. Salsbury was asked to give her views about the current campus situation. She said she liked to take care of all aspects of life in the Bee Hive. That often meant listening to the students, to be their friend, not their mother, "I like to help any student save face if possible." One of her jobs was to page students for phone calls, and she was savvy to their tricks and could easily spot prank calls and pages. Over the past decade she said the students had become more independent, "They probably would like to dispense with all authority and do as they please." She made it clear, however, that in the Bee Hive, "We still maintain rules. There is no smoking, eating or drinking in the Quiet Room. The furniture stays put. And we don't throw things." Although she admitted they were more in vogue, she did not allow four letter words. Her goal was to follow the catalogue description "to produce Christian, cultured men and women at St. Ambrose. I'll continue to try to create order out of chaos. Some days it's a draw."[66]

During those months the sidewalk superintendents were busy overseeing the construction of the new fine arts building. Construction had begun in the fall of 1968 with the hope it would be completed by the fall of 1969. But labor strikes and bad weather delayed construction. Students who walked to the west side of campus to view the progress could be heard saying, "It doesn't look any different than it did a month ago." The building was finally finished in the spring of 1971 and the Music, Art, Speech, Drama, Mass Communications, and Engineering departments moved in.

The building was dedicated the weekend of May 15-16, 1971, with recitals by Roger Ezell, a 1965 graduate, and Lewis Hoy, artist-in-residence at St. Ambrose; a dramatic evening with the actors Ossie Davis and Ruby Dee; and a performance of Mozart's *Mass in C Minor*, with soloists that included Davenport native Helen Spaeth Vanni, from the company of the Metropolitan Opera, and Thomas Fitzpatrick, a 1951 graduate who had studied in Europe on a Fulbright Scholarship. With the opening of the Galvin Fine Arts Center, the third of Menke's planned four buildings was complete. Now only the proposed physical education building remained to be built.[67]

The merger feasability committee met through December and January, preparing for a January 20, 1971, meeting. A week before, both faculties met at St. Ambrose to hear presentations from Menke and Vaccaro. Menke told them that there were two reasons for the merger: First, local businessmen thought the two schools should combine since they were both Catholic; second, a merger could save a considerable amount of money, even though, "mergers are notorious for not saving money." He stated one major problem as the relationship of the diocese with the Sisters of Humility. Vaccaro told the faculties that he had suggested the merger and he wanted it to move quickly, a theme Vaccaro would state repeatedly in the months ahead. The two presidents described the proposed structure of the merged school and took questions from the floor. There were questions about tenure, the number of administrators in the new school, maintenance of the buildings, and whether the merger would really save money. Father McMahan expressed caution and said that the two schools could be merged, but it must be done with "compassion and candor." Sister Elizabeth Anne Schneider said although she hated to see some of the traditions of the two schools disappear, she thought the proposed merger was "exciting."[68] McMahan's and Schneider's views represented many on the two campuses. Both campuses had their share of merger proponents and opponents, but in the months ahead, it would be the Ambrosians who were more cautious.

The sisters were reportedly "generally in favor" of the merger, although some had reservations about the financial aspects; they wondered what voice they would have in the new school; and whether it would be a "vital Christian school." The most "pressing problem" they raised was the retirement fund for the sisters which would prove to be one of their major concerns throughout the merger talks. They said if those questions were not answered adequately, they would be opposed to the merger. Nevertheless, the Marycrest campus was generally more enthusiastic about the merger than the Ambrosians.

The two boards and faculty and student representatives met on January 20, 1971. The students reported that their colleagues on both campuses were in favor of the merger. Schneider reported that the Marycrest faculty who responded to a poll were in complete support of the merger and she presented the opinions of the sisters. Father Hratz said the priests thought the time line was "hasty and premature," and they were generally pessimistic about the merger, especially the "questionable" idea that a merger would solve the financial problems of both schools. St. Ambrose art Professor John Schmits said the faculty was neither overwhelmingly in favor of nor opposed to the merger, but they wanted more details. With that, Bishop O'Keefe thanked the faculty and students and dismissed them from the meeting.[69]

Next, the feasability committee presented its report that a new institution governed by an "Umbrella Board" would achieve three goals: a "superior" academic program; immediate and long-range financial savings; and an institution "more immediately identifiable with the city of Davenport" that would attract more students and gain a "national reputation." In this formulation for the short-term, both college boards would continue to exist and own the property of its college. It addressed the legal questions involved, discussed possible procedures for merging academic departments, and discussed questions of tenure of the faculty and accreditation of the new institution.

Thomas Grady, business manager at St. Ambrose, Edward Henkhaus, business manager at Marycrest, and John Stemlar an accountant from a local firm, presented a financial report. Their statistics showed that St. Ambrose had a total of 1,385 full-time and part-time students; eighty full-time and thirty-four part-time faculty; a 68 percent dormitory occupancy rate; a fee of $2,425 in tuition, room, and board for the current year; and

had a deficit from annual operation in the past year of $220,000. Marycrest had 1,035 students; forty-nine full-time and thirty-two part-time faculty; 84 percent occupancy rate; $2,160 in costs; and a deficit of $110,000 in the previous year. The net worth including properties and investments of St. Ambrose was some $7 million more than Marycrest, but St. Ambrose had $2.6 million in long-term debt and was about to take on another $1 million in debt to finance the current building projects. Marycrest had an outstanding debt of only $224,000. Based on their analysis, the group recommended that the boards should "probably" approve the merger.[70]

Stemlar signed the feasibility document, but in a private letter to Menke, O'Keefe, and Grady two days before the meeting, he said he wanted to "communicate a confidential word of caution about the merger." He noted a "certain urgency" to create the new institution and said that while the merger "may" benefit both schools, he expressed concern that the "umbrella arrangement" could be "detrimental" to St. Ambrose and the new institution. Given St. Ambrose's "uncovered debt" and the operating deficit at Marycrest, Stemlar said the merger should proceed only after all the specifics, including retention of property rights and debt assumption, had been examined.[71] Stemlar, however, did not raise those objections at the meeting.

Following the report, the boards engaged in a long discussion and then approved a motion by John Nagle, the Marycrest attorney, to "accept the feasibility study as a basis for proceeding along general lines." In further discussion, Vaccaro called for a "decision at once" and cited the "anemic and dismal future for both colleges" if the merger did not take place. Schneider said the merger was feasible but steps needed to be taken, including the "directed transfer" of academic departments. Vaccaro warned that if the merger did not take place, Marycrest would become competitive with St. Ambrose for recruiting, fund raising, athletics, and cultural events and he said "certain prominent individuals in the community did not like the present local college competitiveness." Sister Bernadine Pieper said the financial situation could not be rushed, especially the retirement benefits for the sisters, now called the "Peoples' Debt." This money amounted to $1.6 million and stemmed from their custom of "reinvesting part of their salaries in Marycrest, thus accounting for the fact that it now had little debt."

Following a lunch break and more discussion, the Reverend Monsignor Thomas Feeney moved, "That the combined Boards of Marycrest College and St. Ambrose College hereby commit ourselves to a merger of the two institutions and to immediately implement this by a working agreement which would lead to the formation of a new corporate entity by July 1, 1972." The motion carried.[72]

In a press release to announce the agreement, Vaccaro said the boards wanted to make it "very clear that the prime reason for the merger [was] to develop an exciting, growing Christian institution of higher education in the Quad-City area. Any financial considerations of the plan were second to that." Joe Smith wrote in the *Paper SAC* that the merger appeared "inevitable," but that it was at best "a gamble." He said one positive aspect was the opportunity for students to demand curriculum reform and the strengthening of weak departments. SGA president Bill O'Connor urged the students to be involved in merger activities and suggested the formation of an Inter-College Council for that purpose.[73]

A Great and Lasting Beginning

While the members of the various committees dealing with the merger met, another group was meeting to address the criticisms the North Central examiners had made about the curriculum. The current curriculum said that of the 128 hours necessary for graduation, sixty-three were required of all students. The students also had to complete the required courses in a major and also have a minor. The examiners said there was "some rigidity" because the courses taken in the first two years were prescribed and there were few opportunities for the student to explore other areas of study.

Menke had appointed philosophy Professor Joseph McCaffrey to chair a committee consisting of students Carol Lindhom and Michael Linder and faculty members Bertand Miller, physics, Father Smith, history, and Sister Annette Walters, psychology. The committee proposed a set of graduation requirements that preserved the liberal arts core, but gave the student much more freedom in course selection. The committee reorganized the academic structure and created five divisions: science and mathematics, social sciences, professional studies and community services, humanities, and fine and applied arts. Now forty-two hours of general degree requirements had to be met by choosing twelve hours from the division of humanities, twelve from science and mathematics, twelve from social science, and six from fine and applied arts. The number of hours in a student's major could range from twenty-four to forty-two hours. The committee concluded its report by stating that their recommendations were not intended to "abolish, destroy, cripple, or otherwise to endanger the job, Department, or Division of any person or program" at St. Ambrose.[74]

The intent may not have been to abolish or destroy a department, but that was not the perception by some. When McCaffrey presented the report in May, there was reaction from all segments of the campus community. Some supported it as a logical next step in the movement for more independence for students. But some faculty feared that students would avoid their courses which had formerly been required, because they were thought to be unimportant, or too difficult, or were taught by an unpopular or less than competent professor.

But the greatest criticism came in the area of theology. For decades all Catholic students had been required to take one hour of religion every semester. A few years before the students had made their feelings known about those courses; one had said they were "short on insight and long on rigoristic moralism."[75] There had already been some revision, but all Catholic students were still required to take eight hours of theology. The proposed revision put philosophy, theology, and religious students in the Division of Humanities. Since the graduation requirement was for twelve hours in that division, it was possible for a student to choose from the other departments in the division, English and modern and classical languages, and take no philosophy or theology at all.

As a consequence of those objections, the committee revised its proposal. Now there would be six divisions. Philosophy and theology were removed from humanities and joined in a new Division of Theology and Philosophy. Now the student had to choose nine hours from languages and literature, social sciences, and theology and philosophy; eight hours from natural science and mathematics; and six hours from the Division of Arts and/or the Department of Physical Education.[76]

That version was presented to the Academic Senate at a meeting on October 10, 1971 which voted 10-3 to accept the committee report. Next,

the proposal went to the Board of Directors for their approval. O'Keefe was clear about his opinion: he favored retaining the theology requirement. As a "Catholic diocesan college, St. Ambrose owes it not only to the students but to the clergy and people who have supported" it to continue the requirement. Vatican II had called on lay people to play "an increasingly important role in the church," and O'Keefe said colleges like St. Ambrose should provide the education necessary for such leadership. O'Keefe said he was also concerned about the impact the proposed curriculum would have on the seminary. Writing Menke on October 19, he said he resented the action of the Senate and said he would oppose the curriculum changes if it came to a vote of the board at its meeting on October 28. At that meeting, the Board of Directors approved the committee proposal with the proviso that "six hours of theology be required by all students."[77]

Menke explained to the Academic Senate that the board thought that keeping the theology requirement was consistent with the philosophy and goals of the college as stated in the catalogue. The Academic Senate said the Board of Directors had overstepped their authority by requiring six hours of theology. Father Smith was opposed to theology as a requirement, indicating that at a time the college was initiating a curriculum with a great deal of freedom, it was counterproductive to require specific courses. A motion to accept the board's action was defeated 8-7; a motion to ask the board to reconsider its action was carried 11-3.[78]

On December 3, the Board of Directors did reconsider its action of October 28 and it passed the proposed curriculum without the specific theology requirement. That was not what O'Keefe wanted, but he put the best face on it. He wrote the priests of the diocese to explain the new curriculum, especially the new theology and philosophy requirements. He reminded them that while Catholic students had always been required to take religion or theology, non-Catholic students were never required to do so. Now all students were required to take nine hours in the new Division of Theology and Philosophy. O'Keefe also said those Catholic students who did not want to take theology would "no longer need to resort to the expedient of declaring themselves not Catholic." It would be up to the faculty advisors to try to get students to enroll in theology classes and it would be "necessary for the Administration of the college to stress the importance of Theology in achieving the goals of a Catholic College."[79]

The struggle within the faculty and between the faculty and the board brought together several issues then current in Catholic higher education. One was the definition of what constituted a Catholic college. Discussion on that subject had been going on at St. Ambrose since the 1930s when philosophy was seen as the defining discipline. In the 1960s, it had become theology, and the attempts to reform the Sacred Doctrine department were a mark of that change. For O'Keefe and others, it was unimaginable that a college could be called Catholic which did not include the study of theology. Others emphasized that how the Christian life was lived out and proclaimed was equally important, or more important, than classroom work. How much freedom should the students have? That was expressed well by Terry Shelton, editor of the *Paper SAC* and a member of the Academic Senate, who wrote it was "narrow" to presume that six hours of theology would help make St. Ambrose more Christian. He continued, "Perhaps it is time, too, that the school of St. Ambrose assume a true Christian posture in the Davenport community as witnessed by faculty, students and the

The food line in the new South Hall.

administration. If there is to be an education to Christ it will be found in the involvement of a life dedicated and unafraid to speak out for peace against injustices in the area. Let Ambrose make that involvement its only 'requirement.'"[80]

For the faculty, a central question in this struggle was: Who had responsibility for the curriculum? The board seemed content to allow the faculty to set the curriculum except in cases where they perceived the proposed curriculum was contrary to the goals and objectives of the college. But at St. Ambrose, the matter was not clear. The North Central team said in its 1970 review that the power to determine the curriculum had never been formally delegated to the faculty by the board. So in part because of the struggle over the theology requirement, and in part because of the recommendation of the North Central Association, in November 1973, the board enacted "The Faculty Primacy Statement." By this the board delegated to the faculty the "primary responsibility for curriculum, educational policy, graduation requirements, and faculty status," reserving to itself the power of review to be exercised "adversely only in exceptional circumstances, and for reasons communicated to the faculty."[81]

In the fall of 1971, while the merger committees worked and while the faculty discussed the new curriculum and the theology requirement, the students settled into college life. Four hundred of those who responded to a poll that indicated 77 percent had complete satisfaction or satisfaction with St. Ambrose; 80 percent considered the faculty responsive to student needs in the classroom; 67 percent said the dean handled student problems adequately; and the same percentage said those policies were fair. Reflecting the controversy about the curriculum revision, 82 percent said there were too many required courses, and 35 percent said St. Ambrose was oriented too much to one field of student and 86 percent of those said that field was business. Forty percent said in spite of the SGA and the presence of students on committees, they did not think the students had enough voice in decision-making. Only 29 percent said they belonged to an organization of any kind on campus. And for a Catholic college debating requiring the study of theology, only 63 percent of students identified themselves as Catholic; 60 percent of the freshmen who responded said they attended religious services "regularly"; that percentage fell to 43 percent for seniors.[82]

A Great and Lasting Beginning

The decision to merge made in January 1971 resulted in meetings: meetings of the faculties of the academic departments to try and decide how to combine faculty, courses, and office space; meetings of administrators to discuss the administrative structure of the new institution; meetings of student groups pressing to be involved in all decisions; meetings of the priests at St. Ambrose and the sisters at Marycrest to try to understand their unique positions in the current and proposed new institution; and meetings of the two Boards of Directors and the board merger committee.

There was still uncertainty about the merger on the part of the faculties. In March Hratz took a poll of the priests who thought the new institution should be related to the diocese and nearly all of them (sixteen of eighteen polled) said the merged institution should be identified as Catholic. They did not think a cleric needed to be president. They were evenly divided on whether the July 1, 1972, deadline could be met. Ten of them thought the merger was proceeding too rapidly, eight disagreed, which was the same ratio as the St. Ambrose faculty as a whole. They all agreed that the Peoples' Debt should not be placed on the new institution but that all pre-merger debts should be laid on the present corporations. Half of the eighteen polled agreed with the Marycrest sisters that they were not being "welcomed enthusiastically" by the St. Ambrose priests.[83]

In mid-March there was a joint meeting of the priests and sisters. They discussed the nature of the new institution and noted the opinion of the priests that it should be related to the diocese, with the bishop and vicar general on the board. When asked why, the priests cited the support of the people and priests of the diocese over the years and they felt certain such affiliation would be necessary for that support to continue. After discussion, the two groups agreed on a definition of the new school as "a new private, independent, church-related institution of higher education."

Most of the meeting, however, concerned the Peoples' Debt. The Marycrest Board of Directors had recognized the concept and the St. Ambrose board was studying it. Many of the priests raised the issue of their contributed services, taking a priest's lower salary because St. Ambrose was a diocesan institution and they had been assigned to the faculty by the bishop. Eleven of sixteen priests said if there were no relationship to the diocese in the new institution, they would no longer agree to contributed services.[84] But some of the sisters made it clear that they would not stay in the new institution if the matter of the Peoples' Debt was not settled.[85] But the Peoples' Debt was only one issue that faced the boards and committees and if not everyone was pleased with the pace at which the discussions were proceeding, at the end of April, Menke could say, "Definite headway is being made. I think right now we are skirting the edges to nailing this thing down."[86]

Menke was too optimistic, however, and at a meeting in early July it became clear that the two sides were still far apart on the important financial issue, especially the Peoples' Debt. As the discussion continued, a "basic question" emerged: Could the merger occur and could the original July 1, 1972, date be met? A motion was passed by a vote of 6-1 with three not voting, to move the effective date to July 1, 1973. There were still many questions about the merging of academic departments, merging the admissions offices of the two schools, and a proposed fund drive by Marycrest to build a new nursing building. But the finances remained the thorniest problem. At the end of the meeting, Robert Motto moved and Menke seconded a motion that the "Marycrest Board will study the financial obligations toward the Sisters of Humility in regard to payment of retirement funds." The motion carried 5-0 with three abstentions. One other item of business saw the formation of a committee to select a name for the new school.[87]

A new name would not be necessary if the merger could not be effected, and by the fall it was no closer than it had been in July. At a meeting on October 23, 1971, it was decided to accept an offer from the Danforth Foundation to study the various merger proposals. There was also a discussion of the continuing problem of cooperation between the academic departments of the two schools. The meeting ended by passing a motion proposed by Pieper that "the two boards of trustees reaffirm their commitment to work toward the merger . . . and . . . that the division and department chairmen and administrators be informed that cooperation must continue . . . as a necessary step toward merger."[88]

Sister Mary Jeanne Finske, CSC, the academic dean at St. Mary's College, Notre Dame, Indiana, and the Reverend William Kelly, SJ, the executive director of United Colleges of San Antonio, came to Davenport in November and December 1971 and visited with officials from both campuses. They noted that the merger was viewed differently by the "sponsoring bodies of the two institutions." The priests at St. Ambrose viewed it as a way to increase enrollment and that the merger was not the "beginning of a new venture but rather a continuation of what St. Ambrose [had] been." The academic departments at St. Ambrose were not "willingly" moving toward cooperation, and the St. Ambrose faculty as a whole thought the Marycrest faculty would have "difficulty fitting" into the St. Ambrose pattern of education. The sisters were willing to accept the academic aspect of the merger and they believed their presence would complement education at St. Ambrose. But many of them saw the merger as "an absorption by St. Ambrose of a work the Congregation has established at the cost of personal sacrifice over many years."

Moreover, "anxieties [had] developed on both sides" which gave rise to rumors; differences in philosophy "loom as insurmountable obstacles"; "tensions of women's liberation and male or female 'chauvinism' become intermingled" with the legitimate questions about the merger. Those issues confused the goals for the merger and they reminded all parties that the economic goal was the "prevailing and precipitating element of any merger discussion. If there were no economic crisis, there would be no thought of merger." Both schools were under economic pressures, but Kelly thought the St. Ambrose debt was "not unmanageable." In accepting responsibility for the Peoples' Debt, the Marycrest board had put itself in "relatively the same" economic position as St. Ambrose. In conclusion, no one could predict "that a merger will be the salvation of these institutions," but they could hope that the foundation of a viable institution could be laid.[89]

At the same time as the Danforth visitors were on campus, a subcommittee worked to reconcile differences and produce a merger agreement. The subcommittee met with the various groups from each campus and with Finske and Kelly. One of the most important considerations was that the new institution operate in the black and after several drafts of the agreement, the subcommittee reported that "given certain conditions, the newly-merged institution can indeed operate in the black." But they said it would work "only if a true sprit of Christian charity and good will prevails during all phases of the merger." They presented their report at a meeting of the boards on March 11, 1972.[90]

At that meeting the joint boards moved through the merger document point by point, making many amendments. When that process was complete and they had agreed on the amended document, it was moved and seconded that "in light of the subcommittee's report . . . the joint boards approve the merger of St. Ambrose and Marycrest

Ambrosians and Cresters gather to witness the signing of the merger documents. At the table from the left: Dr. Louis Vaccaro, Marycrest president; Sister Bernadine Pieper, CHM, chair, Marycrest Board of Trustees; Mr. John Nagle, Marycrest; Bishop Gerald O'Keefe, chair, St. Ambrose Board of Directors; Msgr. Sebastian Menke, St. Ambrose president.

several names that included Midwest or Midwestern. Another popular name was Newman College for the English nineteenth-century Cardinal John Henry Newman. When the new board met on May 24, five names were presented for discussion: Mid America, Davenport, Newman, Quad City, and LeClaire; and the board added two other names, Maram and Christus. The board members voted by a large margin to choose Newman College.[93]

colleges so that the new institution . . . can be operative by September 1, 1973; this recommendation subject to the ratification of St. Ambrose Board of Trustees and by the Marycrest Board of Trustees." The vote was 6-0 in favor, with six abstentions, and three absent. With the vote taken, each board met separately to decide whether to accept the merger. When they reconvened, each board chairman announced that their board agreed to the merger. The date of March 23, 1972, was chosen for a formal signing ceremony.[91]

Copies of the merger document were signed on each campus using pens from each college. Bishop O'Keefe, chairman of the St. Ambrose board, and Sister Bernadine Pieper, chairman of the Marycrest board, issued a joint statement that emphasized the relationship of St. Ambrose and the Sisters of Humility that went back to 1885 when the first sisters came to St. Ambrose as housekeepers, through to the founding of Marycrest, to the present moment. They said much remained to be done, "and it would be a disservice to lead you to expect any magical, simple panacea to the problems" ahead. Among the immediate steps were the naming of a new Board of Regents, the selection of a new name, beginning the process to select a new president, and the development of a new, all-college senate. The official timetable was to have the new board in place and a name selected by June. Vaccaro had already announced he would leave Davenport in the summer, so the search process for a new president would also begin then. In addition, all the other officers of the new institution would have to be named.[92]

The subcommittee to select a name circulated a questionnaire on both campuses to ask for suggestions on what to call the new school. By early May they had gathered 154 suggestions, from All Saints College through Woksape College. The most common name suggested was the University of Davenport or Davenport University, followed by some combination of St. Ambrose and Marycrest, including Amcrest and the College of Ambrose and Mary. Other frequent suggestions included Antoine LeClaire or some combination that included his name, John Deere Catholic University, and

The college bookstore wasted no time in ordering sweatshirts, beer mugs, pens and pencils, notebooks, and all the merchandise necessary to identify the new college. Long-time Ambrosians and Cresters regretted losing their historic names. But others immediately began to suggest nicknames for the new school. Coach Leo Kilfoy suggested it be the Saints, which he said would be an "appropriate name for a Catholic school, it has a good Dixie Land rhythm that could be easily adapted." John Dooley, a 1972 alumnus, wrote that Bees was no longer appropriate since Cardinal Newman did not have bees swarming around his mouth. Dooley suggested the Gnus: "The *Newman Gnus*. Golly what a ring it has!" He said the African gnu could be the mascot, the newspaper could be the *Newman Gnus*, and basketball fans could cheer, "Let's go Gnu school." He hoped others would get on the "gnu bandwagon."[94]

As classes began at St. Ambrose and Marycrest in the fall of 1972, Newman College was still a long way from realization. The search for a new president proceeded, and by November, had narrowed to three candidates. But the two issues that had been nagging problems during two years of discussions remained: cooperation between the officers and faculty of both institutions and the financial question.

Sister Cathleen Real, CHM, who became president of Marycrest after Vaccaro left, told the Newman Board of Regents that during her four months in office it was "increasingly clear" that the administrators of the two schools approached problems in "dissimilar ways." She said in some way this was healthy but in budgetary and personnel questions it was a handicap. She said the two presidents were "having greater difficulty" in determining procedures and "arriving at mutually satisfactory decisions." She suggested the immediate appointment of a person responsible to the board and she said they could not wait for the new president to be named.[95]

A financial report indicated that the new college would have problems from the moment it started operation. The income estimate of the budget was "optimistic" with no provision for funding the $1 million due the Sisters of Humility for the Peoples' Debt. The estimate was that with available assets, "Newman College would have an operating life of eighteen months." If St. Ambrose and Marycrest were "viable institutions," the report said, it seemed "foolish to proceed with a merger" with "only a limited assurance of viability." The choice was to increase income or reduce expenditures. The report concluded that Newman College could be "made financially viable, but the level of sacrifice has to be far higher than has been proposed thus far."[96]

The Board of Regents discussed those issues at length in a meeting in late December 1972. The St. Ambrose members indicated they favored continuation of the merger if it was fiscally feasible and academically sound. The Marycrest members cited the decision-making process as a "major problem." After discussion, St. Ambrose board member John Figge asked if the board felt it could accomplish financial stability and academic excellence for Newman College based on the projected 1973-1974 budget. Four responded yes, but nine said no. There was then a formal ballot taken to determine the "intent of the individual Board members concerning their willingness to proceed with discussion on the merger." Once again, four said they would proceed, but nine said they would not. The board members decided to make no public statement and to meet again on January 5.[97]

Menke wrote Bishop O'Keefe on December 27 that he thought all were agreed that "some final decision" regarding the merger would take place at the meeting of the Board of Regents scheduled for January 5. He suggested that the St. Ambrose board meet for lunch at noon that day to determine a course of action. He told the bishop there would be new financial information.[98]

O'Keefe agreed that the meeting should take place, although he would be unable to attend. But he told Menke that he would agree with whatever decision the St. Ambrose board made about the merger. If it went ahead, he said he would try to "bring about more harmony. We simply can not continue with the present distrust among us." If the merger was to be discontinued, "It must be done soon." If it was cancelled, "We have to face our own problems which are not financial problems only." Enrollment had dropped for a number of reasons, but "Something is wrong and it must be remedied fast." He listed a number of reasons of concern about the "reputation of the college." He wondered if

the students were ready to accept the "new permissiveness" they had been given, and from what he had read in the *Paper SAC*, "I would judge they are not." O'Keefe concluded: "If the merger is not to be then we must work hard to preserve St. Ambrose. I believe Marycrest stands in a better competitive position than we. Marycrest has a greater support from the sisters than we do from priests; its financial position is better at the moment; its public image is far better than St. Ambrose. We have much to do even to survive. I am convinced that St. Ambrose must survive. We can not let it fail!"[99]

When the Board of Regents met on January 5, they discussed various problems, including the presidential search, the question of North Central accreditation, a new budget forecast that was less optimistic than previous documents, the problem of decision-making before the new president was named, and fund raising for the new institution. Then Robert Motto moved and Sister Jane O'Donnell, CHM, seconded the motion: "Do we wish to merge at this time?" The resulting vote was three yes, ten no. The merger was off. The rest of the meeting concerned the continued programs for students in the current semester and the issuance of a press release.[100]

The possibility of a real merger was questionable from the start. Neither college was in a strong financial position and the insistence of the sisters on the Peoples' Debt only complicated things. The dozens of meetings between academic departments and between administrative groups revealed a difference in operation and educational philosophies that could not be overcome. Both faculties were divided about whether the merger was wise. Both colleges had histories and traditions that became stronger as the moment approached when they would be abandoned. That was especially the case for the two groups who should have been able to bridge that gap, the priests at St. Ambrose and the Sisters of Humility at Marycrest. The level of trust and the willingness to compromise was simply not strong enough to overcome the differences among them.

For many of those same reasons, many of the alumni of St. Ambrose were never in favor of the merger. When the announcement was made that the merger was off, one alumnus took out an ad in the local newspaper that read: "Long Live St. Ambrose."

the CREST

Vol. 34, No. 7   Marycrest College, Davenport, Iowa   Feb. 21, 1973

FIRE Sale   Fire Sale!

CHEAP   NEWMAN   NEWMAN

We have all sizes, but no one to fit them!

I heard it was arson!

It begins on a warm late summer's afternoon. Under green oaks SAGA John serves hamburgers to returning sophomores, juniors, and seniors. You and your new-found roommate move among the people. Your parents are gone, and you feel out of place. But soon you find an oak to lean against. Conversations start. People meet. People talk, people laugh, people live. You gradually get into the swing of things . . . It ends on a warm spring day. Again under green oaks. The president hands you a diploma. It's over. Before you've quite begun, four years have flashed by. Is it possible? As you empty your room out into your car, you feel the slight sadness of parting. People have been leaving Ambrose for nearly a hundred years. You realize you are a small part of that exodus. You realize you are a small part of Ambrose. But Ambrose is a big part of you. Ambrose has molded you into a thinking being. Ambrose has given you four years of unique living. Now St. Ambrose welcomes you to the World.

– Philip Colgan, '75

❧ Chapter Fifteen ❧

The fall semester of 1973 opened with 1,320 students, 144 more than the previous fall, but only 300 more than ten years before. The entire campus was looking forward to the inauguration of a new president. The editor of the *Paper SAC* said there was an "aura of optimism" on campus. It did seem that a perfect storm, created by a combination of student activism, anti-war protests, and the merger, had passed, and the sun had come out again. The *Paper SAC* proclaimed that it was the "main historical document of the college" and that it would offer more news about campus-wide events and not just the "opinions and actions" of particular groups or individuals. Moreover, it hoped to avoid an "abrasive and critical view" that did not contain "constructive" ideas for the community.[1]

The times that Bob Dylan had sung were "a changin'," still were. Three weeks after St. Ambrose and Marycrest announced that the merger was off, the various parties in the Vietnam War signed an agreement to end it. Two months later, nearly 600 American prisoners of war were released and most of the 24,000 American troops still in Vietnam were withdrawn. For the Vietnamese, the war was far from over, but most Americans tried to put it all behind them.

Through the merger talks and the curriculum fight, anti-war advocates on campus continued their campaign: a Peace Moratorium Day for October 1971, sponsored by the Beta Committee to Save Lives, when 125 white crosses were erected in front of the Bee Hive and faculty members were asked to devote time in their classes to Vietnam; a Mass for Peace the next April with a rally and speeches at the LeClaire Park bandshell. Attendance at those events was small; still the student editor said they were indications that "some type of social conscience [was] growing and thriving on campus." With the end of the war, Father Smith announced that peace was "not a dead issue" and he formed the Quad-City Center for the Study of Peace and Non-Violence to "devise and implement alternatives to war and destruction."[2]

During those same years, the number of women on campus increased to about 300. Phi Chi Theta, a national women's business fraternity, was organized as the first "formal organization for women at the college." But there still were few women on the SGA, administrative committees, among the class officers, or on the J-Board. Madelyn Hermiston wrote in the *Paper SAC* that only ten women were present at a recent campus-wide meeting, which she said could lead the male students to believe women were not interested in issues. She said the women needed to "get busy and change their attitudes." Mary Krieger wrote that the SGA was one place where there should be fairness and that "the men on this campus will have to come to the awareness that they are by no means superior to women or better capable of handling the problems of this campus."[3]

The presence of women on campus also impacted the student push to eliminate dormitory hours. For decades the issue had been the time a dormitory resident had to be in at night; now the issue was when or if residents could visit other residents of the opposite sex. As dean, Rogalski had tried to tread the line between allowing students to be responsible for their own actions and the concerns of the college and parents that students would behave inappropriately. The case for some regulation by the college was made by Father Farrell who told the student affairs committee that the college had the right to impose a moral code. He admitted that such a code could inhibit the freedom of some, but he said it was justified if the decision came from a competent authority like the college. For Farrell and others, the issue was directly related to the Catholicity of the college. In the early 1970s, the question of visitation hours was a frequent item of discussion as the students, the administration, the faculty, and the Board of Directors tried to balance individual freedom and the image of a Catholic college.[4]

The oldest continuing social issue at St. Ambrose was student drinking. It had been prohibited in the first set of regulations written by Father Flannagan in 1887, and Schulte and Halligan tried to get the students to join the Cathedral Temperance Society. Bishop Cosgrove and Father Giglinger had carried the temperance crusade to the Davenport community in the 1890s. Iowa was a dry state even before the period of national prohibition from 1920-1933; nevertheless, Ambrosians no doubt took a drink.

In the years after 1933, the sale of alcohol in Iowa was highly regulated, except in Scott County where the law was regularly ignored.

Drinking was part of college culture and St. Ambrose was no different. By the mid-1960s, drinking at campus functions had become an issue for college authorities. In 1967, Dean Rogers explained to the student council the legal aspects of drinking at functions sponsored by campus groups, even if they were not held on campus. The legal drinking age was twenty-one, and anyone who furnished alcohol to those under that age would face penalty under the law.[5]

Then the Iowa General Assembly lowered the drinking age to nineteen beginning July 1, 1972. Now it was legal for most Ambrosians to frequent familiar campus hangouts like the Tiptopper, the Buckhorn, the Fox Den Tavern, TJ's, or

Peace Moritorium Day, October 13, 1971.

Fennelly's Circle Tap, "the Ambrosian cultural and social center." In an attempt to keep them on campus, in September 1972, St. Ambrose became the first college in Iowa to obtain a license to sell beer and opened the Last Class Pub in the back room of the Bee Hive. The Pub operated as a private club for St. Ambrose and Marycrest students and faculty. Some alumni and priests expressed concern about the college serving liquor to students, but the president and the Board of Directors approved the action. Rogalski explained, "What we are trying to do is put the pub in a certain perspective. It's an educational tool, people can socialize and learn responsible drinking." In spite of the fears of some, college business manager Thomas Grady reported that in the first two years there were "no problems whatsoever with the pub."[6]

The J-Board continued to vex the campus community. It had been disbanded in the spring of 1972 when Rogalski said it had become "politi-cized" and that there was a "remarkable disinterest in its guidelines for fines." At the 1972 summer meeting of the SGA, Rogalski proposed to create two boards, one a student board for misdemeanors, and another composed of students, faculty, and administrators for more serious problems. But the SGA objected and an alternate proposal by Rogalski was also rejected. That fall the SGA selected seven students for the J- Board and asked the students for a vote of confidence in the board. Yet in the fall of 1973, it remained controversial. Some students saw it as a "testing ground" for their "rebellion against the disciplinary structure on campus." Others thought it merely enforced the rules of the dean. Some thought it should have the power of judicial review over SGA actions. The SGA continued to discuss the issue of the J-Board and the *Paper SAC* published articles and letters to the editor about it. But just how to deal with student offenses in a way that served justice for the student and the institution and still satisfied the desire of the students for freedom of action remained a "puzzle."[7]

In the years ahead those issues and others would be faced by a new president. Shortly after the announcement that the merger was off, Monsignor Menke resigned the presidency on June 1. He had known for some time that 1972-1973 would likely be his last year because the merger agreement stated that neither sitting president would become the president of Newman College. When the merger failed, Bishop O'Keefe asked Menke to remain as president of St. Ambrose, but Menke declined. He did not want to go back to teaching Latin and Greek; the switch to the vernacular

in the liturgy as a result of Vatican II meant that large numbers of seminarians no longer took Latin. When the bishop offered him the pastorate of Sacred Heart Cathedral, Menke took it. He said later it was a "good move for me and for the college . . . I had been president for nine years during a very difficult period and am happy I made the change."[8]

Menke's characterization of the period as "difficult" understated what he and the college had been through. He oversaw the years of student unrest over the war, the push for student rights, faculty disputes over the curriculum, the onset of co-education, a $6 million building program, and the discussions about the merger. Terry Shelton, the editor of the *Paper SAC*, said he disagreed with some of Menke's decisions but noted his stand for student rights and representation, his paying for unpopular causes from his own pocket, and his "trying to serve in as fair and just a manner" as possible. Shelton hoped Menke's memories of St. Ambrose after a life dedicated to it would be "good memories."

Dr. William J. Bakrow, tenth president of St. Ambrose.

Shelton said it was a time for the campus to "pause to think." As an institution, St. Ambrose was "besieged by problems both internally and externally," either of which could be "fatal." While a new president would not be a "panacea," he could give an "impetus to a sorely sagging faculty morale and possibly introduce a spirit of cohesiveness so necessary if our demise is not to be swift." He urged students to take an active role in the selection process of the new president.[9]

Menke's successor would become the eleventh president of St. Ambrose, and the first to be chosen by someone other than the bishop. At a meeting on February 3, 1973, the Board of Directors established a committee to accept applications, conduct interviews, and recommend a candidate. The committee consisted of four members of the board: Robert Motto who was chosen chair, John Figge, James McLaughlin, and Margaret Tiedemann; three faculty members, Professors Donald Moeller, John Norton, and Prudent Coussens; two students, William Courtright, SGA president, and Teresa O'Connor; and from the administration, the dean of students, Edward Rogalski. Later Bishop O'Keefe was added to the committee. The committee was directed to proceed with a search and recommend a new president by June 1. If that was not possible, the board would appoint an interim president.[10]

The search committee went to work immediately and by April, it had narrowed nearly 130 applications to seven whom it hoped to interview. On May 22, the committee presented four names to the board which voted to offer the presidency to the committee's first choice, Dr. William J. Bakrow.[11] In the meantime, the Reverend Joseph Kokjohn, professor of English and college vice president, was named acting president until Bakrow took office

on September 5.

Bakrow was born in Kansas but grew up in Rochester, New York. He had a Bachelor of Arts Degree from Brown University and Master of Science and Doctor of Education Degrees from Indiana University. He had worked as a newspaper reporter, and then for nearly twenty years as director of development at Canisius College and the University of Buffalo, New York. In 1966, he founded the Motorola Executive Institute in Oracle, Arizona, and served as its director.

In his interview, Bakrow was confident and was not threatened by the difficult situation of St. Ambrose following the failure of the merger. He said it was a hard time for all of private education and told the committee that there was "nothing wrong with this school that a few extra dollars wouldn't cure," and he believed from his experience he could get that money. In the first years of his presidency, he emphasized that "St. Ambrose was a good school, becoming a great one."[12]

On July 27, Bakrow appeared at a joint meeting of the St. Ambrose Board of Trustees and Board of Directors, where he spoke about his "3 R's" to promote the institution: "Recruiting, Refinancing and Raising Money." He told his audience that the trustees were an important part in the development of the college, and asked them for their comments. They said: "Meet more often and keep us in the picture"; "Use us–tell us our responsibilities"; "The college should merchandise [itself] to attract students." He told them he would form board committees to help him promote the mission of the college.[13]

When Bakrow arrived, St. Ambrose was like other Catholic colleges that had dramatically changed in the previous decade. Like the others, the number of lay faculty and staff had increased, with higher salaries and benefit packages than the priests they replaced. A decline in enrollment, or in the case of St. Ambrose, a flat enrollment, meant that income was not increasing. Added to that was an ambitious building program that used the endowment to meet expenses. The social and political turmoil on and off campus had taken its toll on the college community and had further marred the image of St. Ambrose, which was already suspect in the business community. Like other, similar institutions, St. Ambrose turned to an outsider to be its new leader. Bakrow's solution, like other new presidents in similar situations, was to look for government funding for new programs and move into a new market of vocational education, satellite campuses, non-traditional-aged students, and new programs, including graduate degrees. Presidents like Bakrow were "able to bring a sense of urgency, an activist style, an entrepreneurial boldness, and a capacity for fund raising" that made his constituents and the community believe that St. Ambrose was becoming a great college.[14]

A Great and Lasting Beginning

In a wide-ranging interview in the *Paper SAC*, Bakrow said the students should have more committee representation and should also have a vote on those committees. He said the SGA was the principal student organization and he assured the students he would not attempt to weaken it. He hoped to work in a cooperative atmosphere with them and the rest of the campus community. He made it clear, however, that neither students nor faculty should be administrators, for that was his role. He promised to discuss issues with a wide range of people and groups, collect information, investigate problems, but then he would make a decision. When asked what his major goal was, he responded, "academic excellence spearheaded by a talented, motivated faculty, with adequate funding to encourage such dedication." This was not impossible because St. Ambrose College was "on the move." The new editor of the *Paper SAC*, John Stuekerjuergen, said the optimistic atmosphere on campus was because of Bakrow, whom he pronounced was "just what the doctor ordered."[15]

His inaugural address continued many of the same themes. It was a time of "renewal, a time of growing from strength to even greater strength." Renewal meant

The times, they were a changin'. Upper photo, Ron Bohnenkamp, Jerry McMorrow, and Larry LaFebvre were the junior class officers in 1964-1965. Lower photo, Chuck Harmeyer, Sara Fleckenstein, and Dan Temborius were the junior class officers in 1974-1975.

ty of planning and setting goals. He ended on his familiar theme that these were "exciting times" and St. Ambrose was "bordering on greatness."[16]

Most of the campus community was impressed. Bakrow had a "new outlook" and would "do something about things instead of just" sitting and talking about them. He would be "good for the college." Naysayers said the elaborate inaugural ceremony was "overdone," and they adopted a cautious attitude about his plans.[17]

Bakrow wasted no time in making changes. A few weeks following his inauguration, he named Father Frederick McMahan to the newly created position of provost. A long-time faculty member, department head, director of testing, dean of the college, vice president, and two-time acting president, as provost, McMahan was asked to take charge of long-range planning and institutional research. He said planning was a process with questions answered in steps. In the past he said there had been "no managed planning" and often events on campus were controlled by outside circumstances and social and economic conditions. Now the planning process would look to marshal the assets that St.

"having meaning, and values, and a capacity for growth," but renewal was prevented when institutions became prisoners of old habits and attitudes. It was necessary to look ahead, and Bakrow had a five-year plan with four goals. First, he wanted to improve recruitment and increase the size of the student body. Second, there was a need to increase annual support. He saw the local business community as an important source of support, but he realized he had to rebuild a relationship. So he announced that the following summer the college would initiate a management development program for local businesses and industry. Third, to attract new students, it would be necessary to develop new programs. Finally, he spoke about the necessi-

Ambrose possessed that other colleges did not have.[18]

Bakrow named theology Professor Donald Moeller to replace McMahan as academic dean. He said his selection was based on Moeller's "outstanding academic background, his breadth of experience, and his rapport with the faculty." Moeller, who assumed responsibility for the faculty and the curriculum, said the role of the college was to "prepare people for roles of leadership in their times." St. Ambrose was a place "where Catholics can grow in their Catholic experience."[19]

Within weeks Bakrow appointed a long-range planning committee directed by McMahan which consisted of himself, Moeller, Father James

Kelleher, vice president Father Joseph Kokjohn, Edward Rogalski, and board members Robert Motto and Weir Sears. McMahan said the committee had to "know what would be involved in carrying out the plan and the support it would receive. You can't get a ready-made plan for a college."[20]

The committee spent three days training for their new task and then met weekly. By mid-February 1974, it had developed a "tentative" mission statement: "The mission of St. Ambrose College as a diocesan-related institution of higher learning is to provide an excellent experience in the liberal arts, pre-professional, and career education within an institution steeped in the Catholic-oriented Christian view of man that will enable a student to develop his/her personhood morally, mentally, socially, aesthetically, and physically, and equip him/her to use his/her talents in service to one's fellow man." With that in place, the committee spent months discussing how each function of the college lived out that mission and defining the characteristics of the various parts of the college.[21]

During Bakrow's first year, three significant financial gifts came to the college. In late 1973, businessman Wilbur Allaert donated $30,000 to construct a television studio. Allaert had a rendering business in Coal Valley, Illinois, and had made a significant gift to the 1966 campaign to raise funds for the building program. Television had been part of the curriculum since 1949 when it was taught in the old radio studio on the fourth floor of Ambrose Hall. In the mid-1950s, St. Ambrose broadcast a regular "St. Ambrose College Presents" program on local television station WOC. Like the St. Ambrose on the Air radio programs that had periodically been part of local broadcasting since the 1920s, the new television program featured St. Ambrose professors and students debating current topics and musical and dramatic presentations by various St. Ambrose groups. In 1958, St. Ambrose and WOC teamed up to present the nationally syndicated program, "Continental Classroom," where viewers could receive college credit by attending classes and lectures on television. But the means necessary to telecast from campus were not available.[22]

In the meantime, radio at St. Ambrose continued to expand under the leadership of Father Shepler. Shepler was already chair of the new Mass Communications department, the first inter-disciplinary program on campus. Students could choose courses from the fine arts, philosophy, theology, language and literature, natural sciences, mathematics, social science, and new courses in journalism and photography to satisfy the requirements for the fifty-two hour major. Shepler said the objectives were to have the students well-versed in the philosophical and social questions of mankind and be knowledgeable in the mass communications with the ability to apply its tools, which he hoped would make the students "more capable of questioning whether 'everything is black and white.'" Menke said the new major represented a "creative response to a relatively new and rapidly developing force in human society."[23]

Shepler knew the major would be stronger if television could be made a part of the program. The new fine arts building included studios for the radio station, but there was no provision for television until Shepler noticed that the space beneath the raked floor of the auditorium was to have been filled with sand. He went to Menke to ask if the space could be left empty and another way devised to support the auditorium floor. When the archi-

tects said the change could be made, Shepler immediately appropriated the space for a television studio and sought the funding from Allaert.[24]

Even before the television station was built, St. Ambrose had a broadcast outlet when the local cable television company leased space on the roof of the fine arts building for a satellite dish and a relay station for their signal. In return, Shepler persuaded them to give St. Ambrose a channel on cable and to eventually wire every residence hall room and certain classrooms to receive cable television. Now with the Allaert gift, Shepler could begin to build the television studio. He hoped that St. Ambrose television could serve the "3 C's": the campus for he saw television as a means to deliver classes and other educational programming; the community through the cable television channel; and the church for he hoped television could be a means for evangelization to campus and community.[25]

It took several years to build the studio and find the equipment, but on February 8, 1980, on Cox Cable channel 9, the station went on the air showing color bars and lettering to indicate it was St. Ambrose television. The audio portion was programming from St. Ambrose radio station KALA. The first program which appeared on February 19 was a live discussion on "Alcohol Rehabilitation."[26]

The second large donation during Bakrow's first year came from Virginia Galvin-Piper who gave $350,000 to St. Ambrose. In return, the new fine arts center was named for her late husband, Paul V. Galvin, the founder of Motorola. Bakrow, who had worked for the Motorola Company, invited her to visit campus and secured the donation. A ceremony on May 24, 1974, formalized the naming, and it was marked by a small stained glass window designed by Father Catich.

A third large gift that spring came from the family of the late Harry L. McLaughlin who donated a building and land in Moline valued at $425,000.[27] The McLaughlin family had a long-time connection with St. Ambrose. Two brothers, Ray and Henry, had attended the college and another brother, James, graduated from the academy and the college and was a member of the Board of Directors.

At the end of Bakrow's first year, the *Paper SAC* noted the optimism on campus and said Bakrow was a "shrewd, invaluable president" who had been as "successful as his attitude." He had secured several large donations, the television studio was under construction, there had been a number of personnel changes, there was a newly furnished faculty lounge, the athletic field was being rebuilt, and the Executive Institute for Management Development was about to begin. Noting his ability at fund raising, the students gave him a nickname, Dollar Bill Bakrow. The paper said there was no longer a discussion about whether St. Ambrose would survive.[28]

The momentum continued with the June 9 kick-off of the Challenge Grant campaign, an effort to raise $2.3 million. Board members James McLaughlin and John Figge served as co-chairs of the campaign. One million dollars was to be used for basic college programs, another $1 million to pay the balance of the fine arts building, and $300,000 to upgrade the library. That evening lead gifts totaling $1 million were announced: $100,000 from banker V. O. Figge, $100,000 from Wilbur Allaert, the $350,000 gift from Virginia Galvin-Piper, and the $450,000 gift from the McLaughlin family.

The principal speaker of the event was the Reverend Paul Reinhert, SJ, the president of St. Louis University. Reinhert said church schools "suddenly

A Great and Lasting Beginning

are relevant, exciting, and important" since the only way to form character was through religion. He said that schools like St. Ambrose had a great opportunity to "literally change this country and turn it around, for we are in a position to fill the emptiness that gnaws at the very innards of American society today." He urged his audience not to apologize for the Catholicity of St. Ambrose, for the "Christian commitment is your strength, your edge, your greatest selling point." Later at a dinner, publisher Philip Adler said that "Colleges with imagination and foresight will survive. St. Ambrose College is one of them."[29]

As the Challenge Grant campaign got underway, Bakrow received word that the North Central Association had voted to remove the private probation it had imposed following its 1970 visit. St. Ambrose was asked to submit annual reports and schedule the next regular visitation within five years, but for now, the college was in good standing with its principal accrediting agency.[30]

Intramural sports remained popular through the 1960s and 1970s. Students competed in football, basketball, tennis, badminton, volleyball, swimming, golf, horseshoes, table tennis, pool, golf, and the mile-and-one-half turkey trot race. In the 1960s, dozens of individual athletes and teams named the Ramblers, Vikings, Senior Globes, Huns, and Vandals, vied for intramural titles. In the next decade, men's teams named the Owl's Nest, Biz Kids, Davis Style, Duck Inn, Harry's Nuts, Aardvarks, Longballers, and the Brotherhood dominated the field. Reflecting the status of a coed campus, there were also women's intramural teams including the Keggers, Jockettes, Madame Sophie's, Pam's Girls, and Wheel Queens. Some sports had coed teams named the Coeds, Sathrops, Bazoobas, Bogems, Pickers, and Brunzingers.

Rugby, "a ruffian's game played by gentlemen," remained a club sport and was played in front of a "small or non-existent crowd." Father Farrell, a great supporter of the sport, wrote about its "light-hearted seriousness" where there was a spirit of fun and an indifference to the score.[31]

Where there was no organized sport, the students made one up. In the spring of 1973, Ray Kraft and Jim Frick organized an Ashketball league, played by lobbing a tennis ball into an ash can stationed against the wall. In 1975, Mike Waskowiak and Duke Schneider took Joan Stuekerjuergen's idea and organized the first St. Ambrose *Paper SAC* Bicycle Ride Across Campus (SAPSBRAC-I), modeled on the *Des Moines Register's* Annual Great Bike Ride Across Iowa (RAGBRAI). Over one dozen riders began at the corner of Gaines and Locust and wound around campus to South Hall. The *Paper SAC* reported that Beth Wood and Joan Stuekerjuergen "showed good form and came through the ride much better than the guys." Waskowiak said the ride was "real," and provided a "release toward inner peace." At the end of the race, there was already talk about SAPSBRAC-II the next year. In 1976, the *Paper SAC* sponsored the first annual FOLF Fest, a sport that was a combination of frisbee and golf played on a course laid out around campus.[32]

College teams continued to compete in tennis, track, and golf. Baseball returned as an intercollegiate sport in the spring of 1972, the first time since 1948. When athletic director Robert Duax announced the decision to add baseball, he said it was "an important sport which will help round out our

athletic program." The budget was set at $5,000, but no scholarships would be awarded. Ken Blackman, an admissions counselor and professional baseball scout, helped find equipment and solicited money from outside the college. The decision was not without controversy; the *Paper SAC* published a number of letters in opposition to baseball, including one from Professor Wayne DeJohn. DeJohn argued that the proponents of baseball yearned to return to a "stabler, less threatening social world" and channel "otherwise potentially dangerous energies into socially approved directions." Baseball at St. Ambrose was not to be played for the fun of it, rather it was the product of two "overpowering tendencies" in education: "a mindless expansion . . . and a commercializing-booster mentality." He asserted "commercialized quasi-professional athletics" should have no place in an academic institution like St. Ambrose.[33]

Basketball remained as the major intercollegiate sport. In 1974, after eight years as basketball coach, Leo Kilfoy resigned and was replaced by Ron Bohls, who had played for St. Ambrose in the early 1960s. Kilfoy coached teams to five consecutive winning seasons and they were the Midlands Conference champion the two previous years. In 1972, Kilfoy was the NAIA District 15 Coach of the Year and in 1973, he was the Midlands Conference Coach of the Year.[34]

Football was the most popular intramural sport and in spite of Menke's assertion when he became president that it would not return as an intercollegiate sport, there was periodic interest in its comeback. In 1968, most students wanted to bring football back while the faculty thought it would "create many particular evils rather than any general good." When Menke was told that football would create spirit on campus and increase alumni participation, he pointed out that when St. Ambrose had football, those things were not present, even during the 1950s when St. Ambrose had its best teams in history. Moreover, he said the estimated cost of $75,000 could be better spent elsewhere.[35]

Interest in football remained and in October 1973, an SGA poll of 200 students indicated that 85 percent favored a club football program where the students would pay a fee to support the sport. Using that information, the SGA passed a resolution to begin planning for club football. One student praised the decision but asked where the games would be played since the athletic field on the north side of the campus was in bad shape and hardly ready for football. In January 1974, a gift from Robert and Rosemary Motto, in honor of her father, Gerard J. Timmermann, founder of Midwest Timmermann Company, made it possible to rebuild the football field, which became known as Timmermann Field.[36]

One month later Robert Duax announced that a meeting would be held for those interested in either playing or coaching club football. He had put together a five-game schedule with Loras, Marquette, and St. Louis University. Writing in the *Paper SAC*, editor John Stuekerjuergen said that "with the institution of club football, we should see a new sense of pride and spirit that such a sport brings to a college campus."[37]

The first football season in fifteen years began optimistically. Coach Duax said he had "some good talent . . . and real size in the line." Reality set in when the Bees lost the first game to Hanover College, 81-0, and settled for a 0-0 tie in the next game against Marquette. In the third game, against Loras, St. Ambrose scored its first touchdown of the new football era when Rob Avon intercepted a pass and carried it back to set up the

Top row: Ken Berthal, coach, Peggy O'Meara, Linda Lakeman, Debbie Goettsch, Linda Ehelers, Julie Baldwin, Mary Schramm. Bottom row: Katie Dickman, Rosemary Cofield, Linda Frischmeyer, Barb Schneden, Ann Korosec, Cheryl Smith.

touchdown drive; but the Bees still lost the game 18-6. St. Ambrose lost the remaining three games for a season record of 0-5-1.[38]

The next season, Kilfoy took over as coach. He said the current players had more God-given talent than those of his student days, there was better coaching and better equipment, but "Football is still a game of blocking and tackling. The theories are still the same. The fundamentals are still the same."[39] Club football continued for two more seasons while pressure built to resume intercollegiate play.

In the summer of 1974, Edward Rogalski, who had been dean of students since 1968, went on leave to pursue graduate studies. He was replaced as dean by the Reverend George W. McDaniel. A 1966 graduate of St. Ambrose, McDaniel was ordained in 1970 and spent four years in parish ministry before returning to St. Ambrose.

When Rogalski returned to campus in January 1975, he was named vice president for Administration and Student Affairs. He had two priorities: to build a field house and begin a women's sports program. There was a women's tennis team, and now discussions began about basketball, softball, and volleyball. Part of the impetus for a women's sports program came from Title IX of the 1972 Education Act which outlawed discrimination based on sex in any educational program in an institution that received federal funding. Although the act applied to every part of the institution, its application to athletics received the greatest attention. Colleges around the country struggled to deal with the impact of the law on their athletic budgets. Coaches, participants, and fans of male sports, especially the minor sports which were not self-supporting, worried they would not survive a realignment of economic resources. The burden was even greater for historically all-male schools like St. Ambrose which had only become co-educational a few years before.

The first women's intercollegiate contest came on March 30, 1974, when the tennis team defeated Marycrest 6-3. They lost to Augustana 8-0,

but won return matches against Marycrest and Augustana to finish the season with a 3-1 record.

Discussions about a women's basketball team began in the fall of 1974 when about fifteen women indicated they would play if a team were formed. The team came together quickly, and under coach Ken Berthel, played its first game in LeClaire Gymnasium against Marycrest. The Queen Bees won 40-39 on a shot by Barb Schneden with fifteen seconds left in the game. Coach Berthel predicted, "Next year, this is going to be a big thing." The Queen Bees finished their season with a 3-1 record.[40]

The next year women's volleyball and softball were added, coached by Barbara Schuman, an instructor in the Physical Education department. Within a few years, women's teams regularly appeared in state tournaments, and in 1978, the tennis team won the state championship, and the basketball team went to the national NAIA tournament.

Bakrow's early success with special gifts and the Challenge Grant campaign helped to stabilize the financial situation of the college. Another component of financial stability was to increase enrollment. One way to do that was to add programs that tapped into new markets for students. In March 1974, Bakrow appointed Joseph McCaffrey as assistant dean of the college with special responsibilities for curriculum development.[41] Those years saw a number of new programs or the expansion of current programs, many of which were outside the traditional liberal arts core. But that was typical of the new, entrepreneurial presidents taking charge of many American colleges.

In 1972, a new four-year law enforcement major was offered for police officers and others who worked in the criminal justice system. Ten new courses including criminal law, police administration, and criminal investigation were added to the curriculum. In 1974, that program was expanded

A Great and Lasting Beginning

when a new criminal justice major was created. Now students could choose concentrations in general criminal justice, law enforcement, criminal justice administration, and corrections.[42]

In addition to new programs on campus, in the fall of 1974, St. Ambrose began to offer courses outside the city of Davenport. Courses were now taught in Clinton, Muscatine, Fort Madison, and Macomb, Illinois. Students could take classes for personal enrichment or enter a degree program in business administration or criminal justice.[43] Some St. Ambrose students went even farther then eastern Iowa when the college established the International Study-Abroad Foreign Language Program. Offered in conjunction with Central College in Pella and coordinated by St. Ambrose Professor Prudent Coussens, students could spend twelve months abroad and earn up to forty-four credits in programs in Mexico, France, Germany, or

Rev. Jack Smith was one of the leaders of the anti-war movement in the 1960s. He continued his activism with his opposition to ROTC in 1976.

Spain, or choose a nine month, thirty-credit program in London. Moeller stressed that knowledge of a foreign language would help the "businessman, professional or government employee who wants a deeper understanding of what is happening in and to our world." He said it would be a "key" to their success. Maureen Davis, a St. Ambrose junior, was the first student to take advantage of the program when she spent the year at the University of Madrid.[44]

That same year, St. Ambrose began the Career Two Program for non-traditional-aged students or for students whose employment or family obligations kept them from the regular program. Those students could take one or two courses each semester. Dr. Robert Brittingham, the director of the program, noted that colleges were designed for the "single eighteen to twenty-five year old," but educators now realized that the "desire for education is not solely isolated to this type of age grouping." The number of those students grew dramatically; those between the ages of twenty-five and forty had grown from 12 percent of the enrollment in 1970 to 24 percent by 1975. To facilitate that, the college offered baby-sitting services located on the west end of the ground floor of Ambrose Hall.[45]

The growing number of non-traditional students and the larger number of evening and Saturday classes necessitated adjustments of campus routine: those students often had more difficulties communicating with their instructors and dealing with the business and registrar's offices since they kept their regular Monday through Friday office hours. Often restrooms and other campus areas commonly open on weekdays were locked on week-

ends. Parking remained a constant problem. The non-traditional students were assessed the fee all students paid to the SGA for social events, but they complained that they had no interest in those, or because of jobs and family, could not take the time to participate. The SGA proposed to use a portion of the fees for informal events at convenient times for the non-traditional students to meet with faculty, administrators, and one another.[46]

Part of the recent curriculum revision was the creation of a new degree, the Bachelor of Special Studies, intended for students who wanted to earn a degree, but whose previous college work did not fit neatly into the core requirements for the Bachelor of Arts Degree. In 1975, the new degree was made available to nurses who had a three-year RN diploma and were already working in various health care positions. Those students did not study nursing, but in a thirty-hour program, took courses intended to improve their management, business, organizational, communication, and relational skills.[47]

Reaching out for students in another health care field proved to be controversial. In 1975, the school and the Palmer College of Chiropractic reached an agreement that St. Ambrose would offer a pre-chiropractic course. The matter was discussed with the Board of Trustees and the Board of Directors, and both groups approved the arrangement. It also had the support of biology professor Father Carl Rice. McCaffrey said the agreement would bring more new students to St. Ambrose, including the many foreign students who attended Palmer College. Complaints soon arrived from St. Ambrose graduates who were medical doctors. The medical profession had never accepted chiropractic and now those St. Ambrose alumni accused the college of approving this controversial form of treatment. The college responded by pointing out that the courses the Palmer students took were basic science and that no chiropractic courses would be taught at St. Ambrose.[48]

The imbroglio over teaching chiropractic students also complicated fund raising for the recently announced Hauber Chair of Biology, established to honor the late, long-time professor. The goal was to create a $250,000 endowment with donations by the many graduates who had gone on to medical school. But because of the relationship with Palmer College, solicitors found doors slammed in their faces or received only token gifts.[49]

Even more controversial was the decision to add an ROTC program. In March 1976, McCaffrey presented the Special Academic Program in

Military Science to the Academic Council for its approval. The program was to be an extension of the ROTC program at the University of Iowa, which would supply all the instructors. It included two courses in the freshman year; a history course in the second year; and leadership and military organization courses in the last two years. Between the third and fourth years there would be a six-week summer camp.

The Academic Council discussed whether the entire faculty should be consulted to see if there was "possi-

Comedian Bob Hope and Dr. Bakrow share a light moment during the 1976 commencement ceremony.

ble opposition." But the prevailing opinion was that there would be enough publicity that "sufficient opportunity for the expression of opinion" already existed and no other consultation was necessary. The Academic Council approved the program with only one negative vote.

There was opposition, and Bakrow tried to reassure the opponents of the program saying no one would be compelled to take ROTC, and there would be "no arms and no drills on the Ambrose campus." For those who said it was immoral to have ROTC, Bakrow asked if it was immoral for a Catholic school to favor defending the country, and he cited a number of Catholic colleges that had ROTC. He claimed he had received more than one hundred letters with those favoring ROTC outnumbering those who did not by a margin of three to one. He concluded that the "arguments in favor of offering ROTC far outweigh the negative aspects."[50]

The most vocal opponent was Father Smith who wrote Bakrow to express his "strong opposition" to ROTC. He said such a move in the 1950s might have been "less objectionable" given the "naïveté to matters of war and peace and nuclear overkill." But now it was "totally unacceptable, especially for a Catholic college." Smith said St. Ambrose should "remain loyal to its long-standing concern for intellectual excellence and social justice, and more recently, peace as over and against war." Referring to the discussions in recent years about what a Catholic college was, Smith said that there was "little doubt about what a Catholic college *is not*. It is not a part of the military-industrial complex." Bakrow acknowledged that he and Smith were "poles apart" on the issue, but he asked to discuss the matter with him. But Smith was in no mood to discuss, and he resigned from the college on May 3.[51] In spite of the controversy, the ROTC curriculum was published in the 1977-1979 catalogue, but no one enrolled for any of the courses, and the program was quietly dropped.

In his first years Bakrow had been successful in most of his initiatives and as a student wrote, there was a "new atmosphere around the college campus that will let St. Ambrose grow leaps and bounds."[52] But he had misjudged the campus culture and what may have been acceptable in the 1940s and 1950s when Monsignor Burke attempted to bring an ROTC unit to campus, was no longer so.

Spring and summer commencement had marked the end of a student's years at St. Ambrose for generations. On December 19, 1975, the first winter commencement was celebrated for seventy-two graduates. Dr. Neil Waterstreet, a professor of economics who had joined the faculty in 1970 after a long career in business, spoke. Waterstreet was a recent graduate himself, having just completed a PhD begun decades earlier, but which had been interrupted by war and a career.[53]

The spring commencement of 1976 was much more celebratory than the tension-filled commencement of 1970 held in the wake of the strike. The times had changed, but the principal reason for the added excitement was the presence of Bob Hope as the commencement speaker. Scott Oyen, a senior business administration student from Dubuque, had begun the year before to contact Hope to invite him to speak. His persistence paid off and when Hope arrived that Sunday, there were larger than usual crowds. As the procession arrived at the graduation platform and Hope mounted the steps, the St. Ambrose band, led by Professor Charles DCamp, neatly segued from *Pomp and Circumstance* to "Thanks for the Memories." Hope began his talk with a few jokes and references to the fact it was an election year, added some inspirational comments for the graduates, and concluded, "Today you have graduated with Hope. The Faith and Charity are up to you."[54]

In August 1976, Bakrow received word that St. Ambrose had been awarded a $1.5 million Advanced Institutional Development Program (AIDP) grant. To be paid out over five years, the money was used for a variety of academic, student support, and administrative programs. The academic area focused on creating career opportunities and included funding for evening and continuing education course development for non-traditional-aged students; new women's programs; extension courses; and management courses including a new agri-business management program. A second academic area included new interdisciplinary programs; development of computer programs; a new physical education program for teachers of the handicapped; and funding for the new television studio. A third area included funding for support and development of personnel to administer the various new programs.

In the area of service to students, funding was provided for a new learning resource center with an emphasis on non-printed materials for the library; a remedial program to assist those who had difficulties in learning; a new advisory program for student retention; and a testing center that included academic and psychological testing. In all of those areas, there was an emphasis on the non-traditional and minority students.[55]

Bakrow responded to the grant in typical style, "I always said there was nothing wrong

Another campus symbol was created in 1962 when Tom Joyce, a senior from Peoria, dressed as a bee and appeared at basketball games. The student council ran a contest to decide on a name for the new mascot and the winner was Barney the Bee. With the addition of new men's and women's sports, Barney, here portrayed by Rob Avon '75, was busier than ever.

link together humanities with science courses, philosophy and theology with business and technology, and connect all of them to the contemporary world.[57]

From 1885 to 1915, the college catalogue listed the qualifications necessary to earn a Master of Arts or a Master of Accounts Degree. There is no evidence, however, that either degree was ever awarded and they were dropped from the catalogue in 1916. So when a new graduate curriculum leading to a Master of Business Administration (MBA) Degree was announced for the fall of 1977, it was the beginning of graduate education at St. Ambrose. Bakrow said, "The MBA degree today is considered by many as a passport to success. Employment prospects, starting salaries and chances for promotion often are better if you have the MBA."

Dr. Gene Seehafer became the dean of Graduate Management Programs responsible for making the new MBA a reality. Seehafer said the object was to "educate

with the college that one million dollars would not cure. Now we have the million dollars." The grant money was used to fund some new programs already in the planning stages. Other money enabled the college to create new programs: one was the Adaptive Physical Education Program begun in the fall of 1977 with Professor Michael Orfitelli as director. AIDP money was used to adapt the gymnasium and pool area and to purchase new equipment for the program. Other AIDP funds were used to adapt the campus for handicapped accessability.[56]

A new agri-business concentration in the Department of Business Administration was directed to various agricultural-related occupations. According to Professor Wayne Oberle, the program had a "double thrust: for St. Ambrose day students and for those persons currently working in the agri-business world who want to sharpen their skills." New computer equipment was installed in the learning resource center in the library. Anne Lehart was named director of a new Remedial Development Program for students who needed extra help with the academic work. The Women's Program Advisory committee with faculty members from several disciplines was formed to discover ways to integrate women's studies courses into the curriculum. Faculty developed more interdisciplinary courses that would

self-motivated persons in business, governmental or health care organizations." The goal was to teach people "how to earn a living–and how to live," and he said he hoped to include in the curriculum an awareness of moral problems in business and management.[58]

The move to a graduate program in business was a natural next step in the growth of the college. The industries and businesses of the Quad-Cities provided a significant source of potential students which would fulfill Bakrow's goals of increasing enrollment and developing a better relationship with the local business community. To emphasize the connection, a new slogan was used to identify the college: "Ambrose Means Business." The program achieved those goals and two years later, when it was accredited by the North Central Association, the *Quad-City Times* said the college had enhanced its reputation and "St. Ambrose's victory," was another "triumph for the Quad-City area, which continues to come into its own as a metropolitan community."[59]

The Institute for Management Development, begun in 1978, was another program directed to the local business community. This was a non-degree program similar to the Motorola Executive Institute Bakrow had directed before he came to St. Ambrose. Bakrow said he had "dreamed of establishing such a program for the Quad-Cities." Funded by money from the AIDP grant, it had an advisory board of twenty-two local business executives. It was directed to area businessmen and women who were seen as "promotable" by their employers but who lacked some necessary qualifications for promotion. Directed by James van Lauwe, most of the faculty for the program came from the local business community and the courses combined teaching with practical experience. When it began in February 1978, there were so many students, more class sections had to be opened.[60]

There were no major building projects underway in the mid-1970s, although a new field house, the last part of Menke's building program, was under consideration. Other, smaller projects, however, kept sidewalk superintendents busy. Water problems in the chapel that had begun shortly after it was built had continued and badly stained its interior walls. An engineering analysis indicated that the principal cause was a badly designed roof and interior gutter system, as well as ice damage and uncaulked joints around the windows. They recommended a new roof at a cost of about $25,000 and sandblasting the interior stone to clean off the stains. The Board of Directors approved the repairs and appointed board member Margaret Tiedemann to chair a "mini-campaign" to raise money for the restoration of the chapel.[61]

In the fall of 1976, board members Joseph Hanson and Weir Sears were appointed co-chairs of a committee to raise $450,000 to renovate the exterior of Ambrose Hall. Because of the historical character of the building, it had been named to the National Register of Historic Places. To restore its earlier luster, a great deal of work on the exterior was necessary. The decorative cornice along the eave line had originally been painted tin, but had rotted away and needed replacing. The windows needed attention and the brick and stone work needed tuck pointing. When that work was done, new lights were installed along the front of the building to give it a "more friendly appearance," as well as provide security for students walking to and from the library in the evening. To mark the long-time presence of St. Ambrose Academy in the building, the restoration was dedicated to Father John McEniry, who had been principal of the academy for twenty years.[62]

While work progressed on the outside, there were also major renovations on the inside. The ground floor, which had held the kitchens and refectories, was remodeled to accommodate the administration offices which were in the library-administration building. Moving those offices to Ambrose Hall created more space for the library and learning resource center.

The third floor chapel, which had been called the "neatest in the west" when it was dedicated in 1902, had not been in use since the seminarians moved to Hayes Hall in 1968. The altars, altar rail, and other furniture had been removed. The paint was peeling and some of the stained glass windows had pieces missing that allowed pigeons to enter and roost. Now it was restored for use as the John R. Lewis Board Room. A 1913 graduate of the academy, John R. Lewis was the son of Frank Lewis whose gift had made the science hall named for him possible. The broken glass in the windows was replaced and the images restored by a gift from the William F. Novy family. At the dedication, Father Madsen noted its use as a chapel and said it was now a place where the Board of Directors could "continue the process of nurturing young minds with the eternal truths" which had been

taught there while it was the chapel.[63]

Meanwhile the young minds, their professors, and the institution were still rebounding from the turmoil of the early 1970s: the demonstrations, the challenge to power, the curriculum revision, and the failure of the merger. Rogalski noted that the faculty thought moral and educational values were down and they especially did not like the changing sexual mores and the increasing profanity. He said most of the faculty thought the institution should not be "in the lead for social change," and preferred a return to the "bucolic good ol' days," where certain growth of discipline and study were sponsored." Another observer noted that in those years the institution was "very liberal," with strikes and peace marches led by some of the very liberal faculty. But, those "intellectuals nearly dragged St. Ambrose college into non-existence." It was time for a change when Bakrow came and began the change to a "middle-of-the-road" image.[64]

The political stance of the college worried some, while others were concerned about its image as a party school. The claim was that there were parties and a social life "far surpassing that of most schools in the bi-state area." Somewhat defensively, Robin McGraw, the editor of the *Paper SAC*, said he could not understand why "gatherings on the weekends" meant it was a party school. Only about one-fourth of the students lived on campus and he did not believe they were so "full of zest and zeal" that they could party that much and still get to their classes, most of which had strict attendance policies. McGraw said the administration concern about the image was "understandable as they have a reputation to maintain, but they are violating students' rights and expression" if they clamp down.[65]

In November 1978, a *Quad-City Times* reporter visited campus and said there was "hardly a soul in sight." No one was out playing touch football or throwing frisbees. He went to the Bee Hive to find the campus "crazies" but found only students studying. He wondered about the current college campus custom of toga parties or concern about serious issues and was told the most serious issue the SGA had faced that fall was that it had overestimated the number of refrigerators it needed for the students to rent and what it should do about the surplus. SGA president Joe Adam explained the "people are getting scared about the shortage of jobs." Adam said not even the Pub brought in students the way it once did, "Wednesday nights used to be a big night on campus, but it is not any more. Things have changed."[66]

Paper SAC editor Julie Gosma said the article would certainly "please moms and dads." She said students were concerned about grades and jobs but, "Let's be realistic, St. Ambrose is not 'tombsville.'" Students liked to have fun, play loud music, watch the soaps, and there were "crazies" among the students. Socializing was an "important part of any college scene . . . We do have quality students, but we also have quality fun."[67]

Quality fun and campus crazies was not the institutional image that many hoped St. Ambrose would have, and during those years there was a continuing dialogue about how to project the Catholic image of the school. Through the years the college had defined itself from being "thoroughly Catholic," to "operated by the Catholic diocese and oriented to the Christian way of life," to "church-related" to being "in the Judaic-Christian traditions." Now in August 1975, the Board of Directors approved the mission statement developed by the long-range planning committee that called

Homecoming 1978. Dr. Bakrow was joined by homecoming queen Jeanne Rauth (behind him in blue scarf), students and alumni including three long-time Ambrosians: Rev. John McEniry, long-time principal of the academy; Rev. Thomas Lew (in cap), dean of men in the 1930s, and Msgr. Cletus Madsen, professor of music and chaplain.

it a "diocesan-related" college "rooted in the Catholic-oriented view of humankind." As a Catholic college, St. Ambrose should prepare the students "morally, mentally, socially, aesthetically and physically," and equip them to use their talents in the service of "their fellow men and women."[68] This was a vision and mission Bishop McMullen could endorse, but like all mission statements, the difficulty was in realizing those ideals in the daily life of the institution.

Earlier that year, Bishop O'Keefe had been asked by the *Paper SAC* to give his views of Catholicity and the relationship of the college and the diocese. He wrote that the bishops of Davenport had maintained a close association with the college, viewing it as a "valuable assistance in proclaiming the Gospel and the formation of Christian men and women." There were three elements to carrying out this role. First, the teaching of theology was a "most important part," and he said no student should graduate without theology. But he said the present requirement provided only the "barest minimum." The second important element was religious worship. The liturgy should be "attractive and well done," and should prepare the "student to take leadership in his parish and in assisting the parish priests in planning and carrying out the liturgical celebrations." Finally, the college should "reflect the ideals and principles of its founders." It should promote a Christian community on campus based on faith and charity, and it should express concern for others and for "truth, honesty, justice, peace, temperance, purity, generosity." It was the role of the administration to do "all things possible" to generate that community, but it was the students who made that kind of community possible. O'Keefe admitted that many would say that was an "ideal which cannot be attained. I admit it is an ideal; I will not admit that it cannot be attained."[69]

O'Keefe's was one voice in a continuing dialogue about the Catholic character of the college. His was also one voice in a similar discussion among Catholic educators around the country. Speaking at the National Catholic Education Association (NCEA) in 1975, Dr. Frederick J. Crossen, dean of the College of Arts and Letters at the University of Notre Dame, emphasized the importance of the faculty as "the witnesses of a college." Crossen said he did not think the Catholic mission of a college could be carried out unless the faculty was "predominantly" Catholic. But speaking at St. Ambrose the following year, the Reverend Monsignor John F. Murphy, executive secretary of the College Division of the NCEA, said that while the faculty bore the "largest responsibility" for the identity of the institution, there were good reasons that the faculty have "different backgrounds and different insights," but, nevertheless, they should endorse the "institutional objectives."[70]

Those themes were echoed the next summer in an address at St. Ambrose by the Most Reverend Jean Jadot, the apostolic delegate to the United States. Jadot emphasized the necessity to prepare students for their places in the world with a Christian vision and a "firm sense of responsibility and loyalty to the Church." They should fight for social justice, human rights, and combat prejudice. For Jadot the "key to the concept" of a Catholic college was its product, "the students." Each member of the college community was responsible for the development of "fully mature, normal, loving" Christians willing to "contribute the gift of life in the service of God and humankind." Jadot quoted the Vatican II document, *Gadium et Spes* (Joy and Hope), "Our age, more than any of the past, needs such wisdom if all that man discovers is to be ennobled through human effort. Indeed the future of the world is in danger unless provision is made for men and women of greater wisdom."[71]

In the midst of the continuing debate about Catholic identity, O'Keefe and others on campus insisted that a theology requirement was a key component to that identity. The most recent curriculum revision required six hours in theology and philosophy but did not require any specific course. Now Moeller proposed the requirement be raised to nine hours, three of which must be in theology. Many members of the SGA spoke against it: "I think it's a step backward," one said; another said the advisor's program should be strengthened to encourage students to take theology; still another said most students had taken a theology course even though there was no requirement. The faculty was divided on the issue. Moeller argued that St. Ambrose was a Catholic school and a student's search for meaning was incomplete without a religious dimension. Father Dawson defended the 1971 curriculum which had no specific course requirements because it gave the faculty and students more options. Philosophy Professor John Fitzgibbon said a requirement was not necessary and that the commitment to Christianity and Catholicism was best manifested by the attitude of "injecting Christian values into courses where appropriate."[72]

Advocates of a theology requirement won the debate, and beginning in the fall of 1976, nine hours of philosophy and theology were required for graduation along with a new course, introduction to philosophy and theology. There was also a new thirty-hour major in theology. This was intended for laity rather than seminarians and would be useful for religious education coordinators and teachers and for certification for teaching religion in public schools.[73]

In an attempt to bring those ideas together, Bakrow appointed a task force to examine the role of St. Ambrose "regarding its relationship to the various communities" it served. Father Farrell chaired the task force and the members were Sister Ritamary Bradley, philosophy Professor Paul Jacobson, biology Professor Mary Vinje, and college chaplain, the Reverend Drake Shafer. Their position paper acknowledged the college's Christian heritage and said as a religious institution, it had a "commitment to the quest for and expression of truth" within the "accepted tradition of the teaching office of the Roman Catholic Church." It examined the relationship of the college with its students and said it should be obvious they were coming to a Catholic school. It reiterated the importance of the faculty and said the college should be "readily visible" to the larger community. It acknowledged that a university was the "natural home of dissent" and said that had been the case at St. Ambrose, and it emphasized that financial considerations should not make the college abdicate that role. The task force made a number of recommendations to improve the relationship of the college with the students, the faculty, the diocese, and the larger community.[74]

The task force had said that campus ministry was "particularly valuable" in the realization of Catholicity and "ought not be viewed only as one among many student services." In his 1975 article, Bishop O'Keefe had said that ministry should prepare the students to take leadership in their parishes when they graduated. In recent years many of the anti-war and other protest activities had been planned and held in the chapel as chaplains

A Great and Lasting Beginning

Father Dawson and the Reverend William Stratman exercised that ministry. Now Shafer broadened the reach of Campus Ministry and formed a Campus Ministry Council with student committees to plan liturgies, organize social action activities, create fellowship to include all members of the campus community, and provide education for students who wanted to learn more about the faith. Being a Catholic college meant, among other things, an "atmosphere of faith," and it was a priority of campus ministry to make that a reality and "not simply verbiage."[75]

Music ministry was one of the most popular and most visible campus ministry groups. It provided liturgical music that honored the heritage of Catholic worship, but it also reflected its own times. Those goals had been a part of the liturgical renewal led on campus for years by Father Madsen. Now the group of student musicians used keyboards, guitars, and other instruments to accompany their singing at worship.

The group was chosen to represent St. Ambrose when Pope John Paul II came to Des Moines on October 4, 1979. Thirty-nine musicians began their pilgrimage the day before as they boarded a bus to Des Moines. A flat tire on one of the buses delayed their arrival in Des Moines, so with only two hours of sleep, they left for Living History Farms where the Pope celebrated Mass. They sang before the Mass began and then participated from near the altar area. Rogalski had taught them "Sto Lat," a Polish song that wished, "Good luck, good cheer, may you live a thousand years." When the Mass ended, the group began to sing it and the Pope came over and accepted their good wishes. Junior Eileen Lauf said she had "never felt the presence of God so strongly" as that afternoon. Another St. Ambrose student, seminarian Bud Grant, served as the Pope's mitre bearer and could be seen next to him all through the Mass. For Grant it was a "blessing" and a "neat experience."[76]

The task force Bakrow had commissioned said that a Catholic college should provide "service to the intellectual wants of the community." To this end, in 1979, the Reverend Daniel J. Kelly, a 1955 graduate, endowed the Kelly Chair of Theology in memory of his parents, Dr. John and Peggy Kelly. Income from the endowment was used to fund the annual Kelly Chair lecture as well as the work of the faculty of the Theology department. In 1980, Archbishop Jean Jadot returned to campus to deliver the first Kelly Chair lecture. In 1986, the lecture was renamed the Chair of Catholic Studies Lecture.[77]

In April 1979, the campus mourned the sudden death of Fr. Catich. He left a legacy of artwork including this slate of St. Ambrose and the Stations of the Cross that were placed in Christ the King Chapel in 1975. But his greatest legacy was his students who have carried on his work. In 1985, the university opened the Catich Gallery to house his works and serve as a place for the exhibition of the work of other artists.

When the North Central Association removed the private probation status of the college in 1974, it had called for a regular review within five years. That visit took place in the fall of 1977, and Bakrow was notified the next April that full accreditation was continued for a period of ten years. The report cited strengths including the board, the faculty, administration, educational programs, faculty offices and facilities, and the regard for the college within the community. There was concern, however, about the lack of consistent financial support and a managerial structure that did not have a team approach. It suggested more religious programs, more recreational facilities, more minority students, better faculty development opportunities, and more programs to help commuter students participate more fully in the life of the college.[78]

A survey of fifty-one students conducted the next spring reinforced some of the findings of the North Central report. Sixty-one percent of the students said they would come to St. Ambrose knowing what they now knew. Seventy percent said the faculty was good. Thirty percent said Bakrow was either unknown to them or that he stayed behind the scenes. They did, however, give him credit for pulling the college out of financial trouble and they said his relationship with the community was good. Nearly half said the facilities were either "lacking" or poor, especially LeClaire Gymnasium, which one said "looks like it should have been torn down twenty years ago." One student summed up his solution to all the problems of the college: "The library needs to be expanded; more books for research. Athletic facilities need to be expanded. They'd get more kids if they had better facilities. Make it bigger, open more dorms, and lower tuition."[79]

The North Central suggestion for more recreational facilities and the hopes of the students for more athletic facilities made it clear just how inadequate LeClaire Gymnasium was for recreational programs and intercollegiate sports. There was now women's basketball, tennis, volleyball, and softball, and men's basketball, baseball, golf, tennis, club wrestling, and track, and in the fall of 1977, intercollegiate football returned to St. Ambrose. Leo Kilfoy took over as coach and hoped to build on three years of club football. It had been an "excellent way of starting the football program," but Kilfoy thought there were more advantages to intercollegiate football. The first game against Loras ended with a 6-6 tie and the team finished the season with a 2-5-1 record.[80]

A new athletic facility had been part of Burke's post-war plan, it was one of the buildings in Schulte's 1950 campus master plan, it was a part of the Collins development plan of 1957, and in the early 1960s, the student council had called attention to the "overall poor condition of our indoor athletic facilities." In 1966, a student asked if St. Ambrose could continue to "grow and expand without the construction of a new field house in the immediate future," and that year it was one of the four buildings in Menke's development plan.[81] But the expense of the other three buildings in Menke's plan and the upheavals of the period meant it was another ten years before the college could consider a new gymnasium.

In September 1978, Bakrow presented a report to the board making the case for a new athletic facility. The proposed facility would serve the educational and recreational needs of the campus as well as the needs of an expanding intercollegiate sports program. The proposal outlined the inadequacies of LeClaire Gymnasium which had been built in 1916 for a student body of nearly 200. It included statements from the Physical Education department, the Scott County Board of Health which had serious concerns about the pool and locker rooms, and letters from local school officials about what an asset such a facility would be to education in the Quad-Cities. One letter from an alumnus discussed how two of his sons had chosen to attend another college because of the inadequate facilities at St. Ambrose. Based on the proposal, the board passed three motions: that a land-use study be made to determine a location for such a facility; that architect's sketches and cost estimates be presented to the board; and that a feasibility study be undertaken to determine the potential for raising the necessary money to build the facility.[82]

The land-use study began immediately and in December the board was presented with a number of possible locations. They chose the corner of Lombard and Scott Streets on the northwest corner of the campus. The board was told it could build a 45,000 square foot building at an estimated cost of $4 to $5 million. It asked for a study to see if it was feasible to raise $5 million.[83]

Fund raising for the new athletic center became part of a larger campaign, called the Centennial Countdown, planned in conjunction with the celebration of the centennial of the college in 1982. The centennial would be a way to remember the past and look forward to the future. Some recent activities already spoke to that goal. In September 1978, the college observed the first annual Heritage Day when those who had put St. Ambrose in their estate plans were honored. The next year twenty-three former athletes and coaches became the first inductees of the Athletic Hall of Fame. Included were coaches Dukes Duford, Father Joseph Hratz and players from the 1920s through the 1970s.[84]

History Professor Richard Geiger was named centennial coordinator to plan a wide variety of activities to celebrate the event. The plan was to begin the celebration with Mass on the feast of St. Ambrose in December 1981 and close it with the St. Ambrose Mass in December 1982. Bakrow commissioned Father Anthony Farrell to write a centennial history. At first, Farrell was a reluctant historian, since he taught languages and theology, but he admitted that as he progressed, things got "interesting." Bakrow said, "We are going to do ambitious things here. We have a vibrant, dynamic, growing campus." He said the new gymnasium would be a part of the celebration.[85]

The Centennial Countdown campaign began with a luncheon on March 28, 1980, hosted by three co-chairmen, board member John Figge, president of Davenport Bank and Trust; Robert Gerstenberger, senior vice president of Deere and Company; and A. George Forbeck, a 1952 graduate and a member of the Chicago Board of Trade. Their goal was to raise $6.8 million, $3 million of which was designated for the new physical education center. Another $1.8 million was for faculty salary advancement, operational support of the college, money to convert LeClaire Gymnasium to other uses, and a small amount for further work in Ambrose Hall. Another $2 million was for the endowment. At the lunch lead gifts of $1 million were announced which Bakrow said was a "clear signal of the confidence and trust in St. Ambrose as a community resource and leader." As part of the kick-off, a pin oak tree was planted in front of Davis Hall. *Paper SAC* editor Ann Glenn wrote, "Ambrose is on the move! Once again, exciting things are happening at our school." She said $6.8 million was a great deal of money but that was what it would take "to get this school up to par for the competitive, difficult years ahead." While the quality of education was excellent, "We desperately need a physical education center and increased capital and operating budgets."[86]

While the planning was underway for the Centennial Countdown, Ambrosians were watching events in the world. In November 1979, the American embassy in Teheran was attacked and fifty-two Americans were taken hostage, an ordeal that would last for 444 days. Over Christmas, the Soviet Union invaded neighboring Afghanistan, threatening peace in that region. President Jimmy Carter responded with several actions. He imposed a grain embargo on the Soviet Union and cancelled American participation in the summer Olympics in Moscow. He took one other action, however, that had a more direct interest for Ambrosians when he re-instituted the draft. Carter later said he did not need to actually draft anyone into the service, but it was necessary to register them for the draft in the event the situation worsened.[87]

For Ambrosians, Carter's announcement about the draft was a "shocker," and they noted that at some universities the students were "bringing out dusty anti-war music and chanting the old, 'Hell no, we won't go.'" The women on campus were looking at what this might mean for them. One said she would enlist if women had to go, but she would not want to go into combat. Another said, "If it's done to boys, it should be done to girls, and it is the first step towards war." Still another said she was "chicken," and saw her options as going to Canada or getting pregnant, neither of which would be easy, but "getting pregnant would be fun," so she would choose that.[88]

Workshops were held in the chapel basement about the draft, and a vigil was scheduled at the federal building downtown. Some students hung a banner outside the Bee Hive that proclaimed, "Dear Jimmy, draft beer not students." But it was not a return to the activism of a decade before. One student ascribed that to the "harsh realities of economics" as students studied hard to enable them to get jobs which meant that "pragmatism" won out over the "idealism" of the earlier students. The draft was discussed at an SGA meeting in early February before the members went on to other items on their agenda: support for a wrestling club, allocation of money for a pep bus to the Loras game, a report on the Battle of the Bands held the

A Great and Lasting Beginning

previous week, and questions about the food service.[89]

The musical that spring was *Kiss Me Kate*, directed by Father Greene and Andy Reagan with choreography by Mary Lou Dennhardt. Mimi Chouteau and Dave Resnick played Fred and Lilli and their on-stage alter egos Kate and Petruchio; Kelly Pratt was Bianca and John Ruess played Lucentio. The band, led by Professor Charles DCamp, was rehearsing for its first ten-day tour of Europe that summer with

Dr. and Mrs. Bakrow examine the plaque when the library-administration building was named for the founder, Bishop John McMullen.

stops in Austria and Germany including Davenport's sister city Kaiserslautern. The college chorus teamed with music ministry and Father Shafer to celebrate Mass with the premiere of *The Lord's Supper* by John Michael Talbot. Several of the books written and published by Father Catich, who had died suddenly the previous spring, were put on sale. Leslie Bell, one of Catich's students, exhibited photographs in local shows and won first prize in a printmaking competition in Kansas City.

The centennial year began with the celebration of the feast of St. Ambrose with Mass on December 6, 1981. The St. Ambrose Chorus sang Poulenc's *Mass in G*, directed by the Reverend Edmond Dunn. The next day the Reverend John Shea delivered the Kelly Chair Lecture. In the spring Professor Joan Trapp performed a piano recital. The Centennial Faculty Lecture Series began March 2 when Sister Ritamary Bradley lectured on Christian education. She was followed by Professor Ray V. Chohan who spoke on management styles of the eighties and the Reverend Dennis Brodeur who presented a lecture on the foundations of social justice. The spring musical, *Kismet*, was the twenty-fifth musical and featured a reunion of cast members from past shows. Eight students were declared winners of an essay contest held in conjunction with the celebrations, and their essays were published in the new *Journal of Student Research*.

Centennial sidewalk superintendents had a new project when ground was broken for the physical education center that spring. Bakrow optimistically said he hoped the Bees would be able to play basketball by the second half of the next season, but he also gave the disappointing news that a new swimming pool had been dropped from the plans. Bakrow gave credit for the progress on the building plans to Rogalski, whom he said had played a "big role in coordinating and origination of the project," and to Edward

Henkhaus, the vice president for finance since 1979, who had "handled much of the financial duties" of the sale of bonds to finance the construction. As much as anybody, it was Leo Kilfoy who was the driving force for the project. He was involved with every design feature and argued passionately for the best facility possible to serve varsity athletics, intramurals, and the physical education program.

As construction proceeded, however, some former parking areas were no longer available for student parking, and it was suggested that students be allowed to park in the "abundant faculty parking areas." In the meantime, the college was on the "lookout" to buy more property in the neighborhood.[90]

The fall celebrations began with a return to the origins of the college when a convocation with Mass at Sacred Heart Cathedral and a lecture by Dr. Lawrence McCaffrey, a 1949 graduate and professor of history at Loyola University, in the Galvin Fine Arts Center. In September, the library building was named for Bishop John McMullen. The fall Centennial Faculty Lectures were given by Professor Joan Trapp, who lectured on Stravinsky, Professor Patricia Kennedy who spoke on pioneer women in Midwestern fiction, and Professor Wayne Oberle who talked on feeding the world's hungry. Monsignor John Tracy Ellis delivered the Kelly Chair of Theology Lecture on "The Catholic Liberal Arts College: Has It a Future?" Father Farrell's history, *Bees and Bur Oaks: 100 Years of St. Ambrose College*, was published. Bakrow said it was a book "laced with whimsey, humor, reflections, and anecdotes, in addition to its sound and thoroughly researched historical core." The year ended with the Mass to celebrate the feast of the patron on December 5.[91]

Farrell wrote that Bishop McMullen would be "amazed" at what became of his idea for a school for boys. A student body of 2,000 would have "certainly impressed him," and he would perhaps be "a little shocked" at the presence of women students. He would be pleased that the college was still educating young men to be priests, not just for the Diocese of Davenport, but for other dioceses as well. Farrell noted McMullen's concern for social justice and said he would have liked that about the modern St. Ambrose. In the end, Farrell suggested that although McMullen was buried beneath a small stone at Mt. Calvary Cemetery, at one hundred years, St. Ambrose was his real monument.[92]

My first week of college was the beginning of an experience of a lifetime. I think my first impression can be easily stated in one word–Help! But having survived the first few days, I now realize that things are not quite as bad as they seemed. The things that caused the most trouble, surprisingly enough, were the very small things that I didn't even think about. How was I supposed to know that fabric softener sheets go in the dryer and not the washer? . . . Eating here is just like eating at high school, but even better. For one thing, they trust us with knives here. In high school, all we were given were forks and spoons . . . you can try all sorts of yummy sounding things here that mom would never let you try at home, like Captain Crunch in chocolate milk, or a Fruit Loops sandwich. But of course, once you try these, you know why mom would never let you try them at home. I suppose the hardest thing to get used to here is living in a dormitory . . . If you're feeling lonely there is always somebody to talk to just down the hall. But then again, if you're not feeling lonely there is always somebody playing his stereo too loud just down the hall . . . Now don't get me wrong, I like this college . . . But it's going to take a little while longer for me to get the hang of the place, to feel truly "independent," and "out on my own."[1]

❧ Chapter Sixteen ❧

St. Ambrose opened for its 101st year in the fall of 1982 with 2,185 students, 112 more than the previous fall, and an increase of 77 percent since President William Bakrow had arrived on campus in 1973. There were 603 freshmen, the largest freshman class in the history of the school. Registrar Christine Westensee said many colleges in the nation were reporting decreases, and she thought that St. Ambrose was the only Iowa school to show an increase. Bakrow and Professor Donald Moeller attributed the increase to new programs and the quality of the MBA program which had increased from 222 students the previous fall to 280 in 1982.[2] Those students were greeted by 139 faculty members, 77 full-time and 62 part-time; 20 percent were women. Nineteen priests were still listed among the faculty, although six of them, Fathers Pasquale Ferrara, Joseph Hratz, James Kelleher, Carroll McGivern, Carl Rice, and Herman Strub were emeritus. The acorn planted by Bishops McMullen and Cosgrove, Father Schulte, and Mr. Halligan one hundred years before had grown into a mighty oak.

As the college began its 101st year, it had grown with Bakrow, there were more students, a somewhat better financial situation, a better relationship with the business community, and new programs. In his presidential report that summer, Bakrow said that when he had arrived ten years earlier, "managerial excellence was the challenge," but that what was needed now was "leadership, the ability to motivate others, and considerable vision." Bakrow the manager could take a good deal of the credit for that, but now Bakrow the leader would have to build on that if he was to achieve his goal of a "great college."[3]

One consequence of Bakrow the manager and the growth of the college was that the number of administrators had grown. Now there were two senior vice presidents, two vice presidents, two associate vice presidents, four deans, four assistant deans, one associate dean, eighteen directors, four

assistant directors, an administrative assistant, an assistant to the president, a manager, a coordinator, and a registrar. This prompted one student to ask if the rumor was true that there were seventeen vice presidents per student at St. Ambrose.[4] Bakrow and all of those administrators had the responsibility for a more complex college than even ten years before, more students, more buildings, and classes in more places throughout southeastern Iowa.

One of the challenges faced by the college was finding room for the growing number of resident students. A few years before, Davis Hall had been closed to students, but now it reopened floor by floor. The center section of Ambrose Hall, the old Irish Village, was converted into living space for women. Room rates ranged from $340 for a double room and $530 for a single room in Ambrose, East, Hayes, and South Halls. Davis Hall, which was a less desirable residence hall, had rates of $300 for a double and $505 for a single room. Depending on the meal plan, board rates ranged from $465 to $525 a semester.

Tuition for the 101st year was $145 per semester hour. Seventy-five percent of the students at St. Ambrose received some form of financial aid, including federal government loans, Pell grants, and work-study. But once the Reagan administration took office in 1981, it announced it intended to cut back the funding for most of those programs, a move which would likely impact at least 50 percent of the St. Ambrose students. A New York congressman said if enacted, the cuts would force 750,000 college students to leave school. Gerry Werthmann, SGA president, wrote, "These cuts . . . are not small-scale cuts" and the students must make it known that they were "totally unacceptable." He urged a letter-writing campaign to members of congress.[5]

There is no way to know how many Ambrosians wrote their member of Congress about the Reagan cuts, but it was likely that very few did. As colleges entered the 1980s, the political stance of students was moving toward the center. In a nationwide poll of nearly 300,000 students, 60 percent described themselves as "middle of the road." Nearly 22 percent said they were "liberal to far left," a decline of three points from the previous year. Those labeling themselves conservative rose from 17 percent the previous year to 18.3 percent. Over the previous few years students said they were "increasingly concerned" with financial security; and 63.3 percent said "being very well-off financially" was a very important goal in life, up from 60 percent in 1978 and 44 percent in 1967.[6]

Those figures seemed to describe the students at St. Ambrose. Writing in March 1983, Paper SAC editor Pete Cunningham said the world was in need of "student awakening." In the 1960s and 1970s, he believed college students were "people committed to a cause and that they were basically dissatisfied with the status quo." But, he said, times had changed and he no longer associated a college student "with being a campus activist." Now St. Ambrose students had the "narrower concerns [of] materialistic goals and career preparation." Writing a year later, Kelly Keogh, a student from Nashville, said St. Ambrose was "supposed to be a liberal arts

When it was built in 1909, this was the public entrance leading to the auditorium on the third floor. (Photo by John Mohr)

school but it's turning into a business school. Because of the job situation, people are just out to make a buck." Keogh continued that "most of the kids here don't get involved with anything but dances and kegs. Very few of them get their own personal insight into politics, but just vote for whoever their parents are voting for."[7]

❧

Bakrow's goal was to make St. Ambrose a great college. The question for many, however, was what kind of college that would be. Could it continue to represent the values of a liberal arts education in an increasingly specialized world? That issue was expressed in debates among the faculty and students about the curriculum. The 1972 curriculum revision had established divisional requirements, but except for English composition and one hour of physical education which were required of all students, it was up to the

student to choose what courses would be taken to fulfill those requirements. In the ensuing years, two more courses, introduction to philosophy and theology and inter-cultural understanding, were added as requirements. A system of faculty advisors was to ensure that a student took the correct courses to receive a liberal arts education. But experience through the 1970s indicated that the advising system did not work well and students were not choosing well. They chose courses that added to their career path and "found ways of avoiding the liberalizing process which the College's curriculum was intended to guarantee." Faculty critics noted that there was no "synthesis or integration of the diversity in disciplines, skills, and course materials."[8]

In February 1978, Moeller appointed a committee to study the curriculum and suggest possible revisions. He said the goal was to "find out what the educated person should be like in the 1980s and 1990s."[9] The committee's proposal was presented to the community in the fall of 1979. It continued the institutional requirement in theology, currently met by the introduction to philosophy and

theology course, which had been so contentious in the earlier revision. It called for four entry level skills courses in English composition, physical education, public speaking, and mathematics. The most controversial was the elimination of divisional requirements and the creation of seven liberal arts core areas: human nature and human institutions, the scientific study of the physical universe, forms of aesthetic expression, a foreign language or culture, times other than our own, values and the human condition, and formal reasoning. The final course was a three-hour multi-disciplinary problem-solving course.[10] In addition to the core requirements, students would take courses in their academic major. The committee left it to the Educational Policies Committee to decide which courses met the requirement for each core area.

Students thought the proposal was too complex and relied too much on an advising system that had already shown itself to be inadequate. But the principal student objection was stated by Ann Glenn, the editor of the *Paper SAC*. She said there were too many hours not devoted to the requirements for a major, which meant the student would spend "more time being 'liberally educated,' and less time . . . developing skills and understandings basic to getting and keeping jobs." She admitted St. Ambrose was a liberal arts college but it should not ignore "practical courses . . . In today's world we must be able to sell ourselves. As college graduates, we offer a product to American society. We strive to make ours the best product. We must concentrate on gaining practical and conceptual skills." This proposal, she said, "does not allow that."[11]

Most of the faculty believed the core areas were appropriate, but some thought the proposal gave too much power to the Educational Policies Committee in deciding which courses met the distributional requirements. Some objected to the proposal because they feared that their courses might have to be dropped or they might have to create new ones. Others objected because they said it moved away from the freedom of student choice represented by the 1972 revision. Still others disagreed with the basic thematic premise of the distributional requirements. The faculty was divided on whether it would help or hurt enrollment, that other factors like the economy had a greater impact on enrollment. When it came before the faculty, it was defeated on a tie vote.

In 1982, another curriculum review committee began work. Faculty surveys had indicated that something should be done to ensure a broader liberal arts education. Most agreed that there was a lack of a well-rounded educational experience at St. Ambrose, but as two years before, there was disagreement on how to achieve that. Moeller noted the tendency for students to "specialize more and more," and Professor Paul Jacobson, dean of curriculum, said there was "tension between career-oriented fields . . . and liberal arts fields."[12]

The committee worked through the revision process, considered the objections of faculty and students, and finally presented a revision that was accepted. By now more faculty were willing to accept the fact that the students were not doing a good job of choosing their academic program and the college should make some curricular choices for its students. This curriculum required mastery in four basic skills: English, mathematics, public speaking, and library skills. It rejected the thematic divisional requirements in the 1980 proposal and retained the divisional requirements of the earlier 1972 revision which were fulfilled by taking specified general education courses in each department. The new curriculum became effective with the 1985 catalogue.

Pete Cunningham and Kelly Keogh lamented that St. Ambrose students were too concerned with career preparation and lacked the involvement exhibited by students in earlier decades. But there were still some students who continued to raise questions about justice and continued to protest when they discovered injustice. In the spring of 1981, about thirty students and faculty staged weekly demonstrations at the Federal Building to protest American involvement in El Salvador. In November 1981, the American bishops issued a "Statement on Central America," calling for the end to armed conflict and political repression in that region. In response, St. Ambrose Students for Peace planned a series of events to raise awareness about the conflicts in that region.[13]

In March 1982, St. Ambrose students welcomed participants from the World Peace March who were marching from St. Francisco to New York to demonstrate at the United Nations' Special Session on Disarmament. Over 200 people attended a rally in the chapel and then moved to demonstrate at the Rock Island Arsenal. During the demonstration, eight Ambrosians who were distributing leaflets to arsenal workers were escorted from the island and later received letters barring them from the facility. The arsenal continued to be a focus of demonstrations that spring, and in April eleven Ambrosians were arrested for their activities there.[14]

The issues raised by those demonstrations were also part of the curriculum. Father Dawson had taught the ethics of peace and non-violence since 1969. In the first years, the class drew as many as ninety students, but in more recent years there were only ten or fifteen. But Dawson said that in the early 1980s, especially after the American bishops issued a major document, "The Challenge of Peace: God's Promise and Our Response," the numbers were picking up again. That "renewed interest" was "encouraging" to Dawson.[15]

In February 1982, Father Edmond Dunn introduced a new academic minor in peace and justice. Dunn said that around the country similar programs were developed to "counteract the growing militarism in the world" and to raise the consciousness of students about the growing "chasm between the rich and the poor nations of the world." Moeller said this new minor was consistent with the college's "tradition of concern for the social teaching of the church."[16]

Those issues were taken out of the classroom by the Ambrosians for Peace and Justice, a new group formed in 1985. Dunn said it exhibited the same "dedication" as the groups of the 1960s, but with a "quiet impact." Dawson said they were not trying to "shock" people, but to be more "positive and constructive" in advocating the issues. The group divided into three committees to focus on Central American issues, nuclear war, and hunger. They participated in the annual Crop Walk, Hunger Awareness Week, and cooked meals at the Catholic Worker house.[17]

In 1986, twelve members of the group traveled to eastern Kentucky to work at the David School, founded in 1974 in a coal mining region of the state to provide education for Appalachian youth and adults with limited financial resources. Student groups from the Diocese of Davenport had been going there for a few years, and now the David School became the first service project for the Ambrosians for Peace and Justice. They were accompanied by the Reverend Anthony Herold, the spiritual director of the seminary. During their week in David, the Ambrosians worked to help build a new school building.[18]

Dawson's course, and the new peace and justice minor, were consistent with the tradition of St. Ambrose, but other new programs spoke to the concerns expressed by Cunningham and Keogh and represented the new business-oriented values espoused by Bakrow. In November 1982, the MBA program was accredited by the North Central Association which cited its "superb administration" and called it a "good program, filling an education need of the community." At the same time, Dr. James Jensen, a former deputy director of the Army Management Engineering Training Activity at the Rock Island Arsenal, was named the new dean of the program. The program had been offered evenings, and in January 1983, it expanded to add

A Great and Lasting Beginning

a Saturday program. In time, the MBA program, now named the H. L. McLaughlin MBA Program, was taught in Clinton, Muscatine, and Burlington.[19]

In 1982, the college established the Institute of Industrial Engineering, a four-year program which built on the pre-engineering program that was already part of the curriculum. It was created by a task force that included faculty and representatives from local business and industries. Bakrow said this new program was an effort to "market" St. Ambrose and could eventually enroll 300-400 students, which would give it "as large an impact on the college as the MBA." Newton Sacks, who had been director of safety and environment at John Deere, was named to head the institute.[20]

The MBA program and the Industrial Engineering Institute were a response to needs expressed by the local business community and were created by advisory boards that included representatives of the local community. They were academic programs that led to a degree. The earlier Institute for Management Development had been a non-degree program for local executives. In 1985, St. Ambrose and the AAA Travel Agency established the Midwest Travel Institute, a non-degree program, to prepare students for a career in the travel industry. Courses met five days a week for eight weeks and were taught by people in the industry and St. Ambrose instructors.[21]

Some on campus expressed concern about the growing relationship of the college and the corporate world. In an April 1983 letter to the *Paper SAC*, Professors DeJohn and Geiger from history, Dawson from philosophy, and Dunn from theology wrote that the college had to face the truth that St. Ambrose had "become more of a service institution for the corporate world." They admitted that St. Ambrose had always had a business program but the role of "purely vocational or utilitarian programs" had grown "enormously in recent decades." The writers noted that in 1962, forty-eight students (24 percent of the class) had graduated as business and accounting majors; in 1982, those same majors accounted for 166 graduates (48 percent of the class), and that did not count graduates in criminal justice, mass communications, and computer science which had not been taught in 1962.[22]

There were no longer the various literary societies of one hundred years before to help the students learn to speak and to occupy their time on a Friday night. But the centennial students had many other activities from which to choose. As had been the case for decades, student organizations came and went. The SGA continued each year, but often the issues were not great and the interest by the student body was small. The *Paper SAC* and the *Oaks* yearbook both ceased publication in May 1984. They were replaced the next fall by the *Ambrose Magazine*. The *Magazine* was published every other week and came bound like a magazine, with holes punched so students could file the issues in a three-ringed binder. A special year-end issue contained photographs of the seniors and a review of the year's activities.

Several clubs were related to the students' fields of study: Psi Chi, the Psychology Club; FESTA, the future engineers at St. Ambrose; the business fraternity Delta Sigma Pi; the Agri-Business Club; Physical Education Club; the Art Club; and Tri-Beta for biologists. Music Ministry provided music for liturgical services; Alpha Phi Omega was a service fraternity

founded at St. Ambrose in 1980. In 1983, the Student Alumni Organization (SAO) formed "to involve alumni and students in a continuing relationship with St. Ambrose so they feel more a part of the college when they graduate."[23]

There was a series of annual social events beginning with the Mississippi River boat ride at the beginning of the year, then the Woodsie, Oktoberfest, homecoming, Brother-Sister Weekend, Mardi Gras, the Sweetheart's Dance, Springfest, May Day, and the Last Blast. Those events usually included a band, or several bands, sometimes a movie, and often a keg. The possible presence of a keg raised administration concerns about alcohol consumption and liability issues.

The Theatre department had a season of two plays that year, *Tiger at the Gates* and *The Tempest*, the annual children's show was *Winnie the Pooh*, and the spring musical was *Carousel*, which had first been performed at St. Ambrose in 1961. The vocal and instrumental music groups had their usual cycle of concerts each year. One of the high points for the college choir was providing music for the annual Mass to celebrate the feast of St. Ambrose. To celebrate the end of the centennial year in 1982, the choir performed Puccini's *Messa di Gloria* directed by Father Edmond Dunn with the St. Ambrose orchestra and student soloists.

The band's concert season included the Annual All-American concert for Veterans Day and to celebrate the centennial in 1982, there was a special concert performed by alumni members of the band. Three former conductors returned to campus to lead parts of the program: Monsignor Cletus Madsen (he had been made a Monsignor in 1973) had led the band in the 1930s and 1940s; Clarence Kriesa (1947-1965); and Francis Gerzina (1965-1974). They were joined by the current conductor, Dr. Charles DCamp.

The students still focused their attention on the two most consistent issues of student life: food and parking. They complained that snow removal from the parking lots should be better, they paid $12 for a parking permit, but still could not find a place to park, and the neighbors complained if they parked in front of their houses. Suggested solutions included eliminating reserved parking for administrators, prohibiting resident students from bringing cars to campus, telling commuter students they should ride a bicycle or walk to class, and building a parking ramp.[24]

Food in the cafeteria was always a target of criticism, so pizza delivered to their residence hall became an important part of the students' diet. In September 1985, the *Ambrose Magazine* formed a panel of five students to rate local pizza. They approached their task scientifically and ordered from five pizzerias: Happy Joe's, Fat Boy's, Godfather's, the Chef's Hat, and Domino's. They tested texture, thickness, packaging, and delivery time. Four of the five liked Godfather's because of the large amount of cheese, its thick crust, or the large amount of sauce. One liked it because of the little plastic knife that came with it. Kevin Alberhasky, however, liked Domino's because with a "fast delivery and at a great price you can't beat that." The next year, a similar group visited various taco restaurants and rated Martinez Taco House the best.[25]

Neighborhood bars and restaurants drew students away from campus. Some of the most popular were Valentino's on East Kimberly, the Piccadilly Pub, McButts, and the Uptown, which featured pool tables, a large screen TV, and drinks which were "measured liberally." The Circle Tap was only a few blocks west of campus on Locust Street. Owned by Jerry Kelly, a 1963 graduate of St. Ambrose, trays of burgers were put on the bar and customers were trusted to put money down to pay for what they ate. Kelly's attitude was: "Your mom might feed you for free, but I don't. Leave your money on the bar." Riefe's was another block west, and still further west was the Five-Points Donut Shop which featured fresh donuts and other pastries at all hours.[26]

The centennial version of the old Play Hall, the new physical education center, was dedicated on September 30, 1983. The 47,300 square foot building was named the Lee Lohman Arena. Lohman was a 1957 graduate and president of L. B. Benefits, Inc., a Lohman Brother Company based in Geneseo, Illinois. It featured a basketball court with seating for 2,200 spectators, four racquetball courts, two weight rooms, a running track, a training room, and equipment and locker rooms. At the west end of the building on the second floor were classrooms and offices for the physical education faculty and coaches of the varsity sports. Leo Kilfoy said it would be a great advantage to teachers and coaches: "A better athlete wants better facilities and the new gym is more convenient and conducive to good teaching." For years the Bees had played their basketball games at Assumption High School, and Ray Shovlain, the new basketball coach, said the new facility would help recruiting and attendance, since "the on-campus student can now walk to and from the home games."[27]

The principal speaker for the dedication was Richard "Digger" Phelps, head basketball coach at Notre Dame University. Phelps emphasized that education should be the first priority of colleges and warned the Ambrosians not to put too much emphasis on winning and losing in athletics. He said the "most important and biggest game" the students would play would be the "game of life. The only way you're ever going to lose that game is if you beat yourself."[28] SGA president Jim Hannon spoke on behalf of the students. He said he was supposed to thank the college for the new facility but instead, he said the college should thank the students for com-

Rev. Frederick McMahan, Rev. Joseph Hratz, and Rev. Herman Strub had all attended St. Ambrose and graduated in the 1930s. When this photo was taken in 1985, they had a combined total of 101 years of service on the faculty.

ing to St. Ambrose.

The new athletic facility was busy from the day it opened. It housed an expanding intramural program that now included flickerball, tennis, walleyball, volleyball, racquetball, and a St. Ambrose Olympics consisting of ten events. There were men's teams and women's teams in many of those sports as well as coed teams for some.[29]

The intramural program competed for space in the new building with a full fall and winter varsity sports schedule. There were now nine varsity sports: for the men, football, basketball, tennis, golf, and baseball; and for the women, basketball, softball, tennis, and volleyball. That fall, the women's volleyball team won the NAIA District Championship, the Region VII Championship, and was ranked fifth in the nation. The Queen Bees basketball team, under head coach Ken Buckles, finished their first season in Lee Lohman Arena with a 26-3 record and won the District 15 Championship. It was the third 20-win season for coach Buckles and his last season as coach. The next year Lisa Bluder became the women's basketball coach. Women's tennis, coached by Barbara (Walker) Shuman, also won the NAIA District 15 Championship.[30] At the end of the year, the St. Ambrose women's program was named one of the top fifty NAIA programs in the nation.

The football team under second-year coach John Furlong had a 7-3-1 record, the best in more than a decade, and was ranked eighteenth in the nation. The men's basketball team had a new head coach in Ray Shovlain. A 1979 St. Ambrose graduate, Shovlain brought an intensity and new enthusiasm to the program. Shovlain said, "A competitive attitude makes up for a lack of speed, lack of height, or lack of talent," and he began to recruit "our type of player, hard-nosed, who'll dive for loose balls, and be solid defensively."[31] The Bees finished the season with a 12-16 record. The men's golf team won the district title and third-year coach Jeff Griebel was named NAIA Coach of the Year.

In the spring of 1984, the men's tennis team, coached by Shelly Weiner, advanced to the NAIA national tournament for the seventh consecutive

A Great and Lasting Beginning

year. Weiner was named District 15 coach of the year for the seventh consecutive year. The baseball team played to a 20-10-1 season and finished second in the NAIA regional tournament. Plagued by injuries and wet weather, the women's softball team had a 4-10 season.

The athletic program received a new leader in the summer of 1984 when Jim Fox was named athletic director. A legend in Davenport sports, Fox had coached three Central High School football teams and several wrestlers to state championships. A member of three Iowa sports Halls of Fame, Fox brought his broad experience and reputation to the St. Ambrose program.[32]

Unknown to many in the St. Ambrose community, talks had resumed with Marycrest. In May 1979, the St. Ambrose Board of Directors asked Bakrow to select a committee to study the feasibility of "cooperation" with Marycrest. Following a lengthy analysis of the relationship of the two schools, the group recommended that a "full-fledged merger attempt based upon the pre-requisite of sound economics [had] no serious drawbacks." Bakrow presented the recommendation to the board at a meeting on April 21, 1980. The board directed Bishop O'Keefe to write James Tank, the chairman of the Marycrest board, that St. Ambrose wanted to discuss ways in which the two school might cooperate. The board also formed a committee of Monsignor Cletus Madsen, Johnny Lujack, Wier Sears, and Robert Gerstenberger to represent St. Ambrose interests in those discussions. The Marycrest Board of Trustees had also been discussing the "merits of serious consideration to a merger . . . in the very near future." At the least they felt that every effort should be made to "improve communications" and they appointed a committee to meet with the Madsen group.[33]

Three days after the St. Ambrose board meeting, the bishop met with Sister Ann Therese Collins, CHM, the president of the Congregation of the Humility of Mary. She told him that the sisters had no objection to an eventual merger of the two schools, but they would not consider a sale of the Marycrest property. She said the Peoples' Debt was still being paid by the college to the sisters and that would be part of any combination with St. Ambrose. Her view was that the process should begin with cooperation which would allow students from one school to take classes at the other and that after five years, "under this system the schools would in effect be one." She felt there might be "some opposition to retaining [the] present president of St. Ambrose for [the] joint school," but admitted that could change in five years. She told O'Keefe that at the present, "St. Ambrose wouldn't want Marycrest as a gift," which suggested problems at Marycrest that would put a combined institution at a disadvantage. Instead, she favored a "slow, cautious approach to consolidation."[34]

Both groups had hoped to hold their discussions in confidence, but on June 19, 1980, Marycrest interim President Lynn Bryant issued a press release announcing that discussions were under way. Bryant said the community needed to know that the "two schools are not at odds." He admitted that a merger was "years away," but the two schools could exchange students and share courses "tomorrow." Not everyone on either board was pleased that the talks were now public which put unwanted pressure on them to produce results. A *Quad-City Times* editorial said it was "inconceivable" that a city the size of Davenport could support two private liberal arts schools. With two committees in place, the paper said there was reason for

optimism that this time a merger could be effected, "The climate is ripe. The Marycrest-Ambrose Cooperation Committee–or Big MAC, as it has been dubbed–has its work cut out for it."[35]

The newspaper may have thought there was reason for optimism, but the two board groups met a week after the press attention, stressed the need for confidentiality, and said they could do little until the college administrations supplied them with a great deal of information. At the same time Bakrow, Rogalski, and Moeller met a number of times with their counterparts at Marycrest and reported in September 1980 that there had been "no dramatic breakthrough," but they would continue to meet.

One of the difficulties was a perceived difference in the mission of the two schools. Marycrest identified itself as having a "Catholic heritage" while St. Ambrose said it was a diocesan-related Roman Catholic institution. Those two different missions "might or might not be compatible," and Madsen said until that was resolved, other steps should wait. Another difficulty was that the various elements of each campus were divided on the question of the best way for St. Ambrose and Marycrest to relate. In December 1980, Bakrow reported dissension within the Marycrest board and faculty about what course of action to take. On the St. Ambrose campus, there were similar divisions.[36]

Discussions continued for another two years and in September 1982, Madsen told the board there had been little progress. He suggested that the St. Ambrose board adopt a different approach and that an individual from each institution be appointed to explore "any potential for mutual benefits" to the two schools. Professor Joseph McCaffrey was selected to represent St. Ambrose. The Marycrest board was also "not satisfied" with the progress of the talks and members reported that they were hearing from the community that talks should be resumed. They asked Collins to represent Marycrest in discussions with McCaffrey.[37]

McCaffrey and Collins met in December and January and discussed a wide range of options. Collins stressed establishing an exchange of students between the institutions and while McCaffrey did not disagree, he also stressed the need to discuss a possible merger. He told the board committee that there would be "no quick movements" but that talks would continue. As the two continued to meet, they discussed four possible areas of curricular cooperation: foreign languages, theology, sociology-social work, and physical education. They decided to choose sociology-social work and they developed a plan for cooperation between the sociology departments of the two schools.[38]

As their discussions continued, McCaffrey returned to the question of a merger and Collins told him that St. Ambrose could "have" Marycrest, could absorb it so there would be only one college: St. Ambrose. She said, however, that Bakrow would have to go as president. McCaffrey said that would be agreeable but that Dr. Lynn Bryant, the Marycrest president, would also have to resign. Collins agreed and said they had a deal. But when McCaffrey reported this to Bakrow, he told McCaffrey that such a deal was unacceptable, that he had gone too far, and that in fact he did not want any kind of agreement with Marycrest. Subsequently, Bakrow and Bryant met and agreed that the talks had gone too far and should be stopped. Within weeks, further discussions stopped and the two institutions continued to proceed separately.[39]

Another year passed with no further progress, and in the fall of 1985,

Bakrow and Collins, who was now the president of Marycrest, met to discuss the possibility of the two schools coming together. Bakrow said his first choice was to buy Marycrest for $3 to $4 million, his second choice would be a merger and if that failed, cooperation. Collins said her first choice was a consortium from which a merger could evolve. She said a sale of Marycrest would be considered only if the offer was for $12 million. Collins reported the meeting to her board where the consensus was that there was "not much interest at this point" of further talks. Following that meeting, Collins reported the board decision to Bakrow and said the two of them should "continue to search out ways to foster better understanding between" Marycrest and St. Ambrose. But it would be several years before the two groups talked again.[40]

A college's identity is manifested by its mission statement, its curriculum, and its history. The deep sense of identity on the part of St. Ambrose and Marycrest contributed to the difficulties of the merger talks ten years before and

John Morrissey, Sr., created the official mace of the university and carried it at the spring 1984 commencement ceremony.

the more recent discussions about cooperation. Added to formal statements and curricula were the other symbols and customs that students and alumni identified as Ambrosian: the crest created in the 1920s, Bernie Schultz's "Victory March," the alma mater *"Ambrosian Oaks,"* the nickname Bees, the Bee Hive, the Irish Village, graduation under the oaks, the many annual social events that were developed by one generation of students which prospered for a few years only to disappear and be replaced be a new generation of students with new events.

Another of those symbols was added when Bakrow asked John Morrissey, Sr., to create an official mace, an ornamental staff carried at the head of the procession of graduates and faculty as a symbol of the authority of the institution. Morrissey used Brazilian rosewood inset with four slate carvings of a cross, a Eucharistic image of a chalice and host, an oak leaf and an acorn, and the college seal done by Paul Herrera, one of Catich's students. It was topped by a gold acorn. At Bakrow's suggestion, Morrissey carried the mace for the first time at the 1984 spring graduation.[41]

The college symbol with the longest history was the statue of St.

Ambrose, which as David Klise had described years before, had stood on "his pedestal on the front walk imparting his blessing to passersby," for over ninety years. On a November evening in 1985, a visitor to campus jumped up to greet the saint and accidentally pushed the statue off pedestal to the sidewalk below. people gathered to look at the statue lying supine on the side Father Shafer commented, seems much like a death in ily. It was part of college life.

The head was badly damaged although the face was in it appeared that it could be repaired. Neverthless, Anderson, a part-time actor, took up the task of repair it. Anderson through the spring and rebuilt the head, fashioned hand to replace the one that been missing for decades bronzed the entire statue. He made two plaques illustrating in dents from the life of St. Ambrose and another of the college seal for the base. The restored statue was put in place and dedicated at homecoming 1986.[43] In spite of Anderson's work, the refurbished statue began to deteriorate and in 1992, it had to be removed.

The replacement was a statue of St. Ambrose that had stood in the chapel since 1976. This one had come from a church in Cleveland, Ohio. It was slightly shorter than the original and portrayed a different Ambrose. The original had been pastoral, with Ambrose holding a bishop's crozier in the right hand and a book in the left. In the new statue, Ambrose held a sheaf of papers in his right hand and a book in the left, and instead of imparting a blessing to passersby, he looked out at them with a stern stare.

Another statue that had become a campus landmark was the Blessed Mother given by Miss Margaret Meek in 1922. It had originally been in a rock grotto east of Davis Hall, then was moved east of Lewis Hall, and then when the chapel was built, was moved behind Ambrose Hall and sat in a small, wooden shrine. As a result of a gift of $70,000 by board member Johnny Lujack, a new stone grotto was constructed to house the statue. At the dedication in June 1987, Bishop O'Keefe said that the grotto would be a "place where we could go to ask for healing, particularly for a healing of the soul, a place where we might come to find consolation and strength.

A Great and Lasting Beginning

The students who study here are engaged in the search for truth. It is this search for truth which will be aided and brought about by the deepening of their faith."[44]

As class began in the fall of 1984, Bakrow had been president for eleven years. In an interview that fall, he said that with the financial situation of the college "stabilized," it was time to turn to its "academic future." To be sure, the accounts of the first years of the 1980s were in balance, but there were still weaknesses. For one thing, the endowment was too small. It had been $1.6 million in 1981-1982 and increased to $2.4 million the next year, a jump of 49 percent due to an estate designated for scholarships, money from an NEH grant, endowment gifts in the recent campaign, and gains in the stock market. But the audit for 1983-1984 said the endowment, now $3.5 million was "pitifully small," which made the college too tuition-dependent; 90 percent of the annual income came from tuition. It was clear the endowment had to be increased dramatically; Bakrow said it should be $30 million. The auditors suggested increasing annual giving, increasing the size of individual gifts from alumni, and increasing the number of alumni who gave.[45]

To help achieve the financial and academic goals, and to provide a more orderly planning process, in 1984, Bakrow appointed a campus-wide committee to create a strategic plan that looked at the college for the next three years. The committee included the vice presidents, the senior academic officers, and representatives from the faculty, students, alumni, and the Board of Directors. The group used the mission statement developed by the long range planning committee in 1974 which said St. Ambrose was a "private, diocesan-related Catholic institution of higher learning" which provided a combination of instruction in the liberal arts and pre-professional career preparation. The committee agreed that all programs must be compatible with the mission statement; all programs would preserve academic freedom; and all baccalaureate programs would have a liberal arts component. To achieve that, it defined a set of objectives gathered into seven areas: Catholicity, academic excellence, plant and equipment, finances, growth, student services, and college organization. The committee was asked to look three years into the future and develop an action plan to achieve those objectives, along with the estimated cost to achieve each plan.

The planning committee met each year and reviewed the previous plan, made adjustments where necessary in light of changed situations on campus and local economic conditions, and introduced new projects and programs. When the first strategic plan was presented in early 1985, Bakrow said planning was an "evolving procedure based on a projected vision of the College through 1988 . . . Our strategies for efficiency and effectiveness in our mission are simple, intensify, extend, diversify, re-allocate."[46]

Efforts to improve the long-term financial situation of the college, however, faced a significant obstacle in the decade of the 1980s. In the 1970s, the value of farmland in the United States rose dramatically, allowing farmers to expand their operations by borrowing money which created a debt that needed high crop prices to sustain. However, beginning in 1981, prices declined and the value of farmland fell; 1983 saw the "biggest single-year drop in farmland value since the Great Depression."[47] That led to a decline in the production of farm machinery, which was a major segment of the Quad-City economy.

In January 1985, Bakrow told the board there was a "distinct possibility" that the college would have a deficit which could run to "several hundred thousand dollars" for the current academic year. There was a "shrunken pool of students," because of a declining economy in the Quad-City area and more money would have to be spent for financial aid to maintain enrollment levels. He also said the annual fund goal of $600,000 could "fall short." Although the board may have understood the reasons why, they still could not have been happy to hear that the possible deficit could run to "several hundred thousand dollars."[48]

The local economy was also troublesome because the board was considering a major fund raising campaign of at least $10 million, most of which would be designated for the endowment. As preparation for a campaign, Bakrow asked the consulting firm of James W. Frick Associates to survey the board to determine their attitudes and perceptions about the college and their role as members of the board. Part of the survey addressed Bakrow's role as president. Nineteen of the twenty-one members of the board were surveyed and 60 percent believed the college was "well-managed" and attributed that to the president and key administrators. Thirty percent, however, said there was no long-range planning and that the college ran on a day-to-day basis. Others claimed the board had become a "rubber stamp," although that was changing. When Bakrow first spoke to the board in 1973, they asked him to make greater use of them. But the survey found that some board members complained that they should be more involved and there was too much of a "free-wheeling" approach; they felt their meetings tended to be "reactive rather than initiative," and they wanted more information upon which to base decisions. Still, most board members indicated support for Bakrow and saw him as the key to the success of that campaign.[49]

In November 1984, the board had offered Bakrow a four-year contract which said he would remain president until June 30, 1987, and then would become chancellor. As chancellor he would engage in fund raising, especially to increase the endowment. Bakrow accepted the contract and called it a "vote of confidence." He pledged to O'Keefe and the board "a continued, and even augmented effort to make St. Ambrose College–spiritually, academically, and fiscally–an ever-improving institution."[50]

A year later, Bakrow told a reporter for the *Ambrose Magazine* that he would retire when he thought he was "not making important contributions to the college." He said he did not want to stop working, but thought when he left St. Ambrose he would start a small business, perhaps a book store. He made it clear to the reporter that he was not ready to retire yet. But by the time the Frick report was presented to the board on April 10, 1986, Bakrow had apparently decided to retire earlier than the contract date. Writing Bakrow on April 21, James Frick said he knew he had "intended to retire earlier," but he was essential to the success of the campaign and he hoped Bakrow would "give the college two more years, one as president and the other as chancellor." If Bakrow were willing to "extend" his service, Frick felt "reasonably sure" the campaign would be a success. On April 24, Bakrow sent a copy of Frick's letter to the bishop and the two board members who had negotiated his contract. He told them Frick's letter was "self-explanatory . . . He obviously caught a trace of conflict" which had made him write the letter. Bakrow told the bishop if Frick's suggested time frame

A new image of St. Ambrose watches passersby in front of Ambrose Hall. (Photo by Stephen Spartana)

was agreeable to the bishop, it was "satisfactory" to him.[51]

O'Keefe agreed to the terms Bakrow had proposed, but said he was "increasingly uneasy" that the entire board was unaware of the proposed changes in Bakrow's contract. On June 9, 1986, O'Keefe sent a signed contract to Bakrow and although it would be a "breach of confidentiality," told him he intended to inform the board. That same day, the bishop wrote each board member, "As you know, Dr. William Bakrow has been considering retiring from the presidency . . . and has now drawn up a plan for the gradual withdrawal from the office" on June 30, 1987. O'Keefe said he had hoped to call a board meeting to discuss the matter but realized that would not be possible. The bishop included the time table Bakrow had created that included the appointment of Edward Rogalski as executive vice president on approximately July 1, 1986, and the appointment of a search committee for a new president by the end of August. O'Keefe told the board, "I feel that we must honor his request."[52]

When the students returned in September 1986, Bakrow announced that he had asked the board of directors to have his replacement in place by the following June, after which he would serve as chancellor for one year. He said it was good for an institution to periodically have a "changing of the guard," and such a change should come at a time of strength. O'Keefe said the board had agreed to Bakrow's request "with regret." At the same time it was announced that Rogalski had been promoted to executive vice

president, responsible for the day-to-day affairs of the college while Bakrow traveled to raise money for the endowment. In December, the board finalized Bakrow's post-presidential status. With the title of chancellor dropped, he would become president emeritus for a period of one year, responsible for the special gifts component of the endowment campaign.[53]

The bishop appointed the Reverend Monsignor Michael Morrissey, the vicar general, as chairman of the search committee, which included three members of the board, five from the faculty, and two students. The committee hired a search consultant who led them through the process and in April 1987, Morrissey reported to the board that three candidates would be brought to campus.[54]

The search was watched closely on campus. In late April students from a communications class took a survey that found 71 percent of those polled said the main duty of the president was "to ensure the quality of education," others said it was to maintain an open door for students or to increase enrollment. A student member of the search committee said the president should be Catholic, but 39 percent of those surveyed said the religion of the president did not matter. And in what may have been a blow to Bakrow, 34 percent of the students surveyed could not name the current president. The weekly survey conducted by the *Ambrose Magazine* said that Bakrow had two goals when he became president: to have academic excellence and to have a talented, motivated faculty, and it asked if he had achieved those

A Great and Lasting Beginning

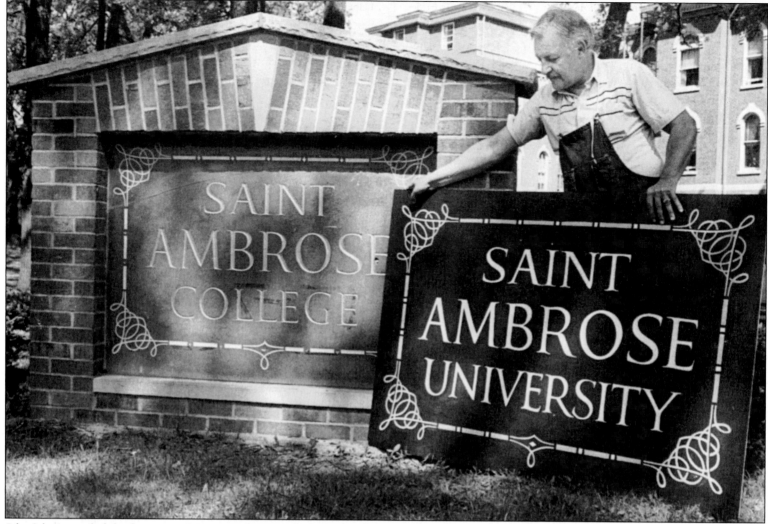

John Schmits marked the change to a university with a new sign using the calligraphy of his teacher, Fr. Catich.

goals. The five students who responded said that business and the business faculty was strong, but that in other fields the faculty was not "enthused," "would rather be somewhere else," and there was "still a ways to go."[55]

At the same meeting that Morrissey reported to the board on the presidential search, the directors took another action that had a far-reaching impact on St. Ambrose when it declared by a unanimous vote that the college was now a university. The impetus for this move had been the announcement that Western Illinois University, a state school eighty miles south in Macomb, Illinois, had planned to open a Quad-Cities campus and offer Bachelor's Degrees in business, accounting, and elementary education. Bakrow and the presidents of Marycrest and Augustana Colleges expressed concern about the possibility of students attending this new campus drawn there by the lower tuition. Bakrow said then that "competition has never bothered" St. Ambrose, but he said expansion of undergraduate programs should be "undertaken collegially," and it would be better for the state to spend money for scholarships so Illinois students could attend colleges already serving the community. At the same time, he said St. Ambrose was too dependent on local students and should move to become a more residential college.[56]

Competition may not have bothered Bakrow, but at the same time he asked his officers to develop a strategy to counter any move Western Illinois made. Their first recommendation was that the Board of Directors announce by July 1, 1987, that St. Ambrose become a university.

Bakrow had not originally supported the idea, but when all his advisors recommended it and the board gave it unanimous approval, he quickly called a news conference to make the announcement. Bakrow explained that the change was necessary to plan for future expansion and to remain competitive with other colleges in the area, especially the recently announced plans by Western Illinois University to expand into the Quad-Cities. St. Ambrose wanted to become a "national rather than a regional institution," and up to now it had been "too dependent on the Quad-Cities," which, given its economic condition, had not been able to "fulfill our ambitions." He said that the new structure would enable St. Ambrose to play a greater role in the economic development of the community through new programs and the enhancement of programs already in place.[57]

To the St. Ambrose community it appeared to be a sudden change: one day the president called a news conference and made an announcement. And it appeared to be that easy. When asked what was involved, the provost, Donald Moeller, said all one did was notify the North Central Association that St. Ambrose was now a university. In fact, the change to university status was not that simple or that casual. The move by Western Illinois was the catalyst, but it reflected changes that had been slowly taking place since the failure of the Marycrest merger fifteen years earlier; and it signaled changes in structure, curriculum, campus life, and culture that would evolve in the years to come. Rogalski said it was a natural move, "We had expanded into so many areas, we were acting like a university without calling ourselves" one. The move would "help clarify our mission, which is to serve a larger segment of the public." Liberal arts remained the core and St. Ambrose's "primary reason for being," and the first college of the university structure would be the college of liberal arts. There would likely be a college of professional studies, a college of business, and Rogalski said others could come later.[58]

The change was received well in the community. *The Rock Island Argus* noted it was "nice' for Quad-Citians to "live in a university community, especially without having to move." But the paper assured its readers that the move was more than "window dressing," that it would help St. Ambrose play an "even larger role in economic development." The *Quad-City Times* said the change meant that St. Ambrose had "a lot in store" for the region, including attracting more students from outside the area which would help the local economy.[59]

Reaction by most on campus was to wait and see what would happen. One faculty wag said now that he taught at a university, the honor was greater, but the pay was the same. Another faculty member suggested changing the school nickname to the "Sages," so they would be known as the "SAU Sages." Most faculty understood that there were many unanswered questions about curriculum, organizational structure, committee structures, and countless other details that would have to be worked out in the coming years. The students were also unsure about what it meant. When the *Ambrose Magazine* asked what changes they expected because the school was now a university, one student said he expected more courses in all fields; another said it would be a more diversified institution; still another thought it would take many years for an answer to the question; others thought it would attract more students; and one said it meant nothing to him right now and he wondered how much it cost to change all the campus signs to say university.[60]

As he neared the end of his presidency, in April Bakrow gave an interview to the *Ambrose Magazine*. He said he and Maree had planned to retire when he was sixty, and he was now 63, so they were "already behind schedule." They wanted to travel and would eventually move back to the east coast to their house in Rockport, Massachusetts. He said they wanted to be catalysts for St. Ambrose alumni gatherings and recruiting and he also hoped to become a consultant on college matters, but he said he would not "look over the shoulder of the new administration." He said he would like to publish articles, and perhaps a book on college administration, especially on the "inter-relationship between business and the academic environment," as he believed the two fields could "learn from each other."[61]

Bakrow became president within months of the failure of the merger, when the college was trying to solve some of the problems that had led it to consider merging with Marycrest. In his first years, he was able to strengthen the financial picture and the enrollment of the college, in part by adding new programs like the MBA and engineering. His background in management led him to establish management training programs which helped to improve the relationship of the college with the Quad-City business community. The college was in better shape when he left than when he arrived, but most of that was the result of work in the first years of his presidency. In his last years, he had begun another planning cycle for the future of the college and a major program for endowment support, but it would remain for others to complete those projects.

Bakrow was awarded an honorary degree and delivered the address at the spring commencement. He reminded the graduates that they were in second grade when he became president of St. Ambrose, and that while they had grown older and wiser, he had grown older. He spoke of the times he had "kicked [the college], screamed at it, pushed it, pulled it, ran pantingly after it, and in general laughed and cried over it." There were times when it seemed to be filled with "wrong-headed students and faculty members, each of whom seemed profoundly dedicated to the notion of disagreeing with everything." But he said there were "more times when it was a marvelously exciting community" with everyone moving "forward together to make it so very special—and you, too, must have come to love it as I do."[62]

On June 5, 1987, Bishop O'Keefe announced the "obvious choice" of Edward Rogalski as the twelfth president of St. Ambrose. "It was like finding a treasure in your own back yard," O'Keefe said, "We have all recognized for a long time the abilities of Dr. Rogalski." Rogalski said he accepted the presidency with "humility and . . . confidence and trust in the people who [had] been so much a part" of his experience at St. Ambrose. He mentioned Madsen who had suggested to Menke in 1968 that he hire Rogalski; he mentioned Menke whom he had served when he was president; and he mentioned the Bakrows. He said his goal for St. Ambrose was to "excel in all we do," in the classroom and in the community. There was a great deal of potential in both, and he said he stood ready "to serve and do my part" to develop that potential.[63]

Rogalski said he would not make any immediate changes to the institution, but would take a year to study before any changes were made. Two projects could not wait however: the formation of colleges for the new university structure and increasing the endowment. Currently at $4 million, Rogalski said the endowment should be at least $20 million to "ensure the near future of St. Ambrose." He assured the campus community that they would all be a part of the planning of those changes and he said he wanted "to devote my energy to try to coordinate human resources: Faculty, students, staff, administration, friends, towards a greater spirited commitment to make St. Ambrose successful."[64]

Rogalski's inauguration was part of a week-long homecoming celebration. The week began Monday evening, October 5, with a powder-puff football game, followed by Monday night football in Stinger's Lounge. Tuesday night there were St. Ambrose versions of popular television game shows. On Wednesday the junior and senior classes sponsored a volleyball party, followed by amateur night on Thursday. Inauguration day on Friday began with Mass celebrated by Bishop O'Keefe and the St. Ambrose priests. That afternoon Rogalski was invested with the symbols of his office by Bishop O'Keefe in a ceremony in front of Ambrose Hall. He was joined on the platform by three former presidents, Monsignor Ambrose Burke, Menke, and Bakrow.[65]

A Great and Lasting Beginning

In his address, Rogalski reflected on the history of the institution, then he spoke of the St. Ambrose he was to lead. He said students were drawn to St. Ambrose because of three strengths: the education of the whole person, a strong faculty, and the tradition of a Christian culture. As a new university, St. Ambrose would not be all things to all people, but it would be the best it could be in teaching, scholarship, and service. To travel this "journey toward excellence," St. Ambrose had to achieve several goals: increase the number of endowed chairs and professorships to make a strong faculty stronger; add substantially to the library which was the heart of the academic enterprise; increase funds for scholarship and grants; and improve the science facilities. He addressed each constituency, the students and alumni; the faculty; the Diocese of Davenport; the neighboring colleges and universities; and the Quad-City community and said each could play a "significant role" in helping St. Ambrose achieve its goals.[66]

At the end of the formal address he spoke about his late

Msgr. Cletus Madsen congratulated Dr. Ed Rogalski upon being named the 12th president of St. Ambrose. It was Madsen who suggested to Msgr. Menke in 1968 that he hire Rogalski as dean of men.

parents, Polish immigrants, "who did not have the benefit of an education themselves but who knew the value of education" for their children. Rogalski's parents were like the parents of the first St. Ambrose students who wanted an education for their sons. The first thirty-three boys who had filed into St. Marguerite's school building one hundred and five years earlier were the sons of those immigrants and now that school was under the leadership of a son of immigrants.

On Friday evening, Ambrosians celebrated around the homecoming bonfire with a pep rally and crowned the king and queen, Chris Lansing and Laura Holzman. The football game at Brady Street Stadium against Northwestern College was a 59-14 victory. Coach John Furlong said it was an "almost perfect" game where the Ambrose scoring was shared by Tim Jackson and Willie Barney who each scored two touchdowns, Todd Sturdy and Rick Solis each scored one touchdown, and kicker Chris Melink had a field goal and eight points after touchdowns.[67] That night there was an alumni social and dinner dance at the Blackhawk Hotel, and on Sunday the

homecoming Mass was celebrated in Christ the King Chapel.

With the inauguration over, the campus community settled into the routine of the fall semester. In addition to the new president, there was also a new dean of students. Stanley Kabat replaced William Rhudy who had held the position for the previous six years and had moved to a new job at Marian College in Fond du Lac, Wisconsin. With a background in counseling and personnel services, for the past three years Kabat had been at Scott Community College. He said his long-term goals were to see the dormitories full and to improve the quality of life on campus for the students. Another staff change occurred with the naming of Sister Judith McKenna, OSF, as the director of campus ministry. McKenna had been co-director with Father Drake Shafer the previous two years and she also served as coordinator of seminary formation. Shafer was taking a leave for advanced studies. McKenna was assisted in sacramental ministry by Fathers George McDaniel and Anthony Herold, the rector of the seminary.[68]

The first strategic plan published in January 1985 contained an objective to develop the impact of the Catholic identity on academic programs. Rogalski had emphasized the Roman Catholic character of the university as expressed by its educational programs and its relationship to the Diocese of Davenport.[69] In 1988, two new programs were introduced to make those goals more real. First was an interdisciplinary minor in Catholic Studies. The minor required a student to take courses in history, English, music, art, philosophy, and theology. The second was the Master of Pastoral Studies for men and women already involved in ministry. The program used an experience-based learning style that drew on their work in parishes or other Catholic institutions.

The football team that had won such a big victory for homecoming finished the season with a 9-2-1 record and advanced to the quarterfinals of the NAIA national playoffs. Lineman Jerry Klosterman was named to the Kodak All-American Team for Division II schools, making him one of the top twenty-two players in the country. Several of his teammates were named to conference and district all-star teams and John Furlong was named District 15 coach of the year. The women's volleyball team won the district championship, and the men's cross country team finished fourth in District 15 and went to the NAIA nationals. The men's golf team finished second in the NAIA district meet.

The Vocal Music department presented a dessert concert, "A Night in Vienna," in November while the band prepared for its annual Veterans Day concert. The band was also busy raising money for its European tour the following summer, the first such trip since 1980. On the stage in Allaert Auditorium, rehearsals were underway for the annual children's show, *Charlotte's Web*, and Professor Michael Kennedy was rehearsing his one-man play, *Edmund Kean: Shakespeare by Lightning*. Non-traditional students now comprised 51 percent of the enrollment. Their student council sponsored a bus trip to Chicago in November and announced they would hold a blood drive in the Bee Hive the next February. The Marriott food service introduced a "Wild Pizza" delivery service for the residence halls each evening from 6:00 to 10:00 p.m. In November and December, presidential candidates Governor Bruce Babbitt, Governor Michael Dukakis, and Congressman Richard Gephardt came to campus seeking votes in the Iowa Caucuses which were held in January.

The possible presence of Western Illinois in the Quad-Cities would continue to vex Rogalski and the board in the years ahead. In a board meeting the day before the inauguration, Moeller asked for guidance on the situation with Western Illinois. He told them the Illinois Higher Education Board would meet in December to consider funding for Western's proposal. Moeller said St. Ambrose had three options: propose an alternative plan, cooperate with Western in some way, let Western go its own way. In its December meeting, the board engaged in a lengthy discussion about the impact of Western Illinois but came to no resolution. In the meantime, St. Ambrose continued to work with Marycrest and Augustana to find ways to "mitigate [a] possible enrollment decline" if Western came to the Quad-Cities.[70]

The next spring the board dealt with two restructuring issues. Rogalski urged them to adopt new by-laws presented to the board in March 1988, and approved the following October. Those new by-laws eliminated the advisory Board of Trustees created in 1969. They also created six standing committees: an executive committee, academic affairs and service, development and university relations, finance and grounds, student life, and a nominating committee. O'Keefe asked each board member to state a committee preference. With regular committee meetings, over time, the board became more engaged in the governing of the university.[71]

The board also approved the division of the university into three colleges: arts and sciences, human services, and business. That same structure had already been approved by the faculty. Next Professor Paul Jacobson was appointed dean of arts and sciences, Professor Daniel Bozik dean of human

services, and Professor James Jensen dean of the college of business. Moeller told the board there was still a great deal to be done, adapting to the new structure would "provide some interesting rubbing of shoulders." But, he said there was a "new dynamism" and he felt confident that they could "reconfigure the resources" already in place to fit the new three-college structure. Moeller assured the board that he was going to fight hard to make sure the requirements of each college contained the liberal arts component of the curriculum.[72]

When classes began for the fall semester 1987, there were 1,549 students, down slightly from the year before. The *Ambrose Magazine* asked students why they came to St. Ambrose. One said he had an opportunity to get a degree in engineering while playing basketball; two cited the small college atmosphere with a good student-to-teacher ratio that made them feel welcome; one said his father had been a graduate; and two said they had relatives who worked at St. Ambrose. A small, welcoming college with a family atmosphere would be themes Rogalski would sound in the years ahead.[73] But the university could not remain small and just how to grow, yet keep that same family atmosphere, was a challenge the new president would have to confront.

Recruiting was one of the keys to increasing the size of the student body and helping the budget remain balanced. As Bakrow had said the previous spring, St. Ambrose had been too dependent on local students, and recruiters had expanded their efforts to Wisconsin, Ohio, Indiana, and Missouri. One consequence of this broader territorial pool was that there were fewer students from Iowa and the Diocese of Davenport.[74]

New scholarship programs were also created. The Ambrose Scholar award gave a tuition scholarship to the top student in a high school graduating class. The Freeman Pollard Minority Scholarship, named for an African-American professor of political science who had recently retired, was awarded to entering freshmen who were African-American, Asian or Pacific Islander, Native American, or Hispanic. Those measures seemed to help. In February 1988, Rogalski reported that there were already 345 applications for the fall semester compared with 232 at the same time the previous year.[75]

The fall of 1987 saw the beginning of a new program of occupational therapy, a profession which helped people to prevent, lessen, or overcome disabilities and lead a more productive life. The department was housed on the third floor of Ambrose Hall in the area that had been the auditorium when it was built in 1908. It had been used last as a theater in 1955 and had become a storage area. In 1973, Mrs. Robert Murphy donated money to remodel the area as an adjunct gymnasium in memory of her husband, a 1954 graduate and member of the basketball team. With the construction of Lee Lohman Arena, Murphy Gym was no longer needed and the St. Ambrose Maintenance department brought in steel beams to divide the space into two floors. The third floor housed occupational therapy and the new fourth floor was eventually turned into classrooms.[76]

In 1990, Ambrose Hall was made more accessible with the construction of an elevator. The elevator car was donated by Bernard J. Hank, Jr., president of Montgomery Elevator and a member of the St. Ambrose Board of Directors. The Friends of St. Ambrose raised the money for the shaft. The elevator was built in the central stairway between the 1885 and 1893 sections of the building and served all floors from the Bee Hive to the Irish Village.[77]

Another avenue that made St. Ambrose more accessible came with the formation of the Office for Students with Disabilities in the fall of 1990. The office served the estimated 5 percent of students on campus with physical or learning disabilities which prevented them from participating fully in the academic program or life on the campus. Scott Howland, the first director, surveyed the campus to find where changes were needed to make the buildings accessible. He called for students to volunteer as note takers or readers to help others in their class work.[78]

The prospect of more students for that fall helped the financial picture, but Rogalski determined that a tuition increase was still necessary. In the previous two years, tuition had increased by just under 6 percent each year. Now for the fall of 1988, tuition was increased by just over 9 percent to $228 a credit hour, or $6,840 for fifteen hours. Room and board was increased by 8 percent. The president said that was an attempt to "maintain and enhance the quality of the educational program," and he assured students that financial aid would increase proportionately.[79]

Raising tuition always involved a risk, but when the *Ambrose Magazine* asked students, 86 percent said they would return the following year in spite of the tuition hike. Sixty percent said the raise was justified to pay competitive salaries and maintain the quality of education. When one was asked if she received her money's worth at the new tuition rate, she responded, "I'd better." But 25 percent said the raise was not justified, instead the university should find more benefactors, save energy, and recruit more students. One said raising money from students should be the last resort for funds, not the first, adding, "The business office spends too much money on mailing." Over half the students said they paid for at least part of their education, with the remainder coming from parents, grants, and loans. Fifty-five percent said they would be in debt when they graduated with estimates from one year to twenty years to repay the loans.[80]

The increase in tuition did not impact enrollment: in 1989, there were 2,278 students, the highest enrollment ever. A significant part of the increase was the number of on-campus students. In the fall of 1989 there were 625 students, 200 more than two years before. Freshmen enrollment was up, a reflection of the more aggressive recruiting program. The number of transfer students also increased, a higher number of students remained at St. Ambrose, and new programs in new sites around the diocese added more students. The greatest factor in the increase was the MBA program which now had over 500 students. There were also new graduate programs in criminal justice, accounting, special education, and pastoral studies.

The increase in student population also created a shortage of classroom space. The Strategic Planning Committee addressed those needs and published an action plan in January 1989 with the objective to develop a master plan that used "present facilities" and included the "possibility of acquisition of additional property for new facilities."[81] The Board of Directors also addressed the problem of residence hall and classroom space when it

formed a Task Force on Size chaired by Monsignor Morrissey that included Rogalski, the university vice presidents, and the deans of the colleges. The group reported to the board on April 10, 1990, that their "initial concern" was to maintain the "quality aspects of a 'small school.'" There were currently 2,148 students, but the university should have a goal of 2,500 students including an increase of 300 more resident students. However, the physical plant was already at 100 percent utilization and to reach that goal, there were immediate needs for dormitory and classroom space, as well as a new library. They estimated it would take $14 to $15 million to accomplish the necessary expansion.

The Task Force told the board, however, that before they made any decision, they judged it "opportune . . . if not absolutely necessary, to resolve 'The Marycrest Question.'" Any further expansion at St. Ambrose could preclude any future arrangements with Marycrest. The Task Force said it might be advantageous to "simply and absolutely take over Marycrest," which could result in a greater efficiency of operation, costs, and scheduling of courses. But they pointed out there were "substantial differences in mission and belief" between the two schools and a "suspicion of the faculties of each other" that remained from the failed merger of nearly twenty years before which could preclude any current merger. Instead they recommended that Bishop O'Keefe meet with the Sisters of Humility and make an "outright purchase offer."[82]

The Board of Directors had asked Rogalski the previous April to find ways to "cooperate rather than compete" with Marycrest, but in October, he informed them that he had been unable to arrange a meeting with Dr. Wanda Bigham, the Marycrest president.[83] Discussions did take place between Moeller and his Marycrest counterpart, Sister Helen Elsbernd, FSPA, about the possibility of cross-registration of students. In an early March meeting, the Marycrest Board of Trustees endorsed the "pursuit of inter-institutional cooperation . . . to establish a cross-registration agreement."[84]

That was the status on April 10 when the St. Ambrose board asked O'Keefe to contact the sisters. O'Keefe met that afternoon with Sister Pauline Tursi, CHM, the president of the congregation and presented in "broad terms" the proposal to buy Marycrest. She replied that she had no objection to the proposal, but neither she nor O'Keefe had any details and she had many questions.[85]

The Marycrest board met on June 9 and expressed surprise at the nature of O'Keefe's proposal of a buy-out and the reluctance by St. Ambrose for a merger. Tursi wrote O'Keefe that they recognized Marycrest had been founded at the request of the bishop of Davenport, and they wished "to be open in response to your request." However, she said the board felt it "must explore all options for the future." Nevertheless, it appointed a committee of three to conduct further meetings with representatives of St. Ambrose.[86]

On June 18, O'Keefe, Rogalski, and Morrissey met with Marycrest board chairman James Victor, Tursi, and Bigham. Rogalski told them that the St. Ambrose campus was full and he was aware that space was available at Marycrest. The St. Ambrose board had recommended that an offer of purchase be made which was directed to Tursi since the Congregation of the Humility of Mary owned the property. Tursi proposed a diocesan university that would include Marycrest and Mt. St. Clare College in Clinton, Iowa. Bigham wondered if St. Ambrose was interested in either cooperation

Dr. Ed Rogalski (second from left) was joined by former St. Ambrose presidents Msgr. Sebastian Menke (left), Dr. William Bakrow, and Msgr. Ambrose Burke at the celebration of his inauguration of their successor.

or a merger but Rogalski said no to both. O'Keefe reminded the group that the previous merger attempts had been unsuccessful and the effort had left the St. Ambrose board with negative feelings. Speaking for Marycrest, Victor said they were not favorably disposed to the St. Ambrose proposal. At the end of the meeting, both groups said they would report back to their respective boards on how to proceed.[87]

A week later, the Marycrest group wrote O'Keefe to thank him for the opportunity to visit on June 18, but that as Marycrest considered how to continue its educational mission, "the termination of our work or the moving of that educational mission to another campus is unacceptable." They believed that a "broader vision" by St. Ambrose could include Marycrest,

but that the Marycrest "family would need to be included in all future considerations."[88]

In response, O'Keefe told the Marycrest group, "If St. Ambrose University is to broaden its vision to include Marycrest," he needed information about the physical plant, the financial condition of the college, the number of tenured faculty with their areas of specialization, and the number of administrators. If that information was received, St. Ambrose would respond "in as much detail as we can about our proposed utilization of the Marycrest 'family' and campus." But O'Keefe was not optimistic about a solution. A week later, he told a correspondent that he had not received a "favorable hearing" from the sisters or from Marycrest. He said he was not

A Great and Lasting Beginning

sure they could find a "satisfactory solution . . . It is possible that Marycrest is pursuing some alternative solution, but I do not know this."[89]

The tension between the two groups was clear, but still they tried to come to some agreement. Through August and September, the academic and financial officers of St. Ambrose reviewed the information and made a recommendation to Rogalski. Acquisition of Marycrest provided some opportunities for St. Ambrose. It would eliminate a local competitor, making St. Ambrose the only Catholic liberal arts institution in the area. It would acquire several programs it did not have including nursing and social work. The two faculties complemented each other; there were only a few instances where a Marycrest faculty member duplicated the area of an Ambrosian. Marycrest had classrooms and residence hall space that was badly needed by St. Ambrose. It was felt that the "greater majority" of Marycrest students would remain at the new institution and that the recruiting position of St. Ambrose would be strengthened in the region. Finally, the general public and many of the alumni of both institutions would be glad to see the two schools come together.

But there were also disadvantages and risks: a college with two campuses created problems for student services and security; integrating the two faculties would have "tensions"; some alumni of both institutions would be "alienated" by bringing the two schools together; and a large amount of money would be necessary for plant improvements on the Marycrest campus. But the "major obstacle" was a "sizable" short-term debt at Marycrest and acquisition under those conditions would create a "tremendous burden" for St. Ambrose. Moreover, a campaign was underway to raise money to renovate Lewis Hall, and a proposal to build a new library was in its early stages, both of which were priorities for Rogalski and St. Ambrose. The financial burden of acquiring Marycrest could significantly delay those two projects.[90]

At the end of September, Bigham presented Rogalski with a list of "selected concerns." She requested that Marycrest tenured faculty be accepted at St. Ambrose and that non-tenured faculty be offered contracts for the next academic year. Marycrest salaries would be raised to the St. Ambrose level. St. Ambrose would accept curricula and faculties of programs it did not currently have. Marycrest students would graduate on their current catalogue, and 1991 and 1992 graduates would receive diplomas from Marycrest. One Sister of Humility and selected other Marycrest board members would join the Ambrose board. The Peoples' Debt would be honored; and if the campus was sold, one-half of the proceeds would go to the sisters.[91]

Rogalski took the analysis of his administrators and Bigham's concerns to a meeting of the St. Ambrose Board of Directors on October 9. The board approved a resolution to authorize the administration to "proceed in good faith to negotiate terms of a consolidation." It agreed to most of Bigham's concerns including the retention of tenured faculty and contracts for the next year for non-tenured faculty. Marycrest curricula would be reviewed for "consistency with the mission statement and philosophy" of St. Ambrose. It agreed to honor the Peoples' Debt and to give the sisters one seat on the St. Ambrose board. But they wanted more financial information, including an audit and data on fund raising and annual gift contributions. Finally the St. Ambrose board suggested that a small committee of directors from each institution address the matter of Marycrest's

short-term debt.[92]

A few days later, Bigham called Rogalski to say that Marycrest was ending the negotiations with St. Ambrose because it had chosen to pursue an "alternative course of action." Within weeks rumors circulated through the Quad-City community that Marycrest was negotiating either a merger or sale with Teikyo University of Japan. No one at Marycrest would confirm the rumors, but on December 10, Bigham announced that the sale had taken place. Rogalski said he had "always envisioned" that the two schools would combine as one stronger university which would relieve space pressures at St. Ambrose and strengthen the "mission of Catholic education" for the diocese and the Quad-City area, but the sale to Teikyo made that "unlikely."[93]

In the weeks ahead, Marycrest, St. Ambrose, and the community struggled to understand the consequences of the failure of St. Ambrose and Marycrest to come together, and the decision by the latter to sell to Teikyo. The *Quad-City Times* said Marycrest should explain why this had been done. It lamented the failure of the talks with St. Ambrose and the fact that the community still had two "relatively small, competing institutions" when it could have had a "single, bigger" and presumably "stronger" one. It said there could be good things with the international affiliation, but for now it admitted "mixed reactions, unless and until Marycrest" provided a better explanation for its actions.[94]

The *Catholic Messenger* expressed regret that the new school meant the death of Marycrest where the Sisters of Humility had done "great good for many years." But it was concerned about the emphasis by Teikyo of educating for a global economy, which was a "narrow view" of education which would only make more workers. Rather it should educate "human beings who can flourish spiritually" and it hoped that the new Marycrest would "highlight some features of the culture which founded it."[95]

St. Ambrose and Marycrest had a long history and whatever good will present in the early decades was deeply strained by the failure of the merger talks in the early 1970s and the similar attempts of the 1980s. For some of the people most intimately involved in the discussions of 1990, it was their third attempt at doing something to bring the two schools together. In addition, the faculties, alumni, and several generations of students had watched and wondered what would happen to the schools and their jobs. In the end it may have been a failure of wills. There were those at St. Ambrose who would accept nothing less than a complete take-over of Marycrest, and those at Marycrest who would accept that from anyone but St. Ambrose. What was missing was the willingness to find a middle ground to serve Catholic education in the region.

In the following weeks, Rogalski and the officers discussed what the failure of the recent negotiations meant. For twenty years the Ambrosians had viewed acquisition of Marycrest as a way to eliminate competition, increase enrollment, bring new programs to St. Ambrose, and add classroom and residence hall space. It was never the best solution, but it was always expedient and it always had to be considered. Now, it was no longer possible as a solution to St. Ambrose's problems, and for the first time, St. Ambrose planners would face their future challenges without the "Marycrest question" as part of their deliberations.

This is a great country and when I am gone, will be a great Catholic country, for a great and lasting beginning is already here.

– Bishop John McMullen, 1881

We have excellent people who are providing a quality educational experience for our students. We are limited by the absence of some resources, primarily monetary, . . . but we have faith and hope and a vision to be the best we can be. Our future focus is unprecedented quality and we are moving there with all our power.

– President Edward Rogalski, 1990

❧ Chapter Seventeen ☙

With the failure of St. Ambrose to purchase Marycrest, the university had to look to its own neighborhood, rather than to property twelve blocks away, as a solution to the problem of providing residence hall and classroom space. As that reality sank in, one officer later recalled, "We really took off." By 1950, the ten acres purchased by Bishop Cosgrove in 1885 had grown to twenty-two acres bounded by Locust, Gaines, Lombard, and Scott Streets. The Scott Street boundary was crossed in 1968 when Cosgrove Hall was built on it. But with the construction of the Galvin Fine Arts building in the early 1970s and the gymnasium in the early 1980s, there was no more room within the current boundaries of the school.

In the next two decades the university purchased a few properties on the block bounded by Scott, Pleasant, High, and Ripley Streets east of Cosgrove Hall, but with no immediate use in mind. But as the student body grew, the Strategic Planning Committee published its January 1989 action plan which suggested the purchase of additional property to accommodate the growing number of students.

The space crisis was also the point of a June 8, 1989, memorandum from Stan Kabat, dean of students, and Father Drake Shafer, vice president for student services. With students wanting more spaces than were available, Kabat and Shafer suggested a major shift of faculty and administrators who occupied offices in Davis Hall to other parts of the campus, opening Davis for student residence.[1] To make room for the faculty moving from Davis Hall, students who had lived in Ambrose Hall were moved out and that space was then occupied by the mathematics and business faculties. That put more pressure on Cosgrove and Rohlman Halls, which were filled, and Davis Hall, which was now renovated to house more students.[2]

Moving personnel around to other spaces in current campus buildings, however, was only a stop-gap measure. That fall, planning began on a $2 million project to buy the remaining property in the block east of Rohlman Hall, and build additional residences. An architect was selected who designed a series of townhouses, arranged in a quadrangle, to house 104 students in thirteen units.[3] Construction began in the spring of 1990 with the hope the houses would be ready for the fall semester, but two major floods that summer delayed completion by several weeks. The new town-

houses were dedicated at homecoming 1990. They were named for John Schneider, Helen Sudbrook, and Majorie V. Andrews, all of whom were long-time supporters of St. Ambrose. The fourth townhouse was temporarily named "D," but in the fall of 2000, would become Strub House, in honor of Father Herman Strub who had asked that the designation not be made until after his death.[4]

The construction of the townhouses in 1990 was an indication that the next fifteen years would be marked by growth in the student population, especially on-campus students, which meant that Dr. Rogalski and his planners would have to provide more residence hall space. In turn, that meant the university had to purchase even more land. Like Catholic institutions around the country, they struggled to understand how the growing institution manifested its Catholicism in the curriculum, student life, and institutional values. That challenged Rogalski and his planners to manage the growth and to be certain St. Ambrose remained true to the vision Bishop McMullen had set out.

As his years as president progressed, Rogalski relied on a core group of officers made up of the college vice presidents. The annual strategic planning process set the parameters for their decisions, but those officers, which some on campus called his "kitchen cabinet," helped him to refine those plans. In 1992 that group included Donald Moeller, provost and dean of the faculty; Edward Henkhaus, vice president, finance; Father Drake Shafer, now vice president for university ministry; Steven Goebel, vice president of university relations, and William Tracy, vice president for academic support services. When Bakrow was president, he met infrequently with those officers as a group, preferring to deal with them individually. But Rogalski trusted and relied on them more and more, and soon scheduled weekly meetings. In 1994, Rogalski added to the group when he appointed Dr. Ann Freeberg as vice president for institutional research, the first woman in the upper-level of university administration.

It was to those officers that Rogalski turned to help solve the need for more residence space and classrooms. Although the endowment was increasing, the annual fund drive raised more money, and there would be

A Great and Lasting Beginning

There were 283 graduates in place for graduation 1993. Since World War II, most spring graduations were held under the oaks. If it rained, the ceremony moved indoors to LeClaire gymnasium, the Assumption High School gymnasium, the Galvin Fine Arts Center, or The Mark of the Quad-Cities. As the size of the graduating classes increased to over 500, in 2004 the university moved the spring graduation to the Mark.

successful special fund raising campaigns, resources were not unlimited, and the officers often had to make difficult decisions about priorities. In the end, it was often Rogalski's "Let's see what we can work out" approach to problems that accounted for the successes of the university.

In his inaugural address, one of Rogalski's goals was the improvement of the science facilities. The occupational therapy program meant more students would be taking science courses in a building that was already inadequate. Chemistry Professor Arthur Serianz acknowledged the need when he said, "For years we've been hampered by the quality" of Lewis Hall, the "oldest un-remodeled building on campus." Acoustics were a problem in many of the classrooms, and inadequate ventilation meant that smells from the chemistry laboratories filtered through the building. Those poor conditions impacted teaching and the recruitment of new science students.

In October 1988, St. Ambrose received a $1.5 million loan from the federal government to renovate Lewis Hall.[5] The university also received a $200,000 grant from the Kresge Foundation and started a fund raising campaign for another $1.6 million. Architect Frederick Ebeling, whose

grandfather had built Lewis Hall sixty years earlier, was hired to reconfigure the interior of the building. During the work, three portable classroom buildings were put on the Galvin parking lot to accommodate some of the classes normally held in Lewis Hall, and other classes were moved to rooms in Galvin.[6]

Work progressed through 1990 and 1991, and the dedication was set for homecoming 1991. The building had a completely new interior. The third floor contained offices for the chemistry faculty and laboratories and classrooms. Biology occupied the second floor and physics was on the first floor. There were additional classrooms and laboratories on the ground floor which now had an entrance on the east end which led to the elevator. The greatest change was the elimination of the old Lewis 111 lecture hall, the site of Theatre III productions and Father Strub's lectures on scripture. Speaking at the dedication, Rogalski said the renovated hall was a "reaffirmation of a continuing . . . commitment to the teaching of the sciences and the educational philosophy" of Monsignor Hauber. Echoing Hauber, Rogalski said science should be a "civilizing influence to help men and women live more abundantly and to elevate society's standards."[7]

Planning for a new library was also underway. For years in periodic polls and articles in the school newspapers, students had complained about the library. They said that often materials they needed were not available, security was lax, it was too noisy, too hot, or too cold. One student said he was "disappointed in the overall quality of our library," and said he often had to go to the public library to find the materials he needed.[8] The Strategic Planning Committee created an action plan in December 1987 to build a new library by 1995. With that in place, a library building committee was formed and a consultant hired to help them.[9] After several months of discussion and planning, the firm of Wollen, Molzan and Partners of Indianapolis was hired to design and build the library.[10] At the same time, planning began for a campaign to raise the estimated $7 million necessary to build it.[11]

The university had changed a great deal since the failure of the merger in 1973, and it would continue to change in the years ahead. One observer of higher education noted, the "willingness to adapt" allowed colleges and universities to "not just survive, but flourish."[12] The university had developed a mission statement in the early 1970s which had been amended a number of times in the intervening years. The heart of the statement declared that it was a "private, diocesan, Catholic institution" which combined instruction in the "liberal arts along with pre-professional, career preparation and a variety of life-long learning programs." It granted undergraduate and graduate degrees, stressed "excellence in teaching and learning" in an environment that fostered "mutual respect," and it encouraged research and public service. Its declared mission was to "enable all its students to develop intellectually, spiritually, ethically, socially, artistically, and physically in order to enrich their own lives and the lives of others."

But in the early 1990s, some on campus began to ask whether St. Ambrose had changed too much and whether it remained true to its heritage and its mission statement. Sociology Professor Ann Freeberg and Father Drake Shafer led the discussion and were joined by Professors Paul Jacobson, Paul Koch, and Marge Legg. The group expanded its membership to eighteen faculty, students, staff, board members, and administrators and they became known as the Values Project Committee. Their hope was to raise campus awareness of the mission values as guides to campus life; identify the values the campus community deemed most important to "proclaim and convey"; and plan programs and strategies to "actualize the core values and best traditions" of the university.[13]

The group used the university mission statement to identify values. To elicit information, the group asked members of the faculty, staff, administration, board, and students to list ways St. Ambrose accomplished its mission; things the school was not doing but should be; things that contradicted the mission; and what values were present at St. Ambrose but were not a part of the mission statement.[14]

The results of the values survey provided a picture of the aspirations of the university and an assessment by a representative sampling of the community whether those aspirations were being met or not. The respondents thought there was wide-spread appreciation for the variety of degrees available at St. Ambrose, but there was concern that the emphasis on career preparation and the rising number of professional degrees were eroding the historic liberal arts heritage of St. Ambrose. The value of life-long learning, one McMullen would have appreciated, was well-served at St. Ambrose, although they were not sure that the public was as aware as it should be of those opportunities.

There was agreement among the responders that the university community had a "shared understanding" of excellent teaching made possible by small class sizes and the ability of teachers and students to have a "one-to-one" relationship. They also recognized the challenges presented in keeping that relationship in a university that was rapidly growing. They were not so sure that there was a common understanding about whether there was excellence in learning and how that should be assessed.

Many said the university worked to foster an "environment of mutual respect" but they admitted that was not apparent to everyone. They cited concerns that respect for the contributions by women were not reflected in salary levels or promotions to higher positions. Others pointed to evidence of racism and a faculty and staff that lacked racial diversity. They recognized another kind of diversity among the student population in the growing number of non-traditionally-aged students and the problems they encountered by a program geared to serve the traditional student population.

The respondents felt that the institution did not do enough to meet the value of encouraging public service. They said there needed to be a greater awareness of the value of public service as a "meaningful part" of the lives of the university community.

The other area that was under-emphasized was the encouragement of research by the faculty. Most of the respondents said St. Ambrose should be "more supportive" of faculty research. The challenge was to strike a balance between the value of research by faculty and the value of teaching. It seemed clear to the Values Committee that the importance of the classroom experience superceded the value of faculty research.

The university mission statement defined St. Ambrose as a private, diocesan, Catholic institution and the respondents to the survey said that the Catholicism of the institution was evident in the presence of clergy, Mass, campus ministry, and theology courses. However, there was a wide divergence on how well each of those facets of the value was observed, with individual respondents suggesting that one or another of them should be emphasized more. The findings suggested that other mission statement values, such as mutual respect, reflected the Catholicity of the university, but they said that more discernment was necessary to make more obvious the Catholic character of the other values of the mission statement. And finally, they noted that defining the Catholic nature of the institution would become more difficult with the growing diversity in the understanding of what being a Catholic meant expressed in the church at large.[15]

The Values Project revealed a tension between the stated mission of the university and the realization of parts of that mission in the life of the campus community. At its core, the Values Project asked, "How was St. Ambrose Catholic?" It answered the question by citing the study of theology and a listing of what the people at St. Ambrose did as a worshiping and service community. But the liberal arts, which previous generations said were the core around which the intellectual and existential life of the university centered, were not mentioned as a part of Catholic identity.

St. Ambrose was not alone in asking those questions. In the 1990s, most

A Great and Lasting Beginning

Catholic colleges were engaged in self-studies which reflected on their Catholic identity. Speaking at a 1994 conference on the "Idea of a Catholic University," the Reverend Brian E. Daley, SJ, professor of historical theology at the Weston School of Theology, noted that being a college "in the Catholic tradition" had to mean more than a historical fact. It had to be reflected in "decisions made and implemented at every level of the college's existence, shaping and expressing its relationship to the wider community of Catholic faith, sacramental communion and ecclesial life." However, Daley admitted there was not agreement on just how that was to take place.[16]

The Values Project looked at how the mission of the university was realized in the actions and activities of the university and its component parts. It ignored a more fundamental question of what a Catholic university was: an intellectual community seeking the truth. In 1990, Pope John Paul II had issued his document on Catholic universities, *Ex Corde Ecclesiae* (From the Heart of the Church). The document created a sensation in higher education because of its insistence on a mandate for those who taught theology, but most of it was a reflection on the role of Catholic higher education. At the beginning the pope wrote, "It is

The SGA 1990-1991. Bottom row (seated): Larry Daigle, Erin Wade, Kristen Delille, Colleen Smith, Alana Redican. Second row: Jen Peters, Christy Vanmeenan, Jolene Jummati, Joe Jummati, Terry Day, Reggie Bates. Third row: Peggy Winke (vice president), Katie Van Blair, Amy Dolan. Top row: Andrea Chlumsky, Becky Maciolek, Mark Allen (president), Reagan Natrop, Rachel Schoenig, Kris Hollarbush.

the honor and responsibility of a Catholic University to consecrate itself without *reserve to the cause of truth.*" Such a university was "distinguished by its free search for the whole truth about nature, man and God . . . a Catholic university is completely dedicated to the research of all aspects of truth in their essential connection with the supreme Truth, who is God."[17] Faculty, administrators, and the curriculum they created should be judged by their "ability to impart truth, and the meaning of truth" to their students.[18]

While the university community looked inward, it also looked outward and watched as the world changed rapidly. In 1989, the domination of eastern Europe by the Soviet Union, which had formed the Cold War context of the previous forty years, began to collapse as communist governments fell to fledgling democracies. In November 1989, the archetype of the political

division of Europe, the Berlin Wall, was brought down. Students watched the events in Berlin on television, but Simone Aull, an exchange student from Kaiserslautern in West Germany, watched with even greater interest as her country changed in one spectacular weekend. She said she had talked with her family several times over that weekend and when asked her reaction to the events in her home country, she replied, "The party was there, and I am here."

If the unfolding events in Europe laid the foundation for a post-Cold War world, events the following fall in the Middle East signaled that it would be the trouble spot of the future. In August 1990, Iraqi leader Saddam Hussein sent his troops into neighboring Kuwait. In response, the United Nations imposed economic sanctions on Iraq and President George H. W. Bush put together an international military force to push the Iraqis out of Kuwait.

In December the Quad-Citians for Peace held a march and peace vigils at the federal building in downtown Davenport. A group gathered each noon on the steps of Christ the King Chapel to pray for peace. The *Ambrose Magazine* asked students whether the United State should use military action in the Persian Gulf. Several responded that the sanctions should be given more time to work; another said if the sanctions did not work, then some sort of military action would be necessary; still another said he did not think the United States should take military action, but he thought it was inevitable. On January 17, 1991, Ambrosians joined people from around the world to watch the bombing of Bagdad live on CNN.[19]

With the war now a reality, a group of about thirty Ambrosians gathered in the Bee Hive to discuss it. Father Digger Dawson, a leader of the antiwar group on campus twenty years before, reminded them of the divisiveness on campus then, but said that expression of opinion was a "responsibility." Professor Richard Geiger, another leader from the Vietnam days, explained the history of the region. Students expressed opposing viewpoints about the war. In summing up the evening, Dawson thanked the participants, adding, "This is what a school's all about. If we can't do something like this, we might as well be dead."[20]

On January 30, the SGA held a forum about the Persian Gulf War.

Speakers included Rogalski; Geiger; Dawson; political science Professor John Norton; biology Professor John Horn, advisor to Amnesty International; economics Professor Rafael Romero; retired Col. John Norton; Leigh Svacina, a financial consultant from Shearson Lehman Hutton; and by telephone, Congressman Jim Leach. SGA president Mark Allen said the purpose of the forum was to "educate ourselves on an event that is changing the world into which we will be released upon graduation." Rogalski opened the forum expressing the hope that all the participants would listen and raise questions. Each speaker in turn discussed the war from his or her own perspective. At the end of the evening, Allen said the forum was a success and that the SGA would organize other events to encourage student participation with war issues.[21] The war continued for another two months and ended when Iraq accepted a cease fire in early March.

The shortness of the war, which ended in what appeared to be a clear-cut victory for the United States, did not produce the kind of divisiveness present on campus during the Vietnam War. The brief flurry of interest by students during the war, however, was an interlude. Unlike their wartime counterparts twenty years before, the Ambrosians of the nineties were less interested in the issues of the day. Even campus activities failed to elicit involvement by most students; while there were many activities, the attendance was small. In October 1992, the *Buzz on Campus*, the new name for the student newspaper which was quickly shortened to the *Buzz*, asked what could be done to get more students involved with campus activities. Most respondents said there should be more publicity, better organization, and more coordination by the various clubs and groups on campus.[22]

The lack of student interest was also reflected in their disinterest in the SGA. A 1994 poll by the *Buzz* indicated that 70 percent of on-campus students and 96 percent of off-campus students did not know who their SGA representative was; 82 percent said they would not take a problem to the SGA for solution; 66 percent said they were not aware of what the SGA was doing.[23] One year the SGA sponsored an open forum for candidates, but no one came, and in many years, most candidates for seats on the SGA ran unopposed.

One complaint that was noted about the SGA was that it was too involved in social activities and ignored campus government. One senator suggested creating a new body to handle social activities, and leaving the other, "political," issues to the SGA.[24] Several SGA members attended the National Association of Campus Activities conference where they learned that St. Ambrose was one of the few schools in the region that had only one board for all student activities. They returned determined to form a new Campus Activities Board (CAB).[25] They wrote a constitution and presented it to the SGA which discussed the matter through the fall of 1994. The proponents faced a number of questions: Who would be eligible to be elected to the CAB? What would the relationship of the CAB be to the SGA? What would be the source of the CAB budget? In the end, they resolved the questions and on December 11, 1994, the SGA voted to create the CAB and give to it some of the functions historically held by the SGA. SGA vice president Ben Zorn congratulated the group and said it had "just made Ambrose history."[26]

As the two groups began operations, however, the prevailing lack of interest in SGA continued. In 1995, the first student elections since the

division of SGA and CAB, Steve Ahrens and Alison Riedel ran for president and vice president without opposition, and the paper noted that their greatest challenge once they were in office was student apathy.[27]

CAB began its first year of activity with Welcome Week events in August 1995. CAB president Chad Burt noted higher than usual attendance at events, and both freshmen and upperclassmen pronounced the week a success. CAB announced future events included a tailgate before the first home football game.[28]

However, some campus issues did elicit strong student opinion and discussion. In the October 1992 *Buzz* article about student involvement, the paper noted that most on-campus students went home on weekends. The students said the dormitory visitation policy and the alcohol policy were too restrictive; one student called St. Ambrose a "high school with dorms" and said that they had more freedom at home.

There was nothing new about student protest against visitation hours and restrictions on the use of alcohol. In the nineteenth century, students found ways to evade the rules, leave the dormitory, and return undetected. The faculty was always vigilant lest a student or an employee brought alcohol into the building. Those customs continued well into the twentieth century. But for most of those years, rule-breaking was just that, teen-aged boys pushing against *in loco parentis* restraints. It was rarely serious, but when it became so, punishment was swift and sure.

Beginning in the mid-1960s, alcohol regulations and visitation hours became focal points for wider student protests against the right of colleges to assume the role of parents. Students argued that at eighteen-years-of-age, they were ready to assume their places in society and make decisions for themselves about their own behavior. College administrators like Menke and Rogalski were forced to balance the competing forces of those student aspirations; of parents, many of whom wanted their children watched over while away from home; the need for order so the proper academic purpose of the college could be fulfilled by both faculty and students; concerns about the health and safety of the students; and the right of a Catholic institution to assert standards of behavior that were consistent with Catholic morality.

Those competing forces remained in the 1990s, but now there were other factors which impacted university policy. Alcohol abuse had become a national epidemic on college campuses. One 1995 study involving 17,000 college students found that more than 40 percent of them engaged in binge drinking, defined for men as five or more drinks consumed in a row one or more times during a two week period. For women the numbers were slightly less. Another study indicated that 75 percent of a typical student body would consume alcohol within a month's time.[29] The numbers were roughly the same in a 1994 poll at St. Ambrose: 79 percent had used alcohol within the past thirty days; 52 percent had consumed five or more drinks at a sitting within the past two weeks.

University administrators concerned about formulating policies took little comfort from another 1995 study that indicated that 33 percent of high school seniors engaged in binge drinking, which meant that students arrived on campus as freshmen already experienced in the use and abuse of alcohol.[30] Moreover, each school year brought news of the death of an

A Great and Lasting Beginning

The pep band encouraged the team and warmed the fans on a cold afternoon in Brady Street Stadium.

American college student by alcohol poisoning. There had been no deaths at St. Ambrose, but occasionally a student was taken to the emergency room.

Prior to 1985, the alcohol policy was simple: those under the legal age of nineteen found drinking in the Pub, at campus events, or in public places would be subject to a fine. Repeated offenses brought more severe penalties.[31]

That year a task force of student service staff, faculty, and students wdeveloped a policy to be in place by the fall of 1985. The new policy was both educative and proscriptive. Its objective was to educate students and employees so they made responsible decisions regarding the use of alcohol; to implement programs, strategies, and regulations to promote responsible decision-making; and to create a support system for those with alcohol or drug problems. It created regulations to tightly control the availability of alcohol at campus events. Drinking was permitted in private rooms by those of legal age, raised to twenty-one in Iowa on July 1, 1986, but no one could consume alcohol in public areas on campus unless it was an approved event. Events where alcohol would be served had to be registered in advance, a controlled area was to be set aside, and only those old enough to drink would be allowed inside that area. In all, the policy for the students, faculty, and staff ran to thirteen pages in the student handbook.[32]

Through those years the educational efforts included an annual Alcohol Awareness Week, which featured casino nights, dances, and other social activities where no alcohol was present. A feature of the week was Mocktails night, where members of the campus community created and served drinks that did not contain alcohol. Many of the educational events were sponsored by BACCHUS (Boosting Alcohol Consciousness Concerning the Health of University Students), a national organization that promoted peer education about alcohol and other health issues.[33]

That formed the basis of the alcohol policy for the next twenty years. Through the decade of the 1990s, students and student groups complained that the policy limited their ability to have social events, and some groups were forced to cancel an event when the organizers failed to comply with the regulations. The students still tried to get around the rules which became a source of tension between them, their organizations, and the dean of students' office. But Rogalski said it was important for the university to provide guidelines and standards for behavior.[34]

The 1986 policy had been created for alcohol and drugs. Because alcohol was legal for some students and was the drug of choice for most Americans, regulation of it on campus became complex. Other drugs were illegal everywhere, and the policy against them was simple: they were forbidden on campus and violations would be controlled by state and federal laws. Nevertheless, a 1994 poll in the *Buzz* found that 20 percent of St. Ambrose students admitted to using marijuana at least once in the previous year; 9 percent had used it within the previous thirty days; and 9 percent had used another illegal drug in the previous year. In February 1996, the dean of students admitted that drug use was "up a bit" in the past semester, but that alcohol was still the drug of choice on campus. Kabat said the alcohol use on campus was higher than the national average but that other drug use was lower than the national average.[35]

Formulating a visitation policy for residence halls was the other area where there was a clash between students' desires for freedom of action and the Catholic university's responsibility to uphold standards of morality and provide a living environment where the students could pursue their studies. In the Values Project, nearly half (forty-three of ninety) of the student respondents to the value, "foster mutual respect," said they felt a lack of trust and respect because they did not have more "power and freedom" in making rules for themselves, especially in regard to visitation policy.[36] But there was also a disquieting increase in violence, including sexual assaults, on and around the campus, even in some instances, in the residence halls. The primary concern was for student safety, but the university could not ignore its potential liability in the event harm was done to a student.

Even more than with alcohol, parents, church leaders, and the public were concerned about the behavior of university students in the residence halls. Since St. Ambrose had become co-educational in the late 1960s, the bishop and the board had taken an active interest in visitation policies. Rogalski reminded the campus community that a visitation policy was an "opportunity to give students an education in the broadest sense in terms of how they could live and how they should live."[37]

The visitation hours had remained essentially the same for twenty years: visitors were not allowed in the women's dormitory, Cosgrove Hall, after 11:00 p.m., and there was a guard on duty beginning at 7:00 p.m. each evening; in the male dormitories, Davis and Rohlman, there was twenty-four-hour visitation. But there was growing pressure by the students to alter those hours. In 1991, Kabat formed a task force of students, faculty, and staff to study the matter. That group surveyed the campus community and asked about three options: twenty-four-hour visitation in all residence halls every day; limited visitation on Sunday through Thursday with no limits on Friday and Saturday; or limited visitation all days of the week. Eighty-five percent said they wanted twenty-four-hour visitation.

On April 9, 1991, Kabat presented a proposal for new hours to the Board of Directors. His proposal called for visitation hours of 8:00 a.m. to midnight Sunday through Thursday and twenty-four-hour visitation on Friday and Saturday in Cosgrove, Davis, and Rohlman Halls. In the townhouses, each unit could set its own hours which could include twenty-four-hour visitation. Hayes Hall, which housed the seminary, had its own, more restricted hours. Students could register overnight guests of the same sex at a security desk and were held responsible for the actions of their guests.[38]

Kabat explained to the board that the first priority for a residence hall was that it have an "academic atmosphere," with the quiet, space, and privacy to allow the student to properly study. Students should also expect to live in a safe and secure environment which meant abiding by the rules and informing any guests about the rules. But he said a residence hall should also reflect the values of the institution and that the personal conduct of the residents "should be reflective of the character of Christian men and women." Following discussion, the board first defeated the proposed hours by a vote of 6-5. The proposal was amended to restrict visitation on Friday and Saturday night to 2:00 a.m., which passed with the provision that the administration would closely monitor how well the new hours worked and report to the board in the fall.[39]

When the students returned in the fall, Kabat explained the new rules. The buildings had been too "open and free" and there was concern about the safety of the students so the new rules "needed to be created." He also announced that a new security desk was established in each residence hall with a guard from the Per Mar security firm. Predictably, many students said the new rules were too strict. One noted that, "Ambrose went from an open campus to a practically restricted one. I don't like it very much and the rules for visiting are a big hassle." But Kabat responded, "Our primary concern is the safety of the students."[40]

Kelli Hoag and Nancy Klosterman, editors for the *Ambrose Magazine*, formulated strategies to get into Rohlman Hall, a male dormitory, after midnight and not get caught. Included in their strategies were: "Tell the Per Mar people that you're from the values committee and just want to see if everyone is tucked snug in their beds with the lights out; Take the intramural course in Kilfoy window climbing; Get out the Windex and pretend you're a window cleaner; Tell them you are the plumber and are there to fix the sink; Dress up as a priest and tell them you're there to absolve souls; Tell the Per Mar people that there is an old lady streaking outside the Blue House, who will distract the students from studying and reading the Bible, thus making entry into Rohlman easier."[41]

Through the next academic year, the faculty academic support committee monitored the visitation policy and in February 1992, suggested an amendment to allow a student to register an overnight guest of the opposite sex. The committee submitted their report to Rogalski who took it to the board in April 1992. The board approved the policy that "some exceptions may allow for guests of the opposite sex to remain beyond visitation hours" but that those exceptions had to be approved by the student services office. However, the board wanted a statement added to express the "values of the Catholic Church regarding values of life, family and the responsibility of the individual."[42] When the Student Handbook was published in the fall of 1992, it included a statement that "As a Catholic university, St. Ambrose University believes that the complete and genuine expression of love through sex requires the commitment to marriage. Therefore, premarital sex is in no way condoned and the visitation policies are in part guided by that value."[43]

The public explanation for limiting visitation in the residence halls had been the safety of the students and an atmosphere that allowed academic work to take place. But the changes permitted by the board in 1992 added the issue of personal morality. One student asked if the policy was about sex or safety? For them, the issue was the freedom to act as they chose, an issue that had resonated through student protests since the 1960s, and they did not like the restrictions. A survey taken in September 1994 indicated that 86 percent of the students strongly disagreed or disagreed with the policy, about the same percentage as the Kabat survey of 1991.[44] The only

A Great and Lasting Beginning

additional change they were able to effect, however, came when the board changed the policy to allow visitors until 2:00 a.m. every day of the week.[45] Still, in 1996, 86 percent of the students said there should be twenty-four-hour visitation.[46]

The visitation policy was not the only source of student comment; so was the food. A September 1994 poll indicated that 74 percent of them said the overall quality of the food service was unsatisfactory or poor. They complained about the variety, the service, and the cleanliness of the cafeteria. The food service was run by Marriott Management Services; in 1986, it had purchased SAGA, the long-time company that provided food to campus. That fall, Allan Hayes took over management and began to make changes. Now students could choose from a wellness menu or a vegetarian menu or from a specialized potato bar, nacho bar, or pasta bar. There were also changes in the snack bar with more variety including pizzas and submarine sandwiches.[47]

For those who still found the food at St. Ambrose inadequate, there were plenty of off-campus sites for food and drink. They could choose from Rookies, heavily Ambrosian, fun and close to campus; or Bleyart's, just around the corner, where Grubby served you; the Filling Station; Pat McGuire's Irish American Grill; or Stickman's, which had good cheeseburgers. The Uptown, a "dive with character," had the names of former Ambrosians carved into the bar. McClellan's Stockade in the East Village had the best jukebox in the Quad-Cities. The Circle Tap remained a favorite, and a block further west, there was still Riefe's, which had good food, but no drinks. If none of those served the purpose, there was Chi-Chi's, the Halftime, Uncle Roscoe's, the Starting Line, Sebastian's, or Mac's Tavern.[48]

The Values Project noted there were "attitudes" reflecting the larger societal "class and group stereotypes" present on campus, specifically involving sexism and racism.[49] The first thirty-three students and their two teachers were white males. Except for the Sisters of Humility who came with the boarders in 1887, St. Ambrose remained a white, male institution for decades. After World War I, Mrs. Helena Bradford Churchill taught drama, and in the 1920s and 1930s, a few women taught as what today would be called adjunct faculty. The female students in the Women's Division of the 1930s were St. Ambrose students, but they were not on campus, so Ambrose remained officially male. The opportunity to change that in the late 1930s was declined, with Marycrest founded as the women's Catholic college. When the St. Ambrose faculty photo was taken in 1939, there were only two women on the staff, but they were not included in the picture. That began to change after World War II when more women entered the faculty. In the 1950s, the Nursing Division brought women to campus and the college came closer to becoming co-educational. When co-education came in the late 1960s, it ended the all-male history and more women on the faculty broke down a bit more that all-male barrier.

In 1992, 110 years after those first thirty-three boys entered, there were 2,417 students, 948 female undergraduates and 275 in graduate courses; there were 768 male undergraduates and 426 graduate students. In the whole student body, the women outnumbered the men 1,223 to 1,194. But the student body was still overwhelmingly white with a few minorities: there were 104 blacks, eighty-eight native American, Asian, and Hispanic students. There were also twenty international students. In 1992, there were 150 faculty members, thirty-one of whom were women. There was one African-American member of the faculty and five others of non-European origin. The upper administration, vice presidents and deans, were all male, and of the twenty-two members of the Board of Directors, Margaret Tiedemann was the only woman.

In a report to the Board of Directors on the third anniversary of his inauguration in October 1990, Rogalski said one of the current challenges was "further diversifying our campus while simultaneously remedying elements of campus sexism and racism."[50] He admitted there were "tensions," but he complimented the students on their "real effort to try to improve the qualities of relationships" among them. But he admitted more needed to be done, especially in recruiting minority faculty.[51]

The Strategic Planning Committee addressed the issue in 1990 with a three-part plan to develop a "campus-wide approach to minority student access and retention; develop a plan for course development and revision to ensure that majority students achieved "multicultural literacy"; and develop resources to achieve "greater diversity in the student population." Included in the plan was a strategy to increase recruitment among minorities.[52] Two years later, a strategic plan was created to address specifically the issue of recruitment of minority faculty.[53]

Rogalski's comments about student efforts to ease racial tension was directed in part to the Black Student Union which was active again after several years of inactivity. In 1990, there were seventeen members who sponsored pizza parties, a talent show, and other social events. According to Willie Barney, the president that year, their goal was to get people to talk about unifying the campus. Over the next few years, the group joined with others to sponsor forums on racism, including the Quad-City Summit on Diversity and Racial Equality that brought 170 community leaders to campus. One year, the group published a column in the *Buzz* with questions and answers about black-white relationships.[54]

Still, there was tension about racial issues. Black students complained that little attention was paid to Black History Month and that there was no recognition of the new Martin Luther King, Jr., national holiday. Others pointed to the fact that in spite of the efforts of the university, there was no increase in the number of black faculty members. And in the late winter of 1994, racial epithets appeared on bulletin boards and the black students said the university had not addressed the racism adequately.[55]

In response, early the next fall, various campus groups joined with campus ministry for a Unity Day Rally. Organizer Lee Ann Davis said, "Certain groups were beginning to feel they didn't fit in" on campus and the rally was an attempt to "understand the differences between people" and to find that their similarities "outweigh the differences." The event began at 9:00 p.m. on the chapel steps with a speech by Rogalski to "be mindful of the forces that attempted to divide us." He said that "anything that threatens the dignity of a single individual on our campus also harms the Ambrose community as a whole." Following speeches by other college leaders, the group staged a candlelight walk around the university campus. When the event was over, Davis said she hoped the groups who organized the rally would

Black Student Union members 1990-1991. Front row: Adaryl Allen, Lisa Owens, Anthony Jackson (treasurer); middle row: Dione Hoarde, Dana Hyatt, Lisa Chapman (vice president), Olivia Boone; top row: Tara Tensley (president), Shawnya Doyle, Josette Epps, Duane Evans, Candace Bailey (secretary), Anita Norwood.

continue to work together throughout the year."[56]

Another of the goals of the strategic plan formulated in 1990 was cultural diversity in the make-up of the campus and in the curriculum. That fall there were students from Korea, Indonesia, Japan, Canada, Panama, Holland, Pakistan, India, Kenya, Ghana, and the Philippines. Two of those students, Geoffrey Ndungu, an industrial engineering student from Kenya, and Ashish Mangalore, a computer science major from India, with Dr. Carol Lyon, the international student advisor, formed the Multi-Cultural Club. Ndungu said the group hoped to have American students join "so they can learn about different cultures." By the next spring there were sixty-nine members and the club sponsored Multicultural Week in March. Each day of the week concentrated on a region of the world, and there were activities about countries in the region every day. The week ended with a Friday night international banquet.[57]

Another way to diversify the campus was to make it possible for St.

Ambrose students to study abroad. The strategic plan for 1989-1991 provided a small amount of money to enable St. Ambrose students to study abroad through a program at Central College in Pella, Iowa.[58] In addition to that relationship, St. Ambrose created opportunities for students by associating with programs at other schools, including the Rome Center of Loyola of Chicago.

Three years later St. Ambrose developed a plan to expand those opportunities by creating its own study abroad program.[59] The first of those came in 1995 when St. Ambrose established a relationship with the Centers for Interamerican Studies in Cuenca, Ecuador. Under the leadership of Professors Arvella Lensing and Beatrice Jacobson, the first students studied in Ecuador in the intersession between the first and second semesters of January 1995.[60] That program expanded when a spring semester program and a faculty exchange were added.

The program in Cuenca continued, and over the next few years, St. Ambrose established programs in Heidelberg, Germany, and Lisbon, Portugal. There had also been faculty-led programs in other places in

A Great and Lasting Beginning

Europe as well as Asia and Latin America.

But the strongest tie was with Ireland. The founder of St. Ambrose was an Irish immigrant and many of the first students were the sons of Irish immigrants. In the late 1990s, some St. Ambrose students studied in Ireland and in the fall of 2001, Professor Jon Stauff, academic director of study abroad, announced a program for the spring of 2002 at Maynooth, just outside Dublin. The St. Ambrose-Ireland connection was strengthened when the Reverend Michael Schaab, a 1966 St. Ambrose graduate who had taught at Carlow College in Ireland, suggested forming a relationship with the Irish school. St. Ambrose already had a connection in Bishop James Davis who had studied there in the nineteenth century. Stauff worked with the Reverend Kevin O'Neill, the Carlow president, Dr. Thomas McGrath, the registrar, and the Reverend Conn O Maoldhomhnaigh, the chaplain, to create a program for St. Ambrose students. The first St. Ambrose students arrived in 2003. Planning was also underway for Carlow students to study at St. Ambrose and other ways to strengthen the relationship between the two schools.

The ties with Ireland were strengthened further when the Department of History and Geography created an Irish Studies Minor. Directed by Professor Ryan Dye, the minor included courses in Irish History, Celtic Spirituality, Irish theatre, Irish music and dance, and the history of the Catholic church in America. The Irish Studies program benefitted from the donation of two large collections of books. One was from Dr. Lawrence McCaffrey, a 1949 St. Ambrose graduate, professor emeritus of history at Loyola University, and one of the foremost scholars of Ireland and Irish America. The other, from Dr. Timothy Walch, the director of the Herbert Hoover Presidential Library, included a broad range of topics on Irish, Irish-American, and American Catholic history.

When St. Ambrose opened in 1882, students chose from a basic liberal arts curriculum or a commercial curriculum which consisted of practical courses like typewriting, shorthand, and bookkeeping that would enable the student to find employment. In the years since, the commercial curriculum evolved into business administration. Those students took liberal arts courses as part of their education; but there was a sense that the liberal arts courses were tolerated in order to graduate, but that the business courses would provide the graduate's livelihood. In the 1970s and 1980s, in part due to the influence of President Bakrow, a number of new academic majors in business were added, as well as some non-degree professional development courses. Those courses contributed significantly to the growing enrollment, and in the 1990s, St. Ambrose added other professional disciplines to the curriculum.

In 1992, St. Ambrose took another step into the health care field with a new physical therapy program. Begun with a $300,000 grant from the Greater Quad-City Hospital Council, the St. Ambrose program was the third in the state of Iowa. Like the occupational therapy program before it, the physical therapy program filled a critical need in a health care profession. The first students entered in the fall of 1992 and the first graduates received their Master of Physical Therapy Degrees in 1997.[61]

In the fall of 1995, St. Ambrose established the Adult College Curriculum for Education and Leadership (ACCEL) program. Modeled after a program at Regis College in Denver, ACCEL was for working adults who wanted a degree for career or personal reasons, but whose work or life situations prevented them from entering traditional educational programs. Applicants had to have completed thirty hours of college work to be admitted and then they took courses which were completed in a five-week workshop format. Within two years there were over 300 ACCEL students working in four degree programs.[62] In 1999, the ACCEL program moved into a new building on Fifty-third Street in Davenport which was built to house the various professional and educational development non-degree programs.[63]

In 1996, planning began to add a Master of Social Work program to the curriculum. Development of the program was assisted by a $150,000 grant from the St. Vincent's Home Corporation, an agency connected to the Diocese of Davenport, which funded local social service agencies. The St. Vincent's Corporation saw the grant as a way to train staff members who would work in the local social service agencies they traditionally funded. Dan Ebener, social action director for the Diocese of Davenport, noted that the "two feet of Christian service are charity and justice," and he hoped St. Ambrose students would be "agents of social change as well as providers of social service."[64] With a faculty in place and the necessary accreditations, the program began to accept students in 1996.

The Master of Physical Therapy, Master of Social Work, the ACCEL program, and the various non-degree professional development programs created in the late 1990s were part of a growing number of new professional degree programs at the undergraduate and graduate levels. New undergraduate majors began in such fields as finance, marketing, sports management, athletic training, radio/television, advertising and public relations, fitness, early childhood education, international business, and exercise science.

In 1996, the MBA, the first graduate program at St. Ambrose, celebrated its twentieth anniversary. Davenport Mayor Pat Gibbs said it was an indication of how St. Ambrose was "improving the quality of the community's work force." Rogalski pointed out that to serve the community even better, a new one-year MBA program had begun classes that day.[65] In the twenty years since the MBA began, new Master's Degrees in accounting, criminal justice, special education, health care administration, organizational leadership, information technology, educational administration, nursing, teaching, and juvenile justice were added to the curriculum. Building on that, in 1998, St. Ambrose introduced its first doctoral program, the Doctor of Business Administration. A second doctoral degree in physical therapy began in 2002.

In late 1999, Rogalski announced that St. Ambrose would establish a Nursing program. He said the decision was made in response to requests from the health care community, that the demand for nurses was great, and that St. Ambrose would help fill that need. The decision was not without controversy, however, since there was still a Nursing program at Marycrest and a former member of that department was hired as a consultant for the new St. Ambrose program. Although Marycrest filed a lawsuit alleging that its program was undermined by St. Ambrose's action, nevertheless, the Iowa Coordinating Council for Post-High School Education and the Iowa Board of Nursing both approved the university's proposal, and classes began in the fall of 2000.[66]

Some of the past Baecke lecturers gathered on November 10, 1993, to hear Rev. George McDaniel deliver the tenth lecture in the series. Left to right: Prof. Richard Geiger (who delivered the lecture in 1985), Dr. Arvella Lensing (1993), Dr. Patricia Kennedy (1986), McDaniel, Rev. Joseph Kokjohn (1987), Rev. Drake Shafer (1990), Prof. Greg Lensing (1988).

Many of the new programs and their students took advantage of the new computer system that was developed through the decade. Some of the administrative offices had used computers since the late 1950s, but in 1977, when Larry Snowden became director of the computer center, the campus community was brought fully into the computer age. Through his leadership, new systems were added as they became available, and new computer labs were established in the library, in Cosgrove Hall, and other areas around campus. With the new technology, a manual was published in 1994 to explain the basic information systems, the hope of which was to "enrich the education of students, to expand the research opportunities of faculty, and to enhance communication across all constituencies of the university."

As final exams approached that semester, the labs were crowded with students writing term papers and doing other end-of-the-semester work. They complained that there were not enough computers and that the hours the labs were open should be extended. Students were handed new "The dog ate my homework" excuses for not having work finished on time: the computer crashed, the printer was down, I couldn't get on-line.[67]

To resolve those limitations, one computer staff member suggested that a system be developed where the students used their own computer and somehow tied into the university system. A Title III Grant for Academic Computing helped the university to make that possible. With the grant, within three years the dormitory rooms had internet access.[68] In the spring of 1995, students opened their own email accounts for the first time. That fall, the first St. Ambrose web page went on-line, and faculty members learned HTML so they could develop their own web pages. Librarian Marylaine Block developed a web site, "Where the Wild Things Are," that pulled together links to research sites in one place. Not everyone was happy about the new easy access to information; when the student directory was put on-line, questions were raised about privacy. But St. Ambrose, like all institutions, developed guidelines for privacy and computer use and tried to keep up with the fast-changing world of computers.

Bishop McMullen had been a prolific writer who was published in several Catholic newspapers and journals of his day. As a student at St. Mary of the Lake, he wrote the campus newspaper and later, when he became

A Great and Lasting Beginning

president of the school, he published the *Monthly*, a journal filled with articles on a variety of topics. Generations of Ambrosians had carried on the tradition of a literary journal. The *Ambrosian Quarterly* was published in the 1920s and 1930s. In the 1950s, students tried to revive the custom when they published the *Facet* but it lasted only one issue. The *Ambrosian Review*, described as a "literary, critical, scientific, and artistic effort," was published briefly in 1966. The *Ambrosian Salad* published a single issue in 1976. In 1982, the *Journal of Student Research*, begun as part of the centennial activities, brought together essays and articles by students. During the years the *Ambrose Magazine* published, it put out an annual creative issue with poetry, short stories, and art but was limited in what it could publish. In 1992, English Professor Carl Herzig and a group of students published the first issue of *Quercus, A Journal of Visual and Literary Art*. The title was the Latin for oak. Published in the spring of each year, *Quercus* contained stories, poetry, and art contributed by students and alumni.[69]

McMullen believed a university should be a place for an exchange of ideas. Through the years speakers had come to campus, there were a variety of forums, panels, and conferences that challenged the campus community. On November 10, 1993, Father George McDaniel delivered the tenth Baecke Chair of Humanities Lecture. The chair had been established in 1981 with a gift from Mr. and Mrs. Albert Baecke. The first occupant was Professor Wayne DeJohn who spoke on the lumber industry in the Mississippi Valley, and topics by subsequent speakers included Medieval Belgium, Shakespeare, the sense of place in American novelists, suicide and the right to die, and Spain. McDaniel spoke on the League for Social Justice, the early 1950s group of Ambrosians and others who carried on the Catholic Action tradition at St. Ambrose.[70]

The Chair of Catholic Studies Lecture continued to bring a wide range of theologians and church leaders to speak. In 2001, the Department of History and Geography established the Richard E. Geiger History Lecture where historians from across the country discussed a wide range of topics from Medieval Europe to contemporary American themes.

In his inaugural address, Rogalski said he wanted more endowed chairs. One of those was the Frank and Jane Folwell Chair in Political Science and Pre-Law, established in 2001. As a result of the chair, the annual Folwell Lecture began with a presentation by Justice Linda Neuman, a member of the Iowa Supreme Court and of the St. Ambrose Board of Directors.

In 1993, Bishop Gerald O'Keefe reached the mandatory retirement age of seventy-five. He had been bishop and chairman of the St. Ambrose Board of Directors since 1967. During those years he was part of the enormous changes at St. Ambrose: co-education, the enlargement of the corporate board to include lay members, the merger attempts, the introduction of graduate programs, and the move to university status. He stood firm to protect those things he felt were important marks of a Catholic university: the teaching of theology, an active campus ministry, good liturgy, and the belief that a Catholic university should prepare its students to take their place as lay leaders in their parishes and institutions. He supported the St. Ambrose Seminary but like bishops around the country, watched with disappointment as the number of seminarians dwindled to only a few.[71]

The new bishop and chairman of the board was William Franklin. Born in Parnell, Iowa, Franklin had grown up in Cedar Rapids and graduated from Loras College. He was ordained in 1956 and spent many of his early years as a teacher and counselor at Wahlert High School in Dubuque. Franklin was installed as Bishop of Davenport on January 20, 1994. He said he recognized "St. Ambrose University as a great source of intellectual life and development of the larger church community," and that he had no plans for any changes, since, "You don't shake up something that is doing very well."[72]

Franklin became bishop just as St. Ambrose was beginning a ten-year period of extraordinary growth. There were new undergraduate and graduate academic programs; the student enrollment increased steadily each year; and the size of the campus grew dramatically. That year the university bought twenty neighborhood properties, almost twice as many as the previous four years combined. Some properties would be used for student housing, but some would be torn down to make room for future buildings.

On April 11, 1994, the university launched the Campaign for St. Ambrose University, chaired by board members John (Jack) L. Bush, chief executive officer of Linwood Mining and Mineral Corporation, and Barry C. O'Brien, retired chairman and chief executive officer of Iowa Illinois Gas and Electric Company, to raise $20.5 million to be used to build the new library and add to the endowment. By the end of the summer, just over $14 million had been raised including a $750,000 challenge grant from the Kresge Foundation.[73] An additional challenge grant of $1 million from the Bechtel Trusts and Foundation of Davenport and a $1 million gift from Arnold and Roselyn Meyer put the total at over $16 million.[74] Ground was broken for the new library following the homecoming Mass on October 9, 1994.[75] Once again sidewalk superintendents gathered to watch the progress of the new library.

But the construction had eliminated a parking lot, and although two other lots had been built which actually increased the total number of parking spaces, there were still complaints that no parking was available close to the buildings. One student said, "I pay $15,000 a year, and I don't even get a free parking spot. That's crazy!" Another asked why he should buy a parking sticker if he could not find a parking space. Still another asked why the teachers got to park close to the buildings when the students could not; after all, the students paid the faculty's salary. Solutions included giving more tickets for improper parking and building a parking ramp.[76]

During those years the number of students increased, putting pressure not only on parking spaces, but also on classroom and residence hall space. Enrollment was 2,417 in the fall of 1992, 2,518 the next year, and 2,584 in 1994; the number of resident students increased from 678 to 835 during those same years. To accommodate the larger number of students, some women were temporarily housed at the St. Paul the Apostle Parish convent and others at the Holiday Inn. At first, those at the Holiday Inn were happy because they had access to the pool and hot tub, but like their counterparts at St. Paul's, they felt disconnected to the campus and were glad to move back when space became available.[77]

In the fall of 1994, the Board of Directors approved Roglaski's recommendation to proceed with planning for a residential facility and a badly needed student center. Rogalski asked Kabat to chair a committee to develop

Photos by Greg Boll & John Mohr

255

A Great and Lasting Beginning

preliminary designs for the two structures.[78] The next spring they had a plan for a residence hall to be built on the east side of the campus.[79] When the plan was presented to the Board of Directors in early April, they were pleased with the location and the concept, but they tabled any further discussion or decision until their meeting in October 1995.[80]

However, in May and June the number of students who wanted to live on campus increased, and Rogalski wrote the board to ask for a special meeting on July 14, 1995, to authorize the construction of a new residence hall for occupancy in the fall of 1996. He told them the anticipated enrollment numbers for the fall and noted that if all of the students who wanted to live on campus actually arrived that fall, "We will be facing a very serious challenge in housing." Moreover, he said enrollment forecasts for the next few years indicated that the student population would continue to increase. He said the most recent master plan had a goal of 1,000 on-campus students by 2005, but that number could be reached by 1996 if space were available.

The board acceded to Rogalski's request, and planning began immediately for a residence hall for 116 students in apartment-style rooms on the corner of Ripley and High Streets. That would be the first of a three-phase project; the second phase was another residence hall at the other end of that block; and the third phase was to connect the two buildings with meeting rooms and lounges.[81] Construction on the first phase began in early November.[82]

Sidewalk superintendents now had two projects to watch, and while work began on the new residence hall, library construction was ahead of schedule. The fund raising was also ahead of schedule. Thanks to large gifts from the Diocese of Davenport, the John Deere Foundation, the Roy Carver Trust, and 2,500 pledges from friends and alumni around the country, the Kresge and Bechtel challenges were met, and slightly over $20 million, just short of the $20.5 million goal, was realized.

The library was finished in late February, and in early March, 350 Ambrosians formed a chain and passed 114 books, one for each year of St. Ambrose, from the old library to the new.[83] The new library opened for the fall semester with the formal dedication at homecoming, October 6, 1996. The day began with Mass where retired Bishop Gerald O'Keefe preached. O'Keefe noted that the "wisdom of the ages" was preserved in libraries, "not only for our own enrichment, our own knowledge, but for the honor and glory of God, the source of knowledge and love." Following Mass, Bishops Franklin and O'Keefe led a procession to the library for the dedication. Chicago Public Library Commissioner Mary Dempsey spoke, calling the day a "proud chapter in St. Ambrose history." The building was named O'Keefe Library, prompting O'Keefe to respond with the words of a grandniece, "That's cool."[84]

Also that fall, construction was underway on a building on Harrison Street that at one time had been a service station and later was the Gallery of Lights. When finished in January 1997, the bookstore moved in and a coffee shop opened.[85] As soon as the library moved out of McMullen Hall, major renovation of it began. The interior was gutted to the outside walls and reconfigured into classrooms and faculty offices. Faculty and students moved into the renovated McMullen Hall in the fall of 1997.

The students wondered about the new residence hall, which at two years of age was still without a name. They called it the new dorm, but asked,

"How long until a new dorm is an old dorm?" They wanted to know if when phase two of the project was completed, it would be called the "newer dorm?"[86] Construction began on the "newer dorm" in the fall of 1999 and it was ready for occupancy the next fall. With that, both buildings were given names. The "new dorm" was named Tiedemann Hall for Margaret and Bud Tiedemann. Both long-time supporters of St. Ambrose, Mrs. Tiedemann was also the first woman on the Board of Directors. The "newer dorm" was named Hagen Hall for James and Mary Hagen. He was a 1956 graduate of St. Ambrose and served on the Board of Directors.[87]

Tiedemann and Hagen featured apartment-style rooms for four to six students. Cosgrove was arranged in suites with two double rooms sharing a common bathroom. Davis, Hayes, and Rohlman Halls were traditional dormitories with single or double rooms and a bath and shower down the hall. At the end of the fall semester of 2000, students were moved out of Rohlman Hall and work began to renovate it into suite-style living. Students moved back in the new Rohlman in August 2001.[88]

The fall semester of 2001 began with a record number 2,271 students, 155 more than the previous fall. There were 1,095 resident students, 109 more than the previous fall, giving rise to rumors of building yet another residence hall. Adequate parking was still a problem, and although there were now 1,300 parking spaces on campus, students and faculty complained that they could never find one. Once again CAB organized Welcome Week that included movies, a concert, Comedy Sportz, and a trip to Wacky Waters. On the first day of classes, Bishop Franklin came to bless the new school year.

Todd Sturdy began his seventh season as football coach. The previous year, the Bees had finished 9-3, won the Midwest Classic Conference Championship, and made the first playoff appearance in thirteen years. The team started well with a 21-14 win over Coe College. The women's soccer team, which had not lost a conference game since 1996, began their season hoping for their sixth consecutive conference championship. The men's team was young and injury-plagued, but second-year head coach, the Reverend Bud Grant, was hopeful that with the best recruiting class in memory, the season could be successful. That semester there were new intramural activities in water aerobics and kickboxing, but Kilfoy football, which was a combination of football, basketball, and soccer, continued as one of the most popular intramural sports.

The morning of September 11, students in the cafeteria were eating a hurried breakfast before their 8:00 class; others were struggling out of bed and would skip breakfast before class; still others rolled over for more sleep before their first classes later in the morning. At 7:46 a.m., an airplane slammed into the north tower of the World Trade Center in New York City. As the morning news programs interrupted their regular programming to cover what most believed to be a terrible accident, students and faculty continued their morning routines. But when a second plane crashed into the south tower of the Trade Center seventeen minutes later, they knew that something unimaginably horrible was taking place.

As they had on December 7, 1941, and November 22, 1963, Ambrosians gathered together to hear the latest reports: President George W. Bush spoke of an "apparent terrorist attack"; a third plane hit the

Pentagon; a fourth crashed in Pennsylvania; all remaining planes in the air were commanded to land at the nearest airport; both trade towers collapsed; tall buildings in Chicago and other cities were evacuated. Appearing on television at noon, Bush asked for prayers for those killed and wounded. As the president spoke, Ambrosians were already gathering in Christ the King Chapel for a prayer service.

The chapel was full, and students held on to one another for comfort and tried to make sense of it all. Dr. Rogalski asked for understanding, the chaplain, Father Chuck Adam, offered prayers, a series of students presented petitions of prayer, and hymns of comfort were sung. It seemed incomprehensible: one student said it was the "first time I saw something on TV and thought I was dreaming." Many said they had never seen anything like it,

Students marked the first anniversary of September 11 with a prayer service and procession around campus. (Photo by John Mohr)

As the days turned into weeks, Ambrosians tried to return to the regular routine of campus life, but not back to normal. It seemed to many that things would not be normal again for a long time, if ever. Still, they tried. Professor Kristin Quinn's 3-D art class built furniture out of books and displayed their work in the library. Campus ministry held its annual Antioch retreat in Sugar Creek. CAB sponsored social evenings, a blood drive, and the Java Jam.

Homecoming was celebrated with a pep rally on Friday night featuring the Dance Team and the cheerleaders. Members of the football team spoke, and Jabari Woods and Jennifer Smith were crowned king and queen. The next day began with the Sixth Annual Killer Bee 5K run, the Taste of Ambrose tailgate party, and a 41-13 victory over St. Francis. All the teams

"Our generation . . . hasn't experienced Pearl Harbor and World War II." Throughout the week there were discussions, more prayer services, a candlelight march around campus and an all-night vigil in the chapel, and a noon-time prayer for peace on the steps of the chapel.[89]

At their next meeting, the SGA passed a resolution expressing their "deepest sympathy and concern" for the tragedies. The resolution said they supported and prayed for "peace through justice." As college students looking to their future, they said they stood "together to end terrorist attacks here in the United States and worldwide, and to do that justly."[90] *Buzz* editor Louis Hare said the "biggest changes" to come out of the tragedy would be tightened security and that the probability of war was high. But he said the world had to come together to solve the problems that led to the attacks, and perhaps in the future, September 11 would be viewed not as the day "thousands of lives ended, but also as the day world peace truly began."[91]

did well that fall, reflected in the fact that twenty-eight players from the football, men's and women's golf, soccer, and cross country teams, were named to all-conference squads.

In November the Theatre Department presented *Anton in Show Business* and then took it to the regional American College Theater Festival in Lincoln, Nebraska. That was the thirteenth year Professor Corinne Johnson took students to the festival. Nine students were selected for the Irene Ryan regional competition. Although that year none went to the national competition in Washington, D.C., the next year Dan Hale was chosen to go on, and two years later, Dan Sheridan had the same honor.[92] In 2005, Johnson was awarded the Regional Acting Coach Award.

Over Christmas break, a group of ten students went to New York to work as volunteers at Ground Zero, the site of the destroyed World Trade Towers. Another group from the Art, Music, and Theatre departments went to New York to see television shows and theater. Members of the chorus with their conductor, Professor Keith Haan, sang at the Cathedral of St. John the Divine. They also visited Ground Zero which was a "life-altering experience."[93]

Another group of students from campus ministry went to Chicago continuing a tradition begun in 1998. Led by Father Bud Grant, the students volunteered at the Chicago Port Ministries, which aided people who were jobless or homeless. The students did manual labor in the house, served meals, worked at a drop-in shelter, and taught English as a Second Language classes. For their efforts the Port Ministries named them the Volunteer Group of the month.[94]

A scene from Anton in Show Business, *standing left to right, Beth Curley, Jill Schmits, Megan O'Connell, seated, Jamie Johnson.*

the previous ten years, hundreds of student-athletes had acted as mentors at local schools, collected books for the Read to Succeed program, provided Christmas gifts for children, worked at the John Lewis Coffee Shop, and brought grade school students to campus for Field Day activities. The women's soccer team was involved with breast cancer awareness programs.[100]

In its third season, the men's volleyball team finished with its first winning season. The baseball team won the conference championship for the first time since 1996 and the women's softball team finished second in the conference. The men's and women's track teams had several representatives on the All-Conference squads.[101]

Students returned for the second semester and learned that Marycrest International University would close at the end of the spring semester.[95] What that might mean for St. Ambrose was unsure, but there had already been inquiries from Marycrest students about transferring to the university.

In February 2002, the *Buzz* published a preliminary drawing of the new university center.[96] Two years before, the Board of Directors had approved a capital fund campaign for the building as part of a $110 million, ten-year campaign.[97] The university center, chapel renovation, and several other building projects were part of phase one of the campaign slated for completion in the first five years. In April 2001, the Kresge Foundation awarded St. Ambrose an $805,000 challenge grant for the university center, and once again major gifts from the Bechtel Foundation and from Jim and Mary Hagen were received. Fund raising had proceeded through 2001 and by the fall, nearly two-thirds of the $18 million goal had been raised.[98]

After spring break the choir, band, and jazz band gave their spring concerts. The jazz concert included the vocal group Stamvoja (St. Ambrose Vocal Jazz) which had been formed four years before by Marti Dunn-Hall, a vocal music instructor. On April 12, the School of Social Work sponsored the Fourth Annual Social Action Conference, with the theme, "Structural Violence: A Multicultural Perspective."

The winter and spring sports schedule was as full as the fall's, with the beginning of one sport's season overlapping the end of another's. The men's basketball team finished with a 20-13 record, coach Ray Shovlain's eleventh 20-win season. In December 1999, Shovlain's teams gave him his 300th coaching victory and in February 2004, he passed 400 wins. The list of All-Conference and All-American players was growing in all of St. Ambrose's sports programs. But Shovlain was proud of the Academic All-Conference and Academic All-Americans; in the 2002-2003 season alone there were nineteen Academic All-Americans and 130 Academic All-Conference players. Shovlain said, "We define winning in a pretty wide perspective. If athletes are doing well academically," he felt they were winning.[99] All the athletes also participated in several community service projects each year. In

It rained on graduation day in May, a fitting end to a year that began under a cloud. Because of the weather, the ceremony was moved to the Mark of the Quad-Cities in Moline. President Rogalski told the graduates that no matter what field they had studied, they were all strengthened for one essential, "the ability to learn and go on learning all of your lives." He said that because of September 11, "our perspective [had] been enlarged beyond our individual concerns. We feel new vulnerabilities, but also new obligations to make a difference." The main speaker, the Reverend Peter Marty, pastor of St. Paul Lutheran Church in Davenport, told the graduates, "Your richest treasure, and your deepest meaning in life, will be found in doing ordinary things in an extraordinary way."[102]

While the campus community of 2001-2002 struggled to understand the new world in which they lived, planning continued for the new university center. Already being referred to as the "hearth and home" or the "living room" of the campus, the building would contain a food court, game room, meeting rooms, offices for student services and student organizations, student health and counseling, the career development center, security, and on the top floor, a large ballroom and other meeting and dining rooms.[103]

At the groundbreaking on September 26, 2002, Rogalski said when he came to campus in 1968, the students gathered in the Bee Hive. But the university had outgrown that facility and now they would be able to gather in the much larger new university center.[104] With the ground broken, construction proceeded through the late winter, spring, and summer of 2003. When the freshmen arrived that fall, most of the steel was up and all Ambrosians could sense just how large the new building would be.

Long-time Ambrosians had grown used to the almost constant construction of recent years. It lent an air of excitement and was a strong signal of growth and prosperity. Rogalski was responsible for a great deal of that. He

A Great and Lasting Beginning

The choir performed for the annual Feast of St. Ambrose Mass in December 2002.

was able to realize his vision for the expansion of programs and the physical campus because of the network of strong support among the alumni and the community he had built. Since he became president, annual giving had nearly doubled, from $596,000 in 1987-1988 to $1.1 million in 2004-2005; the endowment rose from $6 million to nearly $40 million; and successful campaigns raised money for O'Keefe Library and the university center.

When Rogalski greeted the incoming freshmen in the fall of 2003, he told them that he felt a special relationship with their class. They would graduate in the spring of 2007, and he told them he intended to retire that spring so he would graduate with them. The growth of the university had become so identified with Rogalski that some Ambrosians wondered how long that growth would continue. But as they pondered what his retirement meant, the semester began with the usual activities.

On November 7, the last steel beam was raised to the top of the university center with a formal topping-off ceremony. For a week, members of the Ambrose community had the opportunity to sign their names or write a message on the beam. Hundreds of them gathered to watch the beam, with the traditional pine tree and flag attached, as it was hoisted to the top of the building.[105]

In the meantime, as sidewalk superintendents watched the outer walls of the university center go up brick by brick, they looked across the street and watched the construction of the newest residence hall. The need for more residence rooms continued to put pressure on the existing space. The reconfiguration of Rohlman Hall into suites two years before meant there were 100 fewer beds available in the building. The new Tiedemann and Hagen Halls were full, and the students kept coming. Construction began on the new four-story, 128 unit building on the corner of High and Ripley Streets in November 2003.[106]

One of the consistent themes of planners for years had been to renovate Christ the King Chapel. It had been part of the first strategic plan issued in 1985 and had reappeared frequently in subsequent plans. There had been some attempts in the 1990s to fix the roof and clean the interior stone, and there were discussions about how to better adapt it to post-Vatican II liturgical designs. On October 10, 2003, the Board of Directors authorized a fund raising campaign for renovation, which began on December 3, 2003, the fiftieth anniversary of the dedication of the chapel with the Arts and Sciences Lecture, "The Chapels of St. Ambrose University," delivered by Father George McDaniel. Four days later on the feast of St. Ambrose, the campaign began with Solemn Vespers celebrated in the chapel followed by a dinner.

In August 2004, students moved into the newest residence hall, named Bechtel Hall, in honor of the family and the Bechtel Family Foundation. The football season began on September 11 with a victory against Loras College, the first time the two schools had met in twenty years.[107] The highlight of homecoming weekend was the dedication of the university center.

At the ceremony, John Anderson, a 1987 graduate and member of the Board of Directors, announced that the new building was named the Ed and Bobbi Rogalski Center. Anderson said the directors wanted to name the building for someone who "epitomized the St. Ambrose hallmark qualities," and no one did that more than the Rogalskis.[108] It seemed to most that it was appropriate that the "hearth and home" of the university would be named for the couple. In his inaugural address, Rogalski had paid tribute to his parents; his own sons grew up on campus and three of the five of them had graduated from St. Ambrose; and he often used the metaphor of the family when he spoke about the university and its people.

The next week, Rogalski announced that ground would soon be broken on a fourth new residence hall at the south end of Ripley Street in what he now referred to as residence row.

Ed and Bobbi Rogalski (Photo by Gil Cervelli)

Construction continued through the winter and when it opened the next fall, Rogalski announced it would be named Franklin Hall, to honor Bishop William Franklin.

That same month, St. Ambrose and the Genesis Health System announced a partnership to build a new health sciences building. This proposed building would hold the Physical Therapy, Occupational Therapy, and Nursing departments on land donated by Genesis on the corner of West Lombard and Marquette Streets, the former site of Mercy Hospital. Rogalski said bringing the three disciplines together would provide a great opportunity for the students to "engage in a collaborative learning experience."[109] Rogalski hoped ground would be broken for the new building in 2007.

One month after the dedication of the Rogalski Center, the *Buzz* asked students, "How big should SAU get?" Some said the current growth was not excessive and it should get bigger, one there would be "more of a 'university' feel." But most said that it was a "nice size" now; the small classes were appealing; if it got bigger you would lose the "quality of learning and feeling of care"; stay small.[110] Nevertheless, the campus continued to grow. The university owned almost all of the property on the so-called super block between Locust, Gaines, Lombard, and Harrison Streets, a total of nearly forty-one acres. It also had purchased a good deal of the property between Gaines Street and Brown Street, one block further west, which added another seven acres. Cosgrove's original ten-acre purchase had grown to almost forty-eight acres. Some of the houses in the area west of Gaines were used for students and some were torn down. However, by 2006, the only thing constructed west of Gaines Street was a parking lot.

Rogalski and the university he would soon leave were looking to the future and recalling the past. On September 4, 2006, the university began

the celebration of its 125th anniversary with a service in Sacred Heart Cathedral, just a few yards from the location of St. Marguerite's School where McMullen, Cosgrove, Schulte, and Halligan had opened St. Ambrose Seminary. The anniversary was celebrated with special events throughout the year, including the rededication of the chapel on December 10, 2006.

Since Bishop McMullen did not live through the past 124 years of St. Ambrose history, one must be careful to say whether the St. Ambrose of today corresponds to what he envisioned for his school. He would be amazed by the complexity of the world in which his school now operates. The students of McMullen's time came from a homogeneous Catholic culture defined by prayer, the rosary, catechism, Mass on Sunday and Holy Days, fish on Fridays, fasting and abstinence during Lent, Advent, and Rogation Days. The natural rhythms of birth, education, marriage, and death were celebrated in the church. In some cases the Catholicism may have been pro forma, especially for teenagers who attended because of parental pressure. But they went, and they understood the common language and culture of their religion, whether their native language was German or Polish or Italian or English.

When the students came to St. Ambrose, they came to an institution that spoke the same religious language and acted out the same religious culture they experienced at home. Not that everyone through the years agreed about supporting organized labor, or surveying racial prejudice, or taking up a collection for the missions. But there was agreement on the essentials: Mass on Sunday, frequent confession, regular devotions, and there was episcopal and presbyteral concern because the students didn't go to Mass or observe the other elements of that Catholic culture. Those activities defined them as Catholics, and to a large degree, they were what defined St. Ambrose College as Catholic. The liberal arts undergirded that homogeneous Catholic culture, and if the students did not understand that, their priest-professors did, which is why the discussions of the 1930s and 1960s were so important. As the liberal arts gave way to a curriculum with an increased emphasis on career preparation in a market-driven educational environment, it is little wonder that Catholic educators strenuously tried to define themselves and their mission.

In the last forty years, that homogeneous Catholic culture had broken down with "two views of what ails the Church and how it should be corrected." One had a "deep appreciation" for the reforms of Vatican II which, according to its proponents, were never fully implemented. The other view was not as enthusiastic about Vatican II which it said went too far with its reforms and therefore the church was in need of a "cultural correction."[111]

A Great and Lasting Beginning

Bishop Franklin blesses those assembled for the dedication of the Rogalski Center. (Photo by John Mohr)

Those ecclesiastical divisions mirrored the larger divisions in American society taking place at the same time, where the freedoms sought and fought for in the 1960s and 1970s had, in the view of many, become license with no discernable standards of behavior or belief. Those who held that belief yearned for a return to their perception of a pre-Elvis America where the lines of behavior were clear and ideas were well-defined and handed on from generation to generation. Others decried the excesses but still saw the necessity to challenge the status quo and lamented the fact that so few others joined them in those challenges. At St. Ambrose those tensions were part of the struggles over residence hall rules, the battles about the curriculum, and the continuing influence of Roman Catholicism outside the chapel.

McMullen had founded St. Ambrose, in part, to prepare young men as priests to serve his infant diocese. In the years after World War II, the number of seminarians at St. Ambrose and across the country had grown dramatically. By the time Hayes Hall was built in the mid-1960s, however, that growth trend was already beginning to decline. In the decades since, the American church has seen a precipitous decline in the number of seminarians, and as St. Ambrose prepares to celebrate its 125th anniversary, there are very few remaining. But new education programs for lay church leadership and an active campus ministry involving all students reflect the emphasis of the post-Vatican II church on the importance of the laity.

McMullen might be astounded at the changed role of the bishop and the level of control he had over the school. As a university president in the 1860s, McMullen tried to create a school to serve the needs of a burgeoning region of the country. He indicated his willingness to go against the trend, for example, in his belief that seminary and lay students should study together, but he learned that a school begun by a bishop was answerable only to that bishop, and his conflict with Bishop Duggan was a painful lessen. As bishop and founder of his own school, he could have molded it with his own ideas, but his early death precluded that possibility.

Davenport's bishops after McMullen had a mixed record of involvement with the college. From the more passive attitude of Cosgrove, Davis, and Hayes, to the interventionist policies of Rohlman, to the realization of O'Keefe and Franklin that while they were still chairmen of the board, direct control of events on campus was no longer possible and their influence on the college was moral and personal.

The bishops, and to a certain extent, the church, no longer directly controlled St. Ambrose. Outside agencies like the AAUP which defined and monitored the relationship of the faculty to the institution, the federal and state governments who supplied money, and the North Central Association and professional accrediting agencies now defined what the college was. By complying with their guidelines and norms, a St. Ambrose had been created that was not that much different from most other Catholic universities, or most other small, secular universities.

Nevertheless, through the decades, the St. Ambrose community had striven to define itself. The discussions in the 1930s about the liberal arts, the fights over the curriculum in the 1970s, the development and periodic review of mission statements beginning in the 1970s, the Values Project of the early 1990s were all aimed to continue the old and adapt to the new. But as the church and academic world changed, it was a constant struggle to maintain the core identity of St. Ambrose. Rogalski acknowledged that

Ambrosians are marked by their time under the oaks. (Photo by Stephen Spartana)

difficulty when he spoke at the blessing of the new year on August 29, 2005. He said St. Ambrose was an institution "committed to an impartial search for truth," which could be learned in the "Catholic tradition." But those in higher education realized "that there have been tensions in our colleges and universities created by political partisan forces that threaten our academic freedom and thereby our institutional mission." In the face of that, Rogalski reasserted that it was the "faculty and staff, not external characters and actors" who determined the "professional standards for the academy." The dialogue to determine those standards may lead to controversy, but he said that while dialogue was necessary, it must be done in an atmosphere of civility and respect for the opinion of others since, "Academic responsibility and academic freedom must be part of the fuller picture of the search for truth and knowledge."[112]

As an institution of Catholic higher education in the twenty-first century, St. Ambrose was not unique. But it had a history that began with Bishop McMullen's vision, a reputation, and a character all its own. The Values Project of the early 1990s tried to identify and make the campus community aware of the values it espoused so they would be the basis for campus life. Campus ministry developed a phrase to summarize those values: Faith Learning Justice.

At St. Ambrose people of faith still seek ways to live out that faith on campus and in the marketplace. McMullen saw learning as the key to prepare and enrich oneself as a person and as the means to prepare the person for a place in society. Learning is still valued and each fall students and faculty still embark on a journey of discovery about themselves and their world. Ambrosians still have the passion for justice which led McMullen to care for those most in need in his community and which has led Ambrosians to question the powerful and advocate for the powerless.

Ambrosians are marked by their time under the oaks. When McMullen was preparing to leave Chicago to come to his new diocese, he was compared to a gnarled oak tree which sheltered an ivy vine in a storm. Much has changed since Father Cosgrove gave McMullen two rooms to begin his school for boys. But as William Wordsworth observed, "Great changes have been wrought in all the neighborhood. Yet the oak is left." Bishop McMullen's "great and lasting beginning" has extended for 125 years, and is poised to continue his vision into the future.

A Great and Lasting Beginning

Notes

Introduction

1. James J. McGovern, *The Life and Writings of the Right Reverend John McMullen, D.D., First Bishop of Davenport* (Chicago and Milwaukee: Hoffmann Brothers, 1888), 256.
2. *100 Years, The History of the Church of the Holy Name, The Chapel that Became a Cathedral and the Story of Catholicism in Chicago* (Chicago: The Cathedral of the Holy Name, 1949), n.p.
3. *Catholic Messenger*, July 7, 1883.
4. Eliza Allen Starr, "Reminiscences of Bishop McMullen," *The Ave Maria* (July 28, 1883): 595.
5. *100 Years*, n.p.
6. James J. McGovern, *Souvenir of the Silver Jubilee in the Episcopacy of His Grace The Most Rev. Patrick Augustine Feehan, Archbishop of Chicago* (Chicago: 1891), 36, 66; Joseph J. Thompson, *The Archdiocese of Chicago, Antecedents and Development* (Des Plaines, Illinois: St. Mary's Training School Press, 1920), 673. The most complete history of St. Mary of the Lake is D. J. Riordan, "University of St. Mary of the Lake," *Illinois Catholic Historical Review*, 2 (October, 1919): 135-160. See also Harry Koenig, "History of St. Mary of the Lake Seminary," Feehan Memorial Library, University of St. Mary of the Lake/Mundelein Seminary, Mundelein, Illinois; Marcellus James Monaco, "The Foundations of The University of Saint Mary of the Lake" (master's thesis, St. Mary of the Lake Seminary, 1941). Philip Gleason, "Chicago and Milwaukee: Contrasting Experiences in Seminary Planting," Nelson H. Minnich, Robert B. Eno, S.S. & Robert F. Trisco, eds., *Studies in Catholic History in Honor of John Tracy Ellis* (Wilmington, Delaware: Michael Glazier, 1985): 149-174.
7. "Proposals to Establish an Academy at George Town, Patowmack River, Maryland," John Tracy Ellis, ed. *Documents of American Catholic History* (Milwaukee, The Bruce Publishing Company, 1956): 172.
8. Jay P. Dolan, *The American Catholic Experience, A History from Colonial Times to the Present* (Garden City, New York: Doubleday & Company, Inc.: 1985), 249.
9. "The Pastoral Letter of 1833," Peter Guilday, ed., *The National Pastorals of the American Hierarchy (1792-1919)* (Westminster, Maryland: The Newman Press, 1954): 74.
10. Guilday, "The Pastoral Letter of 1840," 135.
11. Joseph M. White, *The Diocesan Seminary in the United States: A History from the 1780s to the Present* (Notre Dame, Indiana: University of Notre Dame Press, 1989), 7, 63.
12. Stafford Poole, C.M., *Seminary in Crisis* (New York: Herder and Herder, 1965), 52.
13. Richard Hofstadter, *Anti-intellectualism in American Life* (New York: Vintage Books, 1962, 1963), 137, 140.
14. Poole, *Seminary in Crisis*, 41.
15. Christopher J. Kauffman, *Tradition and Transformation in Catholic Culture, The Priests of Saint Sulpice in the United States from 1791 to the Present* (New York: Macmillan Publishing Company, 1988), 38ff.
16. Kauffman, *Tradition and Transformation*, 77-85.
17. Edward J. Power, *A History of Catholic Higher Education in the United States* (Milwaukee, The Bruce Publishing Company, 1958), 333-334.
18. Gilbert J. Garraghan, SJ, *The Catholic Church in Chicago, 1673-1871* (Chicago, Illinois: Loyola University Press, 1821), 112,113.
19. Garraghan, *Catholic Church in Chicago*, 114; McGovern, *Souvenir of the Silver Jubilee*, 74; James W. Sanders, *The Education of an Urban Minority, Catholics in Chicago, 1833-1965* (New York: Oxford University Press, 1977), 73; *100 Years*, n.p.
20. McGovern, *Life and Writings*, 13-17.
21. McGovern, *Life and Writings*, 17; Marcellus James Monaco, "The Foundations of the University of Saint Mary of the Lake," (master's thesis, Seminary of Saint Mary of the Lake, 1941), 55.
22. McGovern, *Life and Writings*, 19; Riordan, "University of St. Mary of the Lake," 144.
23. Ellen Skerrett, "The Catholic Dimension," Lawrence J. McCaffrey, Ellen Skerrett, Michael F. Funchion, Charles Fanning, *The Irish in Chicago* (Urbana and Chicago: University of Illinois Press, 1987): 27.
24. McGovern, *Life and Writings*, 144. Ellen Skerrett, "The Catholic Dimension," 28.
25. McGovern, *Life and Writings*, 43; Richard H. Clarke, *Lives of the Deceased Bishops of the Catholic Church in the United States* (New York: Richard H. Clarke, 1888), 593.
26. McGovern, *Life and Writings*, 49.
27. White, *The Diocesan Seminary*, 86.
28. "Catalogo Alumni Pontificio Urbano de Propaganda Fide 1853," 12-13; "Catalogo, 1854," 10-11; "Catalogo, 1855," 8-9; "Catalogo, 1856," 8-9; "Catalogo, 1857," 6-7; "Catalogo, 1858," 4-5; McGovern, *Life and Writings*, 93, 100.
29. McGovern, *Life and Writings*, xviii, xix.
30. *American Celt*, June 3, 1854.
31. McGovern, *Life and Writings*, 117, 122.
32. *American Celt*, February 18, 1854.
33. McGovern, *Life and Writings*, 117.
34. Thomas Darcy McGee to John McMullen, March 28, 1854, Archives of the Archdiocese of Chicago; McGovern, *Life and Writings*, 118.
35. Josephine Phelan, *The Ardent Exile, The Life and Times of Thos. Darcy McGee* (Toronto: The Macmillan Company of Canada Limited, 1951), 141.
36. McGovern, *Life and Writings*, 123; Clarke, *Lives of Deceased Bishops*, 597.
37. Eliza Allen Starr, "Bishop McMullen," *New York Freeman's Journal and Catholic Register*, July 14, 1883.
38. *American Celt*, June 17, 1854.
39. McGovern, *Life and Writings*, 124.
40. Harry C. Koenig, STD, *A History of the Parishes of the Archdiocese of Chicago, Volume I* (Chicago: The Archdiocese of Chicago, 1980), 665.
41. McGovern, *Life and Writings*, 128.
42. Clarke, *Lives of Deceased Bishops*, 606.
43. Suellen Hoy, "Caring for Chicago's Women and Girls, The Sisters of the Good Shepherd, 1859-1911," *Journal of Urban History* 23 (March 1997): 264.
44. Harry C. Koenig, STD, *A History of the Offices, Agencies, and Institutions of the Archdiocese of Chicago, Volume II* (Chicago: The Archdiocese of Chicago, 1981), 894.
45. McGovern, *Life and Writings*, 129.
46. Hoy, "Caring for Chicago's Women and Girls," 265; McGovern, *Life and Writings*, 128- 129.
47. McGovern, *Life and Writings*,134.
48. Koenig, *History of Offices, Agencies, and Institutions*, 902, 986.
49. McGovern, *Life and Writings*, 142; Clarke, *Lives of Deceased Bishops*, 597. Cornelius J. Kirkfleet, *The History of the Parishes of the Diocese of Rockford, Illinois* (Chicago: John Anderson Publishing Company, 1924), 218-219, 331, 401; Edward L. McDonald, *Golden Jubilee History of the Diocese of Rockford* (Waldsmith Illustrators, Publisher, 1958), 145-147, 229-230, 325; Robert R. Miller, *That All May Be One, A History of the Rockford Diocese* (Rockford, Illinois: The Diocese of Rockford, 1976), 156-157, 145, 163-164.
50. Harry Koenig, "History of St. Mary of the Lake Seminary," 31.
51. McGovern, *Life and Writings*, 143, 144.
52. Riordan, "University of St. Mary of the Lake," 145-149.
53. Garraghan, *Catholic Church in Chicago*, 213.
54. James W. Sanders, *The Education of an Urban Minority, Catholics in Chicago, 1833-1965* (New York: Oxford University Press, 1977), 75.
55. Riordan, "University of St. Mary of the Lake," 150; McGovern, *Life and Writings*, 145.
56. McGovern, *Life and Writings*, 145.
57. *Chicago Times*, July 26, 1881.
58. Eliza Allen Starr, *New York Freeman's Journal*, July 14, 1883.
59. *Chicago Times*, July 8, 1883.
60. F. G., "Public Instruction," *Brownson's Quarterly Review* (July 1857): 378, 379, 388.
61. Power, *History of Catholic Higher Education*, 78; Philip Gleason, "American Catholic Higher Education: A Historical Perspective," Robert Hassenger, ed., *The Shape of Catholic Higher Education* (Chicago: The University of Chicago Press, 1967): 27.
62. [Orestes Brownson], "Catholic Schools and Education," *Brownson's Quarterly Review* (January 1862): 84.
63. Monaco, "Foundations," 38.
64. McGovern, *Life and Writings*, 146; Riordan, 151-152; Clarke, *Lives of Deceased Bishops*, 598-599.
65. Riordan, "University of St. Mary of the Lake," 152; McGovern, *Life and Letters*, 147.
66. "Diocesan Theological Seminaries in the Middle West, 1811-1889," John Tracy Ellis, *Essays in Seminary Education* (Notre Dame, Indiana: Fides Publishers, Inc., 1967): 151.
67. Peter Guilday, *A History of the Councils of Baltimore (1791-1884)* (New York: The Macmillan Company, 1932), 106; Lloyd Paul McDonald, "The Seminary Movement in the United States; Projects, Foundations and Early Development (1784-1833)," (PhD diss, The Catholic University of America, 1927), 60, 63.
68. White, *The Diocesan Seminary*, 70, 84, 85, 95-96, 102.
69. Ellis, "Diocesan Theological Seminaries," 127-128.
70. John McMullen, "Clerical Seminaries," *The Monthly, Vol I*, June 1865. Reprinted in McGovern, *Life and Writings*, cix, cxv-cxvi.
71. Riordan, "University of St. Mary of the Lake," 152; Eliza Allen Starr to Cousin Mary, November 27, 1863, James J. McGovern, ed., *The Life and Letters of Eliza Allen Starr* (Chicago: The Lakeside Press, 1895), 199.
72. McMullen to Congregation of the Propagation of the Faith, July 20, 1864, Documents of the Propagation of the Faith, Kenneally 375, Volume 3, 1st Series; Congregation to McMullen, September 1, 1864, Kenneally 1157, Volume 5.
73. Monaco, "Foundations," 23.
74. "Prospectus of 'The Catholic Monthly,'" Documents of the Propaganda of the Faith, June 28, 1864, Kenneally 376, Vol 3.
75. McGovern, *Life and Writings*, 159.
76. James J. McGovern, "Eliza Allen Starr," *The Catholic Encyclopedia*, 1912.
77. Eliza Allen Starr to Mrs. Arrington, May 25, 1871, McGovern, *Life and Letters of Eliza Allen Starr*, 272.
78. McGovern, *Life and Writings*, 159-160; Garraghan, *The Catholic Church in Chicago*, 216; Riordan, "University of St. Mary of the Lake," 153.
79. Ellis, "Diocesan Theological Seminaries," 162.
80. Timothy Walch, *The Diverse Origins of American Catholic Education, Chicago, Milwaukee, and the Nation* (New York and London: Garland Publishing, Inc., 1988), 83.
81. Clarke, *Lives of Deceased Bishops*, 600
82. McGovern, *Life and Writings*, 160.
83. Garraghan, *Catholic Church in Chicago*, 216.
84. McGovern, *Life and Writings*, 160; Riordan, "University of St. Mary of the Lake," 153ff.
85. Koenig, *History of the Offices, Agencies and Institutions*, 1670.
86. McGovern, *Life and Writings*, 179, 182-183; Joseph J. Thompson, *The Archdiocese of Chicago, Antecedents and Development* (Des Plaines, Illinois: St. Mary's Training School Press, 1920), 331; *Davenport Democrat*, July 5, 1883.
87. Daniel Riordan to Richard H. Clarke, March 11, 1885, Richard H. Clarke Papers, I-2-n, Hesburgh Library, University of Notre Dame; Thompson, *The Archdiocese of Chicago*, 47, 105, 108; McGovern, *Life and Writings*, 202, 204; McGovern, *Souvenir of the Silver Jubilee*, 211, 212.
88. Thompson, *The Archdiocese of Chicago*, 48, 215.
89. James P. Gaffey, "Patterns of Ecclesiastical Authority: The Problem of Chicago Succession, 1865-1881," *Church History* 42 (June 1973): 265; "The Notre Dame Scholastic," 12 (June 21, 1879); Charles F. Griffith, "The Erection of the Diocese of Davenport," *Mid-America* 3 (April 1932): 343.
90. *Davenport Democrat*, July 27, 1881; McGovern, *Life and Writings*, 233; *Davenport Democrat*, July 26, 1881; U. A. Hauber, "In Retrospect," *Ambrosian Alumnus*, September 1954.
91. *Chicago Times*, July 28, 1881.
92. *Davenport Democrat*, July 22, 1881; Edward C. Greer, *Cork Hill Cathedral, The Chronicle of St. Margaret's and Sacred Heart Parish Davenport, Iowa 1856-1956* (Davenport, Iowa: Gordon Printing Co., 1956), 52.
93. *Davenport Democrat*, August 1, 1881.
94. *Davenport Democrat*, August 29, 1881.
95. John McMullen, "Catholic Education in Illinois–The Beginning of the End," McGovern, *Life and Writings*, 90, 91.
96. *Davenport Democrat*, September 6, 1881.
97. *Confirmation Ledger, Bishops McMullen and Cosgrove*, Archives, Diocese of Davenport.
98. *Keokuk Daily Gate City*, October 16, 18, 1881.
99. McGovern, *Life and Writings*, 256, 261; *Council Bluffs Nonpareil*, October 30, 1881; Edward M. O'Connor, "Our Diocese and Institutions," *Catholic Messenger*, December 1, 1932.
100. McGovern, *Life and Writings*, 255.

Chapter One

1. The number of students in the first class is different in various sources. The first cash ledger lists thirty-three students who paid tuition that first semester and that is the number I have chosen to use. [Cash

Ledger, Archives, O'Keefe Library.]

2. John McMullen, "Catholic Education in Illinois–The Beginning of the End," McGovern, *Life and Writings*, 91.

3. Power, *History of Catholic Higher Education*, 333-336; Power, "Highlights in the Progress of Catholic Higher Education," *Bulletin, National Catholic Education Association* 60 (August 1963): 129-130.

4. James Howard Plough, "Catholic Colleges and the Catholic Educational Association: The Foundation and Early Years of the CEA, 1899-1919" (PhD diss., University of Notre Dame, 1967), 133.

5. Sebastian A. Erbacher, *Catholic Higher Education for Men in the United States, 1850-1866* (Washington, DC: The Catholic University, 1931), 65.

6. Power, *History of Catholic Higher Education*, 53.

7. *Catholic Messenger*, May 30, 1885.

8. John T. Murphy, CSSp, "The Typical Catholic College: What It Should Teach," *Report of the First Annual Conference of The Association of Catholic Colleges of the United States, Held in St. James' Hall, Chicago, April 12 and 13, 1899* (Washington, DC: Catholic University Press, 1899): 41, 43.

9. Philip Gleason, *Contending With Modernity, Catholic Higher Education in the Twentieth Century* (New York: Oxford University Press, 1995), 29.

10. *Catholic Messenger*, January 6, 1883.

11. Plough, "Catholic Colleges," 48.

12. Gleason, *Contending With Modernity*, 22; Plough, "Catholic Colleges," 39, 42.

13. Andrew M. Greeley, *From Backwater to Mainstream, A Profile of Catholic Higher Education* (New York: McGraw-Hill Book Company, 1969), 13.

14. Joseph Fuhrmann, *Souvenir of the Diamond Jubilee of St. Mary's Church Iowa City, Iowa, 1840-1916* (Iowa City: Joseph Fuhrmann, 1916), 74-75; Anthony Gorham Farrell, *Bees and Bur Oaks: 100 Years of St. Ambrose College* (January 1982),19.

15. John Kempker, quoted in Fuhrmann, *Souvenir*, 76.

16. William F. Dawson, "The Early Years of Saint Ambrose College 1882-1900" (master's thesis, The Saint Paul Seminary, 1956), 32.

17. U. A. Hauber, "In Retrospect," *Ambrosian Alumnus*, February 1956.

18. *Catholic Messenger*, June 22, 1901.

19. *Catholic Messenger*, May 17, 1884.

20. U. A. Hauber, "Sermon for the Funeral of A. J. Schulte," Archives, O'Keefe Library.

21. U. A. Hauber, "In Retrospect," *Ambrosian Alumnus*, February 1951; Hauber sermon, January 22, 1928, Archives, O'Keefe Library.

22. *Davenport Democrat*, December 8, 1938.

23. *Davenport Democrat and Leader*, April 4, 1934.

24. Dawson, "The Early Years," 33.

25. Charles F. Griffith, "Our Anniversaries," *Catholic Messenger*, March 24, 1932.

26. Farrell, *Bees and Bur Oaks*, 21.

27. McGovern, *Life and Writings*, 253.

28. *Davenport Democrat*, July 5, 1883.

29. McGovern, *Life and Writings*, 266, 258.

30. *Davenport Democrat*, June 30, 1882; *Catholic Messenger*, February 25, 1909.

31. *Davenport Democrat*, August 25, 1882; September 4, 1882.

32. Schmidt, *Seasons of Growth*, 111.

33. Boniface Ramsey OP, *Ambrose* (London and New York: Routledge, 1997), 16, 19.

34. F. Homes Dudden, DD, *The Life and Times of St. Ambrose, Volume I* (Oxford: The Clarendon Press, 1935), 66-68.

35. Paulinus of Milan, *The Life of St. Ambrose*, Paragraph 3, Roy J. Deferrari, ed., *The Fathers of the Church,Volume 15, Early Christian Biographies* (U.S.A.: Fathers of the Church, Inc., 1952), 34-35; Ramsey, *Ambrose*, 16-17.

36. Neil B. McLynn, *Ambrose of Milan, Church and Court in a Christian Capital* (Berkeley, Los Angeles, London: University of California Press, 1994), 227, 229.

37. Ramsey, *Ambrose*, 48.

38. F. Homes Dudden, DD, *The Life and Times of St. Ambrose, Volume II* (Oxford: The Clarendon Press, 1935), 495-496.

39. *Davenport Democrat*, October 8, 1882.

40. *Fourth Annual Catalogue of the Officers and Students of St. Ambrose Seminary, Davenport, Iowa, 1885-86* (Davenport, Iowa: Glass & Axtman, Printers and Binders, 1886), 7.

41. U. A. Hauber, "In Retrospect," *Ambrosian Alumnus*, November 1950.

42. Walter J. Burghardt, SJ, "The Intellectual Formation of the Future Priest," *Bulletin, National Catholic Educational Association* 61 (August 1964): 67.

43. John Tracy Ellis, *Essays in Seminary Education* (Notre Dame, Indiana: Fides Publishers, Inc., 1967), 208.

44. *Catholic Messenger*, June 30, 1883.

45. *Fourth Annual Catalogue of the Officers and Students of St. Ambrose Seminary, Davenport, Iowa, 1885-86* (Davenport, Iowa: Glass & Axtman, Printers and Binders, 1886), 11-14.

46. *Catholic Messenger*, February 3, 1883.

47. *Davenport Daily Gazette*, July 6, 1883.

48. *Catholic Messenger*, April 28, 1883, June 23, 1883.

49. Interview, James Dunnion by Charles F. Griffith, December 1926, Archives, Diocese of Davenport.

50. *Catholic Messenger*, July 19, 1884.

51. *Catholic Messenger*, June 30, 1883

52. *Catholic Messenger*, September 8, 1883.

53. *Catholic Messenger*, August 18, 1883, August 25, 1883.

54. *Catholic Messenger*, December 8, 1883, December 6, 1884.

55. *Catholic Messenger*, January 17, 1885.

56. *Catholic Messenger*, April 25, 1885.

57. Interview, Joseph Halligan by Charles F. Griffith, November 1, 1925, Archives, Diocese of Davenport.

58. *Catholic Messenger*, May 9, 1885, April 14, 1932.

59. U. A. Hauber, "In Retrospect," *Ambrosian Alumnus*, September, 1954.

60. *Davenport Democrat*, December 8, 1938; *Catholic Messenger*, May 9, 1885.

61. Interview, Joseph Halligan, by Charles F. Griffith, November 1, 1925, Archives, Diocese of Davenport.

62. *Catholic Messenger*, May 9, 1885.

63. *Davenport Democrat and Leader*, May 30, 1904.

64. Joseph Fuhrmann, *Souvenir*, 76.

65. *Catholic Messenger*, September 5, 1885.

66. *Catholic Messenger*, August 29, 1885.

67. *Davenport Democrat*, July 1, 1885.

68. *Catholic Messenger*, July 11, 1885; *Davenport Democrat*, July 6, 1885.

69. *Catholic Messenger*, July 11, 1885; *Davenport Democrat*, July 6, 1885.

70. *Catholic Messenger*, June 27, 1885, July 4, 1885.

71. Power, *History of Catholic Higher Education*, 114-115.

72. *Catholic Messenger*, July 25, 1885.

73. *Catholic Messenger*, June 30, 1883, July 19, 1884, September 9, 1885, March 12, 1887, March 26, 1887, August 20, 1887.

74. Minutes, Bishop's Council Meeting, May 25, 26, 1886, Archives, Diocese of Davenport.

75. *Catholic Messenger*, September 11, 1886.

76. *Catholic Messenger*, May 14, 1887.

77. Minutes, Bishop's Council Meeting, June 14, 1887, Archives, Diocese of Davenport.

78. Bishop Henry Cosgrove, "Pastoral Letter," June 24, 1887, Archives, Diocese of Davenport.

79. *Catholic Messenger*, July 2, 1887; September 10, 1887.

80. *Catholic Messenger*, August 6, 1887.

81. *The Ambrosian 1913* (Yearbook).

Chapter Two

1. *Catholic Messenger*, November 28, 1896.

2. U. A. Hauber, "In Retrospect," *Ambrosian Alumnus*, November 1949.

3. *Catholic Messenger*, January 7, 1888.

4. Dan Elbert Clark, "The History of Liquor Legislation in Iowa 1878-1909," *The Iowa Journal of History and Politics* 6 (October 1908), 503-608.

5. Marlys Svendsen, *Davenport, A Pictorial History* (Davenport, Iowa: G. Bradley Publishing, Inc., 1985), 42.

6. Frank D. Jackson, Secretary of State, *Census of Iowa for the Year 1885* (Des Moines: Geo. E. Roberts, State Printer, 1885), 246.

7. U. A. Hauber, "In Retrospect," *Ambrosian Alumnus*, November 1951.

8. *Catholic Messenger*, December 21, 1895, February 15, 1896.

9. Sister Mary Henrietta to U. A. Hauber, August 18, 1952, Archives, O'Keefe Library.

10. Thomas S. Harding, *College Literary Societies: Their Contribution to Higher Education in the United States 1815-1876* (New York: Pageant Press International Corp., 1971), 1, 317.

11. *Catholic Messenger*, July 19, 1884.

12. *Fourth Annual Catalogue of the Officers and Students of St. Ambrose Seminary, Davenport, Iowa, 1885-1886* (Davenport, Iowa: Glass & Axtman, Printers and Binders, 1886), 17.

13. Minutes, St. John's Literary and Debating Society, *passim*, Archives, O'Keefe Library.

14. Harding, *College Literary Societies,* 1, 284, 317.

15. *Catholic Messenger*, June 18, 1892.

16. *Fourth Annual Catalogue of the Officers and Students of St. Ambrose Seminary, Davenport, Iowa 1885-86* (Davenport, Iowa: Glass & Axtman, Printers and Binders, 1886), 18.

17. U. A. Hauber, "In Retrospect," *Ambrosian Alumnus*, January 1954.

18. *Catholic Messenger*, December 15, 1894.

19. *Catholic Messenger*, December 14, 1895.

20. *Catholic Messenger*, March 19, 1892, March 26, 1892.

21. Ronald A. Smith, *Sports and Freedom, The Rise of Big-Time College Athletics* (New York: Oxford University Press, 1988), 13, 22-23.

22. Farrell, *Bees and Bur Oaks*, 37-38; Smith, *Sports and Freedom*, 52; U. A. Hauber, "In Retrospect," *Ambrosian Alumnus*, June 1951.

23. *Fourth Annual Catalogue*, 19.

24. *Catholic Messenger*, May 4, 1895; *The Ambrosian 1913* (Yearbook).

25. *Catholic Messenger*, December 23, 1893, December 30, 1893.

26. *Catholic Messenger*, February 6, 1886, February 23, 1895.

27. *Catholic Messenger*, February 24, 1894, February 23, 1895.

28. *Catholic Messenger*, March 3, 1894, November 10, 1894, May 11, 1895, September 21, 1895.

29. *Catholic Messenger*, January 20, 1894.

30. U. A. Hauber, "In Retrospect," *Ambrosian Alumnus*, May 1950.

31. *Catholic Messenger*, October 27, 1888; *Seventh Annual Catalogue of the Officers and Students of St. Ambrose Seminary, Davenport, Iowa, 1888-89* (Davenport, Iowa: H. L. Wagner, 1889), 19.

32. Minutes, Athletic Society, Archives, O'Keefe Library.

33. Minutes, Athletic Society, December 5, 1888, January 9, 1889, January 12, 1889, March 4, 1890, Archives, O'Keefe Library.

34. Minutes, Athletic Society, January 12, 1890, Archives, O'Keefe Library.

35. Smith, *Sports and Freedom*, 131-133.

36. *Catholic Messenger*, September 21, 1889.

37. *Davenport Democrat*, September 6, 1881.

38. *Cosgrove Seminary Accounts, Contributions and Expenditures 1884-1907*, Archives, Diocese of Davenport; Minutes, Bishop's Council, August 16, 1888, Archives, Diocese of Davenport.

39. *Bishop Henry Cosgrove's Account Book, Including Collections for a New Cathedral (1885- 1893)*, Archives, Diocese of Davenport; Minutes, Quasi-Synod, August 24, 1888, Archives, Diocese of Davenport; *Catholic Messenger*, September 21, 1888.

40. U. A. Hauber, "In Retrospect," *Ambrosian Alumnus*, October 1954.

41. Interview, Joseph Halligan by Charles F. Griffith, November 1, 1925, Archives, Diocese of Davenport.

42. Charles F. Griffith, "Some Chapters in the History of the Diocese of Davenport," *Catholic Messenger*, May 19, 1927.

43. Henry Cosgrove to Brother Romuald, December 6, 1889, Brother Paulian Folder, De La Salle Christian Brothers, Midwest District Archives, Memphis, Tennessee.

44. Paulian to Henry Cosgrove, December 10, 1889, Archives, Diocese of Davenport.

45. Minutes, Bishop's Council, January 21, 1890, Archives, Diocese of Davenport.

46. Andrew Trevis to Henry Cosgrove, April 16, 1890, Archives, Diocese of Davenport.

47. Henry Cosgrove to Paulian, April 18, 1890, De La Salle Christian Brothers, Midwest District Archives, Memphis, Tennessee; Paulian to Henry Cosgrove, May 8, 1890, Archives, Diocese of Davenport.

48. Landelin Beck to Henry Cosgrove, February 8, 1890, Archives, Diocese of Davenport.

49. Minutes, Provincial Council, February 19, 1890, Marianist Archives, N.2, Box 1, University of Dayton.

50. Minutes, Provincial Council, February 19, 1890, Marianist Archives, N.2, Box 1, University of Dayton.

51. Beck to Cosgrove, February 18, 1890, Archives, Diocese of Davenport.

52. Minutes, Provincial Council, March 14, 1890, Marianist Archives, N.2, Box 1, University of Dayton.

53. Minutes, Bishop's Council, June 30, 1891, Archives, Diocese of Davenport.

54. Henry Cosgrove to Paulian, March 22, 1893, De La Salle Christian Brothers, Midwest District Archives, Memphis, Tennessee.

55. *Catholic Messenger*, September 12, 1891.

56. *Catholic Messenger*, February 15, 1890.
57. Interview, Joseph Halligan by Charles F. Griffith, November 1, 1925, Archives, Diocese of Davenport.
58. *Catholic Messenger*, March 28, 1891.
59. *Catholic Messenger*, June 27, 1891.
60. *Catholic Messenger*, September 19, 1891.
61. Speech, U. A. Hauber, January 22, 1928, Archives, O'Keefe Library.
62. Funeral Sermon, U. A. Hauber, Archives, O'Keefe Library.

Chapter Three

1. *Catholic Messenger*, October 24, 1891.
2. *Catholic Messenger*, July 25, 1891.
3. *Catholic Messenger*, October 27, 1888.
4. Financial Reports, Nineteenth Century, Archives, Diocese of Davenport.
5. Minutes, Meeting of Bishop's Council, July 12, 1892, Archives, Diocese of Davenport.
6. *Catholic Messenger*, August 6, 1892.
7. Minutes, Meeting of Bishop's Council, June 6, 1893, Archives, Diocese of Davenport.
8. *Catholic Messenger*, July 8, 1893.
9. *Catholic Messenger*, February 24, 1894, February 8, 1902.
10. *Catholic Messenger*, December 9, 1893, May 19, 1894.
11. *Catholic Messenger*, February 18, 1893, December 23, 1893.
12. *Catholic Messenger*, March 10 1894.
13. *Catholic Messenger*, October 5, 1895, October 19, 1895, May 28, 1898.
14. *Catholic Messenger*, March 24, 1894, September 7, 1895, October 5, 1895.
15. *Catholic Messenger*, January 20, 1894, October 20, 1894.
16. *Catholic Messenger*, January 18, 1896.
17. *Catholic Messenger*, June 17, 1893.
18. *Catholic Messenger*, July 1, 1893, June 23, 1894.
19. *Catholic Messenger*, January 27, 1894, February 24, 1894, December 15, 1894.
20. Charles Hoffmann, *The Depression of the Nineties, An Economic History* (Westport, Connecticut: Greenwood Publishing Corporation, 1970), xxix, 4, 109-110, 260.
21. Financial Report 1893-1894, St. Ambrose College, Archives, Diocese of Davenport.
22. *Davenport Democrat*, August 19, 1894.
23. Minutes, Meeting of Bishop's Council, July 12, 1892, Archives, Diocese of Davenport.
24. John Tracy Ellis, *Essays in Seminary Education* (Notre Dame, Indiana, 1967) 149.
25. *Catholic Messenger*, June 16, 1894, August 25, 1894, June 27, 1957; U. A. Hauber, "In Retrospect," *Ambrosian Alumnus*, October 1951.
26. *The Ambrosian 1914* (Yearbook).
27. *Catholic Messenger*, November 24, 1894.
28. *Catholic Messenger*, December 9, 1893.
29. *Catholic Messenger*, February 24, 1894.
30. Minutes, Philalethic Assocation, October 25, 1897, Archives, O'Keefe Library.
31. *Catholic Messenger*, February 19, 1898, March 12, 1898.
32. Minutes, Meeting of St. John's Literary Society, April 9, 1886, November 26, 1886, Archives, O'Keefe Library.
33. U. A. Hauber, "In Retrospect," *Ambrosian Alumnus*, September 1950, October 1954.
34. *Catholic Messenger*, November 17, 1894, November 16, 1895.
35. *Catholic Messenger*, October 20, 1894.
36. *Catholic Messenger*, March 24, 1894, March 31, 1894.
37. *Catholic Messenger*, October 20, 1894, November 3, 1894.
38. *Catholic Messenger*, April 21, 1894, April 28, 1894, May 5, 1894, May 19, 1894, May 26, 1894, June 9, 1894.
39. *Catholic Messenger*, March 22, 1899.
40. *Catholic Messenger*, March 7, 1896.
41. Minutes, Athletic Society, September 30, 1893, February 21, 1894, Archives, O'Keefe Library.
42. *Catholic Messenger*, May 13, 1893.
43. William F. Betterton, "Music in Early Davenport, Bands and Orchestras," *The Palimpsest* 45 (July 1964), 277-278.
44. William F. Betterton, "A History of Music in Davenport, Iowa Before 1900" (PhD diss., University of Iowa, 1962).
45. *Catholic Messenger*, October 27, 1894.
46. *Catholic Messenger*, March 9, 1895.
47. *Catholic Messenger*, October 5, 1895, December 14, 1895, March 7, 1896.
48. Betterton, "A History of Music in Davenport," 187.
49. U. A. Hauber, "In Retrospect," *Ambrosian Alumnus*, September 1950.
50. *Catholic Messenger*, October 19, 1895; U. A. Hauber, "In Retrospect," *Ambrosian Alumnus*, September 1950.
51. *Catholic Messenger*, December 14, 1895.
52. *Catholic Messenger*, June 13, 1896, June 22, 1901.
53. *Nineteenth Annual Catalogue of the Officers and Students of St. Ambrose College, Davenport, Iowa 1901* (Davenport, Iowa: Wagner's Printery, 1901), 8, 19.
54. *Washington, Iowa Democrat*, September 14, 1898.
55. *Catholic Messenger*, February 19, 1898, March 19, 1898, April 30, 1898.
56. *Catholic Messenger*, June 25, 1898.
57. U. A. Hauber, "In Retrospect," *Ambrosian Alumnus*, November 1951.
58. Gleason, *Contending With Modernity*, 33, 36, 50.
59. Gleason, *Contending With Modernity*, 51, 82.
60. Gleason, *Contending With Modernity*, 22.
61. James Howard Plough, "Catholic Colleges and the Catholic Educational Association: The Foundation and Early Years of the CEA, 1899-1919" (PhD diss., University of Notre Dame, 1967), 91.
62. *Catholic Messenger*, April 11,1899.
63. *Report of the First Annual Conference of The Association of Catholic Colleges of the United States, Held in St. James' Hall, Chicago, April 12 and 13, 1899* (Washington, D.C: Catholic University Press, 1899), 18.
64. David P. Killen, "Americanism Revisited: John Spalding and *Testam Benevolentiae*," *Harvard Theological Review* 66 (1973), 413.
65. *Report of the First Annual Conference*, p. 110-111.
66. William L. Bowers, "Davenport, Iowa, 1906-1907 A Glimpse into a City's Past," *Annals of Iowa* 38 (Summer 1966), 364.
67. *Catholic Messenger*, February 10, 1900.
68. St. Ambrose College Reports 1900-1910, Archives, Diocese of Davenport.
69. *Catholic Messenger*, July 20, 1901.

70. Minutes, Meeting of Bishop's Council, May 1, 1901, Archives, Diocese of Davenport.
71. *Catholic Messenger*, April 5, 1902, July 27, 1901, August 31, 1901.
72. *Catholic Messenger*, September 21, 1901; U. A. Hauber, "In Retrospect," *Ambrosian Alumnus*, April 1951.
73. *Catholic Messenger*, December 14, 1901.
74. "Contributions of the Priests of the Diocese for St. Ambrose College Improvements," *Cathedraticum Ledger*, Archives, Diocese of Davenport; Minutes, Quasi-Synod, July 9, 1903, Archives, Diocese of Davenport.
75. *Catholic Messenger*, January 4, 1902 January 25, 1902, February 22, 1902.
76. *Catholic Messenger*, January 11, 1902, February 8, 1902, April 5, 1902, April 26, 1902, May 2, 1902, November 14, 1903.
77. *Catholic Messenger*, March 1, 1902, May 3, 1902.
78. *Catholic Messenger*, May 3, 1902.
79. *Catholic Messenger*, May 3, 1902.
80. *Catholic Messenger*, June 20, 1903.
81. U. A. Hauber, "In Retrospect," *Ambrosian Alumnus*, February 1951.

Chapter Four

1. U. A. Hauber, "Monsignor Hauber's History of St. Ambrose 1900-1905," *Ambrosian Alumnus*, January 1950.
2. U. A. Hauber, "Monsignor Hauber's History of St. Ambrose 1900-1905," *Ambrosian Alumnus*, October 1949.
3. James Howard Plough, "Catholic Colleges and the Catholic Educational Association: The Foundation and Early Years of the CEA, 1899-1919" (PhD diss., University of Notre Dame, 1967), 315.
4. Ed Henneberry, "The '98ers," *The Ambrosian 1915* (Yearbook).
5. U. A. Hauber, Diary, January 25, 1902, Archives, O'Keefe Library.
6. U. A. Hauber, "Monsignor Hauber's History of St. Ambrose 1900-1905," *Ambrosian Alumnus*, December 1949, March 1950.
7. *Catholic Messenger*, December 12, 1907.
8. U. A. Hauber, "Monsignor Hauber's History of St. Ambrose 1900 to 1905," *Ambrosian Alumnus*, December 1949.
9. Minutes, Athletic Society, May 5,1895, Archives, O'Keefe Library.
10. U. A. Hauber, Diary, January 6, 1902, January 25, 1902, Archives, O'Keefe Library.
11. U. A. Hauber, "Monsignor Hauber's History of St. Ambrose 1900-1905," *Ambrosian Alumnus*, April 1950.
12. *Catholic Messenger*, January 27, 1906, February 3, 1906.
13. *The Ambrosian 1915* (Yearbook), *The Ambrosian 1917* (Yearbook), *The Ambrosian 1918* (Yearbook); U. A. Hauber, Diary, 1902, Archives, O'Keefe Library.
14. U. A. Hauber, "Monsignor Hauber's History of St. Ambrose 1900-1905," *Ambrosian Alumnus*, February 1950; Diary, January 11, 1902, February 15, 1902, Archives, O'Keefe Library.
15. Ed J. Coleman to U. A. Hauber, January 29, 1956, Archives, O'Keefe Library.
16. U. A. Hauber, Diary, January 11, 1902, January 12, 1902, January 13, 1902, Archives, O'Keefe Library.
17. U. A. Hauber, Diary, January 24, 1902, Archives, O'Keefe Library; *Catholic Messenger*, March 4, 1909.
18. U. A. Hauber, "Monsignor Hauber's History of St. Ambrose 1900-1905," *Ambrosian Alumnus*, June 1950. *The Ambrosian 1914* (Yearbook).
19. Minutes, Logomachetean Literary Society, October 3, 1903, October 11, 1903, Archives, O'Keefe Library.
20. Minutes, Logomachetean Literary Society, *passim*, Archives, O'Keefe Library, St. Ambrose University.
21. Minutes, *Bonifacius Verein*, Archives, O'Keefe Library.
22. *Catholic Messenger*, November 8, 1910.
23. *Catholic Messenger*, November 7, 1912.
24. *Catholic Messenger*, January 28, 1915, June 10, 1915.
25. *Catholic Messenger*, January 21, 1903.
26. *Catholic Messenger*, June 27, 1903.
27. *Catholic Messenger*, June 20, 1903.
28. *Catholic Messenger*, December 10, 1904.
29. U. A. Hauber, "In Retrospect," *Ambrosian Alumnus*, October 1952; *Catholic Messenger*, August 8, 1903.
30. *Catholic Messenger*, September 16, 1905; U. A. Hauber, "In Retrospect," *Ambrosian Alumnus*, April 1952; *Davenport Democrat and Leader*, April 12, 1938.
31. *Catholic Messenger*, July 19, 1906.
32. Dee Bruemmer to author, July 20, 2005; Bishop Davis Ledger, Expenses at St. Ambrose College, Archives, Diocese of Davenport.
33. *Catholic Messenger*, July 27, 1901, May 3, 1902.
34. *Twenty-Fourth Annual Catalogue of the Officers and Students of St. Ambrose College Davenport, Iowa, 1906*, 54.
35. *Twenty-Third Annual Catalogue of the Officers and Students of St. Ambrose College Davenport, Iowa, 1905*, 53; *Catholic Messenger*, June 17, 1905, July 8, 1905, November 4, 1905, October 18, 1906.
36. *Catholic Messenger*, March 14, 1907, June 20, 1907. *Twenty-Fifth Catalogue of the Officers and Students of St. Ambrose College Davenport, Iowa, 1907*, 58-59.
37. *Catholic Messenger*, May 16, 1907; Ed J. Coleman to U. A. Hauber, January 29, 1956, O'Keefe Library.
38. *Catholic Messenger*, January 10, 1907.
39. Minutes, Bishop's Council, February 26, 1907, Archives, Diocese of Davenport.
40. Minutes, Bishop's Council, February 26, 1907, Archives, Diocese of Davenport.
41. *Catholic Messenger*, June 14, 1906.
42. *Catholic Messenger*, April 25, 1907.
43. *Catholic Messenger*, June 20, 1907.
44. U. A. Hauber, "In Retrospect,"*Ambrosian Alumnus*, February 1952.
45. U. A. Hauber, "In Retrospect," *Ambrosian Alumnus*, December 1951.
46. *Williamsburg Journal-Tribune*, reprinted in *Catholic Messenger*, March 11, 1909.
47. Minutes, Bishop's Council, June 28, 1907, Archives, Diocese of Davenport.
48. Minutes, Bishop's Council, January 21, 1908, Archives, Diocese of Davenport.
49. *Twenty-Sixth Annual Catalogue of the Officers and Students of St. Ambrose College Davenport, Iowa, 1908*, 58-61.
50. *Catholic Messenger*, April 16, 1908, June 18, 1908.
51. *Catholic Messenger*, April 16, 1908, February 25, 1909.
52. *Catholic Messenger*, February 25, 1909
53. "Financial Report of Building Fund of St. Ambrose College," Quasi-Synod Folder, Archives, Diocese

A Great and Lasting Beginning

of Davenport; *Catholic Messenger*, June 24, 1909.

54. *Catholic Messenger*, March 18, 1909.

55. *Catholic Messenger*, August 24, 1911, October 9, 1911.

56. Minutes, Bishop's Council, April 15, 1907, Archives, Diocese of Davenport; Meeting, Board of Managers, St. Ambrose College, January 6, 1908, Archives, Diocese of Davenport.

57. *Twentieth Annual Catalogue of the Officers and Students of St. Ambrose College, Davenport, Iowa, 1902* (Davenport, Iowa: Wagner's Printery, 1902), 11-17.

58. *Report of the Third Annual Conference of The Association of Catholic Colleges of the United States, Held in St. James' Hall, Chicago, April 10, 11 and 12, 1901* (Washington, D.C.: Catholic University Press, 1901), 33.

59. Plough, *Catholic Colleges*, 178-179, 256, 315.

60. *Twenty-Eighth Annual Catalogue of the Officers and Students of St. Ambrose College, Davenport, Iowa, 1910*, 12.

61. *Twenty-Ninth Annual Catalogue of the Officers and Students of St. Ambrose College, Davenport, Iowa, 1911*, 11-12.

62. Minutes, Athletic Society, October 12, 1909, Archives O'Keefe Library.

63. *Catholic Messenger*, February 24, 1910.

64. *Catholic Messenger*, June 25, 1905.

65. Minutes, Logomachetean Society, October 11, 1903, February 13, 1910, January 17, 1909, March 7, 1909.

66. Ronald A. Smith, *Sports and Freedom, The Rise of Big-Time College Athletics* (New York: Oxford University Press, 1988), 83, 84, 92, 96, 192.

67. Charles Macksey, "The Ethical Influence of College Athletics," *Catholic Educational Association, Report of the Proceedings and Addresses of the Third Annual Meeting, Cleveland, Ohio, July 9, 10, 11 and 12, 1906*, 107.

68. Smith, *Sports and Freedom*, 205; *Davenport Daily Times*, September 21, 1910.

69. Minutes, Athletic Society, September 17, 1909, October 15, 1912, Archives, O'Keefe Library.

70. Minutes, Athletic Society, December 12, 1909, June 13, 1910, December 17, 1910, Archives, O'Keefe Library.

71. Minutes, Athletic Society, April 16, 1910, Archives, O'Keefe Library.

72. *Davenport Democrat and Leader*, September 18, 1910.

73. *Catholic Messenger*, October 13, 1910, December 1, 1910.

74. *Catholic Messenger*, October 12, 1911, December 14, 1911, August 15, 1912; Bishop Davis Ledger, Expenses at St. Ambrose College, Archives, Diocese of Davenport.

75. *Catholic Messenger*, March 11, 1909, October 20, 1910, December 8, 1910, December 14, 1911; *The Ambrosian 1915* (Yearbook).

76. William Shannahan, "To the Rt. Rev. Bishop and the Diocesan Consultors," April 18, 1912, College Reports, 1900-1910, Archives, Diocese of Davenport; Minutes, Bishops Council, April 18, 1912, Archives, Diocese of Davenport; A. J. Schulte to James Gillespie, April 27, 1912, College Reports, 1900-1910, Archives, Diocese of Davenport.

77. *Catholic Messenger*, May 16, 1912, May 30, 1912, June 6, 1912, September 26, 1912, July 31, 1913.

78. Minutes, Quasi-Synod, June 20, 1912, Archives, Diocese of Davenport.

Chapter Five

1. David D. Klise to Alumni of St. Ambrose [1963], Archives, Diocese of Davenport.

2. *Catholic Messenger*, June 12, 1913.

3. *Catholic Messenger*, July 10, 1913, July 31, 1913, August 21, 1913.

4. *Catholic Messenger*, July 31, 1913, August 28, 1913.

5. *Catholic Messenger*, December 11, 1913.

6. William H. Cumberland, *The History of Buena Vista College* (Ames: The Iowa State University Press, 1966), 185-186.

7. *Catholic Messenger*, September 18, 1913, September 25, 1913.

8. *Catholic Messenger*, October 2, 1913, October 9, 1913.

9. *Catholic Messenger*, November 13, 1913.

10. U. A. Hauber, "In Retrospect," *Ambrosian Alumnus*, February 1953.

11. *Catholic Messenger*, January 8, 1914.

12. *Catholic Messenger*, September 17, 1914, October 8, 1914, November 16, 1916, December 19, 1918; *The Ambrosian 1920* (Yearbook).

13. *Catholic Messenger*, December 24, 1914, January 21, 1915, October 5, 1916; *The Ambrosian 1915* (Yearbook).

14. *Catholic Messenger*, June 4, 1914.

15. *Catholic Messenger*, June 18, 1914.

16. *Catholic Messenger*, May 27, 1915, June 24, 1915; *The Ambrosian 1916* (Yearbook).

17. *Catholic Messenger*, August 3, 1916.

18. *The Ambrosian 1915* (Yearbook), *The Ambrosian 1916* (Yearbook), *The Ambrosian 1917* (Yearbook); U. A. Hauber, "In Retrospect," *Ambrosian Alumnus*, December 1953.

19. *Catholic Messenger*, December 4, 1913, December 11, 1913, March 29, 1917; *The Ambrosian 1915* (Yearbook), *The Ambrosian 1918* (Yearbook); U. A. Hauber, "In Retrospect," *Ambrosian Alumnus*, December 1953.

20. U. A. Hauber, "In Retrospect," *Ambrosian Alumnus*, September 1950, February 1951, March 1951, April 1951, May 1951.

21. *The Ambrosian 1913* (Yearbook), *The Ambrosian 1915* (Yearbook).

22. *Catholic Messenger*, September 26, 1912.

23. *The Ambrosian 1915* (Yearbook); *Catholic Messenger*, September 30, 1915, October 19, 1916.

24. *Catholic Messenger*, September 30, 1915.

25. *Catholic Messenger*, July 16, 1915; *The Ambrosian 1916* (Yearbook).

26. *The Ambrosian 1915* (Yearbook); *Catholic Messenger*, September 16, 1915, March 16, 1916, July 13, 1916.

27. Plough, "Catholic Colleges," 378, 379.

28. James A. Burns, CSC, "The Condition of Catholic Secondary Education in the United States," *The Catholic Educational Association Bulletin, Report of the Proceedings and Addresses of the Twelfth Annual Meeting St. Paul, Minn., June 28, 29, 30 and July 1, 1915*, November 1915, 379, 380, 394.

29. Plough, "Catholic Colleges," 303; *The Ambrosian 1915* (Yearbook); *Catholic Messenger*, September 14, 1916.

30. *Catholic Messenger*, January 21, 1915.

31. Blueprints, George P. Stauduhar Papers, University of Illinois Archives.

32. *Catholic Messenger*, August 4, 1915, August 12, 1915, August 19, 1915.

33. U. A. Hauber, "In Retrospect," *Ambrosian Alumnus*, September 1955.

34. William L. Hannon, "The Catholic School, A Paper Read Before The Contemporary Club, October 1, 1923."

35. Plough, *Catholic Colleges*, 390.

36. "Report of the Proceedings and Addresses of the Twelfth Annual Meeting St. Paul, Minn., June 28, 29, 30 and July 1, 1915, *The Catholic Educational Association Bulletin* 12 (November, 1915), 149-150.

37. Gleason, *Contending With Modernity*, 50.

38. "Report of the Proceedings and Address of the Fifteenth Annual Meeting San Francisco, Cal., July 22, 23, 24 and 25, 1918, *The Catholic Educational Association Bulletin* 15 (November, 1918); *Catholic Messenger*, November 28, 1918.

39. *Catholic Messenger*, November 4, 1915, July 6, 1916; *Thirty-Fourth Annual Catalogue of the Officers and Students of St. Ambrose College Davenport, Iowa, 1916*, 9.

40. *Catholic Messenger*, November 4, 1915, November 11, 1915, March 9, 1916, April 13, 1916, May 25, 1916, August 31, 1916, October 5, 1916.

41. *Catholic Messenger*, December 14, 1916.

42. *Catholic Messenger*, February 1, 1917.

43. Minutes, Bishop's Council, January 23, 1919, Archives, Diocese of Davenport.

44. Minutes, Bishop's Council, June 20, 1918, Archives, Diocese of Davenport; *Catholic Messenger*, July 5, 1917, August 16, 1917.

45. *Catholic Messenger*, February 11, 1915; *The Ambrosian 1916* (Yearbook), *The Ambrosian 1917* (Yearbook), *The Ambrosian 1919* (Yearbook).

46. *The Ambrosian 1918* (Yearbook), *The Ambrosian 1919* (Yearbook).

47. *Catholic Messenger*, October 8, 1914, March 25, 1915, November 4, 1915.

48. Ralph W. Cram, ed., *History of the War Activities of Scott County Iowa, 1917-1918* (Davenport: The Scott County Council of National Defense, 1918), 26; *Catholic Messenger*, July 13, 1916.

49. *Catholic Messenger*, June 15, 1916.

50. *The Ambrosian 1915* (Yearbook).

51. *Catholic Messenger*, November 8, 1917.

52. *The Ambrosian 1915* (Yearbook), *The Ambrosian 1919* (Yearbook).

53. *Catholic Messenger*, April 12, 1917.

54. *Catholic Messenger*, April 26, 1917.

55. *Catholic Messenger*, May 10, 1917, July 12, 1917; Cram, *History of War Activities*, 26.

56. *Catholic Messenger*, April 25, 1918; *The Ambrosian 1919* (Yearbook).

57. *Catholic Messenger*, March 7, 1918, April 1, 1918, May 16, 1918.

58. *Catholic Messenger*, October 18, 1917, November 15, 1917, January 24, 1918.

59. *Catholic Messenger*, November 1, 1917.

60. *Catholic Messenger*, February 7, 1918, February 21, 1918, March 7, 1918, March 14, 1918.

61. *Catholic Messenger*, February 14, 1918; *The Ambrosian 1918* (Yearbook).

62. *Catholic Messenger*, November 29, 1917, December 6, 1917, June 13, 1918.

63. *Catholic Messenger*, January 20, 1916.

64. Nancy Derr, "The Babel Proclamation," *The Palimpsest* 60 (July/August 1979), 98-115.

65. *Catholic Messenger*, September 5, 1918, September 12, 1918.

66. *Catholic Messenger*, October 3, 1918.

67. John M. Barry, *The Great Influenza, The Epic Story of the Deadliest Plague in History* (New York: Viking Press, 2004), 5, 350.

68. William H. Cumberland, "Epidemic! Iowa Fights the Spanish Influenza," *The Palimpsest* 62 (January/February 1981), 26-32.

69. *The Ambrosian 1919* (Yearbook).

70. *Davenport Democrat and Leader*, October 16, 1918; *Davenport Daily Times*, October 16, 1918; *Catholic Messenger*, October 17, 1918.

71. *Davenport Democrat and Leader*, October 17, 1918; *Davenport Daily Times*, October 17, 1918.

72. *Davenport Democrat and Leader*, October 23, 1918; *The Ambrosian 1919* (Yearbook).

73. Cram, *History of War Activities*, 138; *The Ambrosian 1919* (Yearbook).

74. *Catholic Messenger*, November 21, 1918, November 28, 1918; *The Ambrosian 1919* (Yearbook).

75. Barry, *The Great Influenza*, 374; Cumberland, "Epidemic!" 29.

76. *Catholic Messenger*, December 5, 1918; The *Ambrosian 1919* (Yearbook).

77. Cumberland, "Epidemic!" 31; "Report of the Heath Commissioner," *Annual Report of the City Offices of the City of Davenport 1918-1919*, 104.

78. *Catholic Messenger*, January 2, 1919.

79. *The Ambrosian 1919* (Yearbook).

80. *The Ambrosian 1919* (Yearbook), *The Ambrosian 1920* (Yearbook).

81. *The Ambrosian 1919* (Yearbook); *Catholic Messenger*, May 22, 1919.

82. *Catholic Messenger*, November 13, 1919.

Chapter Six

1. *Catholic Messenger*, October 10, 1929.

2. U. A. Hauber, "In Retrospect," *Ambrosian Alumnus*, September 1955, December 1955.

3. *Catholic Messenger*, February 13, 1919.

4. *Twenty-Sixth Annual Catalogue of the Officers and Students of St. Ambrose College, Davenport, Iowa, 1908*, 58-60.

5. *Thirtieth Annual Report of the Collection for the Support of Ecclesiastical Students of the Diocese of Davenport, 1910-1911*, Archives, Diocese of Davenport.

6. St. Ambrose College Reports, Archives, Diocese of Davenport.

7. *Catholic Messenger*, January 18, 1917.

8. Clark Hall to Joseph J. Meyers, April 11, 1917; Joseph J. Meyers to Clark Hall, May 2, 1917; Clark Hall to Joseph J. Meyers, May 4, 1917, Archives, Diocese of Davenport.

9. Minutes, Bishop's Council, April 12, 1917, Archives, Diocese of Davenport.

10. *Catholic Messenger*, September 5, 1918, October 31, 1918.

11. Minutes, Bishop's Council, January 23, 1919, Archives, Diocese of Davenport.

12. Minutes, Bishop's Council, June 17, 1919, Archives, Diocese of Davenport.

13. Minutes, Meeting of August 20, 1919, Archives, Diocese of Davenport; *Catholic Messenger*, August 21, 1919.

14. "Suggestions for a Sermon on the Endowment Fund," Archives, Diocese of Davenport.

15. James Davis to People of the Diocese of Davenport [1919], Archives, Diocese of Davenport.

16. *Catholic Messenger*, September 11, 1919, November 29, 1919.

17. *Catholic Messenger*, April 15, 1920; U. A. Hauber, "In Retrospect," *Ambrosian Alumnus*, October 1955.

18. *Catholic Messenger*, April 29, 1920.

19. *Catholic Messenger*, May 6, 1920.

20. *Catholic Messenger*, May 20, 1920.

21. Minutes, Bishop's Council, June 28, 1920, Archives, Diocese of Davenport; *Catholic Messenger*, August 12, 1920.

22. Minutes, Bishop's Council, January 12, 1921, Archives, Diocese of Davenport.

23. David E. Hamilton, *From New Day to New Deal, American Farm Policy from Hoover to Roosevelt*,

1928-1933 (Chapel Hill: The University of North Carolina Press, 1991), 10; James H. Shideler, *Farm Crisis 1919-1923* (Westport, Connecticut: Greenwood Press, Publishers, 1976), 49.
24. College Reports 1920s, Archives, Diocese of Davenport.
25. *Catholic Messenger*, July 15, 1920, April 15, 1920.
26. Gleason, *Contending With Modernity*, 79.
27. U. A. Hauber, "In Retrospect," *Ambrosian Alumnus*, May 1953.
28. Joseph F. Kett, *The Pursuit of Knowledge Under Difficulties, From Self-Improvement to Adult Education in America, 1750-1990* (Stanford, California: Stanford University Press, 1994), 285.
29. *Thirty-Fourth Annual Catalogue of the Officers and Students of St. Ambrose College Davenport, Iowa, 1916*, 41-42; *Forty-Second Annual Catalogue of St. Ambrose College Davenport, Iowa*, June 1924, 57.
30. Pope Pius X, *Notre Charge Apostolique* (Our Apostolic Mandate), August 15, 1910.
31. Jay P. Dolan, *The American Catholic Experience, A History from Colonial Times to the Present* (Garden City, New York: Doubleday and Company, Inc., 1985), 344.
32. Martin Cone, "Labor in National Politics Since 1871," (PhD diss., University of Iowa, 1921).
33. St. Ambrose College, *The Endowment Advocate* 1 (September 1922).
34. *Catholic Messenger*, November 6, 1919.
35. *The Ambrosian 1920* (Yearbook); *The Ambrosian 1921* (Yearbook); *The Ambrosian 1922* (Yearbook); U. A. Hauber, "In Retrospect," *Ambrosian Alumnus*, November 1954.
36. Minutes, Building Committee, August 17, 1921, Archives, Diocese of Davenport; Minutes, Bishop's Council, January 25, 1922, Archives, Diocese of Davenport.
37. *The Ambrosian 1922* (Yearbook).
38. "Rules for Davis Hall, October 1924," Archives, Diocese of Davenport; U. A. Hauber, "In Retrospect," *Ambrosian Alumnus*, November 1955.
39. *Catholic Messenger*, November 23, 1922.
40. *Catholic Messenger*, June 8, 1922; *The Ambrosian 1922* (Yearbook).
41. *Catholic Messenger*, November 23, 1922.
42. *Catholic Messenger*, May 31, 1923.
43. *Catholic Messenger*, October 25, 1923.
44. *The Ambrosian 1922* (Yearbook); *The Ambrosian*, March 1923 (Magazine); *Catholic Messenger*, December 2, 1926; St. Ambrose College Student Council to Catholic Students Mission Crusade, December 8, 1926, Archives, Diocese of Davenport.
45. *Catholic Messenger*, November 2, 1922, November 9, 1922; *The Ambrosian 1922* (Yearbook); *The Ambrosian*, Winter 1924 (Magazine).
46. *The Ambrosian 1922* (Yearbook); *The Ambrosian,* Winter 1923 (Magazine); *Catholic Messenger,* May 28, 1925; *The Ambrosian*, Winter 1929 (Magazine).
47. Minutes, Logomachetean Society, January 17, 1923, May 14, 1923, October 21, 1923, February 19, 1924, March 18, 1924, April 1, 1924, Archives, O'Keefe Library.
48. *The Ambrosian 1921* (Yearbook), *The Ambrosian 1922* (Yearbook), *The Ambrosian 1923* (Yearbook).
49. *Catholic Messenger*, January 25, 1923; *The Ambrosian 1923* (Yearbook); *The Ambrosian*, Summer 1928 (Magazine).
50. *The Ambrosian 1923* (Yearbook).
51. *The Ambrosian 1921* (Yearbook), *The Ambrosian 1922* (Yearbook), *The Ambrosian 1923* (Yearbook), U. A. Hauber, "In Retrospect," *Ambrosian Alumnus*, May 1956.
52. *The Ambrosian 1923* (Yearbook); *The Ambrosian*, Winter 1925, Fall 1927, Winter 1927 (Magazine); *Catholic Messenger*, December 12, 1929.
53. *The Ambrosian*, Winter 1925 (Magazine).
54. Minutes, Logomachetean Society, November 6, 1923, Archives, O'Keefe Library.
55. *The Ambrosian*, Winter 1929 (Magazine).
56. Minutes, St. Ambrose Faculty, October 27, 1925, Archives, O'Keefe Library.
57. J. E. (Buck) Turnbull, *The Iowa Conference Story, Forty Years of Intercollegiate Sports, 1922-1961* (Iowa City, Iowa: The State Historical Society of Iowa, 1961), 15.
58. John O'Donnell, "Forrest Cotton," *The Ambrosian*, Autumn 1923 (Magazine).
59. *Catholic Messenger*, November 29, 1923
60. Minutes, Logomachetean Society, December 17, 1924, Archives, O'Keefe Library.
61. *Catholic Messenger*, April 25, 1923.
62. *Catholic Messenger*, October 1, 1925.
63. *The Ambrosian 1921* (Yearbook).
64. Marlys Svendsen, *Davenport, A Pictorial History, 1936-1986* (G. Bradley Publishing, Inc., 1985), 147.
65. Frederick Lewis Allen, *Only Yesterday, An Informal History of the 1920s* (New York: Harper & Row, Perennial Library, 1964), 137.
66. *Catholic Messenger*, February 7, 1924, February 21, 1924; *The Ambrosian*, Spring 1924 (Magazine).
67. St. Ambrose College Reports 1920s, Archives, Diocese of Davenport.
68. Minutes, Meeting of the Iowa State Board of Education, December 2, 1919,143, 151,153, Special Collections, University of Iowa Libraries, Iowa City, Iowa.
69. *Forty-First Annual Catalogue of St. Ambrose College, Davenport, Iowa, June 1923*, 31.
70. St. Ambrose College Faculty to James Davis, February 22, 1924, Archives, Diocese of Davenport.
71. Power, *Catholic Higher Education*, 107.
72. Minutes, St. Ambrose College Faculty, April 9, 1926, Archives, O'Keefe Library.
73. Minutes, St. Ambrose College Faculty, September 23, 1923, Archives, O'Keefe Library.
74. *The Ambrosian*, Spring 1924 (Magazine).
75. Minutes, Bishop's Council, August 6, 1924, Archives, Diocese of Davenport.
76. Faculty of St. Ambrose College to James Davis, October 22, 1924, Archives, Diocese of Davenport.
77. Minutes, Bishop's Council, November 11, 1924, Archives, Diocese of Davenport.
78. Minutes, Bishop's Council, November 11, 1924, Archives, Diocese of Davenport; *Catholic Messenger*, July 28, 1927.
79. Minutes, Bishop's Council, November 11, 1924, Archives, Diocese of Davenport; Arthur H. Ebeling to James Davis, November 14, 1924, Archives, Diocese of Davenport.
80. John P. Fischer, "Our Cover Design," *The Ambrosian*, Autumn 1925 (Magazine), 6, 7; *Catholic Messenger*, April 30, 1925.
81. *The Ambrosian*, Spring 1926 (Magazine).
82. "Standards of Accredited Institutions of Higher Education," *The North Central Association Quarterly* 1 (June 1926): 19-21.
83. St. Ambrose College Reports 1920s, Archives, Diocese of Davenport; U. A. Hauber to the Clergy and Laity of the Diocese of Davenport, February 15, 1927, Archives, Diocese of Davenport; Minutes, Bishop's Council, February 15, 1926, Archives, Diocese of Davenport.
84. Minutes, Bishop's Council, February 15, 1926, Archives, Diocese of Davenport.
85. Report to James Davis, May 21, 1926, Archives, Diocese of Davenport.
86. *Catholic Messenger*, May 13, 1926.
87. *Catholic Messenger,* May 20, 1926
88. *Catholic Messenger,* June 10, 1926.
89. U. A. Hauber, "In Retrospect," *Ambrosian Alumnus*, September 1953.
90. *Catholic Messenger*, August 19, 1926, September 9, 1926, July 28, 1927, August 11, 1927, July 5, 1928, June 12, 1930, June 19, 1930, July 10, 1930.
91. *Catholic Messenger*, July 15, 1926.
92. *Catholic Messenger*, January 13, 1927, April 14, 1927.
93. *Catholic Messenger*, December 2, 1926, June 9, 1927.
94. *The Ambrosian,* Winter 1926 (Magazine).
95. Minutes, St. Ambrose College Faculty, January 13, 1927, Archives, O'Keefe Library.
96. *Catholic Messenger*, March 24, 1927; U. A. Hauber to the Clergy and Laity of the Diocese of Davenport, February 15, 1927, Archives, Diocese of Davenport.
97. "Proceedings of the Commission on Institutions of Higher Education," *The North Central Association Quarterly* 2 (June 1927): 15.
98. *Catholic Messenger*, March 24, 1927; Minutes, St. Ambrose College Faculty, April 7, 1927, Archives, O'Keefe Library, St. Ambrose University.
99. *Catholic Messenger*, March 24, 1927, March 31, 1927.

Chapter Seven

1. *Catholic Messenger*, October 24, 1929.
2. *Ambrosian News*, November 10, 1936.
3. U. A. Hauber to A. J. Schulte, April 27, 1926, Archives, O'Keefe Library.
4. James Burns, CSC, "Failures of our Higher Schools," *The Commonweal*, November 3, 1926, 634-635.
5. U. A. Hauber, "Colleges and the Big Problem, A Paper Read Before the Contemporary Club," September 22, 1941, Archives, O'Keefe Library.
6. U. A. Hauber, *Creation and Evolution, A Catholic Opinion on the Evolution Theory* (New York: The Paulist Press [1925]).
7. U. A. Hauber to A. J. Schulte, April 27, 1926, O'Keefe Library; U. A. Hauber, "Paper for Faculty Seminar," n.d., O'Keefe Library.
8. U. A. Hauber, "To the clergy and laity of the diocese of Davenport," February 15, 1927, Archives, Diocese of Davenport.
9. *Catholic Messenger*, January 6, 1927, July 21, 1927.
10. Gleason, *Contending With Modernity*, 168.
11. *Catholic Messenger*, May 5, 1921.
12. *Ambrosian News*, January 15, 1932, January 21, 1932.
13. M. Jane Coogan, B.V.M., *The Price of our Heritage, History of the Sisters of Charity of the Blessed Virgin Mary, Volume Two, 1869-1920* (Dubuque, Iowa: Mount Carmel Press, 1978), 467.
14. Power, *History of Catholic Higher Education*, 141.
15. Frank J. Lewis to Henry Rohlman, July 23, 1927, Archives, Diocese of Davenport.
16. *Catholic Messenger*, July 28, 1927.
17. Minutes, Faculty Meeting, May 29, 1923, Archives, O'Keefe Library.
18. Henry Rohlman to Diocese of Davenport, August 2, 1927, Archives, Diocese of Davenport; *Catholic Messenger*, August 4, 1927.
19. *Catholic Messenger*, May 28, 1925, June 3, 1926, September 30, 1926, August 19, 1927, August 29, 1929.
20. Minutes, Faculty Meeting, October 4, 1927, Archives, O'Keefe Library; U. A. Hauber, "Paper for Faculty Seminar," n.d., O'Keefe Library; "Proceedings of the Commission on Institutions of Higher Education," *The North Central Association Quarterly* 3 June 1928, 56.
21. *Catholic Messenger*, November 17, 1927.
22. Henry Rohlman to Mother Isabella, BVM, April 17, 1928, Archives, Mount Carmel, Dubuque, Iowa; Henry Rohlman to Mother Isabella, BVM, April 30, 1928, Archives, Mount Carmel, Dubuque, Iowa.
23. Henry Rohlman to Mother Isabella, BVM, April 30, 1928; Sister Mary Benedicta to Henry Rohlman, May 3, 1928, Archives, Mount Carmel, Dubuque, Iowa.
24. *Catholic Messenger*, May 14, 1928, June 28, 1928.
25. Henry Rohlman to Mother Isabella, BVM, May 11, 1928, Archives, Mount Carmel, Dubuque, Iowa.
26. "An Agreement Between St. Ambrose College and Ter-El-Mar Junior College," Archives, Mount Carmel, Dubuque, Iowa.
27. *Catholic Messenger*, August 1, 1929; Sister Mary St. Joan of Arc Coogan, BVM, "History of the Immaculate Conception Academy of Davenport, Iowa and the Foundations of Catholic Education in That City" (master's thesis, Catholic University of America, 1941), 113-115.
28. *Catholic Messenger*, August 8, 1929, September 26, 1929, September 4, 1930.
29. Henry Rohlman to Frank Lewis, January 20, 1928, April 28, 1928, Archives, Diocese of Davenport.
30. *Catholic Messenger*, October 4, 1928; *Forty-Seventh Annual Catalogue of St. Ambrose College, Davenport, Iowa*, April, 1929, 71.
31. *Catholic Messenger*, August 30, 1928.
32. "Statement of the Diocesan Collections of the Diocese of Davenport for the Year Ending December 31, 1936," *Official Bulletin, Diocese of Davenport*, February 1, 1937, Archives, O'Keefe Library.
33. *Catholic Messenger*, May 2, 1929.
34. Minutes, Faculty Meeting, October 9, 1928, February 6, 1929, April 2, 1930, Archives, O'Keefe Library.
35. *The Ambrosian*, Spring 1928 (Magazine), Summer 1928, Fall 1929.
36. Minutes, Faculty Meeting, October 4, 1927, Archives, O'Keefe Library.
37. Minutes, Faculty Meeting, September 23, 1926, Archives, O'Keefe Library; Minutes, Board of Discipline, January 24, 1929, Archives, Diocese of Davenport.
38. Memorandum, T. C. Donohoe, Archives, Diocese of Davenport.
39. Henry Rohlman to U. A. Hauber and Members of the Faculty, May 10, 1929, Archives, Diocese of Davenport.
40. Minutes, Board of Discipline, May 30, 1929, Archives, Diocese of Davenport.
41. Memorandum, U. A. Hauber to Board of Discipline, September 16, 1929, Archives, Diocese of Davenport.
42. Minutes, Board of Discipline, September 16, 1929, Archives, Diocese of Davenport.
43. Henry Rohlman to U. A. Hauber, March 23, 1930, Archives, O'Keefe Library.
44. U. A. Hauber to Henry Rohlman, March 26, 1930, Archives, O'Keefe Library.
45. *Catholic Messenger*, September 13, 1951.
46. Henry Rohlman to U. A. Hauber, April 6, 1930, Archives, O'Keefe Library.
47. Henry Rohlman to Martin Cone, April 9, 1930, Archives, Diocese of Davenport; *Catholic Messenger*, April 10, 1930.
48. Minutes, Faculty Meeting, June 12, 1930, Archives, O'Keefe Library.
49. *Catholic Messenger*, February 6, 1930, June 19, 1930; *The Ambrosian*, Spring 1930 (Magazine).
50. *Catholic Messenger*, May 22, 1930.
51. Henry Rohlman to Frank J. Lewis, September 18, 1931, Archives, Diocese of Davenport.
52. *Ambrosian News*, October 16, 1931, October 23, 1931, October 30, 1931, November 6, 1931, November 30, 1931, November 27, 1931; Paul V. Murray "Are We Losing Historical Perspective in Period of Change?" *Catholic Messenger*, November 28, 1963.
53. Minutes, Faculty Meeting, October 15, 1930, January 14, 1931, Archives, O'Keefe Library.

267 A Great and Lasting Beginning

54. Minutes, Board of Discipline, October 13, 1930, Archives, O'Keefe Library.
55. Minutes, Faculty Meeting, June 12, 1930, Archives, O'Keefe Library; *Catholic Messenger*, May 28, 1931, August 30, 1931, September 10, 1931.
56. *The Ambrosian*, Spring 1928 (Magazine); *The Lens*, March 15, 1930.
57. *Catholic Messenger*, January 22, 1931, May 28, 1931.
58. Paul Murray, *The Ambrosian* Spring 1931 (Magazine).
59. *Catholic Messenger*, March 26, 1931.
60. *Catholic Messenger*, November 26, 1931; *Ambrosian News*, November 13, 1931, November 20, 1931.
61. *Catholic Messenger*, November 26, 1931.
62. "Fr. E. Catich, St. Ambrose Phenomenon," *Acorns and Oaks*, January 1962.
63. *Fifty-First Annual Catalogue of St. Ambrose College Davenport, Iowa*, April 1932, 76.
64. *Catholic Messenger*, October 1, 1931.
65. Data, North Central Association Report, November 18, 1934, Archives, O'Keefe Library.
66. Charles F. Griffith, "Our Anniversaries," *Catholic Messenger*, March 31, 1932, April 7, 1932.
67. *Catholic Messenger*, May 7, 1931.

Chapter Eight

1. *Catholic Messenger*, September 10, 1931, March 19, 1936.
2. Charles Lewis to Mom, September 18, 1935, Archives, O'Keefe Library; Tom Lewis to Mom, May 5, 1936, Archives, O'Keefe Library.
3. Henry Rohlman to Charles F. Griffith, January 28, 1933, Archives, Diocese of Davenport.
4. Minutes, Library Board, October 19, 1934, October 22, 1934, Archives, O'Keefe Library.
5. *Catholic Messenger*, August 3, 1933.
6. *Des Moines Register*, reprinted in *Catholic Messenger*, December 21, 1933.
7. Minutes, Faculty Meeting February 4, 1932, Archives, O'Keefe Library.
8. *Davenport Daily Democrat*, September 28, 1934.
9. *Ambrosian News*, November 1, 1934.
10. *Catholic Messenger*, October 25, 1934; *Ambrosian News*, October 18, 1934.
11. *Catholic Messenger*, August 15, 1935.
12. Francis L. Broderick, *Right Reverend New Dealer: John A. Ryan* (New York: The Macmillan Company, 1963), 278.
13. Daniel Lord, "Sodalities in America and Catholic Action," *Studies* (July 1933): 259, 260.
14. Gleason, *Contending With Modernity*, 152; David J. Endres, "Dan Lord, Hollywood Priest," *America*, Vol. 193, No. 19 (December 12, 2005): 21.
15. Joseph Cardijn, *Laymen Into Action* (London: G. Chapman, 1964), 50, 148, 149.
16. George William McDaniel, "Catholic Action in Davenport: St. Ambrose College and the League for Social Justice," *The Annals of Iowa*, 55 (Summer 1996): 239-272; *Ambrosian News*, February 7, 1935.
17. *Catholic Messenger*, April 5, 1934, April 12, 1934; *Davenport Democrat and Leader*, April 4, 1934.
18. *Ambrosian Magazine*, Winter 1933.
19. *Catholic Messenger*, September 28, 1933
20. Minutes, College Council Meeting, June 6, 1934, Archives, O'Keefe Library.
21. *Catholic Messenger*, July 5, 1933.
22. Coogan, "History of the Immaculate Conception Academy," 115-116.
23. *Ambrosian News*, October 4, 1934.
24. *Ambrosian News*, October 4, 1934, October 25, 1934.
25. *Ambrosian News*, October 11, 1934, November 1, 1934.
26. Minutes, College Council Meeting, April 4, 1935, Archives, O'Keefe Library.
27. Minutes, College Council Meeting, June 6, 1934, Archives, O'Keefe Library; Minutes, Committee on Educational Policy, October 13, 1934, Archives, O'Keefe Library.
28. Minutes, Joint Meeting of College Council and Faculty, October 3, 1934, Archives, O'Keefe Library.
29. Minutes, Joint Meeting of College Council and Faculty, October 3, 1934, Archives, O'Keefe Library.
30. Minutes, Faculty Meeting January 18, 1935, Archives, O'Keefe Library.
31. Henry Takkenberg, "Aims and Purposes of St. Ambrose College," Minutes, Faculty Meeting, January 18, 1935, Archives, O'Keefe Library.
32. Joseph Fenton, "The Ideal of the Catholic College," Minutes, Faculty Meeting, January 18, 1935, Archives, O'Keefe Library.
33. Gleason, *Contending With Modernity*, 139.
34. Minutes, Faculty Meeting, January 18, 1935, Archives, O'Keefe Library.
35. Minutes, Educational Policy Committee Meeting, February 2, 1937, Archives, O'Keefe Library.
36. *Angelicum*, 12 (January-March 1935): 86.
37. *Ambrosian News*, October 25, 1934, November 8, 1934, December 13, 1934, February 14, 1935.
38. *St. Ambrose College, Davenport, Iowa, Fifty-sixth Annual Announcement, March 1938*, 37.
39. *Ambrosian News*, February 23, 1933, November 30, 1933, January 23, 1936, January 7, 1937, March 4, 1937, February 17, 1938, March 31, 1938.
40. *Ambrosian News*, April 14, 1932, March 9, 1933.
41. Minutes, Meeting of the Department of Fine Arts, October 17, 1934, Archives, O'Keefe Library.
42. *Ambrosian News*, November 2, 1933, November 23, 1933.
43. Minutes, Meeting of the College Faculty, January 18, 1935, Archives, O'Keefe Library.
44. *Ambrosian News*, March 14,1935, September 30, 1937, November 4, 1938.
45. *Ambrosian News*, November 4, 1938.
46. *Catholic Messenger*, September 21, 1933.
47. Turnbull, *The Iowa Conference Story, passim.*
48. Turnbull, *The Iowa Conference Story, passim.*
49. *Ambrosian News*, February 8, 1934, February 15, 1934, May 17, 1934, May 5, 1938.
50. *Ambrosian News*, January 15, 1932, February 23, 1933, October 5, 1933.
51. *Ambrosian News*, October 12, 1933, December 14, 1933.
52. *Ambrosian News*, October 27, 1932, October 11, 1934, February 28, 1935, May 2, 1935, March 26, 1936; Report, Department of Modern Languages, October 12, 1934.
53. *Ambrosian News*, October, 26, 1933; Report, Department of Modern Languages, October 12, 1934.
54. *St. Ambrose College, Davenport, Iowa, Fifty-sixth Annual Announcement*, March 1938, 113.
55. *Ambrosian News*, March 10, 1938.
56. Charles Lewis to Mom, October 1, 1935, January 26, 1936, Archives, O'Keefe Library.
57. *Ambrosian News*, March 10, 1938.
58. *Ambrosian News*, October 6, 1938.
59. *Ambrosian News*, October 11, 1934.
60. Charles Lewis to Mom, October 18, 1935, Archives, O'Keefe Library.
61. *Ambrosian News*, October 9, 1931, December 4, 1931, October 25, 1934, November 8, 1934.
62. *Ambrosian News*, November 8, 1934.
63. *Ambrosian News*, September 24, 1936, September 30, 1937, November 4, 1937.
64. *Ambrosian News*, November 19, 1926, December 10, 1936, May 6, 1937.
65. *Ambrosian News*, November 5, 1936.
66. *Ambrosian News*, October 21, 1937, November 4, 1937.
67. *Ambrosian News*, December 9, 1937, December 16, 1937.
68. *Davenport Daily Times*, April 25, 1935.
69. *Davenport Democrat*, April 21, 1935.
70. *Ambrosian News*, May 2, 1935.
71. *Davenport Democrat and Leader*, April 26, 1935; *Davenport Daily Times*, April 25, 1935; *Ambrosian News*, May 2, 1935.
72. *Catholic Messenger*, May 2, 1935.
73. *Ambrosian News*, May 6, 1937.
74. *St. Ambrose College, Davenport, Iowa, Fifty-fifth Annual Announcement*, March, 1937, 79.
75. *Catholic Messenger*, December 11, 1941.
76. *Ambrosian News*, October 24, 1935, October 21, 1938, October 27, 1938.
77. *Catholic Messenger*, October 21, 1937.
78. *Ambrosian News*, September 23, 1937.
79. *Ambrosian News*, November 4, 1938, November 10, 1938; *Clarke Courier*, November 18, 1938.
80. *Catholic Messenger*, December 8, 1938.
81. *Ambrosian News*, January 13, 1938, February 3, 1938.
82. *Catholic Messenger*, June 1, 1933, August 31, 1933.
83. Amleto Cicognani to the Bishops of the United States, May 5, 1935, Archives, Diocese of Davenport; Henry Rohlman to Amleto Cicognani, May 28, 1935, Archives, Diocese of Davenport.
84. *Catholic Messenger*, October 29, 1936; *Ambrosian News*, September 24, 1936, October 22, 1936, October 29, 1936.
85. Amleto Cicognani to the Bishops of the United States, August 20, 1938, Archives, Diocese of Davenport; Edward Mooney to Henry Rohlman, October 31, 1938, Archives, Diocese of Davenport; *Ambrosian News*, November 18, 1938; *Catholic Messenger*, November 24, 1938; Interview with Cletus Madsen, September 25, 1978.
86. Joseph Cardinal Pizzardo to Bishop Henry Rohlman, December 3, 1940, Archives, Diocese of Davenport.
87. Minutes, Meeting of the College Council, April 4, 1935, Archives, O'Keefe Library.
88. Minutes, Meeting of the College Council, January 19, 1936, Archives, O'Keefe Library.
89. Sister Mary Evangela, BVM, to Graduates, August 26, 1936; Sister Mary Evangela to Mother Mary Gervase, BVM, August 27, 1936, Archives, Mount Carmel, Dubuque, Iowa.
90. "Report to the Board of Trustees and the Faculty of St. Ambrose College," December 5, 1936, Archives, O'Keefe Library; Minutes, Meeting of Board of Control and Faculty, December 7, 1936, Archives, O'Keefe Library.
91. Martin Cone to Mother Mary Gervase, BVM, April 6, 1937, Archives, Diocese of Davenport.
92. Mother Mary Gervase, BVM, to Martin Cone, April 14, 1937, Archives, Mount Carmel, Dubuque, Iowa.
93. Interview with Cletus Madsen, September 25, 1978.
94. John P. Gallagher, "The History of Saint Ambrose College 1920-1939," n.d.
95. *Ambrosian News*, September 23, 1937, October 8, 1837, October 14, 1937.
96. *Ambrosian News*, November 11, 1937.
97. *Ambrosian News*, December 2, 1937; *Catholic Messenger*, November 27, 1937.
98. *Ambrosian News*, October 14, 1937.
99. Henry Rohlman, Comments Regarding Marycrest, October 27, 1938, Archives, Diocese of Davenport.
100. Minutes, Meeting with Sisters of Humility and St. Ambrose Officials, January 18, 1939, Archives, O'Keefe Library.
101. Mother Mary Geraldine Upham to Henry Rohlman, March 9, 1939, Archives, Diocese of Davenport.
102. Sister Madeleine Marie Schmidt, CHM, *Seasons of Growth, History of the Diocese of Davenport, 1881-1981* (The Diocese of Davenport, 1981), 201; *Ambrosian News*, March 24, 1938; *Catholic Messenger*, March 24, 1938.
103. "Constitution of the St. Ambrose Alumnae Association," Archives, Diocese of Davenport; Minutes, Meeting of the St. Ambrose Alumnae Association, May 8, 1939, June 5, 1939, Archives, Diocese of Davenport.
104. Minutes, Board of Educational Policy, May 19, 1938, Archives, O'Keefe Library.
105. *Davenport Democrat and Leader*, December 1, 1938.

Chapter Nine

1. Ambrose Burke, Radio Address, October 17, 1940, Archives, O'Keefe Library.
2. Ralph W. Clark to Thomas Lawlor, "Analysis of the Student Questionnaires," October 2, 1939, O'Keefe Library; *Catholic Messenger*, September 28, 1939.
3. *Davenport Daily Times*, September 30, 1939.
4. "Report to the Board of Trustees and the Faculty of St. Ambrose College, December 5, 1936," Archives, O'Keefe Library.
5. *Ambrosian News*, December 9, 1937.
6. Henry Rohlman to Frank J. Lewis, February 10, 1938, Archives, Diocese of Davenport.
7. *Catholic Messenger*, June 22, 1939, September 21, 1939; *Ambrosian News*, October 12, 1939.
8. *Catholic Messenger*, October 5, 1939.
9. *Catholic Messenger*, September 21, 1939.
10. *Catholic Messenger*, July 4, 1935, September 28, 1939, October 5, 1939.
11. *Catholic Messenger*, October 26, 1939.
12. *Catholic Messenger*, October 5, 1939.
13. *Catholic Messenger*, November 2, 1939.
14. *Catholic Messenger*, November 2, 1939; *Davenport Democrat and Leader*, November 1, 1939.
15. Henry Rohlman to Elizabeth Schneider, November 3, 1939, Archives, Diocese of Davenport.
16. *Catholic Messenger*, November 30, 1939, December 28, 1939, April 4, 1940.
17. *Ambrosian News*, October 12, 1939, October 19, 1939.
18. *Ambrosian News*, October 19, 1939, December 14, 1939, March 1, 1940.
19. *Ambrosian News*, October 12, 1939, October 19, 1939.
20. *Ambrosian News*, October 26, 1939; *America* (November 18, 1939): 147.
21. David M. Kennedy, *Freedom From Fear, The American People in Depression and War, 1929-1945* (New York: Oxford University Press, 1999), 387-388, 428.
22. *Catholic Messenger*, September 21, 1939; *Ambrosian News*, October 12, 1939, May 10, 1940; *Davenport Daily Times*, November 7, 1940.
23. Carl Meinberg to Henry Rohlman, December 28, 1939, Archives, Diocese of Davenport.
24. *Catholic Messenger*, January 11, 1940; *Ambrosian News*, January 18, 1940.
25. *Ambrosian News*, January 18, 1940, May 30, 1940.
26. *Catholic Messenger*, February 1, 1940, February 15, 1940; *Oaks 1940* (Yearbook).
27. *Catholic Messenger*, January 18, 1940, January 25, 1949.

28. *Ambrosian News*, February 15, 1940.

29. Henry Rohlman to Ambrose Burke, February 14, 1940, Archives, Diocese of Davenport.

30. *Catholic Messenger*, February 15, 1940, *Ambrosian News*, February 15, 1940.

31. Ambrose Burke, Remarks, n.d., Archives, O'Keefe Library.

32. Minutes, Committee on National Defense, March 17, 1940, Archives, O'Keefe Library.

33. *Ambrosian News*, May 23, 1940.

34. Michael J. Martin to Ambrose Burke, August 17, 1940; Burke to Martin, September 3, 1940, Archives, O'Keefe Library, *Ambrosian News*, October 31, 1940.

35. *Ambrosian News*, October 31, 1940.

36. *Ambrosian News*, March 3, 1939, July 18, 1949, August 8, 1940, October 24, 1940.

37. *Ambrosian News*, October 31, 1940.

38. *Catholic Messenger*, September 5, 1940; *Ambrosian News*, September 26, 1940.

39. *Catholic Messenger*, September 5, 1940; *Ambrosian News*, September 26, 1940.

40. *Ambrosian News*, January 15, 1941, February 5, 1941, February 13, 1941 March 13, 1941.

41. *Ambrosian News*, January 16, 1941; *Catholic Messenger*, December 11, 1941.

42. *Catholic Messenger*, June 5, 1941.

43. *Oaks 1941*.

44. *Oaks 1941*; *Ambrosian News*, October 2, 1941, *Catholic Messenger*, June 12, 1941.

45. U. A. Hauber, "Colleges and the Big Problem," The Contemporary Club, October 20, 1941, 4, 5, 7, 10, 11.

46. *Catholic Messenger*, June 12, 1941.

47. *Catholic Messenger*, June 26, 1941.

48. *Ambrosian News*, December 5, 1941.

49. *Catholic Messenger*, October 23, 1941, October 30, 1921; *Ambrosian News*, October 16, 1941.

50. *Catholic Messenger*, October 23, 1941, October 30, 1941.

51. *Catholic Messenger*, October 30, 1941.

52. *Davenport Democrat and Leader*, December 7, 1941.

53. *Davenport Democrat and Leader*, December 1, 1941.

54. *Ambrosian News*, December 5, 1941, December 11, 1941.

55. *Ambrosian News*, December 5, 1941.

56. *Ambrosian News*, December 11, 1941.

57. *Ambrosian News*, January 16, 1941, February 6, 1941.

58. *Davenport Daily Times*, December 8, 1941

59. *Davenport Times*, December 9, 1941.

60. *Ambrosian News*, December 18, 1941.

61. *Catholic Messenger*, December 23, 1941.

62. *Catholic Messenger*, December 11, 1941, January 22, 1942, March 12, 1942.

63. Mark C. Curran, Heritage Day Speech, June 7, 1997.

64. *Oaks 1941*, *Oaks 1942*; *Catholic Messenger*, April 16, 1942; Mark C. Curran, Heritage Day Speech, June 7, 1997.

65. *Catholic Messenger*, January 15, 1942, January 29, 1942; *Ambrosian News*, January 15, 1942.

66. *Ambrosian News*, April 23, 1942; *Catholic Messenger*, April 23, 1942, June 18, 1942.

67. *Ambrosian News*, November 19, 1942.

68. *Catholic Messenger*, October 8, 1942.

69. *Ambrosian News*, January 14, 1943.

70. *Catholic Messenger*, February 18, 1943; Mark C. Curran, Heritage Day Speech, June 7, 1997.

71. *Ambrosian News*, January 14, 1943; *Catholic Messenger*, May 20, 1943.

72. O. F. Heslar, USNR, to Ambrose Burke, December 8, 1942; Burke to Heslar, December 11, 1942, Archives, O'Keefe Library.

73. Navy Contract, June 12, 1943, Archives, O'Keefe Library; Ambrose Burke to Emmet J. Riley, August 30, 1943, Archives, O'Keefe Library.

74. James G. Schneider, *The Navy V-12 Program, Leadership for a Lifetime* (Boston: Houghton Mifflin Company, 1987), 57.

75. *Catholic Messenger*, May 6, 1943.

76. *Catholic Messenger*, May 27, 1943.

77. *Catholic Messenger*, May 27, 1943.

78. *Catholic Messenger*, June 3, 1943.

79. Ambrose Burke to Michael J. Martin, March 9, 1943, Martin to Burke, March 16, 1943, Archives, O'Keefe Library.

80. *Catholic Messenger*, July 1, 1943, August 19, 1943.

81. *Catholic Messenger*, July 1, 1943, October 14, 1943, February 3, 1944, March 16, 1944, December 7, 1944.

82. Robbins W. Barstow to Ambrose Burke, June 17, 1942; Burke to Barstow, June 19, 1942, Archives, O'Keefe Library.

83. American Friends Service Committee to Ambrose Burke, October 15, 1942; James T. O'Down to Ambrose Burke, January 5, 1943, Archives, O'Keefe Library.

84. Mark C. Curran, Heritage Day Speech, June 7, 1997; Ambrose Burke to John Kamerick, August 19, 1943, Archives, O'Keefe Library; *Catholic Messenger*, July 8, 1943

85. *Ambrosian Newsletter*, April, 1944, December, 1944; *Sea Breez*, December 16, 1943; *Catholic Messenger*, April 6, 1944.

86. Ambrose Burke to Emmet J. Riley, August 30, 1943, Archives, O'Keefe Library; *Catholic Messenger*, October 21, 1943.

87. *Ambrosian Newsletter*, April 1944.

88. *Catholic Messenger*, January 13, 1944.

89. *Ambrosian Newsletter*, October 1944.

90. *Ambrosian Newsletter*, January 1945.

91. *Ambrosian Newsletter*, March 1945.

92. *Catholic Messenger*, June 1, 1944.

93. David M. Kennedy, *Freedom From Fear, The American People in Depression and War, 1929-1945* (New York: Oxford University Press, 1999), 787.

94. Milton Greenberg, *The GI Bill, The Law That Changed America* (New York: Lickle Publishing Inc., 1997), *passim*.

95. *Catholic Messenger*, November 9, 1944; *Ambrosian Newsletter*, November 1944.

Chapter Ten

1. *Catholic Messenger*, February 15, 1945.

2. *Ambrosian Newsletter*, April 1944.

3. *Catholic Messenger*, June 21, 1945.

4. *Catholic Messenger*, September 5, 1946.

5. Ralph Hayes to Ambrose Burke, January 19, 1945, Archives, O'Keefe Library.

6. Ralph Hayes to Francis Griffith, February 14, 1945, Archives, Diocese of Davenport.

7. *Ambrosian News*, December 3, 1948; *Ambrosian Alumnus*, November 1949; *Catholic Messenger*, April 12, 1951.

8. *Catholic Messenger*, August 8, 1946.

9. Ambrose Burke to William Adrian, January 22, 1945; Adrian to Burke, January 29, 1945, Archives, O'Keefe Library.

10. Ambrose Burke to William Adrian, February 3, 1945, Archives, O'Keefe Library.

11. *Catholic Messenger*, August 8, 1946.

12. Jac Treanor to author, June 10, 2006, June 13, 2006, Archives, O'Keefe Library.

13. *Ambrosian Newsletter*, February 1945, March 1945, April 1945.

14. *Sea Breez*, May 12, 1945.

15. L. E. Dengeld to Ambrose Burke, September 21, 1945, Archives, O'Keefe Library.

16. *Catholic Messenger*, October 18, 1945.

17. *Catholic Messenger*, September 20, 1945, October 18, 1945.

18. *Catholic Messenger*, August 16, 1945, September 20, 1945.

19. *Catholic Messenger*, March 14, 1946; Bureau of Naval Personnel to Ambrose Burke, January 11, 1946, Archives, O'Keefe Library.

20. Gleason, *Contending With Modernity*, 209, 215.

21. George M. Marsden, *The Soul of the American University, From Protestant Establishment to Established Nonbelief* (New York: Oxford University Press, 1994), 391, 393

22. *Catholic Messenger*, May 9, 1946, May 23, 1946.

23. *Catholic Messenger*, July 4, 1946.

24. *Catholic Messenger*, July 11, 1946.

25. *Catholic Messenger*, July 11, 1946.

26. *Ambrosian News*, November 8, 1946; *Catholic Messenger*, July 11, 1946, August 29, 1946.

27. Ralph Hayes, Sermon, September 16, 1946, Archives, Diocese of Davenport.

28. *Catholic Messenger*, August 22, 1946, August 29, 1946.

29. *Ambrosian News*, November 8, 1946; *Catholic Messenger*, October 17, 1946, November 11, 1946.

30. *Ambrosian News*, January 30, 1947, March 20, 1947, April 10, 1947.

31. *Catholic Messenger*, October 23, 1947.

32. *Catholic Messenger*, January 29, 1948, November 17, 1949; *Ambrosian Alumnus*, October 1949.

33. *Catholic Messenger*, June 19, 1947.

34. *Ambrosian Alumnus*, October 1949; *Ambrosian News*, February 20, 1948, April 23, 1948, May 6, 1949; *Oaks 1950*.

35. Mark C. Curran, Heritage Day Talk, June 7, 1997.

36. Thomas Donahue to Ambrose Burke, May 8, 1947, Archives, O'Keefe Library.

37. *Ambrosian News*, September 26, 1947; Mark C. Curran, Heritage Day Talk, June 7, 1997.

38. *Ambrosian News*, May 14, 1948.

39. *Catholic Messenger*, August 15, 1946, September 5, 1946.

40. Andrew Corry, "Living Endowment," *Commonweal* (October 19, 1934), 581.

41. Gleason, *Contending With Modernity*, 204.

42. Minutes, Board of Directors, April 23, 1948, Archives, Diocese of Davenport; *Ambrosian News*, May 28, 1948.

43. *Ambrosian News*, October 3, 1946.

44. *Moline Daily Dispatch*, December 10, 1949.

45. *Ambrosian News*, November 5, 1936; *Ambrosian Newsletter*, April 1945; Mark C. Curran, Heritage Day Talk, June 7, 1997.

46. *Catholic Messenger*, September 13, 1951.

47. U. A. Hauber, *Essentials of Zoology* (New York: Appleton-Century-Crofts, Inc., 1949), vii.

48. *Moline Daily Dispatch*, December 19, 1949.

49. Minutes, Board of Directors, October 25, 1946; Ambrose Burke to Ralph Hayes, November 27, 1950; Ralph Hayes to James Gaffney, December 6, 1950, Archives, Diocese of Davenport.

50. U. A. Hauber, "Catholic Education for Rural Living in Iowa," *The Catholic Educator* (September 1952).

51. Vincent A. Yzermans, *The People I Love, A Biography of Luigi G. Ligutti* (Collegville, Minnesota: The Liturgical Press, 1976), *passim*.

52. Luigi Ligutti and John C. Rawe, SJ, *Rural Roads to Security, America's Third Struggle for Freedom* (Milwaukee: The Bruce Publishing Company, 1940), 173.

53. U. A. Hauber, Preliminary Report on Agriculture, September 4, 1945, Archives, O'Keefe Library.

54. U. A. Hauber, Report of the Committee on Agriculture, September 26, 1945, Archives, O'Keefe Library.

55. Ralph Hayes to U. A. Hauber, November 29, 1945, Archives, O'Keefe Library.

56. Ralph Hayes to Priests, December 10, 1945, Archives, O'Keefe Library.

57. Paul Sacco, "A Practical School of Agriculture," *Land and Home* 9 (December 1946), 92.

58. Donald McDonald, "A Rural Life Problem," *Commonweal* (July 7, 1950), 313.

59. *Catholic Messenger*, February 7, 1946, February 14, 1946, February 21, 1946.

60. U. A. Hauber, "Using the School Curriculum to Educate for Catholic Rural Life," An Address Delivered at the National Catholic Rural Life Conference, October 20, 1951.

61. Interview, Joe and Mary Jean Blough with author, July 21, 1993.

62. Ruby Hurley to Richard Kendall, February 5, 1947; Kendall to Hurley, April 19, 1947; Hurley to Kendall, April 30, 1947; Kendall to Hurley, May 8, 1947; Hurley to Kendall, May 13, 1947, NAACP Papers, Youth File, Iowa, Library of Congress.

63. *Ambrosian News*, March 12, 1948.

64. *Ambrosian News*, May 28, 1948.

65. *Ambrosian News*, March 25, 1949, April 29, 1949; *Davenport Daily Times*, April 22, 1949; *Davenport Democrat and Leader*, April 22, 1949.

66. *Catholic Messenger*, January 24, 1952.

67. *Ambrosian News*, February 6, 1948.

68. *Ambrosian News*, February 13, 1948, May 14, 1948, May 21, 1948, December 15, 1950.

69. *Ambrosian News*, November 21, 1947, February 27, 1948; *Catholic Messenger*, April 8, 1948, August 12, 1948.

70. *Catholic Messenger*, April 8, 1948; *Ambrosian News*, January 14, 1949, April 9, 1948.

71. *Ambrosian News*, October 21, 1949, November 4, 1949.

72. *Ambrosian News* May 19, 1950.

73. Interview, Mike Lawrence with author, July 22, 1993.

74. Ambrose Burke to C. W. Anderson, April 2, 1949, Archives, O'Keefe Library.

75. *Davenport Daily Times*, February 16, 1946.

76. Charles J. Darrow to William O'Connor, January 27, 1946, Archives, O'Keefe Library.

77. Edward L. Ruhl to Ambrose Burke, February 21, 1946, Archives, O'Keefe Library.

78. William O'Connor to William Collins, June 28, 1956, Archives, O'Keefe Library.

79. Linna Bresette to Ambrose Burke, November 4, 1948, Archives, O'Keefe Library; Burke to Bresette, November 19, 1948

80. *Ambrosian News*, March 18, 1949; *Davenport Democrat and Leader*, March 20, 1949.

81. *Davenport Democrat and Leader*, March 21, 1949; *Catholic Messenger*, March 31, 1949; *Ambrosian News*, March 11, 1949, March 18, 1949, March 25, 1949.
82. "Constitution of the Catholic League for Social Justice," Archives, Diocese of Davenport.
83. *Catholic Messenger*, May 3, 1951.
84. Interview, Mike Lawrence with author, July 22, 1993.
85. Mary Jean Blough to author, July 27, 1993.
86. Bill Nagle to author, October 7, 1993.
87. Interview, Marvin Mottet with author, July 23, 1993.
88. *Catholic Messenger*, September 2, 1948.
89. *Catholic Messenger*, March 4, 1948; *Ambrosian News*, March 5, 1948.
90. *Ambrosian News*, March 12, 1948, May 6, 1949.
91. *Ambrosian News*, May 16, 1958, May 22, 1959.
92. *Ambrosian News*, April 9, 1948.
93. *Ambrosian News*, February 6, 1948, February 13, 1948, October 29, 1948.
94. *Ambrosian News*, February 21, 1948, January 20, 1950, November 18, 1950, February 8, 1952, October 4, 1957; *The Oaks 1949*, *The Oaks 1950*.
95. Ralph Hayes to Priests, January 24, 1949, Archives, Diocese of Davenport.
96. Ambrose Burke to Priests, January 27, 1949, Archives, Diocese of Davenport.
97. "Do We Need A New Chapel?" Memorandum, Archives, Diocese of Davenport.
98. Memo, Office of the President [mid-March 1949], Archives, O'Keefe Library.
99. Ambrose Burke to John Keating, February 14, 1949, Archives, O'Keefe Library.
100. "Final Report on Pledges from Priests at St. Ambrose," Archives, O'Keefe Library.
101. Ralph Hayes to Priests of the Diocese, April 9, 1949, Archives, O'Keefe Library.
102. *Davenport Democrat and Leader*, January 16, 1950.
103. Ambrose Burke, "Notice to Priests of St. Ambrose," May 13, 1949, Archives, O'Keefe Library.
104. Interview, Charles Shepler with author, September 29, 2003.
105. Edward J. Schulte to Ambrose Burke, November 22, 1949; Burke to Schulte, November 25, 1949, Archives, O'Keefe Library.
106. Ralph Hayes to Harry Toher, December 2, 1949, Archives, O'Keefe Library; *Catholic Messenger*, December 15, 1949.
107. Minutes, Chapel Committee Meeting, December 6, 1949, Archives, O'Keefe Library.
108. Minutes, Chapel Committee Meeting, January 13, 1950, Archives, O'Keefe Library.
109. *Catholic Messenger*, December 15, 1949.
110. John McEniry to Ralph Hayes, February 18, 1949, Archives, Diocese of Davenport; Edward Lew to Ralph Hayes, April 29, 1949; Ambrose Burke to Joseph D. Murphy, April 4, 1949, Archives, O'Keefe Library.
111. Minutes, Priests' Committee, January 25, 1950, Archives, O'Keefe Library; Ambrose Burke to Joseph Schulte, February 27, 1950, Archives, Diocese of Davenport.
112. Ambrose Burke to Edward Schulte, January 5, 1951, Archives, O'Keefe Library; Ralph Hayes to Ambrose Burke, January 8, 1951, Archives, Diocese of Davenport; Ambrose Burke to Edward Schulte, February 27, 1950, Archives, Diocese of Davenport.

Chapter Eleven

1. Ambrose Burke to James Morrin, September 5, 1950, Archives, O'Keefe Library.
2. Ambrose Burke to Edward Schulte, June 9, 1950, Archives, O'Keefe Library; Edward Schulte to Ambrose Burke, June 20, 1950, Archives, O'Keefe Library.
3. Ralph Hayes to Edward Schulte, August 23, 1950, Archives, Diocese of Davenport; Edward Schulte to Ralph Hayes, August 25, 1950, Archives, Diocese of Davenport.
4. *Ambrosian News*, January 12, 1951; *Ambrose Alumnus*, February, 1951; Edward J. Schulte, "Chapel and Seminary Unit," *Church Property Magazine* (March-April 1951), 34-35.
5. Ralph Hayes to Priests of the Diocese, April 4, 1951, Archives, O'Keefe Library.
6. Minutes, Chapel Committee, April 13, 1951, Archives, O'Keefe Library; Ambrose Burke to H. W. Mohr, July 10, 1951, Archives, O'Keefe Library.
7. Ambrose Burke to Edward Schulte, August 24, 1951, Archives, O'Keefe Library; Ambrose Burke to Robert Livingston, August 31, 1951, Archives, O'Keefe Library.
8. *Ambrosian News*, October 22, 1948.
9. *Ambrosian News*, September 26, 1947; *Oaks 1949*.
10. *Catholic Messenger*, May 5, 1949; *Oaks 1948*; *Oaks 1949*; *Oaks 1950*.
11. *Ambrosian News*, January 23, 1948, February 13, 1948; *Catholic Messenger*, March 25, 1948.
12. *Davenport Daily Democrat*, May 22, 1932; *Ambrosian News*, March 14, 1934, April 26, 1934; *Catholic Messenger*, October 10, 1946.
13. *Ambrosian News*, February 12, 1942.
14. *Ambrosian News*, February 18, 1949, *Ambrosian Alumnus*, May 1958.
15. *Ambrosian News*, February 9, 1951, May 18, 1951.
16. *Ambrosian News*, October 24, 1952, March 13, 1953.
17. *Ambrosian News*, October 30, 1953, November 6, 1953, November 13, 1953, November 5, 1954.
18. *Ambrosian News*, March 15, 1957, April 12, 1957; *Ambrosian Alumnus*, April 1957.
19. *Ambrosian News*, May 6, 1955, May 4, 1956, February 8, 1957, May 24, 1957.
20. Edward M. Catich, "The Image of Christ in Art," *The Furrow* 8 (June 1957), 383, 376.
21. *Catholic Messenger*, June 19, 1952; Edward Catich, "The Stations at St. Wenscelaus," Archives, O'Keefe Library.
22. Barb Arland-Fye, "Standing the Test of Time," *Quad-City Times*, May 24, 1998; Alma Gaul, "A Painting for This Time," *Quad-City Times*, December 21, 2003.
23. *Catholic Messenger*, July 24, 1952, July 31, 1952.
24. Amleto Cicognani to Ralph Hayes, September 10, 1955, Archives, Diocese of Davenport; Ralph Hayes to Amleto Cicognani, September 13, 1955, Archives, Diocese of Davenport.
25. *Ambrosian News*, January 12, 1951; *Catholic Messenger*, August 16, 1951.
26. *Catholic Messenger*, August 16, 1951; Ambrose Burke to Cy J. Schlarman, October 9, 1952, Archives, O'Keefe Library.
27. *Catholic Messenger*, October 11, 1951.
28. *Catholic Messenger*, April 12, 1951.
29. Turnbull, *The Iowa Conference Story*, 64, 65.
30. *Catholic Messenger*, April 26, 1951; Turnbull, *The Iowa Conference Story*, 113, 114.
31. Turnbull, *The Iowa Conference Story*, 30-32.
32. Cary Jones to Ambrose Burke; Ambrose Burke to Cary Jones, September 7, 1950; William J. Rogers, Report and Survey, October 9, 1950, Archives, O'Keefe Library.
33. *Ambrosian News*, February 23, 1951; *Catholic Messenger*, February 22, 1951; Ambrose Burke to Burke Hickenlooper, March 22, 1951, Archives, O'Keefe Library.
34. Sister Mary Brigid Conden, *From Simplicity to Elegance: The Story of Mercy Hospital, Davenport 1869-1994* (Davenport, Iowa 1997), 51, 92; Memo Regarding Proposed Nursing Division, February 29, 1952, Archives O'Keefe Library.
35. Conden, *From Simplicity to Elegance*, 94.
36. *Catholic Messenger*, May 31, 1951, November 20, 1952.
37. *Ambrosian News*, October 12, 1951.
38. *Ambrosian News*, February 5, 1954.
39. *Catholic Messenger*, August 16, 1951; *Ambrosian Alumnus*, September 1952.
40. *Ambrosian Alumnus*, February 1954.
41. Ambrose Burke, "The Financial Picture of St. Ambrose Shows Importance of Alumni Living Endowment," *Ambrosian Alumnus*, June 1952.
42. *Ambrosian Alumnus*, May 1955; Minutes, Board of Trustees, September 9, 1957, Archives, Diocese of Davenport.
43. *Ambrosian News*, December 3, 1942.
44. *Ambrosian Alumnus*, April 1950.
45. *Ambrosian News*, April 13, 1956.
46. *Ambrosian Alumnus*, October 1952, September 1953.
47. *Catholic Messenger*, October 13, 1949; *Ambrosian News*, October 14, 1949.
48. Ambrose Burke to John Dauner, May 29, 1950, Archives, O'Keefe Library.
49. Ambrose Burke to Invited Guest [May 1951], Archives, O'Keefe Library.
50. *Time*, April 16, 1951.
51. Ambrose Burke, "The Current Crisis at St. Ambrose College," Archives, O'Keefe Library.
52. Bernard L. Spaeth to Ambrose Burke, June 7, 1951, Archives, O'Keefe Library.
53. *Ambrosian Alumnus*, March 1953; *Ambrosian News*, February 8, 1952, February 15, 1952; *Catholic Messenger*, February 14, 1952, March 13, 1952.
54. *Ambrosian Alumnus*, January 1953.
55. Minutes, Chapel Committee, January 24, 1952, Archives, O'Keefe Library.
56. Ambrose Burke to Edward Schulte, March 5, 1952, Archives, O'Keefe Library.
57. Minutes, Chapel Committee, April 7, 1952, Archives, O'Keefe Library.
58. *Ambrosian Alumnus*, May 1952.
59. *Ambrosian Alumnus*, September 1952; *Davenport Times-Democrat*, September 24, 1952.
60. Ambrose Burke to Edward Schulte, January 14, 1952, Archives, O'Keefe Library; Ambrose Burke to Edward Schulte, November 3, 1952, Archives, Diocese of Davenport; Ambrose Burke to Edward Schulte, December 5, 1952, Archives, O'Keefe Library; Ambrose Burke to Ralph Hayes, January 17, 1953, Archives, Diocese of Davenport; Edward Schulte to Tunnicliff Construction, March 19, 1953, Archives, Diocese of Davenport; Ralph Hayes to Ambrose Burke, April 28, 1953, Archives, Diocese of Davenport.
61. Ralph Hayes to Ambrose Burke, November 3, 1952, Archives, Diocese of Davenport.
62. Ralph Hayes to Ambrose Burke, January 21, 1953, Archives, Diocese of Davenport; Minutes, Chapel Committee, April 16, 1953, Archives, O'Keefe Library; Ambrose Burke to Edward Catich, April 17, 1953, Archives, O'Keefe Library.
63. Ambrose Burke to Edward Schulte, July 16, 1954, Archives, O'Keefe Library.
64. "Notes from Mr. Schulte," Archives, O'Keefe Library.
65. Ambrose Burke to George J. Toher, August 30, 1952, Archives, O'Keefe Library.
66. Ambrose Burke to Robert Livingston, February 3, 1953, Archives, O'Keefe Library.
67. Ambrose Burke to Edward Schulte, January 23, 1953, Archives, O'Keefe Library.
68. *Ambrosian News*, March 20, 1953, May 22, 1953.
69. *Ambrosian News*, October 2, 1953.
70. *Ambrosian Alumnus*, December 1953; *Ambrosian News*, February 5, 1954; *Davenport Daily Times*, December 2, 1953.
71. Samuel Cardinal Stritch, "Dedication of St. Ambrose College Chapel, Davenport, Iowa, December 2, 1953," Archives, Diocese of Davenport.
72. *Ambrosian Alumnus*, December 1953; *Davenport Morning Democrat*, December 2, 1953.
73. David Klise to Alumni, n.d., Archives, O'Keefe Library.
74. *Catholic Messenger*, June 16, 1948.
75. *Ambrosian Alumnus*, October 1951; *Catholic Messenger*, October 11, 1951.
76. *Ambrosian News*, April 27, 1956, May 4, 1956.
77. *Ambrosian Alumnus*, March 1953; *Ambrosian News*, February 20, 1953.
78. *Ambrosian News*, January 18, 1957; *Catholic Messenger*, May 20, 1954; *Ambrosian Alumnus*, November 1953, June 1954.
79. *Ambrosian Alumnus*, January 1954, October 1955.
80. Ambrose Burke to John Kamerick, February 26, 1947, Archives, O'Keefe Library; Ambrose Burke to Ralph Hayes, June 20, 1952, Archives, O'Keefe Library.
81. Minutes, Meeting of Bishop and Pastors, August 4, 1952, Archives, O'Keefe Library; *Ambrosian Alumnus*, January 1954.
82. *Ambrosian News*, February 5, 1954; *Ambrosian Alumnus*, September 1955.
83. *Catholic Messenger*, July 8, 1954; *Ambrosian Alumnus*, June 1954, November-December 1957.
84. Mark S. Massa, SJ, *Anti-Catholicism in America, The Last Acceptable Prejudice* (New York: The Crossroad Publishing Company, 2003), 126; Gleason, *Contending With Modernity*, 290-291.
85. *Catholic Messenger*, November 24, 1955.
86. Hofstadter, *Anti-Intellectualism in American Life*, 140-141.
87. *Ambrosian Alumnus*, May 1953.
88. *Ambrosian Alumnus*, April 1952.
89. *Ambrosian Alumnus*, December 1954, November 1958.
90. *Catholic Messenger*, October 5, 1950.
91. *Catholic Messenger*, February 21, 1952, March 7, 1952, May 3, 1956.
92. *Catholic Messenger*, August 2, 1951.
93. *Catholic Messenger*, April 10, 1952, June 12, 1952; *Sixty-eighth Catalogue, St. Ambrose College*, June 1952, 59.
94. *Catholic Messenger*, April 21, 1955; Paul Sacco to Ralph Hayes, April 1, 1955, Archives, Diocese of Davenport; Ralph Hayes to Paul Sacco, April 18, 1955, Archives, Diocese of Davenport.
95. *Ambrosian Alumnus*, December 1956, February 1957.
96. Ralph Hayes, Memo, November 8, 1955, Archives, Diocese of Davenport.
97. Ralph Hayes to Ambrose Burke, January 17, 1956, Archives, Diocese of Davenport.
98. *Ambrosian Alumnus*, January 1956.
99. Ralph Hayes, February 14, 1956, Archives, Diocese of Davenport.
100. Carl Rice to Martin Casey, January 24, 1963, Archives, O'Keefe Library; Martin Casey to Carl Rice, June 23, 1963, Archives, O'Keefe Library.
101. *Catholic Messenger*, May 31, 1956.
102. *Catholic Messenger*, May 31, 1956.
103. *Catholic Messenger*, July 26, 1956.
104. *Catholic Messenger*, October 29, 1955, July 12, 1956.

Chapter Twelve

1. *Ambrosian News*, February 8, 1957.
2. Charles C. Alexander, *Holding the Line: The Eisenhower Era, 1952-1961* (Bloomington: Indiana University Press, 1975), 100.
3. *Ambrosian Alumnus*, September 1956.
4. *Catholic Messenger*, November 8, 1956.
5. *Ambrosian News*, November 16, 1956.
6. *Catholic Messenger*, June 13, 1957; *Ambrosian Alumnus*, May 1957.
7. *Davenport Daily Times*, November 5, 1957.
8. *Catholic Messenger*, November 28, 1957.
9. *Catholic Messenger*, December 15, 1955.
10. *Catholic Messenger*, December 5, 1957; *Ambrosian Alumnus*, November-December 1957.
11. William Collins to Priests of the Diocese, December 3, 1957, Archives, O'Keefe Library.
12. *Davenport Daily Times*, December 5, 1957.
13. *Davenport Morning Democrat*, December 5, 1957.
14. Ralph Hayes to Prospective Board Members, August 26, 1957, Archives, Diocese of Davenport; *Catholic Messenger*, November 20, 1958; Ralph Hayes to Prospective Board Members, January 23, 1959, Archives, Diocese of Davenport.
15. *Catholic Messenger*, May 15, 1958.
16. Minutes, Board of Trustees, November 18, 1958, Archives, Diocese of Davenport.
17. *Ambrosian News*, February 15, 1957, February 22, 1957, March 8, 1957; *Ambrosian Alumnus*, March 1957, June 1957.
18. *Ambrosian Alumnus*, June 1958.
19. *Catholic Messenger*, October 11, 1951.
20. Registration Statistics, Fall Semesters 1955-1959 Incl., Archives, Diocese of Davenport.
21. *Ambrosian News*, October 19, 1951.
22. *Ambrosian News*, September 30, 1955; Student Personnel Committee to William Collins, May 14, 1958, Archives, O'Keefe Library; *Ambrosian News*, October 7, 1960, October 6, 1961.
23. *Paper SAC*, April 25, 1974.
24. Ambrose Burke to Ralph Hayes, November 3, 1954, Archives, O'Keefe Library; *Ambrosian Alumnus*, September 1955, January 1956.
25. *Ambrosian News*, December 6, 1957, February 7, 1958, February 14, 1957; *Catholic Messenger*, January 23, 1958.
26. *Ambrosian News*, September 26, 1958, October 17, 1958; *Ambrosian Alumnus*, September 1958.
27. *Ambrosian News*, December 4, 1959; *Catholic Messenger*, January 7, 1960.
28. *Catholic Messenger*, May 26, 1960, June 2, 1960.
29. *Davenport Times*, July 8, 1960.
30. *Ambrosian Alumnus*, June 1957, November-December 1957; *Ambrosian News*, October 11, 1957; *Catholic Messenger*, July 3, 1958.
31. *Ambrosian News*, September 30, 1949; Minutes, Board of Trustees, September 9, 1957, Archives, Diocese of Davenport; *Ambrosian Alumnus*, November-December 1957.
32. *Catholic Messenger*, March 13, 1958; *Ambrosian News*, March 7, 1958.
33. Minutes, Board of Trustees, April 25, 1957, Archives, Diocese of Davenport.
34. *Catholic Messenger*, July 3, 1958, December 18, 1958; Minutes, Board of Trustees, February 24, 1959, Archives, Diocese of Davenport.
35. *Ambrosian News*, February 14, 1958.
36. *Ambrosian News*, December 6, 1957, May 9, 1958.
37. *Ambrosian News*, November 29, 1959.
38. John Lewis Gaddis, *We Now Know, Rethinking Cold War History* (Oxford: Clarendon Press, 1997), 238.
39. Lisle A. Rose, *The Cold War Comes to Main Street, America in 1950* (Lawrence, Kansas: University Press of Kansas, 1999), 326.
40. *Ambrosian Alumnus*, April 1957; *Catholic Messenger*, July 24, 1958.
41. *Ambrosian News*, April 10, 1959; *Acorns and Oaks*, Spring 1959.
42. *Ambrosian News*, November 3, 1961, November 10, 1961.
43. *Ambrosian News*, March 6, 1959, November 13, 1959, March 18, 1960.
44. *Ambrosian Alumnus*, October 1953, April 1954, January 1957; *Ambrosian News*, May 14, 1954.
45. *Ambrosian News*, April 20, 1956, May 9, 1958; *Acorns and Oaks*, Summer 1959.
46. *Catholic Messenger*, April 26, 1951.
47. *Ambrosian News*, November 21, 1952.
48. Turnbull, *The Iowa Conference Story*, 175; *Catholic Messenger*, December 26, 1957; *Ambrosian Alumnus*, June 1957.
49. *Ambrosian News*, February 5, 1960.
50. *Ambrosian News*, February 5, 1960.
51. *Ambrosian News*, February 15, 1960.
52. *Ambrosian News*, February 19, 1960
53. William Collins to Ralph Hayes, March 6, 1960, Archives, Diocese of Davenport.
54. *Catholic Messenger*, March 10, 1960; *Ambrosian Alumnus*, March 1960.
55. George Fuller to William Collins, April 12, 1960, Archives, O'Keefe Library; James Junkins, April 6, 1960, Archives, O'Keefe Library;
56. *Ambrosian Alumnus*, March 1960.
57. *Catholic Messenger*, June 2, 1960.
58. *St. Ambrose Free Press*, February 5, 1960, February 19, 1960; *Ambrosian News*, January 22, 1960.
59. *Ambrosian News*, February 15, 1960, January 19, 1962.
60. *Ambrosian News*, October 28, 1960, November 4, 1960.
61. *Ambrosian News*, October 20, 1961, November 3, 1961, February 9, 1962.
62. William O'Connor to Ralph Hayes, February 25, 1958, Archives, Diocese of Davenport; *Ambrosian News*, April 6, 1962, October 18, 1963.
63. *Ambrosian News*, October 9, 1959; *Catholic Messenger*, March 30, 1961, August 17, 1961, August 23, 1962.
64. *Catholic Messenger*, March 1, 1962, March 15, 1962; *Ambrosian News*, April 13, 1962.
65. *Catholic Messenger*, April 5, 1962.
66. *Ambrosian Alumnus*, September 1960; *Ambrosian News*, February 24, 1961, March 3, 1961, March 10, 1961.
67. *Ambrosian News*, November 2, 1962.
68. *Ambrosian News*, November 10, 1960, November 19, 1960.
69. *Ambrosian News*, December 1, 1961, November 30, 1962, November 15, 1963, December 6, 1963.
70. *Ambrosian News*, October 17, 1958; *Acorns and Oaks*, December 1962.
71. *Ambrosian News*, November 6, 1959.
72. *Ambrosian News*, October 14, 1960; *Paper SAC*, January 31, 1974.
73. *Acorns and Oaks*, Summer 1960; *Ambrosian News*, February 24, 1961.
74. *Ambrosian News*, September 29, 1961, November 13, 1964.
75. Carl Rice to Martin Casey, January 24, 1963, Archives, O'Keefe Library.
76. Ralph Hayes to Frederick McMahan, June 15, 1961; *Catholic Messenger*, August 31, 1961.
77. Frederick McMahan to Division Chairs, March 15, 1961, Archives, O'Keefe Library.
78. Mary Brigid Condon, RSM, to Frederick McMahan, May 8, 1961, Archives, O'Keefe Library; Mother Mary Huberta, RSM, to Mary Brigid Condon, RSM, May 15, 1961, Archives, O'Keefe Library.
79. "Proposed Agreement between Saint Ambrose College, Davenport, and the Sisters of Mercy Province of Chicago" [1961], Archives, O'Keefe Library.
80. Mary Brigid Condon, RSM, to Frederick McMahan, April 9, 1962, Archives, O'Keefe Library.
81. Mary Brigid Condon, RSM, to William Collins, June 8, 1962, Archives, O'Keefe Library; Condon, *From Simplicity to Elegance*, 96-97; *Catholic Messenger*, July 12, 1962.
82. "Report of the Committee on Norms and Criteria for Evaluating Members of the Faculty for Advancement in Rank," Archives, Diocese of Davenport; "Tenure Program, AAUP Tenure Committee, March 12, 1962," Archives, Diocese of Davenport; "Faculty Tenure Contract," Archives, Diocese of Davenport.
83. *Acorns and Oaks*, December 1962.
84. *Ambrosian News*, October 26, 1962, November 9, 1962.
85. *Catholic Messenger*, April 13, 1961.
86. *Catholic Messenger*, April 5, 1961.
87. *Catholic Messenger*, July 6, 1961.
88. *Catholic Messenger*, August 1, 1963.
89. Martin Casey to Carl Rice, June 23, 1963, Archives, O'Keefe Library.
90. Ralph Hayes to Frederick McMahan, September 9, 1963, September 10, 1963, Archives, Diocese of Davenport; *Ambrosian News*, September 27, 1963; *Catholic Messenger*, September 12, 1963.
91. *Ambrosian News*, December 6, 1963.
92. *Ambrosian News*, December 6, 1963, December 20, 1963.

Chapter Thirteen

1. Andrew M. Greeley, "A New Breed," *America*, May 23, 1964, 706-709.
2. Arthur M. Schlesinger, Jr., *A Thousand Days, John F. Kennedy in the White House* (Boston: Houghton Mifflin Company, 1965), 606.
3. *Ambrosian News*, March 4, 1966; *St. Ambrose College Alumnus*, March 1967, December 1968.
4. Schmidt, *Seasons of Grace*, 244; *Ambrosian News*, November 30, 1962, December 7, 1962, December 14, 1962, October 16, 1964.
5. *Ambrosian News*, October 9, 1964.
6. *Ambrosian News*, March 26, 1965; *Catholic Messenger*, March 25, 1965; *Davenport Times- Democrat*, March 16, 1965.
7. *Ambrosian News*, March 26, 1965, April 9, 1965, October 15, 1965, May 6, 1966, October 13, 1967.
8. *Ambrosian News*, May 7, 1965, October 29, 1965.
9. *Ambrosian News*, October 22, 1965, October 29, 1965, November 5, 1965.
10. *Ambrosian News*, April 6, 1962.
11. John Mikesch to author, December 1, 2004; Vern Hubka to Frederick McMahan, November 17, 1963, Archives, O'Keefe Library.
12. *Ambrosian News*, January 24, 1964, February 14, 1964, March 4, 1966; *Acorns and Oaks*, November 1967.
13. Gleason, *Contending With Modernity*, 243-244.
14. *Ambrosian News*, December 14, 1962.
15. *Ambrosian News*, April 9, 1963.
16. *Catholic Messenger*, April 11, 1963.
17. *Ambrosian News*, October 25, 1963.
18. Carroll J. Williams to Frederick McMahan, November 20, 1963, Archives, O'Keefe Library.
19. Minutes, National Student Association, November 15, 1963, Archives, O'Keefe Library.
20. *Ambrosian News*, January 24, 1964; *Catholic Messenger*, January 23, 1964.
21. *Ambrosian News*, January 17, 1964, January 24, 1964, February 7, 1964, February 28, 1964; Letters to Frederick McMahan, January 1964, Archives, O'Keefe Library.
22. *Ambrosian News*, January 17, 1964, February 14, 1964.
23. *Ambrosian News*, March 24, 1964.
24. Maurice Dingman to Ralph Hayes, September 5, 1963, Archives, Diocese of Davenport.
25. Student Council to Ralph Hayes, December 4, 1963, Archives, Diocese of Davenport.
26. Maurice Dingman to Ralph Hayes, Undated Memorandum, Archives, Diocese of Davenport.
27. *Catholic Messenger*, June 11, 1964; *Ambrosian News*, June 11, 1964; *Davenport Times- Democrat*, June 12, 1964.
28. *Ambrosian News*, October 9, 1964; *Acorns and Oaks*, March 1965.
29. *Acorns and Oaks*, March 1965.
30. *Ambrosian News*, May 21, 1965; *St. Ambrose College Alumnus*, May 1965.
31. *Ambrosian News*, February 26, 1965; *St. Ambrose College Alumnus*, May 1965.
32. *Ambrosian News*, February 23, 1962.
33. William J. Richardson, SJ, "The University and Christian Formation," Neil J. McCluskey, SJ, *The Catholic University, a Modern Appraisal* (Notre Dame: University of Notre Dame Press, 1970), 175, 167-196 *passim*.
34. *Ambrosian News*, February 26, 1965; *Catholic Messenger*, February 25, 1965.
35. *Ambrosian News*, September 23, 1966.
36. *Ambrosian News*, May 1, 1964.
37. *Ambrosian News*, May 14, 1964.
38. *Ambrosian News*, May 14, 1965, April 1, 1966.
39. *Davenport Times-Democrat*, May 18, 1965.
40. *Ambrosian News*, May 7, 1965, May 14, 1965.
41. *Ambrosian News*, October 1, 1965, October 8, 1965.
42. *Ambrosian News*, December 10, 1965.
43. Gleason, *Contending With Modernity*, 252, 254.
44. Gleason, *Contending With Modernity*, 258, 260.
45. *Ambrosian News*, February 4, 1966, April 1, 1966.
46. *Paper SAC*, January 10, 1969.
47. *Ambrosian News*, April 29, 1966, May 6, 1966.
48. *Ambrosian News*, May 6, 1966, May 13, 1966, October 14, 1966, March 3, 1967, May 12, 1967, September 29, 1967, "Bee-Line 1968-1969."
49. *Ambrosian News*, February 3, 1967, February 17, 1967.
50. *Ambrosian News*, November 4, 1966, February 3, 1967.
51. *Ambrosian News*, March 1, 1968.
52. *Ambrosian News*, October 21, 1966, December 19, 1966, March 3, 1967, May 5, 1967.
53. *Ambrosian News*, November 3, 1967, December 17, 1967.
54. *Ambrosian News*, January 12, 1968; *Catholic Messenger*, April 22, 1965.

A Great and Lasting Beginning

55. *Ambrosian News*, February 10, 1967.
56. *Acorns and Oaks*, July 1967.
57. Menke, "Memoirs and Reflections," 61-62
58. Gleason, *Contending With Modernity*, 317.
59. James Tunstead Burtchaell, *The Dying of the Light, The Disengagement of Colleges and Universities from their Christian Churches* (Grand Rapids, Michigan: William B. Eerdmans Publishing Company, 1998), 595.
60. Martin John Stamm, *The New Guardians of American Catholic Higher Education: An Examination of Lay Participation on the Governing Boards of Roman Catholic-Affiliated Colleges and Universities* (PhD diss, University of Pennsylvania, 1979), 352, 353.
61. Gleason, *Contending With Modernity*, 315.
62. Minutes, Board of Trustees, January 27, 1965, Archives, Diocese of Davenport.
63. *Ambrosian News*, November 29, 1964.64. *Ambrosian News*, November 19, 1965.
65. *Ambrosian News*, October 1, 1965, October 15, 1965, November 19, 1965, December 3, 1965, November 4, 1966.
66. *Catholic Messenger*, March 10, 1966.
67. Minutes, Board of Trustees, January 27, 1965, Archives, Diocese of Davenport.
68. Sebastian Menke, "Memoirs and Reflections of Sebastian G. Menke," unpublished manuscript, 60; *Catholic Messenger*, September 22, 1966.
69. Menke, "Memoirs and Reflections," 59; *Catholic Messenger*, September 22, 1966.
70. *Catholic Messenger*, September 22, 1966, December 1, 1966.
71. Menke, "Memoirs and Reflections," 59.
72. Gerald O'Keefe to Priests of the Diocese of Davenport, November 23, 1966, Archives, O'Keefe Library.
73. *Catholic Messenger*, December 15, 1966.
74. *Ambrosian News*, January 19, 1968.
75. *Ambrosian News*, December 10, 1965; *Catholic Messenger*, October 27, 1966.
76. *Ambrosian News*, February 16, 1968, February 23, 1968.
77. *Ambrosian News*, April 5, 1968.
78. *Acorns and Oaks*, February 1969.
79. Minutes, Board of Trustees, March 18, 1968, Archives, O'Keefe Library.
80. Minutes, Board of Managers, March 29, 1968, Archives, O'Keefe Library.
81. Lawrence Soens to John Franz, April 2, 1968, Archives, Diocese of Davenport.
82. Gleason, *Contending With Modernity*, 227; Burtchaell, *Dying of the Light*, 562.
83. *Ambrosian News*, April 5, 1968.
84. *Ambrosian News*, April 29, 1966, November 18, 1966.
85. *Ambrosian News*, April 7, 1967.
86. *Catholic Messenger*, May 25, 1966; *Ambrosian News*, May 19, 1967.
87. *Catholic Messenger*, May 25, 1966.
88. *Catholic Messenger*, May 25, 1966.
89. *Catholic Messenger*, May 25, 1966.
90. *Ambrosian News*, October 6, 1967.
91. *Ambrosian News*, October 19, 1962.
92. *Ambrosian News*, February 23, 1968.
93. *Ambrosian News*, March 29, 1968, April 5, 1968.
94. *Ambrosian News*, May 10, 1968.

Chapter Fourteen

1. *Acorns and Oaks*, October 1969.
2. *St. Ambrose College Alumnus*, June 1970.
3. *Ambrosian News*, May 5, 1965; David McDaniel to author, May 27, 2004.
4. *Paper SAC*, September 26, 1968.
5. Interview, Edward Rogalski with author, May 28, 2004.
6. *Ambrosian News*, October 7, 1966, November 4, 1966, February 17, 1966, February 24, 1966.
7. *Ambrosian News*, February 9, 1968, February 16, 1968, May 3, 1968, December 5, 1968.
8. *Paper SAC*, February 27, 1969, March 20, 1969; David McDaniel to author, April 22, 2006.
9. *Paper SAC*, October 17, 1968.
10. *Paper SAC*, October 17, 1968.
11. *Paper SAC*, November 14, 1968.
12. *Paper SAC*, May 22, 1969, October 18, 1973.
13. *Paper SAC*, November 21, 1968.
14. *Paper SAC*, December 5, 1968, January 10, 1969.
15. *Paper SAC*, February 27, 1969.
16. *Paper SAC*, January 16, 1969, February 27, 1969.
17. *Paper SAC*, October 2, 1969, November 6, 1969.
18. Gleason, *Contending With Modernity*, 313-314.
19. *Paper SAC*, April 24, 1969.
20. *Paper SAC*, April 24, 1969.
21. *Paper SAC*, May 22, 1969; Bob Dylan, "The Times They Are A-Changin'," Special Rider Music, 1963, 1991.
22. *Paper SAC*, October 9, 1969; Minutes, Board of Trustees, September 15, 1969, Archives, Diocese of Davenport.
23. *Paper SAC*, September 25, 1969, October 9, 1969, October 23, 1969.
24. *Paper SAC*, October 16, 1969, October 30, 1969.
25. *Ambrosian News*, April 28, 1967, May 5, 1967, May 19, 1967; *Paper SAC*, October 2, 1969.
26. *St. Ambrose College Alumnus*, March 1970.
27. Christian G. Appy, *Working-Class War, American Combat Soldiers and Vietnam* (Chapel Hill: The University of North Carolina Press, 1993), 29.
28. *Acorns and Oaks*, February 1970.
29. Minutes, Board of Trustees, September 15, 1969, Archives, Diocese of Davenport; Minutes, Board of Directors, October 28, 1971, Archives, Diocese of Davenport.
30. Robert Leroy Hasenstab, *The Determinants of Board Restructuring in Catholic Higher Education in the United States* (PhD diss, St. Louis University, 1971), 62.
31. *Acorns and Oaks*, February 1970; Minutes, Board of Trustees, May 16, 1966, Archives, Diocese of Davenport; *Ambrosian News*, April 26, 1968.
32. *Paper SAC*, November 21, 1968.
33. *Paper SAC*, January 10, 1969, February 20, 1969.
34. "Constitution and Bylaws, Faculty Association," Archives, O'Keefe Library; "Resume of Saint Ambrose College Faculty Association's action October, 1969 to May 21, 1970," Archives, O'Keefe Library.
35. *Paper SAC*, May 7, 1970.

36. *Paper SAC*, May 14, 1970.
37. *Acorns and Oaks*, July 1970.
38. Minutes, Faculty Association, May 21, 1970, Archives, O'Keefe Library; Minutes Faculty Association, July 8, 1970; *Paper SAC*, September 17, 1970.
39. *Paper SAC*, September 17, 1970.
40. Sebastian Menke to John Schmits, July 14, 1970, Archives, O'Keefe Library; Sebastian Menke to Parents, July 17, 1970, Archives, O'Keefe Library.
41. "St. Ambrose on Strike," History 390 Class Project, Fall 1970, 65-66.
42. *Paper SAC*, October 9, 1969; *Oaks 1970*.
43. *Paper SAC*, February 18, 1971.
44. Norman Burns to Sebastian Menke, July 29, 1970, Archives, O'Keefe Library; "Report of a Visit to St. Ambrose College, Davenport, Iowa, April 20 & 21, 1970 for the Commission on Institutions of Higher Education of the North Central Association of Colleges and Secondary Schools," 1-12, Archives, O'Keefe Library.
45. "Report of a Visit," 9-10, Archives, O'Keefe Library.
46. *Paper SAC*, November 19, 1970.
47. *Paper SAC*, October 30, 1969, November 6, 1969.
48. *Paper SAC*, October 30, 1969, February 26, 1970, October 15, 1970.
49. *Acorns and Oaks*, July 1970; Press Release, St. Ambrose College News Service, July 17, 1970, Archives, O'Keefe Library.
50. News Release, Marycrest College, June 18, 1970, Archives, Diocese of Davenport.
51. Elizabeth Anne Schneider, CHM, to Louis Vaccaro, November 1, 1970, Archives, Diocese of Davenport.
52. Louis Vaccaro to Boards of Directors [Fall 1970], Archives, Diocese of Davenport.
53. Minutes, Joint Board Meeting, December 7, 1970, Archives, Diocese of Davenport.
54. *Paper SAC*, September 13, 1970.
55. *Paper SAC*, September 13, 1970.
56. *Ambrosian News*, May 10, 1968; *Paper SAC*, September 24, 1970.
57. *Paper SAC*, October 22, 1970.
58. Minutes, Administrative Council, October 15, 1970, Archives, O'Keefe Library; Sebastian Menke to Carmichael Peters, October 16, 1970, Archives, O'Keefe Library.
59. *Paper SAC*, December 3, 1970.
60. *Paper SAC*, February 4, 1971.
61. *Paper SAC*, February 4, 1971.
62. *Paper SAC*, February 4, 1971, February 11, 1971, February 18, 1971.
63. *Paper SAC*, May 6, 1971.
64. *Paper SAC*, February 11, 1971.
65. *Paper SAC*, February 11, 1971.
66. *Acorns and Oaks*, January 1971.
67. *Ambrose Magazine*, April 13, 1989; *St. Ambrose College Alumnus*, June 1971.
68. *Paper SAC*, January 14, 1971.
69. Minutes, Joint Board Meeting, January 20, 1971, Archives, Diocese of Davenport.
70. "Feasibility Study, Proposed Reorganization and Merger of Saint Ambrose College and Marycrest College," January 18, 1971, Archives, O'Keefe Library.
71. John Stemlar to Sebastian Menke, January 18, 1971, Archives, Diocese of Davenport.
72. Minutes, Joint Board Meeting, January 20, 1971, Archives, Diocese of Davenport.
73. *Davenport Times Democrat*, January 21, 1971; *Paper SAC*, January 14, 1971, February 11, 1971.
74. *Paper SAC*, April 29, 1971; *Acorns and Oaks*, January 1972.
75. *Ambrosian News*, February 26, 1965.
76. *Paper SAC*, September 23, 1961.
77. Gerald O'Keefe to James Kelleher, October 10, 1971, Archives, O'Keefe Library; Gerald O'Keefe to Sebastian Menke, October 19, 1971, Archives, O'Keefe Library; Minutes, Board of Directors Meeting, October 28, 1971, Archives, Diocese of Davenport.
78. Minutes, Academic Senate, November 4, 1971, Archives, Diocese of Davenport; Sebastian Menke to Academic Senate, October 29, 1971, Archives, O'Keefe Library; John Smith to Joseph Kokjohn, November 2, 1971, Archives, O'Keefe Library.
79. Gerald O'Keefe to Priests of the Diocese, December 6, 1971, Archives, O'Keefe Library.
80. *Paper SAC*, November 11, 1971.
81. Minutes, Board of Directors, November 26, 1973, Archives, O'Keefe Library.
82. *Paper SAC*, September 30, 1971.
83. Priests' Questionnaire, March 5, 1971, Archives, Diocese of Davenport.
84. Joseph Hratz to St. Ambrose Priests, February 2, 1971, Archives, Diocese of Davenport; Priests' Questionnaire, March 5, 1971, Archives, Diocese of Davenport.
85. Minutes, Meeting of Sisters and Priests, March 15, 1971, Archives, Diocese of Davenport.
86. *Paper SAC*, April 19, 1971.
87. Minutes, Merger Committee Meeting, July 2, 1971, Archives, Diocese of Davenport.
88. Minutes, Merger Committee Meeting, October 23, 1971.
89. "Report of Sister M. Jeanne Finske to Danforth Foundation," January 3, 1972, Archives, Diocese of Davenport; William Kelly, SJ, "Report to Danforth Foundation," Archives, Diocese of Davenport.
90. "Final Report on Merger of St. Ambrose and Marycrest Colleges by Sub-Committee of Joint Boards," March 11, 1972, Archives, Diocese of Davenport.
91. Minutes, Joint Board Meeting, March 11, 1972, Archives, Diocese of Davenport.
92. *Paper SAC*, April 13, 1972; *Acorns and Oaks*, April 1972.
93. "Progress Report Name Selection for New Institution," May 12, 1972, Archives, Diocese of Davenport; Minutes, Board of Regents, May 24, 1972, Archives, Diocese of Davenport.
94. *Paper SAC*, October 5, ,1972, October 26, 1972.
95. Cathleen Real, CHM, to Newman Board of Regents, n.d., Archives, Diocese of Davenport.
96. "Financial Considerations for Newman College," n.d., Archives, Diocese of Davenport.
97. Minutes, Newman College Board of Regents, December 22, 1972, Archives, Diocese of Davenport.
98. Sebastian Menke to Gerald O'Keefe, December 27, 1972.
99. Gerald O'Keefe to Sebastian Menke, January 2, 1973, Archives, Diocese of Davenport.
100. Minutes, Newman College Board of Regents, January 5, 1973, Archives, Diocese of Davenport.

Chapter Fifteen

1. *Paper SAC*, September 7, 1973.
2. *Paper SAC*, October 21, 1971, April 27, 1972, October 18, 1973, November 8, 1973, November 15, 1973.
3. *Paper SAC*, September 28, 1972, September 14, 1973.
4. Minutes, Student Affairs Committee, February 27, 1973, Archives, O'Keefe Library.
5. *Ambrosian News*, November 3, 1967.
6. *Paper SAC*, September 8, 1972, September 21, 1972, April 13, 1978.

7. *Paper SAC*, September 1, 1972, February 22, 1973, February 15, 1973, September 14, 1973.
8. Sebastian Menke, "Memoirs and Reflections," 63-64.
9. *Paper SAC*, February 1, 1973.
10. Minutes, Board of Directors, February 5, 1973, Archives, Diocese of Davenport.
11. Minutes, Board of Directors, April 13, 1973, May 22, 1973, Archives, Diocese of Davenport; *Paper SAC*, May 10, 1973.
12. Farrell, *Bees and Bur Oaks*, 258.
13. Minutes, Joint Meeting of Directors and Trustees, July 27, 1973, Archives, Diocese of Davenport.
14. Burtchaell, *Dying of the Light*, 708.
15. *Paper SAC*, September 7, 1973, September 14, 1973; *Acorns and Oaks*, September 1973.
16. *Paper SAC*, October 11, 1973; *Acorns and Oaks*, January 1974.
17. *Paper SAC*, October 11, 1973.
18. *Paper SAC*, October 25, 1973; *Acorns and Oaks*, January 1974.
19. *Paper SAC*, November 8, 1973, December 6, 1973; *Acorns and Oaks*, January 1974.
20. *Paper SAC*, January 24, 1974.
21. *Paper SAC*, February 21, 1974, February 28, 1974, March 28, 1974, April 4, 1974.
22. *Ambrosian News*, January 14, 1949, January 15, 1954, March 5, 1954, October 3, 1958; *Ambrosian Alumnus*, June 1955.
23. *Paper SAC*, September 17, 1971; *Acorns and Oaks*, July 1971.
24. Sebastian Menke, "Memoirs and Reflections," 60-61.
25. *Paper SAC*, September 7, 1973, March 4, 1982.
26. Donald Schneider to author, May 16, 2006.
27. Farrell, *Bees and Bur Oaks*, 259.
28. *Paper SAC*, April 25, 1974.
29. *Ambrose Scene*, Summer 1974.
30. *Paper SAC*, September 5,1975.
31. *Paper SAC*, September 23, 1971, September 19, 1974, November 7, 1974, February 19, 1976.
32. *Paper SAC*, December 13, 1973, September 25, 1975, October 2, 1975, October 9, 1975, April 15, 1976.
33. *Paper SAC*, February 3, 1972, February 17, 1972.
34. *Paper SAC*, March 28, 1974; *Ambrose Scene*, Summer 1974.
35. *Paper SAC*, November 14, 1968, November 21, 1968.
36. *Paper SAC*, October 18, 1973, December 6, 1973; *Acorns and Oaks*, January 1974.
37. *Paper SAC*, November 15, 1973, February 21, 1974.
38. *Paper SAC*, September 5, 1974, October 17, 1974, November 7, 1974.
39. *Paper SAC*, September 18, 1975.
40. *Paper SAC*, November 7, 1974, February 13, 1975, March 6, 1975.
41. *Paper SAC*, March 28, 1974.
42. *Paper SAC*, February 17, 1972, April 20, 1972, February 28, 1974.
43. *Paper SAC*, February 27, 1975, September 18, 1975.
44. *Paper SAC*, February 20, 1975, February 19, 1976, March 25, 1976.
45. *Paper SAC*, November 14, 1974, January 30, 1975, October 24, 1975.
46. *Paper SAC*, October 26, 1978, November 9, 1978, December 7, 1978.
47. *Paper SAC*, September 25, 1975.
48. Minutes, Board of Directors, June 20, 1975, October 28, 1975, Archives, O'Keefe Library; *Paper SAC*, October 24, 1975.
49. *Ambrose Scene*, Summer 1975.
50. *Paper SAC*, August 22, 1976.
51. John Smith to William Bakrow, April 17, 1976, Archives, O'Keefe Library; William Bakrow to John Smith, April 28, 1976, Archives, O'Keefe Library; John Smith to William Bakrow, May 3, 1976, Archives, O'Keefe Library.
52. *Paper SAC*, September 5, 1975.
53. *Paper SAC*, December 12, 1975; *Ambrose Scene*, Summer 1976.
54. *Paper SAC*, March 25, 1976; *Ambrose Scene*, Summer 1976.
55. *Paper SAC*, August 22, 1976, December 9, 1976.
56. *Paper SAC*, November 3, 1977.
57. *Ambrose Scene*, Spring 1978; *Paper SAC*, November 6, 1975, May 11, 1978, October 12, 1978, November 6, 1980.
58. *Paper SAC*, September 9, 1977; *Ambrose Scene*, Fall 1977.
59. *Ambrose Scene*, Spring 1979.
60. *Paper SAC*, February 2, 1978; *Ambrose Scene*, Winter 1978.
61. Minutes, Board of Directors, August 19, 1975, Archives, O'Keefe Library; *Paper SAC*, September 18, 1975.
62. *Paper SAC*, March 25, 1976, October 28, 1976; *Ambrose Scene*, Spring 1977.
63. *Paper SAC*, November 2, 1978; *Ambrose Scene*, Winter 1979.
64. *Paper SAC*, February 22, 1973, September 19, 1974.
65. *Paper SAC*, February 19, 1976.
66. *Quad-City Times*, November 16, 1978.
67. *Paper SAC*, November 16, 1978.
68. Minutes, Board of Directors, August 19, 1975, Archives, O'Keefe Library.
69. Gerald O'Keefe to Robert St. Clair, February 14, 1975, Archives, Diocese of Davenport; *Paper SAC*, February 20, 1975.
70. *Ambrose Scene*, Summer 1976.
71. *Ambrose Scene*, Summer 1976.
72. *Paper SAC*, February 13, 1975, February 20, 1975, February 27, 1975, April 3, 1975.
73. *Paper SAC*, November 6, 1975; *Ambrose Scene*, Summer 1975.
74. William Bakrow to Priests of the Diocese of Davenport, December 22, 1978, Archives, Diocese of Davenport.
75. *Paper SAC*, September 29, 1977, October 5, 1978.
76. *Paper SAC*, September 13, 1979, September 27, 1979, October 11, 1979.
77. *Ambrose Scene*, Summer 1979, Spring 1980.
78. Thurston Manning to William Bakrow, April 21, 1978, Archives, O'Keefe Library; *Ambrose Scene*, Summer 1978.
79. *Paper SAC*, April 27, 1978.
80. *Ambrose Scene*, Fall 1977; *Paper SAC*, September 9, 1977.
81. *Ambrosian News*, October 26, 1962, January 21, 1966.
82. Minutes, Board of Directors, September 22, 1978, Archives, Diocese of Davenport.
83. *Paper SAC*, November 16, 1978; Minutes, Board of Directors, December 18, 1978, Archives, Diocese of Davenport.
84. *Paper SAC*, September 28, 1978; *Ambrose Scene*, Fall/Winter 1979-80.
85. *Ambrose Scene*, Summer 1979; *Paper SAC*, September 13, 1979, November 29, 1979, April 10, 1980.
86. *Ambrose Scene*, Spring 1980; *Paper SAC*, February 28, 1980, March 28, 1980.

87. Jimmy Carter, *Keeping Faith, Memoirs of a President* (New York: Bantam Books, 1982), 482.
88. *Paper SAC*, January 31, 1980.
89. *Paper SAC*, February 7, 1980.
90. *Paper SAC*, February 25, 1982, November 4, 1982.
91. *Ambrose Scene*, Summer 1981, Autumn 1981, Winter 1982, Spring 1982, Autumn 1982; *Paper SAC*, February 25, 1982.
92. Farrell, *Bees and Bur Oaks*, 269-271.

Chapter Sixteen

1. Gregory A. J. Vogel, *Ambrose Magazine*, September 13, 1984.
2. *Paper SAC*, September 17, 1982.
3. "Centennial Year President's Report," Summer 1982; *Ambrose Scene*, Autumn 1981.
4. *Ambrose Magazine*, February 17, 1985.
5. *Paper SAC*, March 26, 1981, February 18, 1982, September 23, 1982.
6. *Paper SAC*, February 12, 1981.
7. *Paper SAC*, March 30, 1983; *Ambrose Magazine*, October 11, 1984.
8. "Report of the Ad Hoc Committee for Curriculum Review," January 1980, Archives, O'Keefe Library.
9. *Paper SAC*, February 9, 1978.
10. "Report of the Ad Hoc Committee for Curriculum Review," January 1980, Archives, O'Keefe Library.
11. *Paper SAC*, October 25, 1979, April 24, 1980.
12. *Paper SAC*, October 14, 1982.
13. *Paper SAC*, February 18, 1982.
14. *Paper SAC*, February 25, 1982, March 11, 1982, April 22, 1982; *Moline Dispatch*, March 2, 1982.
15. *Moline Daily Dispatch*, July 27, 1984.
16. *Paper SAC*, February 4, 1982; *Ambrose Scene*, Winter 1982.
17. *Ambrose Magazine*, December 12, 1985.
18. *Ambrose Magazine*, February 20, 1986.
19. *Paper SAC*, November 4, 1982, November 18, 1982; *Ambrose Scene*, Summer/Fall 1984, Fall/Winter 1984.
20. *Paper SAC*, October 29, 1981, February 4, 1982, September 17, 1982; *Ambrose Scene*, Winter 1982.
21. *Ambrose Magazine*, March 28, 1985.
22. *Paper SAC*, April 28, 1983.
23. *Paper SAC*, March 23, 1984.
24. *Ambrose Magazine*, February 21, 1985.
25. *Ambrose Magazine*, September 26, 1985, December 11, 1986.
26. *Paper SAC*, November 20, 1980, February 12, 1981, May 5, 1983, November 17, 1983.
27. *Paper SAC*, September 22, 1983.
28. *Catholic Messenger*, October 6, 1983.
29. *Ambrose Magazine*, October 11, 1984.
30. *Paper SAC*, December 8, 1983.
31. *Paper SAC*, November 17, 1983, March 1, 1984.
32. *Ambrose Scene*, Spring/Summer 1984.
33. Minutes, Board of Directors, May 4, 1979, April 21, 1980, Archives, O'Keefe Library; Task Force to William Bakrow, April 14, 1980, Archives, O'Keefe Library; Gerald O'Keefe to James Tank, April 22, 1980, Archives, O'Keefe Library; Minutes, Marycrest Board of Trustees, March 7, 1980, Archives, Congregation of the Humility of Mary.
34. Gerald O'Keefe to William Bakrow, April 24, 1980, Archives, O'Keefe Library.
35. *Quad-City Times*, June 19, 1980, June 25, 1980.
36. Cletus Madsen to Board of Directors, February 25, 1981, Archives, O'Keefe Library; Minutes, Board of Directors, April 15, 1983, Archives, O'Keefe Library; William Bakrow to St. Ambrose College Task Force, December 10, 1980, Archives, O'Keefe Library.
37. Minutes, Board of Directors, September 22, 1982, Archives, O'Keefe Library; Minutes, Marycrest Board of Trustees, June 19, 1982, October 23, 1982, Archives, Congregation of the Humility of Mary.
38. Joseph McCaffrey to St. Ambrose College Board of Directors Committee on Cooperation, January 29, 1983, Archives, O'Keefe Library; Minutes, Marycrest Board of Trustees, October 22, 1983, Archives, Congregation of the Humility of Mary; Joseph McCaffrey to Cletus Madsen, March 29, 1984, Archives, O'Keefe Library.
39. Interview, Joseph McCaffrey with author, May 14, 2006.
40. Minutes, Marycrest Board of Trustees, October 12, 1985, Archives, Congregation of the Humility of Mary; Ann Therese Collins to William Bakrow, November 11, 1985, Archives, O'Keefe Library.
41. *Paper SAC*, April 12, 1984; *Ambrose Scene*, Spring/Summer 1984.
42. *Ambrose Magazine*, November 21, 1985.
43. *Ambrose Magazine*, December 12, 1985, September 4, 1986; *Ambrose Scene*, Fall/Winter 1986.
44. *Ambrose Scene*, Fall/Winter 1986, Spring/Summer 1987.
45. *Ambrose Magazine*, October 11, 1984; Minutes, Board of Directors, October 4, 1983, November 2, 1984, Archives, O'Keefe Library.
46. "Strategic Plan, St. Ambrose College, Davenport, Iowa, January 3, 1985," Archives, O'Keefe Library; *Ambrose Scene*, Winter/Spring 1985.
47. Dorothy Schweider, *Iowa The Middle Land* (Ames: Iowa State University Press, 1996), 317.
48. Minutes, Board of Directors, January 3, 1985, Archives, O'Keefe Library.
49. James W. Frick Associates Inc., "A Confidential Report on the Survey of the Board of Directors and Other Members of the Constituency of St. Ambrose College," March 1986, 6, 26, 28.
50. William Bakrow to Gerald O'Keefe, November 5, 1984, Archives, Diocese of Davenport.
51. *Ambrose Magazine*, October 24, 1985; James Frick to William Bakrow, April 21, 1986, Archives, Diocese of Davenport; William Bakrow to Gerald O'Keefe, James McLaughlin, and Weir Sears, April 24, 1986, Archives, Diocese of Davenport.
52. Gerald O'Keefe to William Bakrow, June 9, 1986, Archives, Diocese of Davenport; Gerald O'Keefe to Members of the Board of Directors, June 9, 1986, Archives, Diocese of Davenport.
53. *Ambrose Magazine*, September 4, 1986; *Ambrose Scene*, Summer/Fall 1986; Minutes, Board of Directors, December 19, 1986, Archives, O'Keefe Library.
54. Minutes, Board of Directors, November 5, 1986, April 10, 1987; *Ambrose Scene*, Fall/Winter 1986.
55. *Ambrose Magazine*, April 23, 1987.
56. *Ambrose Magazine*, March 5, 1987.
57. Report of Officers to William Bakrow, February 26, 1987, Archives, O'Keefe Library; Minutes, Board of Directors, April 10, 1987, Archives, O'Keefe Library; *Quad-City Times*, April 23, 1987.
58. *Ambrose Scene*, Spring/Summer 1987.
59. *Ambrose Scene*, Spring/Summer 1987.
60. *Ambrose Magazine*, August 27, 1987.
61. *Ambrose Magazine*, April 9, 1987.
62. *Ambrose Scene*, Spring/Summer 1987.

63. *Ambrose Scene*, Spring/Summer 1987.
64. *Rock Island Argus*, July 31, 1987; *Ambrose Magazine*, September 10, 1987.
65. *Ambrose Magazine*, October 8, 1987, October 22, 1987, November 5, 1987.
66. *Ambrose Scene*, Fall/Winter 1987.
67. *Ambrose Magazine*, October 8, 1987, October 22, 1987.
68. *Ambrose Magazine*, August 27, 1987.
69. "Strategic Plan, St. Ambrose College, January 3, 1985," Archives, O'Keefe Library; *Ambrose Scene*, Fall/Winter 1987.
70. Minutes, Board of Directors, October 8, 1987, December 17, 1987, Archives, O'Keefe Library.
71. Minutes, Board of Directors, March 29, 1988, October 11, 1988, Archives, O'Keefe Library.
72. Minutes, Board of Directors, March 29, 1988, Archives, O'Keefe Library; *Ambrose Magazine*, April 7, 1988.
73. *Ambrose Magazine*, November 29, 1986.
74. *Ambrose Magazine*, February 11, 1988, September 8, 1988.
75. *Ambrose Magazine*, February 11, 1988, August 31, 1988, September 8, 1988.
76. *Paper SAC*, February 15, 1973; *Ambrose Magazine*, April 23, 1987, September 21, 1988, February 23, 1989.
77. *Ambrose Magazine*, December 7, 1989, November 15, 1990; *Ambrose Scene*, Winter/Spring 1990.
78. *Ambrose Magazine*, September 27, 1990.
79. *Ambrose Magazine*, February 11, 1988.
80. *Ambrose Magazine*, April 7, 1988.
81. "1990-1992 Strategic Plan," Archives, O'Keefe Library.
82. Minutes, Board of Directors, April 10, 1990, Archives, O'Keefe Library.
83. Minutes, Board of Directors, April 18, 1989, Archives, O'Keefe Library.
84. Helen Elsbernd, FSPA, to Donald Moeller, February 7, 1990, Archives, O'Keefe Library; Minutes, Marycrest Board of Trustees, March 3, 1990, Archives, Congregation of the Humility of Mary.
85. Gerald O'Keefe to Edward Rogalski, April 16, 1990, Archives, O'Keefe Library.
86. Pauline Tursi, CHM, to Gerald O'Keefe, June 14, 1990, Archives, O'Keefe Library.
87. Edward Rogalski, Meeting Notes, June 18, 1990, Archives, O'Keefe Library.
88. James Victor, Pauline Tursi, CHM, Wanda Bigham to Gerald O'Keefe, Edward Rogalski, Michael Morrissey, June 25, 1990, Archives, O'Keefe Library.
89. Gerald O'Keefe to James Victor, Pauline Tursi, CHM, Wanda Bigham, July 13, 1990, Archives, O'Keefe Library; Gerald O'Keefe to Arnold Meyer, July 25, 1990, Archives, Diocese of Davenport.
90. "Administrative Analysis of Consolidation with Marycrest College," n.d., Archives, Diocese of Davenport; Donald Moeller to Edward Rogalski, September 27, 1990, Archives, O'Keefe Library.
91. Wanda Bigham to Edward Rogalski, September 26, 1990, Archives, O'Keefe Library.
92. Edward Rogalski to Wanda Bigham, October 12, 1990, Archives, Diocese of Davenport.
93. Edward Rogalski to Members of the St. Ambrose University Community, December 10, 1990, Archives, O'Keefe Library; *Quad-City Times*, November 14, 1990, November 15, 1990, December 10, 1990.
94. *Quad-City Times*, December 12, 1990.
95. *Catholic Messenger*, December 13, 1990.

Chapter Seventeen

1. Drake Shafer and Stanley Kabat to Edward Rogalski, Donald Moeller, and Edward Henkhaus, June 8, 1989, Archives, O'Keefe Library.
2. *Ambrose Magazine*, August 30, 1989; *Ambrose Scene*, Fall/Winter 1989.
3. "1991-1993 Strategic Plan," Archives, O'Keefe Library.
4. *Ambrose Magazine*, December 7, 1989, April 12, 1990, August 29, 1990, September 27, 1990; *Ambrose Scene*, Fall/Winter 1990-1991.
5. *Ambrose Magazine*, October 24, 1988.
6. *Ambrose Magazine*, January 25, 1990; *Ambrose Scene*, Winter/Spring 1990.
7. *Ambrose Scene*, Fall/Winter 1991.
8. *Ambrose Magazine*, November 19, 1984.
9. "1989-1991 Strategic Plan," Archives, O'Keefe Library.
10. Corinne Potter to Edward Rogalski, June 22, 1990, Archives, O'Keefe Library.
11. "1992-1994 Strategic Plan," Archives, O'Keefe Library; *Ambrose Scene*, Winter/Spring 1991.
12. Alvin P. Sanoff, "Serving Students Well: Independent Colleges Today," Laura Wilcox, ed., *Meeting the Challenge: America's Independent Colleges and Universities Since 1956* (Washington, D.C.: Council of Independent College, 2006), 39.
13. *Buzz*, October 19, 1991; "Institutional Mission Analysis, A Report on St. Ambrose Community Perceptions of Institutional Values," April 1992, Archives, O'Keefe Library.
14. *Buzz*, October 19, 1991.
15. "Institutional Mission Analysis, A Report on St. Ambrose Community Perceptions of Institutional Values," April 1992, Archives, O'Keefe Library.
16. Brian Daley, SJ, "Introduction," *The Idea of a Catholic University* (University of St. Thomas, 1994), 5.
17. Pope John Paul II, *Ex Corde Ecclesiae*, 1990, No. 4.
18. Gregory J. Coulter, "What Makes a University Catholic?" *The Idea of a Catholic University* (University of St. Thomas, 1994), 18.
19. *Ambrose Magazine*, January 24, 1991.
20. *Ambrose Magazine*, January 24, 1991.
21. *Ambrose Magazine*, February 7, 1991.
22. *Buzz*, October 15, 1992.
23. *Buzz*, February 25, 1994.
24. *Buzz*, February 25, 1994.
25. *Buzz*, October 12, 1995.
26. Minutes, Student Government Association, November 27, 1994, December 4, 1994, December 11, 1994, Archives, O'Keefe Library.
27. *Buzz*, March 25, 1994, March 16, 1995.
28. *Buzz*, August 31, 1995.
29. *Buzz*, February 12, 1998.
30. *Buzz*, February 22, 1996.
31. "Student Handbook, 1984-1986," Archives, O'Keefe Library.
32. "Student Handbook, 1986-88," Archives, O'Keefe Library.
33. *Buzz*, October 21, 1993, October 20, 1994.
34. *Buzz*, April 1, 1993.
35. *Buzz*, February 22, 1996.
36. "Institutional Mission Analysis, A Report on St. Ambrose Community Perceptions of Institutional Values," April 1992, p. 10, Archives, O'Keefe Library.
37. *Buzz*, April 1, 1993.
38. Stanley Kabat to Edward Rogalski, April 1, 1991, Archives, O'Keefe Library.

39. Minutes, Board of Directors, April 9, 1991, Archives, O'Keefe Library.
40. *Ambrose Magazine*, August 19, 1991.
41. *Ambrose Magazine*, October 10, 1991.
42. Minutes, Academic Support Committee, February 6, 1992, Archives, O'Keefe Library; Minutes, Board of Directors, April 14, 1992, Archives, O'Keefe Library.
43. "Student Handbook, 1992-1993," Archives, O'Keefe Library.
44. *Buzz*, September 15, 1994, November 17, 1994.
45. *Buzz*, March 30, 1995.
46. *Buzz*, April 11, 1996.
47. *Buzz*, September 15, 1994.
48. *Buzz*, October 29, 1992, January 28, 1993.
49. "Institutional Mission Analysis, A Report on St. Ambrose Community Perceptions of Institutional Values," April 1992, 4, Archives, O'Keefe Library.
50. Edward Rogalski to Board of Directors, October 9, 1990, Archives, O'Keefe Library.
51. *Buzz*, April 1, 1993.
52. "1992-1994 Strategic Plan," Archives, O'Keefe Library.
53. "1994-1996 Strategic Plan," Archives, O'Keefe Library.
54. *Ambrose Magazine*, March 29, 1990; *Buzz*, September 17, 1992, September 9, 1993, September 15, 1994.
55. *Buzz*, February 11, 1993, February 25, 1994.
56. *Buzz*, September 15, 1994.
57. *Ambrose Magazine*, October 11, 1990, March 7, 1991, March 28, 1991.
58. "1989-1991 Strategic Plan," Archives, O'Keefe Library.
59. "1994-1996 Strategic Plan," Archives, O'Keefe Library.
60. *Ambrose Scene*, Spring 1995.
61. "Strategic Plan 1993-1995," Archives, O'Keefe Library; *Ambrose Scene*, Fall/Winter 1991, Autumn/Winter 1992.
62. *Buzz*, October 26, 1995, October 30, 1997.
63. *Buzz*, March 25, 1999, May 4, 1999; *Ambrose Scene*, Autumn 1999.
64. *Ambrose Scene*, Spring 1997.
65. *Buzz*, August 29, 1996.
66. *Ambrose Scene*, Winter 2000; *Buzz*, December 2, 1999, February 17, 2000, September 28, 2000.
67. *Buzz*, October 6, 1994, December 8, 1994.
68. *Buzz*, February 9, 1995, October 12, 1995, September 12, 1996, November 21, 1996.
69. *Buzz*, November 4, 1993; *Ambrose Scene*, Summer 1993, Spring 2001.
70. *Ambrose Scene*, Summer 1981, Winter/Spring 1994, *Paper SAC*, October 28, 1982.
71. *Ambrose Scene*, Summer 1993.
72. *Buzz*, November 18, 1993; *Ambrose Scene*, Winter/Spring 1994.
73. *Ambrose Scene*, Autumn 1994.
74. *Buzz*, September 1, 1994; *Ambrose Scene*, Spring 1995.
75. *Buzz*, October 29, 1994.
76. *Buzz*, October 20, 1994, November 3, 1994.
77. *Buzz*, August 26, 1993, September 9, 1993.
78. Edward Rogalski to Stanley Kabat, November 2, 1994, Archives, O'Keefe Library.
79. Minutes, Facilities Planning Committee, March 27, 1995, Archives, O'Keefe Library.
80. Minutes, Facilities Planning Committee, April 10, 1995, Archives, O'Keefe Library.
81. Minutes, Facilities Planning Committee, July 19, 1995, Archives, O'Keefe Library.
82. *Buzz*, August 31, 1995, November 9, 1995.
83. *Ambrose Scene*, Spring 1996.
84. *Ambrose Scene*, Spring 1997.
85. *Buzz*, January 31, 1997; *Ambrose Scene*, Summer 1997.
86. *Buzz*, February 26, 1998.
87. *Buzz*, August 31, 2000; *Ambrose Scene*, Spring 2000.
88. *Buzz*, August 31, 2000, September 6, 2001; *Ambrose Scene*, Autumn 2001.
89. *Buzz*, September 20, 2001.
90. *Buzz*, October 4, 2001.
91. *Buzz*, September 20, 2001.
92. *Buzz*, January 31, 2002, January 30, 2003, February 10, 2005.
93. *Buzz*, January 31, 2002.
94. *Buzz*, January 31, 2002, February 14, 2002.
95. *Ambrose Scene*, Spring 2002; *Buzz*, January 31, 2002.
96. *Buzz*, February 14, 2002.
97. Minutes, Board of Directors, March 31, 2000, October 13, 2000, Archives, O'Keefe Library.
98. Minutes, Board of Directors, October 5, 2001, Archives, O'Keefe Library.
99. *Buzz*, December 2, 1999, October 16, 2003, February 12, 2004.
100. *Buzz*, October 16, 2003.
101. *Ambrose Scene*, Summer 2002.
102. *Ambrose Scene*, Summer 2002.
103. *Ambrose Scene*, Autumn 2000, Winter 2001.
104. *Buzz*, October 3, 2002.
105. *Buzz*, November 13, 2003.
106. *Buzz*, September 6, 2001, September 4, 2003, November 13, 2003, October 21, 2004.
107. *Ambrose Scene*, Spring 2004; *Buzz*, September 9, 2004.
108. *Buzz*, October 21, 2004.
109. *Quad-City Times*, October 12, 2004; *Buzz*, October 21, 2004.
110. *Buzz*, November 4, 2004.
111. Melanie M. Morey and John J. Piderit, SJ, *Catholic Higher Education, A Culture in Crisis* (New York: Oxford University Press, 2006), 9-10.
112. *Catholic Messenger*, September 1, 2005.

A Great and Lasting Beginning

A Great and Lasting Beginning

A Great and Lasting Beginning